Wales

THE ROUGH GUIDE

There are more than one hundred Rough Guide titles
covering destinations from Amsterdam to Zimbabwe

Forthcoming titles include
Bangkok • Barbados
Japan • Jordan • Syria

Rough Guide Reference Series
Classical Music • European Football • The Internet • Jazz
Opera • Reggae • Rock Music • World Music

Rough Guide Phrasebooks
Czech • French • German • Greek • Hindi & Urdu • Hungarian • Indonesian
Italian • Japanese • Mandarin Chinese • Mexican Spanish • Polish
Portuguese • Russian • Spanish • Thai • Turkish • Vietnamese

Rough Guides on the Internet
http://www.roughguides.com

Rough Guide Credits

Text editor:	Ann-Marie Shaw
Series editor:	Mark Ellingham
Editorial:	Martin Dunford, Jonathan Buckley, Jo Mead, Samantha Cook, Kate Berens, Amanda Tomlin, Paul Gray, Sarah Dallas, Chris Schüler, Helena Smith, Caroline Osborne, Kieran Falconer, Judith Bamber, Olivia Eccleshall, Orla Duane (UK); Andrew Rosenberg (US)
Online Editors:	Alan Spicer, Kate Hands (UK); Geronimo Madrid (US)
Production:	Susanne Hillen, Andy Hilliard, Judy Pang, Link Hall, Nicola Williamson, Helen Ostick, James Morris
Picture research:	Eleanor Hill
Cartography:	Melissa Flack, Maxine Burke, Nichola Goodliffe
Finance:	John Fisher, Celia Crowley, Catherine Gillespie, Neeta Mistry
Marketing & Publicity:	Richard Trillo, Simon Carloss, Niki Smith (UK); Jean-Marie Kelly, Sorelle Braun (US)
Administration:	Tania Hummel, Alexander Mark Rogers

The Rough Guide to Wales owes a great deal to the many friends and acquaintances, Welsh or otherwise, who happily shared their knowledge, freely voiced opinions and expressed an enthusiasm for Wales which we hope is evident throughout this book. **Special thanks** are due to the staff at tourist offices throughout the country and in particular to the Wales Tourist Board. Also to the Rough Guide crew, especially Jonathan Buckley for helping shape the book in its early stages; Samantha Cook for aid and inspiration this time around; Nicky Twyman for hawk-eyed proofreading; Melissa Flack for beautiful maps; Helen Ostick for affable, unflappable typesetting; and Susanne Hillen and Nicola Williamson for patience and the dogged pursuit of a cover.

Mike Parker would like to thank: Kate Baillie; Emma Clarke at *Buzz!* magazine; Dr Russell Rees; Gruffudd Rowland Williams; Duncan Alexander; Fred, Mo and the Space crew; Adam Price; James and Brigitte; Les (Dr Funkenstein) and Sue; Jane Bell and all at Druidston; Squidge and Sarah; Lynn; Joan Westmacott; Paul Butler and the West Wales Energy Group; Simon Lynch and Patsy; Billy and Ulrike; co-author Paul and editor Annie for limitless patience. A huge *diolch* to Rhian Williams at the Wales Tourist Board for her help, support and unfailing good humour.

Paul Whitfield would like to thank: Sophie Roberts for sharing part of the research trip on the Cambrian Coast; Andy and Jelly for their unending support; Hanna Kjellberg for a Finnish angle on Wales; James, Sarah and the Price family for their indulgence over the Cowbridge account; Mike Day and Sharon Alexander for feedback; and Rhys Mwyn for advice on Welsh music.

This second edition published by Rough Guides Ltd, 1 Mercer Street, London WC2H 9QJ. Previous edition 1994. Reprinted in February 1998.
Distributed by the Penguin Group:
Penguin Books Ltd, 27 Wrights Lane, London W8 5TZ
Penguin Books USA Inc., 375 Hudson Street, New York 10014, USA
Penguin Books Australia Ltd, 487 Maroondah Highway, PO Box 257, Ringwood, Victoria 3134, Australia Penguin Books Canada Ltd, 10 Alcorn Avenue, Toronto, Ontario M4V 1E4, Canada
Penguin Books (NZ) Ltd, 182–190 Wairau Road, Auckland 10, New Zealand
Typeset in Linotron Univers and Century Old Style to an original design by Andrew Oliver.
Printed in the UK by Clays Ltd, St Ives PLC
Illustrations in Part One and Part Three by Ed Briant; illustrations on p.1 and p.427 by Henry Iles.
Mapping is based upon the Ordnance Survey maps with the permission of the Controller of Her Majesty's Stationery Office, © Crown copyright.
© Mike Parker and Paul Whitfield 1997
512pp Includes index

A catalogue record for this book is available from the British Library
ISBN 1-85828-245-4

Wales

THE ROUGH GUIDE

£5

Written and researched by
Mike Parker and Paul Whitfield

THE ROUGH GUIDES

HELP US UPDATE

We've gone to great lengths to ensure that this second edition of the *Rough Guide to Wales* is as complete and up-to-date as possible. However, things do change – places get "discovered", bars and restaurants close, transport connections change – and any suggestions, comments or corrections would be much appreciated.

We'll credit all contributions, and send a copy of the next edition (or any other Rough Guide if you prefer) for the best letters. Please mark all letters *Rough Guide Wales Update* and send to:

Rough Guides, 1 Mercer St, London WC2H 9QJ
or Rough Guides, 375 Hudson St, 4th Floor, New York NY 10014
Or send e-mail to:wales@roughtravl.co.uk

Online updates about this book can be found on Rough Guides' homesite at
http://www.roughguides.com/

THANKS

Thanks to the readers of the last edition who wrote in with helpful comments and suggestions: Ikki Bhogal, Ritalynne Brechner, Frank Brughera & Joel Rubenzahl, Vicky Bullard, Matthew Cooper, J M Evans, Neil Fenton & Suki Moore, Michael Herbert, David W Hope, Rhys H Hughes, Edgar H Locke, Andrew Merchant, Jane R Olmsted, L A Partridge, Linda Price, Hugh Prichard, John Roy, Gary Spinks, Margaret Steyer, Jackie Thomas, Roger Thomas, Gillian Turner, Daisy Williams.

Apologies to anyone whose name has been spelt incorrectly, and to those whose signatures could not be deciphered.

THE AUTHORS

At the age of twelve, **Mike Parker** bought himself a *Teach Yourself Welsh* book and was hypnotized by this ancient land and its diverse culture. Since he started shaving, he has written books on four UK cities and the gay scenes in northern England, Ireland and Scotland, but it is to Wales that he always returns, as much for its pumping party life and rural cosmopolitanism as its crags and castles. At home in Birmingham, England, he combines travel writing with stand-up performing and the odd bit of broadcasting.

Born in England, **Paul Whitfield** spent childhood holidays secreting plastic toys in the sands of Welsh coastal resorts and failing to find them again. It wasn't until twenty years later, after earning a chemical engineering degree in New Zealand and spending a year in Central and South America, that he returned to Britain to make biscuits in Liverpool. Frequent weekend hillwalking and whitewater kayaking trips to Snowdonia kept him relatively sane, but it eventually became too much. Equipped with all the relevant *Rough Guides* he set off to cycle to Morocco, where he decided to write one himself. In between lengthy research trips – mainly to Wales, California and New Zealand – he plugs away at his word processor in Manchester, occasionally getting out to rock climb in Snowdonia and the Lake District.

ROUGH GUIDES
Travel Guides • Phrasebooks • Music and Reference Guides

We set out to do something different when the first **Rough Guide** was published in 1982. Mark Ellingham, just out of university, was travelling in Greece. He brought along the popular guides of the day, but found they were all lacking in some way. They were either strong on ruins and museums but went on for pages without mentioning a beach or taverna. Or they were so conscious of the need to save money that they lost sight of Greece's cultural and historical significance. Also, none of the books told him anything about Greece's contemporary life – its politics, its culture, its people, and how they lived.

So with no job in prospect, Mark decided to write his own guidebook, one which aimed to provide practical information that was second to none, detailing the best beaches and the hottest clubs and restaurants, while also giving hard-hitting accounts of every sight, both famous and obscure, and providing up-to-the-minute information on contemporary culture. It was a guide that encouraged independent travellers to find the best of Greece, and was a great success, getting short-listed for the Thomas Cook travel guide award, and encouraging Mark, along with three friends, to expand the series.

The Rough Guide list grew rapidly and the letters flooded in, indicating a much broader readership than had been anticipated, but one which uniformly appreciated the Rough Guide mix of practical detail and humour, irreverence and enthusiasm. Things haven't changed. The same four friends who began the series are still the caretakers of the Rough Guide mission today: to provide the most reliable, up-to-date and entertaining information to independent-minded travellers of all ages, on all budgets.

We now publish 100 titles and have offices in London and New York. The **travel guides** are written and researched by a dedicated team of more than 100 authors, based in Britain, Europe, the USA and Australia. We have also created a unique series of **phrasebooks** to accompany the travel series, along with an acclaimed series of **music guides**, and a best-selling **pocket guide to the Internet and World Wide Web**. We also publish comprehensive travel information on our two **web sites**: http://www.hotwired.com/rough and http://www.roughguides.com/

LIST OF MAPS

MAP SYMBOLS

Symbol	Description	Symbol	Description
═══	Motorway	⚑	Golf course
──	Major road	◓	Cave
──	Minor road	▲	Mountain peak
----	Path	⅄	Pass
▬▬	Railway	⫰	Waterfall
──	Wall	~~~	Cliff
─ ─	Ferry route	ⓘ	Tourist office
──	Waterway	⊠	Post office
---	Chapter division boundary	★	Bus stop
▬▪▬	Welsh border	▮	Building
✕	Airport	✚	Church
△	Youth hostel	†₊†	Cemetery
Λ	Campsite	▒	Park
�య	Castle	▓	National park
🏛	Stately home	◺	Forest
⌂	Abbey	▒	Sand/beach
♣	Museum	▨	Nature reserve
✿	Country park		

CONTENTS

INTRODUCTION

Wales at its best is the most beguiling part of the British isles. Its soaring mountain ranges, plunging, battered coastline, calm, lush valleys, and old-fashioned market towns all invite long and repeated visits. The culture, too, is compelling, whether in its Welsh or English-language manifestations, in its Celtic or its industrial traditions. If all too many of the British across the border continue to regard Wales as a land of male voice choirs, rugby and grim pit villages, more fool they – and more space to explore for the rest of us.

As you cross the border from England, you are, in fact, immediately aware of the different attitudes and cultures of the two countries. Wales shares many physical and emotional similarities with the other Celtic lands – Scotland, Ireland, Cornwall, Brittany, even Asturias and Galicia in northwest Spain. It shares, too, a desire for an individual political path, which has long been frustrated by English rulers and English-dominated governments. Even in the new, ever more devolved Europe, Wales lacks its own parliament or legislature: a situation that has led to a

WALES AND ITS SHIFTING COUNTY BOUNDARIES

Wales is a small and thinly populated country, and most of the 2.8 million inhabitants congregate in the southern quarter of this land, which stretches 160 miles from north to south and 50 miles from east to west. Only 8000 square miles in all, it is smaller than Massachusetts and only half the size of The Netherlands.

After Henry VIII's Acts of Union in 1536 and 1543, when the Welsh administrative system became formally linked with England's, Wales was divided into thirteen counties or shires, their borders predominantly reflecting those of the baronial domains (or Marcher lordships) they replaced. These counties held fast for hundreds of years: ancient divisions and names familiar to all. In 1974, however, the Local Government Act brought wholesale reorganization of county divisions throughout Britain; in Wales, the original thirteen were streamlined into eight, four of which covered the industrialized southeast (including three separate divisions of Glamorganshire).

Throughout Britain, the "new" counties were never highly regarded, and this was true too of Wales, even though new county boundaries and names – Dyfed, Clwyd, Gwent – corresponded largely with ancient Welsh provinces and kingdoms. In the early 1990s, after twenty years of public discontent, the whole structure of local government was yet again up for grabs, with Wales and Scotland the first to change. After extensive consultation and frequent changes of heart, 22 new unitary authorities came into being, replacing the previous two-tier county and district council structure. Thus, we see the re-emergence of old county names like Denbighshire, Flintshire, Pembrokeshire and Monmouthshire (if not often within the same boundaries as before 1974), the maintenance of post-1974 names such as Powys and Gwynedd, and the creation of a whole new tier of "county boroughs" (such as Cardiff, Neath-Port Talbot, Blaenau Gwent, Caerphilly) in the heavily populated south. Throughout the book, new divisions are used, although some institutions and venues still use the names from the 1974–96 period. It's a confusing situation that will probably settle down in time.

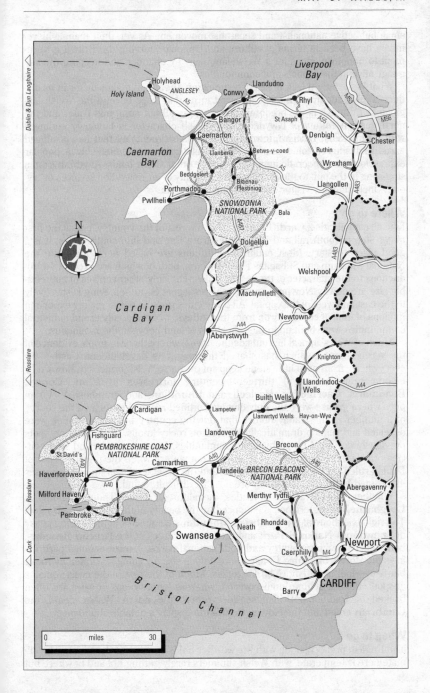

small but active nationalist and separatist movement. As yet, their main achievements have been in terms of culture and language, forcing the British government to honour pledges for a Welsh-language TV channel, and keeping the language alive in the schools and communities.

What Wales might lack in self-determination, though, it makes up for in its distinct cultural identity. This is expressed in myriad ways beyond the Welsh language, as English is the predominant tongue in all but rural mid-Wales and the northwestern county of Gwynedd. The Welsh character is famously endowed with a musicality, lyricism, introspection and sentimentality that has produced bards and singers for centuries. And Welsh culture is undeniably a popular expression – a democratic impulse, as in the other Celtic lands. Anything from a sing-song in the pub to the grandiose theatricality of an eisteddfod involves everyone – including any visitor eager to learn and join in.

Where to go

Like all capital cities, **Cardiff** is atypical of the rest of the country, but as the first major stop on both rail and road routes from England into south Wales, it is a good place to start. Most national institutions are based here, including the National Museum and St Fagans Folk Museum, both of which are excellent introductions to the character of the rest of Wales. The only other centres of appreciable size are dowdy **Newport** and breezy, resurgent **Swansea**, lying respectively to the east and west of the capital. All three cities grew as ports, mainly exporting millions of tons of coal and iron from the **Valleys**, where fiercely proud industrial communities were built up in the thin strips of land between the mountains.

Much of Wales' appeal lies outside the towns, where there is ample evidence of the warmongering which has shaped the country's development. Castles are everywhere, from hard little stone keeps of the early Welsh princes to Edward I's incomparable series of thirteenth-century fortresses of **Flint**, **Conwy**, **Beaumaris**, **Caernarfon**, **Harlech** and **Rhuddlan**, and grandiose Victorian piles where grouse were the only enemy. Fortified residences formed the source of a number of the stately homes that dot the country but many castles were deserted and remain dramatically isolated on rocky knolls, most likely on spots previously occupied by prehistoric communities. Passage graves and stone circles offer a more tangible link to the pre-Roman era when the priestly order of Druids ruled over early Celtic peoples, and the great medieval monastic houses like ruined **Valle Crucis Abbey** are not that difficult to find.

Whether you are admiring castles, megaliths, or Dylan Thomas's home at **Laugharne**, the experience is enhanced by the beauty of the Welsh countryside. The rigid backbone of the **Cambrian Mountains** terminates in the soaring peaks of **Snowdonia National Park** and the angular ridges of the **Brecon Beacons**, both superb walking country and both national parks. A third national park follows the **Pembrokeshire Coast** where golden strands come separated by rocky bluffs overlooking offshore bird colonies. Much of the rest of the coast remains unspoilt, though seldom undiscovered, whereas long sweeps of sand are often backed by traditional British seaside resorts: the **north Wales coast**, the **Cambrian coast** and the **Gower Peninsula** display a notable abundance.

When to go

The English preoccupation with the weather holds equally for the Welsh. The climate here is temperate, with Welsh summers rarely getting hot and nowhere but the tops of mountain ranges ever getting very cold, even in mid-winter. Temperatures vary little from Cardiff in the south to Llandudno in the north, but proximity to the mountains is a different matter: Llanberis, at the foot of Snowdon, gets doused with more than twice as much rainfall as Caernarfon, seven miles away, and is always a few degrees cooler. With rain never too far from the mind of any resident or visitor, it is easy to forget that throughout much of the summer, Wales – particularly the coast – can be bathed in sun. Between June and September, the Pembrokeshire coast can be as warm as anywhere in Britain.

The bottom line is that it's impossible to say with any degree of certainty that the weather will be pleasant in any given month. May might be wet and grey one year and gloriously sunny the next, and the same goes for the autumnal months – November stands an equal chance of being crisp and clear or foggy and grim. Obviously, if you're planning to lie on a beach, or camp in the dry, you'll want to go between June and September – a period when you shouldn't go anywhere without booking your accommodation well in advance. Otherwise, if you're balancing the likely fairness of the weather against the density of the crowds, the best time to get into the countryside or the towns is between April and May or in October. If outdoor pursuits are your objective, these are the best months for walking, June to October are warmest and driest for climbing, and December to March the only times you'll find enough water for kayaking.

PART ONE

THE
BASICS

GETTING THERE FROM THE UK AND EUROPE

Crossing the border from England into Wales is straightforward, with train and bus services forming part of the British national network. High costs and minimal time savings mean flights within Britain will be of little use, with the possible exception of those from Scotland. If you're driving from England, you'll probably be using one of the half-dozen or so roads which all run east to west through Wales. The two providing the quickest access into the heart of the country run along opposite coasts: the M4 motorway in the south, and the A55 dual carriageway in the north. These are both fast and busy roads, and minor routes are more appealing if you aren't in too much of a hurry.

Coming from Ireland **ferries** are definitely the cheapest and easiest way of getting to Wales. From the rest of Europe, there's the choice of flying from various destinations to Cardiff International Airport, or using either the traditional cross-Channel ferry services or the Channel Tunnel to England and making your way onwards from there.

BY PLANE

The only airport of any size in Wales is **Cardiff–Wales International** (☎01446/711111), at which scheduled flights arrive from selected northern European capitals and a few British destinations. The main international carrier is *KLM* (London information on ☎0181/750 9000), which flies into Cardiff from Amsterdam. The only other main carrier is *Manx Airlines* (☎0345/256256), which operates services from Paris, Dublin, Belfast and Edinburgh to Cardiff. These are mostly business flights, timed and priced accordingly, and often not operating at weekends.

In general, from Europe and Ireland you are better off flying into London, Birmingham or Manchester and moving on by bus or train. There are no worthwhile scheduled services from England to Wales or within Wales.

BY TRAIN

After centuries of dreams and plans, the **Channel Tunnel** finally opened for business in 1995. Two operators use the tunnel. **Eurostar** (☎0345/881881) runs hourly **passenger trains** to London Waterloo from Paris and Brussels. Two direct daily connections from Waterloo run along the Alpha Line to Newport and Cardiff, one of which continues to and from stations en route to Swansea and Carmarthen. Prices start at the equivalent of £59 return from Paris to London, £82 return from Paris to Cardiff. **Eurotunnel** runs a frequent **car-carrying train service** that crosses from Calais in northern France to Folkestone in southern England. Buses, cars and motorbikes are loaded onto a freight train, known as *Le Shuttle* (☎0990/353535), which takes 35 minutes to get between the loading terminals at Calais and Folkestone. *Le Shuttle* runs up to every fifteen minutes at peak periods, hourly at the quietest times of the day. Prices, which remain fixed irrespective of the number of passengers in the vehicle, start at the equivalent of £49 for a day return, travelling at night, through to £129 standard return, travelling in the daytime and with the open ticket valid for up to a year. A good-value five-day return starts at £59. Tickets for tunnel services can be bought at train stations, *ABTA*-approved travel agents or on arrival at Paris, Calais or Brussels.

Despite the tunnel, **car ferries** remain well and truly in business, often undercutting the trains and, in the case of the Calais–Dover service, not taking much longer (see "By road", below, for more details).

FROM ENGLAND AND SCOTLAND

Ongoing rail privatization has seen numerous changes in a very short space of time. Some lines

TRAIN INFORMATION

National rail enquiries ☎0345/484950
London Paddington ☎0171/262 6767

and groups of lines – generally speaking, the most profitable ones – have already been taken over by private companies, while others – still part of the dwindling *British Rail* (*BR*) network – have been clumped together in smaller, easy-to-privatize groupings. This fragmentation shouldn't mean anything to you on the ground, though, as **through-ticketing** was enshrined in the privatization legislation, and you should not (at least in

theory) have any trouble in booking a trip that uses two or more operators.

Two main lines provide frequent, fast services **to Wales from London**: the south Wales line from London Paddington via Reading, Swindon and Bristol to Newport, Cardiff and Swansea; and the north coast line to Bangor and Holyhead. Very few direct trains from England go beyond Swansea, although connections at either Cardiff or Swansea link up with trains to Carmarthen and stations in Pembrokeshire. **From other cities in England and Scotland**, you'll probably need to change en route – at Bristol or Bath for the south coast line, at Crewe for the north coast – though

TRAIN FARES AND SAVINGS

Ordinary second-class (Standard Class in *BR*-speak) **fares** are high, and first-class costs an extra 33 percent, but there are six types of reduced fare ticket.

Savers are return tickets that can be used on all trains on Saturdays, Sundays and bank holidays, on most weekday trains outside the morning rush hour for the outward journey, and all trains for the return leg. If you buy a return ticket at any station outside the morning rush hour, you'll routinely be issued with a *Saver* ticket. An **Advance** ticket costs the same as a *Saver* and permits travel on most services over 150 miles, but must be bought before noon on the day before travel, and numbers are limited. **SuperSavers**, cheaper still, cannot be used on Fridays nor on half a dozen other specified days of the year, normally Saturdays in July and August. A **SuperAdvance** ticket costs the same as a *SuperSaver*, has the same limitations as the *Advance* ticket and numbers are even more limited. *Saver* and *SuperSaver* tickets are valid for one month (outward travel has to be within two days of the date on the ticket), and allow a break in the return (but not outward) leg of the journey.

Like the *Advance* and *SuperAdvance* tickets, the even cheaper **Apex** tickets are issued in limited numbers on certain *InterCity* journeys of 150 miles or more, but these have to be bought at least seven days before travelling and you must specify your outward and return departure times. They include a seat reservation in the price. In addition, there is a **Leisure First** ticket which is more expensive than a *Saver*, but allows travel on any train, must be booked before 4pm on the day before you travel and requires outward and return journeys to be separated by a Saturday.

In practice, you can buy *Saver*, *Supersaver* and *Leisure First* tickets to just about anywhere, but other tickets are only available in limited numbers on long, popular journeys. For Wales, that means journeys between London and the main stations on the north and south coast lines.

Children under 5 travel free, those aged 5–15 inclusive paying half the adult fare on most journeys – though there are no discounts on *Apex* tickets. In an apparent effort to dissuade people from using their services, the rail companies now regard skis and large musical instruments as children and charge you for them accordingly. Most long-distance trains now have limited space for **bicycles** and you are required to reserve a place before you travel and pay £3 for each journey.

At weekends, many *InterCity* services have a special deal whereby you can convert your second-class ticket to a first-class one by paying a £5 supplement. This is seldom worthwhile within Wales, but vital if you are travelling to London after a Rugby International match at Cardiff Arms Park and don't want to stand up.

To take the **London–Cardiff** service as an example, an ordinary one-way fare costs £36, more than some of the reduced return fares: a *Leisure First* ticket is £54; a *Saver* is £42; a *SuperSaver* and *SuperAdvance* is £33; and an *Apex* is £24 (via Slough) or £23 (via Salisbury). For a rough idea of *SuperSaver* fares from other British cities, you can expect to pay the following: from Edinburgh and Glasgow to Cardiff £65, or Holyhead £53; from Newcastle to Cardiff and Holyhead, £62 and £52 respectively; from Manchester £35 and £23; and from Birmingham £24 and £33. For all special-offer tickets, you should book as far ahead as you possibly can – many *Apex* tickets are sold out weeks before the travel date.

for south Wales, a semi-fast shuttle runs between Manchester or Birmingham and Cardiff via Hereford or Gloucester.

Mid-Wales is best reached via Birmingham and Shrewsbury, with two lines plunging deep into the heart of the country. The faster route heads through Welshpool, Newtown and Machynlleth, beyond which it divides at Dyfi Junction. The southern spur goes a few miles to Borth and Aberystwyth, the northern one crawls up the coast through Tywyn, Barmouth, Harlech and Porthmadog to Pwllheli. Even slower (but very picturesque) is the second route from Shrewsbury, the **Heart of Wales line**, which limps four or five times daily into Wales, through Knighton, Llandrindod Wells, Llanwrtyd Wells, Llandovery, Llandeilo and a host of tiny halts on the way to Llanelli and Swansea.

Journey times between main centres are remarkably short: London–Cardiff takes under two hours and London–Swansea around three hours. Heading for the north coast, expect the London–Holyhead service to take just over four hours.

BY BUS

Inter-town **bus** services duplicate a few of the major rail routes, often at half the price of the train or less. Buses are reasonably comfortable and often have drinks and sandwiches available on board on longer routes. By far the biggest national operator is **National Express**, whose network covers England and sends half a dozen tendrils into Wales. The chief routes are from London to Cardiff, Swansea and on to Pembroke and Milford Haven; London to Wrexham; London to Aberystwyth and London along the north coast to Holyhead and Pwllheli, both via Birmingham; Birmingham to Cardiff and Swansea; Birmingham to Haverfordwest; Manchester along the north coast; and a cross-country trek from Great Yarmouth, via the East Midlands and Birmingham to south Wales. *National Express* services are so popular that for busy routes and services during weekends and holidays, it's a good idea to buy a reserved journey ticket, guaranteeing a seat.

One-way tickets are usually little cheaper than an **economy return** ticket, which is good for travel on any day except Friday and is valid for three months. If you travel on Friday, expect to pay around thirty percent more. Typical economy return **journey costs** to Cardiff are £23 from London; £45 from Edinburgh, Glasgow or Newcastle; £28

BUS INFORMATION

National Express coach enquiries
(☎0990/808080)

National line to identify local ticket agencies
(☎0990/010104)

National Express on the Internet
(http://www.nationalexpress.co.uk)

from Manchester; and £16 from Birmingham. Manchester–Holyhead return costs £14.

If you are planning to travel extensively throughout Britain by bus, the various *National Express* **discount passes** may save you a lot of money. UK residents under 25, in full-time education or of retirement age can buy a *National Express* **Discount Coach Card** (£7), which is valid for one year and entitles the holder to a thirty percent discount on any fare. All passengers are entitled to buy a **Tourist Trail Pass**, which offers unlimited travel on the *National Express* network. A three-day *Tourist Trail Pass* costs £49 for adults, £39 for students and under-26s; five days' travel in ten cost £79 or £65 respectively; eight days in sixteen cost £119 or £95; and fifteen days in thirty will set you back £179 or £145. In Britain you can obtain both from major travel agents, at Gatwick and Heathrow airports, at the *British Travel Centre* in London (see p.20), or at the main *National Express* office. The main Welsh offices are at Cardiff and Swansea, but tickets are available through a broad network of travel agents. In North America these passes should be available through any travel agent or direct from *British Travel International* (see box on p.11 for address).

For more bus passes for use within Wales and the rest of Britain, see "Getting around", p.22.

BY ROAD: DRIVING

Travelling to Wales by car from England, the main roads into **the north** are the upgraded coastal **A55** route, a dual carriageway all the way from Chester, and the **M56** via Holywell, St Asaph, Colwyn Bay, through a tunnel under the Conwy Estuary and on to Bangor, where it connects with the old trunk route, the A5. The **A5** is still the major road into north Wales from the Midlands and the south of England, best approached from the M6 just north of Wolverhampton, via the fast M54 and new Shrewsbury bypass. Much of the A5 has been improved in recent decades, although there are still traditional bottlenecks at Llangollen and Betws-y-Coed.

The Shrewsbury route is also the best for access into **mid-Wales** as far south as Newtown and Aberystwyth, using the **A458** to Welshpool from the Shrewsbury bypass. Further south, the **A456** from Birmingham, via Kidderminster and Leominster, is occasionally slow when passing through towns, but generally easier than the route through Worcester and Hereford to reach the A44 in Radnorshire and, to the south, the A438/470 to Brecon. This road connects with the swift westbound A40 at the Brecon bypass, best for routes from the Midlands and north of England to southern Cardiganshire and northern Carmarthenshire. An alternative route from the Midlands is via the **M50** "Ross Spur", a quiet motorway off the M5 south of Worcester, meeting the A449 dual carriageway at Ross-on-Wye. The road continues south, dividing at Raglan into the quick A40 for Brecon and the A449 down to Newport, the M4 and all destinations west.

The **M4 from London** makes the most dramatic entry into Wales. The **Severn Bridge** (£3.75 toll) rises high over the mud flats, passing Chepstow, Newport and Cardiff en route to Swansea and the west. A **second Severn River crossing**, a few miles south (same toll), opened in mid-1996, shaving a few miles and minutes off the journey of those travelling from Bristol and England's southern regions. The M4 coasts quickly westwards, although tailbacks are hardly a rarity around Cardiff and Newport. Thankfully, the spectacular new river crossing at Swansea is now open, ending the hideous queues on the old A48 stretch. From here, the M4 mutates into the A48 dual carriageway, connecting with the excellent A40 at Carmarthen, coursing west to Haverfordwest, for connections to Pembrokeshire and southern Cardiganshire.

HITCHING AND LIFT-SHARING

The extensive motorway network and the density of traffic makes long-distance hitching through England and Scotland to the Welsh border and along the M4 to Cardiff and Swansea relatively easy. Key junctions on the edge of metropolitan areas and motorway service stations are the favoured hitching spots, and standing with a sign at the exit produces the best results.

However, **hitching is not generally advised**, especially if you are a woman travelling alone. A way around this impasse is offered by the **lift-sharing** advertisements in the small-ads

paper *Loot*, available daily in London, Manchester and Bristol, with private individuals offering and seeking lifts around Britain. *Freewheelers* (☎0191/222 0090), an established England-based lift-share agency, requires passengers to pay a £10 annual registration fee, plus a £3 fee for each journey and 3.5p per mile as a contribution to the driver's costs – a fraction of the cost of any public transport service.

BY FERRY

Wales has three main ferry ports all serving boats **from Ireland** (see box). Ferries from Dublin, and both ferries and high-speed catamarans from Dun Laoghaire (six miles south of Dublin), arrive at Holyhead on the northwest tip of Wales, while Rosslare, just outside Wexford, is the departure point for ferries and catamarans to Fishguard, and ferries to Pembroke Dock, both in southwest Wales.

Stena Line (☎0990/707070) operates ferries and cats from Dun Laoghaire to Holyhead, and services from Rosslare to Fishguard; *Irish Ferries* (☎0990/171717) runs ferries from Dublin to Holyhead and from Rosslare to Pembroke Dock. **Ferry prices** for the two companies are almost identical, whichever ports you travel between, though for cars, winter fares tend to be a little cheaper from Rosslare, as are high-summer fares to Holyhead. One-way foot passenger fares range from £20 in winter to £26 on summer sailings from Friday to Sunday. Cars with up to five people cost from £84. To save money, avoid weekend sailings from mid-July to mid-September and travel during the day rather than at night. **Catamarans** cost about £5 more as a foot passenger and £10–30 more for a car depending on season. There is also a ferry from Cork to Swansea, operated by *Swansea–Cork Ferries* (☎01792/456116). Most are ten-hour night sailings costing £20–30 for foot passengers and £89–190 for a car and up to four passengers.

There's a much greater choice of **ferries from Europe** to ports in England, the most convenient of which are listed in the box opposite. Competitive pricing, especially since the Channel Tunnel opened, means that unless you are in a hurry lower prices may lure you onto a boat. There are regular crossings with *Hoverspeed*, *Stena Line* and *P&O* from Calais to Dover, the shortest route, for which the lowest fare for a small car and two adults is around £70. For full details of ferry routes and prices, call the ferry companies direct.

FERRY CONNECTIONS

	Company	Frequency	Duration
From Belgium			
Ostend–Ramsgate	*Sally Line* Ferry	6 daily	4hr–4hr 30min
Ostend–Ramsgate	*Sally Lines* Jetfoil	3–6 daily	1hr 40min
From France			
Roscoff–Plymouth	*Brittany Ferries*	1–2 daily	6hr
Cherbourg–Southampton	*Stena Line*	1–2 daily	6–8hr
St Malo–Portsmouth	*Brittany Ferries*	1–7 weekly	9hr
Caen–Portsmouth	*Brittany Ferries*	2–3 daily	6hr
Cherbourg–Portsmouth	*P&O*	1–4 daily	4hr 45min
Le Havre–Portsmouth	*P&O*	2–3 daily	5hr 45min
Dieppe–Newhaven	*Stena Line*	2–4 daily	4hr
Boulogne–Folkestone	*Hoverspeed* SeaCat	4–6 daily	1hr
Calais–Dover	*Stena Line*	25 daily	1hr 30min
Calais–Dover	*P&O*	20–25 daily	1hr 15min
Calais–Dover	*Hoverspeed* Hovercraft	12 daily	45min
Dunkerque–Ramsgate	*Sally Line*	5 daily	2hr 30min
From Ireland			
Dun Laoghaire–Holyhead	*Stena Sealink*	4 daily	3hr 30min
Dun Laoghaire–Holyhead	*Stena Line* Sealynx	4 daily	1hr 50min
Dublin–Holyhead	*Irish Ferries*	2 daily	3hr 45min
Rosslare–Pembroke	*Irish Ferries*	2 daily	4hr 15min
Cork–Swansea	*Swansea–Cork Ferries*	1 daily	10hr
Rosslare–Fishguard	*Stena Line*	2 daily	3hr 30min
Rosslare–Fishguard	*Stena Line* Sealynx	4 daily	1hr 40min
From Spain			
Santander–Plymouth	*Brittany Ferries*	2 weekly	24hr

GETTING THERE FROM NORTH AMERICA

As there are currently no direct transatlantic flights to Wales the range of options for visitors from the US and Canada, is always greatest – and the fares usually lowest – flying into London and covering the rest of the journey overland. Two of London's airports – Heathrow and Gatwick – handle transatlantic flights, and in terms of convenience they're about equal. There are, however, a growing number of direct flights into Manchester or Birmingham, both linked to rail routes into Wales.

Figure on six and a half hours' **flying time** from New York to any of the British airports, eleven and a half hours from the West Coast (it's an hour extra coming the other way, due to headwinds). Most flights cross the Atlantic overnight, reaching Britain the next morning, although a few flights from the East Coast leave early in the morning and arrive late the same evening.

You can rent cars on arrival at the airport, or contact one of the agencies listed on p.27 before you depart for Britain.

> For details on reaching Wales by train, bus or car from the rest of Britain, see p.3 Note that *Eurail* passes are not valid in Britain, though there are specific train and bus passes that are; see p.22 for details of train passes, and p.24 for bus passes available throughout the country.

SHOPPING FOR TICKETS

Given the enormous volume of air traffic crossing the Atlantic, you should have no problem finding a seat – the problem will be sifting through all the possibilities. Basic fares, especially to London, are kept very reasonable by intense competition, and discounts by bulk agents and periodic special offers from the airlines themselves can drive prices still lower. Any local **travel agent** should be able to access airlines' up-to-the-minute fares, although in practice they may not have time to research all the possibilities – you might want to call a few **airlines** direct (see box opposite).

Barring special offers, the cheapest of the airlines' published fares is usually an **Apex** ticket, although this will carry certain restrictions: you have to book – and pay – at least 21 days before departure, spend at least seven days abroad (maximum stay three months), and you tend to get penalized if you change your schedule. There are also winter **Super Apex** tickets, sometimes known as "Eurosavers" – slightly cheaper than an ordinary Apex, but limiting your stay to between seven and 21 days. Some airlines also issue **Special Apex** tickets to people younger than 24, often extending the maximum stay to a year. Many airlines offer youth or student fares to **under-26s**; a passport or driving licence are sufficient proof of age, though these tickets are subject to availability and can have eccentric booking conditions. It's worth remembering that most cheap return fares involve spending at least one Saturday night away and that many will only give a percentage refund if you need to cancel or alter your journey, so make sure you check the restrictions carefully before buying a ticket.

Whatever the airlines are offering, however, you can normally beat it by going through a **specialist flight agent** – either a **consolidator**, who buys up blocks of tickets from the airlines and sells them at a discount, or a **discount agent**, who in addition to dealing with discounted flights may also offer special student and youth fares and a range of other travel-related services such as travel insurance, rail passes, car rentals, tours and the like. Bear in mind, though, that penalties for changing your plans can be stiff. Remember too that these companies make their

MAJOR NORTH AMERICAN AIRLINES

Aer Lingus (☎1-800/223-6537 or 212/557-1110).

Air Canada (in BC, ☎1-800/663-3721; in Alberta, Saskatchewan and Manitoba, ☎1-800/542-8940; in eastern Canada, ☎1-800/268-7240; in US, ☎1-800/776-3300).

Air India (☎1-800/223-7776 or 212/751-6200).

American Airlines (☎1-800/433-7300).

British Airways (in US, ☎1-800/247-9297; in Canada ☎1-800/668-1059).

Canadian Airlines (in Canada, ☎1-800/665-1177; in US, ☎1-800/426-7000).

Continental Airlines (☎1-800/231-0856).

Delta Airlines (☎1-800/241-4141; in Canada, call directory enquiries, ☎1-800/555-1212, for local toll-free number).

Kuwait Airways (☎1-800/458-9248).

Northwest Airlines (☎1-800/447-4747).

TWA (☎1-800/221-2000).

United Airlines (☎1-800/538-2929).

Virgin Atlantic Airways (☎1-800/862-8621).

DISCOUNT AGENTS, CONSOLIDATORS AND TRAVEL CLUBS

Air Brokers International, 323 Geary St, Suite 411, San Francisco, CA 94102 (☎1-800/883-3273 or 415/397-1383). *Consolidator.*

Airtech, 584 Broadway, Suite 1007, New York, NY 10012 (☎1-800/575-TECH or 212/219-7000). *Standby seat broker (mainly from northeastern US cities).*

Council Travel, 205 East 42nd St, New York, NY 10017 (☎1-800/743-1823 or 212/822-2700); 312 Sutter St, San Francisco, CA 94108 (☎415/421-3473); and many other regional outlets. *Student- and youth-oriented travel organization. A sister company,* Council Charter *(☎1-800/223-7402), specializes in charter flights.*

Educational Travel Center, 438 N Frances St, Madison, WI 53703 (☎1-800/747-5551 or 608/256-5551). *Student/youth discount centre.*

Moment's Notice, 7301 New Utrecht Ave, Brooklyn, NY 11204 (☎718/234-6295). *Discount travel club.*

New Frontiers/Nouvelles Frontières, 12 E 33rd St, New York, NY 10016 (☎1-800/366-6387); 1001 Sherbrook East, Suite 720, Montréal, H2L 1L3 (☎514/526-8444); and other branches in Los Angeles, San Francisco and Québec City. *French discount travel firm.*

Now Voyager, 74 Varick St, Suite 307, New York, NY 10013 (☎212/431-1616). *Courier flight broker.*

STA Travel, 10 Downing St, New York, NY 10014 (☎1-800/777-0112 or 212/627-3111; and other branches in the Los Angeles, San Francisco and Boston areas. *Worldwide specialists in discount travel.*

TFI Tours International, 34 W 32nd St, New York, NY 10001 (☎1-800/745-8000 or 212/736-1140), and other offices in Las Vegas and Miami. *Consolidator.*

Travac Tours, 989 Sixth Ave, New York, NY 10018 (☎1-800/872-8800 or 212/563-3303). *Consolidator and charter broker.*

Travel Avenue, 10 S Riverside, Suite 1404, Chicago, IL 60606 (☎1-800/333-3335 or 312/876-6866). *Discount travel agent.*

Travel CUTS, 187 College St, Toronto, ON M5T 1P7 (☎416/979-2406), and other branches all over Canada. *Student/youth travel organization.*

Travelers Advantage, 3033 S Parker Rd, Suite 900, Aurora, CO 80014 (☎1-800/548-1116). *Discount travel club.*

UniTravel, 1177 N Warson Rd, St Louis, MO 63132 (☎1-800/325-2222 or 314/569-2501). *Consolidator.*

Worldtek Travel, 111 Water St, New Haven, CT 06511 (☎1-800/243-1723 or 203/772-0470). *Discount travel agency.*

money by dealing in bulk – don't expect them to answer lots of questions. Some agents specialize in **charter flights**, which may be cheaper than anything available on a scheduled flight, but again departure dates are fixed and withdrawal penalties are high (check the refund policy). If you travel a lot, **discount travel clubs** are another option – the annual membership fee may be worth it for benefits such as cut-price air tickets and car rental.

Don't automatically assume that tickets purchased through a travel specialist will be cheapest – once you get a quote, check with the airlines and you may turn up an even better deal. Be advised also that the pool of travel companies is swimming with sharks – exercise caution and *never* deal with a company that demands cash up front or refuses to accept payment by credit card.

Regardless of where you buy your ticket, **fares** will depend on the season. Regardless of where you buy your ticket, the **fare** will depend on when you travel. Fares to Britain are highest from around early June to mid-September; they drop during shoulder seasons, mid-September to early November and mid-April to early June, and you'll get the best deals during low season, November through April (excluding Christmas). The Christmas–New Year period is a thing unto itself – if you want to travel at this time, book at least two or three months ahead, and be prepared for fares even higher than those in summer.

If Britain is only part of a longer journey, you might want to consider buying a **round-the-world (RTW) ticket**. Some travel agents can sell you and "off-the-shelf" RTW ticket that will stop in about half a dozen cities, of which London is usually one; connections to other parts of Britain will probably have to be added on separately. Others will assemble a route for you, which can be tailored to your needs but is apt to be more expensive. Prices start at around $1400 ($1600 if travelling in summer) for a simple RTW ticket stopping in London.

FLIGHTS FROM THE USA

Dozens of airlines fly from New York to London, and a few fly direct from other East Coast and Midwestern cities. The best low-season fares from **New York** to London hover around $420 round-trip. Low-season fares to London can also start as low as $420 from **Boston**, $520 from **Washington DC** or $550 from **Chicago**; *Delta* flies from **Atlanta** for about $530 and *Virgin* from **Miami** or **Orlando** for $580; *TWA* from **St Louis** for $600; and *Continental* from **Houston** for about $600. For high-season fares, add $150–250.

Don't assume you'll have to change planes when flying from the **West Coast** – *American*, *BA*, *Delta*, *United* and *Virgin* all fly nonstop from Los Angeles. Several carriers connect with flights to London from **Los Angeles** or **San Francisco**, with low-season midweek fares from both cities

starting at around $600. From **Seattle** the price will be more in the region of $650. High-season travel will add at least another $200.

Several airlines also fly direct to UK regional airports, notably **Manchester** (from New York with *American Airlines* and *British Airways*, from Chicago with *British Airways*, from Newark with *Continental* and from Atlanta with *Delta*), and **Birmingham** (*British Airways* from New York and *American* from Chicago).

See "Getting there from the UK and Europe" (p.3) for connections within Britain.

FLIGHTS FROM CANADA

In Canada, you'll get the best deal flying to London from the big gateway cities of **Toronto** and **Montréal**, where low-season midweek fares start at around Can$650 round-trip; direct flights from **Ottawa** and **Halifax** will probably cost only slightly more. From **Edmonton** and **Calgary**, London flights start at Can$950, from **Vancouver** around Can$900. High-season travel will add a premium of Can$300–400 to all these fares.

You can pick up direct flights from many Canadian cities to **Manchester** and **Birmingham** (usually via London), often at no extra cost over the fare to London. Only *Air Canada* flies nonstop to Manchester (from Toronto). Again, see "Getting there from the UK and Europe" (p.3) for connections within Britain.

PACKAGES AND ORGANIZED TOURS

Although you may want to see Wales at your own speed, you shouldn't dismiss the idea of a **package deal**. Many agents and airlines put together very flexible deals, sometimes amounting to no more than a flight plus car or rail pass and accommodation, and these can actually work out better value than the same arrangements made on arrival – especially fly-drive deals, since car rental is expensive in Britain. A package can also be great for your peace of mind, if only to ensure a worry-free first week.

A number of tour operators specialize in travel to Wales. Most can do packages of the standard highlights, and many organize walking or cycling trips through the countryside, with any number of theme tours based around the country's literary heritage, history, gardens – you name it. A few of the possibilities are listed below, and a travel agent will be able to point out others; bear in mind that bookings made through travel agents cost no more than going through the tour operator. For a full listing, contact the *British Tourist Authority* (p.20). Be sure to examine the fine print of any deal, and make sure the operator is a member of the *United States Tour Operator Association* (*USTOA*) or approved by the *American Society of Travel Agents* (*ASTA*). For a list of **operators in Britain** who can book self-catering holidays in Wales, see p.30.

SPECIALIST OPERATORS

BCT (British Coastal Trails) Scenic Walking (☎1-800/473-1210). *Walking trips throughout Snowdonia and central Wales, plus canal trips.*

British Travel International, PO Box 299, Elkton, VA 22827 (☎1-800/327-6097). *Agent for all kinds of independent arrangements including: organizing air tickets, rail and bus passes, hotel bookings, and a comprehensive B&B reservation service.*

Hostelling International (US ☎202/783-6161; Canada ☎1-800/663-5777 or 613/237-7884). *Affiliated with the UK's Youth Hostels Association, organizes walking, cycling and general youth tours.*

Lynott Tours (☎1-800/221-2474). *Special-interest tours, hotel and castle stays, self-drives; agent for Ireland–Wales ferries.*

Sterling Tours (☎1-800/727-4359). *Offers a variety of independent itineraries and some packages.*

Travel Arrangements International, 5123 Roland Ave, Baltimore, MD 21210 (☎1-800/435-4054). *Arranges independent tours of Wales, some packages.*

Travel Bound (☎1-800/456-8656). Virgin Atlantic's *tour arm.*

All these companies' tours can be booked through a travel agent at no extra cost.

GETTING THERE FROM AUSTRALIA & NEW ZEALAND

There are no direct flights to Wales from anywhere in Australia or New Zealand, so you will have to route through London and then travel onward either by connecting flight or overland. For all onward details, see "Getting there from the UK and Europe", p.3.

Daily flights connect London with **Melbourne**, **Sydney**, **Brisbane** and **Perth**, with no great difference in the fares, though competition on the route via Asia usually makes those fares the cheapest; *Garuda, Philippines Airlines, Aeroflot, Britannia, MAS* and *KLM* all offer good deals. More expensive, but worth considering for the extras — such as fly-drive, accommodation packages and free onward travel to Ireland and Europe — are *Thai Airways, Singapore Airlines, Qantas, British Airways* and *Air New Zealand*. Fares obviously depend on the time of year: for most major airlines, low season is October 1 to November 30 and January 16 to February 28; high season is May 16 to August 31 and December 1 to January 15; shoulder season is the rest of the year. The prices quoted below, unless otherwise stated, are the low-season fares published by the airlines (there's no variation in price during the week). On top of a low-season fare you can expect to pay between A/NZ$200 and $400 in

AIRLINES IN AUSTRALIA AND NEW ZEALAND

Aeroflot, 388 George St, Sydney (☎02/9262 2233). *No NZ office.*

Air New Zealand, 5 Elizabeth St, Sydney (☎02/9223 4666); Floor 17, Quay Tower, Customs St, Auckland (☎09/366 2803).

Britannia Airways, Aus-Extras Level 6, 210 George St, Sydney (☎02/9251 1299).

British Airways, Level 26, 201 Kent St, Sydney (☎02/9258 3300); 154 Queen St, Auckland (☎09/356 8690).

Canadian Airlines, 30 Clarence St, Sydney (☎02/9299 7843); Floor 15, Jetset Centre, 44 Emily Place, Auckland (☎09/309 0735).

Garuda, 55 Hunter St, Sydney (☎02/9334 9944); Westpac Tower, 120 Albert St, Auckland (☎09/366 1855).

JAL, Floor 14, Darling Park, 201 Sussex St, Sydney (☎02/9283 1111); Westpac Tower, 120 Albert St, Auckland (☎09/379 9906).

KLM, 5 Elizabeth St, Sydney (☎1-800/505 747 or 02/9231 6333). *No NZ office.*

Malaysian Airlines (MAS), 16 Spring St, Sydney (local-call rate ☎13 2627); Floor 12, Swanson Centre, 12–26 Swanson St, Auckland (☎09/373 2741).

Philippine Airlines, 49 York St, Sydney (☎02/9262 3333). *No NZ office.*

Qantas, Chifley Square, corner Hunter and Phillip streets, Sydney (☎02/9957 0111); Qantas House, 154 Queen St, Auckland (☎09/357 8900).

Singapore Airlines, 17–19 Bridge St, Sydney (local-call rate ☎13 1011); Lower Ground Floor, West Plaza Building, corner Customs and Albert streets, Auckland (☎09/379 3209).

Thai Airways, 75–77 Pitt St, Sydney (☎1-800/422 020 or 02/9844 0999); Kensington Swan Building, 22 Fanshawe St, Auckland (☎09/377 3886).

United Airlines, 10 Barrack St, Sydney (☎02/237 8888); 7 City Rd, Auckland (☎09/307 9500).

DISCOUNT TRAVEL AGENTS

Anywhere Travel, 345 Anzac Parade, Kingsford, Sydney (☎02/9663 0411).

Brisbane Discount Travel, 260 Queen St, Brisbane (☎07/3229 9211).

Budget Travel, 16 Fort St, Auckland; other branches around the city (☎0800/808 040 or 09/366 0061).

Destinations Unlimited, 3 Milford Rd, Milford, Auckland (☎09/373 4033).

Flight Centres, *Australia:* Level 11, 33 Berry St, North Sydney (☎02/9241 2422); Bourke St, Melbourne (☎03/9650 2899); plus other branches nationwide. *New Zealand:* National Bank Towers, 205–225 Queen St, Auckland (☎09/209 6171); Shop 1M, National Mutual Arcade, 152 Hereford St, Christchurch (☎03/379 7145); 50–52 Willis St, Wellington (☎04/472 8101); other branches countrywide.

Northern Gateway, 22 Cavenagh St, Darwin (☎08/8941 1394).

Passport Travel, 320b Glenferrie Rd, Malvern (☎03/9824 7183).

STA Travel, *Australia:* 702–730 Harris St, Ultimo, Sydney (☎1-800/637 444 or 02/9212 1255); 256 Flinders St, Melbourne (☎03/9654 7266); other offices in state capitals and major universities. *New Zealand:* Travellers' Centre, 10 High St, Auckland (☎09/309 0458); 233 Cuba St, Wellington (☎04/385 0561); 90 Cashel St, Christchurch (☎03/379 9098); other offices in Dunedin, Palmerston North, Hamilton and major universities.

Thomas Cook, *Australia:* 321 Kent St, Sydney (☎02/9248 6100); 257 Collins St, Melbourne (☎03/9650 2442); branches in other state capitals. *New Zealand:* Shop 250a St Luke's Square, Auckland (☎09/849 2071).

Topdeck Travel, 65 Glenfell St, Adelaide (☎08/8232 7222).

Tymtro Travel, 428 George St, Sydney (☎02/9223 2211).

---

mid-season and A/NZ$500 and $700 in high season. Students and under-26s are usually able to get a further ten percent off published prices.

Travel agents such as *STA* and *Topdeck* (see box) can often get a further ten percent reduction on the airline's quoted fares.

FLIGHTS FROM AUSTRALIA

The cheapest direct scheduled flight from Sydney to London Heathrow is with *Philippine Airlines*, which flies twice weekly via Manila and Frankfurt from A$1499. *Garuda* flies weekly from Sydney and Brisbane to London Gatwick via Denpasar or Jakarta for A$1550, and from Perth and Darwin for $1459. *MAS* offers a good deal once a week from Cairns via Kuala Lumpur for $1975, while *Aeroflot's* lowest fare from Sydney to Heathrow via Moscow is $1870. At the pricier end of the scale, both *British Airways* and *Qantas* fly daily from Brisbane, Sydney and Melbourne to Heathrow via Bangkok or Singapore, and *Singapore Airlines* flies daily from Sydney, Melbourne and Perth via Singapore; all quote fares of A$2299.

Via North America, *United* offers the cheapest deal: to Heathrow from Sydney or Melbourne via LA and either New York, Washington or Chicago for A$2229. *Air New Zealand* also flies Sydney, Melbourne and Perth to Heathrow via Auckland and LA several times a week for A$2499 ($2699 from Perth), while *Canadian Airlines* departs daily from Sydney and Melbourne for Heathrow via Toronto or Vancouver for A$2499.

Currently the best fare of all is the *Britannia Airways* direct charter to Gatwick and Manchester, via Singapore and Abu Dhabi, which operates from Cairns, Brisbane, Sydney, Melbourne, Adelaide and Perth several times a month between November and March. Fares start at A$1199.

VIA NEW ZEALAND

Both *British Airways* and *Qantas* fly daily from Auckland to London Heathrow, with *Qantas* going via Asia and *BA* via Los Angeles. *Air New Zealand* flies four times a week from Auckland to Heathrow via LA. Several airlines have a stopover or a change of plane at their main city. There is very little difference in price between airlines, with all the major carriers quoting low-season fares of NZ$2399, though booking through a travel agent can get you discounts of up to twenty percent.

United offers the best-value scheduled fares, with a weekly flight to Heathrow from Auckland stopping in LA and Chicago for NZ$2170. The very cheapest fare is *Britannia Airways'* charter flight from Auckland to Gatwick and Manchester (several times a month Nov–March), at NZ$1415.

ROUND THE WORLD FARES

If you're planning a long trip, a **round-the-world** (**RTW**) ticket that includes London can work out very good value. Currently the best deals on offer are *Cathay Pacific/United's* Globetrotter ticket and *Air New Zealand/KLM/Northwest's* World Navigator, both of which offer six stopovers worldwide with limited backtracking for A$2349 (NZ$2999). *Qantas/BA's* Global Explorer ticket is slightly more restrictive, allowing six stopovers but no backtracking within the US, for A$2499 (NZ$2399). For more flexibility, but at a higher price, *Singapore Airlines/TWA's* Easyworld fare (only available in Australia) allows unlimited backtracking for a $3023.

SPECIALIST AGENTS

Adventure Specialists, 69 Liverpool St, Sydney (☎02/9261 2927). *Walking and cycling holidays.*

Destination Adventure, 2nd Floor, Premier Building, corner Queen and Durham streets, East Auckland (☎09/309 0464). *New Zealand agents for Peregrine Adventures.*

Explore Holidays, corner Marsden and Pennet Hills roads, Carlingford, Sydney (☎02/9872 6222). *Accommodation and walking-holiday agent.*

Peregrine Adventures 258 Lonsdale St, Melbourne (☎03/9663 8611); offices in Brisbane, Sydney, Adelaide, Perth and Hobart.

Wiltrans/Maupintour, Level 10, 189 Kent St, Sydney (☎02/9255 0899). *Escorted historic tours.*

YHA Travel Centre, 205 King St, Melbourne (☎03/9670 9611); 36 Customs House, Auckland (☎09/379 4224). *Budget accommodation through-out Britain for YHA members.*

VISAS, CUSTOMS REGULATIONS AND TAX

Citizens of all European countries – other than Albania, Romania, Bulgaria, and the republics of the former Soviet Union (with the exception of the Baltic States) – can enter Britain with just a passport, generally for up to three months. US, Canadian, Australian and New Zealand citizens can travel in Britain for up to six months without a visa. All other nationalities require a visa, from the British Consular office in the country of application.

For stays longer than six months, **US, Canadian, Australian and New Zealand citizens** should apply to the British Embassy or High Commission (see box opposite). In the US, full-time bona fide college students can get temporary work or study permits through the *Council on International Education Exchange (CIEE)*, 205 E 42nd St, New York, NY 10017 (☎212/661-1414).Work permits cost $200 to arrange and are good for six months. Australian and New Zealand citizens need an Entry Clearance Certification for stays of longer than six months; those between the ages of 17 and 26 can stay for up to two years with a Working Holiday Entry Certificate. Extended stays are also possible for those with British grandparents. Applications must be made to the High Commission in person or by post, which takes about three weeks.

CUSTOMS

Since the inauguration of the EU Single Market, travellers coming into Britain directly from another EU country do not have to make a declaration to **customs** at their place of entry and can effectively bring almost as much wine or beer across the Channel as they like – the limits are ninety litres of wine and 110 of beer, which should be enough for anyone. However, there are still restrictions on the volume of **tax- or duty-free** goods you can bring into the country, so you can't invest in a stockpile of cheap cigarettes on your flight, whether you're coming from Paris or New York. The duty-free allowances are as follows:

Tobacco: 200 cigarettes; or 100 cigarillos; or 50 cigars; or 250g of loose tobacco.

Alcohol: Two litres of still wine, **plus** one litre of drink over 22 percent alcohol, or two litres of alcoholic drink not over 22 percent, or another two litres of still wine.

Perfumes: 60ml of perfume plus 250ml of toilet water.

Plus **other goods** to the value of £136.

There are **import restrictions** on a variety of articles and substances, from firearms to furs derived from endangered species, none of which should bother the normal tourist. However, if you need any clarification on British import regulations, contact *HM Customs and Excise*, Dorset House, Stanford Street, London SE1 9PJ (☎0181/202 4227). You are not allowed to bring **pets** into Britain.

VAT

Most goods in Britain, with the chief exceptions of books and food, are subject to **Value Added Tax (VAT)**, which increases the cost of an item by 17.5 percent and is usually included in the quoted price. Visitors from non-EU countries can save money through the Retail Export Scheme, which allows a refund of VAT on goods to be taken out of the country. (Savings will usually be minimal for EU nationals, because of the rates at which the goods will be taxed upon import to the home country). Note that not all shops participate in this scheme (those doing so display a sign to this effect) and that you cannot reclaim VAT charged on hotel bills or other services.

BRITISH EMBASSIES AND HIGH COMMISSIONS ABROAD

Australia British High Commission, Commonwealth Ave, Yarralumla, Canberra, ACT 2600 (☎06/257 1982).

Canada British High Commission, 80 Elgin St, Ottawa ON K1P 5K7 (☎613/237-1530).

Ireland 31–33 Merrion Rd, Dublin 4 (☎01/295 5211).

Netherlands General Koningslaan 44, Amsterdam (☎020/676 43 43).

New Zealand British High Commission, 44 Hill Street, Wellington (☎04/726 049).

USA 3100 Massachusetts Ave NW, Washington DC 20008 (☎202/462-1340).

OVERSEAS REPRESENTATION IN BRITAIN

Australia High Commission, Australia House, The Strand, London WC2B 4LA (☎0171/379 4334); Consulate, Chatsworth House, Lever St, Manchester M1 2QL (☎0161/228 1344).

Canada High Commission, 1 Grosvenor Square, London W1X 0AB (☎0171/258 6600).

Ireland Embassy, 17 Grosvenor Place, London SW1X 7HR (☎0171/235 2171).

Netherlands, 38 Hyde Park Gate, London SW7 5DP (☎0171/590 3200).

New Zealand High Commission, New Zealand House, 80 Haymarket, London SW1Y 4TQ (☎0171/930 8422).

USA Embassy, 24 Grosvenor Square, London W1A 1AE (☎0171/499 9000); Consulate, 3 Regent Terrace, Edinburgh EH7 5BW (☎0131/556 8315).

COSTS, MONEY AND BANKS

The British pound sterling (£; *punt* in Welsh, and widely referred to as "a quid") is a decimal currency, divided into 100 pence (p; in Wales, c for *ceiniogau*). Coins come in denominations of 1p, 2p, 5p, 10p, 20p, 50p and £1. Notes come in denominations of £5, £10 and £20. Shopkeepers will carefully scrutinize any £20 tendered, as forgeries are widespread, and you'd be well advised to do the same. The quickest test is to hold the note up to the light to make sure there is a thin wire filament running through the note from top to bottom; this is by no means foolproof, but will catch most fakes.

It is unlikely, but you may also come across Scottish banknotes which are legal tender in England and Wales, though often refused by traders. They come in the same denominations and have the same value as the British notes but are issued by three different banks; the *Bank of Scotland*, the *Royal Bank of Scotland* and the *Clydesdale Bank.*

CREDIT CARDS AND TRAVELLERS' CHEQUES

You'll find that most hotels, shops and restaurants in Wales are happy to accept the major **credit and charge cards** – *Access/MasterCard, Visa/Barclaycard, American Express* and *Diners' Club* – although they're less useful in the most rural areas, and all over the country smaller establishments, such as B&B accommodation, will often accept cash only. Your card will also enable you to get cash advances from most ATMs, though there will invariably be a minimum amount you can draw – call the issuing bank of your credit card company to get a list of Welsh locations. In addition, you maybe able to make withdrawals using your ATM cash card – your international banking department should be able to advise of this. Make sure you have a personal identification number (PIN) that's designed to work overseas.

The safest, if not the most convenient, way to carry your money is in **travellers' cheques** (in sterling), available for a small commission (normally one percent) from any major bank. The most widely accepted travellers' cheques are *American Express* (*AMEX*), followed by *Visa* and *Thomas Cook* – most cheques issued by banks will be one of these three brands. You'll usually pay commission again when you cash each cheque, normally another one percent or so, or a flat rate – though no commission is payable on *Amex* cheques exchanged at *Amex* branches (see box). Keep a record of the cheques as you cash them, and you can get the value of all uncashed cheques refunded immediately if you lose them.

There are no exchange controls in Britain, so you can bring in as much cash as you like and change travellers' cheques up to any amount.

BANKS AND BUREAUX DE CHANGE

Banks are almost always the best places to **change money and cheques**, and in every sizeable town in Wales you'll find a branch of at least one of the big four: *National Westminster*, *Barclays*, *Midland* and *Lloyds*, the latter being the least common. As a general rule, **opening hours** are Monday to Friday 9.30am to 3.30pm, though branches in larger towns and cities are often open an hour later in the afternooons and on Saturday morning. Outside banking hours, you're best advised to make your way to a **bureau de change**, found in most city centres, often at train stations or airports; try to avoid changing money or cheques in hotels, where the rates are normally the poorest on offer.

If, as a foreign visitor, you run out of money, or there is some kind of emergency, the quickest way to get **money sent out** is to get in touch with your bank at home and arrange for them to wire the cash to the nearest bank. You can do the same thing through *Thomas Cook* or *American Express* if there is a branch nearby (see box). Americans and Canadians can also have cash sent through *Western Union* (☎1-800/325-6000 in North America; ☎0800/833833 in the UK) and *Amex* card holders can use the

American Express MoneyGram (☎1-800/543-4080). Both companies' fees depend on the destination and the amount being transferred, but as an example, wiring $1000 to Wales will cost $75. The funds should be available for collection at the company's local office within minutes of being sent.

COSTS

Wales has become an expensive place to visit, though if you're coming from England, particularly London, prices will seem reasonable in comparison. The **minimum expenditure**, if you're camping and preparing most of your own food, would be in the region of £15 a day, rising to around £20–25 a day using the hostelling network, some public transport and grabbing the odd takeaway or meal out. Couples staying at budget B&Bs, eating at unpretentious restaurants and visiting a fair number of tourist attractions are looking at around £30–40 each per day – if you're renting a car, staying in comfortable B&Bs or hotels and eating well, you should reckon on at least £50 a day. Single travellers should budget on spending around sixty percent of what a couple would spend, mainly because single rooms tend to cost more than half a double. For more detail on the cost of accommodation, transport and eating, see the relevant sections below.

YOUTH AND STUDENT DISCOUNTS

Various official and quasi-official youth/student ID cards are widely available and most will pay for themselves in savings pretty soon. Full-time students over the age of 16 are eligible for the **International Student ID Card** (**ISIC**), which entitles the bearer to special fares on local transport, and discounts at museums, theatres and other attractions; for Americans and Canadians there's also a health benefit (see below). The card costs £5 or the local equivalent, and is available from branches of *Council Travel and Travel CUTS* around the world (see p.9).

The only requirement for a **Go-25 Card** is that you are aged 25 or younger; it costs a pound (or equivalent) less than the ISIC and carries the same benefits. It can be purchased through *Council Travel* in the US, *Hostelling International* in Canada and *STA* worldwide. A university photo ID might open some doors, too.

AMERICAN EXPRESS OFFICES

American Express only operates one office in Wales; also listed are the most convenient English offices.

Cardiff, 3 Queen St, CF1 4AF (☎01222/668858 or 666216).

Bristol, 74 Queens Rd, Clifton BS8 1QU (☎0117/9750750 or 9750751).

Chester, 23 St Werburgh St, CH1 2EQ (☎01244/311145).

London, 445 Oxford St, W1 1DA (☎0171/495 8891).

Shrewsbury, 27 Claremont St, SY1 1QG (☎01743/236387 or 356385).

THOMAS COOK OFFICES

Cardiff, 16 Queen St, CF1 4UW (☎01222/224886).

Cwmbran, 18 South Walk, NP44 1PU (☎01633/869416).

Llandudno, 51 Mostyn St, LL30 2NN (☎01492/860957).

Newport, 144 Commercial St, NP9 1LN (☎01633/256548).

Pontypridd, 109 Taff St, CF37 4UP (☎01443/486161).

Swansea, 3 Union St, SA1 1PJ (☎01792/464311.

Wrexham, 20–21 Hope St, LL11 1BG (☎01978/263170).

INSURANCE AND HEALTH

Wherever you're travelling from, it's a good idea to have some kind of travel insurance to cover you for loss of possessions and money, as well as the cost of any medical and dental treatment. If you're visiting from elsewhere in Britain, you may well be covered by your existing home contents policy, but should you need extra cover, *Endsleigh* is about the cheapest British insurer, offering a month's cover for around £25, and *Frizzell* **and** *Columbus* **are also good value. Whatever your policy, if you have anything stolen, get a copy of the police report, as this is essential to substantiate your claim.**

US and Canadian citizens should also carefully check their insurance policies before taking out a new one. You may discover that you're already covered for medical and other losses while abroad. **Canadian provincial health plans** typically provide some overseas medical coverage, although they are unlikely to pick up the full tab in the event of a mishap. Holders of official **student/teacher/youth cards** (see p.16) are entitled to accident coverage and hospital inpatient benefits – the annual membership is far less than the cost of comparable insurance. **Students** may also find that their student health coverage extends during the vacations and for one term beyond the date of last enrolment. Bank and credit cards (particularly *American Express*) often provide certain levels of medical or other insurance, and travel insurance may also be included if you use a major credit or charge card to pay for your trip. **Homeowners' or renters'** insurance often cov-

TRAVEL INSURANCE COMPANIES

In the UK

Columbus ☎0171/375 0011.
Endsleigh ☎0171/436 4451.

Frizzell ☎01202/292333.

In North America

Access America ☎1-800/284-8300.
Carefree Travel Insurance ☎1-800/323-3149.
Desjardins Travel Insurance – Canada only ☎1-800/463-7830.
International Student Insurance Service

(**ISIS**) – sold by *STA Travel* ☎1-800/777-0112.
Travel Assistance International ☎1-800/821-2828.
Travel Guard ☎1-800/826-1300.
Travel Insurance Services ☎1-800/937-1387.

In Australia and New Zealand

AFTA ☎02/956 4800.
Cover-More ☎02-9202 8000 or 1-800/251 881.

Ready Plan ☎1-800/337 462.
UTAG ☎1-800/809 462.

ers theft or loss of documents, money and valuables while overseas.

After exhausting the possibilities above, you might want to contact a specialist **travel insurance** company; your travel agent can usually recommend one, or see the box above.

The best **premiums** are usually to be had through student/youth travel agencies – *ISIS* policies, for example, cost $48–69 for fifteen days (depending on level of coverage), $80–105 for a month, $149–207 for two months, $510–700 for a year. If you're planning to do any "dangerous sports" (skiing, mountaineering, etc.), be sure to ask whether these activities are covered, as some companies levy a surcharge.

Most North American travel policies apply only to items lost, stolen or damaged while in the custody of an identifiable, responsible third party – hotel porter, airline, luggage consignment, etc. Even in these cases you will have to contact the local police within a certain time limit to have a complete report made out so that your insurer can process the claim.

Travel insurance policies in **Australia and New Zealand** tend to be put together by the airlines and travel agent groups such as *UTAG*, *AFTA*, *Cover-More* and *Ready Plan* in conjunction with insurance companies. They are all similar in premium and coverage, although *Ready Plan* gives the best value. A typical policy for the UK will cost: A$190/NZ$220 for one month,

A$270/NZ$320 for two months and A$330/NZ$400 for three months.

HEALTH

No vaccinations are required for entry into Britain. Citizens of all EU countries are entitled to free medical **treatment** at National Health Service hospitals; citizens of other countries are charged for all medical services except those administered by accident and emergency units at National Health Service hospitals. Thus a US citizen who has been hit by a car would not be charged if the injuries simply required stitching and setting in the emergency unit, but would be if admission to a hospital ward were necessary. Health insurance is therefore strongly advised for all non-EU nationals.

Pharmacists can dispense only a limited range of drugs without a doctor's prescription. Most pharmacies are open standard shop hours, though in large towns some may stay open as late as 10pm – local newspapers carry lists of late-opening pharmacies. Doctor's surgeries tend to be open from about 9am to noon and then for a couple of hours in the evenings; outside surgery hours, you can turn up at the casualty department of the local hospital for complaints that require immediate attention – unless it's an **emergency**, in which case ring for an ambulance on ☎999.

EMERGENCIES AND THE POLICE

As in any other country, Wales' major towns have their dangerous spots, but these tend to be inner-city housing estates where no tourist has any reason to be. The chief risk on the streets – though still minimal – is pickpocketing, so carry only as much money as you need, and keep all bags and pockets fastened. Should you have anything stolen or be involved in an incident that requires reporting, go to the local police station; the ☎999 number should only be used in emergencies.

Although the traditional image of the friendly British "Bobby" has become tarnished by stories of corruption and crooked dealings, the **police** continue to be approachable and helpful. If you're lost in a major town, asking a police officer is generally the quickest way to get help – alternatively, you could ask a **traffic warden**, a much-maligned species of law enforcer responsible for parking restrictions and other vehicle-related matters. They're distinguishable by their flat caps with a yellow band, and by the fact that they are generally armed with a book of parking-fine tickets; police officers on street duty wear a distinctive domed hat with a silver top, and are generally armed with just a truncheon.

EMERGENCIES

For **Police** (*heddlu*), **Fire Brigade** (*brigad dan*), **Ambulance** (*ambiwlans*) and, in certain areas, **Mountain Rescue** or **Coastguard** (*gwyliwr y glaaunn*), dial ☎999.

INFORMATION AND MAPS

If you want to do a bit of research before arriving in Britain, contact the British Tourist Authority (BTA) in your country – the addresses are given in the box on p.20. The BTA will send you a wealth of free literature, some of it just rose-tinted advertising copy, but much of it extremely useful – especially the maps, city guides and event calendars. If you want more hard facts on a particular area, you should approach the Wales Tourist Board offices, also listed overleaf. In general, they are helpful and will provide glossy brochures worth scanning before you set out.

TOURIST OFFICES

Tourist offices (usually called Tourist Information Centres) exist in virtually every Welsh town – you'll find their phone numbers and opening hours in the relevant sections of the *Guide*. The average opening hours are much the same as standard shop hours, with the difference that in

BRITISH TOURIST AUTHORITY HEAD OFFICES

Australia 210 Clarence St, Floor 4, Sydney, NSW 2000 (☎02/9267 4555).

Canada 111 Avenue Rd, Suite 450, Toronto, Ontario M5R 3J8 (☎416/ 961-8124).

Ireland 18–19 College Green, Dublin 2 (☎01/670 8000).

New Zealand Suite 305, Floor 3, Dilworth Building, corner Customs and Queen streets, Auckland (☎09/303 1446).

USA Wales Representative, 551 Fifth Ave, Suite 701, New York, NY 10176 (☎1-800/462-2748 or 212/986-2200 or 2266).

WALES TOURIST BOARD OFFICES

Written requests for information should be sent to: *WTB*, Dept WM1, Davis St, Cardiff CF1 2FU (☎01222/475226).

Mid Wales Tourism, The Station, Machynlleth SY20 8TG (☎01654/702653).

North Wales Tourism, 77 Conway Rd, Colwyn Bay LL29 7BL (☎01492/531731).

Tourism South and West Wales, Charter Court, Phoenix Way, Enterprise Park, Swansea SA7 9DB (☎01792/781212).

Tourism South and West Wales, Old Bridge, Haverfordwest, Pembrokeshire SA62 2EZ (☎01437/766330).

Wales Information Bureau, British Travel Centre, 12 Regent St, London SW1Y 4PQ (no telephone enquiries).

Wales Tourist Board, Head Office, Brunel House, 2 Fitzalan Rd, Cardiff CF2 1UY (☎01222/499909).

summer they'll often be open on a Sunday and for a couple of hours after the shops have closed on weekdays; opening hours are generally shorter in winter, and in more remote areas the office may well be closed altogether. All centres offer information on accommodation (which they can often book – see p.28), local public transport, attractions and restaurants, as well as town and regional maps. In many cases all of this is free, but a growing number of offices make a small charge for their accommodation list or the town guide with accompanying street plan.

Areas designated as National Parks (the Brecon Beacons, Pembrokeshire Coast and Snowdonia) also have a fair sprinkling of **National Park Information Centres**, which are generally more expert in giving guidance on local walks and outdoor pursuits.

MAPS

Most bookshops will have a good selection of **maps of Wales** and Britain; the best can be found in specialist travel bookshops (see oppo-

WALES ONLINE

A growing amount of useful information about Wales can be found on the **Internet**. Obviously, the following list of recommended addresses won't remain current for long, but the network Wales page (http://www.network.wales.org/index.html) gives quick access to most.

Centre for Alternative Technology
http://www.foe.co.uk/cat
Extensive home pages from the pioneering ecological site, with the opportunity to navigate Spaceship earth through the problems of pollution and the environment.

National Trust
http://www.ukindex.co.uk/nationaltrust/
Members' handbook and general information.

This Week
http://www.thisweek.wales.com
The site of *This Week Wales* magazine (see p.37).

Surfers Against Sewage
http://www.sas.org.uk
General information from the hip environmental group, with news reports (much on the *Sea Empress*), a medical database and gruesome photos of besmirched British beaches.

Welsh Tourist Board
http://www.tourism.wales.gov.uk
A rather sanitized Tourist Board site, covering regions, places to visit and events, with a load of small pictures and audio files of vital phrases.

MAP OUTLETS

AUSTRALIA AND NEW ZEALAND

Bowyangs, 372 Little Burke St, Melbourne (☎03/9670 4383).

The Map Shop, 16a Peel St, Adelaide (☎08/8231 2033).

Perth Map Centre, 891 Hay St, Perth (☎08/9322 5733).

Specialty Maps, 58 Albert St, Auckland (☎09/307 2217).

Travel Bookshop, 20 Bridge St, Sydney (☎02/9241 3554).

CANADA

Open Air Books and Maps, 25 Toronto St, Toronto, ON M5R 2C1 (☎416/363-0719).

Ulysses Travel Bookshop, 4176 St-Denis, Montréal (☎514/289-0993).

World Wide Books and Maps, 1247 Granville St, Vancouver, BC V6Z 1E4 (☎604/687-3320).

USA

The Book Passage, 51 Tamal Vista Drive, Corte Madera, CA 94925 (☎415/927-0906).

British Travel Bookshop, 551 Fifth Ave, New York, NY 10176 (☎1-800/448-3039 or 212/490-6688).

The Complete Traveler Bookstore, 199 Madison Ave, New York, NY 10016 (☎212/685-9007); 3207 Fillmore St, San Francisco, CA 92123 (☎415/923-1511).

Forsyth Travel Library, 9154 W 57th St, Shawnee Mission, KS 66201 (☎1-800/367-7984).

Map Link Inc, 25 E Mason St, Santa Barbara, CA 93101 (☎805/965-4402).

Phileas Fogg's Books & Maps, #87 Stanford Shopping Center, Palo Alto, CA 94304 (☎1-800/233-FOGG in California; ☎1-800/533-FOGG elsewhere in US).

Rand McNally,* 444 N Michigan Ave, Chicago, IL 60611 (☎312/321-1751); 150 E 52nd St, New York, NY 10022 (☎212/758-7488); 595 Market St, San Francisco, CA 94105 (☎415/777-3131); 1201 Connecticut Ave NW, Washington, DC 20003 (☎202/223-6751).

Sierra Club Bookstore, 730 Polk St, San Francisco, CA 94109 (☎415/923-5500).

Travel Books & Language Center, 4931 Cordell Ave, Bethesda, MD 20814 (☎1-800/220-2665).

Traveler's Bookstore, 22 W 52nd St, New York, NY 10019 (☎212/664-0995).

*For other locations, or for maps by **mail order**, call ☎1-800/333-0136 (ext 2111).*

ENGLAND AND SCOTLAND

Daunt Books, 83 Marylebone High St, London W1 (☎0171/224 2295).

John Smith and Sons, 57–61 St Vincent St, Glasgow G2 5TB (☎0141/221 7472).

National Map Centre, 22–24 Caxton St, London SW1 (☎0171/222 4945).

Stanfords,* 12–14 Long Acre, London WC2 (☎0171/836 1321); 52 Grosvenor Gardens, London SW1W 0AG; 156 Regent St, London W1R 5TA.

The Travel Bookshop, 13–15 Blenheim Crescent, London W11 2EE (☎0171/229 5260).

*For **mail order** maps, call the Long Acre branch.*

WALES

H K Lockyer Map Shop, 5a Monk St, Abergavenny, Gwent (☎01873/855825).

Lears, 13–17 Royal Arcade, Cardiff (☎01222/395036).

Uplands Bookshop, 27 Uplands Crescent, Swansea (☎01792/470195).

IRELAND

Easons Bookshop, 40 O'Connell St, Dublin 1 (☎01/873 3811).

Fred Hanna's Bookshop, 27–29 Nassau St, Dublin 2 (☎01/677 1255).

Hodges Figgis Bookshop, 56–58 Dawson St, Dublin 2 (☎01/677 4754).

Waterstone's, Queens Building, 8 Royal Ave, Belfast BT1 1DA (☎01232/247355).

---

site). Of the many North American outlets, the *British Travel Bookshop* in New York, in particular, stocks a phenomenal array of maps. *Rand McNally* is also a good bet, with 24 stores nationwide.

Virtually every service station in Britain stocks one or more of the large-format **road atlases** produced by the *AA*, *RAC*, *Collins* and *Ordnance Survey* and others, which cover all of Britain at around three miles to one inch and include larger-scale plans of major towns. The best of these is the Ordnance Survey road atlas which handily uses the same grid reference system as their accurate and detailed folding maps such as the one inch to four mile Travelmaster 7, covering Wales and the West Midlands.

If you want more detail, the most comprehensive maps are again produced by the **Ordnance Survey**, a series renowned for its accuracy and clarity. The 204 maps in its 1:50,000 (a little over one inch:one mile) *Landranger* series cover the whole of Britain in enough detail to be useful for most walkers. The 1:25,000 *Pathfinder* series is more detailed, but most serious hikers favour of the same-scale *Outdoor Leisure* maps which cover only the most frequently walked areas, each sensibly designed to take in a specific area, and even showing fencelines and field boundaries to aid navigation. There are seven *Outdoor Leisure* maps for Wales, three covering Snowdonia from the north coast down to Cadair Idris, two large double-sided ones spanning the Brecon Beacons and Black Mountains, and another two charting Pembrokeshire. *OS* maps are widely available in bookshops, but in any walking district of Wales you can be sure to find the relevant maps on sale locally.

GETTING AROUND

The large cities and densely populated valleys of south Wales support comprehensive train and bus networks, but the more thinly populated areas of mid- and north Wales have to make do with skeletal services. That said, it is rare to find somewhere that isn't reached by an occasional bus, even if it also picks up the local mail. As elsewhere in Britain, the public transport system has suffered cuts over recent years and fares on what services remain are some of the highest in Europe. The present government's pro-car policies have seen new roads carved through the countryside regardless of the environmental cost. However, this does mean that getting about by car is easy, and unless you are planning to spend all your time in Cardiff and Swansea, sheep are likely to be a more persistent problem than other road users.

As a basic rule, if you're using public transport make sure you're aware of all the passes and special deals on offer; and if you're driving, take the more scenic backroads unless you're in a real hurry. Cyclists should skip to the "Outdoor pursuits" section (p.40).

TRAINS

Due to the lack of investment and the government's obsession with privatization, **rail** travel in Wales, and throughout Britain, has been in decline over the past decade. The privatization process is causing great uncertainty and confusion on the railways, with the track and stations now being owned by *Railtrack*, and the trains and services being run by a tangle of private comanies. The logo and name of the rump state company **British Rail** (*BR*), is rarely seen these days except on tickets, which at the time of going to press were still issued by *BR*.

Services in Wales cover all the main cities and an almost random selection of rural towns and wayside halts. The two **major lines** are at opposite ends of the country and connected only by routes though England. In the north, long-distance and local services ply the coastal strip from Chester in England through Conwy, Bangor and on to Holyhead for the Irish ferries. Along the south coast, Newport, Cardiff and Swansea are joined by a fairly fast service extending to London in the east and Fishguard (where you can also pick up boats to Ireland) in the west. The remainder of the routes support an infrequent service, occasionally replaced by buses on Sunday. For all its inconveniences though, the train is one of the best ways to get around Wales: the views are superb and the engineering often impressive. In addition to the mainline network, there are over a dozen volunteer-run train lines (see box on p.25) carrying these two qualities to greater heights. All run steam trains, most on narrow-gauge tracks and predominantly as tourist attractions; the best of them are exceptional.

You can buy **tickets** for trains at stations or from major travel agents – details of the **different types of fare** available are given on p.4, "Getting there from the UK and Europe". For busy long-distance journeys, you can **reserve a seat** for £2 – though this is seldom necessary, even on the main north and south coast routes. At many smaller stations, the ticket offices are closed at weekends, and at some rural halts they've shut for good. In these instances there's sometimes a vending machine on the platform. If there isn't a machine, you can buy your ticket on board – but if you've boarded at a station with a machine or ticket office and haven't bought a ticket, you're liable for an on-the-spot fine of £10.

RAIL PASSES

If Wales is only a part of your wider British travels, foreign visitors might find a **BritRail Pass** a wise investment. The standard pass, which must be bought before you enter the country, is available from *BritRail Travel International* (see box overleaf) and many specialist tour operators outside Britain (see pp. 11 & 13). It gives unlimited travel in England, Scotland and Wales for eight days ($235, Can$289), fifteen days ($365, Can$430), 22 days ($465, Can$535) or a month ($545, Can$625). The **BritRail Flexipass** is good for travel four days out of a month ($199, Can$239), eight days out of a month ($280, Can$349) or fifteen days out of a month ($425, Can$525). Note that with both these passes there are discounts of 10–15 percent

for those under 26 (*BritRail Youth* passes) – the *Flexipass* has a special fifteen days out of two months rate for under-26s ($340, Can$420) –and that one child can travel free on each adult pass. **Australians** and **New Zealanders** can buy *BritRail* passes from branches of *Thomas Cook*: the eight-day version costs A$280/NZ$330, fifteen days A$395/NZ$480, 22 days A$555/NZ$660, and a month A$605/NZ$725; the *BritRail Flexipass* is A$240/NZ$290 for four days out of a month, A$345/NZ$410 for eight days and A$550/NZ$660 for fifteen days. Young people get a twenty-percent discount.

If you are planning to travel widely around Europe by train, then it may be worth while buying a **Eurail Pass** which allows unlimited free train travel in the UK and sixteen other countries. The pass is normally purchased before arrival in Europe but also available from *French Railways*, 179 Piccadilly, London W1 (☎0990/300003) if you can prove foreign residence and have been in Europe for less than six months. The **Eurail Youthpass** (for under-26s) costs £327 (or foreign equivalent) for fifteen days, £468 for one month or £625 for two months; if you're 26 or over you'll have to buy a first-class pass, available in fifteen-day (£409), 21-day (£531), one-month ($798), two-month (£899) and three-month (£1150) increments. You stand a better chance of getting your money's worth out of a **Eurail Flexipass**, which is valid for a certain number of travel days in a two-month period. This, too, comes in under-26/first-class versions: ten days £343/483 and fifteen days £461/636.

There are a number of passes and discount cards available only in Britain itself, to foreign visitors and British nationals alike, from main train stations and some travel agents. The **All-Line Rail Rover** gives unlimited travel on the entire network throughout England, Scotland and Wales for seven (£240) or fourteen consecutive days (£390). Four train passes cover the Welsh lines specifically, the most comprehensive being the **Freedom of Wales** ticket, allowing travel throughout Wales – and the connecting services through England – for a period of seven days (£54 June–Sept; £49 Oct–May). Additional benefits are discounts on some of the narrow-gauge railways and a flat fare of £1 on certain long-distance buses.

The **North and Mid-Wales Rover**, available for seven days (£36) or three days out of seven (£23), covers Welsh routes north of Aberystwyth and the English lines linking them. Tickets also allow free travel on the Ffestiniog Railway (see box

RAIL OFFICES AND AGENCIES ABROAD

NORTH AMERICA

BritRail Travel International, 1500 Broadway, New York, NY 10036 (☎1-800/677-8585).

Canadian Reservations Centre, 2087 Dundas East, Suite 105, Mississauga, ON L4X 1M2 (☎1-800/361-725).

CIE Tours International, 108 Ridgedale Ave, PO Box 2355, Morristown, NJ 07962 (☎1-800/243-7687).

CIT Tours, 342 Madison Ave, Suite 207, New York, NY 10173 (☎1-800/223-7987).

Rail Europe, 226–230 Westchester Ave, White Plains, NY 10604 (☎1-800/438-7245 or 914/682-2999). Specializes in *Eurail* and also sells the widest range of regional passes.

AUSTRALIA AND NEW ZEALAND

CIT, 123 Clarence St, Sydney (☎02/9299 4754); offices in Melbourne, Brisbane, Adelaide and Perth. *No NZ office; all enquiries go through the Australian offices.*

Thomas Cook World Rail *Australia:* ☎1-800/422 747; *New Zealand:* ☎09/263 7260.

opposite) and almost all buses in the region. The same region is covered by the **North and Mid-Wales Day Ranger** (£15.50), and a slightly smaller one by the **North Wales Day Ranger** (£11), both valid after 9.30am weekdays and all day at weekends. There's no special pass for south Wales.

If a rail pass doesn't seem economical, you may be eligible for one of *BR*'s discount cards: the **Young Person's Railcard** costs £16, is valid for a year, and gives 33 percent reductions on all standard *Saver* and *SuperSaver* fares to full-time students and those from sixteen to 25 years. A **Senior Citizens' Railcard**, also £16 and offering 33 percent reductions, is available to those aged sixty or over. The **Family Railcard** costs £20, and gives discounts of between 20 and 33 percent for up to four adults travelling with children. It also allows up to four children aged five to fifteen to travel anywhere in Britain for a flat fare of £2 each (which includes a seat reservation).

STEAM RAILWAYS

With the rising demand for quarried stone in the nineteenth century, quarry and mine owners were forced to find more economical ways than packhorses to get their products to market, but in the steep, tortuous valleys of Snowdonia standard-gauge train tracks proved too unwieldy. The solution was rails of sometimes less than a foot apart, plied by steam engines and dinky rolling stock. The charm of these railways was too much for train enthusiasts, and long after the decline of the quarries, they banded together to restore abandoned lines and locos. Most lines are still largely run by volunteers who have also started up new services along unused sections of standard-gauge

bed. All the lines run steam engines alongside the more economical diesels which tend to predominate during the off-season.

Although run primarily as tourist attractions, several of the **steam railways** operate as public transport and are detailed as such in the text. Tickets are generally sold separately, but eight railways – *The Great Little Trains of Wales* (designated by "GLT" in the box opposite) – offer a *Wanderer Ticket*, allowing either four days' travel within an eight-day period (£25), or eight days in fifteen (£32). Some discounts are also available with main line rail passes (see box above). The ticket is valid all year, but since services are limited outside the summer season it may only be worthwhile from April to October and over Christmas.

BUSES AND COACHES

With the skeletal nature of the train system in Wales, you're going to find yourself relying on buses which provide a much deeper penetration into the countryside. There are a limited number of inter-town buses (known as "**coaches**" in Britain) run by **National Express** (see "Getting there from the UK and Europe"), but for travel within Wales you'll be using **local bus services** run by a bewildering array of companies. In many cases, timetables and routes are well integrated, but it is increasingly the case that private companies compete with each other on the busiest routes, leaving the far-flung spots neglected. Though services are more expensive and less frequent in the rural areas, there are very few places without any service even if it is only a private minibus on market day or one of the "**postbuses**" (see p.26) that also pick up mail.

WALES' STEAM RAILWAYS

The steam railways are listed north to south

Welsh Highland Railway, Caernarfon (☎01766/512340). Not to be confused with the line of the same name in Porthmadog, this new line, along an old trackbed, opens in 1997 and with eventually link Caernarfon to Porthmadog via Beddgelert, 25 miles in all. 24-inch gauge. (See p.362).

Llanberis Lake Railway, Llanberis (☎01286/870549). A short waterside section of the former slate line to Port Dinorwig on the Menai Strait. 24-inch gauge. GLT. (See p.327).

Snowdon Mountain Railway, Llanberis (☎01286/870223). Wales' only rack-and-pinion railway, climbing from Llanberis to the summit café and post office atop Snowdon. 31.5-inch gauge. (See p.332).

Ffestiniog Railway, Porthmadog (☎01766/512340). Wonderful thirteen-mile twisting climb from Porthmadog through the Vale of Ffestiniog to the slate mining town of Blaenau Ffestiniog. Links two standard gauge lines. 23.5-inch gauge. GLT. (See p.345).

Welsh Highland Railway, Porthmadog (☎01766/513402). Flat three-quarter-mile section of what was once the longest and one of the least profitable narrow-gauge lines in Wales. 24-inch gauge. GLT. (See p.345).

Llangollen Railway, Llangollen (☎01978/860951). Rejuvenated six-mile section of the former Ruabon–Barmouth line, running through a gorge-like section of the Dee Valley. Standard 56.5-inch gauge. (See p.245).

Bala Lake Railway, Bala (☎01678/540666). Four-mile lakeside run using the bed of the former Corwen–Barmouth standard-gauge line. 24-inch gauge. GLT. (See p.254).

Talyllyn Railway, Tywyn (☎01654/710472). Slow-climbing one-time quarry line, revived in 1951. The original and one of the best of the volunteer-restored lines, running seven miles at the foot of Cadair Idris. 27-inch gauge. GLT. (See p.287).

Welshpool and Llanfair Railway, Llanfair Caereinion (☎01938/810441). An eight-mile-long descent to the River Banwy with locos used by the German army and a West Indian sugar plantation. 30-inch gauge. GLT. (See p.235).

Corris Railway, near Machynlleth (☎01654/761624). Recently restarted former slate railway using just over half a mile of track but with the rights to extend most of the two miles to the *Centre for Alternative Technology*. 27-inch gauge. (See p.285).

Fairbourne Railway, Fairbourne (☎01341/250362). Diminutive former tramway which brought building materials for the construction of Fairbourne. Linked to the passenger ferry to Barmouth. 12-inch gauge. (See p.291).

Vale of Rheidol Railway, Aberystwyth (☎01970/625819). Stunning twelve-mile run intended for tourists intent on seeing Devil's Bridge. BR's only narrow-gauge and last steam line until it was sold off in 1988. 13.5-inch gauge. GLT. (See p.276).

Teifi Valley Railway, near Newcastle Emlyn (☎01559/371077). A short strip of narrow gauge track along a former standard-gauge route. 23-inch gauge. (See p.267).

Brecon Mountain Railway, Merthyr Tydfil (☎01685/722988). Two-mile narrow-gauge line mostly on the bed of the Brecon and Merthyr Railway which closed in 1963. 24-inch gauge. GLT. (See p.210).

In the **northern** half of Wales, Llandudno-based *Crosville Cymru Wales* (☎01492/596969, in Bangor ☎01248/370236, and in Aberystwyth ☎01970/617951) runs the majority of local services as well as a few scenic long-distance runs. Its network is extensive enough that it might be worth buying a **Day Rover ticket** (£5.70), purchased on the bus and valid for unlimited travel on all Crosville buses except the #701 or #702 services to Swansea and Cardiff. Greater savings can be made with the **Weekly Rover** (£19.50) valid throughout the network for seven days. Visitors concentrating on a smaller area may find use for the **Gwynedd Rover** (£4.20) run by the Caernarfon-based *Bws Gwynedd* (☎01286/679535). Both *Crosville Cymru* and *Bws Gwynedd* push down into mid-Wales where they're joined by services in Ceredigion, Carmarthenshire and Pembrokeshire, which jointly operate the **Bws Dyfed Rover ticket** (☎01267/231817 in

Carmarthen; ☎01437/764551 in Haverfordwest, and ☎01545/570382 in New Quay) charged at £4 for a day, £18 for one week.

In the **southern** section of the country the system is far less unified and only a couple of passes are likely to be of much use. Services west of Cardiff and south of Carmarthen are mostly run by the Swansea-based *SWT* (☎01792/580580) which offers the one-day **Roverbus** pass (£4.50), restricted to Swansea and the Gower, and the weekly **Master Rider** (£13.85) which covers the whole *SWT* network. *Bws Caerdydd* (☎01222/396521), the major company serving Cardiff and the Vale of Glamorgan, offers a wide range of day, evening and weekly tickets; prices depend on the number of zones involved. Perhaps the most useful is the weekly **Cardiff and Penarth** ticket (£8.15) which covers all the local sights. For details of more UK-wide bus passes, see "Getting there from the UK and Europe", p.5. All regions have their own detailed local **timetable**, easily obtained from tourist offices, libraries and stations.

POSTBUSES

In parts of west and mid-Wales, bus services and mail delivery are combined in a network of **postbuses** which cover some of the most remote and beautiful Welsh regions. Few postbuses service destinations of interest to most visitors, but as a way of seeing quiet countryside at low cost (comparable with other bus fares for similar distances) and gaining a small insight into life in rural Wales they can't be beaten. There are currently nineteen postbus routes – the northernmost based at Machynlleth and the most southerly running from Pembroke Dock – usually plied by a morning delivery and an afternoon collection run. Fares are very reasonable, similar to normal bus fares.

For those on a budget who fancy travelling in a group, **Hairy Hog Backpacker Adventures**, Unit 4, Block 1, Fromehall Mill, Lodgemore Lane, Stroud, Gloucestershire GL5 3EH (☎ & fax 01453/751009) offers three-day (£69) and six-day (£120) **minibus tours** around Wales' highlights. Itineraries are flexible, but most focus on the core territory of the Brecon Beacons and Snowdonia, extending out into Pembrokeshire and Anglesey on the longer trips. Beds in **hostels** are booked in advance but not included in the cost.

DRIVING

If you want to cover a lot of the countryside in a short time, or just want more flexibility, you'll need your own transport. England's busy but comprehensive motorway system means that getting to Wales is fairly straighforward, but over the border you'll find there's just one **motorway**: the M4 from London, which crosses into Wales over the Severn Bridge and skirts Newport, Cardiff and Bridgend before petering out just beyond Swansea. An extensive network of dual carriageways and good quality A roads links the major centres but in rural areas you'll often find yourself on steep, winding, single-track (but usually asphalt) lanes with passing places. In very remote areas, you sometimes still have to open gates designed to keep sheep from straying.

In order to **drive in Britain**, you must have a current **driving licence**; foreign nationals will need to supplement this with an **international driving permit**, available from national motoring organizations for a small fee. If you're bringing your own vehicle into the country you should also carry vehicle registration or ownership documents at all times. Furthermore, you must be adequately **insured**, so be sure to check your existing policy.

As in the rest of the UK, you **drive on the left** in Wales, and it can lead to a few tense days of acclimatization for foreign drivers. **Speed limits** are 30–40mph (50–65kph) in built-up areas, 70mph (110kph) on motorways (freeways) and dual carriageways, and 50mph (80kph) on most other roads. As a rule, assume that in any area with street lighting the speed limit is 30mph (50kph) unless stated otherwise. **Fuel** is expensive in comparison with North American prices – leaded four-star petrol (gas) costs in the region of £2.80 per English gallon (4.56 litres), unleaded and diesel slightly less. Prices are increasingly quoted by the litre (around 43–65p/litre) and are generally lowest in the suburbs of cities, where competition is fiercest, and highest at motorway service stations and in remote rural areas.

The *Automobile Association*, the *Royal Automobile Club* and *National Breakdown* all operate 24-hour emergency **breakdown** services. The *AA* and *RAC* also provide many other motoring services, as well as a reciprocal arrangement for free assistance, through many overseas motoring organizations – check the situation with yours before setting out. On motorways the *AA* and *RAC* can be called from roadside booths; elsewhere

MOTORING ORGANIZATIONS

Automobile Association, Fanum House, Basingstoke, Hants RG21 4EA (☎01256/20123).
Royal Automobile Club, PO Box 100, RAC House, 7 Bartlett St, S Croydon CR2 6XW (☎0181/686 0088).
American Automobile Association (AAA), 4100 E Arkansas Ave, Denver, CO 80222 (☎1-800/222-4357).

Canadian Automobile Association. *Each region has its own club – check the phone book for the local address and phone number.*
Australian Automobile Association, 212 Northbourne Ave, Canberra, ACT 2601 (☎06/6247 7311).
New Zealand Automobile Association, PO Box 1794, Wellington (☎04/473 8738).

CAR RENTAL FIRMS

NORTH AMERICA
Alamo ☎1-800/522-9696
Avis ☎1-800/331-1084
Budget ☎1-800/527-0700
Europe by Car ☎1-800/223-1516
Hertz ☎1-800/654-3001
Holiday Autos ☎1-800/442-7737
National Car Rental ☎1-800/CAR-RENT

AUSTRALIA
Avis ☎1-800/225 533
Budget ☎13 2848
Hertz ☎13 3039
Renault Eurodrive ☎02/9299 3344

NEW ZEALAND
Avis ☎09/579 5231
Budget ☎09/375 2220
Fly and Drive Holidays ☎09/529 3790
Hertz ☎09/309 0989

UK
Avis ☎0181/848 8733
Eurodollar ☎01895/233300
Europcar ☎0345/222525
Hertz ☎0990/996699
Holiday Autos ☎0990/300400

ring ☎0800/887766 for the *AA*, ☎0800/828282 for the *RAC* or ☎0800/400600 for *National Breakdown* (calls are free). You can ring these emergency numbers even if you are not a member, although a substantial fee will be charged.

CAR AND MOTORBIKE RENTAL

Compared to rates in North America, **car rental** in Britain is expensive, and, you'll probably find it cheaper to arrange things in advance through one of the multinational chains, or opt for a fly-drive deal. If you do rent a car from a company in Britain, the least you can expect to pay is around £130 a week, which is the rate for a small hatchback from *Holiday Autos*, the most competitive company; reckon on paying £40 a day direct from one of the multinationals, £5 or so less at a local firm. Rental agencies prefer you to pay with a credit card; otherwise you may have to leave a deposit of at least £100. There are very few automatics at the lower end of the price scale – if you want one, you should book well ahead. To rent a car you need to show your driving licence: few companies will rent to drivers with less than one year's experience and most will only rent to people between 21 and seventy years of age.

Motorbike rental is ludicrously expensive, at around £45 a day/£200 a week for a 500cc machine, and around £80/£300 for a one-litre tourer, including everything from insurance to helmets and luggage boxes. If you are travelling to Wales via London, it may be worth trying one of the companies that rent out ex-despatch bikes; for addresses, check the weekly newspaper *Motor Cycle News*, which can also be useful for locating spare parts.

ACCOMMODATION

Welsh tourist accommodation has changed notably in recent decades, from the fearsome guest houses for English holiday-makers in the postwar years, to top-rank international hotels, farmhouse accommodation, hostels and ubiquitous bed and breakfast (B&B) establishments. The change has been for the better, bringing a far greater variety, and considerably better standards, than ever before.

Wales has traditionally been a holiday centre for the millions of English who live within striking distance – particularly those in Birmingham and the Midlands or Manchester, Liverpool and the northwest. This is evident at some of the more faded, tackier seaside resorts in the shape of vast and ugly caravan parks and row upon row of tawdry guest houses. However, with the lower cost of the foreign package holiday, more English people are choosing to fly abroad for their fortnight of sun and sand, freeing up Wales – its spectacular countryside as much as its coastline – for a rapidly increasing number of international visitors.

HOTELS AND B&BS

The **Wales Tourist Board** (*WTB*) operates a grading scheme for **hotels** and **B&Bs**, using crown symbols. One crown indicates a simple, reasonably cheap place with all rooms having at least a washbasin, while anywhere boasting the maximum of five crowns will be luxurious, *en suite* accommodation. The crown grades are based on little more than the number of facilities and generally correspond with the price: a one- or two-crown establishment should cost £20–30 for a double room, a three-crown £30–50, four-crown £40–60 and five-crown anything above that. In addition to the crowns, however, an establishment can receive the badges of (in descending order) Highly Commended, Commended or Merit, which are a better reflection of the kind of service and general comfort you can expect.

The distinction between hotels and B&Bs is blurring all the time. A bad, fully fledged hotel (so-called because of its licensed status) can be vastly inferior to a similarly priced or even cheaper **B&B**, or **guesthouse**, as they're frequently known. This is especially the case amongst the growing army of **farmhouse B&Bs**, which quite often outstrip any hotel for the sheer warmth of welcome and quality of home cooking. B&Bs range from ordinary private houses with a couple of bedrooms set aside for paying guests and a dining room for a rudimentary breakfast, to rooms as well furnished as those in hotels costing twice as much, with delicious home-prepared breakfasts, and an informal hospitality that a larger place couldn't match.

The WTB produces a comprehensive *Farm Holidays* brochure, or consult the *Welsh Rarebits* and *Great Little Places* lists of top hotels, many of which are in old country mansions or rambling farmhouses. These brochures can be obtained free from Prince's Square, Montgomery, Powys SY15 6PZ (☎01686/668030, fax 668029), and there are complete lists of accommodation

---

ACCOMMODATION PRICE CODES

Throughout this guide, hotel and B&B accommodation is priced on a scale of ① to ⑨. Category ① only applies to youth hostels; for the rest, the number indicates the **lowest price** you could expect to pay per night for a **double room in high season**. The prices indicated by the codes are as follows:

① under £20	④ £40–50	⑦ £70–80
② £20–30	⑤ £50–60	⑧ £80–100
③ £30–40	⑥ £60–70	⑨ over £100

throughout Wales available from the *WTB* (see p20).

Official **tourist offices** will only ever give you lists of accommodation that has been "verified" by *WTB* inspectors, which does at least ensure that you shouldn't be short-changed. However, they can sometimes be reluctant to give information about places that haven't paid to advertise in the official local guide: if you don't see something suitable in the guide, don't be afraid to ask if there is anywhere else that matches your requirements for price and location. There are some wonderful establishments well outside of the official verification system; as far as possible we've mentioned such places in the text.

HOSTELS

The network of the **Youth Hostels Association** comprises some 45 properties in Wales, offering bunk-bed accommodation in single-sex dormitories or smaller rooms. A few of these places are spartan establishments of the sort traditionally associated with the wholesome, fresh-air ethic of the first hostels, but many have moved well away from this institutional ambience. Welsh hostels range from some remote, unheated barns in the wilds of mid-Wales and Snowdonia to more cosmopolitan, purpose-built centres in places such as Cardiff. The greatest concentration of hostels, by far, is in Snowdonia, with smaller clusters in Wales' other two National Parks, around the Pembrokeshire coast and in the Brecon Beacons. All cost under £10 a night per person. For a list of all Welsh *YHA* hostels, contact *YHA Wales/Cymru*, Floor 4, 1 Cathedral Rd, Cardiff CF1 9HA (☎01222/396766, fax 237817).

Membership of the *YHA*, which is open only to residents of England and Wales, costs £9.30 per year, £3.20 for under-18s, and can be obtained either by writing to the *YHA* (see box below) or in person at any *YHA* hostel. Members are issued with a directory of all *YHA* hostels and gain automatic membership of the hostelling associations of the sixty countries affiliated to the *International Youth Hostels Federation (IYHF)*. Foreign visitors who belong to any *IYHF* association correspondingly have membership of the *YHA*; if you aren't a member of such an organization, you can join the *IYHF* at any English or Welsh hostel for a £9.30 fee.

At any time of year it's best to **book your place** well in advance, and it's essential at Easter, Christmas and from May to August. Most hostels accept payment by *MasterCard* or *Visa*; if not, you should confirm your booking in writing, with payment, at least seven days before arrival. Bookings made less than seven days in advance will be held only until 6pm on the day of arrival. If you're tempted to turn up on the spur of the moment, bear in mind that very few hostels are open year-round, many are closed at least one day a week even in high season, and several have periods during which they take group bookings only. To give the full details of opening times within this guide would be impossibly unwieldy, so **always phone** – we've given the number for every hostel mentioned. Most hostels are closed from 10am to 5pm, with an 11pm curfew.

Independent hostels and **bunkhouses** – simple affairs close to the mountains designed for

---

YOUTH HOSTEL ASSOCIATIONS

Australia *Australian Youth Hostels Association*, Level 3, 10 Mallet St, Camperdown, Sydney (☎02/9565 1325).

Canada *Hostelling International/Canadian Hostelling Association*, Room 400, 205 Catherine St, Ottawa, ON K2P 1C3 (☎613/237-7884).

England and Wales *Youth Hostels Association* (*YHA*), Trevelyan House, 8 St Stephen's Hill, St Alban's, Herts AL1 2DY (☎01727/855215). *London shop and information office*: 14 Southampton St, London WC2E 7HY (☎0171/836 1036).

Ireland *Youth Hostel Association of Northern Ireland*, 2 Donegall Rd, Belfast BT12 5JN

(☎01232/324733); *An Oige*, 61 Mountjoy St, Dublin 7 (☎01/830 4555).

New Zealand *Youth Hostels Association of New Zealand*, PO Box 436, Christchurch 1 (☎03/799 9970).

Scotland *Scottish Youth Hostels Association*, 7 Glebe Crescent, Stirling FK8 2JA (☎01786/451181).

USA *Hostelling International/American Youth Hostels*, 733 15th St NW, Suite 840, PO Box 37613, Washington, DC 20013 (☎202/783-6161).

walkers, usually providing mattresses and occasionally bedding in communal dormitories – are becoming a more common feature in Wales and, where relevant, are mentioned in the text of the *Guide*.

CAMPING, CARAVANNING AND SELF-CATERING

There are hundreds of **campsites** in Wales, charging from £4 per tent per night to around £10 at the plushest sites, with amenities such as laundries, shops and sports facilities. Some *YHA* hostels (see p.29) have small campsites on their property, for which you'll pay half the indoor fee. In addition to these official sites, farmers may offer pitches for as little as £2 per night, but don't expect tiled bathrooms and hairdriers for this kind of money. Even farmers without a reserved camping area may let you pitch in a field if you ask first, and may charge you nothing for the privilege; setting up a tent without asking is an act of trespass and won't be well received. Note that rough camping is illegal in national parks and nature reserves. That being said, there are a growing number of informal sites in some of Wales' most beautiful spots. These are free to use and have no facilities; details are given in the text.

The problem with most accredited campsites in Wales is that tents have to share the space with **caravans**. Some of Wales' most popular areas – Pembrokeshire, the Wye Valley, the Gower, Snowdonia, the Brecon Beacons – seem to be permanently clogged with these slow-moving, low-tech mobile homes, rumbling inexorably from one park to the next.

As a hangover from the days of thousands of midland holiday-makers decamping to the Welsh coast for a fortnight, many of the traditional seaside resorts are infested with camp upon camp of **permanently sited caravans**, rented out for self-catering holidays. Although these can certainly be cost-effective, with facilities such as bars, shops and discos thrown in, many people prefer to take more robust self-catering holidays in self-contained **cottages, farms, town houses, apartments** or even purpose-built estates. The usual minimum rental period is a week, though long weekend breaks can often be arranged out of season. In midsummer, or over Christmas and New Year, prices start at around £300 for a place sleeping four or six, although in winter, spring or autumn they can dip below £100 for the same property. Some companies specializing in Welsh holiday cottages are listed in the box below; the British Sunday papers generally have exhaustive lists of self-catering holiday companies in their small ads sections.

Detailed, annually revised **guidebooks** to Wales's camping and caravan sites include the *AA's Camping and Caravanning in Britain and Ireland*, which lists their inspected and graded sites, and *Cade's Camping, Tourings and Motor Caravan Site Guide*, published by Marwain. *WTB* produces self-catering and camping directories, available free from its Cardiff address.

SELF-CATERING ACCOMMODATION COMPANIES

Brecon Beacons Holiday Cottages, Brynoyre, Talybont-on-Usk, Brecon, Powys LD3 7YS (☎01874/676446). *Around 100 cottages and other buildings, some decidedly quirky, in the Brecon Beacons.*

Coastal Cottages of Pembrokeshire, Abercastle, Pembrokeshire SA62 5HJ (☎01348/ 837742). *350 cottages, chalets, flats and houses around or near the Pembrokeshire coast.*

Gwyliau Cymreig (*Welsh Holidays*), Snowdonia Tourist Services, Ynys Tywyn, High St, Porthmadog, Gwynedd LL49 9PG (☎01766/513829). *Best, and cheapest, of the many companies offering self-catering accommodation in Snowdonia and the north.*

North Wales Holiday Cottages & Farmhouses, Station Rd, Deganwy, Conwy LL31 9DF (☎01492/582492). *Numerous cottages in Snowdonia and around the north Wales coast.*

Powell's Cottage Holidays, Dolphin House, High St, Saundersfoot, Pembrokeshire SA69 9EJ (☎01834/812791). *250 properties, mainly in south Wales and Gower.*

Quality Cottages, Cerbid, Solva, Haverfordwest, Pembrokeshire SA62 9YE (☎01348/837871). *Coastal cottages throughout Wales, largely around Pembrokeshire and Cardiganshire.*

Wales Cottage Holidays, The Bank, Newtown, Powys SY16 2AA (☎01686/625267). *A varied selection of 500 properties all over Wales.*

FOOD AND DRINK

For many centuries, Welsh cuisine has been considered to be little more than a poor relation of the English culinary art, itself hardly well regarded on the international scene. Restaurants were on the whole uninteresting and the pubs were strictly male-dominated and cheerless. Times have now changed to some extent, for traditional Welsh cuisine is now climbing a slope of resurgence, and this, combined with improved British fare and an eclectic range of international options, has turned eating and drinking throughout Wales into an interesting and enjoyable part of any stay in the country.

EATING

Indigenous British cuisine has taken an upturn in recent years. The pies, cheeses, puddings and meat from all of the regions are being offered in increasing numbers of establishments. Popular British dishes – steak and kidney pies, the ubiquitous fish and chips, cuts of meat with potatoes and vegetables, and stews, for example – are available everywhere in Wales.

Native **Welsh cuisine** is also making something of a comeback. Not surprisingly, such food is frequently rooted in economical ingredients, although this does not mean that it is of a poor quality. Traditional dishes, such as the delicious native lamb (served at its best minted or with thyme), fresh salmon, sewin and other trout can be found on an increasing number of menus, frequently combined with the national vegetable, the leek. Specialities include laver bread (*bara lawr*), a thoroughly tasty seaweed and oatmeal cake often fried with a traditional breakfast of pork sausages, egg and bacon. Other dishes well worth investigating include Glamorgan sausages (a vegetarian combination of local cheese and spices), cawl (a chunky mutton broth), and cockles, trawled from the estuary north of the Gower.

Dairy products, in a predominantly rural country, feature highly, especially in the range of Welsh **cheeses**. Best known is Caerphilly, a soft, crumbly white cheese that forms the basis of a true Welsh Rarebit, when mixed with beer and toasted on bread. Creamy goat's cheeses can be found all over the country. Also stemming from the cheapness of their ingredients are some traditional **sweets and cakes**: Welsh Cakes are flat pancakes of sugared dough, and bara brith, a popular accompaniment to afternoon tea, literally translated as "speckled (with dried fruit) bread". Menus comprising Welsh dishes can be found in numerous restaurants, hotels and pubs, many of which are part of the **Taste of Wales** (*Blas ar Gymru*) scheme to encourage native cuisine. Such establishments generally display a sticker in their windows. *Welsh Food Promotions*, co-ordinator of the *Blas ar Gymru* scheme, publishes a national directory and map (£1) of hotels, restaurants, cafés and shops where indigenous Welsh cuisine can be sampled. Pick it up from tourist offices or bookshops, or direct from them at Cardiff Business Technology Centre, Senghennydd Road, Cardiff CF2 4AY (☎01222/640456, fax 640048).

WHERE TO EAT

Staying in a hotel, guesthouse or B&B, it is likely that a cooked breakfast will be offered as part of the deal. These are generally served between 8am and 9am, with variations according to the establishment in question. A hearty breakfast is usually enough to see most people through the day, with maybe a lunchtime snack around 1pm. Lunch is generally between noon and 2pm, and evening meals from 6pm to 10pm.

Cafés, found absolutely everywhere, are generally the cheapest places to eat, providing hearty, if cholesterol-laden, breakfasts, a solid range of snacks and full meals for lunch and, in a few instances, evening meals as well. Wales' steady influx of hippies and New Agers over the past thirty years has seen the **wholefood café** become a standard feature of most mid- and west Welsh towns. Cheap and usually vegetarian, these rely extensively on fresh local produce and are also frequently an excellent resource centre for alternative and esoteric information about local groups, events, fairs, festivals and even useful things like car-sharing.

Food in **pubs** varies as much as the establishments themselves. In recent years, intense competition has required them to sharpen up their act, and many pubs now offer more imaginative dishes than standard microwaved lasagne and chips. Most places serve food at lunchtime and in the evening (usually until 8.30 or 9pm), and in many towns the local pub is the most economical place to grab a filling evening meal. Recommendations are given throughout the book.

The growth in upmarket **restaurants** has mirrored Wales' increasing sophistication and attraction to the outside world. People of all nationalities have settled in Wales and few towns are without their Indian and Chinese restaurants, joined over recent years by Japanese, French, Thai, American, Mexican, even Belgian and New Zealand establishments. In the larger, more cosmopolitan centres, **bistros** and **brasseries** have sprung up, many offering superb Welsh and international cuisine at thoroughly affordable prices.

Our restaurant listings include a mix of high-quality and good-value establishments, but if you're intent on a culinary pilgrimage, you'd do well to arm yourself with a copy of the *Good Food Guide* (Hodder), which is updated annually and includes detailed recommendations. Throughout this book, we've supplied the phone number for all restaurants where you may need to book a table. Generally speaking, in pubs and cafés you can expect to pay under a tenner per head; in most restaurants and bistros it should be between £10 and £30; only exceptionally will you pay over £30.

DRINKING

As much as in any other part of the British Isles, the **pub** reigns supreme in Wales. Many people imagine that the puritanical "dry" Welsh Sunday is still commonplace: in fact, in the last seven-yearly vote on the matter, the only district to choose to remain alcohol-free on the Sabbath was Dwyfor, covering the Welsh heartland of the

Llŷn peninsula – even this is likely to change, as pressure to abandon the costly poll grows.

Pubs in Wales vary as much as the landscape, from opulent Edwardian palaces of smoked glass, gleaming brass and polished mahogany in the larger towns and cities, to thick-set stone barns in wild, remote countryside. Where the church has faltered as a community focal point, the pub still holds sway, with those in smaller towns and villages, in particular, functioning as a community centre as much as a place in which to drink alcohol. Live music (occasionally improvised) and, this being Wales, singing frequently round off an evening. As a rule of thumb, if the pub has both a **bar** and a **lounge**, the bar will be more basic and frequently very male-dominated, the lounge plusher, more mixed and probably a better bet for a passing tourist. **Opening times** are fairly standard: Monday to Saturday 11am to 11pm, Sunday noon to 10.30pm (with many quieter places closed between 3pm and 6pm throughout the week), with "last orders" called by the bar staff about fifteen minutes before closing time. In general, you have to be 16 to enter a pub unaccompanied, though some places have special family rooms for people with children, and beer gardens where younger kids can run free. The **legal drinking age** is 18.

Beer, sold by the pint (£1.20–2) and half-pint, is the staple drink in Wales, as it is throughout the British Isles. Many pubs are owned by large, UK-wide breweries who sell only their own **bitter** (an uncarbonated, deep-flavoured beer, best when hand-pumped from the cellar), together with a stock of **lagers**, a chilled, fizzy and light drink that corresponds with European and American ideas of beer. Despite being hard to find in England, mild, or **dark** as it is usually known in Wales, is quite common. This is a cheap, very dark and quite sweet beer that tends to pack a bit more of a punch than would be guessed from its taste. Even stronger, sweeter and darker is **porter**, making a welcome comeback in many Welsh pubs. Irish **stout** (*Guinness, Murphy's* or *Beamish*), although never as good as it is in Ireland, is widely available and, if well kept, very tasty.

Among beers worth looking out for are the heady brews produced by Cardiff-based **Brains**, mainly found in the southeastern corner of Wales. Their *Dark* is a superb, rich mild, whilst their *Bitter* and *SA Best Bitter* are amongst the best pints to be had anywhere in the UK. Llanelli-based **Felinfoel** covers the whole southern half of Wales, with *Double Dragon Premium* bitter the aromatic ace in their pack. **Crown Buckley**, also based in Llanelli, produces three excellent bitters and a distinctive mild. The best resource for any serious alehead is the **CAMRA** (*Campaign for Real Ale*) annual *Good Beer Guide*, which should steer you around the best pubs. If you see a recent *CAMRA* sticker in a pub window, chances are the beer will be well worth sampling.

Pubs and off-licences (liquor stores) increasingly stock the growing range of Welsh **whiskies** and other spirits. With Celtic cousins Ireland and Scotland having cornered the market in whisky, the Welsh have hit back with the standard *Swn-y-mor* and a wonderful malt, the *Prince of Wales* (you can visit the distillery in Brecon; see p.202). Welsh gin and *Taffski* vodka can also be found, as

can a number of Welsh **wines**, to be sampled more out of curiosity than anything else. Be warned that wine sold in pubs tends to be slop of the worst order, with the notable exception of pubs serving decent food. Even so, in these establishments and in dedicated **wine bars**, the cost of a bottle can be outrageous.

Pubs are gradually shedding their booze-only image, as more of them serve **tea** and **coffee**, as well as a heavily marked-up range of soft drinks. In more touristy areas, **teashops** have sprung up like fungus, serving tea, snacks and cakes in the daytime. Less twee are the few continental-style **brasseries**, still a rarity out of the main towns, where decent coffee (rarely found in more basic cafés), other drinks and snacks are on offer.

POST AND PHONES

Virtually all post offices (*swyddfa'r post*) are open Monday to Friday 9am to 5.30pm, Saturday 9am to 12.30/1pm; in small communities you'll find sub-post offices operating out of a shop, but these work to the same hours, even if the shop itself is open for longer. Stamps can be bought at post office counters, from the increasingly rare vending machines outside, or from a large number of newsagents and other shops, although often these sell only books of four or ten stamps. A first-class letter to anywhere in Britain (up to 60g; 2.1oz) costs 26p and should arrive the next day; second-class letters cost 20p, tak-

ing two to four days to arrive. Airmail letters of less than 20g (0.7oz) to EU countries also cost 26p, to non-EU European countries 31p, and elsewhere overseas from 43p for 10g. Pre-stamped aerograms conforming to overseas airmail weight limits of under 10g cost 36p from post offices.

Almost all public **payphones** (*teleffon*) are operated by *British Telecom* (*BT*) and there should be one within ten minutes' walk of wherever you're standing, unless you're in the middle of a moor. Many *BT* payphones take only coins (from 10p upwards), but an increasing proportion are being replaced by a new range of sophisticated machines with an LCD instruction panel displaying in six languages, including Welsh. These phones are designed to accept cash, credit cards (with a minimum call charge of 50p) and phonecards available in denominations of £2, £5 and £10 from post offices and newsagents displaying *BT*'s green logo.

Depending on the time of day, calls from payphones cost between two and four times the price of those from residential phones but

OPERATOR SERVICES AND PHONE CODES

Domestic operator ☎100
Domestic directory assistance ☎192
International operator ☎155
International directory assistance ☎153

INTERNATIONAL CALLS

To **call Wales** from overseas, dial the international access code (☎011 from the US and Canada, ☎0011 from Australia and ☎00 from New Zealand), followed in all cases by 44, then the area code minus its initial zero, and finally the number. To call **overseas from Wales** dial ☎00, then the appropriate country code, the area code (without the zero if there is one) and finally the number. Country codes are as follows:

USA and Canada ☎1

Ireland ☎353

Australia ☎61

New Zealand ☎64

generally follow the same charging pattern. Both **inland and international calls** are cheapest during the **reduced rate periods** between 6pm and 8am on weekdays and all day at weekends and on Bank Holidays. Throughout the *Guide*, every telephone number is prefixed by the area code, followed by an oblique slash. The prefix can be omitted if dialling from within the area covered by that prefix. Any number with the prefix ☎0500 or ☎0800 is free to the caller; ☎0345 and ☎0645 numbers are charged at the local rate; while ☎0891 numbers (information services) and ☎0898 numbers (usually salacious entertainment lines) are charged at the exorbitant "premium rate".

OPENING HOURS AND HOLIDAYS

General **shop hours** are Monday to Saturday 9am to 5,30/6.00pm, although there's an increasing amount of Sunday and late-night shopping in the larger towns, with Thursday or Friday being the favoured evenings. The big supermarkets also tend to stay open until 8 or 9pm from Monday to Saturday and open on Sunday from 10am to 4pm, as do many of the stores in the shopping complexes springing up on the outskirts of major towns. Many provincial towns still retain an "early closing day" when shops shut at 1pm – Wednesday is the favourite. Note that not all service stations are open for 24 hours, although you can usually get fuel around the clock in the larger towns and cities. Also, most fee-charging sites are open on Bank Holidays, when Sunday hours usually apply.

PUBLIC HOLIDAYS IN WALES

January 1

Good Friday – late March to mid-April

Easter Monday – late March to mid-April

First Monday in May (this public holiday may soon be replaced by a date in October)

Last Monday in May

Last Monday in August

December 25

December 26

Note that if January 1, December 25 or December 26 falls on a Saturday or Sunday, the next weekday becomes a public holiday.

ADMISSION TO MUSEUMS AND MONUMENTS

Many of Wales' most treasured sites – from castles, abbeys and great houses to tracts of protected landscape – come under the control of the privately-run UK-wide **National Trust** or the state-run **CADW, Welsh Historic Monuments** (see box for addresses) whose properties are denoted in the guide by "NT" and "CADW". Both organizations charge an entry fee for most places, and these can be quite high, especially for the more grandiose NT estates. If you think you'll be visiting more than half a dozen NT places or a similar number of major CADW sites, it's worth taking out **annual membership** (NT £26, under-23s £12; CADW £18, students £13), which allows free entry to their properties. NT membership covers you throughout Britain, and though CADW sites are restricted to Wales, membership allows half-price entry to sites owned by *English Heritage* and *Historic Scotland*. In addition CADW offers the **Explorer Pass** which allows free entry into all CADW sites for three consecutive days (£9), or seven days (£14) and, like the annual passes, are also available with a vast array of family, senior and youth concessions.

A few Welsh **stately homes** remain in the hands of the landed gentry, who tend to charge in the region of £5 for edited highlights of their domain. Many other old buildings, albeit rarely the most momentous, are owned by the local authorities, and admission is often cheaper. Municipal **art galleries** and **museums** are usually free, though this doesn't hold true for either the National Museum of Wales or the Welsh Folk Museum, both in Cardiff. Although a donation is usually requested, **cathedrals** tend to be free, except for perhaps the tower, crypt or other such highlight, for which a small charge is made. **Churches** are increasingly kept locked, except for services, but when they are open, entry is free. Wales also has a number of ventures exploiting the country's **industrial heritage**, mostly concerned with mining for coal, slate, copper or gold. A short tour supplemented by a video should cost a couple of quid while the full underground interactive "experience" can be up to £10.

Entry charges given in the *Guide* are the full adult rates, but the majority of the fee-charging attractions located in Wales have 25–35 percent **reductions** for senior citizens, the unemployed and full-time students, and 50 percent reductions for children under 16, with under-5s admitted free almost everywhere. Proof of eligibility is required in most cases. In addition, there is frequently a family ticket, usually priced just under the rate for two adults and a child and usually valid for up to three kids; those offered by CADW are particularly good value. Most attractions are open daily in summer and closed one or two days a week in winter, though major sites are open daily all year – full details of opening hours are given in the *Guide*.

Finally, foreign visitors planning on seeing more than a dozen stately homes, monuments, castles or gardens might find it worthwhile to buy a **Great British Heritage Pass**, which gives free admission to some six hundred sites

---

THE NATIONAL TRUST AND CADW

The National Trust (Head Office), 36 Queen Anne's Gate, London SW1H 9AS (☎0171/222 9251).

The National Trust (North Wales), Trinity Square, Llandudno LL30 2DE (☎01492/860123).

The National Trust (South Wales), King's Head, Bridge Street, Llandeilo SA18 3NL (☎01558/822800).

CADW Brunel House, 2 Fitzalan Rd, Cardiff CF2 1UY (☎01222/500200).

throughout the UK. Over sixty of these are in Wales, including Penhow Castle in Chepstow, Tredegar House at Newport and Cardiff Castle, as well as all National Trust and CADW properties. The pass can be purchased for periods of seven days (£25), fifteen days (£36) or a month (£50) through *British Airways*, if booked in advance, major tourist offices or the *British Travel Centre* in London. North Americans can buy it in advance from the *British Travel Bookshop*, 551 Fifth Ave, New York, NY (☎212/490-6688), or *Red Seal Tours*, 170 Evans Ave, Suite 201, Toronto, ON M8Z 5Y6 (☎1-800/668-4224 or 416/503-2233) for $39 (Can $52) for seven days, $58 (Can$72) for fifteen days, or $85 (Can$100) for a month.

THE MEDIA

The media that you will encounter in Wales is a predictable hybrid of Welsh and Britain-wide information. Although the London-based UK media attempts to cover life in the other corners of Britain, few people would agree that Wales, Scotland and the northern regions of England receive a fair share of coverage in any medium. Of all the solely Welsh media, newspapers are probably the weakest area, and radio or TV coverage the strongest and most interesting.

NEWSPAPERS AND MAGAZINES

Of the **British daily newspapers**, all available in Wales, the vast majority are fearsomely right-wing and Londoncentric – news of Wales is not terribly well covered. The London-based **tabloid newspapers** – known otherwise, and with good reason, as the "gutter press" – are the papers you are most likely to see read in any part of Britain. Specializing in prurient gossip and scandal, the two leaders in this field are the right-wing *Sun* and the damply leftish *Daily Mirror*. Slightly more upmarket, adding in a bit more news but always filtered through a severely right-wing analysis, are the *Daily Mail* and *Daily Express*. Best of the quality broadsheet papers are the vaguely left-leaning *Guardian*, the right-wing *Daily Telegraph* and the generally robust but financially struggling *Independent*. The only quality **Welsh daily** is the *Western Mail*, an uneasy mix of local, Welsh, British, and a token smattering of international news, with populist competitions and features on TV stars. It does, however, maintain an upbeat Welsh slant on everything, although this can sometimes be little more than a ludicrous angle given to a British story on the strength of some tenuous Welsh connection. A recent revamp has made it far brighter and more visually appealing,

but, with a few honourable exceptions, the quality of writing and analysis veers too easily towards the lightweight. Of the **regional dailies**, north Wales' *Daily Post*, published and printed over the border in Liverpool, is best for details of local news and events and the nearby *Wrexham Evening Leader* is dependable and newsworthy. In the Cardiff area you'll come across the *South Wales Echo*, from the *Western Mail* stable; in Gwent, the evening *South Wales Argus*; and out in Swansea and the southwest, the *Swansea Evening Post*, Dylan Thomas' old sheet, a lively, community-centred read. All areas have their own long-standing **weekly papers**, generally an entertaining mix of local news, parish gossip and events listings. Wales' national **Sunday paper**, *Wales on Sunday*, from the same family as the *Western Mail*, has descended somewhat into tabloid trivia, but it's still worth buying, for its bright, colourful take on Welsh life and occasional hard-hitting exposés and campaigning journalism. It's also very good on Welsh sport.

Go into any bookshop in Wales, and you'll be surprised by the profusion of Welsh **magazines**, in both English and Welsh. For a broad overview of the arts, history and politics, it is hard to beat *Planet*, an English-language bimonthly that takes a politically irreverent line, combining Welsh interest with a wider cultural and international outlook. The more serious English-language monthly *New Welsh Review* is steeped in Wales' political, literary and economic developments, while *Poetry Wales* is an excellent publication of new writing. The liveliest insight into Welsh politics and debate is provided by the monthly *Red Kite* (*Y Barcud Goch*), incorporating perspectives from all centre and centre-left politicos. For a wider view of Welsh social issues, with insights into "alternative" culture from a non-party political basis, together with creative writing and a hearty infusion of cynical humour, pick up *The Big Issue Cymru*, sold by homeless vendors on the streets of major towns and cities. It's the fortnightly little sibling of England's *Big Issue* magazine, launched to runaway success in 1991. The monthly *Chalice* magazine is your best bet for news and features of New Age, spiritual and esoteric Wales, complete with thorough listings of meetings, classes, courses and festivals – you'll find it in most independent bookshops, hippie emporia and health-food places. If you're half-proficient in Welsh, the weekly news digest *Y Cymro* is an essential read, or, if you're attempting to master the language, try *Prentis* magazine and the weekly news file *Golwg*, both aimed at learners.

For **listings** and news of arts events, pick up free copies of *Buzz!* or *finetime* in Cardiff, *What's On* in and around Swansea, *Meter* in west Wales, and the quarterly *This Week Wales* in the north. The Pembrokeshire National Park also produces an excellent free newspaper, *Coast to Coast*, covering events in the region.

TELEVISION AND RADIO

It is in TV and radio that the Welsh media becomes most distinct from its London-based counterparts. Cardiff is the home of Britain's second-largest concentration of TV and radio stations, both Welsh arms of devolved broadcasting organizations like the mighty BBC and indigenous Welsh operators such as S4C and HTV. The wholehearted way in which UK-wide TV and radio has moved out of southeast England is in marked contrast to the Londoncentric print media.

The state-funded British Broadcasting Corporation (BBC) operates two **TV** channels in Wales – the mainstream **BBC Wales on 1** and the more esoteric **BBC Wales on 2**. Although these official titles make the stations sound avowedly Welsh, the vast majority of programming is UK-wide, with Welsh programmes, principally news and sport but also features, political and education programmes, slotted into the regular schedules of documentaries, soaps, arts and music shows, quizzes, quality drama and imports. This is even more the case with **HTV** (Harlech Television), the Welsh holder of the licence to broadcast on the commercial, and determinedly populist, ITV network. The principal Welsh channel is **S4C** (*Sianel Pedwar Cymru*, verbally abbre-

viated to "*ess pedwar eck*"), whose existence is owed to the protesters (including the Plaid Cymru president) who refused to allow the government to renege on its commitment to a Welsh fourth channel alongside the planned UK-wide Channel 4 The station has grown from these shaky beginnings in the early 1980s to become a major player in the European media network and sponsor of diverse projects, including Welsh animation and feature films, notably the 1994 Oscar-nominated *Hedd Wyn*. It broadcasts Welsh-language programmes at lunchtime and for five or six hours every evening, although nearly all of them are subtitled in English for those with the Teletext system. In between, the output is in English, culled from the robust minority-aimed programming on the Channel 4 that broadcasts in England, Scotland and Ireland. S4C's programming is slick, confident and occasionally controversial, and includes a nightly dose of the BBC's longest-running TV soap, *Pobol y Cwm* (*People of the Valley*).

Augmenting the terrestrial stations, **satellite** dishes are an increasingly familiar sight on the side of houses, pubs and hotels in Wales. These tune into a vast array of European pap networks and Rupert Murdoch's **British Sky Broadcasting** (BSkyB) – numerous channels of consumer-oriented dross interspersed with expensive sports programming and a surprisingly good 24-hour news service.

The BBC is also a major player in **radio**, with five UK networks, all broadcasting in Wales: Radio One combines pop with an increasingly confident interpretation of youth culture, Two is dull easy-listening, Three classical, Four a passionately loved ragbag of magazine shows, current affairs, drama, arts and highbrow quizzes, and Five Live a constant, entertaining mix of news and sport. It also operates two stations in Wales alone: **BBC Radio Wales**, an extremely competent, if gentle, English-language service of news, features and music, and **BBC Radio Cymru**, which has made great efforts of late to become the voice of Welsh-speaking youth, much to the disapproval of older listeners who don't warm to the "Yo! People of Wales" manner of characterful DJ Eifion Jones.

Of the commercial stations, the brashest is Radio One soundalike **Red Dragon Radio**, serving Cardiff and around, together with **Touch AM**, its twin for news, features and easy-listening music. Better in the capital is **Bay FM**, a laid-back multicultural community station from Cardiff Bay, currently on a restricted licence but aiming for permanence. **Swansea Sound**, whose reception extends west towards Pembrokeshire, is solid and frequently interesting, but the best local station is the bilingual **Radio Ceredigion**, more communi-ty-based than any of the others. In the north, **Radio Maldwyn** is the cheap and cheerful station for Montgomeryshire, while **BBC Radio Clwyd**, **Marcher Coast** (bland pop) and **Marcher Gold** (old pop) battle it out in the northwest corner.

ANNUAL EVENTS

The most obviously unique events in Wales are the ***eisteddfodau*** (singular *eisteddfod*), a term that originally meant "a meeting of bards". Nowadays it covers anything from a small village festival, where prizes of a couple of pounds are awarded for poetry and song, to two vast cultural orgies: the **International Eisteddfod**, held on a purpose-built fixed site at Llangollen in early July, and the roving **Royal National Eisteddfod**, in the first week of August, whose venue is proclaimed a year and a day in advance by the Gorsedd of Bards from within a stone circle. The similar **Urdd Eisteddfod**, for young people, takes

EVENTS CALENDAR – JANUARY TO EARLY JUNE

February–March: Five Nations rugby championship. Welsh success perhaps seems unlikely at the moment, but – as they showed by stealing a surprise win in 1994 – anything can happen.

End of February: Llandudno Beer Festival.

March 1: St David's Day. *Hwyrnos* and celebrations all over Wales.

Early March: Llanwrtyd Wells Folk Festival (☎01591/610666).

April: Time to Care in Cardiff (☎01222/343030). A month of fun and fund-raising (in aid of Cardiff Body Positive) around the city's lesbian and gay scene.

Mid-April: Swansea Beer Festival.

Early May: Llandrindod Wells Drama Festival at the Albert Hall theatre (☎01597/822283).

Early May: Llantrisant Free Festival, Llantrisant Common, Vale of Glamorgan. New Age and music bash.

May–October: Festival of the Countryside, mid-Wales (☎01686/625384). An assortment of events, guided walks, music and demos of rural crafts throughout the summer.

Mid-May: Tredegar House Folk Festival, Newport (☎01633/815612).

Mid-May: Pontrhydfendigaid Eisteddfod, Dyfed. One of the largest, best regional *eisteddfodau*.

Mid-May: Europa Caerdydd (☎01222/871922). A four-day burst of street entertainment, music, cabaret and fireworks around The Hayes, Cardiff.

Late May: Spring Fair (Ffair Wanwyn), Llanfair Clydogau, near Tregaron (☎01239/698313). Magical music fest, with art, dance, theatre and natural therapies.

Late May: Hay-on-Wye Festival of Literature (☎01497/821217). London's literati flock to the borders for a week.

Late May: Cardiff International Animation Festival at St David's Hall (☎01222/878444). Europe's largest gathering of animators in Britain's liveliest centre of the craft.

Last week in May: St David's Cathedral Festival (☎01437/720804). Superb setting for classical concerts and recitals.

End of May–first week in June: Eisteddfod Genedlaethol Urdd (☎01269/845705). Vast and enjoyable youth *eisteddfod* – the largest youth festival in Europe – alternating between north and south Wales. In Waunfawr Park, Crosskeys, near Newport 1997, Llŷn peninsula 1998, Lampeter 1999.

Early June: Gwyl Beaumaris, Anglesey (☎01248/750057 ext 110). One of the best arts festivals, combined with a regatta and fringe.

Mid-June: Cardiff Singer of the World competition (☎01222/342611 ext 235 or 227). Huge, televized week-long festival of music and song, with a star-studded list of international competitors.

Mid-June: Man Versus Horse Marathon, Llanwrtyd Wells, Powys (☎01591/610236). A 22-mile race between runners, cyclists and horses. If a human beats a horse (it has come tantalizingly near to happening), he or she stands to pocket around £15,000.

Mid-June: Criccieth Festival (☎01766/522778). Music, theatre and art.

Late June: Gwyl Ifan (folk dance festival), various locations in and around Cardiff (☎01222/563989).

Late June: Drovers' Walk, Llanwrtyd Wells, Powys (☎01591/610236). Waymarked walks recreate the old drovers' routes, with an ex-drovers' inn reopening just for the day.

Last week in June: Gregynog Festival, near Newtown, Powys (☎01686/650224). Classical music festival in the superb country house surroundings of Gregynog Hall.

July 1: Annual commemorative march by nationalists in Abergele, Clwyd, to remember the two inept protesters who accidentally blew themselves up on the occasion of the Investiture of the Prince of Wales in 1969 (see p.357).

Early July: Beyond the Border, the Wales International Storytelling Festival at St Donat's Castle, Vale of Glamorgan (☎01446/794848). Relaxed, entertaining few days in a fabulous setting.

Second week in July: Llangollen International Music Eisteddfod (☎01978/860236). Over twelve thousand participants from all over the world, including choirs, dancers, folk singers, groups and instrumentalists.

Second weekend in July: Gŵyl Werin y Cnapan, Ffostrasol, near Lampeter, Dyfed (☎01239/858955 or 711374). The best folk and Celtic music festival held anywhere in the world.

Mid-July: Royal Welsh Show, Builth Wells, Powys (☎01982/553683). Massive agricultural show and sales fair.

Mid-July: Gower Music Festival (☎01792/207924).

Late July: Welsh Proms at St David's Hall, Cardiff (☎01222/878444).

Late July: Ras yr Wyddfa (☎01286/870721). A one-day race from Llanberis up Snowdon, attracting masochists from the world over.

Last week in July–first week in August: Cardiff Street Festival. Includes the Butetown Carnival, a loud, multiracial celebration and party by the bay.

First week in August: Royal National Eisteddfod (☎01222/763777). Wales' biggest single annual event: fun, very impressive and worth seeing if only for the overblown pageantry. Bardic competitions, readings, theatre, TV, debates and copious help for the Welsh language learner. At Bala 1997, Bridgend 1998, Anglesey 1999 and Llanelli 2000.

Mid-August: Brecon Jazz Festival, Powys (☎01874/625557). Widely regarded as one of the best in Britain.

Late August: Pontardawe Music Festival, West Glamorgan (☎01792/864192). Folk, ceilidhs, international music and dance.

Late August: Cilgerran Coracle Races, Dyfed (☎01239/614204).

Late August: Llandrindod Wells Victorian Festival, Powys.

Last week in August: Gŵyl Machynlleth (☎01654/703355). Wide-ranging arts festival, with a solid programme of chamber music at its core.

August Bank Holiday weekend: Harvest Fair, Tregroes Moor, near Fishguard (☎01994/419323). Superb music and arts festival, spanning a wide New Age and dance range of events. Ran into some financial trouble in 1996, so its days may be numbered.

August Bank Holiday Monday: World Bog Snorkelling Championships, Llanwrtyd Wells, Powys (☎01591/610236). Plus a mountain-bike bog-leaping contest.

First two weeks in September: Excalibur Celtic Festival, Swansea and the Gower area (☎01792/232359). Sporting challenges, endurance tests, a triathlon and music events.

Late September–early October: Cardiff Festival (☎01222/236244). Themed annual festival that is one of the UK's largest. Incorporates music, art, drama, opera and literature.

October: Swansea Festival of Music and the Arts (☎01792/302432). Concerts, jazz, drama, opera, ballet and art events throughout the city.

December 31: 6km race in Mountain Ash, Mid Glamorgan, in memory of local eighteenth-century shepherd Guto Nyth Brân, who died after running 12 miles in 53 minutes.

December 31: Fancy-dress costume night in New Quay, Dyfed.

December 31: New Year Walk-In, Llanwrtyd Wells, Powys. A boozy stagger round the town.

place in early June. *Eisteddfodau* are the most Welsh of events, incorporating theatre, dance, music from rock to choirs, debate, ceremony, competitions and exhibitions. However, provision is made throughout for non-Welsh speakers, who are always welcome to what have become Europe's largest indigenous cultural festivals.

Many towns and cities now have annual **arts festivals** of some kind, mentioned throughout the *Guide* and, in the case of the major events, in the box on p.39. Aside from these, the old working traditions of Wales have spawned such occasions as the annual Cilgerran **coracle races** and Llanwrtyd's **drovers' runs**. Some of Wales' events have a distinctly bizarre background and appearance; for instance the snorkelling competition in peat bogs and the pilgrimages for *Prisoner* fans to the surreal village of Portmeirion. If you want to explore the odd customs and traditions of Britain in greater depth, read Martin Green's *Curious Customs* (Impact Books). Finally, New Age **fairs** and **festivals** are a common feature of summer throughout Wales; these are usually publicized by handbills, posters in wholefood shops and cafés, and by word of mouth. A few, however, have broken through to annual, and permanent, respectability.

OUTDOOR PURSUITS AND SPECTATOR SPORTS

No matter where you are in Wales – even in the more populated valleys and coastline of the south – you're never far from a stretch of countryside where you can lose the crowds on a brief walk or cycle ride. For tougher specimens, there are long-distance footpaths and skyline ridge walks, as well as some of the best rock climbing and potholing (caving) in Britain. On the coast and many of the country's inland lakes, you can follow the pursuits of sailing and windsurfing, and there are plenty of fine beaches for less structured fresh-air activities.

WALKING

There's nowhere in Wales that you can't be out of a built-up area into some decent walking country in half an hour or so, but three areas are so outstanding they have been designated **national parks**. Almost the whole of the northwestern corner of Wales is taken up with the **Snowdonia National Park** (see p.307), a dozen of the country's highest peaks separated by dramatic glaciated valleys and laced with hundreds of miles of ridge and moorland paths. From Snowdonia, the Cambrian Mountains stretch south to the **Brecon Beacons National Park**, with its striking sandstone scarp at the head of the south Wales coalfield, and lush, cave-riddled limestone valleys to the south. One hundred and seventy miles of Wales' southwestern peninsula make up the third park, the **Pembrokeshire Coast National Park**, best explored by the **Pembrokeshire Coast Path**, one of Wales' increasing number of designated **Long-Distance Paths** (see box opposite).

Unless you are doing your walking on weekdays out of season, don't expect to be on your own.

SAFETY IN THE WELSH HILLS

Welsh mountains are not high by world standards, but the fickle weather makes them extremely dangerous and they should be treated with respect. You can easily find yourself disoriented in the low cloud and soaked by unexpected rain, so if the weather looks like it is closing in, get down fast. It is essential that you are properly equipped – even for what appears to be an easy expedition in apparently settled weather – with proper warm and waterproof layered clothing, supportive footwear, adequate maps, a compass and food. Always tell someone your route and expected time of return – and call when you get back so they know you're safe.

Walking has become very popular in all the national parks and finding solitude can require some effort.

Many of the best day walks in the country are detailed in this *Guide*, but for more arduous mountain walks, you'll benefit from a specialist walking guide, easily available in the appropriate walking area. The best are listed in *Contexts* and there's more information available from *The Ramblers' Association* (1–5 Wandsworth Rd, London SW8 2XX; ☎0171/582 6878, fax 587 3799), Britain's main countryside campaigning organization and self-appointed guardian of the nation's footpaths and rights of way.

RIGHTS OF ACCESS

Although they are managed by committees of local and state officials, all three Welsh national parks are in fact predominantly privately owned. There is **no general right of access**, but both the National Trust and the Forestry Commission, the principal landowners, normally allow free recreational use of their land. For how long this will be the case is currently under some doubt, as the government is considering selling off Forestry Commission land.

Access to other land is restricted to **public rights of way**: **footpaths** (pedestrians only) and **bridleways** (pedestrians, horses and bicycles) that have seen continued use over the centuries. Historically, these are often over narrow mountain passes between two hamlets, or link villages to mines or summer pasture land. Rights of way are marked on Ordnance Survey maps and are indicat-ed with a Public Footpath (*Llwybr Cyhoeddus*) sign; any stiles and gates on the path have to be maintained by the landowner. Some less scrupulous owners have been known to block rights of way by destroying stiles – and with some walkers wilfully straying from official rights of way, some resentment is perhaps understandable. Disputes are still uncommon but your surest way of avoiding trouble is to meticulously follow the right of way on an up-to-date map. Ordnance Survey maps also indicate routes with **concessionary path** or **courtesy path** status; though these are usually open for public use they can be closed at any time.

A new departure by the map makers – after years of badgering by *The Ramblers' Association* – is the latest edition of the "Dolgellau" *Landranger* map. For the first time, minor tracks – some following ancient drovers' roads – which were previously shown without any right of access, are now included as "other routes with public access". Though no changes have been made to the rights of access, the new awareness has opened up several possible walking and mountain-biking routes, particularly across large tracts of *Forestry Commission* land.

THE LONG-DISTANCE PATHS

Defined as any route over twenty miles long and waymarked at frequent intervals by a recognizable symbol (acorn), **Long-Distance Paths** have enjoyed a boom in recent years: *The Ramblers' Association* recognized no less than six new long-distance paths in its 1996 yearbook including the

---

THE TOP LDPS

Wales' Long-Distance Paths are detailed where appropriate throughout the *Guide*. What follows is a brief rundown of the most popular.

Cambrian Way (274 miles). Wales' longest and most arduous path, cutting north–south over the remote Cambrian Mountains.

Dyfi Valley Way (108 miles). Brand-new creation which traces both sides of the beautiful Dyfi Valley and estuary, described in Laurence Main's path guide (see "Books" in *Contexts*).

Glyndŵr's Way (128 miles). A lengthy meander amongst the remote mountains and lakes of mid-Wales from Welshpool to Knighton via Machynlleth.

Landsker Borderlands Trail (60 miles). Slightly contrived circular walk around the Landsker region, starting from Canaston Bridge in Pembrokeshire.

Offa's Dyke Path (168 miles). From north to south Wales, largely tracing the line of the eighth-century earthwork along the English border.

Pembrokeshire Coast Path (186 miles). Dips into quiet coves and climbs over headlands with sweeping ocean views around the Pembrokeshire Coast.

Wye Valley Walk (107 miles). From Chepstow to Rhayader following the River Wye and partly through England.

Landsker Borderlands Trail and the Taff Trail (in box on p.41). Some of the walks – the Pembrokeshire Coast Path and Offa's Dyke Path in particular – use a strong unifying theme for their route; others are a mite esoteric though this seldom detracts from the quality of the walk. LDPs are usually well supplied with youth hostels, though you may need a tent for some of the more heroic hikes. *Stilwell's National Trail Companion* (see "Books" in *Contexts*) currently lists handy accommodation along Glyndŵr's Way, the Offa's Dyke Path and the Pembrokeshire Coast Path.

More information is available from *The Ramblers' Association* or the *Long Distance Walkers' Association* (9 Tainters Brook, Uckfield, East Sussex, TN22 1UQ).

ROCK CLIMBING AND SCRAMBLING

As well as being superb walking country, Snowdonia offers some of Britain's best **rock climbing** and several challenging **scrambles** – ascents that fall somewhere between walks and climbs, requiring the use of your hands. One or two of the tougher walks included in the text have sections of scrambling, but for the most part this is a specialist discipline, well covered in the walking books listed in *Contexts*.

There are a couple of noted climbing spots around the Pembrokeshire coast and in the Brecon Beacons, but the vast majority are in **Snowdonia**. A predominance of low-lying crags and its easy access make the area particularly popular, and on any sunny weekend you'll spot brightly coloured figures hanging off almost every cliff face. The principal areas to head for are the Llanberis Pass, the Ogwen Valley, Tremadog, near Porthmadog, the sea cliffs around South Stack near Holyhead, and the desperately difficult Pen Trwyn on the Great Orme at Llandudno. The best general guide for experienced climbers, *Rock Climbing in Snowdonia* by Paul Williams (Constable), is stocked in the region's numerous climbing shops.

Beginners should contact *Plas-y-Brenin: The National Mountaineering Centre*, Capel Curig, LL24 0ET (☎01690/280366), which runs residential courses and two-hour samplers, or the *British Mountaineering Council*, 177–179 Burton Rd, Manchester M20 2BB (☎0161/445 4747).

CYCLING

Despite the recent boom in the sale of mountain bikes, **cyclists** are treated with notorious disrespect by many motorized road users and by the people who plan the country's traffic systems. There are few proper cycle routes in any of Wales' big towns, so if you're hellbent on tackling the congestion, pollution and aggression of city traffic, get a **helmet** and a secure **lock** – cycle theft is an organized racket. Prospects are brighter in rural areas, where the back roads along river valleys or climbing mountain passes have a sufficient density of pubs and B&Bs to keep the days manageable. Steep gradients can be a problem but ascents are never long, with Wales' highest pass barely reaching 1500ft. Your main problem is likely to be finding spare parts – for anything more complex than a tyre or inner tube, you'll need a specialist shop. The CTC (see below) lists places in its annual handbook.

One beacon of hope in the madness of Britain's transport policy is *Sustrans*, 35 King St, Bristol BS1 4DZ (☎0117/9290888), an organization committed to forming a national cycle network predominantly using existing quiet roads and disused railway lines. The main north–south Welsh leg, **Lôn Las Cymru**, opened in 1996 covering three hundred hilly miles from Anglesey, through Snowdonia, the Brecon Beacons and the industrial valleys of the south, to the Severn Bridge. *Sustrans* publishes two maps of the route (£5 each), 8a covering Holyhead to Builth Wells and 8b from there to Chepstow and Cardiff.

Off-road cycling is becoming increasingly popular in the highland walking areas, but cyclists should remember to keep to rights of way designated on maps as bridleways, BOATs ("Byways Open To All Traffic") and RUPFs ("Roads Used As Public Footpaths"), and to pass walkers at considerate speed. Footpaths, unless otherwise marked, are for pedestrian use only. In deference to walkers, access to certain bridleways has been restricted, particularly around Snowdon: bikes are not allowed on the approaches to the summit between 10am and 5pm from June to September. With no book specifically geared to the off-roader in Wales, the best one to buy is the Britain-wide *Fifty Mountain Bike Rides* (Crowood) by Jeremy Evans, featuring ten 2–7hr rides in Wales, complete with sketch maps, riding conditions and details of pubs and cafés along the way.

Transporting your bike by **train** is a good way of getting to the interesting parts of Wales without a lot of stressful pedalling. At present, bikes are carried free on suburban trains outside the weekday rush hours of 7.30am–9.30am and 3.30–6.30pm; on most inter-town routes bikes are carried at £3 per journey. Book early, as many trains only have space for one bike. **Bike rental** is available at bike shops in most large towns and many resorts, but the specimens on offer are often pretty derelict – all right for a brief spin, but not for any serious touring. Expect to pay in the region of £8–10 per day, £40–60 per week.

Britain's biggest cycling organization is the **Cyclists' Touring Club** or CTC (Cottrell House, 69 Meadrow, Godalming, Surrey GU7 3HS; ☎01483/417217) which supplies members with touring and technical advice, as well as insurance. Its free sheets for members cover 35 routes through Wales. Those planning their own touring routes would do well to buy the OS 1:250,000 (4 miles to an inch) Wales and West Midlands maps. These are detailed enough to show relief and almost all tarmacked roads – and you won't find yourself cycling across a whole map in one day. The Ordnance Survey's excellent series of regional *Cycle Tour* guides, though presently covering just England, is planned to extend to Welsh regions in the near future.

For those who want a guaranteed hassle-free cycling holiday, various companies offer easy-going tours where you ride from hotel to hotel, and a van carries your bags. One of the most professional outfits is *Country Lanes*, 9 Shaftsbury St, Fordingbridge, Hants SP6 1JF (☎01425/655022) – with excellent food and accommodation but a steep price tag at £700 for a six-day excursion. More manageable is *Bicycle Beano*, Erwood, Builth Wells, Powys LD2 3PQ (☎01981/560471) which offers weekend or week-long cycling holidays through the heart of the Welsh countryside.

BEACHES, SURFING AND WINDSURFING

Wales is ringed by fine **beaches** and **bays**, many of the best of which are readily accessible by public transport – though of course this means they tend to get very busy in high summer. With most of the Welsh coast influenced by the currents of the North Atlantic Drift, water temperatures are higher than you might expect for this latitude, but only the truly hardy should consider swimming outside the warmer June to October period. For swimming and sunbathing, the best areas to head for are the Gower Peninsula, the Pembrokeshire Coast, the Llŷn Peninsula and the southwest coast of Anglesey. Though it has more resorts that

any other section of Wales' coastline, the north coast certainly hasn't got the most attractive beaches, nor is it a place to swim.

Wales' southwest-facing beaches offer the best conditions for either board or kayak **surfing**, with decent, but by no means Hawaiian-sized, waves at several key spots. In the south this means Rhossili, at the western tip of the Gower, and Whitesands Bay (Porth-mawr), near St David's. The surfing scene in north Wales centres on the long sweep of Porth Neigwl (Hell's Mouth), near Abersoch on the Llŷn, and Rhosneigr on Anglesey. **Windsurfers** tend to congregate at these major surf beaches and at Barmouth, Borth, around the Pembrokeshire Coast and at The Mumbles. For more information, call the **Welsh Surfing Federation**, 71 Fairway, Port Talbot SA12 7HW (☎01639/886246).

With raw and partly treated effluent still being discharged off many Welsh beaches, it has to be said that they are not the cleanest in Europe, many of them falling well below EU standards. Steps are being taken to improve the situation and *Welsh Water*, which manages water treatment throughout Wales, is committted to ending the dumping of raw sewage, but far too many stretches of the coastline are contaminated by seaborne effluent and rubbish. Europe awards a Blue Flag to designated beaches which pass nineteen tests for water quality and 24 land-based criteria for beach facilities: Wales currently has four such beaches – Pembrey Country Park at Cefn Sidan, Tenby North, St David's/Whitesands and Trearddur Bay.

Don't be fooled, incidentally, by the yellow flags (with a deceptively large areas of blue) you'll see on many other beaches. These are awarded to beaches that meet just two of the basic measures of cleanliness by the government's tourist-conscious Tidy Britain Group. For annually updated, detailed information on the condition of British beaches, the *Good Beach Guide*, compiled by the *Marine Conservation Society* (David & Charles), is the definitive source.

KAYAKING AND RAFTING

Board riders constantly have to compete for waves with the surf ski riders and **kayakers** who frequent the same beaches. Paddlers, however, have the additional run of miles of superb coastline, particularly around Anglesey, the Llŷn and the Pembrokeshire coast. The northern coasts are amply detailed in Terry Storry's slightly dated

Snowdonia White Water Sea and Surf (Cicerone), which also also contains maps and notes on Snowdonia's myriad short, steep bedrock rivers, many of which can only be paddled just after a deluge. The same author's more up-to-date *British White Water* (Constable) covers the hundred best rivers in Britain, including all those in his Snowdonia book, plus some in south Wales, though without river maps.

As equipment improves, paddlers have become more daring and Victorian tourist attractions such as Swallow and Conwy falls, both near Betws-y-Coed, are now fair game for a descent. Most of the kayaking is non-competitive but on summer weekends you might catch a slalom either on the River Dee at Llangollen or at the **National Whitewater Centre** on the River Tryweryn, near Bala, where you can also ride the rapids in rubber rafts.

Without your own kayak or canoe, it's still possible to get on the water with tour companies, who can be contacted through the **Welsh Canoeing Association**, Canolfan Trwweryn, Fron Goch, Bala, Gwynedd LL23 7NU (☎01678/521199).

PONY TREKKING

Wales' scattered population and large tracts of open land make it ideal for **pony trekking**, now a major business with approaching a hundred approved riding centres and many smaller operations. Don't expect too much cantering over unfenced land: rides tend to be geared towards unhurried appreciation of the scenery from horseback and are often combined with accommodation on farms. Mid-Wales has the greatest concentration of stables but there are places all over the country, amply detailed in the brochures supplied by the *Wales Trekking and Riding Association*, 9 Neville St, Abergavenny, Gwent NP7 5AA (☎01873/858717). Riding schools checked and approved by the *WTB* get billing in the free *Discovering Wales on Horseback* leaflet; these typically run two-hour morning and afternoon sessions, charging around £8–10 an hour.

RUGBY

Rugby (or more formally, Rugby Union) is a passion with the Welsh, and their national game. Support is strongest in the traditionally working-class valleys of the south Wales coalfields, where the fanaticism has traditionally been fuelled by the national side's success. But despite winning the

1994 **Five Nations Championship** – a tournament where Wales, England, Scotland, Ireland and France all play each other – Wales has seen some lean seasons of late. Its team has struggled to keep up with the standards of arch rival England, let alone match the power and attacking panache of the all-conquering southern hemisphere sides, Australia, New Zealand and South Africa.

The glory days of Welsh rugby were the 1970s, when Wales turned out some of the best sides ever seen. The scarlet jerseys struck fear into their opponents and Wales won six out of the ten championships – three of them **Grand Slams**, where all four of the Five Nations opponents were beaten individually. Players making Wales so formidable included fearless fullback J P R Williams, the country's most-capped player; elusive and magical outside-halves, Barry John and Phil Bennett; and the world's highest try-scoring scrum-half, Gareth Edwards.

But victories were harder to come by in the 1980s, and by 1991 the national side reached its nadir with its worst-ever international loss of 63–6 at the hands of Australia. That year also saw Wales' highest point scorer, Paul Thorburn, quit the international game disillusioned. Wales' recovery to a dominant side in Rugby Union has been hampered by the loss of many players poached by the rival professional code, Rugby League, chiefly played in northern England and Australasia. It wasn't until 1995 that Rugby Union finally woke up to the fact that amateur status was costing it players, and the code turned professional worldwide. Welsh golden boy Jonathan Davies, who defected to the Widnes League side has now signed for newly salary-paying Cardiff, hopefully heralding a wave of players returning to their Union roots.

In September 1999, Cardiff is due to host the **Rugby World Cup** – a four-yearly tournament between all the major rugby-playing nations – using the national stadium, Cardiff Arms Park, as the prime venue. Throughout 1997 and 1998 Wales' international fixtures will be played elsewhere – sometimes in England – as the stadium is drastically remodelled and its capacity boosted to 75,000. In the meantime, unless you are affiliated to one of the Rugby Union clubs or are prepared to pay well over the odds at one of the ticket agencies, getting to see a major international is nigh on impossible. Most tickets are allocated months before a match, and touts will often be found selling tickets for hundreds of pounds outside the gates on the day. Away from the international arena, a thriving rugby scene exists at club level, with some 178 clubs and 40,000 players taking to the field most Saturdays throughout the season (September to just after Easter). The four top teams, which usually feature a smattering of international players, are Neath, Swansea, Cardiff and Llanelli, with Pontypridd snapping at their heels. It's often worth going to a match purely for the light-hearted crowd banter – if you can understand the accents. Check with individual clubs for fixtures and ticket prices, which start at well under £10.

FOOTBALL

Compared to rugby, **football** (soccer) is seen as a minority sport, but in fact there are just as many Welsh footballers who prefer not to pick up the ball and run with it. The three top sides in the country are Cardiff City, Swansea City and Wrexham, which all play in the English Football League. In recent years, Wrexham have held their position in the Second Division (behind the Premier and First Divisions) while Cardiff and Swansea have dropped into the Third. The rest of the clubs play in the lackustre (but improving) **League of Wales**.

Spurred on by goal-mouth terriers such as Leeds' ageing Ian Rush, Chelsea's Mark Hughes and Manchester United's electrifying Ryan Giggs, the national team came very close to being the only British side in the 1994 World Cup, only to be thwarted in the end by Romania. Under new manager Bobby Gould, it also made a less than promising start to the qualifiers for the 1998 championship.

DISABLED TRAVELLERS

Britain has numerous specialist **tour operators** catering for physically disabled travellers, and the number of non-specialist operators who welcome clients with disabilities is increasing. For **information** on operators and facilities, get in touch with the *Royal Association for Disability and Rehabilitation* (*RADAR*), 12 City Forum, 250 City Rd, London EC1V 8AF (☎0171/250 3222, minicom 4119); or its Welsh equivalent, *Disability Wales*, Llys Ifor, Crescent Rd, Caerphilly, Mid Glamorgan CF8 1XL (☎01222/887325). There's also the *Holiday Care Service*, Floor 2, Imperial Buildings, Victoria Rd, Horley, Surrey RH6 7PZ (☎01293/774535, fax 784647, minicom 776943), which provides extensive lists of inspected accommodation, major sites and caravan parks. Though they're not specifically geared up with visitors in mind you might also try getting in touch with the *Wales Council for the Deaf*, Maritime Offices, Woodland Terrace, Maescoed, Pontypridd, Mid Glamorgan CF37 1DZ (☎01443/485687, minicom 485686), the *Wales Council for the Blind*, Shand House, 20 Newport Rd, Cardiff CF2 1YB (☎01222/473954). The *Disabled Motorists' Federation* (☎01743/761181) will furnish you with a free road route plan and map tailored to your specific needs.

In **North America** contact *Mobility International* at PO Box 10761, Eugene OR 97440 (☎503/343-1284); the *Society for the Advancement of Travel for the Handicapped* 347 Fifth Ave, New York, NY 10016 (☎212/447-7284), a non-profit travel industry referral service that passes queries on to its members; and the *Travel Information Service*, Moss Rehabilitation Hospital, 1200 W Tabor Rd, Philadelphia, PA 19141 (☎215/456-9600), a telephone information and referral service.

Disabled travellers in **Australia** can get information and advice from *ACROD*, PO Box 60, Curtin, ACT 2605 (☎06/682 4333); those in **New Zealand** should try the *Disabled Persons Assembly*, PO Box 10, 138 The Terrace, Wellington (☎04/472 2626).

Should you go it alone, you'll find that Wales is still years behind the advances towards independence made in North America and Australasia. **Public transport** companies are only just starting to make any effort to help disabled people. Some rail services now accommodate wheelchair users in comfort and some assistance is available at stations if you call in advance, preferably 48 hours ahead (see box overleaf). Wheelchair users and blind or partially sighted people are automatically given 30–50 percent reductions on train fares. People with other disabilities are eligible for the **Disabled Persons Railcard** (£14 per year), which gives a third off most tickets. There are no bus discounts for the disabled, while, of the major **car rental** firms, only *Hertz* offer models with hand controls at the same rate as conventional vehicles, and even these are in the more expensive categories. With **accommodation** it's much the same story: modified suites are available at the odd B&B, but mostly only at higher-priced establishments. Exceptions include five wheelchair-accessible *YHAs*: Broad Haven, Manorbier, Newport, Pen-y-Pass and Conwy.

In some areas of Wales where **public toilets** need to be locked to avoid vandalism, local authrities have joined the National Key System (NKS) in which disabled people are able to gain access to facilities with a standard key obtainable from *RADAR* for £2.50 along with a booklet detailing locations. Tourist offices also sometimes hold a key which you can borrow.

Access to **monuments and museums** is improving all the time. The National Trust produces its annual *Information for Visitors with Disabilities* guide detailing accessibility to NT sites throughout England and Wales, and CADW allow wheelchair users and the visually handicapped, along with their assisting companion, free entry to all monuments. Access to theatres, cinemas and other public places is slowly improving.

LOCAL RAIL CONTACT NUMBERS IN WALES

By calling the appropriate number below, you should be able to reserve a seat and arrange assistance at any stations where you need to transfer, as well as at the beginning and end of your journey.

Cardiff *Great Western* ☎01222/499811 ext 2554
Valley Lines ☎01222/499811 ext 2714
Mid Wales ☎01743/458099
North Wales ☎01244/356310
Swansea ☎01792/632206

mation covering everything from transport and restaurants to beach access and parking. It also classifies all accredited accommodation into three accessibility grades, and categorizes restaurants and sites using nationally recognized **accessibility symbols**. Even the *WTB*'s guide to *Discovering Wales on Horseback* features riding schools which cater to the disabled.

Other useful publications include the *Access* series by the *Pauline Hephaistos Survey Projects*, and *RADAR*'s annually updated *Holidays in the British Isle: A Guide For Disabled People*. And look out for *The World Wheelchair Traveller* by Susan Abbott and Mary Ann Tyrrell (AA Publications), which includes basic hints and advice.

PUBLICATIONS

The most helpful **publication** is the free *Discovering Accessible Wales* booklet published by the *Wales Tourist Board* and packed with infor-

LESBIAN AND GAY WALES

Homosexual acts between consenting males was legalized in Britain in 1967, but it wasn't until 1994 that the **age of consent** was finally reduced from 21 to 18 (still two years above than that for heterosexuals), and hopes are high that equality can be won in the coming few years. Lesbianism has never specifically been outlawed, apocryphally owing to the fact that Queen Victoria refused to believe it existed.

With such a rural culture, it's perhaps not surprising that Wales is less used to the lesbian and gay lifestyle than its more cosmopolitan English neighbour. Although Plaid Cymru itself has always supported lesbian and gay rights, there still exists a hard strain of nationalist who believes that gay emancipation is incompatible with true Welsh patriotism. At the 1993 National Eisteddfod in

Llanelwedd, Powys, the stall of the national Welsh-speaking lesbian and gay organization, *Cylch*, was trashed one night – an action that was widely condemned.

The Welsh scene is muted, to say the least. The main centres of population – Cardiff, Newport and Swansea – have a number of pubs and clubs, with Cardiff especially beginning to see a worthy and confident gay scene more in keeping with the capital's size and status. Details are given in the text of the *Guide*. Out of the southern cities, however, gay life becomes distinctly discreet, although university towns such as Lampeter and Bangor manage support groups and the odd weekly night in a local bar, while Aberystwyth boasts a gay pub and a high-profile annual film festival with a very definite queer strand. Cardiff's lesbian and gay **switchboard** operates five evenings a week (see Cardiff listings) and is the most up-to-date source of information on places, events, accommodation and contacts throughout Wales. Alternatively, there are some informal but well-established networks, especially amongst the sometimes reclusive alternative lifestylers found in mid- and west Wales. **Border Women** (who should surely have called themselves Offa's

Dykes) is a well-organized network for mid-Wales, with house meetings and monthly discos. They can be contacted via PO Box 42, Ludlow, Shropshire SY8 1WD. **Cylch** organize a variety of events – contact them at Bwlch Swyddfa Bost 23, Aberystwyth, Dyfed SY23. The UK-wide monthly *Gay Times* (£2.50) has thorough listings and contact information, together with the best directory of the half-dozen or so **gay hotels** throughout Wales.

ALTERNATIVE, NEW AGE AND GREEN WALES

Possibly more than any other part of Britain, Wales – the mid and west in particular – has become something of a haven for those searching for alternative lifestyles. This process dates back nearly a century, but it was the 1960s that saw mass migration west, something that has continued unabated since. Permanent testimonials to this include the **Centre for Alternative Technology** (CAT), near Machynlleth, now one of the area's most visited attractions, and **Tipi Valley**, near Talley, a permanent community in Native American tipis who run a regular public sweat lodge. Both institutions were founded in the idealistic mid-1970s and have prospered through less happy times. For the most part, it's been a fairly smooth process, although antagonism between New Agers and local, established families does break out on occasion.

The legacy of this for visitors is evident everywhere. Even in some of the smallest rural Welsh towns, you'll often find a health-food shop, wholefood café, somewhere flogging esoteric ephemera or an alternative resource centre. Any of these will give you further ideas and contacts for local happenings, places, groups and individuals. We've tried to give details of such places throughout the *Guide*. Other manifestations of such prolific non-mainstream activity include a robust **free party scene** in the rural parts of north, mid- and west Wales. These are often held in spectacularly beautiful settings – by lakes, on beaches –and take place virtually every weekend throughout the summer. Keep your eyes and ears peeled for information and don't hesitate to ask people for guidance. To complement the free events, there's a plethora of good **festivals** from spring to autumn, ranging

ORGANIZATIONS RUNNING RETREATS AND HOLIDAYS

Centre for Alternative Technology, Machynlleth, Powys (☎01654/703743). Residential courses on green themes like self-built homes and organic gardening.

Cerridwen, near Llandysul, Ceredigion (☎01559/370211). Residential courses and breaks, most for women only.

Cwm Bedw Barns, Abbeycwmhir, Llandrindod Wells, Powys LD1 6PH (☎01597/851929). Monthly meditations and regular retreats.

Dreamweavers (☎01974/298920). Residential workshops (on Celtic Shamanism, for instance) at their Morningstar Lodge.

Head For The Hills, Garth, Builth Wells, Powys (☎01591/620388). Guided walking and camping breaks, examining the ancient land-

scape, with communal vegetarian cuisine and campfires.

The Light Centre (☎01267/202264). Residential healing retreats and energy workshops in Carmarthenshire.

Marion Violets (☎01570/493641). Celebratory and spiritual outings and residentials around West Wales, including some for women only.

Penquoit Centre, Lawrenny, Pembrokeshire (☎01646/651666). Retreats in tipis and single cells, plus hostel and camping, for space or courses on anything from expressive dance to coracle building.

Vajraloka Buddhist Meditation Centre, Corwen, Denbighshire (☎01490/460406). Regular retreats for men.

from big folk and blues bashes to smaller gatherings in remote fields, with little more than a couple of banging sound systems. Again, information for smaller events travels best by word of mouth, although for larger, more organized and larger events, you'll see adverts and fliers months in advance. Especially in the wake of the vicious 1995 Criminal Justice Act, there are now far stronger laws against trespass and free parties, although their imposition is sketchy. If you run into any problems, there is a **Travellers' Legal Advice Service** operating in Cardiff (☎01222/874580).

For ecologically minded tourists, there are now numerous package deals that include walking, cycling, dancing and healing holidays and retreats in remote centres, usually with vegetarian and vegan food as part of the deal. Some of these are static, many are in temporary sites, while others keep you on the move. Again, we have included many of these within the body of the *Guide*, and some further ones are listed below. Alternatively, pick up a copy of the monthly magazine *Chalice* (£2.50), which contains listings and adverts on many such places and is a great way to plug into the extensive networks around Wales; buy it at health-food and hippie shops, or from PO Box 164, Newport NP9 8YA (☎01633/281238).

DIRECTORY

Drugs It is most unwise to go through customs carrying any illegal substances. Once in the country, being caught in possession of a small amount of marijuana resin, grass, ecstasy (E) or mushrooms will usually get you no more than a fine, though possession of larger quantities or of "harder" narcotics could lead to imprisonment or deportation.

Electricity In Britain the current is 240V AC. North American appliances will need a transformer and adaptor; Australasian appliances will only need an adaptor.

Laundry Coin-operated laundries (laundrettes) are to be found in Welsh towns of any size and are open about twelve hours a day from Monday to Friday, with shorter hours at weekends. A wash followed by a spin or tumble dry costs about £2, with "service washes" (your laundry done for you in a few hours) about £1 more.

Smoking The last decade has seen a dramatic change in attitudes towards smoking and a significant reduction in the consumption of cigarettes. Smoking is now outlawed on most public transport and in just about all public buildings, and many restaurants and hotels have become non-smoking establishments. Smokers are advised, when booking a table or a room, to check that their vice is tolerated there.

Time Greenwich Mean Time (GMT) is in force from late October to late March, when the clocks go forward an hour for British Summer Time (BST). GMT is five hours ahead of the US Eastern Standard Time and ten hours behind Australian Eastern Standard Time.

Tipping and service charges In restaurants a service charge is usually included in the bill; if it isn't, leave a tip of 10–15 percent unless the service is unforgivably bad. Some restaurants are in the habit of leaving the "total" box blank on credit-card counterfoils, to encourage customers to add another few percent on top of the service charge – if you're paying by credit card, check that the "total" box is filled in before you sign. Taxi drivers expect a tip in the region of 10 percent. You do not generally tip bar staff – if you want to show your appreciation, offer to buy them a drink.

Toilets Public toilets are found at many train and bus stations and are signposted on town high streets. In urban locations, a fee of 10p or 20p is usually charged.

Videos Visitors from North America planning to use their video cameras in Britain should note that Betamax cassettes are less easy to obtain in Britain, and VHS is the most common format.

PART TWO

THE

GUIDE

CHAPTER ONE

SOUTHEAST WALES

Home to almost 1.8 million people, sixty percent of the country's population, the southeastern corner of Wales, comprising the counties of Monmouthshire and Glamorgan, is one of Britain's most industrialized regions. Both population and industry are most heavily concentrated in the sea ports and former mining valleys, although quiet hills and beaches are always just a matter of miles away.

Monmouthshire (formerly Gwent and often still referred to as such) is the easternmost county in Wales, starting at the English border in a beguilingly rural way, the **River Wye** criss-crossing between the two countries from its mouth at the fortress town of **Chepstow**; here, you'll find one of the most impressive castles in a land where few towns are without one. In the Wye's beautiful valley lie the spectacularly placed ruins of **Tintern Abbey**, downstream of the old county town of **Monmouth**. To the north, the foothills of the Black Mountains rise up out of the fertile river plains, making market towns such as **Abergavenny**, and the quieter valleys to its north, popular walking and outdoor pursuits centres.

Monmouthshire becomes increasingly industrialized as you travel west, with the **River Usk** meandering through the middle of the county and spilling out into the Bristol Channel at **Newport**, Wales' third-largest conurbation. Although it is hardly likely to feature on a swift tour of Wales, the town has an excellent museum and the remains of an extensive Roman settlement at **Caerleon**, a northern suburb of the town.

To the west and north are the world-famous **Valleys**, once the coal- and iron-rich powerhouse of the nation. This is the Wales of popular imagination: hemmed-in valley floors packed with lines of blank, grey houses, their doors and sills painted in contrasting gaudy brightness, slanted almost impossibly towards the pithead. Although nearly all of the mines have since closed, the area is still one of tight-knit towns, with a rich working-class heritage that displays itself in some excellent museums and colliery tours, such as the **Big Pit** at Blaenafon and the **Rhondda Heritage Park** in Trehafod. The valleys follow rivers coursing down towards the coast, where great ports stood to ship their products all over the world. The greatest of them all was **Cardiff**, once the world's busiest coal port, now Wales' upbeat capital. Excellent museums, a massive castle, exciting rejuvenation projects and Wales' best cultural pursuits make the city an essential stop. Lying to the immediate west, and a world away from the industrial hangover of the city and valleys, is the lush, conservative **Vale of Glamorgan**, dotted with stoic little market towns and chirpy seaside resorts – most notably **Barry** and **Porthcawl**.

The west of Glamorgan is dominated by Wales' second city, **Swansea**, rougher, tougher and less anglicized than the capital. Like Cardiff, Swansea grew principally on the strength of its docks, and sits on an impressive arc of coast that shelves round from the belching steel works of **Port Talbot** in the east to **Mumbles** and **Oystermouth**, holiday towns of amusement arcades, pubs and

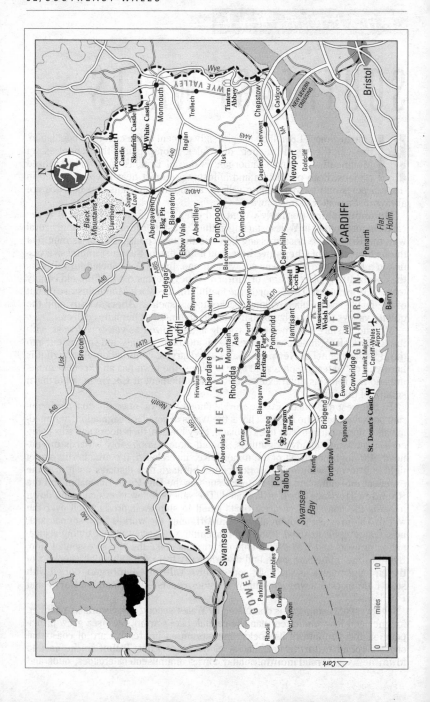

ACCOMMODATION PRICE CODES

Throughout this guide, hotel and B&B accommodation is priced on a scale of ① to ⑨. Category ① only applies to youth hostels; for the rest, the number indicates the **lowest price** you could expect to pay per night for a **double room in high season**. The prices indicated by the codes are as follows:

① under £20	④ £40–50	⑦ £70–80
② £20–30	⑤ £50–60	⑧ £80–100
③ £30–40	⑥ £60–70	⑨ over £100

---

chip shops, on the jaw of the delightful **Gower peninsula** in the west. Gower – one of the country's favourite playgrounds – juts out into the sea, a mini-Wales of grand beaches, rocky headlands, bracken heaths and ruined castles.

Getting around

Southeast Wales is by far the easiest part of the country to travel around. Swift new dual carriageways connect with the M4, bringing all corners of the region into close proximity. **Public transport** is similarly thorough: this is the only part of Wales with a half-decent train service, and most suburban and rural services interconnect with Cardiff, Newport and Swansea, as well as further afield to Gloucester and the Midlands; Monmouth was long ago cut off from the train network, although it is easily reached by car and bus. Bus services fill in virtually all of the gaps.

The Wye Valley

Perhaps the most anglicized corner of Wales, the **Wye Valley** – along with the rest of Monmouthshire – was only finally recognized as part of Wales in the local government reorganization of 1974, before which the county was officially included as part of neither England nor Wales, so that maps were frequently headlined "Wales and Monmouthshire". Most of the rest of the county is firmly and redoubtably Welsh, but the woodlands and hills by the meandering River Wye share more similarities with the landscape over the border. The two main towns are decidedly English in flavour: **Chepstow**, at the mouth of the Wye, with its massive castle radiating an awesome strength; and **Monmouth**, sixteen miles upstream, a spruce, old-fashioned town with the lingering air of an ancient seat of authority.

Six miles north of Chepstow lie the inspirational ruins of the Cistercian **Tintern Abbey**, worth catching first thing in the morning or into the evening when the crowds of coach-trippers have evaporated. Surrounding the abbey are some beautiful walks through bluebell woods and old oak forests on a spit of land sandwiched by the river bend, rising high above the ruins. Running parallel to the river, albeit on the English side of the border, the southern segments of the **Offa's Dyke** earthworks are closely followed by a long distance footpath.

Chepstow

Of all the places that call themselves "the gateway to Wales", the old border town of **CHEPSTOW** (Cas-Gwent) has probably the greatest claim, being the first town on the main road into Wales on the immediate Welsh side of the border.

Situated on the western bank of the River Wye, just over a mile from where its tidal waters flow out into the muddy Severn estuary, Chepstow is a sturdy place with little of the immediate charm or quirkiness of many other Welsh market towns. This is partly due to the scale of soulless modern developments in the town centre that have combined to overwhelm the remaining buildings in streets still laid out in an identifiably medieval pattern.

The Town

Chepstow's position as a former port is evident in the thirteenth-century **Port Wall**, encasing the castle precincts and the town centre in their loop of the river. The fifteenth-century **West Gate** bisects the **High Street**, a handsome thoroughfare sided by Georgian and Victorian buildings and sloping down from the gate towards the river. Here, an elegant five-arch cast-iron **bridge**, built in 1816, is still in use for cross-border traffic into England. To the southeast, a walk along the Wye leads past the **Willow Tea Room**, where a plaque commemorates the quay as the site from which the three leaders of Newport's Chartist March of 1839 were dispatched to Van Diemen's Land (Tasmania). Opposite, a Union Jack flag is provocatively daubed on the English side of the river cliffs – a feature since 1935 and regularly repainted.

Bridge Street leads from the old bridge up towards the main entrance of **Chepstow Castle** (April–Oct daily 9.30am–6.30pm; Nov–March Mon–Sat 9.30am–4pm, Sun 11am–4pm; £3; CADW). As a strategic siting, the castle can scarcely be bettered. Built tight into a loop of the River Wye, it guards one of the most important routes into Wales. Chepstow was the first stone castle to be built in Britain, with its first Norman incarnation, the Great Tower keep, rising in 1067, just one year after William the Conqueror's victory at Hastings. William had realized the importance of subduing the restless Welsh, creating borderland Marcher Lordships and encouraging the title holders to expand into Welsh territory: a succession of Chepstow's lords attempted this, necessitating renewed and increasingly powerful fortification of their castles over the ensuing two hundred years. Ownership of both title and castle passed to the earls of Norfolk and then Pembroke, who retain the fortress to this day.

The walled castle is comprised of three separate enclosures, the Lower Ward being the largest and dating mainly from the thirteenth century. Here, you'll find the **Great Hall**, home to a wide-ranging exhibition on the history of the castle, incorporating genuine and replica armour from various stages of the castle's past, with particular emphasis on the English Civil War years, when Royalist Chepstow was twice besieged.

Twelfth-century defences separate the Lower Ward from the Middle Ward, which is dominated by the still imposing ruins of the **Great Tower**, whose lower floors include the original Norman keep. Beyond the Great Tower is the far narrower Upper Ward which leads up to the Barbican **watch tower**, from which there are some superlative and vertiginous views looking back over the castle and down the cliff to the mudflats of the river estuary.

Opposite the castle is a crimson-painted Georgian town house containing the **Chepstow Museum** (March–Oct Mon–Sat 11am–1pm & 2–5pm, Sun 2–5pm; £1). The displays concern themselves with local life, with nostalgic photographs and paintings of the trades supported in the past by the River Wye, and records of Chepstow's brief life in the early part of this century as a shipbuilding centre.

Once you've exhausted the charms of Chepstow, you could follow the fairly challenging, two-hour **Wye Valley Walk** to Tintern Abbey (see below), which starts from the castle car park. A map is advisable, as the path tucks and meanders around and above the twisting Wye. You could return along the other side of the river on the Offa's Dyke Path (see p.228), which reaches its southern end at Sedbury Cliffs, a mile or so east of town on the English side of the border.

Practicalities

Chepstow's **train station** is five minutes' walk to the south of the High Street; its **bus station**, busy with *Stagecoach Red and White*'s (☎01633/266336) regular Tintern and Monmouth services, is on Thomas Street on the other side of the West Gate. The **tourist office** is located in the castle car park, off Bridge Street (Easter–Oct daily 10am–6pm; Nov–Easter daily 10am–1pm & 2–4pm; ☎01291/623772). **Bike rental** is available over the border at *Pedalabikeaway Cycle Centre* in Cannop Valley (☎01989/770357). They'll deliver if they're not too busy.

There's budget B&B **accommodation** at the *Coach and Horses* pub on Welsh Street, north from the West Gate (☎01291/622626; ③), and *Ashburne House*, 33 Bridge St (☎01291/625747; ②), which also has a good tea room. There are pricier beds up the road at the cheerful *Castle View Hotel*, 16 Bridge St (☎01291/620349; ④), which also serves great food, and at the stately *George Hotel* in Moor Street, next to the West Gate (☎01291/625363; ④). Heading out of town, a mile east over the Wye in Sedbury Lane, is *Upper Sedbury House* (☎01291/627173; ③), a wonderful, friendly B&B in a converted jailhouse.

The town is blessed with some good **pubs**. The cosy *Coach and Horses* (see above) has real ale, the town's best bar food and regular live folk and rock, while the riverside *Boat Inn*, along the quay walk from the bridge, is enormously convivial with a good, vegetarian-friendly menu. In the High Street, by the West Gate, the grimy but welcoming *White Lion* boasts a bowling alley, and at the bottom of the cobbled Hawker Hill Street, down from the High Street, is the cheery and very local *Five Alls*. For full-on **eating**, the plush *Beaufort Hotel* at the bottom of the High Street serves satisfying Welsh lunches and dinners, and *Afon Gwy*, at 28 Bridge St (☎01291/620158), a smart conservatory restaurant overlooking the river, floodlit bridge and the castle, serves excellent mid-priced European and Welsh dishes.

Tintern Abbey

Six miles north of Chepstow alongside some of the River Wye's most spectacular stretches, **Tintern Abbey** (April–Oct daily 9.30am–6.30pm; Nov–March Mon–Sat 9.30am–4pm, Sun 11am–4pm; £2.20; CADW) has inspired writers and painters for over two hundred years, ever since the Reverend William Gilpin published a book in 1782 extolling the picturesque qualities of the abbey and its valley. On a quiet day, the sight of the soft, roofless ruins is hugely uplifting; the "tall rock/The mountain, and the deep and gloomy wood" written about by Wordsworth are still evident today. Such is the abbey's enormous popularity, however, that in the middle of a summer's day, the magic can all but evaporate: it is better to go out of season or at the beginning or end of the day when the crowds have thinned out.

The abbey lasted as a monastic settlement from its foundation by the Cistercian order in 1131 to its dissolution in 1536, and the original order of monks was brought wholesale from Normandy, its members establishing themselves as major local landholders and agriculturalists. This increased the power and wealth of the abbey, attracting more monks and necessitating a massive rebuilding and expansion plan in the fourteenth century, when Tintern was at its mightiest. Most of the remaining buildings date from this time, after which the influence of the abbey and its order began to wane. Upon dissolution, many of the buildings were plundered and stripped, leaving the abbey to crumble into advanced decay. Its survival is largely thanks to its remoteness, as there were no nearby villages ready to use the abbey stone for rebuilding. From the eighteenth century onwards, travellers searching for a picturesque rather than religious experience have been attracted to the romantically placed, ivy-clad ruins; and a trip to Tintern was essential for the Romantics – Wordsworth and Turner amongst them.

The centrepiece of the complex was the magnificent Gothic **church**, built at the turn of the fourteenth century to encase its more modest predecessor. The bulk of the building remains, with the remarkable tracery in the west window and intricate stonework of the capitals and columns firmly intact; amazingly, these details withstood plundering raiders over four hundred years, as well as the elements. Behind the great east window lie the sharply rising slopes of the wooded valley, forming a perfect backdrop.

Around the church are the less substantial ruins of the **monks' domestic quarters**, mostly reduced to one-storey rubble. Rooms are easily distinguishable, however, including an intact serving hatch in the kitchen and the square of the monks' **cloister**. The course of the abbey's waste disposal system can be seen in the **Great Drain**, an irregular channel that links kitchens, toilets and the Infirmary with the nearby Wye. The **Novices' Hall** lies handily close to the Warming House, which, together with the kitchen and Infirmary, would have been the only heated parts of the abbey, suggesting that novices might have gained a falsely favourable impression of monastic life before taking their final vows. In the dining hall, you can still see the **pulpit door** that would once have led to the wall-mounted pulpit, from which a monk would read the scriptures throughout each meal.

The best way to appreciate the scale and splendour of the abbey ruins is by taking a walk on the opposite bank of the Wye. Just upstream from the abbey, a bridge crosses the river, from where a path climbs a wooded hillside. Views along the way and from the top are magnificent, framing the gaunt shell of the abbey in its sylvan setting.

Four miles northwest of the ruins, the sleepy hilltop settlement of **TRELLECH** was one of the largest boroughs in the vicinity. Reminders of its ancient status abound: there's a thirteenth-century steepled church on a seventh-century site, and, nearby, the curious **Tump**, an ancient mound that, legend has it, cannot be disturbed without deadly reprisal. A few hundred yards further south, by the B4293 Llanishen road, are the three **stones** of the village's name. Also known as Harold Stones, the straining fingers of rock, around 3500 years old and thrusting up in the middle of a sheep-filled field, are thought to be aligned with the Skirrid mountain, Monmouthshire's holiest. Off the lane to Tintern, you'll find the **Virtuous Well**, long a place of pilgrimage, with reputed healing qualities that probably stem from the water's high iron content.

Practicalities

The tiny village of **TINTERN** (Tyndyrn) is now cluttered with teashops and overpriced hotels, strung along the main road around the loop of the river. The principal **visitor centre** (April–Oct daily 10.30am–5.30pm; (☎01291/689566) is located another few hundred yards towards Monmouth at the **Old Station**. Amongst the amenities there are an interesting exhibition about the old Wye Valley railway and a good selection of leaflets on local walks, including sections of the Offa's Dyke path (see p.228) and cliff rambles above the meandering river. B&B **accommodation** is available locally at the excellent *Wye Barn* on The Quay (☎01291/689456; ③), or slap opposite the abbey, in the sumptuous *Beaufort Hotel* (☎01291/689777; ⑥). *Parva Farmhouse Hotel*, on the main road (☎01291/689411; ④), is deservedly renowned for its **food**, while at Trellech you can eat well at both the *Lion Inn* and the *Village Green* restaurant (☎01600/860119).

Monmouth

Enclosed on three sides by the rivers Wye and Monnow, **MONMOUTH** (Trefynwy) retains some of its quiet charm as an important border post and one-time county town. Now bypassed by the A40 dual carriageway which shoots along the banks of the Wye, Monmouth has few reminders of the twentieth century, save for its occasionally traffic-choked streets.

The centre of the town is **Agincourt Square**, a large and handsome open space at the top of the wide, shop-lined Monnow Street, gently descending to the thirteenth-century bridge over the River Monnow. The cobbled square is dominated by old coaching inns either side of the arched Georgian **Shire Hall**, embedded in which is an eighteenth-century statue of the Monmouth-born King Henry V, victor at the 1415 Battle of Agincourt, which brought Normandy, and soon afterwards France, under the rule of the English crown. In front of the Shire Hall is the pompous statue of another local, the Honourable Charles Stewart Rolls, the first man, in 1910, to pilot a double-flight over the English Channel, and also the co-founder of the mighty Rolls-Royce empire.

Almost opposite Shire Hall is **Castle Hill**, which you can walk up to glimpse some of the ruins of the **castle**, founded in 1068, rebuilt in stone in the twelfth century and almost annihilated in the Civil War. The only notable part of the castle still to be seen is the Great Tower, in which Henry V was probably born in 1387. Next to the castle, the gracious seventeenth-century **Great Castle House**, built out of the castle bricks, now serves as the headquarters of the Royal Monmouthshire regiment, but the building is out of bounds to civilians.

Priory Street leads north from Agincourt Square to the town's **museum** (Mon–Sat 10am–1pm & 2–5pm, Sun 2–5pm; £1), located in the market hall complex. The most comprehensive exhibit is the **Nelson Collection**, which attempts to portray the life of one of the most successful seafaring Britons through use of the Admiral's personal artefacts, including his sword, medals, intimate letters and china, together with pictures, prints and naval equipment of the day. Charles Rolls' mother, Lady Llangattock, was an ardent admirer of Nelson and a voracious collector of related memorabilia, and it is her collection now on display in the museum.

At the very bottom of Monnow Street, a couple of hundred yards from Agincourt Square, the road narrows to squeeze into the confines of the seven-hundred-year-old **Monnow Bridge**, crowned with its hulking stone gate of 1262, that served both as a means of defence for the town and a toll collection point. Just over a mile east of the town, a steep road climbs up to **The Kymin**, a fine viewpoint over Monmouth and the Wye Valley. It's crowned by the crenellated Georgian Round House and a Neoclassical **Naval Temple**, built in 1801 to cheer Britain's victories at sea.

Practicalities

Buses operate from the **bus station** behind *Kwik Save* at the bottom of Monnow Street, and the **tourist office** is in the Shire Hall, Agincourt Square (Easter–Oct daily 10am–6pm; ☎01600/713899). **Bike rental** is available from the nearby *Monmouth Cycle Centre*, 5 Beaufort Arms Court (☎01600/772779). You'll find **accommodation** at the intimate and cheerful *Riverside Hotel* on Cinderhill Street over the Monnow Bridge (☎01600/715577; ⑤), or in B&Bs like *Red Lion House*, 16 Draybridge St (☎01600/713633; ③), and the welcoming *Old Gaol* at 11 Hereford Rd (☎01600/712463; ③). The **youth hostel** is right in the heart of town in Priory Street School (March–Oct; ☎01600/715116; ①), a converted fifteenth-century priory used as a school for two hundred years until 1970. Two miles south in the village of Mitchel Troy is the excellent *Church Farm* B&B (☎01600/712176; ③). The nearest **campsite** is the tent-friendly *Monmouth Caravan Park* (☎01600/714745) on Rockfield Road, just past the fire station.

The main Monnow Street contains an assortment of fast-food joints; more substantial and tasty lunchtime and evening **food** is available at the *Punch House* in Agincourt Square; cheaper lunches can be had at the *Green Dragon* in St Thomas Square, down by the Monnow Bridge. The *French Horn* (☎01600/772733), handsomely situated at 24 Church St, is a good bistro for Welsh and continental dishes.

Monmouth is also home to a staggering number of **pubs**: worth trying are *The Bull* in Agincourt Square, the young and lively *Nag's Head*, at the bottom of Whitecross Street in St James' Square, and the *Robin Hood*, at the bottom of Monnow Street near the bridge, where Shakespeare is said to have drunk.

If transport is no problem, a superb pub lies three miles south of Monmouth off the A466 in the Wye Valley: *The Boat*, in the hamlet of Redbrook, must be reached by stumbling over the River Wye and the English border, courtesy of a dizzying footbridge stapled to the side of the disused rail bridge. The bizarre journey is worth it, for the pub is home to some amazing characters, liable to strike up a live jazz or folk session at the drop of a woolly hat.

Mid-Monmouthshire

The confrontational past of the middle tranche of Monmouthshire, long-disputed border country, can be gleaned from the castles that dot the landscape with dependable regularity. This section of the county is noticeably more "Welsh" than the border country of the Wye Valley. Stretching up from the wide-skied marsh-land that falls gently into the Severn estuary, the land reaches the flat, ugly settlement of **Caldicot**, only notable for its over-restored castle. The A48 runs from the border into south Wales, connecting **Caerwent**, a near-deserted village that was once a great Roman town, and **Penhow**, crowned by a homely fortified manor that guarded the quiet valley.

To the north is an undulating land of forests and tiny villages, criss-crossed by winding lanes that offer unexpectedly delightful views around each corner. The contours shelve down in the west to the valley of the **River Usk**, the former border of Wales as decreed in the sixteenth century by Henry VIII. Today, the A449 road roars through the valley, bypassing lanes, villages and the peaceful small town of **Usk**, home of the excellent Gwent Rural Life Museum, before joining the A40 near the spectacular ruins of **Raglan** castle.

Caldicot

Sandwiched between the main motorway and rail links between south Wales and London, **CALDICOT** is a sprawling, overgrown village of modern housing and little interest. The only possible exception is the heavily restored **castle** (March–Oct Mon–Sat 10.30am–5pm; £1.50), on the eastern side of the village. Built in the twelfth century as one of the Norman Marcher castles, constructed to keep a wary eye on the Welsh, the buildings crumbled in the years leading up to the 1800s, before being rebuilt by a wealthy Victorian barrister, Joseph Cobb. The only original parts are a large fourteenth-century round tower and elaborate gatehouse, situated either side of a grassy courtyard, whose centrepiece is one of Nelson's battle cannons from his *Foudroyant* flagship. The castle buildings contain exhibitions of local history, together with an impressive furniture collection from the seventeenth to the nineteenth centuries. Rather pricey medieval banquets (☎01291/424447) take place throughout the summer. Caldicot is the first sight of Wales for train travellers using the main line from London, and now for drivers using the brand-new second Severn bridge crossing (£3.75 toll), which connects up to the M4 westwards and Bristol on the English side of the estuary. Planned access roads threaten one of Wales' most unexpected landscapes to the southwest of Caldicot: the pancake-flat lushness of the **Caldicot Levels**, great for gentle cycling, walking and poking around the tiny villages and ancient churches that loom large on the landscape. The best place to appreciate the area's tranquillity is at **Goldcliff**, a straggle of houses petering out by the mudflats of the estuary. Here, you can walk along the sea walls and watch diving sea birds and fishermen competing for the same catch.

Caerwent

Two miles northwest of Caldicot lies the apparently unremarkable village of **CAERWENT**, from which the former county of Gwent took its name. Almost two thousand years ago, the village was known by the Romans as *Venta Silurum*, the "market town of the Silures", a local tribe forcibly relocated here from a nearby hillfort by the conquering Romans in around 75 AD, after 25 years of battle.

Venta Silurum is an unusual Roman remain, for this was a domestic market town, not, as was far more common, a military base. The most complete remnants of the Roman town are the crumbling **walls** which form a large rectangle around the modern village. Access is easiest from the steps next to the *Coach and Horses* inn, leading you up onto stone ramparts that still command melancholic views around the quiet valley. The South Wall is the most complete, still maintaining its fourth-century bastions, and it continues around to the old West Gate. Halfway along, a lane cuts up towards the rather ugly tower of the village **church**, in whose porch are maps and diagrams explaining the site of the village, as well as examples of artefacts that have been dug up. Here, you can also see two inscribed stones, one a dedication from the Siluri tribe to their Roman overlord, Paulinus, and another, dedicated to Ocelus Mars, demonstrating the odd merging of Roman and Celtic gods for worship. Opposite the church, on the village's main street, the remains of a Roman temple are currently being excavated. Nowadays, Caerwent sits on top of an altogether more contemporary military occupation, as the home of Europe's largest American rocket base at the neighbouring RAF station.

Penhow

There's another castle three miles west of Caerwent in the hamlet of **PENHOW**, whose neat church sits next to a fortified moated manor house on top of a grassy hillock. The manor house is known as **Penhow Castle** (Easter–Sept Wed–Sun 10am–5.15pm; Oct–Easter Wed 10am–4pm; £3.15), and its buildings are an accumulation of styles from the twelfth to the fourteenth centuries. The house is privately owned and claims to be the oldest lived-in castle in Wales, originally built for the St Maur family, a name later corrupted to Seymour. You can tour it with a headset commentary, starting with the impressive, thick-set Norman keep, the castle's oldest section and the family's private apartments from 1129, now filled with period trimmings such as rush lights and sporting clubs to give a credibly authentic feel. The tour continues through a tiny, narrow defile into the fifteenth-century Great Hall, complete with a minstrel gallery decorated with the Seymour family wings. Steps lead up to the Seymour bedchamber, with one step deliberately built an inch higher than the others, a common ploy in medieval days to trip up intruders. The tour concludes chronologically, passing through some of the Regency-style lodging rooms and finally through into a cluttered Victorian kitchen and nursery.

Usk

Bypassed by the main A449 is the orderly little town of **USK** (Brynbuga), astride the river of the same name. Pastel-painted houses, shops and some great pubs and restaurants line narrow Bridge Street, which leads up from the river and crosses towards the castle, looming up on a hilltop to the left. Opposite the ivy-clad ruins is the hub of the town, **Twyn Square**, where buses stop amongst the copious garish flower boxes that surround the twee restored clock tower. At the top of the square is a thirteenth-century **gatehouse**, once part of a Benedictine nunnery, and now guarding the passage to the impressive twelfth- and thirteenth-century church. There are surviving features from its days as a nunnery in the 1200s, including the nave and the slightly later tower.

Forking to the right off Bridge Street near the river is New Market Street, which runs past the **Gwent Rural Life Museum** (April–Oct Mon–Fri 10am–5pm, Sat & Sun 2–5pm; £1.50), housed in a converted eighteenth-century malt barn and specializing in the period from the early 1800s up until the end of World War II. Of all such places, this is one of the most fascinating, as the enormous collection has been put together over many decades by hundreds of local residents. Aspects of farming are explained in a pleasantly haphazard way: everything from animal-castrating implements to recreations of domestic and farming interiors – including a dairy, brewery, laundry, thatcher's and carpentry workshop – are packed into every available corner, and outdoor barns continue the exhibition with farm carts, stagecoaches and an exhibition about the Great Western Railway. Give yourself a good few hours to take it all in.

Practicalities

Usk is a quietly enjoyable place to **stay**, with good pubs for evening entertainment. For central **accommodation**, try the upmarket *Nag's Head* in Twyn Square

(☎01291/672820; ④), or the smart, spacious *King's Head* on Old Market Street (☎01291/672963; ③). Cheapest accommodation is the hostel-style *Usk Centre of Agriculture* (☎01291/672311, ext 25; ①), a mile from town on the A472 Pontypool Road. High above this road, three miles west of Usk, *Pentwyn Farm* (☎01495/785249; ③) at Little Mill is a great farmhouse B&B, with superb optional dinners and an outdoor pool. There are **campsites** two miles southeast of Usk at the *Grass Ski Centre* in Llanllowell (☎01291/672652), and four miles north at *Cwm Farm*, in Bettws Newydd (☎01873/840263).

Most of the town pubs serve **food** – the best being the *Nag's Head* (see above) and the cheap and immensely cheerful *Inn Between* at 53 Bridge St. Otherwise, Bridge Street is lined with small cafés, delis, the excellent, moderately priced Italian bistro *Rocco Italia* at no. 7 (☎01291/672459; closed Sun) and the reasonable *Bush House* at no. 15 (☎01291/672929), serving French, Mediterranean and Welsh dishes, with vegetarian options. For down-to-earth **drinking**, try the *Inn Between* or the genial *White Hart*, on the corner of Bridge and Maryport streets.

Raglan

Numerous buses leave Usk every day for **RAGLAN** (Rhaglan), seven miles to the north and also easily reached from Monmouth. An unassuming village wallowing in the folds of the hills, Raglan is worth visiting for its glorious **castle** (April–Oct daily 9am–6.30pm; Nov–March Mon–Sat 9.30am–4pm, Sun 11am–4pm; £2.20; CADW), whose fussy, and comparatively intact, style makes it stand out from so many other crumbling Welsh fortresses. The last medieval fortification built in Britain, Raglan was begun on the site of a Norman motte in 1435 by Sir William ap Thomas, whose design combines practical strength with ostentatious style. Various descendants added to the castle after his death, and building carried on into the late sixteenth century.

The **gatehouse** is still used as the main entrance, and the best examples of the castle's showy decoration appear in its heraldic shields, intricate stonework edging and gargoyles. Inside, stonemasons' marks, used to identify how much work each man had done, can be seen on the walls. Ap Thomas' grandson, William Herbert II, was responsible in the mid-fifteenth century for the two inner courts, built around his grandfather's original gatehouse, hall and keep. The first court is the cobbled **Pitched Stone Court**, designed to house the functional rooms like the kitchen (with two vast double-flued chimneys) and the servants' quarters. To the left is **Fountain Court**, a well-proportioned grassy space surrounded by opulent residences that included grand apartments and state rooms. Separating the two are the original 1435 **hall**, the **buttery**, the remains of the **chapel** and the dank, cold **cellars** below.

Off Fountain Court, through the South Gate, is the pristine **bowling green**, standing on twelve-foot-high walls above the Moat Walk, and reached by a flight of stone steps from the green. The moated yellow ashlar **Great Tower**, off Fountain Court, demonstrates continental influences in its construction, and gives it a surprisingly contemporary appearance. Two sides of the hexagonal tower were blown up by Cromwell's sidekick Fairfax after an eleven-week onslaught against the Royalist castle in 1646. The tower can still be climbed, however, right to its peak, giving phenomenal views over the green water of the moat, the intricate masonic detail of the castle and the smooth hills beyond.

Abergavenny and North Monmouthshire

Of all the towns in Monmouthshire, **Abergavenny** is the best base for a holiday. As well as a fine range of places to eat, drink and stay, the lively market town has a delightfully whimsical Museum of Childhood and a town museum in the ugly keep of the castle. Abergavenny is surrounded by commanding hills, a magnet for cyclists and walkers, of which the **Sugar Loaf** and the legend-infused **Skirrid** are deservedly the most popular.

The town is also a good base for the pastoral border country to the east, most commonly visited to see **White**, **Skenfrith** and **Grosmont** castles, known collectively, if unimaginatively, as the **Three Castles**, and first built in the later Norman years as William the Conqueror's field marshals battled continuously to impose their authority on the rebellious Welsh. Of the three, White Castle is the most imposing, although all three are in sufficiently good repair to warrant a visit.

A pointing finger of the north of the county stretches from Abergavenny along the **Vale of Ewyas** and the Honddu River at the bottom of the stark **Black Mountains**. Lost in rural isolation are the astounding churches at **Partrishow** and **Cwmyoy**, a couple of miles below **Llanthony Priory**, which has many features in common with Tintern Abbey, although with a fraction of the crowds. The road twists up to **Capel-y-ffin**, whose crumbling monastery was colonized in the 1920s by Eric Gill's artistic commune, and on through the **Gospel Pass** to some of Wales' most invigorating mountain scenery, before dropping once more down to the Wye Valley and the border town of Hay (see p.213).

Getting around in this largely rural patch of Monmouthshire can be difficult. Abergavenny is easy to reach from all destinations by train or bus, but, once up into the mountains of the north, public transport completely dries up; with bike and car rental available in Abergavenny, this need not be too much of a problem.

Abergavenny

Although only a couple of miles and a few hills from the iron and coal towns of the northern valleys, **ABERGAVENNY** (Y Fenni) grew because of its weaving trades and markets, giving it an entirely different feel. Despite Neolithic finds and the certainty that a small Roman outpost was situated here, the first main settlement in the town was around the Norman castle, which was built by the English king Henry I's local appointee, Hameline de Ballon, with the express aim of securing enough power to evict local Welsh tribes from the area, an important through route into Wales. Hostility to the Welsh reached its peak at Christmas 1175, when William de Braose, then lord of the town, invited Gwent chieftains to the castle, only to to murder them all. The town grew, shaken badly by the Black Death (1341–51) and a routing by Owain Glyndŵr in 1404, but continued to prosper, thanks largely to the weaving and tanning trades that developed from the sixteenth century. The industries of Abergavenny prospered alongside its flourishing market, still the focal point for a wide area, drawing many people up from the valleys every Tuesday. In World War II, Hitler's deputy, Rudolf Hess, was kept in the town's mental asylum as a prisoner after his plane crash-landed in Scotland in 1941. He was allowed a weekly walk in the nearby hills, growing, it is said, to love the Welsh countryside. This combination of urban amenities and vastly rewarding upland scenery is Abergavenny's main attraction today.

Arrival and information

Abergavenny is well connected to the national rail network, its **train station** (☎01873/852393) lying on the well-used line between Newport and Hereford. Buses depart from Swan Meadow **bus station** in all directions. The **tourist office** (Easter–Oct daily 10am–6pm; ☎01873/857588) and **Brecon Beacons national park office** (Easter–Oct daily 9.30am–5.30pm) are in the same building in the Swan Meadow car park. The latter is especially good for planned walking routes and leaflets on local wildlife, flora and fauna, while **maps** are best bought at the redoubtable *H K Lockyer Map Shop*, 5a Monk St (☎01873/855825). *Brook Bikes*, 9 Brecon Rd (☎01873/857066), **rents cycles**, while the British Waterways office at nearby Govilon (☎01873/830328) arranges **boat** rental along the Monmouthshire and Brecon Canal. **Concerts** and **theatre** take place in the spiky Victorian town hall on Cross Street (☎01873/852721).

Accommodation

Apart from those listed below, there are numerous cheap B&Bs on the Monmouth Road, between the town centre and the station, and the Brecon Road, on the western side of town.

Angel, Cross Street (☎01873/857121). Smart and quiet town-centre hotel. ⑥.

Great George, Cross Street (☎01873/854230). Opposite the *Angel*, although more animated, and hosting regular live music. ④.

Guest House, 2 Oxford St (☎01873/854823). Friendly town-centre B&B, adjoining the popular local *Mansel Restaurant*. ③.

King's Arms, Neville Street (☎01873/855074). A surprisingly cheap and well-appointed town-centre pub, situated between Castle and High streets. ③.

Lower House Farm, Pantygelli (☎01873/853432). Bunkhouse accommodation under the slopes of the Sugar Loaf a couple of miles north of town. ①.

Maes Glas, Raglan Terrace, Monmouth Road (☎01873/854494). Great B&B close to the town's train station. ③.

Park Guest House, 36 Hereford Rd (☎01873/853715). Plush B&B in a beautiful Georgian town house, near the station and town centre. ③.

Pentre Court, Brecon Road (☎01873/853545). Cheerful B&B a mile out of town, with an outdoor swimming pool. ②.

Pentre House, Brecon Road (☎01873/853435). Roomy, friendly Georgian country house at the turning for Sugar Loaf mountain. Lovely gardens and a very welcoming atmosphere. ②.

The Town

From the train station, Monmouth Road rises gently into the town centre, becoming Cross Street and, finally, High Street. Off to the right are Monk Street and, next to the blue-turreted Victorian Gothic town hall, Market Street, running down past the sites of the frenetic Tuesday (livestock) and Friday (produce) markets to the austere redbrick chapel that now houses the **Museum of Childhood and the Home** (Mon–Sat 10am–5pm, Sun 1–5pm; £2), an unashamed wallow in nostalgia, from Victorian dolls (plus an Edwardian one saved from the *Titanic*) and a reputedly haunted doll's house, to cigarette cards, rocking horses, needlework samplers, clockwork toys and cribs. Well-to-do children's playrooms from the Edwardian and Victorian eras have been recreated, contrasting with the far less sophisticated interior of a contemporary Welsh farmhouse. Underneath the chapel is an excellent small **coffee shop**.

Any street heading left off Cross or High streets leads to Castle Street, where the dark, fragmented remains of Abergavenny's medieval **castle** moulder. The castle's keep was entirely remodelled in the nineteenth century, and left to sit in the middle of the shabby ruins like an incongruously ugly Lego model. The castle's only real saving features are its serene position near the River Usk, at the bottom of the bowl of surrounding hills, and its mildly interesting **town museum** (March–Oct Mon–Sat 11am–1pm & 2–5pm, Sun 2–5pm; Nov–Feb Mon–Sat 11am–1pm & 2–4pm; £1). Displays cover the town's history, using photographs and billboards, and recreated interiors including a saddlery and a sanitized Border farmhouse kitchen of 1890.

Abergavenny's parish **church of St Mary**, behind the Swan Meadow car park, contains some superb effigies and tombs that span the entire medieval period. Originally built as the chapel of a small twelfth-century Benedictine priory, the existing building goes back only as far as the fourteenth century, although some of the monuments within predate the building. There are effigies of members of the notorious de Braose family, along with the tomb and figure of Sir William ap Thomas, founder of Raglan Castle and Dr David Lewis (died 1584), the first Principal of Jesus College, Oxford.

Eating and drinking

There are places to **eat** everywhere in Abergavenny – from the legion of takeaways in Cross Street, Market Street and along the Brecon Road, to excellent lunchtime and evening food in virtually all of the town's pubs.

Great George, Cross Street. Young and lively pub, especially for the weekend discos and live music on Sun evenings.

Great Western, Station Road. Nostalgia-soaked railway pub next to the station, with inexpensive, dependable food.

Greco, Cross Street. A huge place, great for piles of cheap cholesterol. Open until 7.30pm daily.

Greyhound Vaults, Market Street (☎01873/858549). Opposite the *Museum of Childhood*, this is great for a wide range of tasty, moderately priced Welsh and English specialities, including the best vegetarian dishes in town.

Hen and Chickens, Flannel Street, off High Street. Staunchly traditional pub, with the best beer in town and a separate dining room for food.

Somerset Arms, Victoria Street, by the junction of Merthyr Road. Soothingly old-fashioned locals' pub with cheap, hearty food.

Sue's Coffee House, Flannel Street (☎01873/856255). Good for daytime snacks of the sandwiches, soups and salads variety.

Swan, behind the tourist office on Cross Street. Endearingly shabby town-centre hotel pub, with a good bar menu.

Walnut Tree Inn, on the B4521 at Llanddewi Sgyrrid, two miles north of town (☎01873/852797). Legendary foodies' paradise, drawing diners from all over Britain. It's exorbitantly expensive (especially in the evening), but the food, from the owner's native Italy, is astounding.

Blorenge, Sugar Loaf and The Skirrid

Standing in the quiet grounds of Abergavenny Castle, the surrounding skyline is dominated by three southern outposts of the Black Mountains climbing out of the river plain. To the southwest is **Blorenge** (1834ft), a corruption of "Blue Ridge", accessible from the road that strikes off the B4246 a mile short of Blaenafon. The open road climbs the shale- and sheep-covered slopes to the car parks near the radio masts. An easy walk from here leads across boggy heathland to the long cairn at the summit, from which there are some glorious views south over the old mining region and north over the Usk valley, Abergavenny and the Black Mountains. Clinging to the lower contours of Blorenge is the **Monmouthshire and Brecon canal**, built into its own ridge as it glides through beech woods above the Usk valley. The canal, built around the turn of the nineteenth century to support coal mining, iron ore and limestone quarrying, is a marvellous feat of engineering, successfully steering a 25-mile lock-free stretch (the longest in Britain) through some of the most mountainous terrain. There is a steeper ascent of the Blorenge from **Llanfoist**, a mile southwest of Abergavenny, which cuts past the church and under the canal before zigzagging up the mountain.

The broad and smooth cone of **Sugar Loaf** (1955ft) commands the Black Mountains foothills to the northwest of Abergavenny (see p.62). Falling away from its summit are paths that scour the windswept slopes before descending to tiny villages in the valleys of the Usk, the Grwyne Fawr and the Grwyne Fechan. The easiest ascent is from the south, taking the right fork of Pentre Lane off the A40, half a mile west of Abergavenny, and following the road to Mynydd Llanwenarth. A longer, but fairly easy climb goes from the Rholben of Den Spurs, to the immediate east of the Mynydd Llanwenarth; but perhaps the most glorious ascent is the longest, on the north side of the mountain, from the Fforest Coal Pit, down by the Grwyne Fawr.

The Skirrid (Ysgyryd Fawr), at 1595ft, is the most eye-catching and mysterious mountain in the area. Shooting up from the Gavenny valley, three miles northeast of Abergavenny, the hill almost seems man-made, as the gentle green fields climb about halfway up before stopping suddenly in favour of purple scrub and bracken. The best path, although it is still a steep ascent, leads from the lay-by on the B4521 just short of the *Walnut Tree Inn*. The almighty chasm that splits the peak is said to have occurred by the force of God's will when Christ died, drawing Saint Michael and legions of ensuing pilgrims to the bleak spot. A few boulders lean on the summit, sole remains of the forbidden chapel built by persecuted Catholics in this most inhospitable but breathtaking spot.

The Three Castles

The fertile, low-lying land between the Monnow and Usk rivers was important as an easy access route into the agricultural lands of south Wales, and the Norman invaders built a trio of strongholds here to protect their interests. **Skenfrith, Grosmont and White castles** (all CADW) were founded in the eleventh century, and lie within an eight-mile radius of each other.

The size and splendour of the castles demonstrates their significance in protecting the border lands from both the restless English and disgruntled Welsh, who first attacked nearby Abergavenny Castle in 1182, prompting King Ralph of Grosmont to rebuild the three castles in stone. In July 1201, the three were presented as a unit by King John to Hubert de Burgh, who fought extensively on the continent and brought back sophisticated new ideas on castle design to replace earlier castles with square keeps. He rebuilt Skenfrith and Grosmont, and his successor as overlord, Walerund Teutonicus ("the German"), worked on White Castle. In 1260, the advancing army of Llywelyn ap Gruffydd began to threaten the king's supremacy in south Wales, and the three castles were refortified in readiness.

Gradually, the castles were adapted more as living quarters and royal administrative centres than military bases, as the Welsh began to adapt to English rule. The only return to military usage came in 1404–05, when Owain Glyndŵr's army pressed down to Grosmont, only to be defeated by the future King Henry V. The castles slipped into disrepair, and were finally sold by the Duchy of Lancaster to the Duke of Beaufort in 1825. The Beauforts sold the three castles off separately in 1902, the first time since 1138 that the three had fallen out of single ownership.

White Castle

White Castle (Castell Gwyn; May–Sept 10am–5pm; £1.70, free access at other times) lies about eight miles north of Raglan and six miles east of Abergavenny, just north of the village of Llantilio Crossenny. This most awesome of the three is sited in open, rolling countryside with some superb views over to The Skirrid mountain and the hills surrounding the River Monnow. A few patches of the white rendering that gave the castle its name can be seen on the exterior walls. Entering the grassy Outer Ward, enclosed by a curtain wall with four towers, gives an excellent view over to the brooding mass of the castle, situated neatly in a moat on the Inner Ward. A bridge leads over the moat into the dual-towered Inner Gatehouse, where the western tower, on the right, can be climbed for its sublime vantage point. Here, you can appreciate the scale of the tall twelfth-century curtain walls in the Inner Ward. The arrow slits in the walls are unusually cross-shaped, a distinctive feature of the castle's thirteenth-century rebuilding. Of the domestic buildings within the walls, only the foundations and a few inches of wall remain. At the back of the ward, there are massive foundations of the Norman keep, demolished in about 1260 and unearthed once more in the early part of this century. The southern wall that took the place of the keep was once the main entrance to the castle, as can be seen in the postern gate in the centre, on the other side of which a bridge leads over to the Hornwork, one of the castle's three original enclosures, although now no more than a grassy mound.

Skenfrith Castle

Seven miles northeast of White Castle, alongside the River Monnow, is the thirteenth-century **castle** (free access) in the centre of the tiny border village of **SKENFRITH** (Ynysgynwraidd), dominated by the circular keep that replaced an earlier Norman incarnation. Whilst not as impressive as White Castle, Skenfrith is in a pretty riverside setting on the main street of an attractive village.

The castle's walls are built of a sturdy red sandstone in an irregular rectangle. In the centre of the ward is the 21-foot-high round keep, raised slightly on an earth mound to give archers a greater firing range, and containing the vestiges of the private apartments of the castle's lord on the upper floors; most notable are the huge fireplace and private latrine. Along the west curtain of the wall are the excavated remains of the Hall Range of domestic buildings, including an intact thirteenth-century window, complete with its original iron bars.

Grosmont Castle

Five miles upstream of Skenfrith, right on the English border, the most dilapidated of the Three Castles, **Grosmont Castle** (Castell y Grysmwnt) sits on a small hill above the village of **GROSMONT** (free access). Entering over the wooden bridge above the dry moat, the first ruins you pass through are those of the two-stage gatehouse. This leads into the small central courtyard, dominated on the right-hand side by the ruins of a large Great Hall, dating from the first decade of the thirteenth century. The ground floor rooms were lit by lancet windows with widening stepped sills, as can still be seen. The village **church** is also worth a look, with some impressive Norman features, most notably the nave arches and the font. A memorial in the nave is popularly believed to be of John Kent, a fifteenth-century bard and magician sometimes believed to have been Owain Glyndŵr in hiding.

Practicalities

The Three Castles can only reached by walking, cycling (bike rental is available in Abergavenny) or driving. A circular route of all three castles is described in a *Green Guide* leaflet (35p) available from Abergavenny tourist office, where you can also pick up a more detailed eighteen-mile walk leaflet (£1).

Accommodation in the area is largely in farmhouse B&Bs, many of them excellent. Half a mile north of White Castle is the very friendly *Great Tre-Rhew Farm* (☎01873/821268; ②). One mile south is the slightly posher *Mrs Ford's* at Little Treadam (☎01600/780326; ③), just north of Llantilio Crossenny. Of the village pubs, pride of place goes to the *Hostry Inn* in Llantilio Crossenny (☎01600/780278; ③) for B&B lodging and excellent food. If they're full, they'll sort you out for the night in a local farm. For other nearby accommodation and amenities, see the Abergavenny account (p.62).

The Vale of Ewyas

In total contrast to the urban blights in the north valleys just a few miles away, the northern finger of Monmouthshire, stretching along the English border, is one of the most enchanting and reclusive regions in Wales. The main A465 Hereford road leads north out of Abergavenny, passing the surreal mound of The Skirrid on the right-hand side. Six miles out of town, the road bypasses the village of **Llanfihangel Crucorney**, where a lane diverges off to weave along the bank of the Honddu River past the remote village of **Cwmyoy**, with its wonky, subsided church, and on to the crumbling old religious institutions of **Llanthony Priory** and **Capel-y-ffin**. Parallel to the Honddu, a couple of miles and some impressive mountains to the west, is the **Grwyne Fawr**, a sparkling river that flows through the heart of some of Wales' most peaceful and gentle countryside, a patchwork of lush fields moulded along improbably shaped hills. Folded amongst the contours is one of the country's most perfect small churches at **Partrishow**.

Llanfihangel Crucorney, Partrishow and Cwmyoy

The place most geared up to suck in the tourists around these parts is the graceless village of **LLANFIHANGEL CRUCORNEY** (*Llanfihangel Crucornau*, the Holy Place of Michael at the Corner of the Rock), named after the tales of St Michael and The Skirrid (see above). On the main village street, quietened by the new bypass, are the odd fifteenth-century **church**, whose tower is divided from the nave by an abandoned roofless section, and the less-than-hospitable **Skirrid Inn**, which makes bold claims to be the "oldest pub in Wales", a fact singularly difficult to prove.

On the southern outskirts of Llanfihangel Crucorney, the exquisite *Penyclawdd Court* (☎01873/890719; ③) is a rambling Tudor manor house where meals can be taken by candlelight in the ponderous oak dining room. It is supposedly only open to the public on summer Sunday afternoons, although, if you telephone first, you can usually get to see the place and its recreated herb and knot garden at other times. Meals for non-residents, including period Tudor feasts, are also available on Sundays and other nominated days – call for details. Just north of the village, the Georgian *Great Llwyn Farm* (☎01873/890418; ③) overlooks the river valley.

From here, the main road through the valley heads north into the beautiful **Vale of Ewyas**, along the banks of the Honddu River. After a mile, a lane heads west towards the enchanting valley of the **Grwyne Fawr**, lost deep in the middle of quiet hills. The road is well worth following, if only for the discovery of the hamlet of **PARTRISHOW**, where a bubbling tributary of the Grwyne Fawr trickles past the delightful **church** and **well** of St Issui. First founded in the eleventh century, the tiny church was refashioned in the thirteenth and fourteenth centuries, with major restoration work needed in 1908 to prevent it collapsing. The church interior's finest feature is the lacy fifteenth-century rood screen carved out of solid Irish oak, and adorned with crude symbols of good and evil – most notably in the corner, where an evil dragon consumes a vine, a symbol of hope and well-being; the rest of the whitewashed church breathes simplicity by comparison. Of special note are the wall texts painted over the doom picture of a skeleton and scythe – before the Reformation, such pictures were widely used in the hope of teaching an illiterate population about the scriptures, until King James I ordered that such "Popish devices" should be whitewashed over and repainted with scripture texts. Here, the ghostly grim reaper is once again seeping through the whitewash. Encased in glass by the pulpit is a rare example of a 1620 Bible in Welsh.

Back on the main road, it winds its way on the valley's western side, past the fork at the *Queen's Head* (☎01873/890241; ②), excellent for B&B and pony trekking, and a good place to **camp**. It's well worth taking the little lane that peels off the main road, as it dips down over the river and into the village of **CWMYOY**, where all eyes are drawn to the amazing spectacle of the parish **church of St Martin**, whose age and history are shrouded in uncertainty, and which has substantially subsided due to geological twists in the underlying rock. Nothing squares up: the tower leans at a severe angle from the bulging body of the church and the view inside from the back of the nave towards the sloping altar, askew roof and straining windows is unforgettable.

Llanthony

Four miles further up this most remote of valleys is the hamlet of **LLANTHONY**, nothing more than a small cluster of houses, an inn and a few outlying farms around the wide open ruins of **Llanthony Priory** – a grander setting, and certainly a quieter one, than Tintern. With origins swaddled in myth and hearsay, the priory is believed to have been founded around 1100 on the site of a ruined chapel by Norman knight William de Lacy, who, it is said, was so captivated by the spiritual beauty of the site that he renounced worldly living and founded a hermitage, attracting like-minded recluses and forming Wales' first Augustine priory. The church and outbuildings still standing today were constructed in the latter half of the twelfth century. Roving episcopal envoy Giraldus Cambrensis visited the emerging priory church in 1188, noting that "here the monks, sitting in their cloisters, enjoying the fresh air, when they happen to look up at the horizon behold the tops of mountains, as it were touching the heavens". Now that this same church, with its row of wide, pointed transitional arches and squat tower, is roofless, the heavens and the sheep-speckled Black Mountains (see p.208) are even nearer. The *Abbey Hotel* here (☎01873/890487; ④), fashioned out of part of the tumbledown priory, was built in the eighteenth century as a hunting lodge. A path behind the ruins winds up to the Offa's Dyke path, straddling the England–Wales border on its lofty, windy ridge.

Though on a scale far more modest than Tintern Abbey, Llanthony has the edge in many respects. Whereas Tintern has grown into a mini-industry, supporting garish restaurants and shops around the ruins, Llanthony remains much as it has been for 800 years, retaining a real sense of spirituality and peace, against a superior backdrop of river and mountain. A hundred yards along the road from the priory is the thick-set *Half Moon Inn* (☎01873/890611; ②), home of superb beer, good-value food and comfy beds.

Capel-y-ffin and the Gospel Pass

From Llanthony, the road climbs slowly alongside the narrowing Honddu River before coasting gently along by ruined farmhouses for four miles to the isolated hamlet of **CAPEL-Y-FFIN**, just yards over the Monmouthshire border in Powys. Locked in the middle of sheer hills, Capel-y-ffin has a strangely devotional feel, due principally to the fact that the village is made up of little more than two chapels and a curious ruined monastery. The minute, whitewashed eighteenth-century chapel on the main road has an apt text inscribed into one of its windows: "I will lift up mine eyes unto the hills from whence cometh my help" – at Capel-y-ffin, you can barely help doing anything else. A lane forks off by the phone box, leading up to the ruins of the privately owned (and confusingly named) **Llanthony Monastery**, founded in 1870 by the Reverend Joseph Lyne. The religious order failed to survive his death in 1908, but the place later became a self-sufficient outpost of the art world when, in 1924, it was bought by English sculptor, typeface designer and mild eccentric Eric Gill, whose commune, a motley collection of artists and their families, drew much of their creative inspiration from the tiny valley of Nant y Bwch, the stream that runs by the lane, which can be followed all the way to its source underneath the commanding heights of **Rhiw Wen**.

From here, the road narrows as it weaves a tortuous route up into the **Gospel Pass** and onto the glorious roof of the Black Mountains (see p.208). A howling, windy moor by **Hay Bluff**, five miles up from Capel-y-ffin, affords vast views and terrific walking over spongy hills, punctuated by bleak crags and the distant view of tiny villages. The road drops just as suddenly as it climbed, descending five miles into Hay-on-Wye (see p.213).

Facilities are scarce around here; *The Grange* (☎01873/890215; ③) is a comfortable B&B in whose extensive grounds (including a portion of Offa's Dyke) you can pitch a tent. Capel-y-ffin **youth hostel** (☎01873/890650; ①; closed Dec & Jan, which also has **camping**, lies a mile up the valley from the hamlet itself).

Newport and around

The westernmost slice of Monmouthshire is the most stark in terms of contrast, from the lofty and windswept peaks of the northern segment around Abergavenny to the grit and industry of the valley towns in the south. Dominating the latter is **NEWPORT** (Casnewydd-ar-Wysg), Wales' third-largest town, a downbeat, working-class place that grew up around the docks at the mouth of the Usk.

Its rich history has been largely swept away by the twentieth century, but isolated nuggets remain, whether in the scant ruins of the riverside **castle**, or the church of St Woolos, high on a hill over the town and elevated to cathedral status in 1921. The superb municipal **museum** draws together the strings of the town's vibrant past, including a memorable and informative section on the nineteenth-century **Chartist movement**, formed to fight for universal franchise. **Caerleon** – the "old port" on the River Usk – has become little more than a northern suburb of the town, although it predates Newport by at least a thousand years as one of the most important Roman military stations in Britain and, reputedly, as the base of King Arthur.

The Town

Scything the town in two is the River Usk, foul and muddy as the tidal waters flow down to the Severn estuary, three miles away. Wedged in between the rail and main road bridges are the pathetic remains of the town's **castle**, first built in 1191, rebuilt in the fourteenth century, sacked by Owain Glyndŵr in 1402 and refortified later in the same century. Apart from its remarkably uncongenial position, the castle is notable for the sheer drop down to the mudflats of the estuary and the vaulted ceiling still retained in the central tower.

On the other side of the Newport Bridge, a walkway leads along the river bank past Peter Fink's giant red 1990 sculpture, **Steel Wave**, a nod to one of Newport's great industries. The main route into the town centre proper is up the pedestrianized High Street, which shortly meets up at the main crossroads of Newport and Westgate squares. Here stands the **Westgate Hotel**, an ornate Victorian successor to the hotel where soldiers sprayed a crowd of Chartist protesters with gunfire in 1839, killing at least a dozen. The hotel's original pillars still show bullet marks.

Commercial Street, leading south from Westgate Square, is Newport's main shopping thoroughfare, lined with tatty shops, but beautifully framing the town's famous Transporter Bridge (see p.72). One hundred yards along Commercial Street, the pedestrianized **John Frost Square** (named after a former mayor and one of the 1839 Chartist leaders) lies to the left. Although no more than an ugly 1960s precinct, the square does contain the distinctly quirky **Newport clock**, originally built for the 1992 Garden Festival at Ebbw Vale. Every hour, the silver mock-temple shudders, shakes, splits, smokes and comes near to apparent collapse, usually drawing an appreciative audience. In front of the clock is the town's library, tourist office and imaginative civic **museum** (Mon–Thurs 9.30am–5pm, Fri 9.30am–4.30pm, Sat 9.30am–4pm; free). Starting with the origins of Gwent, the displays look at the county's original occupations and early lifestyles, and includes a section on mining with a roll call of those killed in local pit accidents – 3508 men between 1837 and 1927. Newport's spectacular growth from a small Uskside dock in 1801 with a population of 1000 to a grimy port town of 70,000 people by the turn of this century is well charted, through the use of photographs, paintings and contemporary documents. The two most interesting sections deal with the Chartist uprising and the Roman mosaic remains excavated at Caerwent, and on the top floor the **Wait Collection** of Edwardian kitsch is most noted for its three hundred-plus teapots.

The other road that heads south from Westgate Square is **Stow Hill**, one of Newport's few handsome thoroughfares of Victorian and Georgian town houses. A ten-minute walk up the hill leads to **St Woolos Cathedral**, a curious jigsaw of

NEWPORT

ACCOMMODATION
1 Kepe Lodge
2 Queen's Hotel
3 St Etienne

0 yds 300

architectural styles and periods. The tiny, whitewashed twelfth-century Lady Chapel leads through a superb Norman arched doorway – supported by columns reputedly of Roman origin from Caerleon – into the Norman nave, notable for its clerestory windows, bounded by two fifteenth-century aisles. The modern east end of the cathedral harmonizes well, with a circular east window in a swirl of autumn colours locked in a marbled round-headed arch that harks back to the Norman features.

Dominating the Newport skyline is the 1906 **Transporter Bridge** (Mon–Sat 8am–6pm, Sun 1–5pm; car toll 50p, free for cyclists and pedestrians), built to enable cars and people to cross the river without disturbing the shipping channel, hoisting them high above the Usk on a dangling platform. Its comical, spidery legs flare out to the ground, connecting the aptly named Brunel Street on the west bank (reached down Commercial Street and its continuation, Commercial Road) and Stephenson Street opposite. The pristine blue cage that slides across the estuary looks like something from the drawing board of an eccentric Victorian designer.

Tredegar House

Buses #3, #15 and #30 go out to the westerly suburbs of Newport and **Tredegar House** (house April–June & Sept Wed–Sun noon–6pm; July & Aug Tues–Sun noon–6pm; Oct Sat & Sun noon–6pm; park daily 9am–dusk; house tour & gardens £4, walled gardens & park £1), just off junction 28 of the M4. The home of wealthy local landowners, the Morgan family, from 1402 until 1951, Tredegar and its grounds have been transformed into a recreation park complete with boating and fishing lake, craft workshops and donkey rides. The house itself is an unassuming seventeenth-century pile in warm red brick, built to replace the Morgans' earlier home, and its interior is in the process still of restoration to an approximation of its Regency heyday, when Tredegar was one of Wales' most fashionable and exclusive mansions, where royalty and politicians mingled right up to the years preceding World War II. Of the rooms in the tour, the first-floor Gilt Room is the most memorable: an explosion of glittering fruit bosses, an intricate gilded marble fireplace, mock-walnut panelling and an elaborate painted stucco gold ceiling. The formal walled gardens are behind the housekeeper's shop and are in the process of being re-laid in patterns culled from eighteenth-century designs.

THE CHARTISTS

During an era when wealthy landowners bought votes from the enfranchised few, the struggles of the Chartists were an historical inevitability. Thousands gathered around the 1838 People's Charter that called for universal male franchise, a secret (and annual) ballot for Parliament and the abolition of property qualifications for the vote. Demonstrations in support of these principles were held all over the country, with some of the most vociferous and bloodiest taking place in the radical heartlands of industrial south Wales. On November 4, 1839, Chartists from all over Monmouthshire marched on Newport and descended Stow Hill, whereupon they were gunned at by soldiers hiding in the *Westgate Hotel*, killing around 22 protesters. The leaders of the rebellion were sentenced to death, which was commuted to transportation, by the self-righteous and wealthy leaders of the town. Queen Victoria even knighted the mayor who ordered the random execution.

Practicalities

Newport's **tourist office** is in the museum complex in John Frost Square (Mon–Thurs 9.30am–5pm, Fri 9.30am–4.30pm, Sat 9.30am–4pm; ☎01633/842962), a hundred yards from Kingsway **bus station** (town enquiries ☎01633/263600, other services ☎01633/265100), and a quarter-mile from the **train station** (☎01633/842222).

Accommodation is abundant and generally reasonable. For hotels, try the informal, pink *Queen's Hotel*, 19 Bridge St (☎01633/262992; ③), the central, if starchy *Westgate Hotel*, at the bottom of Commercial Street and Stow Hill (☎01633/244444; ⑤), or the genteel *St Etienne*, 162 Stow Hill (☎01633/262341; ④). At the western end of Bridge Street, Caerau Road rises up sharply to the south, passing the relaxed, hospitable *Kepe Lodge* at no. 46a (☎01633/262351; ③). There is a **campsite** at *Tredegar House* (☎01633/815880); see above for bus services.

There are plenty of chain **food** outlets along Bridge and Commercial streets, and nearby *Rocky's* serves individualistic burgers on the tiny Baneswell Road, off Bridge Street (closed Sun evening). Up by the cathedral, the *Ristorante Vittorio*, 113 Stow Hill (☎01633/840261), is a popular and traditional Italian trattoria. The *Westgate Hotel* has a reasonable daytime café-bar open in the small alley alongside in Commercial Street, next to the *Scrum Half* café, excellent for cheap and filling breakfasts and lunches.

Despite the profusion of **pubs**, none is terribly special: the 1530 *Olde Murenger House*, on the High Street, has a beautiful Tudor frontage spoiled by a tatty interior, the *Queen's Hotel*, on Bridge Street, is large and unremarkable, and the cosy *Lamb* just down the road at no. 6 is popular. The most spirited pub in the town centre has to be the *Hornblower*, 127 Commercial St, though it's not a place for the faint-hearted, a raucous biker's pub with some heavy choices of music. Newport is, however, one of the major centres of the buoyant Welsh **rock and dance music** scene. Legendary try-out pub venue *TJ's* is at 14 Clarence Place (☎01633/216608), or for a bit of later dancing try *Heights 2000* (☎01633/250978) at 40 Stow Hill or the studenty *Cotton Club* (☎01633/252973) on Cambrian Road.

Caerleon

Half-hourly buses wind their way along the three-mile journey north of Newport to **CAERLEON** (Caerllion), whose compact town centre is situated to the immediate northwest of the town bridge over the River Usk. The remnants of the Roman town lie scattered throughout the present-day centre.

It was the Usk (Wysg) that gave Caerleon its old Roman name of Isca, a major administrative and legionary centre built by the Romans to provide ancillary and military services for the smaller, outlying camps in the rest of south Wales. Its only near equivalents in Roman Britain were Chester, servicing north Wales and northwest England, and York, dealing with the Roman outposts up towards Hadrian's Wall and beyond. Founded in 74 AD, lasting until its abandonment late in the fourth century, Isca was a garrison housing up to six thousand members of the Second Augustan Legion in a neat, rectangular walled town. Although the town fell gradually into decay after the Romans had left, there were still some massive remains standing when itinerant churchman and chronicler Giraldus Cambrensis visited in 1188. In his effusive writing about the remains, he noted with evident relish the "immense palaces, which, with the gilded gables of their roofs, once rivalled the magnificence of ancient Rome". Although time has had an inevitable corrosive effect on the remains since Giraldus' time, the excavated bath house and preserved amphitheatre still retain a powerful sense of ancient history.

At the back of the *Bull Inn* car park are the Roman **fortress baths** (April–Oct daily 9.30am–6.30pm; Nov–March Mon–Sat 9.30am–4pm, Sun 2–4pm; £1.70; £2.85 joint ticket with Legionary Museum; CADW). The bathing houses, cold hall, drain (in which teeth, buttons and food remnants were found) and communal pool area are remarkably intact and beautifully presented, with highly imaginative uses of audio-visual equipment, sound commentary and models. On the High Street, the Victorian neo-classical portico is the sole survivor of the original **Legionary Museum** (April–Sept Mon–Sat 10am–6pm, Sun 2–6pm; Oct–March Mon–Sat 10am–4.30pm, Sun 2–4.30pm; £2, £2.85 joint ticket with baths), now housed in a modern building behind. There are hundreds of artefacts dug from the remains of Isca and the smaller fortress at nearby Burrium (Usk). These include some intricately carved gemstones, lamps, tools, dental equipment, belt buckles, soldiers' amulets, personal hygiene items such as tweezers and nail cleaners, dice and game counters. The museum's new **Capricorn Centre**, although aimed squarely at school parties, is interesting for the recreated Roman barrack where you can try on a typical soldier's armour plating.

Opposite the Legionary Museum, Fosse Lane leads down to the hugely atmospheric Roman **amphitheatre** (same times as the baths; free), the only one of its kind preserved in Britain. Hidden under a grassy mound called King Arthur's Round Table until excavation work brought it to light in the 1920s, the amphitheatre was built around 80 AD, the same time as the Colosseum in Rome; legions of up to six thousand would take seats to watch the gory combat of gladiators, animal baiting or military exercises. The oval shape of the amphitheatre is backed by grassy stepped walls, on which the members of the legion would sit, tightly packed in, to watch activities in the middle. Over the road, alongside the school playing fields, are the scant foundations of the legion's **barracks**. The belief that Caerleon was the seat of King Arthur's court is a longstanding one. Lord Tennyson came here to research the rumours, and today, you can do no better than wander around the sublime **Ffwrrwm Centre** (most shops daily 9.30am–5.30pm), off the High Street, and talk to the various traders there who subscribe passionately to the belief. Whatever, the Ffwrrwm is a very special place: stunning courtyard sculptures draw their inspiration from ancient Celtic and Arthurian lore, surrounded by some great craft and New Age shops and a wonderful café-cum-bistro. Near the entrance to the complex, you can even clasp the gold horns of a Welsh fertility bull, an act that is supposed to lend you untold powers of procreation.

Practicalities

Caerleon's spanking new **tourist office** (Easter–Sept daily 10am–1pm & 2–6pm; ☎01633/422656) lies next to the legionary museum. A far wider range of information can be found in the various outlets in the Ffwrrwm Centre (see above), notably in the gateside antique shop and the delightful *Celtic Spirit* shop.

Staying in Caerleon is a more amenable option than nearby Newport. You can follow in the footsteps of Lord Tennyson by staying at the comfortable *Hanbury Arms* (☎01633/420361; ④), at the bottom of the High Street above the river. Alternatively, there's a great B&B at *Clawdd Farm* on Bullmoor Road (☎01633/423250; ②). The Caerleon campus of the *Gwent College of Higher Education* (☎01633/430088; ②) has decent en-suite rooms. By far the best place to **eat** is the *Oriel* bistro (☎01633/430238) in the Ffwrrwm courtyard, with outdoor seating in summer and a roaring fire in winter. It's normally a daytime venue, but will open in the evenings for group bookings, if telephoned in advance. Alternatively, the *Olde Bull Inn* on the High Street is good for food, drink and live entertainment.

The Valleys

No other part of Wales is as instantly recognizable as **the Valleys**, a generic name for the string of settlements packed into the narrow cracks in the mountainous terrain to the north of Newport, Cardiff and Swansea.

Coming through Monmouthshire, the change from rolling countryside to sharp contours and a post-industrial landscape is almost instantaneous. Each of the valleys depended almost solely on coal mining which, although nearly defunct as an industry, has left its mark in the staunchly working-class towns, where row upon row of brightly painted terraced housing, tipped along the slopes at some incredible angles, are broken only by austere chapels, the occasional remaining pithead or the miners' old institutes and drinking clubs.

This is not traditional tourist country, and yet is without doubt one of the most interesting and distinctive corners of Wales. Some of the former mines have re-opened as gutsy and hard-hitting museums – **Big Pit** at Blaenafon and the **Rhondda Heritage Park** at Trehafod being the best. Other civic museums, at **Pontypool**, **Pontypridd** and **Merthyr Tydfil**, have grown up over decades, chronicling the lives (and, all too frequently, the deaths) of miners and their families. A few older sites, such as vast **Caerphilly Castle** and the sixteenth-century manor house of **Llancaiach Fawr**, have been attracting visitors for hundreds of years. But it is beyond the mainstream sights that the visitor can gain a more rounded impression of valley life, whether in the Utopian workers' village at **Butetown**, the roundhouses at **Nantyglo**, fortified against an anticipated workers' uprising, the iron gravestones at **Blaenafon**, the dignified memorials found in almost every community to those who died underground or, in the heart-rending case of **Aberfan**, when a loose slag tip buried a primary school, and nearly 150 people, in 1966. South Wales, perhaps more than any other part of Britain, demonstrates the true cost of being the world's first industrialized nation.

Now much cleaned up, the Valleys combine unique sociological and human interest with staggering beauty in the sheer hills that rise behind each community. As a result of the formidable terrain, each valley was almost entirely isolated. Canals, roads and train lines competed for space along the valley floor, petering out as the contours became untameable at the upper end. Not until the 1920s were any connecting roads built, and even today, transport is frequently restricted to the valley bottoms, with roads and train lines radiating out through the south Wales coalfield like spokes on a giant wheel.

This section covers the Monmouthshire and Glamorgan valleys from Pontypool in the east to Cwm Afan and Port Talbot in the west. For the account of the Vale of Neath, see p.117.

Some history
The land beneath the inhospitable hills of the south Wales valleys had some of the most abundant and accessible natural seams of coal and iron ore to be found, readily milked in the boom years of the nineteenth and early twentieth centuries. In many instances, wealthy English capitalists came to Wales and ruthlessly

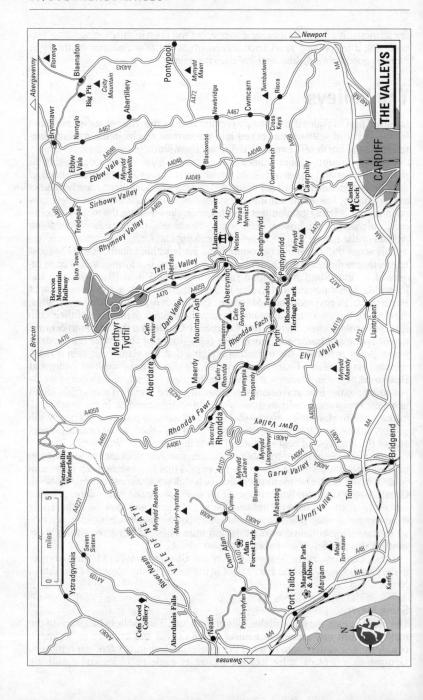

THE VALLEYS

stripped the land of its natural assets, while simultaneously exploiting those that were paid lowly amounts to risk life and limb in the mines. The mine owners were in a formidably strong position – thousands of Welsh peasants, bolstered by their Irish, Scottish and Italian peers, flocked to the Valleys in search of work and some sort of sustainable life. The Valleys – virtually unpopulated at the turn of the nineteenth century – became blackened, packed with people, pits and chapels by the turn of the twentieth.

In 1920, there were 256,000 men working in the 620 mines of the south Wales coalfield, providing one-third of the world's coal resources. Vast Miners' Institutes, paid for out of a wages' levy, jostled for position with the Nonconformist chapels, whose fervent brand of Christianity was matched by the zeal of the region's politics, trade-union-led and avowedly left-wing. Great socialist orators rose to national prominence, cementing the Valleys' reputation as a world apart from the rest of Britain, let alone Wales. Even Britain's pioneering National Health Service, founded by a radical Labour government in the years following World War II, was based on a Valleys community scheme by locally born Aneurin Bevan.

The Valleys' decline has taken place in rapid bursts, with over half of the original pits closing in the harsh economic climate of the 1930s. A Welsh cabinet secretary proposed in the mid-1930s that losses could be cut by the wholesale flooding of the Rhondda valleys as part of a massive hydroelectricity scheme. World War II saw a brief respite in the closure programme, which continued even more swiftly in the years immediately after. As coal seams have been exhausted and the political climate changed, the number of men employed in the industry has dipped down into four figures, precipitated by the aftermath of the 1984–85 miners' strike. No coalfield was as solidly behind the strike as south Wales, whose workers and families responded wholeheartedly to the call to defend the industry which their trade union, the National Union of Mineworkers (NUM), claimed was on the brink of being decimated. The year-long war of attrition between the intransigent Thatcher government and Arthur Scargill's NUM was bitter, finally seeing the government victorious as the number of miners returning to work outnumbered those staying out on strike. Just over a decade on, and all of the south Wales pits – bar one, temporarily reprieved in April 1994, and since very profitably run as a workers' cooperative – have closed.

The Valleys without coal seemed unthinkable. Some of the areas – the larger, better-populated valleys – have staged considerable recovery, with units of Japanese hi-tech industries moving into industrial estates hewn out of smoothed-out slag heaps. Alongside are new sports centres and shiny new museums fashioned out of the old pit sites. But many of the smaller, more isolated valleys have seen their population dwindle, with shops, chapels and pubs closing as young people have fled to leave an older, ex-pit generation behind that may well prove to be the last major group of inhabitants in some towns.

Pontypool

The first identifiably Valleys town – although never a coal-mining centre – heading west is **PONTYPOOL** (Pontypŵl), on the Llwyd River that winds up from the Usk at Caerleon. A sprawling, hilly town, it's hardly likely to keep you busy for long, although it's worth finding time for a short stop at the **Valley Inheritance Museum** (Feb–Dec Mon–Sat 10am–5pm, Sun 2–5pm; £1.20), housed in a Georgian stable block at the western entrance of Pontypool Park. The building was part of the estate of a mansion belonging to the Hanbury family, local landowners and industrial pioneers, and the museum casts a wide net over the town's history and trades, all of which seems to have sprung from the one family. Founding father Richard Hanbury (1538–1608), the exhibition drily notes, was a true entrepreneur, "but on occasion his enterprise led to prison sentences for fraud". The Hanburys established Pontypool's staple tinplate-making industry which led, in turn, to elaborate japanning and thence to ironworking.

A rare surviving feature of Valleys towns can be found in Pontypool, in the shape of the steamy *Mario's Café* at the bottom of Broad Street. Italian emigrants flocked to south Wales in the nineteenth century, many shunning mining and opening quite grand chrome-plated coffee houses. As successive generations have abandoned the family business, cafés have closed all over the Valleys.

The **train station** (☎01633/842222) is inconveniently sited over a mile to the east of the town centre, making **buses**, which stop by the handsome Victorian town hall, a far easier option.

Blaenafon and around

Road and river continue six miles north from Pontypool to the iron and coal town of **BLAENAFON**, at the source of the Llwyd River. It has a very different feel to many valley towns, its lofty hillside position making it feel far less claustrophobic, but its decline is testified by a shrinking population of little more than 5000, a quarter of its nineteenth-century size. The town's Victorian boom can be seen in its architecture, most notably the impressively florid **Working Men's Hall** that dominates the town centre, and where miners would pay a halfpenny a week for the use of the library and other recreational and educational facilities. The parish **church of St Peter** is a good example of what became known as Enginehouse Churches – an enginehouse being the sole type of building familiar to local masons. The church door, font and some of the gravestones are all constructed from iron.

Blaenafon's **ironworks**, just off the Brynmawr Road (May–Sept Mon–Sat 11am–5pm, Sun 2–5pm; group tours all year; £1.20; CADW; ☎01495/752036), were founded in 1788, although iron smelting in this area dates from the sixteenth century. Limestone, coal and iron ore – ingredients for successful iron smelting – were abundant locally, and the Blaenafon works grew to become one of the largest in Britain in the early nineteenth century, finally closing in 1900. The remains on the site offer a thorough picture both of the process to produce iron, and the workers' lifestyles that went with it. At the **museum**, housed in the Stack Square cottages (built for the foremen and craftsmen between 1789 and 1792), there are exhibitions on the history of iron and steel making in the Llwyd Valley. Unless you're on a pre-booked guided tour, you'll have to content yourself with staring from the viewing platform at the awesome sight of the line of late Georgian blast furnaces and the adjoining water-balance lift, used to collect water from a diverted stream to lift the iron from the site onto tramlines and thence to the canal.

Big Pit

Just as it is now possible to visit the scene of Blaenafon's iron industry, the town's defunct coal trade has also been transformed smoothly into a tourist attraction: **Big Pit** (March–Nov daily 9.30am–5pm, last underground tour 3.30pm; £5.50, surface tour only £2.50) lies three-quarters of a mile west of the town in wide, open countryside; a half-hourly shuttle bus runs from Blaenafon. The colliery closed exactly a century after its 1880 opening. Of all the mining museums in south Wales, Big Pit brings the visitor closest to the experience of a miner's work and life, as you descend 300ft, kitted out with lamp, helmet and very heavy battery pack, into the labyrinth of shafts and coal faces for a guided tour. The guides – most of whom are ex-miners – lead you through explanations and examples of the different types of coal mining, from the old stack-and-pillar operation, where miners would manually hack into the coal face before propping up the ceiling with a wooden beam, to more modern mechanically worked seams. Constant streams of rust-coloured water flow by, adding to the dank and chilly atmosphere that must have terrified the small children who were once paid twopence for a six-day week (of which one penny was taken out for the cost of their candles) pulling the coal wagons along the tracks. Back on the surface, the old pithead baths, blacksmiths, miners' canteen and winding engine house have all been preserved and filled with some fascinating displays about the local and south Wales mining industries, including a series of characteristically feisty testimonies from the miners made redundant here in 1980.

Out on the rolling moorland by the entrance of the pit, the old mine train line has been brought partly back into use and is now known as the **Pontypool and Blaenafon steam railway** (April–Sept Sun & Bank Holiday Mon only 11am–4pm; £1.50), worth taking for the couple of hundred yards to the evocative **Whistle Inn**, once the main pub for the miners, but now dependent on tourists. The atmosphere is unashamedly nostalgic, with a vast collection of miners' tin lamps hanging from the ceiling.

The Sirhowy Valley and Ebbw Vale

West of Pontypool and Blaenafon, the settlements of the **Ebbw Vale** are hemmed in by some of the Valleys' best forest scenery. Particularly popular is the **Cwmcarn Forest**, reached from the main A467 in **CWMCARN** village, two miles north of workaday **RISCA** (Rhisga), where the Sirhowy and Ebbw valleys divide. There's a successful forest drive around Cwmcarn, affording magnificent views over the old pit towns and the distant sparkle of the Severn estuary. Along the route, near Car Park 7, is the Iron Age hillfort of **Twmbarlwm**. A small cairn on the summit suggests its earlier use as a Bronze Age burial ground and the site's defensive position was also exploited by Roman and Norman settlers. The forest is home to a **campsite** (☎01495/272001), near the **visitor centre** (April–Sept daily 10am–6pm; Oct–March daily 10am–5pm; ☎01495/272001).

The Ebbw valley divides into two just short of **ABERTILLERY**, which sits at the foot of the Ebbw Fach, the smaller of the two valleys. High above the divide, a mile to the east, is the twelfth-century hilltop church of **St Illtyd**, commanding superb views all round. There's little to keep you in Abertillery itself, although you might consider continuing through to the sprawling upland settlement of **NANTYGLO**, four miles north. Signposted on the western edge of the town are two remarkable nineteenth-century fortified **roundhouses**, built by the local iron master, Joseph Bailey, an English Anglican renowned for his harsh treatment of workers. So fearful was he of insurrection, he built these mini-castles in 1816, complete with four-feet-thick walls and iron plate doors with musket holes.

From Risca, the Sirhowy River winds west past the village of **CWMFELIN-FACH**, before turning north to run parallel with Ebbw Vale. The obligatory **country park**, on the forested slopes to the south of the village, offers some good walks and a **camping barn** (☎01495/270991). The main entrance lies off the big roundabout at the suburb of **Crosskeys**, where the valleys divide. Three miles north, the Sirhowy town of **BLACKWOOD** (Coed Duon) is home to one of the most splendid of the Valleys' many **Miners Institut**es (☎01495/227206), now the well-restored home of theatre, choirs and music, including (in this, the birthplace of the Manic Street Preachers) numerous rock and dance events.

The Rhymney Valley

Travelling west, the next valley you come across is the **Rhymney Valley**, gathered around a river that reaches its first major settlement at **CAERPHILLY** (Caerffili), seven miles north of Cardiff. A flattened and colourless town, the only feature of any interest is its **castle** (April–Oct daily 9.30am–6.30pm; Nov–March Mon–Sat 9.30am–4pm, Sun 2–4pm; £2; CADW), notable for its sheer bulk and for being the first castle in Britain built concentrically, with an inner system of defences overlooking the outer ring. Looming out of its vast surrounding moat, the medieval fortress with its cock-eyed tower occupies over thirty acres, presenting an awesome promise not entirely fulfilled inside. On the site of a Roman fort and an earlier Norman fortification, the castle was begun in 1268 by Gilbert de Clare, who wanted to protect the vulnerable coastal plains around Cardiff from the warring of Llywelyn the Last. Two years later, Llywelyn largely destroyed the castle, which was swiftly rebuilt, but for the next few hundred years, Caerphilly was little more than a decaying toy, given at whim by kings to their favourites – most notably by Edward II to his minion, and possibly lover, Hugh le Despenser, in 1317. The Civil War necessitated the building of an armoury within the castle, which prompted Cromwell to seize it, drain the moat and blow up the towers. By the turn of the twentieth century, Caerphilly Castle was in a sorry state, sitting amidst a growing industrial town that saw fit to build in the moat and the castle precincts. Houses and shops were demolished to allow the moat to be reflooded in 1958.

You enter the castle through a great **gatehouse** that punctuates the barbican wall by a lake, much restored and now housing an exhibition about the castle's history. A platform behind the barbican wall exhibits medieval war and siege engines, pointing ominously across the lake. From here, a bridge crosses the moat, part of the wider lake, to the outer wall of the castle itself, behind which sits the hulking inner ward. On the left is the southeastern tower, outleaning its rival in Pisa, a great cleft buried deep in its walls where Cromwell's men attempted to blow it sky high. With the exception of the ruined northeastern tower, the other corner turrets have been blandly restored since the Civil War, with the north-western tower housing a reasonably interesting exhibition designed to give a thorough overview of Welsh castles, their methods of construction and some speculative facts and figures about the day-to-day life of their medieval inhabi-tants. More interesting is the massive eastern gatehouse, which includes an impressive upper hall and oratory and, to its left, the wholly restored and reroofed **Great Hall**, largely built around 1317 by Hugh le Despenser.

Caerphilly is also, of course, known for its crumbly white **cheese**, which is made the traditional way at the *Courthouse* inn on Cardiff Road, a few minutes' walk from the castle, and served as part of numerous dishes, including a great-value ploughman's.

Butetown

The Rhymney becomes increasingly industrialized as it steers through the contours to the north of Caerphilly, past a seamless succession of small towns and rotting industry. At the very head of the valley, a mile beyond **RHYMNEY** town and just short of the A465 Heads of the Valleys road, is **BUTETOWN** (Drenewydd), a tiny settlement utterly different from any other in the area. Built as a model workers' estate in 1802–03 by the Marquess of Bute, a member of Wales' richest land- and resource-owning family, the town was originally conceived as the beginning of a whole new, airy workers' community. His idealism was unusual amongst the ironmasters and coal owners of the day and, sadly, only the central grid of houses was built. Two ironworkers' cottages in the main street have been converted into a small local **museum** (April–Sept daily 2–5pm; £1; other times by appointment on ☎01685/843039), detailing life for nineteenth-century employees, still arduous in such uplifting surroundings.

A mile east of Butetown, the **Bryn Bach Country Park**, on the northern edge of the close-knit little town of **TREDEGAR**, has camping and bunkhouse **accommodation** (☎01495/711816).

The Taff and Cynon valleys

Like the Rhymney, the River Taff also flows out into the Bristol Channel at Cardiff, after passing through a condensed couple of dozen miles of industry and population. The first town in the Taff vale is **Pontypridd**, one of the most cheerful in the Valleys, and where the Rhondda River (see p.85) hives off west. Continuing north, the river splits again at **Abercynon**, where the Cynon River flows in from Aberdare, site of Wales' only remaining deep mine. Just outside Abercynon is the enjoyable sixteenth-century **Llancaiach Fawr** manor house. To the north, the Taff is packed into one of the tightest of all the Valleys, passing **Aberfan** five miles short of the imposing valley head town of **Merthyr Tydfil**.

Pontypridd

PONTYPRIDD's quirky arched **bridge** of 1775 was once the largest single-span stone bridge in the world. It was built by local amateur stonemason William Edwards, whose previous attempts had crumbled into the river below. His final effort stands to this day, its three holes either side designed to lessen the bridge's overall weight and allow gusty winds through.

On the other side of the river is **Ynysangharad Park**, where Sir W Goscombe John's gooey double statue in honour of Pontypridd weaver Evan James and his son represents allegorical figures of music and poetry. In 1856, James composed the stirring *Mae Hen Wlad Fy Nhadau* (*Land of My Fathers*) that has become the Welsh national anthem.

By the bridge at the end of Taff Street, the **Pontypridd Historical and Cultural Centre** (Mon–Sat 10am–5pm; June–Aug also Sun 2–5pm; 25p) is housed in what was the town's typically austere 1861 chapel. This is one of the best museums in the Valleys – a real treasure trove of photographs, video, models and exhibits that succeed in painting a warm and human picture of the town and its outlying valleys. The interior of the old *tabernacl* itself has been lovingly restored, with ornate ceiling bosses, pillars, pulpit, stained-glass window and tinny organ all contributing to the atmosphere. There are exhibitions of old

Pontypridd in photographs and paintings, transport in the area, and records from the nearby Albion colliery, at which 290 men and boys died in an underground explosion in 1894. Pontypridd is the home town of crooner Tom Jones and opera star and actor Sir Geraint Evans, both celebrated amongst the exhibitions here.

Near the elegant and impressive train station, **John Hughes' Grogg Shop** on Broadway caricatures legions of rugby stars and Welsh celebrities in oddball sculpture, and a short walk past the pubs at the bottom of Taff Street brings you out parallel to Market Street and the chaotic bustle of the old-fashioned **market** spilling out into the surrounding streets and squares.

Pontypridd is one of the best bases in the Valleys, as it is well connected to bus, train and road networks. The **train station** is a ten-minute walk south of the old bridge on The Graig. The **tourist office** (Mon–Sat 10am–5pm; June–Aug also Sun 2–5pm; ☎01443/409512) is in the *Historical and Cultural Centre* on Bridge Street. **Accommodation** is rather scarce: try the lively *Millfield Hotel* in Mill Street (☎01443/480111; ④) or the *Morning Star* B&B on The Graig (☎01443/486594; ②), both near the station, or, right in the thick of the action, the bustling *Market Tavern* in Market Street (☎01443/485331; ③). The **youth hostel** at Llwynypia (see p.87) is only four short stops up the valley rail line. **Food** options are fairly basic: from the Italian coffee-house atmosphere of *Merengi's* in the Taff Vale precinct, and the hearty café in the *Muni Arts Centre* on Gelliwastad Road, above Taff Street, to a huddle of cheap takeaways and restaurants opposite the station. **Pubs** are more Pontypridd's style, with the musical *Globe* up on Graig High Street, behind the station, the lively *New Inn* on Market Street and, just over the bridge from the Heritage Centre, the *Llanover Arms* on Bridge Street.

Llancaiach Fawr

The river divides at **Abercynon**, four miles up the Taff valley, with the Cynon River flowing in from Aberdare in the northwest. Abercynon is a stark, typical valley town of punishingly steep streets lined with blank, grey houses, fading out into a coniferous hillside. Two miles east of Abercynon, just north of the village of **NELSON**, is the sixteenth-century **Llancaiach Fawr** (Mon–Fri 10am–5pm, Sat & Sun 10am–6pm; £3.75; ☎01443/412248), a Tudor house, built around 1530, that has been transformed into a living-history museum set in 1645, the time of the Civil War, with all of the guides dressed as house servants, speaking the language of seventeenth-century Britain. Although there is great opportunity for the whole experience to be nightmarishly tacky, it is quite deftly done, with well-researched period authenticity and numerous fascinating anecdotes from the staff; visitors are even encouraged to try on the master of the household's armour. Special tours – candlelit, murder-mystery and seventeenth-century evenings – are also available. Regular buses from Pontypridd, Cardiff and Ystrad Mynach station pass the entrance. If you want to **stay** nearby, the delightful *Llechwen Hall* (☎01443/742050; ④) sits high on the hills to the south of Nelson, while, almost opposite Llancaiach Fawr, the *Fairmead* guesthouse (☎01443/411174; ③) is low-key but reliable.

Aberfan

North of Abercynon, the Taff valley contains one sight that is hard to forget: the two neat lines of distant arches that mark the graves of the 144 people killed in October 1966 by an unsecured slag heap sliding down a hill and onto the Pantglas primary school in the village of **ABERFAN**. Thousands of people still make the pilgrimage to the village graveyard, to stand silent and bemused by the enormity of the disaster. The human cost – including 116 children who died huddled in panic at the beginning of their school day – is beyond comprehension. Amongst the gravestones that strive to rationalize the tragedy, one of the most humbling and beautiful valedictions is to a ten-year-old boy, who, it simply records, "loved light, freedom and animals". Official enquiries all told the sorry tale that this disaster was an almost inevitable eventuality, given the cavalier approach to safety so often displayed by the coal bosses. Gwynfor Evans, then the newly elected first Plaid Cymru MP in Westminster, spoke with well-founded bitterness when he said "let us suppose that such a monstrous mountain had been built above Hampstead or Eton, where the children of the men of power and wealth are at school . . .". That, of course, could never have happened.

Merthyr Tydfil

MERTHYR TYDFIL sits at the top of the Taff valley, on the cusp of the industrial Valleys to the south and the grand, windy heights of the Brecon Beacons to the north. Merthyr's strategic site was first exploited by Romans as an outpost of their base at Caerleon (see p.73), then in 480 AD, Tydfil, Welsh princess and daughter of Brychan, Prince of Brychianog, was captured as she rode through the area, and murdered for her Christian beliefs. She became St Tydfil the Martyr, and her name was bestowed on the scattered population of the area.

In the seventeenth century, the village became a focal point for Dissenters and Radicals, movements which, through poverty and crass inequality, gained momentum in the eighteenth century as the town's four massive ironworks were founded to exploit the abundant seams of iron ore and limestone. Merthyr became the largest iron-producing town in the world, as well as by far the most populous town in Wales – in 1831, the town had a population of 60,000, more than Cardiff, Swansea and Newport combined. Workers flocked from all over Britain and beyond, finding themselves crammed into squalid housing whilst the ironmasters built themselves great houses and palaces on the better side of town. Merthyr's radicalism bubbled furiously, breaking out into occasional riots and prompting the election of Britain's first socialist MP, Keir Hardie, in 1900. It was here that the first red flag was raised, when rioters in 1831 gathered around a standard dipped in the blood of a killed calf.

However, the town's precipitous development saw it peak and trough earlier than other places: of the four mighty ironworks, only one was still open at the end of World War I, and that closed in the 1930s. In 1939, a Royal Commission suggested that the town be abandoned and the inhabitants shifted to the coast. The plan was forgotten when war broke out.

Although the twentieth century has been a story of decline for Merthyr, it's still a robust and enjoyable town, good for forays into the Valleys or the Beacons and with a fascinating, and unique, pedigree of its own.

The Town

The town centre is wedged in between the High Street and the River Taff, but the sights listed here are all around the Taff to the immediate northwest. The **Ynysfach Engine House** (March–Oct Mon–Fri 11am–5pm, Sat–Sun 2–5pm; Nov–Feb Mon–Fri 10am–4pm, Sat & Sun 1–4pm; £1) was once the powerhouse behind the mighty Cyfartha ironworks. Costumed mannequins portray scenes from Merthyr's past as a centre of iron and steel making, coupled with an entertaining video about the town's industrial history. The overall effect is gritty, with a special look at the social conditions in the urban chaos of the nineteenth century.

Half a mile further up the River Taff, tucked amongst modern houses just off Nant-y-Gwenith Street, the lower end of the Neath Road, is **Chapel Row**, a line of skilled ironworkers' cottages built in the 1820s, one of which holds composer **Joseph Parry's Birthplace** (March–Oct daily 2–5pm; free), though this is most interesting as a social record of slightly better-than-average workers' domestic conditions of the nineteenth century. Parry's music, including the national favourite *Myfanwy*, is piped between rooms, and the upstairs section of the house is given over to a display of his life and music.

Back across the other side of the river, just beyond the Brecon Road, is a home in absolute contrast to Parry's humble and cramped birthplace: **Cyfartha Castle** (April–Sept Mon–Fri 10am–6pm, Sat & Sun noon–6pm; Oct–March closes 5pm; £1), built in 1825 as an ostentatious mock-Gothic castle for William Crawshay II, boss of the town's original ironworks. The castle is set within an attractive, 160-acre park which slopes down to the river and afforded Crawshay a permanent view over his iron empire. It's a great museum: going through the well-recreated Valleys Italian café takes you down into the old wine cellars for a gutsy history of the town. Starting with tales of the martyr Tydfil, the Penydarren Roman fort and ruined Morlais Castle, the narrative soon leads into Merthyr's industrial and political heritage. Merthyr's place in working-class history is well examined, with an interesting set of panels and pamphlets on the 1831 riot. Other exhibits look at Aberfan, the 1984–85 miners' strike, pubs and the temperance movement and the beleaguered 1980s Sinclair C5 car, constructed here at the Hoover plant – "built by Hoover, driven by suckers" as the local phrase had it.

Upstairs, the castle's opulent main rooms, all chandeliers and acres of curtains, now house a superb collection of Welsh and international art. Welsh highlights include an uncharacteristically gentle study of *The Elf* by monumental sculptor Goscombe John, and paintings by local Penry Williams, Augustus John, Cedric Morris, Kyffin Williams and Alfred Jones, whose double portrait of Salome is quite mesmerizing. Works by other artists – Jack Yeats and Edward Burne-Jones among them – complement mementoes from Crawshay's empire.

The surrounding park contains landscaped walks, a nursery, café, bowling green, tennis courts, a pitch-and-putt course and a stage set next to the main lake. You can rent a bike here, too.

Practicalities

The **train station** (☎01222/228000) is on the east of the town centre, a minute's walk from the High Street. North from here is Glebeland Street and the **bus station** (☎01633/266336), where services depart for all points of south and mid-Wales. The **tourist office**, 14a Glebeland St (Mon–Sat 9.30am–5.30pm; ☎01685/379884), is behind the bus station. Municipal **bike rental** (☎01685/725000 or 371555) is available in the summer from Cyfartha Castle.

Accommodation is varied, including the unpretentious *Tregenna Hotel* in Park Terrace, next to Penydarren Park (☎01685/723627; ④); there are humbler surroundings at the *Hanover Guest House*, 31 Hanover St (☎01685/379303; ②), or the *Penylan*, 12 Courtland Terrace (☎01685/723179; ②). There's a **campsite** four miles north of town in the beautiful surroundings of *Grawen Farm*, Cwmtaf, near Cefn-Coed (☎01685/723740).

There are plenty of daytime **food** outlets in the main shopping area of the town centre, with a few cafés, Chinese and Indian restaurants open into the evening along the High Street. Pubs serving food include the *Harp Inn* on Swansea Road, the *Tregenna Hotel* in Park Terrace, or the historic *Three Horseshoes Inn*, Dynevor Street, where up to three hundred Chartists used to cram into the small bar. Any of these will also prove amenable for a night's **drinking**, as will the downbeat *Belle Vue* and lively *Narrow Gauge*, both on Glebeland Street.

The Rhondda

For many people, the **Rhondda** – sixteen miles long and never as much as a mile wide – is the quintessential Welsh Valleys, and though others may grumble it's still here you'll find the region's quintessential heritage distilled into straggling hillside communities. Hollywood played its part in promoting the area, with the Oscar-winning weepie *How Green Was My Valley*, although the story was based on author Richard Llewellyn's early life in nearby Gilfach Goch, strictly speaking outside the valley. Whatever, the Rhondda was the heart of the massive south Wales coal industry, an industry that, at its peak, provided around one-third of the entire world's consumption.

In 1860, tentative mining explorations had taken place in Rhondda's quiet, fertile land, and the two valleys housed around 3000 people. By 1910 nearly 160,000 were squeezed into the available land, in ranks of houses grouped around sixty or so pitheads. The Rhondda, more than any other of the Valleys, became a self-reliant, hard-drinking, chapel-going, deeply poor and terrifically spirited breeding ground for radical religion and firebrand politics. The Communist Party ran the town of Maerdy (nicknamed "Little Moscow" by Fleet Street in the 1930s) for decades. The 1984–85 miners' strike saw solidarity in the Welsh pits on a greater scale than any other part of Britain. But the last pit in the Rhondda, the epicentre of the coal-mining industry, closed four days short of Christmas in 1990. Left behind is not some dispiriting ragbag of depressing towns, but a range of new attractions, cleaned-up hillsides and some of the friendliest pubs and working men's clubs to be found anywhere in Britain. Hillwalking, with astounding views over the tight little towns, is now serious business.

The Rhondda starts just outside **Pontypridd**, winding through the mountains alongside train line, road and river for a few miles to **Trehafod** and the colliery museum of the **Rhondda Heritage Park** (daily 10am–6pm, last admission 4.30pm; £4.45), formed by locals when the Lewis Merthyr pit closed in 1983. You can explore the engine winding houses, lamp room, fan house and a new trip underground, with stunning visuals and sound effects, recreating 1950s and late nineteenth-century life (and death) through the eyes of colliers. A chilling roll call of pit deaths and a final narration by Neil Kinnock about the human cost of mining – especially for the Valley women – are very moving. Nearby, in Warwick House on Trehafod Road, is the **Kingmaker Coal Craft** studio and shop (Mon–Sat 9am–5.30pm), where the "black gold" of the Rhondda is fashioned into amazing figurines and models.

Although it's not always recognized, the Rhondda is in fact two valleys which divide at the solid town of **PORTH** ("Gateway"), a mile beyond the museum. The **Rhondda Fach** (Small Rhondda) River twists its way northwards through the smaller and frequently forgotten valley, passing endless quintessential Valleys towns like Ynyshir, Pontygwaith, Tylorstown, Ferndale and Maerdy – row after row of tiny houses clinging grimly to sheer valley walls. **Rhondda Fawr (**Big Rhondda) stretches from the outskirts of Pontypridd to Blaenrhondda and is blessed with a train line, a decent swift road and most of the sights.

The first notable settlement is **TONYPANDY**, birthplace of Lord George Thomas, former honey-toned Speaker of the House of Commons, a mile short of **LLWYNYPIA**, wedged in by walkable forested hillsides and home to the Rhondda's excellent **youth hostel** (see below). From here, a steep two-mile climb leads up to **Mynydd y Gelli**, where remains of an Iron Age hut settlement and a Bronze Age burial chamber and stone circle can be seen.

On the other side of the valley from Llwynypia, a sheer path climbs up to the notorious 1960s hilltop estate of **PENRHYS**, built as a lofty antidote to the wedged-in valley settlements all around. Unfortunately, the Sixties optimism rapidly disintegrated, leaving a sink estate with bad services, terrible weather and numerous social problems. On the hillside looking down into the Rhondda Fawr, you can see the grotty Catholic shrine and well of **St Mary** by the main road in Penrhys. The road, river and train line wind tortuously past an endless stream of towns to **TRE-ORCHY** (Treorchi), one of the most famous mining towns in Wales, largely due to the international status of its **Royal Male Voice Choir**, the oldest in Wales. Visitors are welcome to rehearsals, which take place each Sunday, Tuesday and Thursday (Mr Morgan on ☎01443/435852) at the Treorchi Primary School in Glynocli Road. Treorchy is also home of the splendid **Parc and Dare Hall** (☎01443/773112 or 775654) and theatre. The Hall houses an exhibition about Paul Robeson, "honorary Welshman" and black American spiritual singer and civil rights activist.

From Treorchy, the A4601 branches off the valley road and heads west up the mountainside, twisting its way around Mynydd Maendy and Mynydd Llangeinwyr. One of the most spectacular roads in Wales, it divides to head west down the Cwm Afan and south for the Cwm Ogwr Fawr. At the top of the Rhondda

---

MALE VOICE CHOIRS

Fiercely protective of its reputation as a land of song, the voice of Wales is most commonly heard amongst the ranks of **male voice choirs**. Although they can be found all over the country, it is in the southern, industrial heartland that they are loudest and strongest. The roots of these choirs lie in the Nonconformist religious traditions of the seventeenth and eighteenth centuries, when Methodism in particular swept the country, and singing was a free and potent way of cherishing the frequently persecuted faith. Throughout the breakneck industrialization of the nineteenth century in the Glamorgan valleys, choirs of coal miners came together to praise God in the fervently religious way that was typical of the packed, poor communities. Classic hymns like *Cwm Rhondda* and the Welsh national anthem, *Mae Hen Wlad Fy Nhadau* (*Land of My Fathers*), are synonymous with the choirs, whose full-blooded interpretation of them continues to render all others insipid.

The collapse of coal mining in the twentieth century has left a few choirs perilously short of members, although most continue to practise with almost religious devotion, performing in Wales and abroad with regularity. Each small Valleys town has its own choir, most of whom happily allow visitors to sit in on rehearsals. The Wales Tourist Board issues a leaflet, available from tourist offices, which gives contact phone numbers for each choir's secretary. Contact them directly, and take the chance to hear one of the world's most distinctive choral traditions in full, roof-raising splendour.

Fawr is **TREHERBERT**, its straggle of houses continuing up the valley at **BLAENCWM** and **BLAENRHONDDA**, two communities effectively bypassed since the new road was built in the 1930s by unemployed miners, connecting Treherbert to the forests and lakes of Hirwaun Common en route to Brecon.

Spectacular walks abound in the Rhondda. A mildly difficult two-mile hike from Blaencwm, for instance, leads to the remarkable mound of **Penpych**, sitting sentinel over the Rhondda Fawr, while a diversion east at Ferndale passes the remains of a Roman marching camp, **Twyn-y-Briddallt**, and **Old Smokey**, a huge pile of colliery spoil with excellent views, before winding up at the isolated little village of **LLANWONNO**, home to remote glades, an ancient church and a good village pub. At the top of the valley, from the vast site of Maerdy colliery (the last Rhondda pit), a path edges along the infant river, past the rocky height of **Castell Nos**, an old border defence castle, and on up to the Lluest Wen reservoir.

Practicalities

A **train** line, punctuated with stops every mile or so, runs from Pontypridd to its terminus at Treherbert, the entire length of the Rhondda Fawr. **Buses** also cover the route, continuing up into the mountains and the Brecon Beacons. The Llwynypia **youth hostel**, in the Glynocornel Centre opposite the station (closed Nov & mid-Dec to mid-Feb; ☎01443/430859; ①), is well placed for residential environmental studies and walking. Other **accommodation** includes the chintzy *Heritage Park Hotel*, next to the Rhondda Heritage Park at Trehafod (☎01443/687057; ④), and, just opposite, the *Village Inn* (☎01443/688204; ③). In Porth is the scruffy but friendly *G&T's*, 64–66 Pontypridd Rd (☎01443/685775; ③), which also serves winning **food**. Nearly a mile up from Llwynypia is **Ystrad**, where the cosy *Greenfield* pub in William Street serves good food and beer. Although, for the most part, eating options in the Rhondda towns mean a range of chip shops, Chinese takeaways and pickled eggs in the pubs, some of the **pubs** and **working men's clubs** (which you'll generally need to be invited into, although there are many people more than happy to do this for you) serve food.

The Ogwr, Garw and Llynfi valleys

Running west from the Rhondda, these three valleys are less harsh in appearance than the others: the contours are slightly softer, the open spaces wider and the towns smaller and lower key. The **Ogwr Valley** plunges south from the Rhondda Fawr's Treorchy, through the sleepy villages of **Nant-y-moel** and **Ogmore Vale**, before the main road forks at **Pont-yr-awel** for the branch road over to the Garw Valley. High between the two is the one-horse hamlet of **LLANGEINOR**, little more than a fine medieval church, circular village green, good country pub and numerous paths radiating out over the upland moors.

The Ogwr Valley descends through orderly little townships en route into **BRIDGEND** (Pen-y-bont ar Ogwr), an ancient settlement that guards the entrance to the three valleys. Consequently, it was deemed important enough to house two Norman castles, either side of the river. The "old castle" survives only in the name of the suburb on the town-centre side of the river, while opposite, the scant remains of the "new castle", high on a wooded hill above the A4063 Maesteg road, are notable mainly for the surviving late-Norman decorated gateway. That aside, there's not much to occupy you in Bridgend, although it's a useful transport interchange, with a good selection of shops and a few handsome buildings. Just over a mile northeast of the town are the more substantial remains of **Coity Castle** (free access; CADW), built around the end of the twelfth century by one of the earliest Norman knights in the area, who, it is said, married the daughter offered to him by the local Welsh chieftain. A large outer ward encloses the original keep and some domestic buildings dating from the fourteenth to the sixteenth centuries. Bridgend is also very handy for Porthcawl, Ewenny Priory and beyond – see the Vale of Glamorgan section (p.110).

The **Garw Valley** seems a world apart; it is one of the dead-end valleys that consists of one road, river and railway crammed in on the valley floor, before they all peter out into the wooded hillsides. Although scarred by mine workings, the valley is surprisingly pretty and, as it's well off any tourist track, very rewarding for good walks and congenial company in the pubs and shops. At the lower end of the valley, the **Bryngarw Country Park** (daily dawn–dusk) is a pleasant diversion. Landscaped gardens, exceptional flower collections and mature woodlands are gathered around a **visitor centre** (April–Sept daily 10am–6pm; ☎01656/725155) and the restored Bryngarw House, which now houses a bistro and conference centre.

With the restored train line from Bridgend, through Tondu and up the Llynfi valley to Maesteg, there are now plans (and money) to link the old line up the Garw Valley from Tondu, and deploy steam trains on the route. For now, road transport is the only option. Just short of **PONTYCYMER**, where you can stop for refreshments at the *Ffaldau Arms* or *Station Café*, are the chimneys and deserted outhouses of the abandoned Lluest colliery. The valley pushes on to its head at **BLAENGARW**, whose old **Workmen's Hall** has metamorphosed into a remarkable new community space with a cinema, workshop, new technology and performance areas (details on ☎01656/871911); even the hall's typically austere frontage has been transformed with stunning murals and mosaics. In this, the butt-end of one of the most remote valleys in south Wales, it's a remarkable symbol of confidence in the future.

The **Llynfi Valley**, stretching up from Bridgend and Tondu along the A4063, is broad-bottomed and leafy, the main settlement being the downbeat town of **MAESTEG**, struggling to find replacements for its lost collieries. Although this is true of many towns in the Valleys, it is in these more westerly corners of the region that the pinch is being felt most keenly. There is understandable resentment here that the better-known valleys, particularly the Rhondda, Cynon and Taff, have soaked up so much of the area's publicity and available funds. Continuing through Maesteg, the main road links up with the A4107 at Cymer, for Cwm Afan.

The only **accommodation** in this area is at *Bryngarw House* (☎01656/729009; ⑤ including dinner) in the country park, although this is usually for pre-booked conferences, wedding parties and the like. A mile east, over the hill in the Llynfi valley, there's B&B at *Chestnut Ways* (☎01656/724665; ③) on the main A4063 in Coytrahên. If you're exploring the area, or want to catch something at the Blaengarw Workmen's Hall, telephone them for suggestions as to someone local who might offer B&B. Otherwise, there are numerous fine sites to pitch a **tent**.

Cwm Afan, Port Talbot and Margam

Although not as idyllic as its optimistic tourist-board tag – "Little Switzerland" – would have it, **CWM AFAN**, winding its way between the top of the Llynfi valley and the coast at Port Talbot, is nonetheless a bucolic spot, all traces of industry long expunged, and warrants exploration. The valley's main attraction is the **Afan Forest Park**, 9000 acres of hilly forest land around an excellent **countryside centre** (April–Sept daily 10.30am–6pm; Oct–March daily 10.30am—5pm; ☎01639/850564), three miles west of dour little **CYMER**. The centre houses the **South Wales Miners' Museum** (same times; 50p), where an informal collection of mining memorabilia, looking at miners' home and working lives, religion and dangers, fills numerous glass cases. X-rays and lung segments show the horrific effects of silicosis and pneumoconiosis. On a more uplifting note, there's also an impressive longitudinal diagram of the south Wales coalfields in stained glass. The centre also has **camping** and **bike rental** facilities, and organizes regular events and walks.

The valley descends towards the sea, reaching the floor village of **PONTRHY-DYFEN** in a couple of miles. Actor Richard Burton was born in a house at the foot of one of the impressive viaducts that slice through the village. From here, roads either side of the river continue south to the industrial sprawl of **PORT TALBOT**, still dominated by its massive steel works. It's a town in which you're unlikely to linger, though a few Victorian touches remain in the largely modern town centre, and the docks, including the impressive modern deep-water harbour with its mile-long breakwater, provide plenty of action. A suburb of the town, **Aberavon** has a long and sandy, if fairly featureless, seafront lined with a few fun pubs, nightclubs and the ever-popular *Afan Lido* (☎01639/875214), site of big concerts, events, sports and the swish new *AquaDome*, a leisure pool with all of the trimmings.

A couple of miles southeast of Port Talbot, just the other side of junction 38 of the M4, lies **MARGAM**, originally a Cistercian settlement before becoming the home of various industrial magnates. The first left turn after the motorway junction leads to the impressive **Abbey church**, the sole remaining Cistercian house of worship in Wales. The harmonious Italianate frontage is largely due to nineteenth-century restoration, although original twelfth-century features can be seen here and inside. Note particularly the solid arcades. The neighbouring **Margam Stones Museum**, housing numerous important Roman, Celtic and medieval standing stones, is currently closed and plans for its future are uncertain.

Lying just the other side of the Abbey church, and accessed by car along the next turn off from the main road, is **Margam Country Park** (attractions April–Sept daily 10.30am–5pm, park 10am–7pm, last entry 4pm; £3.50; Oct–March park only Wed–Sun 10am–5pm, last entry 3pm; £1), centred around the nineteenth-century Gothic pile of **Margam Castle**. There's a lot to see and do within the grounds: walks up to the ruined hilltop Capel Mair, around Mynydd-y-Castell Iron Age fort and through the superb floral grounds, dotted with some exciting contemporary sculpture by some big names like Barbara Hepworth and Elizabeth Frink. Tucked in by the Abbey church walls are the impressive remains of the original Cistercian abbey, most notable for the surprisingly intact vaulting of the twelve-sided chapter house, which survived the Dissolution of the Monasteries only to have its roof collapse under the weight of weed and plants in 1799. Nearby is Margam's showpiece **orangery**, a splendid Georgian outhouse, built in 1790 and 327ft long. Tucked in the same corner are a kids' "fairyland" play area and a great box-hedge maze. Waterfalls, sculpture and some splendid shrubbery fill the spaces around the ceremonial boardwalk, leading up to the castle. The mansion was gutted by fire in 1977, although you can wander into the lobby and peer up the octagonal lantern tower and see a few models and photos. In the courtyard, there's a café, shop and unbelievably crass display of replica Crown Jewels.

Practicalities

Again, there is very little tourist **accommodation** in these parts – once again, those **camping** have it easiest with a dedicated site at the Afan Forest Park and numerous quiet unofficial spots. In Cymer village, *Brynteg House* (☎01639/851820; ②) is a decent small B&B and teashop. Better still, *Ty'n-y-Caeau* (☎01639/883897; ③) is a seventeenth-century vicarage just off the main road in Margam village, on the other side of the motorway junction from Margam Park. There are numerous cheap and stodgy **cafés** in Port Talbot and Aberavon, or you can find food in the *St Oswald's* bar on Station Road.

Cardiff

Official capital of Wales since only 1955, the buoyant city of **CARDIFF** (Caerdydd) has swiftly grown into its new status, and although the country is still without any directly elected government or assembly of its own, the increasing number of Welsh Office subsections in Cardiff, together with new, progressive developments, are beginning to give the city the true feel of an international capital.

Many of the city's rivals – amongst them Machynlleth, seat of Glyndŵr's parliament, Swansea, a large, sprawling and unmistakably Welsh city, and even Ludlow, an English border town once the seat of the Council of the Marches – dismissed Cardiff as a young upstart. True, the civic charter incorporating Cardiff dates only from 1905 and, before the coal-exporting explosion during the nineteenth century, it was an insignificant fishing village. The "not very Welsh" charge is also frequently levelled at the city: in some ways, this is perhaps justified – if compared with Swansea, Cardiff is very anglicized, and you will rarely hear *Cymraeg* on the city's streets. But, Cardiff's standard-bearers argue, what sort of snobbery is it that decrees a young and vibrant city should *not* be the nation's capital? Cardiff is an exciting city that is still developing and, unlike Edinburgh or London, which rest on their wistful and long histories, Cardiff pushes on, as one of Europe's largest regeneration projects transforms the old dockland around Tiger Bay into a vast freshwater marina bounded by a new opera house, spruce waterfront buildings, new museums and transport systems.

Some history

It is known that some of the Roman tribes from Isca settled in Cardiff, building a small civilian village alongside the military fort. The fort is thought to have been uninhabited from the Romans' departure until the Norman invasion, when William the Conqueror offered Welsh land to his knights if they could subdue the local tribes. In 1093, Robert FitzHamon built a simple fort on a moated hillock that still stands today in the grounds of the castle. A town grew up in the lee of the fortress, becoming a small community of fishermen and farmers that remained a quiet backwater until the end of the eighteenth century. The Bute family, lords of the manor of Cardiff, instigated new developments on their land, starting with the construction of a canal from Merthyr Tydfil (then Wales' largest town) to Cardiff in 1794. The second Marquis of Bute built the first dock in 1839, opening others in swift succession. The Butes, who owned massive swathes of the rapidly industrializing south Wales valleys, insisted that all coal and iron exports used the family docks in Cardiff, and it became one of the busiest ports in the world. By the turn of the twentieth century, Cardiff's population had soared to 170,000 from its

1801 figure of around 1000, and the spacious and ambitious new civic centre in Cathays Park was well under way.

The twentieth century has seen the city's fortunes rise and plummet. The dock trade slumped in the 1930s, and the city suffered heavy bombing in World War II, but with the creation of Cardiff as capital in 1955 – widely felt to be long overdue – optimism and confidence in the city have blossomed. Many large governmental and media institutions have moved here from London, and the development of the dock areas has provided a positive boost to a flagging cityscape. Unlike so many British cities, there is an almost tangible feeling here of optimism.

Arrival, information and getting around

Cardiff–Wales international **airport** is ten miles southwest of the city on the other side of Barry. Hourly buses #X91 (Mon–Sat) and #145 (Sun) operate from the main terminal into the city **bus station** on the southwestern side of the city centre, which serves all *National Express* buses, local and trans-Wales bus routes. Across the fore-court is Cardiff Central **train station**, for all *InterCity* services (including a speedy hourly shuttle to London), as well as many suburban and *Valley Line* services. **Queen Street station**, at the eastern edge of the centre, is for local services only.

The **tourist office** is in the forecourt of Cardiff Central station (April–Sept Mon–Sat 9am–6.30pm, Sun 10am–4pm; Oct–March Mon–Sat 9am–5.30pm, Sun 10am–4pm; ☎01222/227281). It will book accommodation, provide good free maps of the city and give details of walking and bus tours. You should also be able to pick up a copy of *Buzz!*, a free, occasionally ribald monthly guide to arts in the city; the arts and events freesheet *finetime* performs a similar function. For more alternative information, try some of the shops in the Castle and High Street arcades (see below).

City transport

Cardiff is an easy and compact city to walk around, as even the bay area is within twenty minutes' stroll of Central station. Once you're out of the centre, however, it's best to fall back on the extensive **bus network**, most reliably operated by the garish orange *Cardiff Bus* (*Bws Caerdydd*) company. It operates sales offices and information kiosks at the bus station in Wood Street (Mon & Fri 8am–5.30pm, Tues–Thurs & Sat 8.30am–5.30pm), in the *Littlewoods* store in St David's Shopping Centre on Working Street (open store hours) and in front of the Old Library in The Hayes (Fri 8am–5.30pm, Sat 8.30am–4.30pm). The city is divided into four colour-coded **fare zones**, and prices depend on the number of zones crossed, from 30p off-peak in one zone to £1 in the rush hour across all four. A **Capital ticket** (£3), bought from a sales office or on the bus, gives unlimited travel around Cardiff and Penarth for a day, and **multi-ride tickets** are available for a minimum of a week, starting at £7.50 for Cardiff and Penarth only, with prices around £10 that combine this area with the Vale of Glamorgan, the Caerphilly district, Barry or Newport. Destinations further afield, such as Penarth and the Valleys, are well served by local rail services, with regular connecting buses.

The **last buses** leave the city centre at around 11.20pm, meaning that if you're staying out of town you may well need to get a **taxi**. These can be found in ranks at Central station, Duke Street by the castle and Queen Street station. Alternatively, reliable cab companies include *Capital Cars* (☎01222/777777), *Metro Cabs* (☎01222/464646) and *West Cars* (☎01222/487171).

ACCOMMODATION

1 Acorn Lodge
2 Angel Hotel
3 Arosa House
4 Cardiff Bay
5 Cardiff Hotel
6 Courtfield Hotel
7 Ferriers
8 Georgian Hotel
9 Glenmor Hotel
10 Jury's Hotel
11 Maxine's
12 Metropole
13 Park Hotel
14 Ramblar Court
15 Rosanna House
16 Town House
17 Ty Gwyn

Accommodation

The main belt of guesthouses and hotels lies along the genteel and leafy Cathedral Road, in the suburb of Pontcanna, and is easily reached by foot from the city centre. The other main area for accommodation is around the Newport Road, heading northeast out of the city centre through Roath, about fifteen minutes' walk from the centre. Alternatively, you might consider staying in the breezy resort of Penarth (see p.110), a ten-minute train hop around the bay.

Hotels

Angel Hotel, Castle Street (☎01222/232633). Cardiff's grandest and best-known hotel, opposite the castle. ⑧.

Cardiff Bay, Schooner Way, Atlantic Wharf, Cardiff Bay (☎01222/465888). Grand Victorian building transformed into a smart hotel in an area that is slowly coming together as part of the great plan for the old docks. ⑦.

Cardiff Hotel, 138 Newport Rd, Roath (☎01222/491964). Informal and well-placed small licensed hotel. ③.

Churchills Hotel, Cardiff Road, Llandaff (☎01222/562372). Mock-Edwardian hotel in a quiet part of the city near the cathedral of Llandaff. ⑥.

Courtfield Hotel, 101 Cathedral Rd, Pontcanna (☎01222/227701). Popular and lively hotel with a large gay clientele and a good restaurant. ④.

Georgian Hotel, 179 Cathedral Rd, Pontcanna (☎01222/232594). Good value in a comfortable small hotel. ④.

Glenmor Hotel, 150–152 Newport Rd, Roath (☎01222/489545). Peaceful, moderately priced hotel; all rooms have en-suite facilities. ④.

Jury's Hotel, Mary Ann Street (☎01222/464141). Large and plush modern hotel opposite the new International Arena. ⑥.

Town House, 70 Cathedral Rd, Pontcanna (☎01222/239399). Elegantly restored small hotel, run by an irrepressibly cheerful American couple. ④.

Park Hotel, Park Place (☎01222/399309). Just off Queen Street in the centre, the *Park Hotel* is large and formal, with all rooms swathed in floral designs. ⑧.

Guesthouses

Acorn Lodge, 182 Cathedral Rd, Pontcanna (☎01222/221373). Pleasant, quiet B&B near Pontcanna Fields, a 15-min walk from the city centre. ③.

Arosa House, 24 Plasturton Gardens, Pontcanna (☎01222/395342). Lying next to the city centre, the *Arosa* is very friendly and reasonably priced. ③.

Ferriers, 130 Cathedral Rd, Pontcanna (☎01222/383413). Best-value B&B in Cardiff, welcoming, inexpensive and with excellent service. ③.

Hotel Metropole, 175 Newport Rd, Roath (☎01222/464642). Downbeat, but reasonable, large guesthouse. ③.

Maxine's, 150 Cathedral Rd, Pontcanna (☎01222/220288). Cosy low-cost B&B. ③.

Ramblar Court, 188 Cathedral Rd, Pontcanna (☎01222/221187). Good-value, welcoming guesthouse with a few en-suite rooms. ③.

Rosanna House, 175 Cathedral Rd, Pontcanna (☎01222/229780). Very cheap, reflected, to some extent, in the decor of the place. Handy for the city and the river. ②.

Ty Gwyn, 7 Dyfrig St, off Cathedral Road, Pontcanna (☎01222/239784). Close to the city centre and well placed for Pontcanna Fields and the River Taff. Friendly and quiet. ③.

Hostel, self-catering and campsites

Cardiff Youth Hostel, 2 Wedal Rd, Roath Park (☎01222/462303). Large, purpose-built red-brick building, situated just underneath the A48 Eastern Avenue flyover at the top of Roath Park, almost two miles from the city centre. Buses #78, #80 or #82 go from the central bus station. No curfew. Closed Dec. ①.

Lavernock Point Holiday Estate, Fort Road, Lavernock, near Penarth (☎01222/707310). Buses #P4, #P5 and #P8 pass within a mile of Lavernock Point, a sadly run-down piece of coast just south of Penarth. It has a campsite and also caters for touring caravans.

Pitman Cottage and **Dogo Street**, off Cathedral Road, Pontcanna (☎01446/772773). Three well-equipped self-catering flats in central Cardiff, each sleeping four. From £165–195 for a week.

Pontcanna Fields Campsite, off Cathedral Road, Pontcanna (☎01222/398362). Limited tent spaces, so booking advised in high season.

University of Wales College, Cathays (☎01222/874027). Over 100 en-suite rooms in self-catering flats near the city centre. A good and cheap option. ③.

The City

Cardiff's sights are clustered around fairly small, distinct districts. The **commercial centre**, compact and easily navigable on foot, is bounded by the River Taff – source of the nickname of generations of expatriate Welsh – on the western side. The Taff flows past the walls of Cardiff's extraordinary **castle**, an amalgam of Roman remains, Norman keep and Victorian fantasy. Nearby is the great ribbed stadium of **Cardiff Arms Park**, home of Welsh rugby and the nation's soccer team. By the southeast tip of the castle walls is the crossroads of Cardiff, where great Edwardian shopping boulevards Queen Street and High Street conceal a world of arcades, great stores and predictably bland malls. North of the castle are a series of white Edwardian buildings – the spacious **civic centre** around **Cathays Park**, home of the **National Museum**, **City Hall** and **University College**.

A mile south of the commercial centre is the area around **Cardiff Bay**, once the city's liveliest district. With the construction of the barrage to form a vast freshwater lake, the bay has been spruced up considerably, and now houses the excellent **Welsh Industrial and Maritime Museum**.

The other city area that is most likely to detain you is the elegant suburb of **Llandaff**, two miles northwest of the city centre above the banks of the Taff, and still feeling like a closely knit village built around the city's patchwork **cathedral**.

The commercial centre

The commercial centre of Cardiff is roughly square-shaped, bordered by the castle, Queen Street station, the International Arena and Central station, making a surprisingly compact city.

Between Central station and Castle Street is the fat bowl of **Cardiff Arms Park**, the home of Welsh rugby on the banks of the Taff. With its giant ribs and curving sides, the Arms Park is as obvious a Cardiff landmark as any, even if the national team's performance slipped into the doldrums before the unexpectedly successful 1994 Five Nations Championship. Even so, the atmosphere in the Park, or in the pubs and streets of the city, when Wales have a home match – particularly against old enemy England – is charged with good-natured beery fervour. The national stadium will host the 1999 Rugby World Cup, which Wales unexpectedly captured

CENTRAL CARDIFF

N

yds 0   200

ARCADES
A Andrew's
B Castle
C Dominions
D Duke Street
E High Street
F Morgan
G Royal
H Wyndham

ahead of South Africa, and is to undergo a massive facelift in readiness. Between now and then, the whole area is likely to resemble a huge building site.

Running up from Central station to the castle walls is **St Mary's Street**, one of the city's grandest boulevards of ornate Victorian and Edwardian shop frontages, leading north to become the **High Street**, off which is the elegant, turn-of-the-century **indoor market**. Along both streets, Edwardian arcades, cleaned up and with some of the city centre's most interesting shops inside, lead off between the buildings. Of these, the **High Street** and **Castle arcades**, at the top of High Street, are the most rewarding, packed with great club clothes shops, quirky gift places and a range of esoteric emporia from which you can pick up fliers for clubs and events. Further down the High Street towards Central station, the glorious Morgan Arcade and its near neighbour, the Royal Arcade, run east to the bottom of **The Hayes**, a pedestrianized street of disparate restaurants and some great pubs. A few yards to the south, The Hayes meets up at a junction of five streets by the belching towers of the **Brains brewery**, opposite the **Wales National Ice Rink**, home to one of Britain's top ice hockey teams, the Cardiff Devils. At the junction, Bridge Street runs away to the east and into the elegant Regency part of the city centre around David and Charles streets. At 31 Charles St is **Ffotogallery** (times variable), one of the country's foremost galleries for bold and often hard-hitting photographic exhibitions. Slicing off south from The Hayes, opposite the *Marriott* hotel, is atmospheric Mill Lane, Cardiff's **café quarter**.

The Hayes leads north to the beautifully sandblasted and colonnaded frontage of the **Old Library**, recently closed as a craft centre and awaiting redevelopment. Here the road divides, with both left and right prongs heading either side of the fifteenth-century grey limestone parish **church of St John**. The most notable feature – the slender tower – is difficult to appreciate with the cluster of buildings around it, although the light and graceful interior is worth seeing, especially for the floridly pompous altar in the south aisle by prolific Victorian sculptor, Goscombe John. The right turn at the Old Library is **Working Street**, a very busy shopping area, especially around the entrances to the gargantuan **St David's Centre** and the **St David's Hall** complex, which, between them, have succeeded in obliterating a huge section of the old city centre, although St David's Hall serves as a much-needed concert and entertainment venue.

Queen Street is Cardiff's most impressive shopping thoroughfare, now pedestrianized with many of the fine nineteenth-century buildings spruced up. At its western end, a typically pugnacious statue of **Aneurin Bevan**, postwar Labour politician and classic Welsh firebrand, stands aloof from the bustle. First left off Queen Street is the Friary, at the end of which is **Oriel** (Mon–Sat 9am–5.30pm), Cardiff's best selection of modern art and sculpture exhibitions, both international and Welsh (*Oriel* is Welsh for "gallery"). It's also the local branch of Her Majesty's Stationery Office (great for maps and travel paraphernalia), and the capital's prime stockist of Welsh-interest publications. The showpiece oval glass and brick mound at the bottom of Churchill Way is the **Cardiff International Arena**, host of massive concerts, trade fairs and conferences.

Cardiff Castle

The political, geographical and historical heart of the city is **Cardiff Castle** (daily May–Sept 10am–6pm with tours every 20min; March–April & Oct 10am–5pm with tours every 30min; Nov–Feb 10am–4.30pm with tours at 10.30am, 11.45am, 2pm & 3.15pm; £3.70 full tour, £3 shorter tour, £2.30 grounds only), an intriguing, appealing hotchpotch of remnants of the city's history. The fortress hides inside a vast walled yard, each side measuring well over 200 yards long and corresponding roughly to the outline of the original fort built by the Romans, Cardiff's first inhabitants. A few dozen yards of **Roman wall**, the sole reminder of their presence, has been unearthed to the immediate right of the entrance in the thirteenth-century Black Tower on Castle Street, and is now lit and labelled, along with some excellent three-dimensional murals depicting life in a Roman fort. Tucked into the southeastern corner wall beyond the Roman segment are the dry **regimental museums** of the Welsh Regiment and the Queen's Dragoon Guards, filled with a starchy collection of military memorabilia. From here, walkways lead along the **battlements**, offering some excellent views over the city and the gracious Portland-stone buildings of Cathays Park.

Occupying the northwestern corner of the castle grounds is a neat Norman motte crowned with the eleventh-century **keep**, with views down onto the turrets and towers of the **domestic buildings**, dating in part from the fourteenth and fifteenth centuries, but much extended in Tudor times, when residential needs began to overtake military safety in terms of priority. Ultimately, it was the third Marquis of Bute (1847–1900), one of the richest men on the globe, who lavished a fortune on upgrading his pile, commissioning architect and decorator William Burges (1827–81) to aid him. With their passion for the religious art and the symbolism of the Middle Ages, they systematically overhauled the buildings, adding a spire to the octagonal tower and erecting a clock tower; but it was inside that their imaginations ran free, and they radically transformed the crumbling interiors into palaces of vivid colour and intricate, high-camp design. These buildings can only be seen as part of the guided tour, making the extra fee well worthwhile.

The tour starts in the square cornered **clock tower**, running through the **Winter Smoking Room** at the bottom, up to the **Bachelor's Bedroom** and bathroom and, above that, the **Summer Smoking Room**. All are decorated in rich patterns of gold, maroon and cobalt, with many of the images culled from medieval myths and beliefs. From here, the tour goes through the 1878 **Nursery**, with hand-painted tiles and silhouette lanterns depicting contemporary nursery rhymes, the 1881 **Arab Room**, decorated by imported craftsmen, and into the grand **Banqueting Hall**, which dates orginally from 1428, but was transformed by Bute and Burges with the installation of a riotously kitsch fireplace to commemorate Robert the Consul, Earl of Gloucester and late Norman lord of the castle. In all the rooms, fantastically rich trimmings complement the dizzily gaudy style so beloved of two nineteenth-century eccentrics, and it's worth remembering that, as one of over sixty residences owned by the Butes in Britain alone, Cardiff was only lived in for six weeks of the year.

The last point of note in Cardiff Castle can only be seen from outside the precincts. The **Animal Wall**, where stone creatures are frozen in impudent poses, was another tongue-in-cheek nineteenth-century creation, running all along the route of Castle Street west to the river bridge.

Cathays Park and the civic centre

On the north side of the city centre, only a hundred yards from the northeastern wall of the castle precinct, is the area known most commonly as **Cathays Park**. The park itself is really the large rectangle of greenery that forms the centrepiece for the impressive Edwardian buildings of the **civic centre**, but the term Cathays Park is generally used for the whole complex. Dating from the first couple of decades of this century, the gleaming white buildings arranged with pompous Edwardian precision speak volumes about Cardiff's self-assertion, even half a century before it was officially declared capital of Wales. The processional **Boulevard de Nantes**, named after Cardiff's twin city in Brittany, fronts the complex on the city-centre side.

Centrepiece of the complex is the magnificent, domed, dragon-topped **City Hall** (1905), an exercise in ostentatious civic self-glory that reaches a peak in the first-floor Marble Hall is particularly showy: all Sienese marble columns and statues of Welsh heroes. Amongst the (all male) figures are twelfth-century chronicler Giraldus Cambrensis, thirteenth-century native prince of Wales, Llywelyn ap Gruffydd, fifteenth-century national insurgent and perpetual hero, Owain Glyndŵr, Welsh king Henry Tudor and tenth-century architect of Wales' progressive codified laws, Hywel Dda (Howell the Good). Overseeing them all is the figure of Dewi Sant himself, the national patron saint, St David.

The low-key **Law Courts** (1906), stand to the left of the City Hall, with the **National Museum of Wales** (see below) balancing the view on the right-hand side. Behind them, two ruler-straight boulevards, evidently designed with ceremonial splendour in mind, run through the rest of the civic centre, arranged in symmetrical precision around **Alexandra Gardens** in the middle. At the very centre of the park is the colonnaded circular **National War Memorial** (1928), a popular and surprisingly quiet place to sit and contemplate the rush of civic and governmental duty all around. At the north end of the western boulevard, **King Edward VII Avenue**, is the **Temple of Peace** (1938), dedicated just before the outbreak of World War II to Welsh men and women the world over who were fighting for peace and relief of poverty. The eastern road, **Museum Avenue**, runs past an assortment of buildings belonging to the University of Wales College of Cardiff. At the northern head of Cathays Park is the ugliest and most foreboding building of them all: the principal Cardiff departments of the **Welsh Office**.

National Museum of Wales

The **National Museum of Wales** (Tues–Sun & Bank Holiday Mon 10am–5pm; £3.25) is one of Britain's finest. Housed in a large, white, domed Portland-stone building that was constructed in sections from 1912 through to 1992, it manages to carry off the illusion of a singular *grand projet*. As a national museum, it attempts both to tell the story of Wales and reflect the nation's place in the wider, international sphere.

The most obvious crowd-pleaser, starting on the ground floor at the back of the entrance lobby, is the epic **Evolution of Wales** gallery, a natural history exhibition packed with hi-tech gizmos and a staggering amount of information. It starts with a stirring large-screen video presentation, *Dyma Gymru* (This is Wales), pumped full of stunning aerial footage taken over mountains, waterfalls and other natural Welsh wonders. It then goes on to explain, through fossils, rocks and footage of volcanoes, earthquakes and the galaxies, the slow beginnings of life on earth. Dinosaurs and the early mammals get a good look in, a main attraction being a terrific tyrannosaurus rex skull.

The environmental education continues in the adjacent **Natural History** galleries, with a magnificent collection of sparkling crystals, recreations of assorted environments – mountain, wetland, seashore, dunes – and some great interactive technology and interpretive boards. It then heads upstairs with a display entitled "Man and the Environment", featuring numerous animals and their habitats, and culminates in the world's largest leatherback turtle, caught off Harlech in 1988 and condemned to spend the rest of eternity frozen in a curious diving position, half-smile still lingering. Displays looking at the effect of mankind on our changing environment complete the gallery.

To the right of the main lobby are various temporary exhibitions and an extensive **botany collection** which ranges from simple classifications of major Welsh flower species to a detailed analysis of conservation, pollution and responsible tourism in the ecologically delicate countryside and coast of Wales. The museum was one of the first anywhere to commission intricate plant and flower models (in materials like silk, wax and paper), resulting in one of the best such collections in the world.

The first floor houses the excellent **archeology galleries**, whose treasures include intricate gold torques from the Bronze Age and the dazzling 3000-plus-year-old **Caergwrle Bowl**, a gold votive container in the shape of a boat. Leading off is an unusually interesting **coin** collection, with some good panels on the history of Welsh and British minting, and, at the back, an inspirational collection of 23 stones and 14 casts, spanning the earliest carved fragments (around the fifth century), through Celtic and early Christian standing stones to the more elaborate examples of the early medieval age.

THE ART COLLECTIONS

The Evolution of Wales and Natural History galleries occupy the entire western and central flank of the ground and first floors. The eastern side of the building is home to the **art galleries**. Galleries One to Ten examine Wales' artistic heritage, starting with a marble altar from the first century BC and taking in works from the medieval Renaissance, including some stunning pieces from the studios of Botticelli and El Greco. There's a strong collection from the **eighteenth-century** British and Italian schools, inevitably rich in the work of Wright, Gainsborough and Reynolds. This was perhaps Welsh art's heyday, and the three main protagonists – Richard Wilson, William E Parry and Thomas Jones – are well represented. Wilson's skill in capturing the unique light of Wales can be seen to lustrous effect in his studies of castles at Caernarfon, Dolbadarn and Pembroke, as well as more emotionally intense pieces such as the beautiful *Pistyll Cain*. One of Wilson's protégés, William Hodges, also makes an appearance, most notably in his gentle evocation of *Llanthony Priory*.

Scattered throughout the first ten rooms is an intriguing, eclectic ragbag of British art of the last 150 years: Frank Brangwyn's teeming canvases, a typically rich and detailed collection of Pre-Raphaelites, and an astonishingly gaudy gold, silver and enamel table centrepiece given by the people of Wales to the Duke and Duchess of York (later King George V and Queen Mary) for their wedding in 1893. Welsh painters are well highlighted: you'll find cool, blanched portraits by Gwen John, and her brother Augustus' measured, intensely poetic depictions of *Dylan Thomas* and Newport "supertramp" *W H Davies*. There's also a superb, and growing, collection of **ceramics**, one of Wales' most prolific areas of applied art.

But the most exciting artworks are contained in Galleries Eleven through Fifteen, kicking off with a fabulous **sculpture** collection, including many by the celebrated one-man Welsh Victorian statue industry, Goscombe John. Far better here than on the dreary municipal plinths they usually adorn, his male studies verge on the homoerotic and his female forms are exquisite.

Mesmerizing pieces by Rodin pepper the building, particularly in Gallery Twelve, where a copy of *The Kiss* and his original *Eve* (the downcast figure such a contrast to the life-affirming lovers) share space with the watery landscapes of Boudin, Renoir's coquettish *The Parisienne*, and numerous works by Manet, including the intricately observed *Effect of Snow at Petit Montrouge*.

Gallery Thirteen houses what is arguably the museum's strongest suit, its collection of **Impressionists**, the bequest of two local wealthy sisters, Margaret and Gwendoline Davies. The sisters' favourite was Cézanne, whose work features alongside artists such as Sisley (including his view of Penarth), Carnière, Degas and Pissarro. Van Gogh's stunning *Rain at Anvers* – angry slashes of rain run right across the otherwise harmonious canvas – was painted just weeks before his suicide. Gallery Fourteen includes Postimpressionists, Futurists and Surrealists such as Magritte, Sickert, Sylvia Gosse, Harold Gilman's colourful London scenes and studies by Edward Morland Lewis, including a bold depiction of *The Strand, Laugharne*. Finally, Gallery Fifteen houses a hearty collection of British **abstractionism**, with a strong Welsh bent. Highlights include some stunning and wild pieces by Welsh supremo Ceri Richards, Evan Walters' piercing 1936 portrait of a *Welsh Miner*, Josef Herman's rousing *Miners Singing* and Kyffin Williams' brooding Welsh skies and jagged landscapes. Some sculpted pieces, including some fine works by Henry Moore, among them *Upright Motif*, and Barbara Hepworth's haunting *Oval Sculpture*, complete the room.

Cardiff Bay

Although you can get there by train and bus (#7 or #8), it's only a thirty-minute walk south from Central station to the **Cardiff Bay** area. It's soon to become an even pleasanter stroll, when Bute Street – the ruler-straight connecting road running through tatty Butetown – is transformed into a swish ceremonial avenue, complete with trams and trees. Cardiff Bay is on the up, and nothing is being allowed get in the way of its rapid gentrification.

The Cardiff Bay area – the spicier tag of **Tiger Bay** (immortalized by locally born chanteuse Shirley Bassey) being rarely used these days – comprises two distinct parts. **Butetown**, to the east, is home to much of the city's ethnic population, stretching from the low-slung 1960s estates alongside Bute Street to the tarted-up Victorian and Edwardian buildings at the head of the docks; **Grangetown**, to the west, is another old, now firmly multiracial, working-class suburb on the other side of the Taff.

The first impression of the area is one of immense and rapid change. New roads and roundabouts are being cut through rusted wasteland, riotous Victorian and Edwardian frontages have been swabbed clean, and soulless new buildings – with a couple of honorably spirited exceptions – are spreading like advanced fungus. Cardiff Bay has become one of the world's biggest regeneration projects, aiming to transform the seedy (but quite appealing) dereliction of the old docks into a designer heaven. However, all involved in the project want to make clear that Cardiff Bay will not become a Welsh version of London's yuppified white elephant, Docklands.

Central to the whole project is the controversial **Cardiff Bay Barrage**, due to be built right across the Ely and Taff estuaries, transforming a vast mudflat into a freshwater lake. Opponents say that this will have serious ecological implications in disturbing one of Britain's most important habitats for wading birds and that the rise in the water table could well destabilize the foundations of buildings and homes around the bay. Supporters claim that the project is the single biggest catalyst in the total transformation of the area, and that the vast new marina will prove an invaluable addition to the city. Central to the proposals has long been the creation of a brand-new waterfront opera house, but infighting and controversy have so far scuppered any concrete plans (see box overleaf).

For now, Butetown and the docks are among the most fascinating parts of Cardiff, where ostentatious Victorian shipping company headquarters rub shoulders with spruced-up dockers' housing. The architectural highlights of the whole area are detailed in a 40p **leaflet**, *Butetown Walkabout*, which can be picked up in the tourist office or any of the local museums.

Overlooking the bay, with its imaginative street art designs and offbeat maritime touches, is the central site of the **Welsh Industrial and Maritime Museum** (Tues–Sun 10am–5pm; £2), mainly made up of a series of modern buildings purpose-built around the giant engines and boats that form a major part of the exhibition. Wales' great industries, particularly coal and iron-ore mining, are explained through the use of video, photographs and exhibits, including some entertaining

---

CARDIFF BAY OPERA HOUSE

Planned and serenaded as the showpiece for the Cardiff Bay development, a national **Opera House** was hoped to do for Cardiff what Sydney's had done for that city. With the outstanding international success of the Welsh National Opera, a suitably monumental permanent home (the cramped confines of the city's New Theatre barely suffice) was seen as the final seal on Wales' choral and operatic reputation.

As part of the hype surrounding the project, an international architecture competition was launched in the late 1980s and won by radical Iraqi architect, Zaha Hadid with a startling design known as the "crystal necklace", a square of thrusting, angular glass containing a central courtyard. From here, things went downhill. Initially enthusiastic, the distinctly illiberal Welsh press became increasingly hostile towards the unconventional Ms Hadid and succeeded in stirring up considerable public antipathy towards both the design and, ultimately, the entire concept of an opera house. Rumblings about elitism and lack of consultation began to surface, fuelled by the leader writers of the *Western Mail* and *South Wales Echo*. The notoriously conservative London architecture and media establishments also weighed in, sneering at Cardiff's brash presumption and Hadid's lack of credentials (she was previously known only for a striking-looking but malfunctioning fire station in Germany).

By mid-1995, the project was in trouble. Open warfare about the opera house was breaking out all over and even considerably modified designs by Hadid failed to staunch the flow of criticism. The final nail in the project's coffin came three days short of Christmas 1995, when the Millennium Commission, awash with money from the UK National Lottery, turned down any funding to the Welsh National Opera House. This had never been seen as a possible hurdle: the only explanation must be that the criticism-conscious Commission got cold feet over the mounting hysteria being whipped up over this project.

The shambles that this tale became lives on, however, in the rumbling discussions about what should replace the aborted house. Agreed on – though again subject to the vagaries of lottery and other public funding – is the plan for a multi-purpose arts and cultural centre, designed more conventionally and with a wider remit than just opera. The fact that Hadid's opera house would have fulfilled many such functions anyway seemed to prove the hypothesis that this was not an argument about the elitism of opera; rather a small-minded, reactionary response that has damaged Wales' reputation considerably in the international cultural sphere. Plans are once again under way for this new centre, including the mid-1996 launch of a brand-new architecture competition; Zaha Hadid has declined to enter. Hopes to have the building up by the year 2000 have disappeared and Cardiff people are unsurprisingly sceptical about the revamped project. In the meanwhile, the big hole at the end of Bute Place will continue to gape and moulder.

facts and photos about the pit ponies that were once such a feature of the coalfield. Cardiff's nautical heritage is represented in exhibits like the transplanted bridge of an ocean-going steamship and buxom figureheads that once ruled the waves. The **Hall of Power** contains working models of the methods of power that drove south Wales into massive industrialization, right from the waterwheel to contemporary methods of energy conservation. Outside are numerous railway locomotives, including an impressive replica of Richard Trevithick's engine that made the world's first train journey in 1804 up the Taff valley. Other forms of transport on display include a steam tugboat and an air-sea rescue helicopter. On a reconstructed rail bridge, telescopes enable superb viewing across the marshes and the bay.

The museum's temporary activity centre, **Q-shed** (same times and prices as museum), was converted out of a Victorian shipping warehouse facing the bay; behind it is Stuart Street and **Techniquest** (Mon–Fri 9.30am–4.30pm, Sat & Sun 10.30am–5pm; £4.50), a stunning new building of metal and glass crowned with a wonderful arc roof. It's by far the largest and most impressive "hands-on" science museum in the UK, packed full of exhibits, experiments and numerous chances to play like a five-year-old. It also includes a planetarium (75p) and science theatre.

On the other side of WIMM is the **Pierhead Building**, which has beckoned ships into Cardiff port since its construction in 1896. A typically rich Victorian neo-Gothic terracotta pile, it was built for the Bute Dock Company and perfectly embodies the wealth and optimism of the Bute family and their docks.

From the Pierhead, a path leads down along the waterfront to a park dotted with some great pieces of public art and sculpture and the gleaming white, stumpy-spired **Norwegian church** (Mon–Sat 9.30am–5.30pm), an old seamen's chapel converted into a café and exhibition space. Just behind the church is the park's most startling piece: a giant tubular eye peering out over the bay. This is the **Cardiff Bay Visitor Centre** (Mon–Fri 9.30am–4.30pm, Sat & Sun 10.30am–5pm; free), a thinly disguised PR job for the more controversial developments taking place hereabouts. Despite that, it's well worth a look, if only for the fabulous scale model of the entire docks area, illuminated to show different infrastructure developments at the touch of a button.

Back from the waterfront are some interesting places to wander. James Street, behind Techniquest, is the main commercial focus, while the sandblasted, cleaned-up old buildings around Mount Stuart Square are impressive, particularly the mammoth **Exchange Building**. Built in the 1880s as Britain's central Coal Exchange, the building saw the world's first £1 million deal struck in 1911 and is now used as a conference and exhibition centre. A few yards away, on the corner of West Bute Street, the old church of St Stephen has been converted into a superb new performance space, **The Point** (see p.107). At the top of West Bute Street, opposite Cardiff Bay station, is a small branch of the WIMM, **126 Bute Street**, housed in the old *Frazer's Ship Chandlery* shop. It's mainly used for school groups and researchers, but is open to the public on WIMM Steam Days, held on the first Saturday of the month between April and October (☎01222/481919).

From Bute Park to Llandaff

Between Cardiff Castle and the River Taff lies **Bute Park**, once the private estate of the castle, and now containing an **arboretum**, superb flowerbeds, the foundation remains of an old priory and some pleasant walks along the Taff banks. The main road crosses over the river at Cardiff Bridge, with a right turn leading up into the coolly formal **Sophia Gardens**. A quarter of a mile along the river is the multi-purpose **Welsh Institute of Sport**, the national sports centre and, beyond that, the home of Wales' sole first-class cricket team, Glamorgan, and the less formal open spaces of **Pontcanna Fields**, which lead along the Taff for a couple of miles to the suburb of Llandaff.

Llandaff is a small, quiet ecclesiastical village two miles northwest of the city centre along Cathedral Road. The church that has now grown up into the city's **cathedral** is believed to have been founded in the sixth century by St Teilo, but was rebuilt in Norman style from 1120 and well into the thirteenth century. From the late fourteenth century, the cathedral fell into an advanced state of disrepair, hurried along by the adverse attention of Cromwell's soldiers during the Civil War. In the early eighteenth century, one of the twin towers and the nave roof collapsed. Restoration only began in earnest in the early 1840s, and Pre-Raphaelite artists such as Edward Burne-Jones, Dante Gabriel Rossetti and the stained-glass firm of William Morris were commissioned for colourful new windows and decorative panels. Llandaff is evidently not a lucky cathedral, however, for in January 1941 a German landmine destroyed whole sections of it. Faithful and painstaking restoration was finally completed in 1960.

The fusion of different styles and ages is evident from outside, especially in the mismatched western towers. The northwest tower is by Jasper Tudor, a largely fifteenth-century work with modern embellishments, whilst the adjoining tower and spire were rebuilt from nineteenth-century designs. Inside, Jacob Epstein's overwhelming *Christ in Majesty* sculpture, a concrete parabola topped with a circular organ case on which sits a soaring Christ figure, was the only entirely new feature added in the postwar reconstruction, and dominates the nave today. At the west end of the north aisle, the **St Illtyd Chapel** features Rossetti's cloying triptych *The Seed of David*, whose figures – David the shepherd boy, David the King and the Virgin Mary – are modelled on Rossetti's Pre-Raphaelite friends. Along a little further, in the south presbytery, is the tenth-century Celtic cross that is the cathedral's only pre-Norman survivor.

At the far end of the cathedral is the elegantly vaulted and beautifully painted **Lady Chapel**, notable for its gaudy fifteenth-century reredos on the back wall that contains, surrounded by golden twigs and blackthorn in each niche, bronze panels with named flowers (in Welsh) in honour of Our Lady. Over two dozen flowers take their Welsh names from the Virgin Mary.

Eating

The city's long-standing internationalism, particularly its Italian influence, has paid handsome dividends in its range of **restaurants**. Most places are within easy walking distance of the city centre, although a few of the better cafés and restaurants are in the cheaper corners of Cathays and Roath (particularly the curry houses along Crwys, Albany and City roads), a stone's throw from the centre beyond the university, and some of the old dockers' haunts around Cardiff Bay. The speed of change and gentrification here means that many have undergone metamorphosis into expensive showpiece bars and restaurants.

For bargain-priced **takeaways** in the city centre, your best bet is Caroline Street, between St Mary Street and the bottom of The Hayes. St Mary Street, especially the lower end towards the station, is the home of numerous reliable pizza and pasta chains.

Breakfast, snacks and sandwiches

Bwyty Hayes Island, The Hayes. In the thick of things outside the Old Library, this popular outdoor snack bar is a great place to while away half an hour on a pleasant day.

Café Bon Appetit, Castle Arcade. Right opposite the castle's main entrance, a trendy café great for huge breakfasts (including veggie options), cheap, wholesome snacks, or just hanging out.

Celtic Cauldron, Castle Arcade. On the other side of the arcade from *Café Bon Appetit*, is this friendly daytime café, dedicated to bringing a range of simple Welsh food – soups, stews, laver bread, cakes – to an appreciative public.

Servini's, 3 Wyndham Arcade, off Mill Lane. Tasty sandwiches and salads to take away or eat in.

Welsh and British

Armless Dragon, 97 Wyvern Rd, Cathays (☎01222/382357). Unusual and enjoyable restaurant, with a good range of Welsh dishes amongst a wider bill of fresh fish and game. Decent choice for vegetarians, too. Prices range from moderate to expensive. Closed Sun.

Best of Wales, the *Marriott Hotel*, Mill Lane (☎01222/399944). Brasserie with a slightly sterile environment, but great food including some sturdy Welsh classics. Handy for the bars of the café quarter, bang opposite.

Blas ar Gymru, 48 Crwys Rd, Cathays (☎01222/382132). Meaning "taste of Wales", this is a comfortable restaurant with a highly imaginative, moderately priced menu made up of delicious traditional recipes from every corner of Wales. Leave room for the selection of Welsh cheeses. Closed Sun.

Louis Restaurant, 32 St Mary St. Charming old-fashioned tea rooms with a clientele of genteel old ladies and bargain-hungry students. Food is basic, cheap, lavish in quantity and superb in quality. Last orders 7.45pm Mon–Sat; closed Sun.

New Harvesters, 5 Pontcanna St, Canton (☎01222/549866). Small restaurant with a limited menu of fresh and extremely well-cooked Welsh and British food. Closed Sun. Moderate.

Italian

Giovanni's, The Hayes (☎01222/220077). One of Cardiff's best-reputed Italian restaurants, *Giovanni's* is lively and enormously friendly, with a wide menu of old favourites and some unusual house specialities. Closed Sun.

Pizzeria Villagio, 73 Merthyr Rd, Whitchurch (☎01222/522483). Family-run trattoria, with a solid selection of cheap pizza, pasta and Italian main dishes. Simple and authentic.

Saverio, 110–112 Caerphilly Rd, Heath (☎01222/623344). Busy, friendly, traditional Italian trattoria in the north of the city.

International

Bombay Brasserie, 175 City Rd, Roath (☎01222/494779). Affordable Indian restaurant, among the best of many in the area.

La Brasserie, 60 St Mary St (☎01222/372164). Extremely loud and lively, with beautifully prepared, moderately priced French food and a speciality of charcoal grills.

Las Iguanas, 8 Mill Lane (☎01222/226373). Lively and enjoyable Mexican restaurant in the heart of the café quarter, with fair-priced portions of well-cooked classics.

Minsky's, Cathedral Walk, off Charles Street. New café-showbar tucked behind *Debenhams*, a bit heavy on the loud music, but reliable for good-value snacks and meals.

Noble House, 9–10 St David's House, Wood Street (☎01222/388317). A great, reasonably priced Chinese restaurant, with an excellent range of Peking and Szechuan dishes.

Tang's, 15–23 Westgate St (☎01222/227771). Quite pricey, but the best all-round Chinese restaurant in the city centre, whose owners have a long pedigree in Cardiff cuisine.

Taste of India, 103–105 Woodville Rd, Cathays (☎01222/228863). Well-priced Indian restaurant, frequented by students.

Thai House, 23 High St (☎01222/387404). A great range of Thai dishes, with good bargains.

Drinking

Cardiff's pub life has expanded exponentially over recent years, and includes some atmospheric Edwardian palaces of etched smoky glass and deep red wood. Don't forget Cardiff's own beer, *Brains*, whose Bitter is pale and refreshing and whose Dark is a deep mild that should not be missed on a visit to its home city.

Chapter, Market Road, Canton. Three bars in the arts complex, far better than the traditional rather downmarket arts centre bar. Good choice of real ale and whisky.

Duke of Wellington, corner of Caroline Street and The Hayes. Over-restored Edwardian city pub, serving excellent beer, piped all the way from the brewery next door.

Flyhalf & Firkin, Westgate Street. Opposite the Arms Park, and dripping with rugby memorabilia. Gets heaving at times, especially on international match days.

Golden Cross, 283 Hayes Bridge Rd. Laid-back restored Victorian pub, a few hundred yards from the *Duke of Wellington* but richer in atmosphere and a far better bet for an unhurried pint. Has some beautiful tiled pictures of yesteryear Cardiff.

Model Inn, 14–15 Quay St. The main pre-club watering hole for the beautiful youth.

Mulligan's, corner of St Mary's and Caroline streets. Packed Irish pub with regular live music sessions.

Old Arcade, Church Street. Small, old-fashioned arcade bar next to the market, opening its lounge bar on busy nights only. Popular with rugby fans for its game memorabilia.

Rummer Tavern, 14 Duke St. Opposite the castle entrance, a dark, wooden city pub attracting shoppers in the day and a young crowd at night.

Nightlife

Top-flight **concert venues** such as *St David's Hall* and the *Cardiff International Arena* have brought internationally acclaimed orchestras and performers to the city, although these sterile environments are no match for the sweatier gigs and traditional rock found in some of Cardiff's earthier pubs and clubs. The burgeoning Welsh rock scene, both English- and Welsh-language, breaks out regularly in the capital, as does a club and dance scene that is verging on serious trendiness.

Venues and clubs

Astoria, 43–45 Queen St (☎01222/227717). Humungous great offshoot of the famous London club, with a packed party atmosphere and a range of mainstream and Ibizan house and trance. Licensed until 4am, sometimes later.

Clwb Ifor Bach, Womanby Street (☎01222/232199). A sweaty and massively fun live music and dance club with nightly gigs, sessions or DJs. The acid jazz *Juice Joint* (Thurs) and live bands, often Welsh-speaking (Tues & Sat), are the highlights.

Dog and Duck, Womanby Street (☎01222/224754). Late-night beer-swilling music club.

The Emporium, 8–10 High St (01222/664577). Reliable dance club, popular for techno, rap, garage and the whole spectrum of house music.

Gassey Jacks, 39–41 Salisbury Rd, Cathays (☎01222/239388). Loud, boisterous and enjoyable pub and club, with nightly live R&B, blues, soul and jazz in a studenty environment.

Hip'po Club, 3–7 Penarth Rd (☎01222/341463). Hardcore dance nights, live music, late licence and even a garden. Pulls in a few big-name DJs and has a great atmosphere.

Royal Oak, 200 Broadway, Newport Road (☎01222/473984). Odd live-music pub, with something of a fetish for boxing memorabilia – there's even an old boxing ring.

Sam's, 63 St Mary St (☎01222/345189). Lively mixed bar-cum-club, with everything from live heavy metal, through drag and comedy shows to pumping house DJs. Good for the 5–8pm happy hour when you can hang outside and check the pulse of the café quarter.

Student Union, Park Place (☎01222/396421). Big-name live bands in an impressive club complex, open to non-students.

Time Flies at the City Hall (☎01222/382830). Legendary monthly dance event that's Cardiff's biggest night out, drawing in punters from miles around.

Toucan Club, Castle Street (☎01222/388681). Midweek live bands, weekend cabaret, DJs, Latin American dance and comedy.

The lesbian and gay scene

Although the scene in the city is far from massive, it has grown in both size and confidence over the last few years. The best source for current information and advice is **Friend** (Tues–Sat 8–10pm; ☎01222/340101) or **Lesbian Line** (Tues 8–10pm; ☎01222/374051). Alternatively, as virtually everywhere is in Charles Street (just off Queen Street in the city centre), it doesn't take too much to discover what's going on. All venues are for men and women.

Club X, 39 Charles St (☎01222/645721). Stylish and popular gay club, open until 2am Wed–Sat. Above is the *Pride Café,* a cracking daytime eatery that reverts to being part of the club at night.

Exit Bar, 48 Charles St. Opposite *Club X*, this is where most people have their pre-club drinks. Late-opening (until midnight) disco bar, with loud music and frantic atmosphere.

King's Cross, Hayes Bridge Road/Caroline Street. Large and long-established gay pub, with few frills but a friendly atmosphere.

Theatre, cinema and classical music

Theatre in Cardiff encompasses everything from the radical and alternative at *The Point* and the *Chapter* to big, blowzy productions at the *New Theatre*, home of the *Welsh National Opera*. Classical music is best heard at *St David's Hall*, although the newly opened *Cardiff International Arena* is likely to siphon off some of the more prestigious shows.

Theatre

Bute Theatre, *Welsh College of Music and Drama*, North Road (☎01222/372175). Student, amateur and travelling productions.

Chapter Arts Centre, Market Road, Canton (☎01222/399666). Home of fine British and touring theatre and dance companies in a multi-functional arts complex.

New Theatre, Park Place (☎01222/394844). Splendid Edwardian city centre theatre that plays host to big London shows.

The Point, West Bute Street, Cardiff Bay (☎01222/499979). Performance space newly converted from an old church. Good for experimental theatre, music and dance, as well as more mainstream events.

Sherman Theatre, Senghennydd Road, Cathays (☎01222/230451). An excellent two-auditorium repertory theatre hosting a mixed bag of new and translated classic Welsh- language pieces, stand-up comedy, children's entertainment, drama, music and dance. Many plays on Welsh themes in both English and Welsh.

St Stephen's Theatre, West Bute Street, Cardiff Bay (☎01222/498885). Experimental theatre from the resident *Moving Being* company, as well as visiting performers.

Cinema

Capitol Odeon, *Capitol Shopping Centre*, Queen Street (☎01426/915487).

Chapter Arts Centre, Market Road, Canton (☎01222/399666). Cardiff's main art-house and alternative film centre, with two screens.

MGM, 63 Queen St (☎01222/231715).

Odeon, 55 Queen St (☎01426/915487).

Classical music

Cardiff International Arena, Harlech Court, Bute Terrace (☎01222/224488). Mighty impressive new development, rising high over the city centre's southern streets. Occasional venue for visiting international orchestras and operas.

Cardiff Male Voice Choir, c/o 577 Cowbridge Rd East (☎01222/563488). Regular performances in the city and twice-weekly rehearsal nights (Wed & Fri), to which members of the public are welcome. Phone first for details.

St David's Hall, The Hayes (☎01222/878444). Part of the massive St David's shopping centre, this large and glamorous venue is possibly the most architecturally exciting building in town. Home to visiting orchestras and musicians from jazz to opera, it's frequently used by the excellent *BBC Welsh Symphony Orchestra and Chorus*.

University Concert Hall, Corbett Road, Cathays Park (☎01222/874816). Home of public concerts by university and local orchestras, jazz groups and easy-listening ensembles.

Welsh National Opera – see *New Theatre*, p.107.

Listings

Airlines *Cardiff Air Travel* for general information (☎01446/711777); *Manx Airlines* (☎01222/342797).

Airport Cardiff International, out at Rhoose, near Barry (☎01446/711111).

Bike rental *Taff Trail Cycle Hire*, Forest Farm Country Park, Whitchurch (Easter–Oct daily 10am–6pm; ☎01222/751235). Located on the other side of the river footbridge from Radyr station.

Books *Dillons* at 1–2 St David's Link, The Hayes; *Lear's* at 37 St Mary St, and in the Cardiff Students' Union in Senghennydd Rd, Cathays.

Bus enquiries *Cardiff Bus* (☎01222/396521); *National Express* (☎01222/344751).

Car rental *Avis*, 4 Saunders Rd, Station Approach (☎01222/342111); *Crwys Auto Service*, 59 Crwys Rd (☎01222/225789); *Hertz*, 9 Central Square (☎01222/224548).

Dentist Emergency dental work at *Riverside Health Centre*, Wellington Street, Canton (☎01222/371221).

Exchange *American Express*, 3 Queen St (☎01222/665843); *Thomas Cook*, 16 Queen St (☎01222/224886), and in the tourist office at Central station.

Football Cardiff City, Ninian Park, Sloper Road (☎01222/398636).

Hospital *Cardiff Royal Infirmary*, Newport Road (☎01222/492233).

Laundries *Launderama*, 60 Lower Cathedral Rd; *GP*, 244 Cowbridge Rd, Canton; *Drift Inn*, 104 Salisbury Rd, Cathays Park.

Left luggage At Central station (Mon–Fri 10am–9pm, Sat 10am–8.30pm).

Newspapers and magazines The Cardiff-based daily *South Wales Echo* is a fairly uninspiring read, although it does have some good listings, especially for films in the city. For a wider overview of arts and events, pick up the free monthly publications *Buzz!* or *finetime*.

Pharmacy *Boots*, 5 Wood St (Mon–Sat 8am–8pm, Sun 6–7pm; ☎01222/234043).

Police *Cardiff Central Police Station*, King Edward VII Avenue, Cathays Park (☎01222/222111).

Post office The Hayes (Mon–Fri 9am–5.30pm, Sat 9am–12.30pm; ☎01222/227305).

Rugby International games at Cardiff Arms Park (☎01222/390111) and club matches next door on the Arms Park smaller pitch (☎01222/383546).

Swimming pools *Wales Empire Pool*, Wood Street (☎01222/382296); *Welsh Institute of Sport*, Sophia Gardens (☎01222/397571).

Train enquiries ☎01222/228000 (daily 8am–10pm).

Travel agencies *Campus Travel* in the YHA shop, 13 Castle St (☎01222/220744); *John Cory Travel*, Park Place (☎01222/371878); *Welsh Travel Centre*, 240 Whitchurch Rd, Cathays (☎01222/621479).

Around Cardiff

On the edge of the Cardiff suburbs, the thirteenth-century fairy-tale fortress of **Castell Coch** stands on a hillside in woods. West of the city, the massively popular **Museum of Welsh Life** tells the country's history with bricks and mortar, with a sundry collection of buildings salvaged from all over Wales. The museum lies in the grounds of the rambling Elizabethan country house of **St Fagans Castle**, restored over the centuries by its various owners.

Castell Coch

Four miles north of Llandaff is the plain village of **TONGWYNLAIS**, above which the coned turrets of **Castell Coch** (April to mid-Oct daily 9.30am–6.30pm; mid-Oct to March Mon–Sat 9.30am–4pm, Sun 11am–4pm; £2.20; CADW) rise mysteriously out of the steep wooded hillside, a ruined thirteenth-century fortress that was rebuilt and transformed into a fantasy castle in the late 1870s by William Burges for the third Marquess of Bute. With its working portcullis and drawbridge, Castell Coch is the ultimate wealthy man's medieval fantasy, isolated on an almost Alpine hillside, yet only a few hundred yards from the motorway and Cardiff suburbs. Many similarities with Cardiff Castle can be seen here, notably the outrageously lavish decor, culled from religious and moral fables, that dazzles in each room. Lady Bute's bedroom, at the top of one of the three towers, comes complete with a fabulously painted double dome, around which are 28 panels depicting frolicking monkeys, some of which were considered lascivious for their day. Bus #136 from Central station turns round at the castle gates, or the #26 drops in Tongwynlais, from where it's a ten-minute climb.

The Museum of Welsh Life and St Fagans Castle

Separated from Cardiff by only a sliver of greenery, the village of **ST FAGANS** (Sain Ffagan), four miles west of the city centre, nonetheless has a rural feel that is only partially disturbed by the busloads of tourists that roll in regularly to visit the **Museum of Welsh Life** (July–Sept daily 10am–6pm; Oct–June daily 10am–5pm; £5), a branch of the excellent National Museum of Wales constructed around **St Fagans Castle**, a country house built in 1580 on the site of a ruined Norman castle and furnished in early nineteenth-century style, complete with heavy oak furniture and gloomy portraits. The mansion's formal gardens and eighteenth-century fishponds have also been restored to something akin to their original design.

A collection of buildings from all corners of Wales have been carefully dismantled and rebuilt on this site since the museum's inception in 1946. The most impressive element is the fifty-acre **outdoor collection**, particularly the diminutive whitewashed 1777 **Pen-Rhiw Chapel** from Dyfed, the pristine and evocative Victorian **St Mary's Board School** from Lampeter and the ordered mini-fortress of a 1772 **Tollhouse** that once guarded the southern approach to Aberystwyth. Many of the domestic buildings are farmhouses of different ages and styles – compare, for example, the grandeur of the seventeenth-century red-painted **Kennixton Farmhouse** from the Gower or the homely Edwardian comforts of **Llwyn-yr-Eos Farm** with the threadbare simplicity of the Gwynedd farmworkers' **Llainfadyn Cottage**.

The best demonstration of how life changed over the years for a section of the Welsh population comes in the superlative **Rhyd-y-car** ironworkers' cottages from Merthyr Tydfil. Built originally around 1800, each of the six houses, with their accompanying strip of garden, has been furnished in the style of a different era – stretching from 1805 to 1985. Even the frontages and roofs are true to their age, offering a wade through working-class Welsh life over the past century. Next door are the Victorian **Gwalia Stores** from the mining community of Ogmore Vale, whose smell of polished mahogany is as evocative as the starchy-aproned assistants and jars of boiled sweets on sale. A large and interesting variety of workplaces, including a stinking **tannery**, a **pottery**, three **mills**, a **bakehouse** and a **smithy**, most of which house people demonstrating the original methods, make up a large number of the remaining buildings. Hourly bus #32 (and the irregular #C1) leaves Central station for the village.

The Vale of Glamorgan

The bowl of land at the very bottom of Wales is known as the **Vale of Glamorgan**, a rich, pastoral land of gentle countryside shelving down to a cliff-ridden coastline, punctuated by long, sandy beaches. The Vale does not feature on many visitors' itineraries, as they speed through from Cardiff to Swansea, the Gower and the west. This really is their loss, for the quiet and pretty towns, together with the sheer profusion of excellent beaches and tumbledown castles, warrant a good couple of days' exploration. Brash seaside resorts at **Porthcawl** in the west and **Barry** to the east contrast with the far more refined, breezy atmosphere of **Penarth**, a crusty seaside town clinging to the coat-tails of Cardiff. In between lie yawning wide bays, bracing cliff walks and spectacular ruins. At the western tip of the Vale coast is **Kenfig**, a vast, grass-spotted desert of coastal dunes and nature reserves.

Inland, the lower parts of the Vale are a curious mix of urban reminders such as Wales' major **airport** at Rhoose and occasional looming factories, set against rolling green pasture land sprinkled with charming, if scarcely thrilling, market towns like **Cowbridge**, **Llantrisant** and, most pleasing of all, **Llantwit Major**.

Its proximity to Cardiff makes the Vale easy to explore using **public transport**. The mainline train route through the Vale has a stop at Bridgend, a useful interchange for bus services to the coast and some of the larger inland settlements, although buses from Cardiff reach most places. Barry and Penarth, almost suburbs of Cardiff, are easily reached by bus and train.

Penarth and around

Considering itself a cut above the boisterous capital of Cardiff and the downbeat resort of Barry, **PENARTH** is a quietly enjoyable town wedged between the two. The Cardiff Bay developments over on the other side of the Ely estuary are lending benefits to the town, and new roads are drawing Penarth ever more inexorably into the big city's net, despite the actions of locals to ensure the independence of this half plush suburb, half seaside resort. In any event, it's an easy, enjoyable day out from Cardiff, and a reasonable place to stay.

The Town

Penarth is the end of the train line from Cardiff, receiving half-hourly shuttle trains that ply their way from here, through the capital, and out into the valleys. From the train station, a path on the right leads up to Stanwell Road, which continues into the clean-cut Edwardian shopping streets of the town centre.

The redbrick **Turner House Art Gallery** (opening times and prices variable; ☎01222/708870) is on the Plymouth Road, and houses temporary exhibitions, usually brought out from the National Museum of Wales' vast collection.

The Dingle path runs down the left-hand side of the Turner House, leading into the showy civic **Alexandra Park**, from whose oceans of flowerbeds, benches full of elderly inhabitants and bandstand it is easy to glean Penarth's character. This picture only intensifies on continuing down the hill onto the charmingly fusty **Esplanade**, with the amusement arcade in the green bubble of a hall on the pier, which also houses the seasonal tourist office and a few fish-and-chip stands. The overall effect, even in the garishly painted wrought-iron seafront, is sedately pleasing.

Flat Holm and Lavernock Point

Two miles due south of Penarth is **Lavernock Point**, jutting out into the Bristol Channel, a forlorn setting for campsites and pubs, but notable as the place in which conversation was first heard by means of radio waves. This – as a plaque on the wall of the dismal Victorian chapel notes – took place on May 11, 1897, when Guglielmo Marconi sent the immortal words "Are you ready?" over to his assistant George Kemp on the island of **Flat Holm**, three miles out in the Bristol Channel. From Penarth or Lavernock, it is easy to see that Flat Holm (Welsh) and its near neighbour, Steep Holm (English) live up to their names, with Steep Holm jutting proudly out of the water like a great whale and Flat Holm, by contrast, looking like a large dirty plate tipping gently into the waves, crowned with a lighthouse.

Flat Holm has been used as a Viking anchorage, a cholera hospital, a lighthouse and a lookout point. Today it's an interesting and beautifully remote nature reserve, the nest of thousands of gulls and shelducks. **Boats** depart daily in season, and irregularly in the winter, from Barry Harbour. Overnight stays are possible in the small **hostel** on the island. Both the boats and the hostel are operated by the Flat Holm Project in the Old Police Station on Harbour Road in Barry (☎01446/747661; ①).

Lavernock Point is a fifteen-minute walk from the bus stop on the B4267. Half-hourly bus #P4 operates from Cardiff and Penarth, dropping just near the mildly diverting **Comeston Medieval Village**, a tourist board excuse for an attraction that need not delay you too long.

Practicalities

Penarth's **tourist office** kiosk (April–June & Sept Fri–Sun 10am–6pm; July & Aug daily 10am–6pm; ☎01222/708849) is at the head of the pier on the Esplanade. For those wishing to see Cardiff without the bustle of city life, staying in Penarth is a good option – **accommodation** ranges from the well-placed *Croeso* guesthouse, 13 Plymouth Rd, near the station (☎01222/709167; ②), with the *Alandale* at no. 17 (☎01222/709226; ②), to the frillier surrounds of the Victorian *Raisdale House Hotel* on Raisdale Road, off the Plymouth Road (☎01222/707317; ③). The dingy *Lavernock Point Holiday Estate* (☎01222/707310) has tent pitches. For a day in the lap of luxury, *Avalon* on Beach Road (☎01222/531131) is a great, if pricey, leisure, health and beauty centre where you can use the sauna, sunbeds, Turkish bath, spa pool and indoor swimming pool.

Along Penarth Esplanade are a number of pricey **restaurants**. Cheapest for hearty English and Italian snacks is *Rabaiotti's*. Pizza and pasta are available at *Villa Napoli* in the *Glendale Hotel*, 10 Plymouth Rd, or there's the *Prince of India* (closed Sun) at 13 Ludlow Lane, tucked behind the main shops on Windsor Road. For **pubs**, try the enjoyably scruffy and youngish *Railway*, behind the station on Plymouth Road.

Barry and around

Good only as a day trip, the brashest seaside resort in south Wales is **BARRY** (Barri), whose speciality of loud, chip-swallowing, beer-swilling seaside fun is a million miles from the effete coastal charms of Penarth, or any of the small villages further along the Vale coast. However, until the 1880s, when it was developed as a rival port to the Bute family's Cardiff, Barry was a small fishing village, and line upon line of neat, genteel avenues – many with cheap B&Bs – still run down to the town's quieter, stonier beach at **The Knap**; here, you'll find an old-fashioned open air **lido pool** (Easter–Sept school holidays, Sat & Sun 10am–6pm; term time daily noon–6pm, weather permitting). A short walk from the centre of town, in the Memorial Hall on Gladstone Road, the **Living Archive Centre** (April–Sept Tues–Fri 10am–4pm, Sat 10am–6pm, Sun noon–6pm; Oct–March Tues, Thurs & Fri 10am–4pm, Wed 1–4pm; £1) is a model of its kind: videos, permanent and changing exhibitions and regular drama, dance and music performances tell some hoary tales of the area's long and turbulent history.

Most of the resort's activity centres on **Barry Island** (Ynys y Barri), an odd-shaped stump of land that sticks out from the town along Harbour Road, a riotous sprawl of funfairs and chip shops, interspersed with a rollerdrome, laser centre and crazy-golf green, all pinned out along a cheerfully pristine prom. Bang opposite is the **Pleasure Park** (daily Easter–June; Sept & Oct 1–10pm; July & Aug 11am–10pm), a shabby collection of rides, arcades and fairground attractions. To the left is the enormous residential **Barry Island Resort** (Easter–Oct daily 10am–11.30pm; £5 for non-residents for the day), an ex-Butlin's holiday camp that has all of the allure and architectural appeal of a prison camp, but which is stuffed to the gunwales with rides (free after you've paid the entrance fee), tacky end-of-the-pier entertainment by small-time TV personalities, pools with slides and glitzy theme bars around every corner.

The resort stretches out behind barbed-wire fences along one headland that frames the eastern end of the main beach, **Whitmore Bay**. Running behind the sands is a promenade, much-smartened but still awash with fun pubs, cheap cafés and bleeping, flashing amusement arcades. At the back of the prom is the **tourist office** (April–Sept daily 10am–6pm; ☎01446/747171). Trains rattle through Barry Docks and Barry stations before terminating at Barry Island.

Dyffryn Gardens and Llanerch Vineyard

The A4226 heads north from Barry, past the kids-oriented **Welsh Hawking Centre** (daily 10.30am–5pm; £3), with over 250 birds of prey to be seen and held. Off to the right, lanes descend to the hamlet of **DYFFRYN** and the magnificent **Dyffryn Gardens** (April–Oct daily 10am–5.30pm; March Sat & Sun 10.30am–4.30pm; £2), set around the Victorian home of a local merchant. Seldom busy, the gardens offer everything from formal lilyponds and billiard table-smooth lawns to joyous bursts of floral colour and the russets, golds and greens of an arboretum. By the lane junction just south of the gardens you'll find the **St Lythan Long Cairn**, over four thousand years old. It's nowhere near as impressive, however, as its near neighbour, the **Tinkinswood Long Cairn**, a huge, capstoned burial chamber, around 4500 years old. Legend has it that anyone who sleeps beneath the fifty-ton monolith for a night will either die, go raving mad or become a poet. You'll find it on the other side of the Dyffryn Gardens entrance, just beside the wooded lane between Dyffryn and **St Nicholas**, a village on the A48 just two miles from Cardiff's Culverhouse Cross roundabout.

Four miles northwest of St Nicholas is **Llanerch Vineyard** (Easter–Christmas daily 10am–5pm; £2.50), a mile from junction 34 of the M4. This is Wales' major vineyard, with a full capacity of 30,000 bottles of white and rosé *Cariad* wine per annum. You can wander through vineyards and woodland and past lakes, tour the wine production plant and try the finished product.

Practicalities

Accommodation in Barry town is plentiful enough, although not very enticing. Best bets are the chintzy *Knights Hotel*, 59 Colcot Rd (☎01446/747496; ③), or the cheerful *Haylings Guest House*, near the beaches and Barry Island at 1 Romilly Rd (☎01446/748614; ②). Out of town, there's a fabulous farmhouse B&B two miles southwest of the Llanerch Vineyard at *Cartreglas Farm* (☎01446/772368; ③), just north of the village of Welsh St Donats. Off the A4226 north of Barry, a mile and a half short of the junction with the A48, *Whitton Rosser Farm* (☎01446/781427; ①) has **hostel** accommodation that's mainly geared towards groups. There's **bike rental** in central Barry at *The Bike Rack* 116 Park Crescent (☎01446/737470).

The Vale coast

West of Barry, the **coast of the Vale** of Glamorgan alternates between craggy cliffs and wide, white sand beaches. Considering its location between Wales' two great cities, it's surprisingly quiet and you can easily lose all signs of civilization along some of the excellent cliff and beach walks. Until **Kenfig**, you aren't even aware of the industrialized nature of the area, as most of the old-fashioned little towns and seashore villages seem to have escaped the worst – a few garish caravan parks notwithstanding.

Llantwit Major

On first impressions, **LLANTWIT MAJOR** (Llanilltud Fawr) is mundane, as the rickety winding streets at its heart have been surrounded by modern housing estates and rows of ugly shops. Despite this, the town has an ancient pedigree, and is most noted as the centre of St Illtud's ministry around 500 AD. Here, the scholarly Illtud educated a succession of young men at his monastery, giving the town the chance to claim the title of Britain's earliest centre of learning. Amongst Illtud's pupils were St David himself and St Patrick, who was abducted from the monastery by Irish pirates to become their patron saint.

Buses drop passengers behind the 1960s Napoleon Way precinct, from where it's a short walk down East Street or Station Road into the town centre. A miniature Italianate **town hall** sits just before the main town square and was built in the fifteenth century as the replacement of one destroyed by Owain Glyndŵr; it now serves as council offices and a **tourist office** (Mon–Fri 9am–1pm & 2–4pm; Easter–Sept also Sat 9am–5pm, Sun 2–5pm; ☎01446/796086). From here, Burial Lane winds its way past the triangular pub-lined village square and down to the front of the magnificent **parish church**, sheltering in a hollow next to the trickle of the Col Huw River.

The first thing that strikes you about the church is its size: it is, in fact, two churches joined at the tower. The older west church, nearer the stream, dates from around 1100, and in the twelfth and thirteenth centuries aisles were added to transform it into the nave of a new church. The west church is notable for the collection of decorative Celtic crosses and stones arranged haphazardly inside. Prize amongst these is the exquisitely carved eighth-century boulder at the back of the church, on which the letters ILT and half of a U (remains of ILTUD) can still be made out. A guidebook (£2) about the church and its history is available from *Harvest Pottery*, opposite the front entrance on Church Street.

At the junction at the top of Burial Lane, Colhugh Street descends for a little over a mile along the scrubby valley of the Col Huw River to the partially sandy **beach**, starting point for some wonderful walks along the caves and inlets of the stratified cliffs and back into the rolling countryside. The best route to take is the path that runs west along the clifftops for two miles to **St Donat's Bay**, dominated by a mock-Gothic castle, dating back to the fourteenth century, that was bought and restored by US tycoon Randolph Hearst in the 1930s, and is now an international college and multi-purpose **arts centre** (information ☎01446/792151, box office 794848) easily at the forefront of Welsh efforts to internationalize local culture. As well as theatre, film, dance, exhibitions and community outreach, the centre hosts the excellent **Wales International Storytelling Festival** (July) and the **Vale of Glamorgan Festival** (Sept). Halfway along the route, a path dips down to the beach at **Tresilian Bay**, from where you can return to Col Huw cove along the beach.

Llantwit Major is blessed with good pubs and recreational facilities, making it pleasant enough to **stay**. Try the quiet *West House Country Hotel* (☎01446/792406; ③), between the parish church and the castle ruins; for B&B there's the friendly *Curriers Guest House* in the main square (☎01446/793506; ③), peaceful *Mrs Plested's*, 2 Anchor Cottages on Colhugh Street (☎01446/792727; ②), or *Kenilworth House* on Station Road (☎01446/796900; ③). *Rose Dew Farm* on Ham Lane South has the *Acorn* **campsite** (☎01446/794024).

For **food**, there are cheap takeaways along East Street and its continuation, Boverton Road, or, in the old town centre, try the daytime *Truffles* café in Church Street, where you should leave plenty of room for the sublime home-made chocolates. The best restaurant in town is *Italian Joe's* on Colhugh Street (☎01446/792321), or, for something cheaper, most of the town centre **pubs** do food at lunchtime and in the evening. Of them all, the *Old White Hart* on the Square is best for food and has a nice enough atmosphere, although the nearby *Tudor Tavern* is more of an earthy drinking hole.

Southerndown and Ogmore

West of Llantwit Major, the coast ducks and dives past remote, sandy beaches and cliffs, punctuated by small streams trickling in from the lush farmland behind. **SOUTHERNDOWN** is a diffuse holiday village of touristy pubs and one excellent restaurant – *Frolics* on Beach Road (☎01656/880127; closed Sun & Mon), with a creative, wholesome and fairly expensive menu dictated entirely by seasonal specialities – but the real reason for coming here is **Dunraven Bay**, a beautiful, wide beach backed by jagged cliffs with perfectly defined different layers of limestone and shale. In the busy car park by Dunraven Beach is the **Heritage**

Coast Centre (☎01656/880157), a small information point about walks and dri-ves along this splendid part of the south Wales coastline. This is the western end of a magnificent five-mile **coastal walk**, dipping down into tiny, wooded valleys and up across wide stretches of cliff and sand.

The village of **OGMORE** (Ogwr) is a straggling, windswept sort of place, but lies close to the remains of **Ogmore Castle**, situated about a mile north along the coast from Southerndown. The castle's position is stunning, in the very bottom of a flat valley, sided by tree-clad hillsides and peaks of dunes behind them. The castle dates from the Norman Conquest in around 1100, and its solid central stone keep, in which a few original windows are still intact, was added later in the twelfth century.

Ewenny Priory

Two miles further up the B4524 is **EWENNY**, a village whose main draw is the towering remains of Benedictine **Ewenny Priory**, tucked away down leafy lanes, three-quarters of a mile to the east of the village. Founded in 1141, the priory's formidable fortress-like walls were intended to protect against the hostile Welsh, who saw the Benedictines as little more than lapdogs of the Norman invaders. The walls, strengthened continuously throughout the thirteenth century, are still very much intact today, broken only by the two huge gateways in which the portcullis holes can still be seen. The priory was dissolved during the Dissolution of the Monasteries, shortly after which a private house was built in the precincts, and it is not possible to visit.

The priory **church**, on the other side of the mansion, is squat and powerful, brooding over the ecclesiastical remains scattered around it. It is divided into two sections by a plain early medieval rood screen. On the western side (nearest to the rest of the priory) is the nave, whose damp, cold interior includes some splen-did Norman windows. This nave served as the parish church, as opposed to the eastern chancel, which housed the monastic chapel.

Merthyr Mawr

On the banks of the Ogmore River two miles west of Ewenny, the small village of **MERTHYR MAWR** seems a rural haven of unexpected beauty. A narrow lane steers around into the village of neat thatched and whitewashed cottages. The lane continues along a wooded glen to its end on the edge of the great dune desert of Merthyr Mawr, stretching over miles to the distant sea. By the car park is the gaunt ruin of **Candleston Castle**, a fifteenth-century fortified manor house that was abandoned last century as the shifting sands came too close. There is a **campsite** (☎01656/652038) for those seeking solitude.

Porthcawl

Once one of Wales' most popular seaside resorts, **PORTHCAWL** has been on a downward slide for years. Tatty bungalows and depressing caravan parks announce entry into the town, now little more than a retirement centre. Recent years have seen concerted attempts to re-ignite the spark of the town with limit-ed success: half-decent entertainment tends to bypass the place and, apart from the usual clutch of tacky seaside shops, cheap B&Bs and pubs alongside some safe, sandy beaches, there is little here to excite the adventurous visitor.

Half-hourly **buses** connect Bridgend with Porthcawl, depositing travellers at the top of the pedestrianized John Street in the town centre. A two-minute walk straight down the street leads to the Old Police Station, housing the less-than-friendly

tourist office (April–Sept Mon–Sat 9.30am–5.30pm; ☎01656/782211), where you can pick up a fairly useful free town guide, and a sporadically open local history **museum**. John Street continues down to the Esplanade, a typical line of Victorian and Edwardian hotels along a rocky beach, and where you'll find the domed **Grand Pavilion**, home to assorted seaside entertainment shows, pantomimes and the like. East, the Esplanade runs to a lifeboat station at the harbour before veering north with the coast as Eastern Promenade. Here are the solid seaside attractions: the **Coney Beach amusement park** behind whelk stalls and candy floss shops that look out over the donkey rides on Sandy Bay, and two vast caravan parks perched over this cove and neighbouring Trecco Bay. On the northwest side of town, a twenty-minute walk from the centre, is the far quieter and more beautiful **Rest Bay**.

Accommodation in Porthcawl is plentiful, cheap and concentrated around Mary Street, Gordon Road and Esplanade Avenue: right in the centre are the *Collingwood Hotel*, 40 Mary St (☎01656/782899; ③), the slightly plusher *Minerva Hotel*, 52 Esplanade Ave (☎01656/782428; ③), *Rossett House*, 1 Esplanade Ave (☎01656/771664; ②), and the welcoming *Rosedale Guest House*, 48 Esplanade Ave (☎01656/785356; ②). There are dozens of places to **eat** in the hotels, pubs and cafés strewn around the town centre; one of the best, surprisingly, is *Pizza R Us*, 108 John St (☎01656/773900), serving a sturdy range of good pizzas. Of the many **pubs**, the *Rock Hotel*, 98 John St, has decent beer and generous food.

Kenfig

The cliffs and beaches north of Porthcawl stop at the one-time fishing port of **KENFIG** (Cynffig), two miles along the coast, where a thriving community founded in the Bronze Age was finally overwhelmed by the shifting sand dunes in the sixteenth century – they have obliterated whole swathes of land, burying houses and the church in its path; the only surviving remains of the town are the miserable stumps of the **castle**. Today, the dunes of Kenfig Burrows have been stabilized by marram grass plantations, and the whole site is open as a **nature reserve** (summer daily 10am–5pm; winter Sat & Sun 2–5pm), with a small display about local wildlife, and advice for those who want to go walking or bird-watching at the hide by the freshwater **Kenfig Pool**. Apart from the inevitable gulls, frequent visitors here are oystercatchers, ringed plovers and redshanks. Most remarkable is the reserve's backdrop: firstly the smoking stacks of the Port Talbot steelworks and secondly, the great, hazy curve of Swansea Bay stretching for dozens of miles to the Gower. Don't miss the historic *Prince of Wales* inn over the road from the nature reserve, the main survivor of the old port.

The inland Vale

Although the scenery is not as startling as the coast, the rural land of the Vale of Glamorgan is speckled with some interesting towns, villages and ruined castles, connected by small, high-hedged lanes. **Llantrisant**, a hilltop market town just off the M4, sits astride the border of mountainous valley and rural vale, while **Cowbridge**, seven miles south, nestles firmly in a green patchwork of countryside, secure in its quiet charms as the unofficial capital of the Vale.

Llantrisant

LLANTRISANT perches dramatically between two peaks that rise suddenly out of the flattened valley of the rivers Ely and Clun, ten miles west of Cardiff, and was once encircled by fortifications to exploit its natural position as a watching post over the Vale of Glamorgan.

The centre of the small town is the **Bull Ring**, where there's a suitably wild-eyed statue (donated by the Cremation Society) of **Dr William Price** (1800–93), dressed in his favoured druid's outfit of moons, stars and a fox fur on his head. Dr Price subscribed to some precocious beliefs – vegetarianism, nudity, republicanism, the unhealthiness of socks, anti-smoking, free love and the potential environmental disasters from mass industrialization. He is best remembered for cremating his dead infant son, Iesu Grist (Welsh for "Jesus Christ"), in a makeshift service on Llantrisant Common in January 1884, burning the small body in an oil drum. He was arrested and, in a sensational trial at Cardiff, acquitted, after which cremation was made legal.

Overlooking the Bull Ring is the **Model House Craft and Design Centre** (Jan–April Wed–Sun noon–5pm; May–Dec Tues–Sun 10am–5pm; free), which serves as one of the region's best centres for exhibitions, workshops and conventions. It also houses a shop where local crafts are sold, the excellent *Workhouse* café (this was once the town workhouse) and a permanent display on the work of the **Royal Mint**, moved here from London in 1967. All British coins are now minted at Llantrisant, and the small display runs through some of the historical background that produced one national mint, including examples of coins from the eighteenth and nineteenth centuries and some of the heavy old machinery that once had to be employed.

Cowbridge

The A48 now bypasses **COWBRIDGE** (Y Bont Faen) – and you might want to do the same – although the smugly prosperous town boasts an interesting range of architectural styles and numerous good pubs and restaurants. The town's Norman street pattern, focusing on the main thoroughfare, is still evident, stretching for almost a mile in a virtual straight line. On the south side of the High Street, Church Street leads under the narrow gatehouse that is the sole remainder of the town's fourteenth-century walls. One-third of a mile further east along the High Street is *Basil's Brasserie*, a good place to eat.

A little more than a mile out of town, down a quiet lane fringed with high hedges, there is a tiny lay-by opposite the Regency finery of Howe Mill. A path opposite leads along the bank of the River Thaw for quarter of a mile to the gauntly impressive ruins of **Beaupre Castle**, largely an Elizabethan manor house. Built by the local noble family, the Bassetts, Beaupre is a huge shell of ruined Italianate doorways and vast mullioned windows in the middle of a quiet Glamorgan field.

The Vale of Neath

The **Vale of Neath** likes to think of itself as a world apart from the Valleys, looking more towards Cymric Swansea than anglicized Cardiff. **Neath**, focal point of the Vale, is a curious town with antiquities from the Roman, Norman and medieval periods, all set in grim industrial surroundings that somehow make them all the more remarkable. The River Neath flows in from the northeast, past **Aberdulais**, with its impressive, industrial waterfalls. The falls are on the Dulais River, which heads north to the **Cefn Coed Colliery Museum**. The valleys to the east of the Vale of Neath are dealt with in the Valleys section (p.75).

Neath

Recently cleaned up, the town of **NEATH** (Castell-Nedd) has overcome its past as a centre of copper smelting to become a spacious, pleasantly ordinary place that is much overshadowed by near neighbour Swansea. The tumbledown **castle** ruins (closed to the public) sit unhappily in a corner of the *Safeway* car park, and the most picturesque corner of town is Church Place, where the borough **museum** (Tues–Sat 10am–4pm; free), a mildly interesting ramble through Neath's history over the past six thousand years, is housed in the splendid surroundings of the Old Mechanics' Institution. Just outside of town on the A465 are the remains of **Neath Abbey** (free access; CADW). The ghostly, dark silhouette of the abbey, founded in the early twelfth century, is wedged in amongst an industrial estate and oily canal. In the sixteenth century, a chunk of the abbey was converted into a mansion, which later metamorphosed into a copper-smelting works.

Aberdulais and around

Two miles further up the River Neath (accessible by hourly bus from Station Square in Neath) is the village of **ABERDULAIS**, where the River Dulais tumbles over the scoops and platforms of the **Aberdulais Falls** (April–Oct Mon–Fri 10am–5pm, Sat & Sun 11am–6pm; £2.80; NT). The natural power of the site was first harnessed in 1584 for a copper works that developed into a corn mill, ironworks and a tin-plating unit in the nineteenth century. One hundred and sixty million litres of deep-green water course over the rocks every day, gouging out bowls of rock and pouring over precarious lips jutting out over the spume below. In the old stable block, an excellent **interpretive centre** contains a glass-fronted window onto one of the falls' subterranean channels, where pounding water can be seen rushing by, inches away. It also contains replicas of some of the many paintings of the falls, a venue beloved of eighteenth- and nineteenth-century landscapists, including Turner.

The area outside the Falls is currently a huge building site for the upgraded A465, disturbing the tranquillity of the **canal basin**, just beyond the Falls car park. It's quite an interesting spot; there's the canal fed by a curious low-slung aqueduct over the wide River Dulais, and the four-mile towpath walk up to the basin at **Resolven** is beautiful, as the man-made waterway criss-crosses the route of the river at the bottom of the Vale of Neath.

The main A465 heads up the Vale from Aberdulais, with the A4109 branching off north to the **Cefn Coed Colliery Museum** (April–Sept daily 10.30am–6pm; Oct–March daily 10.30am–4pm; £1.50), four miles away. Although not as impressive as the Rhondda Heritage Park or Big Pit, Cefn Coed includes a huge working winding engine and some well-presented exhibitions about the site, once the deepest anthracite mine in the world. There are also some glorious signposted walks from the museum up into the surrounding wooded hills.

Four miles further up, by the side of the A4109, is the unusual attraction of a community-founded **sawmill** in the unassuming village of **SEVEN SISTERS** (Blaendulais). You can see the wood being felled, watch it being worked on and buy some astonishingly good-value end products, from garden benches to bird houses. On site, there's also a mock Wild West town, **Gunsmoke** (April–June Sat, Sun & school holidays 11am–5pm; July & Aug daily 11am–5pm; £1.50), aimed squarely at the nippers.

Swansea

Over forty years ago, local boy Dylan Thomas called **SWANSEA** (Abertawe) an "ugly, lovely town". No-one has described the city so neatly or accurately since. Large, sprawling and boisterous, Swansea is the second city of Wales, with great aspirations to be the first. It's far more of a Welsh town than Cardiff, and you'll hear *yr iaith*, the Welsh language, spoken daily on its streets.

Thomas' scathing but affectionate epithet rings true at every turn. A jumble of tower blocks and factory units dot the sloping horizons, gathered around the concrete city centre, massively rebuilt after devastating bomb attacks in World War II. But multifarious charms show themselves on closer inspection: some intact old corners of the city centre, the spacious and graceful suburb of Uplands, a wide seafront overlooking the huge sweep of Swansea Bay and a bold marina development around the old docks. Spread throughout are some of the best-funded **museums** in Wales. Another great bonus is the city's position on the fringe of the ever-popular Gower, with the seaside resorts of **Mumbles** and **Oystermouth** (for both, see p.127), now little more than salty suburbs.

Some history

The city's Welsh name, Abertawe, refers to the settlement at the mouth of the River Tawe, a grimy ditch that is slowly being teased back to life after centuries of use as a sewer for Swansea's metal trades. The English name is believed to have been prompted from Viking sources, suggesting that a pre-Norman settlement existed in the area. The first reliable origins of Swansea came in 1099, when a Norman castle was built here as an outpost of William the Conqueror's empire. A small settlement grew near the coalfields and the sea, developing into a mining and shipbuilding centre that, by 1700, was the largest coal port in Wales.

Copper smelting became the area's dominant industry in the eighteenth century, soon attracting other metal trades to pack out the lower Tawe valley, which grew into a five-mile stretch of rusting, stagnant land and water that has only recently begun to be re-landscaped. With the town's flourishing metal trades, a swiftly growing port and the arrival of the Swansea Canal, thousands of emigrants moved to the city from all over Ireland and Britain. By the nineteenth century, the town was one of the world's most prolific metal-bashing centres.

Smelting was already on the wane by the turn of the twentieth century, although Swansea's port continued to flourish. Britain's first oil refinery was opened on the edge of the city in 1918, with dock developments growing in its wake. Civic zeal, demonstrated best in the graceful 1930s Guildhall dominating the west of the city, was reawakened after the establishment of an important branch of the University of Wales here in 1920, but World War II had a devastating effect on Swansea, with thirty thousand bombs raining down in three nights in 1941. The rebuilding of the centre has left a series of soulless concrete streets and underpasses weaving between shopping centres, although now, with a population of around 200,000, Swansea is undergoing something of a renaissance. With a resurgent music and club scene, the sparkling new National Literature Centre, *Tŷ Llen*, and some spirited redesigns of streets and squares in the city centre, Swansea is bouncing back.

Arrival, information and getting around

Swansea is the main interchange station for services out to the west of Wales and for the slow line across the middle of the country to Shrewsbury in Shropshire. The **train station** is at the top end of the High Street, a ten-minute hike from the bus station, from where local and national services fan out to all corners of south Wales and beyond. The **bus station**, complete with a highly efficient information office, is sandwiched between the Quadrant shopping centre and the *Grand Theatre*. On the northern side of the Quadrant is Singleton Street, where you'll find the municipal **tourist office** (Mon–Sat 9.30am–5.30pm; ☎01792/468321), where you can pick up the comprehensive monthly magazine*What's On*. For information on clubs, festivals and less mainstream events, try the music, clothes and hippie shops in the Picton Arcade, between The Kingsway and Oxford Street, near the *Grand Theatre*.

As most of the sights are within walking distance of each other, **getting around** Swansea is easy. Popular suburbs, such as Uplands and Sketty, near the University, are a bracing half-hour walk from the centre, although *SWT* buses cover the suburbs thoroughly, and run out into Mumbles and the Gower.

Accommodation

As a lively city on the edge of some of Wales' most popular and inspirational coast and rural scenery, Swansea makes a logical base. Transport is good out into the surrounding areas, and **beds** in the city are less expensive than those in the more picturesque Gower – dozens of dirt-cheap hotels and B&Bs line the seafront Oystermouth Road, pitched at those catching the Swansea–Cork ferry. There's one city-edge **campsite** – *Ynysforgan Farm*, yards from junction 45 of the M4 in Morriston (☎01792/775587) – but you're better off heading for the Gower.

Hotels

Cefn Bryn, 6 Uplands Crescent, Uplands (☎01792/466687). Cheery enough, family-run hotel in Swansea's most elegant suburb. Good reputation for food. ③.

Forte Crest, Kingsway (☎01792/651074). In the city centre, overlooking The Kingsway traffic island, with all of the usual *Forte* facilities. ⑤.

Glengariff, 372 Oystermouth Rd (☎01792/458137). Pleasant, if fairly basic seafront hotel. ②.

Oyster, 262 Oystermouth Rd (☎01792/654345). Small and friendly hotel, serving great local cuisine. ②.

Oystercatcher, 386 Oystermouth Rd (☎01792/456574). Cheap and cheerful place with a slightly wider range of facilities than many others in this price band. ②.

Parkway, 253 Gower Rd, Sketty (☎01792/201632). Quiet and extremely comfortable hotel in a comparatively salubrious area. ④.

St James, 76b Walter Rd, Uplands (☎01792/649984). Small, welcoming hotel in an airy Victorian house. ③.

Southview, 392 Oystermouth Rd (☎01792/651720). Agreeable hotel overlooking the bay. ③.

Guesthouses

Channel View, 17 Bryn Rd, Brynmill (☎01792/466834). Friendly and unpretentious guesthouse almost next to the St Helen's cricket and rugby ground. ②.

Crescent, 132 Eaton Crescent, Uplands (☎01792/466814). Large, pleasant, well-converted Edwardian guesthouse with superb views over the city and the bay. ③.

SWANSEA

△ Cardiff & M4

River Tawe

Ferry Port

△ Carmarthen & M4

Train Station

GRENFELL PARK ROAD
PENTRE GUINEA ROAD
NEW CUT ROAD
STRAND
HIGH STREET
CASTLEWIND STREET
ORCHARD ST
DYFATY ST
PRINCESS WAY
QUAY PARADE
THE KINGSWAY
MANSEL ST
PAGE ST
CROMWELL STREET
MOUNT PLEASANT
TERRACE ROAD
WALTER ROAD
ST HELEN'S ROAD
WESTBURY ST
ST JAMES CRESCENT
ARGYLE ST
BEACH ST
OYSTERMOUTH ROAD
KING EDWARDS ROAD
ST HELEN'S AVENUE
BRYN-Y-MOR ROAD
BRYN-Y-MOR CRESCENT
EATON CRESCENT
UPLANDS CRESCENT
UPLANDS
FINSBURY RD
BRUNSWICK ST
BERNARD STREET
GLANBRYDAN AVENUE
GLANMOR ROAD
GLANMOR PARK ROAD
SKETTY ROAD
PARC WERN ROAD
PANTYCELYN ROAD
DYFED AVENUE
PANT-Y-CELYN ROAD
TOWNHILL ROAD
COCKETT RD
CAPCOCH ROAD
VIVIAN ROAD
GOWER ROAD
DELA BECH ROAD
BRYNMILL LANE
BRYN ROAD
MUMBLES ROAD
SKETTY PARK LANE

Plantasia
Castle
Tŷ Llen
Swansea Museum
Dylan Thomas Theatre
Maritime & Industrial Museum
Leisure Centre
St David's Square
Bus Station
Market
Grand Theatre
Glyn Vivian Art Gallery
Swansea F.C.
Dylan Thomas Birthplace
Guildhall
Patti Pavilion
Cwmdonkin Park
Singleton Park
University College of Swansea

N

0   yds   500

HOTELS
1 Cefn Bryn
2 Forte Crest
3 Glengariff
4 Oyster
5 Oystercatcher
6 Parkway
7 St James
8 South View

GUESTHOUSES
8 Channel View
9 Crescent
10 Hariton
11 Uplands Court

△ Gower

▷ Mumbles

Harlton, 89 King Edward Rd, Brynmill (☎01792/466938). Budget guesthouse near to the university and cricket/rugby ground. ②.

Uplands Court, 134 Eaton Crescent, Uplands (☎01792/473046). Enjoyable guesthouse within a gracious Victorian villa in a pleasant area. ③.

The City

Swansea's train station faces out onto the morose **High Street**, which heads south into Castle Street and past the remains of the **castle**. The most obvious landmark of the ruins are the semicircular arcades, built into the wall between 1330 and 1332 by Bishop Gower to replace a Norman predecessor. The castle enjoys a new, improved setting against the recently overhauled **Castle Square**, a pleasant amphitheatre of steps surrounding a fountain. The ragbag of architecture around it, however, is still postwar Swansea at its most unadventurous – particularly the dull 1950s block entirely given over to *McDonald's*. Swansea's new municipal street furniture, in a sort of distressed turquoise and purple, is certainly eye-catching, even if many of the angular purple flower stands are usually mistaken for litter bins. Whether the wholesale redesign will survive the current wave of bitter complaint in the local paper remains to be seen.

A block behind the High Street, the retail park on the Strand includes the great glasshouse of **Plantasia** (Tues–Sun & Bank Holiday Mon 10am—5pm; £1.50). Tropical plants, butterflies, snakes, an aquarium and numerous insects fill the huge glass pyramid, one of the best of its breed.

Alexandra Road forks right off the High Street immediately south of the station, leading down to the **Glynn Vivian Art Gallery** (Tues–Sun 10.30am–5.30pm; free), on the corner of Clifton Hill, a road so steep that the pavement gives way to steps every few yards. This delightful Edwardian gallery houses an inspiring collection of Welsh art including works by Gwen John, her brother Augustus, whose mesmerizing portrait of *Caitlin Thomas*, Dylan's wife, is a real highlight, and Kyffin Williams; the grimy mining portraits of Josef Herman; and a whole room of the huge, frantic canvases of Ceri Richards, Wales' most respected twentieth-century painter. In the early nineteenth century, Swansea was a noted centre of fine porcelain production, of which the gallery houses a large collection, together with pieces of contemporary works from Nantgarw, near Cardiff.

Belle View Way, off Alexandra Road just south of the gallery, leads to the ugly traffic island that acts as a focus for Swansea's shopping districts, with Orchard Street, a pedestrian link to the High Street, The Kingsway and Princess Way all converging on the same gloomy spot. The main shopping streets lie to the southwest, bounded by The Kingsway and Princess Way. Sheltering underneath the Quadrant Centre, the curving-roofed **market** makes a lively sight, with plenty of bustle, colourful stalls and the smells of flowers, fresh baking and food. On sale are local delicacies such as laver bread, a delicious savoury made from seaweed, as well as cockles trawled from the nearby Loughor estuary, typical Welsh cakes, fish and cheeses.

The Maritime Quarter

The spit of land between Oystermouth Road, the sea and the Tawe estuary has been christened the Maritime Quarter – tourist-board-speak for tarted-up old docks – with a centrepiece of a vast marina surrounded by legions of unsold modern flats.

Entering the area from the east, the main road bridge over the Tawe now houses a World War II ack-ack gun that stands as a memorial to the Luftwaffe decimation suffered by Swansea. The city's old South Dock, now cleaned and spruced up, features the **Swansea Museum** (Tues–Sun 10.30am–5.30pm; free), or more properly the Royal Institution of South Wales, on Victoria Road. Wales' oldest public museum was founded in 1835, and much of it is still enticingly old-fashioned, although recent revamping has glitzed up many of the displays. The biggest draw is a wizened Egyptian mummy, but there's also an interesting stroll through the history of the heavily industrialized Lower Swansea valley, comprehensive collections of archeological finds, local porcelain and pottery and some good natural history exhibits. A small grid of nineteenth-century streets around the museum has been thoughtfully cleaned up, and now houses some enjoyable cafés, pubs and restaurants.

Tucked behind the museum in Somerset Place is the new **Tŷ Llen** (Tues–Sun 10.30am–5pm; free), the National Literature Centre for Wales. Opened on St David's Day 1995 as part of Swansea's UK City of Literature celebrations, and properly named the *Dylan Thomas Centre*, it boasts a theatre space, two galleries, a restaurant, bookshops and craft shops. An impressive enough structure, combining the much spruced-up nineteenth-century Guildhall with a honeyed modern extension, it would have been even more striking had the original design – a sweeping glass creation by Wil Alsop, winner of the high-profile competition launched around the proposal – not been scrapped in an unfortunate precursor to the wrangles with Cardiff's planned Opera House (see p.102).

A hundred yards or so west, behind the *Evening Post* building, the city's **Environment Centre** (daily 10am–4pm; free) is housed in the old telephone exchange on Pier Street. It holds recycling facilities, information points and regularly changing exhibitions on a green theme.

From here, Burrows Place leads down to the marina and the superb **Maritime and Industrial Museum** (Tues–Sun 10.30am–5.30pm; free). Taking Swansea's seaside position as its starting point, the museum presents a lively history of the city, with an especially compulsive section on the horrors of the Blitz. The many vehicles include an old tram that once rattled along the seafront to Mumbles and a rare example of Gilbern cars, Wales' principal (and long-dead) contribution to the motor industry. The museum's tramshed annexe houses a lively history of the Mumbles railway, built in 1804 as the world's first passenger-carrying railway and closed in 1960, with numerous fact-filled wall displays and a great video showing scratchy footage of the big red beasts in action.

The Maritime Museum faces out onto a flotilla of yachts bobbing in the marina. Close by stands John Doubleday's statue of Dylan Thomas, dubbed "A Portrait of the Artist as Someone Else", due to its remarkable lack of resemblance to the poet. Just behind the statue, on Gloucester Place, is the mural-splattered warehouse that has now become the **Dylan Thomas Theatre**, which intersperses productions of his work with visiting and local companies' offerings. Slap opposite is the **Swansea Arts Workshop** (daily 11am–5pm; free) in a beautifully converted old chapel. Changing exhibits complement a small shop space of local crafts, many of them excellent.

West Swansea

West of the city centre, St Helen's Road dips down to the seafront near the tall white tower of the **Guildhall** and Walter Road, staying inland until the airy suburb of **Uplands**. The Guildhall, a typically soaring example of 1930s civic architecture, contains **Brangwyn Hall** (☎01792/301301 for access), named after painter Sir Frank Brangwyn (who painted the eighteen enormous British Empire Panels that line the hall), and a frequent venue for some excellent classical concerts. Immediately behind the Guildhall, down by the coast road, is **Victoria Park**, whose most prominent feature is the **Patti Pavilion**, a graceful green-roofed hall with glass sides, a gift from opera singer Adelina Patti, brought here from her home at Craig-y-nos in the Brecon Beacons (see p.208). The pavilion – used for concerts, variety shows, gigs and even raves – was rebuilt with the help of the BBC TV show *Challenge Anneka*. Unfortunately, planning permission had not been sought and a predictable rumpus ensued before retrospective permission was granted.

The drab postwar achitecture of **Swansea University**, three-quarters of a mile further, enjoys a commanding position over the bay stretching to Mumbles Head. Within the complex is the eclectic **Taliesin Arts Centre**, Swansea's most imaginative performance space, together with the **Ceri Richards Gallery** (Mon 11am–5pm, Tues–Fri 11am–6pm, Sat noon–6pm; free), specializing in touring exhibitions, frequently by contemporary Welsh and Celtic artists.

Hourly buses leave the Quadrant depot to trundle along Walter Road in the direction of Uplands, which is otherwise a half-hour walk from the city centre. North of the main road, leafy avenues rise up the slopes past the sharp terraces of **Cwmdonkin Park**, at the centre of which is a memorial to Dylan Thomas inscribed with lines from *Fern Hill*, one of his best-known poems. From the park, the views over huddles of houses down to the curving shoreline are breathtaking. On the eastern side of Cwmdonkin Park is Cwmdonkin Drive (reached from the main road via The Grove), a sharply rising set of solid Victorian semis, notable only for the blue plaque on no. 5, Thomas' birthplace.

Eating, drinking and nightlife

Swansea's metamorphosis from a sturdily working-class, industrial city into a would-be tourist centre is manifest in its pubs, restaurants and entertainment centres. Many of the grittier, older establishments survive, but increasing numbers are being steadily gentrified. This leaves a fairly stark choice between grotty, if more interesting, places and some rather sterile newer developments. For nightlife, the city is well placed as a major centre in Wales, with most passing performing artists obliged to make a stop here.

Restaurants and cafés

Bengal Brasserie, 47 Walter Rd (☎01792/643747). Best of the many Indian restaurants in Swansea, well worth the ten-minute hike from the city centre.

Bizzie Lizzie's, 55 Walter Rd (☎01792/473379). Relaxed and informal cellar-bar bistro, with a good range of cheapish Welsh, international and vegetarian dishes.

Casa Reba, 8 Craddock St, off The Kingsway (☎01792/643526). Spanish eatery with a reasonable lunch menu and a more extensive, expensive, evening selection.

Eleo's Brasserie, 33 The Kingsway (☎01792/648609). Gloriously tacky mock olde-worlde bistro, with pub classics and pasta dishes in large quantities at reasonable rates.

Footlights Coffee Bar, Grand Theatre, Singleton Street. Good daytime meeting space with a delicious, inexpensive lunch menu, including some imaginative vegetarian options. Also has a good restaurant extension for lunchtimes and evenings.

Hwyrnos, Green Dragon Lane, off Wind Street (☎01792/641437). Fixed Welsh evening menu plus harp-twanging entertainment in an extremely convivial, bordering on boozy, atmosphere. More sedate lunchtime menu also available. Prices are moderate.

New Capriccio, 89 St Helen's Rd (☎01792/648804). Popular Italian restaurant, with bargain lunch menu. Closed Sun evening and Mon.

Ribcage Brasserie, 18 Anchor Court, Victoria Quay, Swansea Marina (☎01792/648555). Lively, inexpensive eatery, serving steaks, burgers, Tex-Mex, salads and so on, popular with a young, pre-club set.

The Schooner, 4 Prospect Place (☎01792/649321). Excellent, moderately priced fish restaurant, with a speciality of local catches. Closed Sun evenings.

Steak by Night, 10 Craddock St, off The Kingsway (☎01792/466810). Late-opening, standard-priced and lively steakhouse, with a dependable menu.

Tŷ Llen restaurant, Somerset Place (☎01792/465392). Fine, relaxing restaurant in the National Literature Centre, with a good range of fair-priced local specialities.

Bars, pubs and clubs

Adam and Eve, 207 High St. Traditional pub, with a great atmosphere and varied clientele. Well known for the excellence of its beer.

Bush Inn, High Street. Only worth mentioning in warning: don't be deceived by the charmingly olde-worlde exterior – inside, it's a loud, video-filled nightmare.

Cardiff Arms, 53 The Strand. Boisterous and packed live rock pub, with visiting bands and a laid-back atmosphere. Sat afternoon blues sessions.

Celtic Pride, 49 Uplands Crescent, Uplands (☎01792/645301). Good local pub with almost nightly live music, including jam sessions and Welsh music.

Duke of York, Princess Way. Swansea's best venue for jazz and blues music, as its *Ellington's* club (small fee payable) hosts nightly gigs.

Escape Club, Northampton Lane (☎01792/290504). Enormous, purpose-built rave club, encouraging glitzy dressing and "sexual sophistication".

No Sign Bar, 56 Wind St. A narrow frontage leads into a long, warm pub interior with a rather soulless restaurant at the back. The etymology of the pub's name is explained in depth in the window.

Palace, 154 High St (☎01792/457977). Gay club open seven nights a week, 5-min walk north of the station. Mixed men and women.

Queen's Hotel, Gloucester Place, near the marina. Large old seafaring hotel and pub, with good snack lunches and Sun roasts. Regular evening live music and quizzes.

Tramp's, 15 The Kingsway (☎01792/476520). At the heart of Swansea's cheesier clubland, *Tramp's* is OK for handbag and other more mainstream house music.

Theatre, cinema and classical music

Brangwyn Hall, The Guildhall, South Road (☎01792/302489). Vastly impressive music hall in the Art Deco civic centre. Hosts regular concerts by the *BBC Welsh Symphony Orchestra* and others.

Dylan Thomas Theatre, Gloucester Place, by the marina (☎01792/473238). Reruns of Thomas' classics, intertwined with other modern works.

Grand Theatre, Singleton Street (☎01792/475715). One of Britain's best provincial theatres, with a wide-ranging diet of visiting high culture, comedy, farce and music.

Patti Pavilion, Victoria Park (☎01792/477710). Well-restored former opera hut of chanteuse Adelina Patti, home to numerous musical and theatrical performances.

Taliesin Arts Centre, Swansea University (☎01792/296883). Welsh, English and international visiting theatre, music and film, including offbeat and alternative fare.

UCI Cinema, The Strand (☎01792/645005). Ten-screen multiplex.

Listings

Bike rental *M&P Cycles*, 31 St Helen's Rd (☎01792/644204).

Books *Uplands Bookshop*, 27 Uplands Crescent (☎01792/470195); *Waterstones*, Oxford Street.

Bus enquiries *SWT* office in the Quadrant Centre bus station, Plymouth Street (Mon–Fri 8.30am–5.30pm, Sat 8.30am–5pm) or telephone enquiries (Mon–Sat 8.30am–6pm, Sun 10am–6pm; ☎01792/475511).

Car rental *Brisco*, Dyfatty Street (☎01792/457338); *Europcar*, 187–9 Lower Oxford St (☎01792/650526).

Ferry enquiries *Swansea–Cork Ferries* (☎01792/456116) runs daily crossings of the Irish Sea.

Festivals The annual Swansea Festival of music and the arts takes place around October, and the city's *Beer Festival* occupies the Patti Pavilion in mid-April; details of both from the tourist office.

Hospital *Singleton Hospital*, Sketty Park Lane, Singleton, West Swansea (☎01792/205666).

Laundries *Brynmill Launderette*, 121 Rhyddings Terrace, Brynmill; *Lendart*, 71 Uplands Crescent, Uplands.

Pharmacies *Dragon Pharmacy*, 13 Orchard St (both Mon–Sat 10am–6pm); *Evans Taylor*, 56 The Kingsway.

Police Main station is near the train station on Orchard Street (☎01792/456999).

Post office 35 The Kingsway (☎01792/655759).

Rugby Swansea Rugby Club, one of Wales' premier sides, play at St Helen's Park in Uplands (☎01792/648654).

Soccer Swansea City FC at the Vetch Field (☎01792/474114).

Surfing Information and equipment for watersports and other outdoor activities from the *High Adventure* shop, 6 Wind St (☎01792/648712).

Train enquiries ☎01792/467777.

Gower

A fifteen-mile peninsula of undulating limestone, **GOWER** (Gŵyr) points down into the Bristol Channel to the west of Swansea. The area is fringed by sweeping yellow bays and precipitous cliffs, caves and blowholes to the south, and wide, flat marshes and cockle beds to the north; brackened heaths with prehistoric remains and tiny villages lie between, and castle ruins and curious churches are spread evenly around. Out of season, the winding Gower lanes afford opportunities for exploration; but in the height of the summer, they are congested with caravans shuffling between one overpriced car park and the next.

Gower can be said to start in Swansea's western suburbs, along the coast of Swansea Bay that curves round to a point in the pleasantly old-fashioned resort of **Mumbles** and Mumbles Head, which marks the boundary between the sandy excesses of Swansea Bay and the rocky inlets that dip and tuck along the serrated coastline of southern Gower. This southern coast is punctuated by sites exploited for their defensive capacity, best seen in the eerie isolation of the sand-bound **Pennard Castle**, high above **Three Cliffs Bay**. West, the wide sands of **Oxwich Bay** sit next to inland reedy marshes, beyond which is the glorious village of **Port Eynon**, home to an excellent youth hostel and a beautiful beach. West of Port Eynon, the coast becomes a wild, frilly series of inlets and cliffs, topped by a five-mile path that stretches all the way to the peninsula's glorious westernmost point, **Worms Head**.

Rhossili Bay, a spectacular four-mile yawn of sand backed by the village of Rhossili, occupies the entire western end of Gower from Worms Head to the islet of Burry Holms. The northern coast merges into the tidal flats of the estuary, running past the salted marsh of Llanrhidian, overlooked by the gaunt ruins of Weobley Castle, and on to the famous cockle beds at Pen-clawdd.

Getting around

Apart from the coastal track to Mumbles, no train line has been built on Gower. With its proximity to urban Swansea, however, bus transport is comprehensive, with at least hourly connections from Swansea to Mumbles, Pennard, Oxwich, Port Eynon, Rhossili, Pen-clawdd and regular journeys to the northwestern corner around Llanrhidian, Weobley Castle and Llangennith. Driving around Gower in peak season can be frustratingly slow and parking chronically expensive. Cycling, together with walking, are ideal ways to tour the area, as the peninsula's attractions are all within a short distance of each other and, in many cases, well off-road. Rent a bike in Swansea (see opposite) or, on Gower, at *Clyne Valley Cycles* in Walters Row, Dunvant (☎01792/208889), and in Mumbles from *Swansea Bay Cycle Hire* on Village Lane (☎01792/814290), in front of the *Antelope Hotel*.

Mumbles and Oystermouth

At the far westernmost end of Swansea Bay, Mumbles (Mwmbwls) derives its name from the French *mamelles*, or "breasts", a reference to the twin islets off the end of Mumbles Head, and is now used as the name for all of the loose sprawl around OYSTERMOUTH (Ystumllwynarth). Here, the seafront is an unbroken curve of budget hotels, breezy pubs and cafés leading down to the old-fashioned pier and funfair towards the rocky plug of Mumbles Head. Behind the promenade, a busy warren of streets climb the hills, lined with souvenir shops, department stores and a glut of fine restaurants – Mumbles is deservedly renowned for its cuisine. Around the headland, reached either by the longer barren coast road or a short walk over the hill, is the district of Langland Bay, with a sandy beach quite popular with surfers.

The small seafront tourist office (April to mid-May & Sept daily 10am–4pm; mid-May to Aug daily 9.30am–5.30pm; ☎017792/361302 or accommodation 363392) lies opposite Newton Road, which leads up to the hilltop ruins of Oystermouth Castle (April–Oct daily 11am–5.30pm; £1). Founded as a Norman watchtower, the castle was strengthened to withstand attacks by the Welsh, before being converted into a residence during the fourteenth century. Today you can see the remains of a late thirteenth-century keep next to a more ornate three-storey ruin incorporating an impressive banqueting hall and state rooms. The surrounding parkland affords spectacular views over the Mumbles headland, Swansea and its sweeping bay.

Midway between Swansea city and Mumbles are the Clyne Gardens at Blackpill, a putative Welsh Kew Gardens, if the city council have their way. The old estate of the Vivian family, the fifty-acre gardens contain some lovely walks: through rhododendron glades, bog gardens, woods, meadows and past a few follies.

Practicalities

Mumbles is a lively and enjoyable alternative base to Swansea, its position on the cusp of Gower making it even more attractive. With a diverse range of seaside entertainment, some fine restaurants and the legendary Mumbles Mile of pubs, there's plenty to do as well. **Accommodation** is plentiful: try the shorefront *Tides Reach*, 388 Mumbles Rd (☎01792/404877; ②), the brassy *Carlton Hotel*, 654–656 Mumbles Rd (☎01792/360450; ③), or the *Osborne Hotel*, high on a clifftop in Rotherslade Road, Langland Bay (☎01792/366274; ③). Overlooking Langland Bay, on Langland Court Road, is the mock-Tudor *Langland Court Hotel* (☎01792/361545; ④) and, up the road in Higher Lane, the delightful *Hillcrest House Hotel* (☎01792/363700; ④) – the food at both is good, at the latter it's exceptional. Elsewhere, good **restaurants** abound – not for nothing is Mumbles twinned with Kinsale, Ireland's culinary capital. Highlights include the cosy *Quo Vadis*, 614–616 Mumbles Rd (☎01792/360706), and *CJ's*, down the road at no. 135 (☎01792/361246), while several pubs and wine bars, like *PA's*, 95 Newton Rd, are also good for food.

Scores of seafront pubs constitute the **Mumbles Mile**, one of Wales' most notorious pub crawls. Of them all, *The Antelope*, the *Oystercatcher* and the *White Rose* are the most enjoyable, if most touristy, alternatives. Most tourists feel that they have to have a pint in *Dylan's Tavern*, which, when it was known as the *Mermaid*, was the young writer's most regular haunt. Unsurprisingly, it's now packed full of Dylan Thomas kitsch and memorabilia.

The south and west Gower coasts

From Mumbles Head, the limestone crags of the **southern Gower coast** twist and delve the fifteen miles or so to Worms Head, at the bottom of Rhossili Bay. Many of the sandy bays that rupture the cliffs are easily accessible by car, although they tend to be crowded in peak season.

From Mumbles Head to Three Cliffs Bay

The first few miles of the southern Gower coast are highly developed, with stern hotels and beach huts backing some fine sands. Best locally is **Langland Bay**, a fifteen-minute stroll from the middle of Mumbles. A good gash of sand between two headlands, it's very popular with surfers. **Caswell Bay**, a mile west, is to be avoided – best crack on around the stunning cliff path to the tiny and remote **Brandy Cove**, an old smugglers' haunt, or pebbly **Pwlldu Bay**, owned by the National Trust, and backed by a wooded ravine that offers many stunning walks. Brandy Cove and Pwlldu Bay are inaccessible by car; park in Bishopston village and walk the last mile or so.

Three miles along, huge **Three Cliffs Bay** is one of Gower's finest beaches, a silent valley fringed by dunes and the eerie ruins of **Pennard Castle**. Although justifiably popular, its relative inaccessibility ensures that it's never too packed. The easiest approach is from the car park at **Southgate**, half a mile away, then along spectacular clifftops. Otherwise, you can try one of the paths that fan out along the tufty valley of the Pennard Pill from **PARKMILL**, a tourist honeypot on the main A4118. Here, the twee charms of the **Gower Heritage Centre** (daily 10am–6pm; £2) are forced on passing visitors and are only worth it if you've not yet clocked a working Welsh craft mill.

A mile north of Parkmill (reached by the lane that heads past the Heritage Centre) is the Neolithic (3000–1900 BC) burial chamber known, in honour of the thirteenth-century lords of Oystermouth Castle, as **Parc le Breos**. Although not intrinsically fascinating, as it has been much restored, the roofless chamber is impressive, if only because of its age and sheer size – seventy foot long and divided into four separate chambers. In 1869, the skeletons of two dozen people were found in it. Just beyond the chamber and to the right, a deep fissure in a limestone outcrop marks the position of the dank and musty **Cathole Rock Cave**, in which flint tools, dated at over 12,000 years old, have been found.

The best local **B&B** is *Lunnon Farm* (March–Oct; ☎01792/371205; ②), a welcoming farmhouse just north of Parkmill. Otherwise, there's the cheerful *Parc-le-Breos House* to the northwest (☎01792/371636; ③), or, in Bishopston village, the *Winston Hostel* at 11 Church Lane (☎01792/232074; ③). There's decent **self-catering** accommodation at *Home From Home*, 2a Queens Rd, Mumbles (☎01792/360624), and **camping** at *North Hills Farm* (April–Oct; ☎01792/371218), overlooking Three Cliffs Bay between Parkmill and Penmaen.

Oxwich

One of the most curious landscapes in Gower is the reedy **nature reserve** around **Oxwich Burrows**, a flatland of salt and freshwater marshes reached via the lane that forks left off the A4118 at the ruined gatehouse of the privately owned **Penrice Castle**. The marshes are dotted with pools and bounded by ancient woodland and, down by the coast, sweeping dunes. Close by on the coast, the scattered village of **OXWICH** is grouped next to the gaping sands of Oxwich Bay. Despite a couple of (possibly unconnected) incidents of serious illness befalling a few Oxwich Bay surfers in 1994, the sands and sea regularly receive awards – including the coveted EU blue flag – for their quality, and this is certainly one of Gower's most popular resorts. The squat church of St Illtud sits alone, away from the village, at the top of the beach. A quieter beach can be found just over a mile away at **Slade Sands**, reached along the lane that climbs from the Oxwich crossroads past the ruins of a Tudor manor, known as **Oxwich Castle** (May–Sept daily 10am–5pm; £1.70; CADW). It's a fine example of Tudor gentrification, as Sir Rice Mansel (member of a powerful Welsh dynasty) upgraded his ancestral home into what we see today between 1520 and 1538. His son Edward added the multi-windowed eastern range, a pile of rooms together with a highly fashionable long gallery that fell into ruin shortly afterwards.

The popularity of Oxwich is evident in its plentiful **accommodation**: numerous B&Bs, include *Little Haven* (☎01792/390940; ②) and *Woodside* (☎01792/390791; ②), both on the main street, while the *Oxwich Bay Hotel* (☎01792/390329; ③) enjoys splendid isolation by the sands near the parish church. The *Oxwich Camping Park* on the Penrice road (April–Sept; ☎01792/390777), has a swimming pool and laundry on site.

Horton and Port Eynon

The rocky cliffs from Oxwich Point fade into wide stony bays towards the quiet village of **HORTON**, with a decent beach, and brasher **PORT EYNON**, busy and touristy by comparison, with a clutch of seafood restaurants, chip shops and the laid-back *Ship Inn*. The villages' sands and dunes are sheltered by a prominent headland, easily reached by a series of paths that wind their way along the shore from the car park, past the Victorian lifeboat station, now the youth hostel, and above the bleak ruins of the old shoreline salt house and oyster pools. The headland, owned by the National Trust, is a wild and windy spot, where tufted grass gives way to sharp limestone crags. A natural cave at the tip can be seen from above, a great dome-shaped chasm that plummets into the hillside. Around the headland to the west is the more ordered and accessible **Culver Hole**, built into the cliffs. A man-made cave, it may originally have been a stronghold for the long-gone Port Eynon castle, and has served its time subsequently as a smugglers' retreat, dovecote and armoury.

The lichen-spattered limestone headland casts good views over the curve of Port Eynon Bay and the cliffs round to Rhossili, five miles west. This **coastal path** is the most spectacular walk on Gower, veering along crags above thundering waves for five miles, and the only real beach in this stretch is the secluded **Mewslade Bay**, just short of Rhossili, accessible by the path from Pitton. Along the coast walk, about midway between the two villages, is **Paviland Cave**, the site of an astonishing find in 1823: the skeleton of a Stone Age hunter, dated at least 19,000 years old. At **Thurba Head**, on the eastern side of Mewslade Bay, there are a few scant remains of an Iron Age hillfort sited magnificently a few hundred feet above the waves.

Port Eynon hogs the accommodation limelight. Its **youth hostel** (mid-Feb to Nov; ☎01792/390706; ①) is welcoming, and its warden passionately knowledgeable about the area. Otherwise, there's the *Culver House Hotel* (☎01792/390755; ③), or **camping** at *Carreglwyd Park* (☎01792/390795) and *Bank Farm*, off the A4118 towards Horton (☎01792/390228).

Rhossili and Worms Head

The village of **RHOSSILI** (Rhosili), at the western end of the Gower, is a centre for walkers and beach loungers alike. Dylan Thomas described the terrain to the west of the village as "rubbery, gull-limed grass, the sheep-pilled stones, the pieces of bones and feathers", and you can tread in his footsteps to **Worms Head**, an isolated string of rocks with the spectacular appearance of a basking Welsh dragon, accessible for only five hours at low tide. At the head of the road, near the village, is a well-stocked, helpful **National Trust information centre** (April–Oct daily 10.30am–5.30pm; Nov–Dec Sat & Sun 11am–4pm; ☎01792/390707). It posts the tide times outside for those heading for Worms Head, and holds details of local companies renting surfing and hang-gliding equipment.

Below the village, a great curve of white sand stretches away into the distance, a dazzling coastline vast enough to absorb the crowds, especially if you are prepared to head north along it towards **Burry Holms**, an islet that is cut off at high tide. The northern end of the beach can also be reached along the small lane from Reynoldston, in the middle of the peninsula, to Llangennith, on the other side of the towering sandstone **Rhossili Down**, rising up to 633ft. **Surf instruction** and rental are available from *PJ's* at Llangennith (☎01792/872686).

In Rhossili village, there are reasonable **B&Bs** in *Broadpark* (☎01792/390515; ②) and *Sunnyside* (☎01792/390596; ②). **Campsites** can be found at *Pitton Cross Park* (☎01792/390593), a mile short of Rhossili off the B4247 and *Hillend* (☎01792/386204), at the end of the southern lane from Llangennith, behind the dunes that bump down to the glorious beach. Evening **drinking** and **food** in Rhossili is largely down to the bar of the friendly *Worms Head Hotel* (☎01792/390512; ④) in the middle of the village.

Mid and north Gower

The great sweep of land that rises to the north of the main Gower road does not attract anything like the number of visitors that the south and west do, solely due to the lack of comparable coastline: the northern fringe of the Gower is a flattened series of marshes and mudflats merging indistinguishably with the sands of the

Loughor estuary. Wading birds, gulls and bedded cockles can all be found amongst the flats, dunes and inlets burrowing into the land from the estuary.

Gower's central plateau is often ignored, with much of the countryside nothing more than a pleasant patchwork of pastoral farmland. The great ridge, Cefn Bryn, stretched across the centre of the peninsula, is savage and impressive, its wiry peat and grass dotted with hardy sheep, ancient stone cairns and holy wells. The best views over the peninsula are from the road brushing over its roof.

From Llanrhidian to Llanmadoc

The small and unremarkable village of **LLANRHIDIAN** sits above the great marsh of the same name, a largely inaccessible goo of mud and water virtually indistinguishable from the sands of the Loughor estuary. Views from the village pub, the *Welcome to Town*, are superb. An unclassified road weaves west for two miles towards **Weobley Castle** (April–Oct Mon–Sat 9.30am–6.30pm, Sun 2–6.30pm; Nov–March Mon–Sat 9.30am–4pm, Sun 2–4pm; £1.70; CADW). Gaunt against the backdrop of the marsh and the estuary, the castle was built as a fortified manor in the latter part of the thirteenth century.

The lane continues for two miles to the village of **Cheriton**, with its charming thirteenth-century church, and then on to **LLANMADOC**, where you can park and venture onto the land spit of **Whitford Burrows**, a soft patch of dunes now open as a nature reserve. Paths lead from Llanmadoc village up the steep hump of **Llanmadoc Hill** to the south. **The Bulwark**, a lonely and windy hillfort, can be seen at the eastern end of Llanmadoc Hill's summit ridge.

The **Cefn Bryn** ridge of sandstone, stretched out across the middle of Gower, climbs over five hundred feet to give some astounding views to both coasts of the peninsula. It is most easily explored from the quiet village of **REYNOLDSTON**, grouped around a sheep-filled village green. The village's pub, the *King Arthur Hotel* (☎01792/391099; ③), hosts live folk and rock music nights. From Reynoldston, a dramatic road rises up the slope of Cefn Bryn before skating across its summit in a perfect, straight line. A small car park lies next to a path across the boggy moor to **King Arthur's Stone**, a massive and isolated burial-

---

KING ARTHUR'S STONE

Gower, more than any other concentrated landscape in Wales, is littered with dolmens, standing stones and other prehistoric remains. The most celebrated of them all – indeed, the most well known in Wales – is **King Arthur's Stone**, just north of the lane that climbs out of Reynoldston across Gower's central ridge.

Anything up to 6000 years old, the dolmen – a thrusting capstone resting on six supporting stones – is mentioned, often as *Maen Ceti*, in documents dating back a thousand years. It is said to be a thirsty stone, occasionally making a nocturnal flit to Port Eynon for a drink in the sea. Alternatively, the reputation possibly arises from its alleged position over an underground stream – certainly there are many surfacing around it.

From King Arthur's Stone, a line leads across the road to the Lady's Well, a spring deemed holy and now enclosed in a hut, and through to Penmaen's ruined chapel and Neolithic burial chamber, some three miles southeast. The line passes numerous stones and mysterious remains and is a well-worn route, charged with a special energy, that features in some curious photographs with streaks and dots in hitherto clear skies.

chamber capstone dating from at least 4000 BC and weighing over 25 tons. Paths lead off the road in all directions, giving clear views to both Gower coasts.

Local **B&Bs** include the *Britannia Inn* (☎01792/386624; ③) and the smoke-free, vegetarian-friendly *Bryn-y-Mor* (☎01792/386603; ②), both in Llanmadoc, and *Greenways Hills Farm* in Reynoldston (☎01792/390125; ②). A mile northwest of Reynoldston, the luxurious *Fairyhill* (☎01792/390139; ⑤) is a gorgeous country-house hotel, with a superb restaurant open to the public. There's a great **campsite** in Llanmadoc (☎01792/386202), and another, *Hillend* (☎01792/386204), a mile west of Llangennith, overlooking the northern stretches of Rhossili Bay.

travel details

Unless otherwise stated, frequencies for trains and buses are for Monday to Saturday services, Sunday averages 1–3 services though the main routes are more frequent and some routes have no Sunday service at all.

Trains

Cardiff to: Abergavenny (hourly; 40min); Barry Island (every 20min; 25min); Birmingham (8 daily; 2hr 20min); Bridgend (every 30min; 20min); Bristol (every 30min; 45min); Caerphilly (every 30min; 20min); Carmarthen (8 daily; 2hr); Chepstow (hourly; 30min); Crewe (hourly; 2hr 40min); Haverfordwest (6 daily; 2hr 40min); Llwynypia (every 30min; 45min); London (hourly; 2hr); Maesteg (hourly; 50min); Manchester (8 daily; 3hr 20min); Merthyr Tydfil (hourly; 1hr); Neath (hourly; 40min); Newport (every 15–30min; 12min); Penarth (every 20min; 15min); Pontypool (every 2hr; 30min); Pontypridd (every 15min; 30min); Swansea (hourly; 50min); Trehafod (every 30min; 35min); Ystrad Rhondda (every 30min; 50min).

Newport to: Abergavenny (hourly; 25min); Birmingham (8 daily; 2hr 10min); Bristol (every 30min; 35min); Caldicot (hourly; 13min); Cardiff (every 15–30min; 12min); Chepstow (hourly; 20min); Hereford (hourly; 50min); London (hourly; 1hr 50min); Pontypool (every 2hr; 15min); Swansea (hourly; 1hr 5min).

Swansea to: Cardiff (hourly; 50 min); Carmarthen (hourly; 45min); Ferryside (10 daily; 40min); Fishguard (3 daily; 2hr 30min); Haverfordwest (9 daily; 1hr 45min); Kidwelly (10 daily; 30min); Knighton (5 daily; 3hr); Llandeilo (5 daily; 1hr); Llandovery (5 daily; 1hr 20min); Llandrindod Wells (5 daily; 2hr 30min); Llanelli (hourly; 20min); Llanwrtyd Wells (5 daily; 1hr 45min); London

(hourly; 2hr 50min); Milford Haven (9 daily; 2hr); Narberth (every 2hr; 1hr 15min); Newport (hourly; 1hr 5min); Pembroke (every 2hr; 2hr); Tenby (every 2hr; 1hr 35min); Whitland (hourly; 1hr 5min).

Buses

Abergavenny to: Brecon (hourly; 1hr); Cardiff (hourly; 2hr); Clydach (hourly; 25min); Crickhowell (hourly; 20min); Llanfihangel Crucorney (6 daily; 15min); Merthyr Tydfil (hourly; 1hr 20min); Newport (hourly; 1hr 10min); Pontypool (hourly; 25min).

Bridgend to: Blaengarw (hourly; 35min); Cardiff (hourly; 50min); Cowbridge (every 30min; 20min); Cymer (hourly; 1hr); Kenfig (hourly; 40min); Llantrisant (hourly; 50min); Llantwit Major (9 daily; 40min); Margam Park (hourly; 15min); Ogmore (9 daily; 15min); Pontypridd (hourly; 1hr 20min); Porthcawl (every 30min; 25min); Southerndown (9 daily; 20min); Swansea (hourly; 50min).

Cardiff to: Abergavenny (hourly; 2hr); Aberystwyth (2 daily; 4hr); Bangor (3 daily; 8hr); Barry Island (hourly; 50min); Birmingham (5 daily; 2hr 30min); Blaenafon (hourly; 1hr 40min); Caernarfon (1 daily; 7hr 40min); Caerphilly (every 30min; 40min); Cardiff youth hostel (every 30min; 15min); Cardiff–Wales Airport (hourly; 30min); Cowbridge (every 30min; 35min); Heathrow Airport (8 daily; 2hr 45min); Lampeter (2 daily; 3hr 10min); Llandrindod Wells (1 daily; 2hr 30min); Llantwit Major (hourly; 1hr); London (6 daily; 3hr 10min); Machynlleth (1 daily; 5hr 30min); Merthyr Tydfil (every 30min; 45min); Nelson (hourly; 35min); Newport (every 30min; 45min); Penarth (every 30min; 30min); Pontypridd (hourly; 25min); Senghenydd (hourly; 50min); Swansea (hourly; 1hr); Welshpool (1 daily; 4hr 30min).

Chepstow to: Caerwent (hourly; 25min); Monmouth (11 daily; 55min); Newport (hourly; 1hr); Penhow (hourly; 35min); Pontypool (every 2hr; 1hr 30min); Tintern (8 daily; 20min); Usk (6 daily; 45min).

Merthyr Tydfil to: Abergavenny (hourly; 1hr 20min); Brecon (7 daily; 40min); Cardiff (every 30min; 45min); Swansea (hourly; 1hr).

Monmouth to: Chepstow (11 daily; 55min); Newport (every 2hr; 1hr); Raglan (every 2hr; 20min); Ross-on-Wye (8 daily; 40min); Tintern (9 daily; 30min); Trellech (4 daily; 20min); Usk (every 2hr; 30min).

Neath to: Aberdulais (hourly; 15min); Cymer (hourly; 35min); Pontrhydyfen (hourly; 25min).

Newport to: Abergavenny (hourly; 1hr 10min); Abertillery (every 30min; 55min); Birmingham (5 daily; 2hr); Blaenafon (every 30min; 1hr 10min); Brecon (every 2hr; 2hr); Caerphilly (every 30min; 40min); Caerwent (hourly; 40min); Cardiff (every 20min; 45min); Chepstow (hourly; 1hr); Holyhead (1 daily; 8hr 30min); London (5 daily; 2hr 45min); Monmouth (every 2hr; 1hr); Pontypool (every 30min; 45min); Pwllheli (1 daily; 9hr); Raglan (every 2hr; 45min); Usk (every 2hr; 30min).

Swansea to: Aberdulais (hourly; 45min); Aberystwyth (2 daily; 3hr); Brecon (3 daily; 1hr 30min); Cardiff (hourly; 1hr); Dan-yr-ogof (3 daily; 55min); Llangennith (3 daily; 1hr 20min); Merthyr Tydfil (hourly; 1hr); Mumbles (every 10min; 15min); Neath (every 30min; 30min); Oxwich (every 2hr; 1hr); Pennard (hourly; 35min); Port Eynon (every 2hr; 1hr 10min); Rhossili (every 2hr; 1hr 15min); Uplands (hourly; 10min).

CHAPTER TWO

SOUTHWEST WALES

The most westerly outpost of Wales, the counties of **Carmarthenshire** and, in particular, **Pembrokeshire** attract thousands of visitors. The principal draw is the glorious coastline, sweeping and flat around **Carmarthen Bay** and rocky, indented and spectacular around the **Pembrokeshire Coast National Park** and its 186-mile path.

The last remnants of industrial south Wales peter out at **Llanelli**, before the undistinguished county town of **Carmarthen**. Of all the routes that converge on the town, the most glorious is the winding road along the Tywi Valley, past ruined hilltop forts on the way to **Llandeilo** and Wales' most impressively sited castle at **Carreg Cennen**, high up on the dizzy plug of rock of the Black Mountain. Burrowing further into the sparsely populated countryside, broken only by endearing small market towns such as **Llandovery**, leads to remote hills and tiny valleys, home to the gloomy ruins of **Talley Abbey** and the Roman gold mines at **Dolaucothi**.

The wide sands of southern Carmarthenshire, just beyond Dylan Thomas' adopted home town of **Laugharne**, merge into the popular south Pembrokeshire bucket-and-spade seaside resorts of **Tenby** and **Saundersfoot**. Tenby sits at the entrance to the south Pembrokeshire peninsula, divided from the rest of the county by the Milford Haven and Daugleddau estuary, which brings its tidal waters deep into the heart of the pastoral county. The peninsula's turbulent, rocky coast is ruptured by some remote historical sites, including the Norman baronial castle at **Manorbier** and **St Govan's chapel**, a minute place of worship wedged into the rocks of a sea cliff near Bosherston. At the top of the peninsula is the old county town of **Pembroke**, dominated by its fearsome castle, across the Milford Haven estuary from small seaside villages and tiny islands along the rugged curve of **St Bride's Bay**, inland of which is the market town and transport interchange of **Haverfordwest**, dull but seemingly difficult to avoid. St Bride's Bay's rutted coastline is one of the most glorious parts of the coastal walk, leading north to brush past the impeccable city of **St David's**, whose exquisite cathedral shelters from the town in its own protective hollow. St David's, founded by Wales' patron saint in the sixth century, is a magnet for visitors; aside from its own charms, there are opportunities locally for spectacular coast and hill walks, hair-raising dinghy crossings to local islands and numerous other outdoor activities.

The coast turns towards the north at St David's, becoming the southern stretch of Cardigan Bay. Sixteen miles away by road, and well over thirty by rugged nips and tucks of the coastal walk, is the pretty port of **Fishguard**, terminus for ferries to Rosslare in Ireland. The northernmost section of the Coast Path, from Fishguard to the outskirts of Cardigan and past the delightful little town of **Newport**, is the most dramatic and remote. To the south and southeast are the eerie **Mynydd Preseli**, relic-spattered mountains, overlooking windswept plateaux of heathland and isolated villages – none more remote than along the leafy **Cwm Gwaun**, a lovely and much-bypassed valley cutting through the hills.

Getting around

Despite the remoteness of much of the southwestern part of Wales, public transport is surprisingly efficient and comprehensive. Direct **train** services connect Cardiff and Swansea with Llanelli, Carmarthen, Tenby, Haverfordwest, Milford Haven and Fishguard. The Heart of Wales line shuffles out of Swansea and Llanelli to Llandeilo and Llandovery, before delving into Powys. Connecting bus services out to the smaller towns and villages are regular and dependable, especially to the more popular destinations of Laugharne, Saundersfoot, Broad Haven and Dale on St Bride's Bay, and St David's.

Bus services are more thorough in peak tourist season, when most coastal villages have a fairly regular operation. Carmarthen and Haverfordwest are the principal bus terminuses, with services radiating out from Tenby, Pembroke and Fishguard. Only in the deserted lanes of northern and eastern Pembrokeshire does bus travel become difficult, although it's excellent walking and cycling country, and there are ample places to rent **bikes** throughout the area. Off the mainland, most of the islands are connected by regular (seasonal) **boat** services, although few of these allow for overnight stops.

ACCOMMODATION PRICE CODES

Throughout this guide, hotel and B&B accommodation is priced on a scale of ① to ⑨. Category ① only applies to youth hostels; for the rest, the number indicates the **lowest price** you could expect to pay per night for a **double room in high season**. The prices indicated by the codes are as follows:

① under £20	④ £40–50	⑦ £70–80
② £20–30	⑤ £50–60	⑧ £80–100
③ £30–40	⑥ £60–70	⑨ over £100

From Llanelli to Carmarthen

LLANELLI, reached from Swansea on a new road and rail bridge over the muddy River Loughor (Afon Llwchwr), marks the informal border between anglicized southeast Wales and the *bro*, Welsh Wales, where the native language can frequently be heard in everyday conversation. Once known as Tinopolis after its major industry, it's a downbeat town of refineries and the dominant *Felinfoel* and *Buckley* breweries, famous both for its beer and its rugby. If neither appeal, there's little to keep you here. In any case, it's a good half-mile walk through monotonous streets from the train station to the town centre, much rebuilt in recent years but with little to distinguish it from any other comparably sized settlement. Half a mile north of the centre, off the A476 Felinfoel Road, the graceful upland houses of the metal masters surround the pleasant glades of **Parc Howard**, with superb views down to the sea. The park centres on the Victorian home of Sir Stafford Howard, tinplate merchant and Llanelli's first mayor. This is now the town **museum** (Mon–Fri 11am–1pm & 2–4pm, Sat & Sun 2–4pm; free), a diverting enough collection of civic artefacts, old photos and paintings of the district, a load of Llanelli pottery and a few surprises, such as a nightdress and chemise belonging to Queen Victoria. Llanelli also has a **rugby club** (☎01554/774060), known as the Scarlets, one of the country's most famous and successful teams, who play at

Stradey Park out on the A484 to Burry Port. And that's about it as far as the town goes. In fact, you can visit the best thing about Llanelli before you even get there: a left turn when the bridge enters Carmarthenshire leads to the excellent **Penclacwydd Wildfowl and Wetland Centre** (Easter–Sept daily 9.30am–6pm; Oct–Easter daily 9.30am–5pm; £3.60), a salt marsh dotted with bird hides and landscaped walkways. With birds from all over the world and well-developed visitor facilities, it's easy to lose most of a day here.

The most notable **accommodation** in Llanelli is the *Hotel Miramar*, 158 Station Rd (☎01554/754726; ③), whose speciality Portuguese restaurant is excellent. The *Awel y Mor* guesthouse, 86 Queen Victoria Rd (☎01554/755357; ②), is also good. For **food**, there are a few cheap Indian and Chinese restaurants on Station Road.There are a number of good boozy **pubs** around: try Murray Street for a variety, including the cheery local *Queen Victoria*.

Burry Port and Pembrey

Four miles west, along the sands of the Loughor estuary, is the undistinguished town of **BURRY PORT** (Porth Tywyn), whose harbour, a ten-minute walk south of the station, is a pleasant surprise, as the town shows no sign of any nautical connection – a few theme pubs notwithstanding. It was here that Amelia Earhart, the first woman to fly the Atlantic, landed after a journey of nearly 21 hours in June 1928 – there's a memorial stone by the harbour.

The village of **PEMBREY**, a mile west along the A484, is virtually indistinguishable from Burry Port. To the east of the village, the flat expanse of **Pembrey Burrows** forms an area of alternating wetland and dunes, now featuring a family-oriented **country park** (daily dawn–dusk; £3), with an adventure playground, miniature train, pony trekking, bike rental and nature trails. There's a short dry **ski slope** on site (May–Sept Mon–Wed, Sat & Sun 10am–6pm, Thurs & Fri 10am–9pm; Oct–April Mon–Fri 2–10pm, Sat & Sun 10am–6pm; details ☎01554/834443), and **camping** (☎01554/834369) by the main entrance. The country park leads down to the seven-mile **Cefn Sidan** sands, a gentle slope of beautiful beach curving around the end of the Burrows. At the northern end of the Burrows, an old airfield has been recently converted into the **Welsh Motor Sports Centre** (☎01554/891042), a venue for Formula Three racing, a rally school and numerous motorcycling and driving events.

Kidwelly

The next stop up the train line from Llanelli is **KIDWELLY** (Cydweli), a sleepy little town dominated by an imposing **castle** (April–Oct daily 9.30am–6.30pm; Nov–March Mon–Sat 9.30am–4pm, Sun 11am–4pm; £2.20; CADW), on a steep knoll over the River Gwendraeth. The castle, and an accompanying priory since demolished, were established around 1106 by the Bishop of Salisbury as a satellite of Sherborne Abbey in Dorset. Kidwelly's strategic position, overlooking vast tracts of coast, was the main reason for its construction. On entering through the massive fourteenth-century gatehouse, you can still see portcullis slats and murder holes, through which noxious substances could be tipped onto unwelcome visitors. The **gatehouse** forms the centrepiece of the impressively intact semicircular outer ward walls, which can be climbed for some great views over the grassy courtyard and rectangular inner ward above the river. This is the oldest surviving part of the castle, dating from around 1275, with the upper storeys added in the fourteenth century by warlord Edward I's nephew. Views from the musty solar and hall, packed into the easternmost wall of the inner ward, show the castle's defensive position at its best, with the river directly below. Although the whole castle is long since roofless, the remains are some of the most intact of any medieval Welsh castle that has not been extensively restored. As well as climbing the walls of the outer ward, stairs in the inner ward also lead into the upstairs rooms, largely domestic quarters.

A fourteenth-century town **gate**, just above the medieval bridge of the same age, shields the castle approach from the main through road. More entertaining, the small-scale **Industrial Museum** up Priory Street (June–Sept Mon–Fri 10am–5pm, Sat & Sun 2–5pm; £1) is housed in an old tinplate works on the northwest edge of the town. Many of the works' old features have been preserved, including the rolling mills where long lines of tin were rolled and spun into waferthin slices.

On the other side of the train station from the town is the old **quay**, cleaned up and restored into an appealingly remote and forlorn picnic area and nature reserve. From here, there are views of wading birds skimming over the nearby mudflats and old saltings of the Gwendraeth estuary, once an important port for the medieval town.

In Kidwelly, there's decent pub **accommodation** at the *Old Malthouse*, by the castle (☎01554/891091; ③), and B&B at 21 Ferry Rd (☎01554/891368; ②), off the main street towards the Carmarthen Bay **campsite** at *Tanylan Farm* (☎01267/267306), which perches alongside the estuary between Kidwelly and Ferryside. Good food and drink are available at the cosy *Boot and Shoe*, 2 Castle St.

St Ishmael and Ferryside

As the train leaves Kidwelly and hugs the side of the River Towy's estuary, the views out across the water are magnificent. You'll pass by a tiny chapel at **ST ISHMAEL** that served a medieval village completely destroyed in a storm three hundred years ago, and now buried deep beneath the flats; another storm in 1896 briefly revealed the remains of houses. A mile further on, **FERRYSIDE** (Glanyfferi) is a tranquil village that grew as a day-trip destination by train for Valley miners. Although the station still remains, Ferryside is far quieter today, its narrow streets facing Llansteffan Castle across the calm waters and circling sea birds. A yacht club, fishing centre and sandy beach make up the village facilities, together with a handful of pubs and restaurants. **Accommodation** can be found at *Beach Cottage* on Foreshore (☎01267/267507; ②), and there's good food and drink in the main square at the *White Lion Hotel* and the earthier *Ship Inn*.

Carmarthen

The ancient and unquestioned capital of its region, **CARMARTHEN** (Caerfyrddin) does not entirely live up to the promise of its status. Although it's a useful transport interchange and lively market town, with some excellent shops and sixty pubs for 15,000 inhabitants, there's an undeniably down-at-heel and cheerless atmosphere which doesn't encourage you to stay for long – fortunately, with so many beautiful and interesting places nearby, there's little need to. It's the first major town in west Wales, where the native language is heard at all times, and was once – in the early eighteenth century – the largest town in all Wales.

Founded as a Roman fort, Carmarthen's most popular moment of mythological history dates from the Dark Ages and the supposed birth of the wizard Merlin (Myrddin, in Welsh, gives the town its name) just outside the town. In the late eleventh century, the Normans began a castle near the remains of a Roman fort, extending its walls to encompass a growing village. In 1313, Carmarthen was granted its first charter by Edward I, helping the town to flourish as an important wool centre, and was taken by Owain Glyndŵr in the early years of the fifteenth century. An eisteddfod was founded in the mid-fifteenth century, and is still used as the basis for today's National Eisteddfod. The importance of the town grew, attracting trade and new commerce, industrial works, a key port and a position as a seat of local government, a status still held by Carmarthen as the county town of Carmarthenshire.

Arrival, information and accommodation

The **train station** (☎01267/235803) lies over the Carmathen Bridge on the south side of the river. All **buses** terminate at the bus station on Blue Street, and many connect with trains at the station. The town's **tourist office** is in Lammas Street, close to the Crimea Monument (Easter–Oct daily 9.30am–5.30pm; Nov–Easter daily 10.30am–4.30pm; ☎01267/231557), although more esoteric information on the alternative scene can be found in *Aardvark Wholefoods* in Mansel Street, *Jackdaw* hippie gear shop on Heol y Bont, between the Guildhall and the river or, for Welsh-language events, *Siop y Pentan* in the market square. For **bike rental**, go to *Ar Dy Feic* at 20b Heol y Brenin (☎01267/221182).

There's lots of **accommodation** in town, especially on Lammas Street, where you'll find the *Boar's Head* (☎01267/222789; ④), one of the town's grandest old coaching inns, the rather anodyne *Falcon Hotel* (☎01267/237152; ④), and the low-key *Drovers' Arms* (☎01267/237646; ③). B&B is best at *Y Dderwen Fach*, 98 Priory St (☎01267/234193; ②), and the *Old Priory* guesthouse, 20 Priory St (☎01267/237471; ②), both out along the main road to Lampeter and Llandeilo.

The Town

The stern facade of the early twentieth-century **County Hall** shields the rambling streets of the town centre when you approach from the train station, and largely swallows up the uninspiring remains of Edward I's **castle** off Nott Square. The most picturesque eighteenth- and nineteenth-century part of town lies spread out at the base of the castle, around King Street and Nott Square, the town's main shopping hub.

Lying just off Nott Square is the town's handsome eighteenth-century **Guildhall**, the other side of which leads you out on to Darkgate and Lammas Street, a wide Georgian thoroughfare flanked by coaching inns, some interesting local shops and branches of all the main banks. Mansel Street leads north off Lammas Street to the indoor **market**, a great centre for local produce, secondhand books, endearingly useless tat and cheap cafés. On the main market days – Wednesday, Friday and Saturday – stalls spill outside into a slate-grey modern square.

From Nott Square, King Street heads northeast towards the sturdy tower of **St Peter's church**, architecturally undistinguished but well placed amongst the trees and surrounding town houses. Inside, Carmarthen's status as one of the most important Roman towns in Wales is evident from the altar in the western porch. Opposite is the Victorian School of Art that has now metamorphosed into the excellent **Oriel Myrddin** (Mon–Sat 10.30am–4.45pm; free), a craft centre and art gallery that acts as an imaginative showcase for many local artists. Half a mile further east, just off Priory Street, lie the insubstantial remains of a **Roman amphitheatre**, excavated in the late 1960s. In contrast with the atmospheric bowl at Caerleon, Carmarthen's remnants, surrounded by modern housing, are no more than a few grass humps.

Eating, drinking and entertainment

You can get great daytime **snacks** at the old-fashioned *Morris Tea Rooms*, almost opposite the Lyric Theatre in King Street, and the vegetarian café in the *Waverley Stores* health-food shop, 23 Lammas St. Most of the busy town centre pubs offer reasonable lunches – for evening food, try the smartish but inexpensive *Hamilton's Wine Bar*, 11–12 Queen St (☎01267/235631), or, right next door, *The Queens*, a friendly, oak-panelled pub. Slightly scruffier, although excellent value, is the *Blue Boar* in Water Street, off Lammas Street, and, in the same street, *Morgan's* chip shop and pizzeria, which closes at 8pm. The best-value pub food can be found at the *Boar's Head* on Lammas Street. Just off Nott Square, *MP's Pizzeria*, 20b Bridge St, is unremarkable, but offers a huge range of pizzas every evening until just after pub closing time. For a pricier treat, there's the truly superb new *Quayside Brasserie* on the Tywi quay (☎01267/223000), great for fresh local meat, fish and seafood.

Some of the town's many **pubs** get a little raucous at times. The more sedate include the *Drovers' Arms* in Lammas Street, an unpretentious place with some superb beers, while the *Granby* in King Street is the quiet, friendly haunt of several good characters. There's often **live music** at the *Boar's Head* on Lammas Street or in the Civic Hall at the Nott Square end of King Street. The **Carmarthen Festival** (tickets from the creaky old *Lyric Theatre*, ☎01267/232632), a varied stew of music, art, poetry and dance, takes place at the end of June and beginning of July.

The Tywi Valley

The **River Tywi** curves and darts its way east from Carmarthen through some of the most magical scenery in south Wales. The thirty-mile trip to **Llandovery** is punctuated by gentle, impossibly green hills topped with ruined castles. It's not hard to see why the Merlin legend has taken such a hold in these parts – the landscape does seem infused with a kind of eerie splendour.

The year-round tourist office in Carmarthen (see p.139) has a great deal of **information** about the Tywi Valley and surrounding area. There's a smaller office in the Crescent Road car park at **Llandeilo** (Easter & May–Sept Mon–Sat 10am–5pm; ☎01558/824226). There is a regular **bus** service from Carmarthen to Llandeilo, with the majority of the buses using the A40 via Nantgaredig and Pontargothi, and a couple daily heading off at Nantgaredig down the B4300 via Llanarthne.

From Abergwili to Llanarthne

The severe grey Bishop's Palace at **ABERGWILI** was the seat of the Bishop of St David's between 1542 and 1974, and now houses the **Carmarthen County Museum** (Mon–Sat 10am–4.30pm; 50p), a spirited amble through the history of the area. This surprisingly interesting exhibition covers the history of Welsh translations of the New Testament and Book of Common Prayer – both translated for the first time here in 1567. Local pottery, archeological finds, wooden dressers and a lively history of local castles are presented in well-annotated displays. The upstairs section looks at local police and crime, geology, the origins of Wales' first eisteddfod in Carmarthen in 1450, the local coracle industry and education.

A mile east of Abergwili, the main A40 road passes the sharp slopes of **Merlin's Hill** (Bryn Myrddin), reputedly the sleeping place of the great wizard. Close by, the quiet roadside hamlet of **WHITEMILL** (Felinwen) has value accommodation and decent pub food at the *Whitemill Inn* on the main road (☎01267/290239; ②). In the hamlet of **NANTGAREDIG**, just over three miles from Abergwili, there's little apart from the welcoming *Cwmtwrch Hotel* (☎01267/290238; ④), complete with swimming pool and leisure club; a good mile north is the superb and beautifully remote *Pantgwyn Farm* (☎01267/290247; ③), justifiably famous for its lavish breakfasts. Nearby **PONTARGOTHI** has the slightly touristy *Cresselly Arms* and the chintzier, but more locally frequented *Cothi Hotel* (☎01267/290251; ③); a few miles north of the village is *Plâs Alltyferin* (☎01267/290662; ②), a cosy B&B in a Georgian farmhouse that does excellent food.

The village of **LLANARTHNE** lies south of the main A40, and has two superb pubs: the *Golden Grove Arms* (☎01558/668551; ③), which serves up hearty food and has extremely comfortable accommodation, and the delightfully wacky *Paxton Inn*, home of live jazz and innumerable guest beers.

High above the village, accessible by a steep twenty-minute walk or a more leisurely drive around the lanes, is **Paxton's Folly**, a castellated tower, providing an exhilarating viewpoint over the rural patchwork below. Sir William Paxton, a London banker, built the folly after trying to bribe the electors of Carmarthen to make him MP with one of the most expensive campaigns in history, and the promise to pay for a bridge over the Tywi at Dryslwyn if successful. When the electors rejected him, he refused to build the bridge and constructed his folly overlooking the proposed site.

Four miles east of Llanarthne is the luscious estate of the **Gelli Aur Country Park** (daily dawn–dusk; parking £1), built around an 1824 baronial mansion. Gelli Aur, which translates as "Golden Grove", offers some elegantly coiffured gardens, a deer park, nature trails and an impressive arboretum.

Dryslwyn and Dinefwr castles

Despite William Paxton's petulance, there is now a bridge over the Tywi from below the tower over to **DRYSLWYN** and its forlorn **castle** (open all hours), straddling the top of a mound next to the river. Dryslwyn was built by Rhys ap Rhys Gryg, one of the Welsh princes of Deheubarth, in the thirteenth century, overlooking an important crossing point of the river. He had originally sided with Edward I before turning against him, incurring the king's wrath and an 11,000-strong army to besiege him in the castle in 1287. The collapsed stone walls surround a desolate inner courtyard, currently being restored as part of the castle's renaissance. Although the remains of the castle are barely worth the climb, the views are delightful.

The strategic importance of the Tywi Valley is underlined by the presence of the tumbledown ruins of **Dinefwr Old Castle**, reached through the extensive parkland of Plas Dinefwr, which forms a spectacular isolated spot on a wooded bluff over the river. Currently under restoration, and due to reopen in 1997 (information from CADW, ☎01222/500286), the castle was built in the twelfth century by Lord Rhys, who successfully united the warring Welsh princes against the Normans. The vital site had been used for a previous castle, built as a royal fortress in the ninth century and used by Hywel Dda, "Hywel the Good", king of Deheubarth and codifier of Welsh laws (see p.150).

By 1523, the old castle had become ill-suited to the needs of the descendants of Lord Rhys, who aspired to something a little more luxurious. The "new" castle, now named **Newton House** (April–Oct daily 10.30am–5pm; £2; NT), was built in 1660 half a mile north of the old castle, added to over the ensuing centuries and given a new limestone facade in the 1860s. The National Trust is currently restoring the house, and visitors are allowed to see increasing numbers of the gracious period rooms. The library, lined by Rhys (or Rice) family portraits, sits pretty beneath a remodelled seventeenth-century plaster ceiling. More of Lord Dinefwr's paintings are on display in the drawing room, including a bizarre portrait of canal builder and industrialist Thomas Keymer dressed as a Chinaman. Visitors can also climb a splendid stairwell to a viewing platform that was added when buttresses were needed to prop the house up in the nineteenth century. The spectacular parkland (open all year) was landscaped mainly in the 1770s by George Rhys, whose work was much admired and slightly enhanced by Capability Brown, following a visit in 1775. It now contains rare white cattle, fallow deer and a woodland nature reserve.

Llandeilo and Carreg Cennen Castle

A mile further on from the Dinefwr castles, the main street – Rhosmaen Street – of the handsome small market town of **LLANDEILO** climbs up from the Tywi bridge, behind which are the tourist office (see p.141) and the train station. Although there is little in the way of actual sights in the town, Llandeilo is brilliantly situated in a bowl of hills amidst the Tywi Valley and on the edge of the magnificent uplands of the Black Mountain (see p.206). It's a quiet, rustic little place, whose few streets cluster around the main thoroughfare and the unusual raised graveyard (split by the main road) of the parish **church of St Teilo**. Down by the river bridge, a waterside path leads into Dinefwr Park and to the isolated **Llandyfeisant chapel**, operating until recently as a Dyfed Wildlife Trust information centre, but currently closed.

There are numerous places to **stay** in Llandeilo, including inexpensive B&Bs like *Mrs Denton*, 7 Thomas St (☎01558/822950; ②), the more upmarket *Brynawel*, 19 New Rd (☎01558/822925; ③), or town pubs such as the *Cawdor Arms* on Rhosmaen Street (☎01558/823500; ③). For good **food**, try *Fanny's*, 3 King St by the churchyard, by day, or *Cadw Clecs* bistro (☎01558/822199), on Rhosmaen Street, by night. Llandeilo is positively stuffed with **pubs**: the supposedly haunted *Three Tuns Inn* on Carmarthen Street (between King and Rhosmaen streets) is good for live music, the imposing *Castle Hotel*, opposite *Cadw Clecs* on Rhosmaen Street, brews its own *Watkins* beer, serves food and lays on entertainment, while for plain old beer and good food, head down the road to old coaching inn, the *White Horse*.

Pick up information on less mainstream local happenings at the excellent Friends of the Earth-run *Green House*, opposite *Barclays Bank* on Rhosmaen Street. For details of gigs, raves and festivals, check the noticeboard of *Siop-y-Fedwen*, a couple of doors up.

Carreg Cennen Castle and around

Isolated in the rural hinterland four miles southeast of Llandeilo is the most magnificently sited castle in the whole of Wales: **Carreg Cennen Castle** (daily May–Sept 9.30am–7.30pm; Oct–April 9.30am–4.30pm; £2.20; CADW), just beyond the tiny hamlet of Trapp. It was first constructed on its fearsome rocky outcrop in 1248, although Sir Urien, one of King Arthur's knights, is said to have built his fortress here first. Built primarily as a Welsh stronghold, Carreg Cennen fell to the English in 1277 during Edward I's initial invasion of Wales. The castle lasted as an inhabited fortress until 1462, when it was partially destroyed by the Earl of Pembroke, William Herbert, who believed it to be the base of a group of lawless rebels.

The most astounding aspect of the castle is its commanding position, three hundred feet above a sheer drop down into the green valley of the small Cennen River. The car park and **rare breeds farm**, catering primarily for children with rare species of cows, sheep and goats, are at the bottom of a long path that climbs sharply up, opening out quite astounding views towards the uncompromising purple lines of the Black Mountain, in utter contrast to the velvet greenery of the Tywi and Cennen valleys. The castle seems impenetrable, its crumbling walls merging with the limestone on which it defiantly sits. The highlights of a visit are the views down the sheer drop into the river valley and the long descent down into a watery, pitch-black cave that is said to have served as a well. Torches are essential (50p rental from the excellent tea room near the car park), although it is worth continuing as far as possible and then turning them off to experience absolute darkness. The tea room near the car park has a superb selection of home-cooked Welsh dishes, and you'll find B&B in nearby **TRAPP** at *Tŷ Isaf* (☎01558/822002; ③), in a farmhouse and its outlying cottages. The village also boasts a good pub, and the superb **Trapp Arts & Crafts Centre** (March–Christmas Tues–Sun 10.30am–6pm), the region's best showcase for local artisans, where imaginative temporary exhibitions complement the main business of selling.

The A40 and train line trail one another to the northeast of Llandeilo, through a pastoral landscape, in which biblical reminders, testimony of the Welsh fervour in the Christian faith, can be seen in the hamlets of **BETHLEHEM**, where the friendly village shop and tea room will keep your Christmas cards ready to be franked with the blessed postmark, and nondescript **SALEM**, either side of the main road. **LLANGADOG**, halfway between Llandeilo and Llandovery, is a pretty little town under the glowering bluff of the Black Mountain. Three miles southwest of the town is **Garn Goch**, a massive Iron Age hillfort spread over fifteen acres, as impressive for its bleak position of isolation as for the remaining earthworks and stone rampart. On the main A40, just after the Llangadog turning, there's a decent **campsite** at *Abermarlais Park* (☎01550/777868 or 777797).

Llandovery and around

Twelve miles beyond Llandeilo, the town of **LLANDOVERY** (Llanymddyfri) has architecture and a layout that have changed little for centuries. Like so many other mid-Wales settlements, an influx of New Agers from the 1960s has had a discernible effect on the town: there's a thriving independent theatre, and bookshops and wholefood stores abound. Alongside this more alternative flavour, Llandovery is still a major centre for cattle markets every other Tuesday. Around the town, there are good excursions out into breathtaking countryside to the Dolaucothi Gold Mine and Talley Abbey to the west, Rhandirmwyn and Llyn Brianne to the north and the Black Mountain to the southeast (this last covered in the Powys and Dee Valley chapter, p.206).

Arrival and accommodation

Llandovery is a natural base for exploring the Tywi Valley, being well connected by bus and train, and containing numerous good pubs, guesthouses and eating places. The **train station** sits on the main A40 just before Broad Street, and **buses** leave from Broad Street and the Market Square. The **tourist office** in the new heritage centre on Broad Street (Easter–Sept daily 10am–5.30pm; ☎01550/720693) is combined with an excellent Brecon Beacons National Park office, stocking numerous leaflets on local walks and natural history. Local guides and books are stocked in the *Old Printing Office*, near the war memorial on Broad Street. Information on more esoteric events can be found at the *Llandovery Theatre* on Stone Street (☎01550/720113), or in the *Iechyd Da* health-food shop in Broad Street.

The best **accommodation** is at the *King's Head Inn* in the Market Square (☎01550/720393; ③), a friendly, popular pub-cum-restaurant. Slightly more expensive is the colonnaded *Castle Hotel*, Broad Street (☎01550/720343; ④), where the nineteenth-century travelling writer George Borrow lodged for a night. Cheap B&Bs include *Mrs Billingham's*, Pencerrig New Road (☎01550/721259; ②), *Cwm Gwyn Farm*, Llangarreg Road (☎01550/720410; ②), and *Ashgrove*, Llangadog Road (☎01550/720136; ②). The nearest **campsite**, a mile east of Llandovery off the A40, is the *Erwlon* (☎01550/720332).

The Town

On the south side of the main Broad Street, a grassy mound holds the scant remains of the town's **castle**. There are good views from the ruins over the shallow waters of the Bran River, which splits from the Tywi a mile short of the town, and the huddled grey buildings that make up Llandovery itself.

Broad Street has been the main through route for years, as can be seen from the solid early nineteenth-century town houses and earlier inns that line it; the road widens up towards the cobbled, rectangular Market Square, crowned by a clock tower. This thoroughfare has changed little since George Borrow visited the town in 1854 as part of his grand tour of Wales, remembering it as the "pleasantest little town in which I have halted in the course of my wanderings". Above the tourist office, the community-run **Llandovery Heritage Centre** (Easter–Sept daily 10am–5.30pm; £1) is an excellent example of its kind. As well as the everyday artefacts of local people, there are some excellent depictions of local legends such as the Lady of the Lake from Llyn y Fan Fach and hero bandit Twm Sion Cati, the "Welsh Robin Hood". Other displays look at the drovers and their Black Ox bank (which became a part of the present-day *Lloyds* bank), the Heart of Wales railway, hymn-writer William Williams and seventeenth-century vicar Rhys Prichard, author of *Canwyll y Cymry* ("The Welshmen's Candle").

Stone Street heads north from the Market Square, past some slightly tattier pubs and up to the redoubtable **Llandovery Theatre**, home of part of the theatre bookselling operation of Hay-on-Wye's Richard Booth, as well as a coffee shop – an excellent place in which to pick up an update on events in the area.

Eating and drinking

The best places to **eat** in Llandovery are the numerous pubs. The *King's Head* in the Market Square offers delicious lunchtime and evening food, as do the *Castle Hotel* on Broad Street (slightly more expensive) and the *White Swan* in the High Street. The town has a number of daytime cafés and tea rooms, mainly around the Market Square, where the *Drovers' Restaurant* (☎01550/721115) is good for a slightly pricer treat. Out of Llandovery, the *Royal Oak Inn* in Rhandirmwyn (see p.146), is well worth the hike for its imaginative menu of well-cooked classics.

For **drinking**, the eccentric and bizarrely old-fashioned *Red Lion*, a red, colonnaded house nestled in an easy-to-miss corner at 2 Market Square, can't be beaten. If you can't find it, or if – as frequently happens – the landlord has chosen to close early, try the nearby *King's Head*, or, round the corner, the young and sporty *Greyhound* (*Y Milgi*) in Stone Street.

The Dolaucothi Gold Mine, Talley Abbey and Brechfa Forest

The countryside to the west of Llandovery is blissfully quiet, with just a handful of main roads and lanes rarely containing traffic of any volume. The principal route off the A40 between Llandeilo and Llandovery, the A482 heads towards the straggling village of **PUMSAINT** (Five Saints), whose etymology is explained in the stone seen near the entrance of the **Dolaucothi Gold Mine**, half a mile off the main road (site April–Sept daily 10am–5pm, £1.50; underground tour & panning May–Sept daily 10.30am–5pm, £4.50; NT): the indentations in the rock are said to be the marks left by five sleeping saints, who rested here one night.

Pumsaint is the only place in Britain where the Romans definitely mined gold, laying complicated and astoundingly advanced systems to extract the precious metal from the rock, and remains of Roman workings – a few water channels and an open cast mine – can still be seen from the self-guided walk around the site. After they left in 140 AD, the mine lay abandoned until 1888, when the promise of gold opened the mine once more; further probes unearthed gold, but not enough to justify costs, and the mines closed once again. Today, the underground tour goes deep into the mine workings and usually allows visitors, equipped with the mine's panning dishes, to prospect for gold themselves.

A mile to the north of Pumsaint, a characteristically straight road heads north above the valley of the Twrch River. This is a segment of **Sarn Helen** (Sarn y Lleng), a trans-Wales Roman road built between forts at Caernarfon and Carmarthen, often crossing some of the country's bleakest terrain. Its whimsical name may be a corruption of the Welsh, meaning Causeway of the Legion, although it is more popularly held to refer to Helen, the Welsh wife of a Roman chieftain in Britain.

Southwest of Pumsaint is the village of **TALLEY** and the landmark crumbling tower of its twelfth-century **abbey**, sited spectacularly alongside the reeds and lily pads of two gloomily dark lakes. Established in the late 1100s, Talley was Wales' only Premonstratensian abbey, lasting as such only into the next century. Adjoining the distinctly unimpressive ruins is the serene **church of St Michael**, intact from its foundation in 1773 and still including its original box pews.

Just north of Talley, the B4310 winds west from **Llansawel** to plunge into the valley of the Afon Cothi, surrounded by the towering conifers of the **Brechfa Forest**, one of the best spots for guaranteed solitude in Wales and the starting point for many good walks. You can pitch a **tent** by the forest streams or at a good serviced site at the *Red Dragon Inn* (☎01558/685527) in Rhydcymerau, on the B4337, deep in the the forest's northern fringe. Otherwise, the best base is the cheerful village of **BRECHFA**, with the superb, welcoming *Tŷ Mawr* country hotel (☎01267/202332; ⑤), the *Glasfryn* B&B (☎01267/202306; ③), and a great pub, the *Forest Arms*. Other local **accommodation** includes the *Brunant Arms* (☎01558/650483; ②) in **Caio**, a mile east of the gold mine, a characterful pub which also offers mouthwatering food, loads of board games and regular debates. If money's not too tight, *Glanrannell Park Hotel* (☎01558/685230; ④), just south of Pumsaint in Crugybar, is a fine place: acres of grounds, an informal, jolly atmosphere and knowledgeable local hosts.

Towards Llyn Brianne

The land to the north of Llandovery – mostly near the northern banks of the Afon Tywi – is equally remote, and even more spectacular, with walks following the river valley and fanning out over the hills. The old lead-mining hamlet of **RHANDIRMWYN**, above the winding river and with some of the best views in mid-Wales, is a good base, reached by daily postbuses from Llandovery. Here you'll find the popular *Royal Oak Inn* (☎01550/760201; ③), for great food, drink and B&B. Just below the village, there's a riverside **campsite** (☎01550/760257), and, a mile or so above, accessible by a steep path, there's the fabulously remote, *Bryn Poeth Uchaf* gas-lit **youth hostel** (April–Sept; ☎01550/750235; ①). You should book in with the warden at *Hafod-y-Pant* farm, three-quarters of a mile away by track, on the lane that winds up the slopes from Cynghordy train station and under the spectacular 102-foot-high viaduct that curves its way over the little valley of the Afon Brân. Midway between the viaduct and Hafod-y-Pant, there's the delightful farmhouse B&B of *Llanerchindda* (☎01550/750274; ③), base for many a Cambrian Way walker (see p.400).

The lane that clings to the Tywi's right bank continues north from Rhandirmwyn, through wooded glades and past gnarled shoulders of mountain, with the glittering river always in view. Three miles beyond Rhandirmwyn, there's a car park at the Ystradffin chapel for the RSPB's **Dinas Nature Reserve**, deep within which is the reputed hideout cave of Twm Sion Cati (see p145). You're discouraged from seeking out the bandit's cave – slightly up the hill from the riverside path and still waymarked by arrows on posts – lest you disturb the red kites, woodpeckers, nuthatches, redstarts and pipits, but even so this is a delightful spot: wooden walkways traverse the ancient woodland, a burst of flowers, butterflies, water and twisted trees. Once through, you can walk along the banks of the fast-flowing Tywi up to its confluence with the Afon Doethie.

A mile beyond Dinas, lanes widen for the traffic that bustles towards **Llyn Brianne**, at whose southern end are a car park and visitor facilities. Considering the reservoir was only built in the 1970s (to supply Swansea), it has folded well into the contours of the land and there are some good shoreline walks. Despite the increase in industry and visitors, it's still a remarkably peaceful area. Walks around the lake and beyond link up to isolated youth hostels and camping sites along the Abergwesyn Pass (see p.218).

South Carmarthenshire

Frequently overlooked in the stampede towards the resorts of Pembrokeshire, **southern Carmarthenshire** is a quiet part of the world, with few of the problems of mass tourism suffered by more popular parts of Wales. The coastline is broken by the triple estuary of the Tywi, Taf and Gwendreath rivers, forking off at right angles to each other; between the Tywi and Taf is a knotted landscape of hills and tiny, winding lanes. One decent, dead-end road penetrates this slip of land, petering out at **Llansteffan**, a village cowering below the hilltop ruins of its castle.

On the other side of the Taf estuary, the village of **Laugharne** is the area's sole big tourist attraction, on the strength of its position as a place of pilgrimage for Dylan Thomas devotees. A curious and insular village, Laugharne was the last home of the Thomases, whose boathouse has been turned into a loving museum to the writer, and whose regular drinking hole is as much a part of the pilgrimage as the house. Laugharne's recently reopened castle is a further incentive to visit.

The A40 continues into **Whitland**, an architecturally unremarkable town, but historically significant as the site of the first parliament in Wales. Roads descend south from Whitland to the coast at **Pendine**, a popular resort due to its seemingly endless sweep of sand, venue for an assortment of land speed record attempts.

Regular trains connect Carmarthen with Whitland and the west. Buses fill in the gaps, with a service from Carmarthen and St Clears to Laugharne and Pendine. Another service also leaves Carmarthen for Llansteffan.

Llansteffan

The impressive ruins of a **castle** (free entry) loom above the seemingly forgotten village of **LLANSTEFFAN** (sometimes anglicized to "Llanstephan"), on the opposite bank of the Tywi estuary from Ferryside. It's a ten-minute walk up from the tawdry beach car park to the solid castle gatehouse, the most interesting survivor of this Norman ruin, which was built between the eleventh and thirteenth centuries by the Anglo-Norman de Camille family, attracting the occasional wrath of the Welsh as a result.

The entrance used today is not the original gatehouse, which was converted into living quarters in the fourteenth century: the bricked-up entrance is obvious from outside. In both gatehouses, however, the portcullis and murder holes can still be seen. A couple of other towers, in considerably more advanced states of dereliction, punctuate the crumbling walls that surround the D-shaped grassy courtyard in the middle. From the top of the towers, it's easy to appreciate the importance of this site as a defensive position, with far-reaching views in all directions. It's no surprise that, before the present castle, there was an Iron Age promontory fort here, known to have been occupied from 600 BC.

From the castle, descend the path down towards Wharley Point, past *Parc Glas*, formerly a milk-and-rum tavern, and continue down the lane towards the beach. The door in the wall on the right conceals **St Anthony's Well**, with its supposed powers of healing for lovesickness.

Informal **tourist information** for the Llansteffan area, including lists of accommodation, is available at the friendly **post office** in the village of Llangain (☎01267/241487), halfway between Carmarthen and Llansteffan. In Llansteffan, there are **B&B**s at *Brig y Don* on The Green (☎01267/241349; ②), and, two miles short of the village from Carmarthen and with superb views over the estuary, at *Pantyrarthro Manor* (☎01267/241226; ②). There's a **campsite** at *Church House Farm* in Llangain (☎01267/241274). A couple of miles beyond Llansteffan, overlooking Laugharne and the Taf Estuary, there's very good **bunkhouse** accommodation at *The Holt* on *Mwche Farm* (☎01267/241782).

The best sources of reliable budget **food** are the *Sticks Inn* on Main Street, and the *Wern Inn* in Llangynog, five miles north of the town.

Laugharne

The village of **LAUGHARNE** (Talacharn), on the other side of the Taf estuary from Llansteffan, is being increasingly taken over by the legend of Dylan Thomas, the nearest thing Wales has to a national poet. Along an excruciatingly narrow lane (not suitable for cars) bumping along the estuary, you'll stumble across the **Dylan Thomas Boathouse** (Easter–Oct daily 10am–6pm; Nov–Easter daily except Sat 10.30am–3.30pm; £1.75), the simple home of Thomas, his wife Caitlin and their three children from 1949 until he died from "a massive insult to the brain" (spurred by numerous whiskies) on a lecture tour in New York four years later. It's an enchanting museum with a feeling of inspirational peace above the ever-changing water and light of the estuary and its "heron-priested shore". The upstairs is given over to a selection of local artists' views of the estuary and the village – none so rewarding as the one from the windows. Downstairs, the family's living room has been preserved intact, with the rich tones of the man himself reading his work via a period wireless set. Numerous artefacts are encased or on display, and contemporary newspaper reports of his demise show how he was, while alive, a fairly minor literary figure: the *Daily Mirror* manages a small obituary on page five, while even the *Carmarthen Journal* relegates the story to second place behind the tale of a missing local farmer. A small tea room and outdoor terrace give views over the water and a welcome chance for refreshment. Back along the narrow lane, you can peer into the blue garage where he wrote: a gas stove, curling photographs of literary heroes, pen collection and numerous scrunched-up balls of paper on the cheap desk suggest quite effectively that he is about to return at any minute. The poet is buried in the graveyard of the parish church in the village centre, marked by a simple white cross.

Laugharne is probably the closest to the original of Llareggub, Thomas' fictional town of darkly rich characters in *Under Milk Wood* – an honour, it is claimed, that is shared with New Quay in Cardiganshire. Whichever village he really meant, Laugharne has numerous Thomas connections and plays them with curiously disgruntled aplomb – none more so than the great alcoholic's old boozing hole, **Brown's Hotel** on the main street, where, in the nicotine-crusted front bar, Dylan's cast-iron table still sits in a window alcove, although the brusque landlord is loath to discuss the poet and his work. *Brown's* is a tight, secretive, locals' pub, but one that is on the receiving end of thousands of visitors.

The main street courses down to the ornate ruins of **Laugharne Castle** (May–Sept daily 10am–5pm; £1.70; CADW). Built in the twelfth and thirteenth centuries, most of the original buildings were obliterated in Tudor times when Sir John Perrot transformed it into a splendid gentleman's mansion. The mix of medieval might and Tudor finery is an intriguing one, especially in the impressive Inner Ward, dominated by two original towers, one of which you can climb for some good interpretive displays and, from the domed roof, sublime views over the huddled town. Like so many Welsh castles, Laugharne, built as an Anglo-Norman lookout over the sea, was taken by the Welsh princes Llywelyn the Great (in 1215) and Llywelyn the Last (in 1257), who also captured the then lord of the manor, Guy de Brian IV. The "castle brown as owls" (Dylan Thomas) has a connection with another famous Welsh writer, Richard Hughes, who lodged in the adjoining Castle House between 1934 and 1942. His *Danger* (1924), about a disaster in a Welsh mine, was the world's first radio drama, although he remains best known for his novel, *A High Wind in Jamaica*. There's a little exhibition on him in the shore-facing gazebo in the castle's delightful gardens, landscaped to their Victorian specifications.

Opposite the castle entrance is the tiny toytown **Town Hall**, topped by a white-washed Italianate bell tower, which served as a one-cell prison.

Practicalities

Laugharne has surprisingly little B&B **accommodation**: try the *Runnymede* guesthouse on Clifton Street (☎01994/427367; ②), the main road as you come in from St Clears, which becomes Market Street as it continues into the village centre. By the very comfortable *New Three Mariners* pub (☎01994/427426; ③), Newbridge Road heads down to the *Cors* (☎01994/427219; ③), a gracious small country house that doubles up as a decent restaurant. Alternatively, there are numerous cheap places down the road in Pendine (see p.151), or a **campsite** at *Waunygroes* in Llanybri (☎01267/241250). On the Pendine side of Laugharne is the *Ants Hill* camping park (☎01994/427293).

For **eating**, the choice is a little wider, although not a great deal better. *Brown's Hotel* (see above) serves large, stodgy meals until 8.30pm, guaranteed to fill anyone. The *Mill House Diner* on Wogan Street takes food orders until 10pm (Tues–Sat; 9pm Sun & Mon), but offers an uninspiring menu. Unless you're prepared to eat in the *Under Milk Wood Bar* (formerly *Dylan's Diner* and originally the *Rose and Crown* pub), just across the road, there isn't much option. The best **drinking** hole in Laugharne is the effortlessly cheery *New Three Mariners*.

DYLAN THOMAS

Dylan Thomas (1914–53) was the quintessential Celt – fiery, verbose, richly talented and habitually drunk. Born into a snugly middle-class family in Swansea's Uplands district (see p.123), Dylan's first glimmers of literary greatness came when he was posted, as a young reporter, on the *South Wales Evening Post* in Swansea, from which some of his most popular tales in *Portrait of the Artist as a Young Dog* were inspired. Thomas' wordy enthusiasm is well demonstrated in a passage describing his gulping down a pint of beer, waiting for the senior reporter to join him for a pub crawl: "I liked the taste of beer, its live, white lather, its brass-bright depths, the sudden world through the wet brown walls of the glass, the tilted rush to the lips and the slow swallowing down to the lapping belly, the salt on the tongue, the foam at the corners."

Rejecting the coarse provincialism of Swansea and Welsh life, Thomas arrived in London as a broke 20-year-old in 1934, weeks before the appearance of his first volume of poetry, which was published as the first prize in a *Sunday Referee* competition. Another volume followed shortly afterwards, cementing the engaging young Welshman's reputation in the British literary establishment. He married in 1937, and the newlyweds returned to Wales, settling in the hushed, provincial backwater of Laugharne. Short stories – crackling with rich and melancholy humour – tumbled out as swiftly as poems, further widening his base of admirers, although they remained numerically small until well after his death and, like so many other writers, Thomas has only gained star status posthumously. Despite his evident streak of hedonism and his long days in Laugharne's *Brown's Hotel*, Thomas was a surprisingly self-disciplined writer, honing his work into some of the most instantly recognizable poetry written this century, mastering both lyrical ballads of astounding simplicity and rhythmic metre, as well as more turgid, difficult poetry of numerous dense layers. Perhaps better than anyone, he writes in an identifiably Celtic, rhythmic wallow in the language. Although Thomas knew little Welsh – he was educated in the time when the native language was stridently discouraged – his English usage is definitively Welsh in its cadence and bold use of words.

Thomas, especially in public, liked to adopt the persona of what he perceived to be an archetypal stage Welshman: sonorous tones, loquacious, romantic and inclined towards a stiff tipple. Playing this role was particularly popular in the United States, where he journeyed on lucrative lecture tours. It was on one of these, in 1953, that he died, poisoned by a massive whisky overdose. Just one month earlier, he had put the finishing touches to what many regard as his masterpiece: *Under Milk Wood*, the "play for voices". Describing the dreams, thoughts and lives of a straggling Welsh seaside community over a 24-hour span, the play has never dipped out of fashion and has lured Wales' greatest stars, including Richard Burton and Anthony Hopkins, into the role of chief narrator. The small town of Llareggub (misspelt Llaregyb by the po-faced BBC, who couldn't sanction the usage of the expression "bugger all" backwards) is loosely based on Laugharne, New Quay in Cardiganshire, and a vast dose of Thomas' own imagination.

Whitland and Pendine

Heading west down the A40 from Laugharne, you soon come across **WHITLAND** (Y Hendy Gwyn), a small town dominated by a hulking dairy complex, an important place in the history of Wales. It was here – in 930AD – that Hywel Dda (Hywel the Good), king of Deheubarth, called together representatives from all the other

Welsh kingdoms to the first all-Wales assembly, designed to pull together disparate bands of legislation in order to codify common laws between them for the whole of Wales. There, they set up an elaborate and exhaustive code of egalitarian laws for their kingdoms, including the right of bastard children to be equal to legitimate siblings, the ending of marriage by common consent, the equal division of land between man and wife upon separation, and the equal division of land amongst all children upon the death of the parents. Many of these customs survived until the Tudors conquered Wales, and Welsh people today still hold great pride in the fairness and lack of oppression in a once independent Wales. The tales of Hywel Dda are told at a **commemorative centre** (Easter–Sept Mon–Sat 10am–5.30pm), where Hywel Dda's laws are inscribed (in Welsh) on stone tablets around the walls. It's located two minutes from the station on St Mary Street.

Due south of Whitland, the tatty seaside resort of **PENDINE** (Pentywyn) is home to a mass of caravan parks, souvenir shops, cheap cafés and vast tracts of out-of-bounds military land, but the crowning glory is the six-mile-long stretch of sand that sweeps away to the east. In 1927, Malcolm Campbell set a new world land speed record of 174.88mph here; Welsh rival J G Parry-Thomas tried to better Campbell's record a month later, dying gruesomely when he was decapitated by a loose part of the car. The *Beach Hotel* displays photographs and mementoes of the record attempts, and the star exhibit of the new **Speed Museum** on the seafront (April–Sept daily 10am–5pm; free) is *Babs*, Parry-Thomas' car that was retrieved from the sands after his death. True to its history, you can even drive on Pendine Sands, although it'll cost you £1.20 for the privilege, and the maximum speed limit is 10mph – boy racers beware.

If you want a **base** in these parts, you can do no better than the delightful B&B (with excellent optional dinners) of *Brunant Farm* (☎01994/240421; ③), high on the hills two miles southeast of Whitland.

Tenby and around

On a natural promontory of great strategic importance, the beguilingly old-fashioned resort of **TENBY** (Dinbych-y-Pysgod) has a long pedigree. First mentioned in a ninth-century bardic poem, the town grew under the twelfth-century Normans, who erected a castle on the headland in their attempt to colonize south Pembrokeshire and create a "Little England beyond Wales" – an appellation by which the area is still known today (see box overleaf).

Three times in the twelfth and thirteenth centuries the town was ransacked by the Welsh; the last time, in 1260, by Prince Llywelyn himself. In response, the castle was refortified and the stout town walls that largely still exist were built. Tenby prospered as a major port for a wide variety of foodstuffs and fine goods between the fourteenth and sixteenth centuries, but decline followed, and, with the arrival of the train in the mid-nineteenth century, the town became a fashionable resort. Lines of neat, prosperous hotels and expensive shops still stand haughtily along the seafront.

Although the town is extremely conservative, with a large population of retired people, there is plenty of entertainment and a huge number of pubs and restaurants to attract visitors of any age. In the middle of summer, it can seem full to bursting point, with heavy traffic restrictions and a considerable rush on decent accommodation.

"LITTLE ENGLAND BEYOND WALES"

Ever since the Normans stormed their way through Wales, securing their positions with powerful castles in strategic places, Pembrokeshire has been effectively divided. But the origin of the colonized southern section of the county goes back even further, to the days when Viking raiders came in by sea and snatched the best land – the sandy southern coast and the fertile pasture of the Daugleddau estuary. The Normans only continued an already established practice, intermingling with the existing Vikings (to produce a very English racial mix) and keeping the Celtic Britons (ie the Welsh) to the northern part of the county.

Today, the racial divide of the past is still evident. **"Little England Beyond Wales"** is the name given to an area that falls south of what has become known as the **Landsker Line**, an easily traceable invisible boundary through the heart of Pembrokeshire. Along the line, you'll find some sixteen castles or castle tumps (such as Roche, Haverfordwest, Llawhaden, Narberth). Either side, and village names are demonstrably Welsh or incongruously anglicized. This strange history dictates much: the south of the county has developed mass appeal to English migrants and tourists, whilst the north tends to attract fellow Celts and other Europeans. Politically, the Tenby and Pembroke area has inclined towards the most Unionist of UK parties, the Conservatives (who hold very little sway in the rest of Wales), whilst the north dallies between the old Liberal tradition and modern Welsh nationalism in the shape of Plaid Cymru. The bottom line to this is that south Pembrokeshire can be something of a po-faced disappointment, while the northern part of the county is wilder, more rugged and far less predictable – a truly Welsh experience.

Tenby is also one of the major stopping-off points along the **Pembrokeshire Coast Path** (see p.159), a welcome burst of glitter and excitement amidst mile upon mile of undulating cliff scenery. The **national park** boundary skirts around the edge of the town, and further along the coast are the two picturesque sandy stop-offs of **Amroth** and **Saundersfoot**. A couple of miles offshore from Tenby, the old monastic ruins of **Caldey Island** make for a pleasant day trip.

Arrival, information and accommodation

The **train station** (☎01834/842248) is at the western end of the town centre, at the bottom of Warren Street. Some **buses** stop at South Parade, at the end of Warren Street, although most (including *National Express* coaches) call at the bus station on Upper Park Road. The **tourist office** faces the North Beach on The Croft (daily July & Aug 10am–9pm; Easter–June, Sept & Oct 10am–6pm; Nov–March Mon–Sat 10am–4pm; ☎01834/842402). It has details of day trips by bus to St David's that cannot be done on public transport. *Equinox* on St Julian Street sells a curious combination of hippie ephemera alongside painfully twee gifts; posters on the walls also detail local gigs and festivals.

Accommodation

As a major resort, there are dozens of hotels and B&Bs in Tenby, and although prices are a little higher than you might expect, decent and reasonable **accommodation** is not hard to find.

HOTELS AND GUESTHOUSES

Ashby House, 24 Victoria St (☎01834/842867). A comfortable, low-key hotel next to the Esplanade and the South Beach. ③.

Atlantic, The Esplanade (☎01834/842881). One of the better hotels along the South Beach, with a high standard of rooms and even a small indoor pool. ④.

Caldey View, St Julian Street (☎01834/842126). Good-value B&B, with showers in all rooms. ③.

Castle View, The Norton (☎01834/842666). Well located, staring out over Castle Hill and the harbour, a friendly hotel with en-suite rooms. ③.

Coach Guest House, 11 Deer Park (☎01834/842210). Cheery, welcoming hotel near the train station. ③.

Fourcroft, The Croft, North Beach (☎01834/842886). The only remaining hotel on the northern esplanade, a cheerful family place with jacuzzi, sauna and small outdoor pool. ③.

Glenthorne Guest House, 9 Deer Park (☎01834/842300). Large guesthouse, well reputed and excellent value. ②.

Lyndale Guest House, Warren Street (☎01834/842836). Welcoming small B&B near the station, happy to cater for vegetarians. ②.

Myrtle House, St Mary's Street (☎01834/842508). Non-smoking hotel in the town centre, and known for its fine food. ③.

Tall Ships, 34 Victoria St (☎01834/842055). Bright, airy place near the South Beach. ③.

Tenby House, Tudor Square (☎01834/842000). Pleasantly old-fashioned town centre pub-hotel with well-appointed en-suite rooms. ④.

HOSTELS AND CAMPSITES

Kiln Park campsite, Marsh Road (☎01834/844121). This campsite is a mile west of Tenby off the A4139 to Pembroke. Closed Nov–Feb.

Meadow Farm, Northcliff (☎01834/844829). On the northern fringes of town, a small and semi-official site that's a great alternative to the family fun parks. Closed Oct–March.

Pentlepoir youth hostel, Old School, Pentlepoir (☎01834/812333). A YHA hostel right on the A478 near Saundersfoot station; take bus #350. ①.

Red House Farm, New Hedges (☎01834/813918). Pleasant and cheap campsite midway between Tenby and Saundersfoot, just off the A478. Closed Oct–March.

Skrinkle Haven youth hostel, Skrinkle Haven, near Manorbier (☎01834/871803). Bright and modern YHA hostel four miles west of Tenby overlooking the cliffs. Situated near the Manorbier bus route from Tenby. Tent spaces available. ①.

The Town

Tenby is shaped like a triangle, with two sides formed by the coast meeting at Castle Hill. The third side is formed by the remaining town **walls**, which are reached from the train station after a ten-minute walk straight up Warren Street. South Parade runs alongside the massive twenty-foot-high wall, first built in the late thirteenth century and massively strengthened by Jasper Tudor, Earl of Pembroke and uncle of the future king, Henry VII, in 1457. Further refortification came in the 1580s, when Tenby was considered to be in the frontline against a possible attack by the Spanish Armada. In the middle of the remaining stretch is the only town gate still standing at **Five Arches**, a semicircular barbican that combined practical day-to-day usage as an entrance for the town's citizens and peacetime visitors, with hidden lookouts and angles acute enough to surprise invaders. The wall continues south to the Esplanade, with a long line of snooty hotels facing out over the smarter and far less commercialized South Beach.

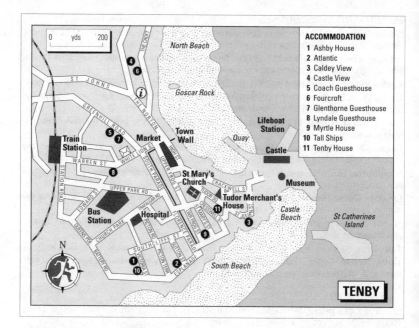

The centrepiece, and most notable landmark, of the town centre is the 152-foot spire of the largely fifteenth-century **St Mary's church**, between St George's Street and Tudor Square. A pleasantly light interior shows the elaborate ceiling bosses in the chancel to good effect, and fifteenth-century tombs of local barons demonstrate Tenby's important mercantile tradition. On the western side of St Mary's runs Frog Street, home of numerous craft shops and an indoor **arcade market**, containing craft stalls and gift shops.

Wedged between the town walls and the two bays, the **old town** makes a thoroughly enjoyable place to wander, with many interesting and unusual shops tucked away down small alleyways and steps. Many of the original medieval lanes are still intact in the immediate area around the parish church. **Sun Alley** is a tiny crack between overhanging whitewashed stone houses that connects Crackwell and High streets. Due east, on the other side of the church, **Quay Hill** runs parallel, a narrow set of steps and cobbles tumbling down past some of the town's oldest houses to the top of the harbour. Wedged in a corner of Quay Hill is the **Tudor Merchant's House** (April–Sept Mon–Fri 10am–5pm, Sun 1–5pm; £1.60; NT), built in the late fifteenth century for a wealthy local merchant at the time when Tenby was second only to Bristol as an important west coast port. The rambling house is on three floors, packed with period furniture from the sixteenth century (with later additions), although more notable are the examples of a prominent local weakness, tapering Flemish-style chimneypieces. The walls are adorned with three surviving Tudor religious frescoes.

Crackwell and Bridge streets run down to the picturesque **harbour**, which can look idyllic if it's not too crowded. Sheltered by the curving headland and fringed by handsome pastel-shaded Georgian and Victorian town houses, it is a great place to stroll around on a warm evening. During the day, it's the scene of considerable activity as the departure point for numerous excursion boats, the most popular being the short trip over to Caldey Island (see below). Above the harbour is the headland and **Castle Hill**, where paths and flowerbeds have been planted around the sparse ruins of the Norman **castle**. A surviving gatehouse is the most impressive remain, although fragments of walls, an archway and windswept tower are scattered around the site, impressive if only for the all-round views that it offers. Now, the breezy grass slopes are covered with a proud collection of rampant Victoriana in the form of ornate benches, vast beds of bright flowers (notably Tenby's indigenous small daffodil in springtime), a pompous memorial to Prince Albert, a bandstand, and the town **museum** (Easter–Oct daily 10am–6pm; Nov–Easter Mon–Fri 10am–noon & 2–4pm; £1), founded in 1878. Doubling up as a small, but impressive, art gallery, the museum is typical of Tenby: slightly ponderous and municipally minded, but interesting. Right at the entrance is an eye-catching contemporary photo of Tenby's north beach after the *Sea Empress* oil spill of February 1996 (see p.175). Compare the glutinous black beach with its golden present and it's hard not to be impressed by the scale and speed of the cleanup. In the museum proper, the geology section includes a five-foot mammoth tusk found near Milford Haven, ancient axes and a woman's skull dated from around 1300 BC. The local history gallery is entertainingly presented, but it is in the Wilfred Harrison art collection that the museum really shines, with strong pieces by Augustus and Gwen John, and locally born Nina Hamnett. The room next door is temporarily home to a major collection bequeathed to the county by English artist **Graham Sutherland** (1903–80), who considered Pembrokeshire perpetually "poised on the brink of some drama". The savage beauty of the westernmost tip of Wales was a direct influence on the artist – "I came here, I was hooked and obsessed," he wrote – and it appears in many of his abstracted landscapes. A permanent home is currently being sought for the collection, likely to be in St David's (see p.178). On the stairs up to the floor above, there are some mesmerizing studies of Caldey Island by Eric Gill and David Jones of the artists' commune at Capel-y-ffin in the Black Mountains (see p.69). Upstairs, there's an interesting room of pristine stuffed animals, including a terrifying golden eagle, a collection of lifeboat and shipping memorabilia and a room that, until Easter 1998, is housing a collection of artefacts from Caldey.

From the top of Castle Hill, there are great views over the more sedate South Beach and to the tiny **St Catherine's Island**, cut off at high tide but otherwise reached by way of the beach. The remains of the **fort** that can be seen on the islet date only from 1869, when Lord Palmerston constructed a chain of similar defences to be built as a protection for the Admiralty docks at Pembroke.

Caldey Island

Looming large over Tenby's seascape is **Caldey Island** (Ynys Pyr), a couple of miles offshore due south of the Esplanade. Celtic monks first settled here in the sixth century, perhaps establishing an offshoot of St Illtud's monastery at Llantwit Major (see p.113). The exact duration of this Celtic settlement is unclear, although the ninth-century Latin inscription on the island's sixth-century Ogham stone would indicate that the community was still thriving then. Nothing is then known of the island until 1113, when English king Henry I gave it to Norman nobleman, Robert Fitzmartin, who in turn gave it to his mother. In 1136, it was given to the Benedictine monks of St Dogmael's at Cardigan, who founded their priory here. Upon the Dissolution of the Monasteries in 1536, the Benedictine monks left the island and a fanciful succession of owners bought and sold it on a whim, until it was, once again, sold to a Benedictine monastic order in 1906 and subsequently to an order of Reformed Cistercians. The island has been a monastic home almost constantly ever since.

Boats leave Tenby Harbour every fifteen minutes in season (mid-May to mid-Sept Mon–Fri 9.45am–4pm; Easter to mid-May & mid-Sept to early Oct occasional sailings; school summer holidays also Sat 1–4pm; ☎01834/842402; £5). Tickets (not tied to any specific sailing) are sold at the kiosk in Castle Square, directly above the harbour. On landing at Caldey's jetty, a short walk leads through the woods to the island's main settlement.

The village itself is the main hub of Caldey life. As well as a tiny post office and popular tea room, there's a **perfume shop** selling the herbal fragrances distilled by the monks from Caldey's abundant flora. The narrow road going to the left leads down to the heavily restored **chapel of St David**, whose most impressive feature is the round-arched Norman door. Opposite is the gathering point for daily (menonly) tours of the garish twentieth-century **monastery**, a white, turreted heap that resembles a Disney castle. In peak season, tours take place every couple of hours.

A lane leads south from the village to the old **priory**, abandoned at the Dissolution and restored at the turn of this century. Centrepiece of the complex is the remarkable twelfth-century **St Illtud's church**, marked out by its curiously blunt (and leaning) steeple. This houses one of the most significant pre-Norman finds in Wales, the sandstone **Ogham Cross**, carved with an inscription from the sixth century and added to, in Latin, during the ninth, found under the stained-glass window on the south side of the nave. The church's rough flooring is largely comprised of pebbles from the island's beaches. The lane continues south from the site, climbing up to the gleaming white island **lighthouse**, built in 1828. Views from here are memorable.

Eating and drinking

There are dozens of **cafés** and **restaurants** around the town – in high season, the beaches (especially the North Beach) are packed in by cheap places. Many of the restaurants in the narrow streets of the town centre are tourist traps, overpriced and less than memorable – once again, pub food is often far better value.

Restaurants and cafés

Bay Tree, Tudor Square. Smartish, but not too expensive, bistro with a slightly more imaginative selection of meat and vegetarian dishes than in most places nearby.

Charney's, High Street. Popular café, with some imaginative menu choices.

Chortles, High Street. Informal bistro, with some unusual local dishes amongst the more pedestrian fare. Good for grills and Sun lunches. Inexpensive.

Fecci and Sons, Upper Frog Street. Genuine Italian snackery and ice-cream parlour, with over sixty speciality ice creams. Inexpensive.

La Cave, Upper Frog Street (☎01834/843038). Relaxed and impressive restaurant, with well-cooked local specialities. Moderate.

Munchies, Crackwell Street. Daytime wholefood takeaway. Inexpensive.

Pam Pam, Tudor Square. Just about the best of the avowedly "family" restaurants, serving good-value portions of everyone's favourite dishes.

Plantagenate, Quay Hill (☎01834/842350). Cosy and thoroughly enjoyable restaurant serving local specialities, tucked next to the *Tudor Merchant's House*. Apparently, it's the oldest house in Tenby – you can see a thirteenth-century Flemish chimney en route to the loo.

Pubs

Coach and Horses, Upper Frog Street. Lively and with a young crowd who appreciate the good beer and reasonable bar snacks.

Five Arches Tavern, St George's Street. Snooty and upmarket, but pleasant enough, and with good food.

Lamb, High Street. Reasonably priced bar food makes up for the slightly pricey drinks in this convivial, mixed-age pub.

Lifeboat Tavern, Tudor Square. Popular and enjoyable young people's pub.

Normandie Hotel, Upper Frog Street. Old-fashioned pub, which suffers from being too bright and loud. Good food available at all times.

Tenby House, Tudor Square. Another young favourite, which borders on the rowdy of a weekend evening. Good for live music.

Three Mariners, St George's Street. Home of good beer and regular live music.

Listings

Bike rental *Broadmoor Garage*, Kilgetty (☎01834/813266).

Car rental *Five Arches Garage*, South Parade (☎01834/842244).

Cinema The elegant *Royal Playhouse*, White Lion Street (☎01834/844809).

Exchange The main banks are on Tudor Square and have currency-changing facilities.

Festivals The fairly highbrow Tenby Arts Festival (☎01834/845180 or 842291), in late Sept, has a rowdy and lively Fringe.

Hospital Trafalgar Road (☎01834/842040).

Laundry Broadwell Hayes, near the viaduct.

Leisure centre Marsh Road (☎01834/843574), including a swimming pool.

Pharmacies *Boots*, High Street; *Craven*, White Lion Street.

Police Warren Street (☎01834/842303).

Post office Warren Street.

Taxis *Dai's* (☎01834/843096); *Tudor* (☎01834/844301).

Amroth and Saundersfoot

AMROTH marks the easterly end of the 170-mile **Pembrokeshire Coast Path**, which winds and darts its way around every cove and cliff in the county, right the way around to St Dogmael's, just outside Cardigan. It's a pleasant village, without being especially exciting: the beach is good, with south-facing sands ensuring maximum sunshine. For those starting or finishing the path at Amroth, a bed for the night might be a welcome necessity: the best places in the village are the *Ashdale* (☎01834/813853; ②) and *Beach Haven* (☎01834/813310; ②). The *New Inn* is right next to the beach and is an enjoyable place to eat and drink, if generally packed come the summer. From the centre of Amroth, a signposted walk (*The Knights' Way*), or a drive around the steep lanes, leads up to the **Colby Woodland Garden** (April–Oct daily 10am–5pm; £2.60; NT), about a mile, as the crow flies, above the village. The estate, wedged deep into a wooded valley, was, until the last century, mined extensively for anthracite and iron ore. It's very pleasant, if hardly spectacular: highlights include the sloping walled garden and, in May and June, the explosion of colour in the rhododendron bushes. There's also a local art and craft gallery containing some fine pieces amongst the landscapes and flower prints.

The coast between Amroth and Tenby is one long line of caravan parks, broken only by the picturesque harbour of **SAUNDERSFOOT**, built originally for the export of local anthracite and coal. The town has been attracting visitors for centuries, and is a lively, good-natured place; now all the industry has folded, the harbour and the wide yawn of sand are used purely for recreational purposes. The main focus of activity is the large **harbour** area, where there is a predictable clutch of cafés, tawdry shops, a faded crazy-golf course and boisterously fun pubs. You can also rent a powerboat for either a day (starting at £34) or a week (£170), or try out waterskiing: the best starting point is *Jones & Teague*, on the far end of the harbour wall (☎01834/813429).

Saundersfoot's **train station** is located a mile outside town, a journey up a winding wooded hillside road. The excellent Pembrokeshire National Park **information office** (Easter–Sept Mon–Sat 9.30am–1pm & 2–5.15pm) is in a small, white building on the harbour, although it doesn't book accommodation. If you want to **stay** in the village, try the airily pleasant *Harbour Light Hotel*, 2 High St (☎01834/813496; ②), or the small *Hurst Lea* B&B on St Bride's Lane (☎01834/812339; ②). A mile north of Saundersfoot, the thoroughly enjoyable *Wiseman's Bridge Inn* (☎01834/813236; ②), is a pub with B&B facilities and gloriously isolated **camping**, though the best proper site is a mile south of Saundersfoot at *Trevayne Farm* (April–Aug; ☎01834/813402), just short of Monkstone Point, which has excellent views over Saundersfoot and the great arc of sand that sweeps round to Amroth and Pendine. There's a **youth hostel** in the Old School at Pentlepoir (☎01834/812333; ①), on the A478 near Saundersfoot station.

Saundersfoot contains copious **places to eat**: the best bets are the charming *Old Chemist Inn* on The Strand and, around the main harbour square, the *Royal Oak* on Wogan Terrace. In Pentlepoir village, just the other side of Saundersfoot station, you can often find live music at the *Fountainhead* pub.

South Pembrokeshire coast

The southern zigzag of coast that darts west from Tenby is a strange mix of caravan parks and Ministry of Defence shooting ranges, above some spectacularly beautiful bays and gull-covered cliffs. From Tenby, the A4139 passes through **Penally**, little more than an extended suburb of the town, before delving down past the **Lydstep Haven** beach. A road dips south, past **Skrinkle Haven** and into the winding streets of **Manorbier**, whose ghostly castle sits above a small bay. Three miles inland from here is the quintessentially pretty village of **St Florence**, its narrow lanes crowned by a profusion of Flemish chimneys.

The coast nips and tucks in past some excellent, and comparatively quiet, beaches, passing the tourist magnet of **Freshwater East** before rising up to some impressive cliffs en route to the beautiful **Barafundle Bay** and the National Trust's **Stackpole Head**. Behind Stackpole, and the neighbouring **Broad Haven** beach, is the picturesque village of **Bosherston** and its lily lakes. Between Bosherston and the coast is the first MOD artillery range, which has to be crossed if you want to see the remarkable and ancient **St Govan's chapel**, squeezed into a rock cleft above the crashing waves.

THE PEMBROKESHIRE NATIONAL PARK AND COAST PATH

Of the ten national parks in England and Wales, the **Pembrokeshire Coast** is the only one that is predominantly sea-based, hugging the rippled coast around the entire western section of Wales. Established in 1952, the park is not one easily identifiable mass, rather a series of occasionally unconnected patches of coast and inland scenery. Starting at its southeastern corner, the first segment clings to the coast from Amroth through to the Milford Haven waterway, an area of sweeping limestone cliffs and some fabulous beaches. The second, and by far the quietest, part courses around the inland pastoral landscape of the Daugleddau estuary, which plunges deep into the rural heart of Pembrokeshire southeast of Haverfordwest. The third part is superb for cliff walking and scenery, around the beaches and resorts of St Bride's Bay, where the sea scoops a great chunk out of Wales' westernmost land. In the north of the county, the boundary of the park runs deep inland to encompass the Mynydd Preseli, a barren but invigoratingly beautiful range of hills dotted with ancient relics.

Crawling around almost every wriggle of the coast, the **Pembrokeshire Coast Path** winds 186 miles from St Dogmael's near Cardigan in the north to its southern point at Amroth. For the vast majority of the time, the path clings precariously to clifftop routes, overlooking seal-basking rocks, craggy offshore islands, unexpected gashes of sand and shrieking clouds of sea birds. Only on the southwestern end of the Castlemartin peninsula does it veer inland for any major length, as the coast is given over to army training camps and rifle ranges; the path also ducks inland along the Milford Haven estuary, where the close proximity of belching great oil refineries and the huge expanse of hill-backed water provide one of the many surprises around the route.

The most popular, and ruggedly inspiring, segments of the Coast Path are around St David's Head and the Marloes peninsula, either side of St Bride's Bay, the stretch from the castle at Manorbier to the tiny cliff chapel at Bosherston along the southern coast and, generally quieter, the undulating contours, massive cliffs, bays and old ports along the northern coast, either side of Fishguard. These offer miles of windswept walking amongst great flashes of gorse, heather and seasonal plants, as well as the opportunity to study thousands of sea birds at close quarter. Basking seals are frequent visitors to some of the more inaccessible beaches, particularly around the time when pups are born in the autumn. This is reckoned to be one of the major causes of accidents along the route, as people try to gain better views of the creatures and consequently tip over the edge.

Few walkers appreciate the danger of the path, on which there is a grim annual death toll, mainly through those falling over the cliffs. Of all the seasons, perhaps spring is the finest for walking as the crowds are yet to arrive and the clifftop flora is at its most vivid. There are numerous publications available about the Coast Path, of which the best is Brian John's *National Trail Guide*, which includes section 1:25,000 maps of the route. The national park publishes a handy *Coast Path Accommodation* guide, detailing B&Bs and campsites the entire length of the route, available from tourist and national park offices and bookshops. It also publishes the excellent free newspaper, *Coast to Coast*, which contains exhaustive listings of special walks, boat trips and other events, and which you can pick up from the various national park offices listed throughout this chapter. A further path has been created around the haunting Daugleddau estuaries, inland from the Milford Haven. For details of both the national park and the Coast Path, contact the Information Officer at the Pembrokeshire Coast National Park Authority, Winch Lane, Haverfordwest, Pembrokeshire SA61 1PY (☎01437/764591 ext5135).

On foot, you can get closer to the best of the scenery, by way of the Pembrokeshire Coast Path's four-mile walk west, brushing along the top of some of Wales' most dramatic cliffs, with the **Stack Rocks** and limestone arch that mark the last point of access on this part of the coast. All around, and to the west, are artillery ranges, forcing the Coast Path inland to avoid snipers. The next point of access on the coast is the west-facing **Freshwater West**, a wide beach popular with surfers, reached across windy grass dunes and heathland. The peninsula tapers out to the west, a long finger of rugged coastline pointing out towards the main part of the county. The westernmost village is **Angle**, sitting on the edge of its bay that faces out across the Milford Haven towards the grim reminders of industrialization in the shape of a vast oil refinery.

Penally, Manorbier and St Florence

Just over a mile down the A4139 from Tenby, the dormitory village of **PENALLY** is unremarkable save for the vast beach, a wide and sunny sprawl of sand that runs right up to become Tenby's South Beach a mile further up. The coastal path hugs the clifftop from the viewpoint at Giltar Point, just below Penally, reaching the glorious privately owned beach at the 54-acre headland of **Lydstep Haven** after two miles (a fee being charged for the sands); it's a beautiful spot, with limestone caverns to explore in the craggy Lydstep Point. Although some of the caverns are only accessible at low tide, the Smuggler's Cave is safe at all times. A mile further west is the cove of **Skrinkle Haven**, reached via steep steps from the car park at the end of the little lane off the Manorbier road. Above the beach is an excellent **youth hostel** (☎01834/871803; ①), where you can also **camp**, or you can find **B&B** at *Myrtle House*, near the Penally train station (☎01834/843623; ②), or the slightly superior *Hillgarth*, in Skrinkle village (☎01834/871266; ③). There's another campsite at *Whitewell Farm* (☎01834/871569), sandwiched between the main road and train line just west of the town. Of the pubs, the lively *Cross Inn*, near the station, is best.

Manorbier

The next part of the Coast Path heads inland to avoid the artillery range that occupies the beautiful outcrop of **Old Castle Head**, then leads straight into the quaint village of **MANORBIER**, pronounced "Manner-beer" (Maenorbŷr), birthplace in 1146 of Giraldus Cambrensis, Gerald of Wales (see p.350), who described the castle here as "excellently well defended by turrets and bulwarks, and . . . situated on the summit of a hill extending on the western side towards the sea". Founded in the early twelfth century as an impressive baronial residence, the **castle** (April–Sept daily 10.30am–5.30pm; £2) sits above the village and its beach on a hill of wild gorse. The Norman walls are in a very decent state of repair, surrounding an inner grass courtyard in which the extensive remains of the castle's chapel and state rooms jostle for position with the nineteenth-century domestic residence, whose TV aerial strikes a note of contemporary discord. Views from the ramparts are wonderful: you can see the corrugated coastline, bushy dunes, deep-green fields, and smoking chimneys of the tinted village houses. In the walls and buildings are a warren of dark passageways to explore, occasionally opening out into little cells with lacklustre wax figures, purporting to illustrate the castle's history. Needless to say, prime position goes to a waxwork of Gerald himself.

The lane below the castle leads past the curious, elongated tower of the parish church down to Manorbier's shell-shaped **cove**, a sandy break in the red sandstone cliffs. For a more secluded bathe, follow the path on the left of the beach (as you face the sea) up over the headland known as the Priest's Nose, past the Neolithic crom-lech (burial chamber) known as the **King's Quoit**, with its lopsided capstone, and round for just over half a mile to the steep steps down to often-deserted **Precipe Beach**. At high tide, the beach is entirely flooded, so check times carefully.

In Manorbier, you'll find **accommodation** at the smart, comfortable and no-smoking *Old Vicarage* (☎01834/871452; ③), or camp at *Park Farm* (☎01834/871273) on the northern side of the village, just off the B4585 towards Manorbier station. The *Castle Inn* hosts live music on Saturdays.

Swanlake Bay and Freshwater East

The lanes and Coast Path wriggle ever westwards, the path skirting across the top of the beautifully remote, and always quiet, **Swanlake Bay**, a mile from Manorbier; car drivers will find it almost impossible to find a place to park, although just off the small lane from Manorbier to Hodgeston, the farmers at East Moor Farm and *West Moor Farm* (☎01834/871204; ③), where you are also able to **camp**, usually allow a few people to park and walk the remaining distance. Swanlake is a far better option than the next beach along, close to the garish village of **FRESHWATER EAST**, whose magnificent sheltered beach is spoiled by the profusion of hideous sprawl-ing holiday developments in the village that backs it.

St Florence

Three miles north of Manorbier is the delightful little village of **ST FLORENCE**, whose whitewashed stone cottages, many with their original medieval Flemish chimney stacks, are huddled around the tiny lanes. The Ritec stream, along whose banks there is a beautiful walk which takes you east of the village, was once an inlet, and St Florence an important port during the Middle Ages before the stream retreated. If you want to **stay** here, the country-house atmosphere of *Elm Grove* (☎01834/871255; ③) comes at a very reasonable price. The village pubs are also excellent: the wonderful *New Inn* is the first amongst equals in this village of good boozers.

From Stackpole Quay to Angle

The rocky little harbour at **Stackpole Quay**, reached via the small lane from Freshwater East through East Trewent, is a good starting point for walks along the breathtaking cliffs to the north, or half a mile south to one of the finest beach-es in Pembrokeshire: **Barafundle Bay**. Clear water and a soft beach are fringed by wooded cliffs; south of the beach is a spectacular stretch of the Coast Path leading to **Stackpole Head**, a tufted plateau on craggy arches jutting into the sea.

The path continues around the coast, through the dunes of **Stackpole Warren**, to **BROAD HAVEN**, where a pleasant small beach overlooks several rocky islets, now managed by the National Trust. Basing yourself here gives good access inland to the nearby **Bosherston Lakes**, three fingers of water artificially created in the late eighteenth century, but beautifully landscaped. The western-most lake is the most scenic, especially in late spring and early summer when the lilies that form a carpet across its surface are in full bloom. Not far from the main car park for the lakes, the **Stackpole Centre** (☎01646/661425) has a decent pro-gramme of live music and theatre, especially in summer. Near Stackpole Quay car park are some lovely National Trust holiday cottages (☎01225/791199).

Another lane dips south from the village of **BOSHERSTON**, a mile inland from Broad Haven, across the MOD training grounds peppered with warning signs reminding that "military debris may explode and kill you", and at times access to the land is altogether banned, as indicated at National Park information offices and other points like Bosherston post office. Persevere through the series of unwelcoming gates down the lane running for just over a mile to a spot overlooking the cliffs where **St Govan's chapel** is wedged: it's a remarkable tiny, grey chapel, known to be at least eight hundred years old (and possibly as much as fourteen hundred). Legend has it that Saint Govan chose this spot to be buried when a gang of hoodlums was attacking him on the clifftop, and the cliffs opened up and folded gently around him, protecting him from certain death. The steps descend straight into the sandy-floored chapel, now devoid of any furnishings, save for the simple stone altar. At its side, steps lead into a small cell honed from the rock, containing the fissure that is supposed to have sheltered Saint Govan. Steps continue down to the spume of the sea hurtling at the rocks. Here, you get a magnificent close-up of the precarious crags, caves and arches, deep turquoise water, rigidly straight rock strata and limestone worn and washed by the sea. Good-value **accommodation** is found at the enjoyable *St Govan's Inn* in Bosherston village (☎01646/661311; ③), which also has reasonably priced food.

All the land to the west of St Govan's chapel is dominated by the dugouts and abandoned shells and tanks of the army and, apart from the narrow strip of clifftop land on which the Coast Path runs, is entirely out of bounds. The path skirts along the top of the cliffs to the west for four miles, past the striking cleft in the rocks known as **Huntsman's Leap**, two isolated beaches at **Bullslaughter** and **Flimston Bay** to the **Stack Rocks**. Alternatively, a lane – with restrictive times of opening – runs down to the Stacks from near Merrion on the B4319, passing the mourning little chapel of **FLIMSTON** village, a hamlet forcibly abandoned to the army.

The Stack Rocks jut out of the sea like a series of tall, lichen-spattered stepping stones. A hundred yards further west (and as far as you're allowed to go) is a graceful, curving limestone arch rising out of a wave-flattened platform of rock, known as the **Green Bridge of Wales**. On a quiet day, the only company you will have are the shrieking gulls, guillemots and kittiwakes swooping around before perching on the limestone ledges. The land to the west, appropriated by the military, contains some of the most spectacular coastal scenery in the county, as well as some superb dunes and important ancient remains. **Climbers** eager to see the caves of Linney Down and the stacks and caves of the southern coast should apply in writing to The Commandant, RAC Castlemartin, Merrion, Pembroke SA71 5EB. Permits to enter the 5884-acre "West Range" are given between mid-August and January only, and you must specify the cliffs you want to climb.

Castlemartin, Freshwater West and Angle

Forced to turn inland here, the Coast Path continues back up the lane to Merrion and follows the B4319 through the village of **CASTLEMARTIN** – whose church houses an organ once owned by Mendelssohn. Here you'll find a few places to **stay**: the *Court Farm* (May–Sept; ☎01646/661228; ②), and *West Farm*, Castlemartin's old vicarage (April–Sept; ☎01646/661227; ③), where you can also **camp**. The Coast Path follows the B4319 a couple of miles to **Freshwater West**, a west-facing beach resort that's excellent for surfing, although the currents can be too strong for swimming. The desolation of the wind-battered dunes behind the beach make for interesting walking.

THE PEMBROKESHIRE ENERGY INDUSTRIES

On both sides of the magnificent Milford Haven waterway, the most prominent features on the landscape belong to the refineries and power station that fringe the waters. Storage tankers, observation towers and security fences litter the Coast Path here, the most blighted stretch being the five miles between the west side of the Pembroke River estuary and Angle Bay. On the estuary's north side, the path passes alongside a vast Gulf refinery, and much land around the southwestern corner of Pembrokeshire is in the strict custody of the Milford Haven Port Authority (MHPA).

As well as occasional disasters such as the dreadful *Sea Empress* episode (see p.175), the presence of so much polluting and potentially hazardous industry in this rural corner of Wales has many ramifications. A few years ago, a huge fire at the *Texaco* refinery on the south side of the Haven prompted many residents of Rhoscrowther and Pwllcrochan to leave the area, and forced eviction of these villages occasionally surfaces as an option, hardly helping the remaining residents' confidence.

A new threat has arisen through the planned conversion of Pembroke power station into an orimulsion plant. This controversial fuel, which power station owner National Power (NP) admits has a "kill factor" some 442 times greater than ordinary crude oil, has been burned elsewhere, notably at the now-closed Richborough station in Kent, England, where local crops suffered drastically, land was poisoned and car paint blistered – pure coincidence, says NP. It threatens to close Pembroke power station altogether, unless consent is given for its conversion. There are strong advocates on both sides: NP has gained the support of some local trade unions and councillors, for whom the jobs and prosperity argument is uppermost. In an area with few employment prospects, this is powerful, and opponents to the scheme have been painted as middle-class outsiders with little concern for the local economy. The local press has pitched in enthusiastically, swallowing NP's statements with little analysis – a typical headline recently read "ORIMULSION OR BUST!"

The B4319 meets the B4320 from Pembroke near the **Devil's Quoit**, a Neolithic burial chamber topped by an impressive capstone. The road continues west into the last finger of the peninsula, reaching the remote village of **ANGLE**, at the western end of a wide curve of mud, known as **Angle Bay**. Angle consists of one long street, bounded by old, coloured cottages and some impressive pubs. Better for swimming is **West Angle Bay**, a secluded spot a mile to the west of the main village, overlooking another of the Lord Palmerston protective forts on **Thorn Island**, now converted into the most secluded of **hotels**, the *Thorn Island Hotel* (June–Aug; ☎01646/641225; ④), where the price includes dinner. You can stay at the *Timothy Lodge* (☎01646/641342; ②) in the middle of Angle, or camp at *Castle Farm* (☎01646/641220) just behind the village church. For **eating and drinking**, try the colonnaded, crenellated *Globe Hotel*, centrepiece of the village, or the nearby *Hibernia Inn*, a hundred yards west, good for food and convivial company. A ten-minute hike east along the shore brings you to the delightful, remote *Point House* inn, whose fire is said to have burned continuously for over three hundred years.

Pembroke and around

The old county town of **PEMBROKE** (Penfro) and its fearsome **castle** sit on the southern side of the Pembroke River, a continuation of the massive Milford Haven waterway, described by Nelson as the greatest natural harbour in the world. The slightly over-restored castle is nonetheless an essential sight, dominated by its vast 75-foot Norman keep. But aside from that, and the town's wonderful **Museum of the Home**, Pembroke is surprisingly dull, with one long main street of attractive Georgian and Victorian houses, some intact stretches of medieval town wall and little else to catch the eye.

The town grew up solely to serve the castle, the mightiest link in the chain of Norman strongholds built across southern Wales. The walled town, drawn out along a hilltop ridge, flourished as a port for Pembrokeshire goods to be exported throughout Britain and to Ireland, France and Spain. The main quay was situated alongside the waters below the imposing walls of the castle.

Cromwell attacked the town in 1648 during the English Civil War. By this stage, the castle was partially derelict and it was only the strength of the recently repaired town walls that enabled the citizens to withstand the worst of the onslaught. They were beaten, however, by a 48-day siege and by the Parliamentarian troops seizing the water supply, after which Cromwell ordered the continued demolition of the castle and walls.

Pembroke developed as a centre of leather making, weaving, dyeing and tailoring, never really regaining its former importance. In the twentieth century, the small town was on a serious slope of decline, its port long since overtaken by neighbouring sites. One fortunate result of this is that the town is mercifully free of postwar development in the centre, although the fringes around the main street are largely modern and bland.

Around the town are several noteworthy sights, the most interesting being the ruined Bishop's Palace in **Lamphey**, a country residence for the bishops of St David's in the thirteenth century, and a couple of miles further on, the attractive town of **Carew**, with its Celtic cross and castle. **Pembroke Dock**, a couple of miles north of Pembroke, grew up in a grid pattern during the nineteenth century to serve its parent town as a naval dockyard.

The Town

The **Pembroke River**, a tidal mass of mud, flows in from the Daugleddau to frame the northern side of Pembroke town centre. Running parallel to the southern bank is the long **Main Street**, which stretches from the train station (as Station Road) in the east to the mighty lines of the castle.

Opposite the castle walls at 7 Westgate Hill (the continuation north of the Main Street) is the delightfully eccentric **Museum of the Home** (May–Sept Mon–Thurs 11am–5pm; £1.50), an all-encompassing name for the thousands of objects packed into a steep town house. It's a collection of utterly ordinary items from the eighteenth to the twentieth centuries, loosely gathered into themes – the dairy, toiletries, personal and smoking accessories, kitchen equipment, bedroom accessories and children's games. The enthusiasm of the owners, who show people around with illuminating conversation and great interest, makes the sensation somewhat akin to being let loose in a small stately home.

From the museum and the castle gates, Main Street widens out past multi-coloured shop frontages of eighteenth- and nineteenth-century construction, dipping down for over half a mile towards the towered **St Michael's church**, heavily, and unsympathetically, restored by the Victorians. Blackhorse Walk turns north, running down to the Mill Pond and the most impressive remnants of the thirteenth-century town **walls** running between the demolished East Gate and Barnard's Tower, a medieval towered house attached to the walls.

The castle

Pembroke's history is inextricably bound up with that of the **castle** (April–Sept daily 9.30am–6pm; Oct–March daily 10am–4pm; £2.50), founded as the strongest link in the chain of fortresses built by the Normans across south Wales to tame and subjugate the people. In the early years following the Norman invasion, the people of Deheubarth (west Wales) avoided the conquest, thanks to a tacit agreement between Rhys ap Tewdwr and the Norman victors. Upon his death in 1093, however, Norman lord Roger de Montgomery didn't hesitate for a moment in charging into the area and capturing it by force from the surprised natives. Pembroke's powerful bulk, protected by a hill on its southern side and water on the other three, proved impregnable to the Welsh, who attempted to besiege it. But to no avail; it has never been under the control of the Welsh. The earldom of Pembroke, created in 1138, was passed down to the Marshals, or local landowners awarded an earldom, who almost entirely rebuilt the castle between 1189 and 1245, and over the ensuing three centuries enforced the feudal rule of "Little England Beyond Wales" (see p.152), a primitive (but successful) way of ensuring Welsh subservience to the English in the farthest-flung corner of the country, by establishing firm English military rule from the chain of powerful castles built in a string across Pembrokeshire. In 1452, Henry VI granted the title and castle to Jasper Tudor, whose nephew Harri (or Henry) was born here and became king, as the Lancastrian heir to the throne, after defeating Yorkist Richard III at Bosworth Field in 1485. During the Civil War, Pembroke was a Parliamentarian stronghold until the town's military governor suddenly switched allegiance to the King. Cromwell's troops sacked the castle after besieging it for 48 days.

Despite Cromwell's incessant battering and centuries of subsequent neglect, Pembroke still inspires feelings of awe at its sheer, bloody-minded bulk, even if it is largely due to extensive restoration over the last century. Entering through the soaring gatehouse brings the visitor into the large, grassy courtyard, around which the battlements are broken up by great hulking towers. These marked the positions where the town walls formerly attached themselves to the fortress.

At the back of the courtyard is the inner ward, grouped around the castle's most eye-catching feature: the vast, round Norman **keep**, 75ft high and with walls 18ft thick, crowned by a dome. The intact towers and battlements contain many heavily restored communal rooms, now empty of furniture (and to a large extent, atmosphere too), although the walkways and dark roofed passages that connect them give the visitor ample chance to chase around spiral stairways into great oak-beamed halls. Some of the rooms, mainly in the gatehouse, are used to house some excellent displays on the history of the castle and the Tudor empire.

In the keep, the view of the dank, dripping interior is quite disorientating, as the tower seems to taper upwards. Even better is the eerie view into the yawning innards from the top, which can be reached via steps in the massive walls. The tower was probably built at the beginning of the thirteenth century by William Marshal. One clue to its age comes in the two contrasting windows in its side – one round-headed and Norman, the other pointed and Perpendicular – suggesting that the construction spanned the transitional period between the two architectural ages.

Alongside the keep is a cluster of domestic buildings, largely ruined and unrestored, and seeming insignificant in comparison with the sheer bulk of the rest of the castle. Apart from a dungeon tower – complete with grille to peer through into the gloomy cell below – there's a Norman Hall, where the period arch has been disappointingly over-restored and reinforced, next to the Oriel or Northern Hall, a Tudor recreation of an earlier antechamber. A set of steps at the side of the Northern Hall leads down and down into a huge natural cavern, dank and slimy, way below the castle, where light is beamed in through a barred hole in the wall that looks out over the waterside path.

Practicalities

Pembroke's **train station** (☎01646/684896) is on the easternmost side of the town centre on Station Road. From there, head left out of Station Drive, over the roundabout and down the Main Street into the town centre. A new **tourist office** is on Commons Road (Easter–Sept daily 10am–5.30pm; Feb–Easter Tues, Thurs & Sat; ☎01646/622388), parallel to Main Street, and provides a useful free town guide. At the entrance to the castle is a small **National Park information centre** (Easter–Sept Mon–Sat 9.30am–1pm & 2–5.30pm; ☎01646/682148).

Accommodation ranges from cheap B&Bs such as the *Connaught*, 123 Main St (☎01646/684655; ②), and the real ale *Old Cross Saws* pub (☎01646/682475; ②) along the road at no. 109, to slightly plusher hotels like the *King's Arms*, also on the Main Street near the castle (☎01646/683611; ④), and the *Moat House* on The Commons (☎01646/684557; ⑤).

Food is easy to find in Pembroke: try *The Pantry*, 4 Main St, near the castle, for stodgy and cheap daytime and early evening snacks, the excellent *Woodhouse* restaurant (☎01646/687140), with a limited, but beautifully cooked, menu of local produce, or the bar food at the *King's Arms Hotel*, also on Main Street. In Pembroke Dock, the food at the *Welshman's Arms* on London Road is excellent, as is the pricier continental *La Brasseria* in Law Street (☎01646/686966).

There are dozens of **pubs** – the best in Pembroke is the *Old Cross Saws* on Hamilton Terrace (see above), although it's hard to beat a summer evening on the verandah, overlooking the Mill Pond, at the *Waterman's Arms*, over the bridge on Northgate Street. The *Castle Inn*, 17 Main St, is dowdy, but friendly and entertaining enough. Near the ferry terminal in Pembroke Dock on Pembroke Street, the friendly *White Hart* is good value all round.

Pembroke Dock

Built as a result of a local argument that developed when Milford Haven refused to provide a home for a naval dockyard, the town of **PEMBROKE DOCK** (Doc Penfro), a couple of miles north of its parental city, grew up almost instantaneously in the nineteenth century. Constructed on a rigid grid plan with some handsome Victorian buildings flanking the wide streets, its fortunes have fluctuated severely between recession and boom, but today, thanks to the oil refineries and the development of a deep-water dock, the town is on a firmer footing than it has been for decades.

Pembroke Dock's **train station** leads out on to Water Street. To the right, Pier Road heads down to Hobbs Point, a spectacular viewpoint over the boats and smoking stacks of the Daugleddau River, and the departure point for *Tudor Line* **leisure cruises** along the waterway (☎01646/685627). Down on the harbourside, off Front Street, a rickety bridge leads to the **Gun Tower** (April–Oct Mon–Sat 10am–5pm; free), a converted Victorian military defence post, one of numerous fortifications built to guard the Milford Haven waterway. It now houses a few moderately diverting exhibits on its history, and a **tourist office** (☎01646/622246). Immediately west is the imposing dockyard, sheltering behind high walls and containing the **ferry terminal** for *Irish Ferries* trips to Rosslare, Ireland (☎0990/329543).

Carew

A tiny village that can become unbearably packed in high season, **CAREW** (Caeriw), four miles east of Pembroke by the Carew River, is a pretty place. Just south of the river crossing, by the main road, is the village's **Celtic cross**, erected as a memorial to Maredydd, ruler of Deheubarth, who died in 1035. The graceful, remarkably intact taper of the shaft is covered in fine tracery of ancient Welsh designs.

A small hut beyond the cross serves as the ticket office for **Carew Castle** and **Mill** (Easter–Oct daily 10am–5pm; £1.50 castle only, £2 castle & mill). The castle, a hybrid of Elizabethan fancy and earlier defensive necessity, is reached across a field. Explanatory models illustrate the development of the site, which is an excellent example of the organic nature by which castles grew, from the Norman tower believed to be the original gatehouse, through the thirteenth-century front battlements, to the newer Tudor gatehouse and the Elizabethan mansion grafted onto them all. A few hundred yards west of the castle is the **Carew French Mill**, the only mill powered by the shifting tides in Wales. The impressive eighteenth-century exterior belies the pedestrian exhibitions and self-guided audiovisual displays of the milling process at different stages.

Lamphey

The humdrum village of **LAMPHEY** (Llandyfai), two miles east of Pembroke, is best known for the ruined **Bishop's Palace** (unrestricted access; CADW), off a quiet lane to the north of the village. This was a country retreat for the bishops of St David's, dating from at least the thirteenth century and abandoned at the Reformation in the mid-sixteenth century, although it was in use as Crown apartments for a few decades afterwards.

Stout walls surround the palace ruins, scattered over a large area, with many of the palace buildings having long been lost under the grassy banks. Most impressive are the remains of the Great Hall across the entire eastern end of the complex, with fourteenth-century Bishop Gower's hallmark arcaded parapets on its top, similar to those that he built in the Bishop's Palace of St David's (see p.182). The gloomy hall beneath the Great Hall has the feeling of a crypt, lit as it is only by narrow slits.

Lamphey is a pleasant place in which to linger: it's on the train line to Pembroke, there's charming **accommodation** at the *Court Hotel* (☎01646/672273; ④), a graceful white Georgian mansion opposite the Bishop's Palace ruins, and the *Dial Inn* on the Ridgeway does superb local food.

Mid-Pembrokeshire

Pembroke Dock lies on the southern banks of the magnificent **Daugleddau** river estuary, the continuation of one of the world's greatest natural harbours, the **Milford Haven**. This spawned an eponymous Quaker community on the northern bank, which now seems, rather sadly, to be searching for a new post-industrial identity by ploughing vast sums into the development of some dubious tourist features. Seven miles to the north, the chief town of the region, **Haverfordwest**, makes an important market and transport centre that, despite some handsome architecture, remains rather soulless. A few miles northeast of town, **Scolton Manor** houses the county museum.

The A40 arrives in Haverfordwest from the east, brushing through an unspectacular, but effortlessly pleasant, rural landscape on the way. Just south of the road, five miles from town, **Picton Castle** sits above the wide, tidal waters of the Daugleddau, a river estuary flooding the valleys of inland Pembrokeshire and providing a surprisingly maritime feel amidst such impressively rolling countryside. Dotted around the muddy estuary are creaky little villages and some fine walks and pubs. The main road roars on, bypassing the stout little town of **Narberth**, self-appointed capital of the **Landsker borderlands**, a revived name for the imaginary, but effectively real, line that divides the anglicized corner of south Pembrokeshire from its Welsh-speaking neighbour (see p.152). Near the town are some big-time tourist attractions, among them the mighty **Oakwood** theme park, home to Europe's largest wooden roller coaster.

A branch train line leaves the *InterCity* Fishguard route at Whitland, calling at Narberth en route to Pembroke and Pembroke Dock. The train line divides again at Clarbeston Road, with the Milford Haven-bound branch calling at Haverfordwest. A reasonable bus service throughout the area has most routes starting at either Pembroke or Haverfordwest.

Milford Haven

One of the most impressive sights in this part of Wales is the view from the 1970s **Cleddau Bridge** (car toll 75p), which curves out of Pembroke Dock over to **NEYLAND** on the opposite bank. Pedestrians can also try it: the views over the jutting headlands are magical, the masts of boats far below and the full skies reflected in the clear water. Even the refineries look attractive from this far up. Even better, try to synchronize your journey over the bridge with a decent sunset, when the glowing sun dips perfectly into the estuary mouth.

The waterway below – the Milford Haven — is one of the world's great natural harbours, recognized even by William Shakespeare:

> ...how far it is
> To this same blessed Milford; and, by the way,
> Tell me how Wales was made so happy as
> To inherit such a haven.
>
> (Imogen in *Cymbeline*, Act III, scene 2)

Taking its name from the waterway, **MILFORD HAVEN** (Aberdaugleddau), four miles west of Neyland, was founded in the late eighteenth century by a group of early American settlers from Nantucket, who were imported as whalers. The grid pattern they imposed survives today – principally three streets rising sharply parallel to the waterway – when new civic and religious buildings were founded. Despite a magnificent site and interesting heritage, Milford Haven has a dead-beat atmosphere, due largely to the town attractions being relocated around a horribly sterile dock development, now given the misnomer of the Marina. The waterside is impressive though, with tugs and steamers ploughing up the glittering waters of the Haven, stretching out below the pleasant gardens.

The waterside road is Hamilton Terrace, which skirts around to the tarted-up **docks**, home of an assortment of museums – the child-oriented **discovery centre**, *Kaleidoscope* (daily 10am–6pm; £4), a tawdry **Dockside Gallery**, some unpleasant cafés and restaurants, and the genuinely interesting town **museum** (Easter–Oct Tues–Sun 11am–5pm; £1), housed in an eighteenth-century warehouse, built to store whale oil. Exhibits include photographs and mementoes from the fishing trade, an explanation of the modern oil industry, details of the Quaker beginnings of the town and some fascinating archive material of Milford Haven in wartime.

On the western side of the docks and estuary, **Fort Hubberston** is the most explorable of Pembrokeshire's nineteenth-century Palmerston defence forts. Built between 1860 and 1865, the barracks was home to 250 men in the late nineteenth century, and, although rickety and somewhat vandalized, is an eerie and interesting place to poke around. Nearby is the ruined octagonal dome of the **Hakin Observatory**, the sole remaining relic of town founder Charles Francis Greville's dream to build a "mathematical college".

Practicalities

Milford Haven **train station** is located under the Hakin road bridge, next to the docks. The docks **information office** (daily 10am–6pm) is not an official one, but sells an all-in-one ticket to the town's sights, apart from the museum (£5) – for the official information office, head up to 94 Charles St (April–Sept Mon–Sat 10am–5pm; ☎01646/690866). The town is home to west Wales' only professional **theatre**: the *Torch* on St Peter's Road, at the end of Charles Street (☎01646/695267).

Accommodation includes the classy *Belhaven House Hotel*, 29 Hamilton Terrace (☎01646/695983; ③), the *Pebbles Guest House*, 15–18 Pill Fold (☎01646/698155; ②), and in the western suburb of Hakin, the *Kings Arms* pub (☎01646/693478; ③); there's a **campsite** at *Sandy Haven*, near Herbrandston, two miles west of town (☎01646/693180). For **food** and **drink**, the *Wanderer Bistro* in Hamilton Terrace (☎01646/697594) serves an excellent range of local and continental dishes.

Haverfordwest and around

In the seventeenth century, the town of **HAVERFORDWEST** (Hwlffordd), lying in the valley of the Western Cleddau seven miles northeast of Milford Haven, was created as the county town of Pembrokeshire, replacing the old settlement of Pembroke. Haverfordwest itself is an old town, having grown up around one of Gilbert de Clare's castles, the remains of which dominate the town to this day. The town prospered as a port and trading centre in the seventeenth and eighteenth centuries, its homely architecture reflecting the richness of the age. Despite all the natural advantages, Haverfordwest's half-empty modern shopping centre seems to reflect the lack of pride in the place these days, and it's scarcely a place to linger.

Castle Square is the epicentre of the town, and it's from here that a small alley-way to the right of *Woolworth's* ascends to the **castle**, unfortunately failing to live up to the expectations created by views of it from down below; all there is to see is a dingy shell of the thirteenth-century inner ward. Next to the castle, in the imposing governors' house, is the **district museum** (April–Oct Tues–Sat 11am–5pm, Sun 11am-4pm; Nov–March Tues, Thurs & Sat 11am-4pm; £1), a motley collection of minor art pieces and some fairly interesting local history. Back down below, the Riverside Shopping Centre follows the river from Castle Square up to the Old Bridge, next to the bus terminus and tourist office, and adjoining the centre is a lively indoor **market** (Mon–Sat). The more interesting parts of Haverfordwest lie up the handsome High Street, rising from the River Cleddau. Opposite the commanding **St Mary's Church**, founded in the thirteenth century, are the preserved remains of a Georgian town-house vault, on the corner of Market Street, the town's most interesting shopping thoroughfare, full of craft, antique and book shops.

Practicalities

The **train** station is a ten-minute walk east of the town centre, while **buses** come and go from the depot at the end of the Old Bridge, near the **tourist office** (May–Sept Mon–Sat 10am–5.30pm; Oct–April Mon–Sat 10am–4pm; ☎01437/763110). Next to the tourist office, the *Holiday Information Centre*, at 2 Riverside Quay, houses a booking agency for the excellent self-catering *Coastal Cottages of Pembrokeshire* (☎01437/765765) and a bureau for the many outdoor pursuits under the *Activity Wales* banner (☎01437/766888), and there is also an excellent **national park office** at 48 High St. There's more alternative information at *Sacred Space*, opposite the tourist office, the *Pembrokeshire Primrose Company* and *Celtic Gift Shop* at 24 Market St, and *Swales Music Centre*, by St Mary's church.

Accommodation is provided at the solidly Georgian *Castle Hotel* in Castle Square (☎01437/769322; ⑤), or, a little cheaper, the *College Guest House*, 93 Hill St (☎01437/763710; ③), and the *Villa House*, St Thomas Green (☎01437/762977; ③). There's a **campsite** two miles northwest on the A487, at the *Rising Sun Inn* in Pelcomb Bridge (☎01437/765171). The *Hotel Mariners* is an old coaching inn in Mariners' Square, and offers the best bar snacks in the town, along with a pricier **restaurant**. The *Carmarthen Arms*, near the station, is low-key, but enjoyable enough and with a good bar menu.

Picton Castle and Scolton Manor

The main A40 heads east out of Haverfordwest, past the train station. After two or three miles, signs point south towards **Picton Castle** (mid-July to mid-Sept Thurs & Sun noon–5pm; £4), a graceless building, something of a hybrid of architectural styles from the fourteenth to the eighteenth centuries, but sited in glorious **grounds** (April–Sept Tues–Sun 10.30am–5pm; £2.50) with views over the Eastern Cleddau and its valleys.

Four miles northeast of Haverfordwest, along the B4329, **Scolton Manor** (April–Oct Tues–Sun & Bank Holidays 10am–4pm; £1) is a modest stately mansion, dating from 1840, which forms the nucleus of the Pembrokeshire County Museum. It's a good place to appreciate the lifestyle of a rich Victorian family: the rooms of gilt, brocade and fine furnishings in total contrast with the perfunctory cellar, larder and laundry below. There's a fine collection of prints and maps detailing some of the lost Picturesque estates of Wales, a Carriage House filled with traps, a steam engine on a short strip of track and a wealth of illumnating local artefacts. There's a good **café** on site and a surrounding **country park** (open all year) with an environmentally aware visitor centre.

Narberth and the Landsker Borderlands

In contrast to Milford Haven and Haverfordwest, the area now known as the **Landsker Borderlands** forms a quiet, charming part of mid-Pembrokeshire, broken by some beautiful villages that are still well off the beaten tourist track. *Landsker* is a Norse word meaning "frontier", here used as a definition of the division between Cymric north Pembrokeshire and the anglicized south (see p.152). Although the division is ancient, going back to the Norman colonization of the south of the county, the name, despite sounding sufficiently archaic, is a comparatively recent sobriquet – first mentioned, in this context, in the 1930s.

The "capital" of the borderlands is **NARBERTH** (Arberth), a pleasing little town on the train line to Tenby, just off the main A40; this is supposed to be the court of Pwyll in the *Mabinogion*, a collection of pre-Norman Welsh folk tales and legends, and in reality, its ruined **castle** was the old home of the Welsh princes.

At the far eastern end of the town is the **train station**, at the top of Station Road, which runs down to St James Street, and connects with the market square and the bottom of the town's neat High Street. Dividing the High Street is the curious, spiky **town hall**, built in the 1830s to mask the municipal water tank underneath. Upstairs is the **tourist office** (see overleaf), and the **Landsker Visitor Centre**, which aims to illustrate local history interwoven with the lurid tales of the *Mabinogion*, which it describes as a "window on the Iron Age". At the top end of the High Street, **Queen's Hall** (☎01834/861212) is one of the best emerging venues in Pembrokeshire, hosting world music concerts, trance to techno raves, theatre, art exhibitions and more.

Water Street runs down from behind the town hall to the **Wilson Museum** (Easter–Sept Mon–Sat 10.30am–5pm; 60p), housed in an old town pub – the entrance lobby is the barely altered front parlour. Much of the collection comes from local people, the net result being a beguiling slice of Narberth life over the past couple of centuries. There are themes, such as local transport, religion and education, but these are soon forgotten in the pursuit of yet more trivia. Completely unrelated to Narberth, but interesting nonetheless, the museum also has a rare 1925 stuffed velvet Mickey Mouse, complete with his early rat-like features. The museum opens out into a great little bookshop and coffee shop, giving onto the market square. Next door, there's a new high-tech, interactive gallery (unnamed at the time of writing), where you can play on the Internet and attend workshops, as well as look at pictures.

Blackpool Mill and Oakwood

Narberth lies to the east of the most impressive scenery around the Daugleddau estuary. The tidal reach of the Eastern Cleddau River goes as far as **Blackpool Mill** (Easter–Oct daily 11am–6pm; £2), four miles west of Narberth. An elegant four-storey stone block, the mill was built in 1813 to grind wheat using water power, although this source was replaced at the beginning of this century by turbines. Much of the machinery has been restored and can be seen throughout the building, alongside replica workshops filled with bland wax models. Below the mill, a series of caves have also been filled with models, this time replica brown bears, cavemen, wolves and a huge Welsh dragon in a fanciful attempt to depict life in prehistoric Wales.

The A4075 heads south from Blackpool Mill, past two big local attractions. First is the **Oakwood** theme park (April–June & Sept–Oct daily 10am–5pm; July & Aug daily 10am–11pm; £8.95), Wales' largest such site and a good day out. The star attraction is the new *Megaphobia*, Europe's largest wooden roller coaster, but there's also toboganning, water rapid rides, boating, go-karting, a Wild West town and numerous smaller rides. Immediately south, the **Canaston Centre** (daily 10am–11pm; free entry, then various prices) is firmly family-oriented, with garish "fun" restaurants amidst sundry attractions, top of which is the *Crystal Maze*, a series of interactive challenges from the television programme of the same name.

On the banks of the Eastern Cleddau

Fanning out to the west of Blackpool Mill are the quiet lanes that wind down towards the muddy banks of the Claddau estuary. It's a charming landscape of small, inconsequential settlements and, along the eastern bank at least, great walking.

The well waymarked path (the Landsker Borderlands Trail) runs the entire length of the Eastern Cleddau, starting from the lonesome northernmost hamlet of **LANDSHIPPING**, whose desolate **quay**, a mile south, was once a busy ferry point and coal port. Here, the two Cleddau (*dau gleddau*, or "two swords") rivers diverge, with the main estuary plunging southwards through wooded hillsides. **LAWRENNY** village, four miles south, is a pretty place, dominated by the four-storey tower of the magnificent twelfth-century **St Caradoc's church**. A track alongside the church winds up to the site of Lawrenny's old castle, now a picnic area with tremendous views over the confluence of the Cresswell and Carew rivers at **Lawrenny Quay**, about half a mile from the village. This is the starting or finishing point for the best short walk along the estuary – a water's-edge stroll past ancient oak woodlands with views of the almost Toytown **Benton Castle** (privately owned) on the other bank.

The path hugs the northern bank of the Cresswell for two miles before reaching tiny **CRESSWELL QUAY** (Cei Cresswell), home to the *Cresselly Arms*, a wonderful, waterfront pub where beer comes in frothing jugs, and the *Penquoit Centre* which offers inspirational **accommodation** (see below) and hosts a range of courses and special interest groups. A mile west of Cresswell Quay, the old limestone quarrying village of **WEST WILLIAMSTON** is the gateway to **Williamston Park** (free access), a National Trust/Dyfed Wildlife Trust nature reserve jutting out into the folds of the rivers Cresswell and Carew.

North of Narberth, the most spectacular scenery is along the rich, non-tidal valley of the Eastern Cleddau, especially in the idyllic and steep village of **LLAWHADEN**, whose ghostly **castle** (free access, collect key from post office if locked) sits on a bluff above the river. Once a residence of the Bishop of St David's, the castle's remains reflect its later role more as a luxurious home than as a defensive fort. Most impressive is the decorative, square fourteenth-century gatehouse, dating from the castle's major transformation into a bishop's palace.

Practicalities

The **tourist office** in Narberth is open at the same times as the Landsker Visitor Centre (April–Oct Mon–Sat 10am–5pm; summer school holidays also Sun; Nov–March Thurs–Sat 10am–1pm; free; ☎01834/860061) and stocks a wide selection of free leaflets on local villages and walks.

Accommodation in Narberth itself is woefully lacking, and although there are a handful of occasional B&Bs along Station Road, Spring Gardens, St James Street and into the Market Square, these are unreliable – it's best to have a look when you arrive. There are a couple of nearby **camping** options: *Noble Court* (☎01834/861191), half a mile north on the B4313, and, on the northeastern fringe of town, *Dingle Farm* on Jessie Road (☎01834/860482).

If you want guaranteed B&B, you're better off in neighbouring **ROBESTON WATHEN**, just over a mile northwest, where both *Traethgwyn* (☎01834/860598; ②) and *Canton* (☎01834/860620; ③) are central. Elsewhere in the area, *Knowles Farm*, a mile north of Lawrenny village (☎01834/891221; ③), is a great farmhouse B&B well placed for some wonderful walks. In Cresswell Quay, the *Penquoit Centre* (☎01646/651666; ①–③) offers a private hostel, single retreats (riverside cells for single visitors), tipis and caravans. For camping along the Daugleddau, there's the peaceful *New Park Farm* (☎01834/891284), a mile from the river's edge near Landshipping. There's **bike rental** at the *Highgate Cycle Centre* (☎01834/891213), just off the A4075 nearly a mile south of Cross Hands.

There's good **food** in Narberth at the café in the *Queen's Hall* arts venue (see p.171), or over the road in *Lillabette's* teashop. Pub **food** is best at the *Coach and Horses* at the top of the High Street, or the *Angel Inn* further down by the town hall. **Drinking** is easy, with a multitude of good pubs: try the jolly locals' *Eagle Inn*, behind the Wilson Museum at the bottom of Water Street, or the memorabilia-bedecked *Kirkland Arms* on St James Street. The *Bridge Inn* at Robeston Wathen hosts regular **jazz** nights (information ☎01834/861408), while the *Cresselly Arms* (see opposite) is always convivial.

St Bride's Bay

The most westerly point of Wales – and the very furthest you can get from England – is one of the country's most enchanting areas. The coast around **St Bride's Bay** is broken into rocky crops, islands and broad, sweeping beaches curving around between two headlands that sit like giant crab pincers facing out into the warm Gulf Stream amidst the crashing Atlantic. The southernmost headland winds around every conceivable angle, offering calm, east-facing sands at **Dale**, sunny expanses of south-facing beach at **Marloes** and wilder west-facing sands at **Musselwick**. Between the latter two, the peninsula descends to its dramatic end at the **Deer Park**, just beyond **Martin's Haven**, where boats for the offshore islands of **Skomer**, **Skokholm** and **Grassholm** depart.

The middle scoop of the bay combines the typical ruggedness with a little more in the way of golden sands, backed by teeming, popular holiday villages such as **Little Haven**, **Broad Haven** and **Newgale**. From here, the spectacularly lacerated coast veers to the left and the **St David's peninsula**, along stunning cliffs interrupted only by occasional gashes of sand. Just north of **St Non's Bay**, the tiny cathedral city of **St David's**, founded in the sixth century by Wales' patron saint, is a justified highlight. Rooks and crows circle above the impressive ruins of the huge **Bishop's Palace**, sitting beneath the delicate bulk of the **cathedral**, the most impressive in Wales. The St David's peninsula, more windswept and elemental than any other part of Pembrokeshire, tapers out just west of the city at the popular **Whitesands Bay** and the hamlet of **St Justinian's**, staring out over the crags of **Ramsey Island**.

Bus transport to most corners of the peninsula radiates out from Haverfordwest: a twice-weekly service to Dale and Marloes, a daily service to Broad and Little Haven and an hourly service to Newgale, Solva and St David's.

Marloes, Dale and the offshore islands

DALE is a popular yachting and windsurfing centre, fourteen miles from Haverfordwest. In the peak season, it can become unbearably crowded, the village car park at the top of the shingle beach filling up with alarming speed. Although not an especially attractive village and blighted by views of oil refineries, its east-facing shore makes it excellent for watersports in the lighter seas. Equipment and instruction for windsurfing, sailing, surfing and even mountain biking are available on the seafront from *West Wales Windsurfing & Sailing* (☎01646/636642).

The calm waters of Dale are deceptive, and as soon as you head down further towards **St Ann's Head**, one of the most invigoratingly desolate places in the county, the wind speed whips up, with waves and tides to match. Blasted by some of the highest winds in Britain (gale force on about 32 days in an average year), buffeted by extraordinarily strong tide-races and virtually frost-free throughout the winter, it's a fine, invigorating spot for a walk, despite being the site of the 1996 *Sea Empress* wreck (see box opposite). Thankfully, most visible reminders of the spill have now vanished. The Coast Path sticks tight to the undulating coastline, passing tiny bays en route to the St Ann's lighthouse. Tucked in the eastern lee of St

---

A SHORT CIRCULAR WALK AROUND ST ANN'S HEAD

Note: The OS Outdoor Leisure 1:25,000 map #36 (South Pembrokeshire) is recommended

The start and finish point is the free National Trust car park on the site of the old radar centre at **Kete** (SM 803042), just over a mile down the lane from Dale village. From the car park, turn left onto the lane and take the path that forks sharply right after a few yards. This path follows the edge of a couple of fields, before joining the Coast Path proper at a stile. Turn left (south), passing the scant bumps of an old Iron Age fort on **Little Castle Point**, where the path veers east, meandering past Vomit Point. Views west are spellbinding, especially over the rocky humps of islands out in the bay. Before long, the buildings of St Ann's Head loom into view and the path briefly joins the lane that terminates at the lighthouse. To the right is a viewpoint, worth a short diversion, over Cobbler's Hole, a spectacularly folded and fissured set of cliffs.

The path runs alongside the lane as it approaches the lighthouse, but doubles back on itself just before reaching it. You are now heading north again, past old walled cottage allotments and down some steps, built in 1800 to ease the arrival of materials for the new lighthouse that was being built at the time. Mill Bay looms into view on the right, and the path skirts around the top of the mainly shingle beach, nipping up and down before settling into another pleasant stretch as it heads towards the mighty modern beacons erected to warn of problems in the Haven. Just beyond is the old Palmerston fort at West Blockhouse Point, now a Landmark Trust holiday property. A few hundred yards later, the main path splits into three. Left leads up to a farm track and, ultimately, back to the car park at Kete, whilst right descends gently to the safe, sandy beach of **Watwick Bay**, one of the most pleasant – and crowd-free – anywhere on the Pembrokeshire coast.

THE *SEA EMPRESS* OIL SPILL

Nothing has jettisoned Pembrokeshire into the headlines as much as the grounding of the oil tanker, *Sea Empress*, off the rocks of St Ann's Head on February 15, 1996. Bound for the Texaco refinery at Milford Haven, the tanker was carrying 130,000 tonnes of North Sea crude oil when it ran aground less than ten miles short of its destination. The ensuing crisis, with local residents evacuated and kept ill-informed and conflicting news stories emerging, was handled badly from the start. It quickly became evident that Pembrokeshire's tourist industry – the staple of the local economy – was under serious threat, so damage-limitation exercises were drawn up immediately by the county council, the National Park authority and the Wales Tourist Board.

A full nine days after the initial spill, a salvage operation finally cranked into life to pump the oil out. By this time, prevailing southerly and easterly winds had caused the black slick to spread along the south Pembrokeshire coast, reaching even the beaches of Carmarthenshire and the Gower. Tens of thousands of sea birds died, beaches were smothered and much of Pembrokeshire's unique coastal flora was damaged. The cleanup, however, has been remarkable. Although the long-term effects of the detergent sprayed on the sea will take years to be assess, its efficacy cannot be doubted. By the summer of 1996, all of the beaches and cliffs had been exhaustively scrubbed and the sea had returned to its usual sparkling turquoise. Considering how ham-fistedly much of the initial crisis was handled, this is an astonishing turn of events.

Beyond the ecological tale, the *Sea Empress* disaster has had significant political ramifications in Pembrokeshire. Schoolchildren have worked on projects about the spill, exhibitions have been drawn together and local residents formed new campaigning organizations, groups and links. For an ongoing assessment of the implications of the spill, together with an irreverent view of Pembrokeshire politics and happenings, pick up a copy of *Rebekah*, a small radical free paper. If you can't find one, contact PO Box 206, Haverfordwest SA62 3YF.

Ann's Head is **Mill Bay**, where Henry VII landed in 1485, marching the breadth of his native Wales and gathering a loyal army to face Richard III at Bosworth Field.

Marloes and around

The coast turns and heads north from St Ann's Head, reaching the sandstone-backed **West Dale Bay**, less than a mile from Dale on the opposite side of the peninsula. Warnings are usually given about the unpredictability of the currents and hidden rocks in the sea here, and you may find the broad sands of **MARLOES**, a mile from the village, a safer place to swim. This is a superb beach that never gets crowded – its size alone prevents that. A great curve of sand dissected by rocky spills, Marloes Sands is best known for its stunning cliffs of grey, gold and purple folds of rock, alternate layers of grey shale and old red sandstone. The most impressive way to appreciate the difference is by seeing the **Three Chimneys**, two-thirds of the way along the sands. These three vertical lines of hard Silurian sandstone and mudstone were formed horizontally and forced up by the Armorican earth movements. There was a fourth "chimney" which crumbled in a severe storm in 1954. The beach is crowned at its western end by **Gateholm Island**, accessible at mid-tide and below. It's a site of great importance: over 130 Iron Age hut circles, pottery and pieces of jewellery have been found here, and it's thought to have been an ancient monastic community. Today, it's powerfully atmospheric and a great place to **camp**. The easiest access is from the Runwayskiln hostel (see below), a hundred yards before which is a large National Trust car park.

A rough track leads from the north of the car park to meet the lane to **MARTIN'S HAVEN**, a cluster of houses and a car park on a slim neck of the peninsula that faces out to Skomer island. If you're walking, the mile-long Coast Path walk from the Gateholm end of Marloes Sands is wonderful, with easy access to a couple of tiny, deserted coves. Inexplicably ignored by the Coast Path is the sublime **Deer Park** (which incidentally has no deer, and probably never did), the very far tip of this peninsula, reached by a small gateway in the wall just beyond the car park. Paths radiate out all over the headland, all with stunning views over the offshore islands and the entire yawn of St Bride's Bay: if you can catch a decent sunset here, you'll see none better. There's a small Dyfed Wildlife Trust information point at Martin's Haven, the principal departure point for **boats** to the offshore islands of Skomer, Skokholm and Grassholm.

Skomer (boats April–Oct Tues–Sun 10am, 11am & noon; £6) is a 722-acre flat-topped island that dominates the near horizon of Martin's Haven. It has the finest **sea bird** colonies in northern Europe, the remains of hundreds of ancient hut circles, a stone circle, collapsed defensive ramparts and settlement systems and, near the narrow neck where the boats land, a Bronze Age standing stone, *Harold's Stone*. Of all the sea birds on Skomer, perhaps the most noted are there 200,000-plus Manx shearwaters, but there are also puffins, gulls, guillemots, storm petrels, cormorants, shags and kittiwakes. Land birds include buzzards, skylarks, jackdaws, chough, owls and peregrine. If you head to the north of the island, facing out over the Garland Stone, there's a good chance of seeing basking grey seals, especially in the autumn. In spring and early summer, wild flowers carpet the island.

Two miles south of Skomer is the 240-acre island of **Skokholm** (boats June–Aug Mon 10am; £15.50; booking essential on ☎01437/781412), whose warm red sandstone cliffs are a sharp contrast to Skomer's grey severity. Britain's first bird observatory was founded here in the 1930s, and the island is still rich in birdlife. The boat trip includes a guided tour by the island's warden.

The final boat trips head out to the tiny outpost of **Grassholm** (boats June–Sept landing trip on Mon, evening tour Thurs; round trip Fri £20), over six miles west of Skomer – a rough, two-hour journey if the weather's not good. From the mainland, Grassholm looks like a small icing-covered cake: the "icing" is, in fact, a swarming mass of 70,000 gannets, one of the largest colonies in the Northern Hemisphere, that covers well over half the island.

All of the boat trips are operated on the *Dale Princess*. No booking is required for Skomer trips and Grassholm Thursday trips, although this can be done, if desired, at National Park information centres. Monday and Friday Grassholm trips are bookable on ☎01646/601636. Accommodation is also available on Skomer and Skokholm – see below for details.

Back on the mainland, the Coast Path continues round to **Musselwick Sands**, a beautiful and unspoilt beach less than half a mile from the village of Marloes (can be dangerous at high tide). Further north along the peninsula is the narrow **St Bride's Haven**, at the end of the lane that peters out by the tiny chapel of St Bride, whose cemetery is on the way to the beach, a tiny, but beautiful inlet, well sheltered from the winds. There are some good rockpools around the beach.

Practicalities

For **accommodation**, the most reasonable option in Dale is *Point Farm* (☎01646/636254; ③), a wonderful sea-facing farmhouse quarter of a mile along the road to the Dale Fort Field Studies Centre, due east of the village. Pricier, but good, is the *Post House Hotel* (☎01646/636201; ④), in the middle of the village. Marloes is well stocked for B&Bs: pick from the *East End* guesthouse (☎01646/636365; ②), *Foxdale* (☎01646/636243; ②) or *Greenacre* (☎01646/636400; ②). The **youth hostel** at Runwayskiln (April–Sept; ☎01646/636667) consists of a series of converted farm buildings overlooking the northern end of Marloes Sands. **Camping** is possible at *Greenacre* or *Foxdale* (see above), near the youth hostel at Runwayskiln (☎01646/636257), or at *West Hook Farm* (☎01646/636424) near Martin's Haven. To stay on Skokholm (fully catered) and Skomer (self-catering), contact the Dyfed Wildlife Trust (☎01437/765462). **Food** and **drink** are available at the *Griffin Inn* or the bistro by the beach in Dale, and at the *Foxes Inn* in Marloes.

From Little Haven to Solva

Altogether flatter and more easily walked by tourists, the coast north of **LITTLE HAVEN** can be disappointingly blighted by tacky seaside developments. Little Haven village is the exception – a picturesque old fishing village and coal port that descends in steep streets to a sheltered stony beach, extremely popular with divers and swimmers in summer. At low tide, walks along the beach towards Broad Haven are superb: you can explore caves and rockpools or just enjoy the full westerly skies. **Accommodation** centres on the *Little Haven Hotel* (☎01437/781285; ③), or there's *Mount Pleasant* at 6 Settlands Hill (☎01437/781439; ②), and, a mile above the village, *Bower Farm* (☎01437/781554; ③), a very friendly farm B&B. The nearest **camping** is at *Howelston Farm* (☎01437/781253), up the hill south of Little Haven. The most noteworthy place to **eat** here is the redoubtable *Swan Inn* by the harbour, with bar snacks available each day, and an excellent restaurant specializing in local seafood (Wed–Sat; ☎01437/781256). If you can't afford that, cross the harbour for great meals at the *Castle Inn*.

Quite different from Little Haven are the garish charms of neighbouring **BROAD HAVEN**, a mass of fun pubs and caravan parks above a wide, popular beach fringed by some remarkably fissured and shattered cliffs. There's a National Park **information office** here (April–Sept daily 9.30am–5pm; ☎01437/781412), the major booking office for trips out to Skokholm, Skomer and Grassholm islands, and the village is also well off for **B&Bs** – try *Glenfield*, 5 Atlantic Drive (☎01437/781502; ②), *Ringstone*, on Haroldstone Hill (☎01437/781051; ③), half a mile north, or the breezy, large *Broad Haven Hotel* (☎01437/781366; ④). The **youth hostel** is next to the National Park office (☎01437/781688; ①), and there's **camping** at the tacky *Broad Haven Holiday Park* (☎01437/781277). *Haven Sports* on Marine Road (☎01437/781354), just behind the *Galleon Inn*, rents out windsurfing equipment (tuition available) and mountain bikes.

The Coast Path goes it alone from here, occasionally coinciding with a stray country lane that opens out sublime views through the wind-flattened gorse and trees. Worth seeking out a couple of miles north is the quieter sandy beach at **DRUIDSTON HAVEN**, hemmed in by steep cliffs and reached along small paths at the bottom of the sharply sloping lane from Broad Haven. Easiest access to this delightful beach is from *Druidston Hotel* (☎01437/781221; ③), a popular, easy-going place with a cellar bar that spills out on to the clifftops. Self-catering cottages, including an old circular croquet pavilion, are also available on site. Just before the hotel, a lane heads inland for a few hundred yards to the tiny hamlet of **DRUIDSTON**, where you can **camp** at *Shortlands* (☎01437/781234).

Nolton Haven and Solva

NOLTON HAVEN, a mile along the coast, is little more than a picturesque cluster of houses and caravans around a sheltered shingle cove. Part of the tracks of long defunct tramway that brought coal down to the jetty from the nearby Trefrane colliery can be seen here. **Accommodation** in the village includes the harbour-front *Mariner's Inn* (☎01437/710469; ④), which serves excellent, if pricey, dinners, and *Nolton Haven Farm* (☎01437/710263; ②). For camping, there's *Longlands* (☎01437/710234), a third of a mile short of the village on the Druidston side. Just inland is the village of **Nolton**, in the centre of which is *Celtic Corner* in North Nolton Farm (☎01437/710254), with nights of raucous harp-twanging, boozing, local delicacy devouring and even a bit of dancing.

A cliff path and small lane climb out of Nolton Haven, after a half-hour walk descending to the southern end of the vast west-facing **Newgale Sands**, popular with families and surfers alike. The southern end of the beach, away from the main Haverfordwest–St David's road and the tawdry little village of **NEWGALE**, is a better bet for seclusion. Brandy Brook, disgorging onto the beach just beyond Newgale's *Duke of Edinburgh* pub, marks the boundary of "Little England Beyond Wales" (see p.152) and the extent of Norman colonization of Pembrokeshire.

The coast turns west, rising abruptly to spectacular riveted cliffs beyond Newgale, a wilder, somehow more Celtic landscape than that of southern Pembrokeshire. The Coast Path from Newgale to **SOLVA** (Solfach), three miles west, is great, with easy clifftop walking, magnificent views over the rippled coast and, in the lee of the Dinas Fach headland, a secluded sandy beach at **Porthmynawyd**. Solva is a pleasant, if heavily touristed, village sitting at the top of its own inlet that runs down to the sea by the **Gwadn beach**, on the east side of the river. Above the beach, the **Gribin Headland** stands wedged between the valleys of the Solva and Gribin rivers – as well as the superb views, it's worth climbing for the impressive Iron Age earthwork on its summit.

In Solva, it's better to **stay** in the picturesque Lower Village, at the head of the inlet. There's the *Harbour House Hotel* (☎01437/720013; ③) by the car park or, on the main street, two reliable choices in the *Old Pharmacy* (☎01437/721881; ③) and *Llys Aber* (☎01437/721657; ②). The nearest **campsite** is a fifteen-minute walk above Upper Solva at *Llanungarfach Caravan Park* (☎01437/721202). In the centre of the village, *Le Papillon Rouge* (☎01437/720802) serves excellent **meals** with imaginative use of local seafood and meats, and a good vegetarian choice. The *Cambrian Hotel* is dependable enough for a **drink**, although geared heavily to tourists.

St David's

ST DAVID'S (Tyddewi) is one of the most enchanting and evocative spots in Britain. This miniature city clusters around its purple- and gold-flecked cathedral at the very western point of Wales on a windswept, treeless peninsula of awesome ruggedness. It is the country's spiritual and ecclesiastical centre, totally indepen-

dent of Canterbury, and the granting of official city status in 1995 has only reinforced its importance.

Traditionally founded by the Welsh patron saint himself in 550 AD, the see of
St David's has drawn pilgrims for a millennium and a half – William the
Conqueror included – and by 1120, Pope Calixtus II decreed that two journeys to
St David's was the spiritual equivalent of one to Rome. The surrounding city – in
reality, never much more than a large village – grew up in the shadow cast by the
cathedral, and St David's today still relies on the imported wealth of newcomers
to the area, attracted by its savage beauty, together with the spending power of its
visitors. With numerous historical sites, outdoor pursuit centres, good cafés,
superb walks, bathing and climbing, St David's and its peninsula are an absolute
must for anyone who wants to experience Wales at its wildest.

Arrival and information

From the bus terminus in New Street, the friendly and efficient **tourist office**
(Easter–Oct daily 9.30am–5.30pm; ☎01437/720392) is just a short walk away in
City Hall on the High Street. Local **boat companies** organize trips to the outlying islands: *St David's Adventure Days* (☎01437/721611 or 0800/132588), behind
the *Coastal Trader* café on the High Street, offers one-hour tours around Ramsey
Island (£10), and runs various outdoor activities for which it also rents equipment.
Across the square at the top of The Pebbles, *Thousand Island Expeditions*
(☎01437/721686) offers an exhilarating two-hour ride (£16.50) around the coast
of Ramsey Island, darting into caves and seeing seals, sea birds, porpoises and
the towering sea cliffs. It also runs trips out to Grassholm, multi-island tours and
a thunder through white water in the Bitches, a precarious string of rocks
between the mainland and Ramsey. An absolute soaking is guaranteed. If you
want to land on Ramsey, try *Ramsey Island Pleasure Cruises* (☎01437/720285 or
eves 721423), at the St Justinian's lifeboat station, just over a mile west of the city.

Apart from the adventure centres, **bike rental** is available from *St David's
Cycle Hire*, behind the *Coastal Trader* (☎01437/720057 or 720354).

Accommodation

There are numerous places to **stay** on the St David's peninsula, with prices fairly
high in season at the larger hotels, but coming down dramatically for the rest of
the year. Campsites abound in and around the city. For accommodation on
Ramsey Island, see p.183.

HOTELS AND GUESTHOUSES

Alandale, 43 Nun St (☎01437/720333). Small, friendly and central guesthouse. ③.

Mr & Mrs Davies, Upper Treginnis, near St David's (☎01437/720234). A comfortable farmhouse B&B a mile southwest of the town, above the valley of the River Alun. Tent pitches also
available. ②.

Old Cross, Cross Square (☎01437/720387). Comfortable, creaky hotel with decent-sized
rooms and a good restaurant. Closed Nov–Feb. ④.

Pen Albro, 18 Goat St (☎01437/721865). Cheery B&B next to the *Farmers Arms*, St Davids'
liveliest (and only) nightspot. ②.

Ramsey House, Lower Moor (☎01437/720321). Excellent small hotel on the road to Porth
Clais, with superb Welsh cuisine. ③.

St Non's, Goat Street (☎01437/720239). Rambling old-fashioned country hotel near the
River Alun. ④.

Whitesands Bay, Whitesands (☎01437/720403). Family-oriented beach hotel with outdoor pool, above the very popular beach. ④.

Y Glennydd, 51 Nun St (☎01437/720576). Town-centre B&B in a converted Victorian house. ③.

HOSTELS AND CAMPSITES

Caerfai Farm, Caerfai Bay (☎01437/720548). Best campsite near St David's, a 15-min walk from the city. Closed Oct–April.

Glan-y-mor, Caerfai Road (☎01437/721788). The nearest campsite to town, also offering diving instruction.

Llaethdy youth hostel, Llaethdy (☎01437/720345). Large and popular hostel, two miles northwest of St David's near Whitesands Bay. ①.

Lleithyr Farm, Whitesands Bay (☎01437/720245). Campsite and caravan park just off the B4583, half a mile short of Whitesands Bay.

Pencarnon Farm, off St Justinian's Road (☎01437/720324). One of the best campsites in the area, in a fantastic setting above a virtually private beach. All facilities.

Rhosson Ganol, St Justinian's (☎01437/720361). Popular year-round campsite, handy for the boats out to Ramsey Island.

Twr-y-Felin Hostel, Caerfai Road, St David's (☎01437/720391). Wonderful outdoor activity centre, lively and friendly, with a wide range of sporting pursuits alongside decent hostel accommodation. You can also camp here.

The Town

The main road from Haverfordwest enters St David's inauspiciously, past a petrol station and a ragbag of hotels. Becoming the High Street, the road courses down to Cross Square, a triangular city centrepiece around a **Celtic cross**, and continues under the thirteenth-century **Tower Gate**, which forms the entrance to the serene **Cathedral Close**, backed by a windswept landscape of distant farms and knobbly rock, a heathland almost devoid of trees.

The cathedral lies down to the right, hidden in a hollow by the River Alun. This apparent modesty is explained by reasons of defence, as a towering cathedral, visible from the sea on all sides, would have been vulnerable. On the other side of the babbling Alun lie the ruins of the Bishop's Palace. New Street heads north past the enjoyable **Oceanarium** (daily 10am–6pm; Oct–March closes 4pm; £3), complete with a shark tank overlooked by a viewing gallery. A few hundred yards beyond, on the northern fringe of town near the rugby club, the excellent **St David's Farm Park** (April–Oct daily 10am–5pm; £3.50) is a collection of animals and rural crafts aimed squarely at the kids, but fun for adults too. Throughout St David's, there are numerous small commercial **art galleries** and craft outlets: a few are dreadful, but most reflect the quality of the many artists attracted to this unique corner of Wales. Worth singling out is the excellent *St David's Studio Gallery* at 28 High St, good both for crafty giftware and the prints and paintings of its exuberant owner, Stan Rosenthal.

The cathedral

Approached down the Thirty-Nine Articles (or steps) that run from beyond the powerfully solid **Tower Gate** – the only remaining medieval gate of four – the gold and purple stone cathedral's 125-foot tower has clocks on only three sides (the people of the northern part of the parish couldn't raise enough money for one to be constructed facing them), and is topped by pert golden pinnacles that seem to glow a different colour from the rest of the building. You enter the **cathe-**

dral through a porch in the south side of the low twelfth-century nave, although the line of the former higher roof can be clearly seen outside of the tower. The most striking feature of the nave is the intricate latticed oak **roof**, built to hide sixteenth-century emergency restoration work, when the nave was in danger of collapse. The nave floor still has a discernible slope and the support buttresses inserted in the northern aisle of the nave look incongruously new and temporary.

At the end of the nave, an elaborate **rood screen** was constructed under the orders of fourteenth-century Bishop Gower, who envisaged it as his own tomb. Behind the rood screen and the organ, the choir sits directly under the magnificently bold and bright lantern ceiling of the tower, another addition by Gower. The round-headed arch over the organ was built in Norman times, contrasting with the other three underpinning the tower, which are pointed and date from the rebuilding work that took place in the 1220s. At the back of the right-hand choir stalls is a unique **monarch's stall**, complete with royal crest, for, unlike any other British cathedral, the Queen is an automatic member of the St David's cathedral Chapter. A new card sign – "Reserved for the Sovereign", as if she might just pop in unannounced – underlines the point. The misericords under the choir seats display some ribald medieval humour; there's one of a chaotic wild boar hunt and another of someone being seasick. Behind the left-hand choir stalls, the **north transept** contains the tomb of St Caradoc, with two pierced quatrefoils, in which it is believed people would insert diseased limbs in the hope of a cure. Off the north transept, steps from St Thomas' chapel lead up to the **Chapter Library** (July & Aug Mon–Fri 2–4pm; Sept–June Mon only; 50p), which includes the Royal Charter of June 1995 that granted St David's city status.

Separating the choir and the presbytery is a finely traced, rare **Parclose screen**. The back wall of the **presbytery** was once the eastern extremity of the cathedral, as can be seen from the two lines of windows. The upper row has been left intact, while the lower three were blocked up and filled with delicate gold mosaics in the nineteenth century, surrounded by over-fussy stonework. The colourful fifteenth-century roof, a deceptively simple repeating medieval pattern, was extensively restored by Gilbert Scott in the mid-nineteenth century. At the back of the presbytery, around the altar, the **sanctuary** has a few fragmented fifteenth-century tiles still in place. On the south side is a beautifully carved sedilla, a seat for the priest and deacon celebrating mass. To its right are thirteenth-century tombs of two bishops, Iorwerth (1215–31) and Anselm de la Grace (1231–47), and on the other side of the sanctuary is the disappointingly plain thirteenth-century tomb of St David, largely destroyed in the Reformation.

Behind the filled-in lancets at the back of the presbytery altar is the Perpendicular **Bishop Vaughan's chapel**, crafted out of a soft honeyed stone, with an exquisite fan tracery roof built between 1508 and 1522. Bishop Vaughan's statue occupies the niche to the left of the altar. To the right is an effigy of Giraldus Cambrensis, Gerald of Wales, his mitre placed not on his head, but at his feet – a reminder that he never attained the status of bishop for which he was evidently desperate. Opposite, facing west, a peephole looks into the presbytery. Around the opening, the four crosses may well predate the Norman church. The bottom cross is largely obscured by a casket that reputedly contains some of the intermingled bones of St David and his friend, St Justinian. Behind the chapel is the ambulatory, off which the simple **Lady Chapel** (with some sentimental Edwardian stained glass) leads. Either side of the Lady Chapel are tombs in wall niches: the one on the left was originally believed to have been for Bishop Beck

(1280–96), the builder of St David's Bishop's Palace, but now houses Bishop Owen (1897–1926), whose devoted service to the Church in Wales and the Welsh nation is symbolized by the roaring dragon above him.

The Bishop's Palace

From the cathedral, a path leads over the tiny, clear River Alun to the splendid **Bishops' Palace** (April–Oct daily 9.30am–6.30pm; Nov–March Mon–Sat 9.30am–4pm, Sun 2–4pm; £1.70; CADW), built by bishops Beck and Gower around the turn of the fourteenth century. The huge central quadrangle is fringed by a neat jigsaw of ruined buildings in extraordinarily rich colours: the distinctive green, red, purple and grey tints of volcanic ash, sandstone and many other types of stone. The **arched parapets** that run along the top of most of the walls were a favourite feature of Gower, who did more than any of his predecessors or successors to transform the palace into an architectural and political powerhouse. Two ruined but still impressive halls – the **Bishops' Hall** and the enormous **Great Hall**, with its glorious rose window – lie off the main quadrangle, above and around a myriad of rooms adorned by some eerily eroded corbels. Underneath the Great Hall are dank vaults containing an interesting exhibition about the palace and the indulgent lifestyles of its occupants. The destruction of the palace is largely due to Bishop Barlow (1536–48), who supposedly stripped the buildings of their lead roofs to provide dowries for his five daughters' marriages to bishops.

Eating, drinking and entertainment

With only one pub to its name, St David's can hardly be said to rock. Entertainment is otherwise limited to the annual **classical music festival** held at the end of May in the cathedral, and regular **craft fairs** in the Cathedral Hall; the tourist office has details. There are, however, several reasonable places to eat.

Cartref, Cross Square (☎01437/720422). Enjoyable, swish restaurant with a menu of well-cooked, moderately priced local dishes. Open March–Dec.

City Inn, New Street. Large and relaxed hotel bar with a selection of inexpensive home-cooked Indian delicacies.

Coastal Trader, 1 High St. Great snackerie that's also a good place in which to hang out and meet the travelling crowd for which St David's has become something of a scene.

Farmers Arms, Goat Street. The city's only pub. Young, lively and very friendly; especially enjoyable on the terrace overlooking the cathedral on a summer's evening.

Foster's Bistro, 51 Nun St (☎01437/720576). Small restaurant with a menu of reasonably priced local dishes and international favourites. Open April–Oct.

La Patisserie, Nun Street. Daytime bakery with some local delicacies.

Morgan's Brasserie, 20 Nun St (☎01437/720508). A charming restaurant specializing in locally caught fresh fish. Prices are moderate to expensive.

St David's Peninsula

Surrounded on three sides by inlets, coves and rocky stacks, St David's is an easy base for some excellent walking around the headland of the same name. A mile due south, accessed along the signposted lane from the main Haverfordwest road just near the school, popular **Caerfai Bay** provides a sandy gash in the purple sandstone cliffs, rock from which was used in the construction of the cathedral. To the immediate west is the craggy indentation of **St Non's Bay**, reached from St David's down the tiny rhododendron-flooded lane, signposted to the *Warpool*

Court Hotel, that leads off Goat Street. Saint Non reputedly gave birth to Saint David at this spot during a tumultuous storm around 500 AD, when a spring opened up between Non's feet, and despite the crashing thunder all around, an eerily calm light filtered down onto the scene.

St Non's received pilgrims for centuries, resulting in the foundation of a tiny chapel in the pre-Norman age, whose successor's thirteenth-century ruins now lie in a field to the right of the car park, beyond the sadly dingy well and coy shrine where the nation's patron saint is said to have been born. The 1934 **chapel**, built in front of the austere 1929 **Retreat House** (details of stays and courses from Father Timothy on ☎01437/720224), was constructed in simple Pembrokeshire style from the rocks of ruined houses, which, in turn, had been built from the stone of ancient, abandoned churches.

The road from St David's to St Non's branches at the *St Non's Hotel*, where Catherine Street becomes a winding lane that leads a mile down the tiny valley of the River Alun to its mouth at **PORTH CLAIS**. Supposedly the place at which Saint David was baptized, Porth Clais was the city's main harbour, the spruced-up remains of which can still be seen at the bottom of the turquoise river creek. Today, commercial traffic has long gone, replaced by a boaties' haven.

Running due west out of St David's, Goat Street ducks past the ruins of the Bishop's Palace and over the rocky plateau for two miles to the harbour at **ST JUSTINIAN'S**, little more than a ruined chapel, lifeboat station, car park and ticket hut for the boats over to Ramsey Island, which leave here with great regularity during the summer. As well as the tours based in St David's itself (see above), *Ramsey Island Pleasure Cruises* (April–Oct ☎01437/720285 or eves 721423) operate trips to Ramsey.

Under the extremely able stewardship of the RSPB since 1992, **Ramsey Island** itself, a dual-humped plateau less than two miles long, is quite enchanting. Birds of prey circle the skies above the island, whose feathered population is better known for the tens of thousands of sea birds that noisily crowd the sheer cliffs on the island's western side. On the beaches, seals laze sloppily below the deer paths beaten out by a herd of red deer.

Thousand Island Expeditions boats for Ramsey depart not from St Justinian's, but instead from **Whitesands Bay** (Porth Mawr), two miles to the north and reached from St David's via the B4583 off the Fishguard road (see "Arrival and information", p.179). Campsites and cafés line the shore, one of the most popular in all Pembrokeshire, and as Whitesands faces west, surfing is good. Far less crowded, and spectacularly beautiful, is **Porthmelgan**, a narrow slip of cove reached by a fifteen-minute walk northwest along the Coast Path from Whitesands car park. **St David's Head**, a thin spit of rock and cliff juts out into the ocean, less than a mile to the west. Rising behind Whitesands and Porthmelgan, the gnarled crag of **Carn Llidi** tops a pastoral patchwork of fields.

From St David's to Fishguard

The north-facing coast that forms the very southern tip of Cardigan Bay is noticeably less commercialized and far more Welsh than the touristy coasts of south and mid-Pembrokeshire. From the crags and cairns above St David's Head, the Coast Path perches precariously on the cliffs, where only the thousands of sea birds have access. The first point of contact with the sea for humans is the black sand beach at **Abereiddi**, half a mile short of the quieter sands of **Traeth Llyfn**.

A CIRCULAR WALK AROUND ST DAVID'S HEAD

OS 1:25,000 Outdoor Leisure map #35 (North Pembrokeshire) is advised for this walk

The tapering finger of rock that tumbles down from the slopes of Carn Llidi is one of the most mysterious and magical places in Wales. Evidence of ancient civilization is everywhere, and numerous mystics and seers have pinpointed the area as a focus of the earth's natural energies.

Starting from the Whitesands Bay car park, double back on yourself up the lane to St David's. Go past the twin semis and take the left track opposite the caravan park. Where the lane forks, take the right turning, signposted to Upper Porthmawr. Take the track between the two farmhouses and continue climbing, following the right track at the National Trust sign. Ascend to the rocky top of Carn Llidi (595ft) on the obvious track, passing two cromlechs – capped burial stones – on the lower slope. At the top, you get mesmerizing views over the whole of St Bride's Bay, the patchwork of the Dewisland peninsula, the cathedral, the rocky outcrops of Ramsey, Skomer and Grassholm, the dips of the coast north up to Strumble Head, Whitesands Bay and miles of glittering sea.

Retrace your steps down the hill, past the cromlechs, and take the first obvious right path. This leads swiftly down to a hedge-backed green lane, turn right and keep walking as it curves gently round. On reaching the kissing gate, turn right into the peaceful little valley below the craggy carns. The slope on the right has been excavated to reveal the extensive remains of an Iron Age field and settlement system, although this will be hard to see if the bracken is high. Take the first left path before the valley reeds, cross the peaty brook and bridleway, continuing up to meet a green road and then the main Coast Path. Turning left towards the headland brings you along and above some superb cliffs, speckled with wild flowers and squawking sea birds. After a few hundred yards, above the path to the left, you should spot *Carreg Coetan Arthur* (Arthur's Quoit), a 6000-year-old capstoned burial chamber. The path strikes on towards the end of the headland. Shortly, a line of broken wall indicates the first line of defence of *Clawdd-y-Milwyr* (The Warrior's Dyke), an Iron Age fort that occupied the very tip of this promontory. Although the Coast Path now ducks down to the other shore, you can continue over the dyke and see the three lines of defensive ditches crossing the headland.

Turning south, walk along the clifftop with the sandy cove of Porthmelgan down below. The path bumps gently down to the beach, a pleasant alternative to the crowds and ice creams of Whitesands. At mid-tide and lower, there are even some great caves to poke around in. From here, the Coast Path climbs back to Whitesands Bay. Just before reaching the car park, a memorial stone records the fact that there once stood a St Patrick's chapel here, built between the sixth and tenth centuries. St Patrick, a Welshman who became the patron saint of Ireland, is said to have sailed from here for Ireland in the late fourth century AD.

Although the major income from this part of west Pembrokeshire is now tourism, the stumpy remains of old mines, quarries and ports at Abereiddi and **Porthgain** bear witness to the slate and granite industries that once employed hundreds. Industry dies down towards **Trefin** and up to the more remote beaches and inlets that punctuate the coast as it climbs up to the splendid knuckle of **Strumble Head**. To the east is **Carregwastad Point**, the site of the last invasion of Britain in 1797. The event is also remembered in **Fishguard**, where local soldiers tricked the invading French into unconditional surrender at the *Royal Oak*

Inn in Upper Fishguard's neat little centre. Immediately either side of the upper town lie **Goodwick**, where ferries leave for Ireland, and cutely picturesque **Lower Fishguard**, most famous as the set for the glitzy 1971 movie version of *Under Milk Wood*, with the immortal coupling of Richard Burton and Elizabeth Taylor.

Abereiddi to Abercastell

A quiet lane leaves St David's and runs parallel to the coast across the rocky Pembrokeshire plateau, where the few trees have been blasted into spooky shapes by the relentless gusts off the Irish Sea. A small lane turns left five miles from St David's and tumbles down into the bleak hamlet of **ABEREIDDI**, at the head of its stony, black sand beach. You can find tiny fossilized animals in the shale on the beach, which can become extremely crowded in mid-summer. Above the beach are remains of workers' huts, industrial units and a tramway that once climbed over the hill to Porthgain, all part of the village's slate quarry that closed in 1904. Beyond the ruins, the old quarry was blasted for safety, producing an inland lagoon where the seawater, combined with the minerals, has turned a violent shade of bright blue, but is unfortunately not suitable for swimming in. Near Abereiddi is the homely and welcoming *Cwmwdig Water Guesthouse* (☎01348/831434; ③), tucked between the two lanes from Llanrihan and Croes-goch. A mile along the lane to Croes-goch is *Bank House Farm* (☎01348/831305; ②).

Following the Coast Path past the Blue Lagoon brings you down to **Traeth Llyfn**, about half a mile away; car drivers can take the track through *Barry Island Farm* halfway down the lane between Llanrihan and Porthgain. Traeth Llyfn is sandier and more peaceful than the beach at Abereiddi, although heed the warnings that currents are deceptively strong and can be perilous for mediocre swimmers.

The lane parallel to the coast passes the hamlet of Cwmwdig Water and leads to tiny **LLANRIHAN**, from where a left-hand turn descends over a mile or so to the rambling village green of **PORTHGAIN**, a fascinating old port that grew up around its slate works, the stumpy remains of which, together with an old brick-works, lime kiln and eerie ruins of workers' cottages, are huddled around the tiny quay. It also has the best pub in the county: the marvellous *Sloop Inn*, an eighteenth-century stone house with excellent beer, good food and numerous wall-mounted photographs of the old port in its sepia heyday. For pricier fare, the *Harbour Lights* (☎01348/831549) has a far-flung reputation for well-cooked local seafood and vegetables.

Two miles further east, where the lane intersects with the coast for the only time, is **Aber Draw**, a small and rugged beach just short of the village of **TREFIN** (Trevine). The natural rock chair by the village water pump used to be employed as the seat of a mock-mayor, elected annually from amongst the villagers. Trefin is well blessed with **B&Bs**: there's the *Hampton Stores* (☎01348/837701; ②) in the village centre or, opposite the old chapel on the main street, the superb *Old Court House* (☎01348/837095; ③), which also offers hearty vegetarian meals, pick-ups from Haverfordwest or Fishguard and all-in walking holiday packages. There's a YHA **hostel** in the old school on Ffordd-y-Avon (March–Oct; ☎01834/831414; ①) and, a few yards beyond, there's good B&B and **camping** at *Park Court Farm* (☎01834/831217; ②).The *Ship Inn* is good for food.

The coastal lane continues east to **ABERCASTELL**, past the 4500-year-old **Carreg Samson** cromlech (burial chamber), topped by a sixteen-foot capstone, at Longhouse. The vast capstone and its precarious supporting stones make for an awesome sight as you approach from Longhouse, framed as it is by lush hills, rocky inlets and the sea. If you're walking, continue past the cromlech and down to the coast path into Abercastell, whose harbour, once used for the export of limestone and coal, is now an attractive and popular spot, just above a muddy beach. From Abercastell, one of the best parts of the Coast Path zigzags east along the wild, vertiginous cliffs to the point at **Trwyn Llwynog**, about two miles away.

Mathry to Carregwastad Point

Deserted lanes and a beautiful stretch of Coast Path meander around the coast from Abercastle to the secluded bay at **Aber Mawr**, two miles directly north of the inland village of **MATHRY** (Mathri), where the ancient *Farmers Arms* (☎01348/831284; ③) does great B&B and excellent food and drink. Bang opposite the pub, **Jim Harries Woodturners** (workshop Mon–Fri 10am–12.30pm & 1.30–5pm; shop Mon–Fri 9.30am–6pm, Sat & Sun 10am–4pm) gives you the chance to see local craftsfolk at work and buy the finished products. It's pricey and aimed squarely at passing coach parties, but there are some decent affordable bits to be found. In the wooded valley above Aber Mawr, the *New Mill* (☎01348/891637; ②) at Tregwynt, near St Nicholas, is popular with Coast Path walkers. **Bike rental** is available from *Preseli Mountain Bikes* (☎01348/837709), at Parcynole Fach on the road between Mathry and St Nicholas.

Two miles east of the village of Mathry is **CASTLEMORRIS** (Casmorys), to the north of which is **Llangloffan Farm** (May–Sept Mon–Sat 10am–12.30pm; April & Oct Mon, Wed, Thurs & Sat 10am–12.30pm), whose homespun cheesemaking process is demonstrated to visitors. A mile and a half further north, the **Felin Tregwynt Woollen Mill** (free entry) is an old whitewashed stone place, where you can see wool being spun and processed and mooch around the inevitable gift shop. There are some interesting modern sculptures in the grounds.

The headland – known as **Pen Caer** – that rises to the north, peaking at **STRUMBLE HEAD**, is delightful: tiny hedge-backed lanes bump around between rocky cairns, fields of wild flowers and sudden glimpses of the shimmering sea. This is the closest the Welsh mainland gets to Ireland, and from its lofty heights you can usually see the ferries and hydrofoils zipping across the waters en route to and from Fishguard.

The Coast Path running up the west side of Pen Caer is remote and spectacular, affording a full panorama of views. Between the sandy stretch of Aber Mawr and the craggy Strumble Head, the only semi-accessible beaches are **Aber Bach**, immediately north of Aber Mawr, and the west-facing gash of **Pwllcochran**, a mile further north. There's a superbly sited **youth hostel** (April–Oct; ☎01348/891233; ①) above the strands of **PWLL DERI**, nearly two miles further north. **Camping** is also allowed here. Looming large on the inland side of the hostel are the three crags of **Garn Fawr** (699ft), most easily reached from the car park on their eastern edge, on the lane up to Strumble Head. Garn Fawr is easy to climb and well worth the effort: there are some impressive remains of ditches, ramparts and hut circles from its days as an early Iron Age fort, and, on a good day, you can see as far as the Wicklow Mountains of Ireland and the Llŷn peninsula and Snowdon in north Wales. Even if visibility doesn't allow such sights, the views over the headland and coast are quite gorgeous.

Strumble Head, a mile or two due north of Garn Fawr, is reached either by the rugged coast path – with astounding views over the two-mile long "wall" of cliffs to the south – or the far more gentle perambulation of a floral country lane. The

THE "SAINTS & STONES" TRAIL

Leaflets available from all local tourist offices describe this excellent **car or bike** trail, which leads around some of northern Pembrokeshire's most remote and atmospheric little **churches**. In each one, you'll find good information, a leaflet on the church and occasionally even a kettle and a tin of biscuits. The saints to whom the churches are dedicated are generally some of the lesser-known Celtic heroes; stones date from around the fifth century. Many of the sites predate Christianity as important places of worship, some as far back as the Bronze Age. You can follow the trail without deviation (a steepled church icon on a brown sign indicates the route) or dip into parts of it as you head around the lanes of north Pembrokeshire.

last farm before the headland is *Fferm Tresinwen* (☎01348/891621), a good place to **camp** for great walks along the promontories and coves of this enchanting stretch of coast. At the headland, the 1908 **lighthouse** is perched atop **Ynys Meicel**, connected to the mainland by a foreboding metal footbridge. It's a peaceful, invigorating spot: great for sea bird spotting and idly watching jet vapour trails in the sky (this is one of the principal routes into London's Heathrow Airport).

Between Strumble Head and the coat-tails of Fishguard, the riveted coast is best known for an historical quirk. This is the site of the last attempted invasion of Britain, by a rabble of Franco-Irish soldiers in 1797 (see also Fishguard for more detail). After having landed at **Carregwastad Point** (where the event is marked by a headstone), the disorganized army made its base at **Trehowel Farm**, midway between Strumble Head and the quiet little hamlet of **LLANWNDA**. Trehowel was stocked up with food and drink for an imminent family wedding, and a recent shipwreck had meant that most local farms were full of contraband liquor. The would-be conquerors set to the victuals with gusto, swiftly becoming too drunk to threaten an acquiescent doormouse. Their sole moment of derring-do came in attacking the idyllic little **church of St Gwyndaf** in Llanwnda, stealing some of the silver plate within. Although there are no mementoes of the church's most bizarre episode, it's well worth a visit, for its charming setting, ancient history that winds back beyond the eighth century and collection of pre-Norman carved stones, embedded in its walls. The mile-long path from Llanwnda to Carregwastad Point is a fabulous walk, as it coasts gently down fields and across the top of a craggy cwm. Go over the stile and along the path on the other side of the track from the church entrance.

Fishguard

The coast road runs around the bay, along The Parrog and past the 900-yard East Breakwater, before climbing sharply up Gas Works Hill to **FISHGUARD** (Abergwaun), occupying its own lofty headland. This is an enjoyably attractive town in its own right, with good views from its easy coast walk, but, unfortunately, is seldom seen as anything more than a brief stopping-off place to the ferries, which leave regularly for Rosslare in Ireland from the suburb of **Goodwick** (Wdig).

The road from Goodwick becomes West Street, which meets up by the town hall with the High Street and Main Street, and it's along these three streets that most of the town's shops, banks, pubs and restaurants lie. Near the town hall is the **Royal Oak Inn**, the scene of the Franco-Irish surrender in 1797 (see above). The hapless forces arrived to negotiate a ceasefire, which was turned by the assembled British into an unconditional surrender. Mementoes of the event can be seen in the pub. Part of the invaders' low morale – apart from the drunken farces in which they'd become embroiled – is said to have been sparked off by the sight of a hundred local women marching towards them. The troops mistook their stovepipe hats and red flannel dresses for the outfit of a British Infantry troop and instantly capitulated. Even if that is not true, it is an undisputed fact that 47-year-old cobbler Jemima Nicholas, the "Welsh Heroine", single-handedly captured fourteen French soldiers. Her grave can be seen next to the uninspiring Victorian **parish church**, St Mary's, behind the pub.

Main Street winds northeast before plummeting down around the coast towards **Lower Fishguard** (Cwm), a cluster of old-fashioned holiday cottages around a muddy, thriving pleasure-boat port – a total contrast to the vast operation on the other side of the town at Goodwick, where the ferries leave for Ireland. Views from Lower Fishguard over the town headland and to the port breakwater are superb.

Practicalities

Fishguard's **tourist office** (June–Aug daily 10am–5.30pm; April & May, Sept & Oct daily 10am–5pm; Nov–March Mon–Sat 10am–4pm; ☎01348/873484) is in the old town, at the bottom of Hamilton Street on Main Street, and local books, together with information on Ireland, can be found in the *Seaways* bookshop on West Street. **Buses** stop by the town hall in the central Market Square. A subsidiary tourist office (same times as main office; ☎01348/872037) has opened by the Goodwick ferry terminal.

The road arrives in the unprepossessing surroundings of Goodwick, where the **ferries** leave twice daily for Rosslare in Ireland (☎0990/707070); see p.6. The **train station** is next to the ferry terminal on Quay Road.

Accommodation is plentiful and cheap, with most places well used to visitors coming and going at odd times for the ferries. Next to the port is the faded elegance of the *Fishguard Bay Hotel* on Quay Road (☎01348/873571; ③). Up in Fishguard proper, the *Hamilton Guesthouse* (☎01348/874797; ①/②), at 21–23 Hamilton St, a minute's walk from the tourist office, offers cheerful B&B and a backpackers' dorm. Also central is the *Manor House Hotel* on Main Street (☎01348/873260; ③), with a restaurant serving wonderful local dishes. The nearest **camping** is at *Tregroes Touring Park* (☎01348/872316), a mile southwest of Fishguard just off the A40. This is very near Tregroes Moor, venue for the laid-back, music-oriented **Harvest Fair** festival (information on ☎01994/419323), which takes place over the late-August bank holiday.

Fishguard is well served for places to **eat** and **drink**. In the main town, there's the superb restaurant in the *Manor House Hotel* (see above), or, for cheaper daytime snacks, the splendid *Annie Francis Caffi Pobydd* on the roundabout by the town hall. Pub food is plentiful and reliable: try the nautically themed *Bennett's Navy Tavern* on the High Street or the upmarket, historical *Royal Oak*. For plain old drinking, try the earthy and beery *Fishguard Arms* on Main Street or the staunchly traditional *Cambrian Arms* on Hamilton Street. Tuesday is folk night at the *Royal Oak* – participants are especially welcome. Down in Lower Fishguard, the eccentric *Ship Inn* is unmissable, with good food and lots of interesting clutter all over the walls and ceiling.

Mynydd Preseli

In a county celebrated for some of the most magnificent coastal scenery in Britain, Pembrokeshire's interior is frequently overlooked. The **Mynydd Preseli** (Preseli Hills) occupy a triangle of land in the north of the county, roughly bounded by the coast in the north, the B4313 to the west and the A478 to the east, and flecked with prehistoric remains. After miles of sea bird-swirling coastline, the rickety walled lanes and gloomy bare hills come as a refreshing change.

From Fishguard, the Gwaun River wriggles southeast through its cwm, Europe's oldest glacial vale. It's a surprising slash of lush greenery through the barren, stone- and sheep-spattered hills, the tiny villages and remote churches seemingly untouched by the modern age. Indeed, residents of the Cwm Gwaun retain an attachment to the pre-1752 Julian calendar, celebrating New Year in the middle of January.

The main A487 coast road is the only major **bus** route hereabouts, cruising from Fishguard to Cardigan through the delightful small town of **Newport**, a fine and friendly base for the area. Just south of the town, the Preseli's most impressive and historic peak, **Carn Ingli**, beckons. Further south, the brooding mountains shelter innumerable standing stones, stone circles, hill forts, cairns and earthworks. Ancient sites – whether in the reconstructed Iron Age settlement at **Castell Henllys** or the bucolic church at **Nevern**, complete with 1500-year-old inscribed stones and a "bleeding" yew tree – are the mainstay of a visit to this powerful corner of Wales. As a further incentive, it's all close enough to the final (or first) stretch of the Pembrokeshire Coast Path. The cognoscenti's favourite part of the path is that between Newport and St Dogmael's, blessed with awesome solitude, abundant natural life and stunning coastal features, especially the cliff formations.

Newport, Nevern and the coast

The A487 skims all too quickly through **NEWPORT** (Trefdraeth), an ancient and proud little town, with a good deal to be proud about. Set on a gentle slope that courses down to the estuary of the Afon Nyfer, Newport still elects a mayor annually, a legacy of its days as the capital of the Norman Marcher Lordship of Cemmaes. One visible manifestation of this heritage is the annual custom, in August, of the "Beating of the Bounds", when the Mayor, the Lord Marcher and the local MP beat out the town's boundaries on horseback. Today, it's a quietly enjoyable place, with great shops, superb accommodation, food and drink, welcoming inhabitants and a selection of fine coastal and hill walks on the doorstep.

The Town and Carn Ingli

From the main street, Long Street and Lower St Mary Street head down to the tidal banks of the Afon Nyfer. A path hugs the southern shore of the estuary, over which squawking sea birds circle and skim the water's edge. Turn east (or take the Parrog Road in a car) for a gentle stroll along to the **Parrog**, Newport's nearest beach, complete with sandy stretches at low tide. The best nearby beach is the vast dune-backed **Traethmawr**, on the other side of the estuary, reached over the town bridge down Feidr Pen-y-Bont. Just short of the bridge, on the town side, **Carreg Coetan Arthur**, a well-preserved capped burial chamber, can be seen behind the newish holiday bungalows. The footpath that runs along the river either side of the bridge is marked as the Pilgrims' Way. Follow it eastwards for a delightful riverbank stroll to Nevern (see below), a couple of miles away. On Lower St Mary Street, the old school has metamorphosed into a spanking new youth hostel (see "Practicalities") and the excellent **Newport Eco House** (Mon–Fri 9.30am–4.30pm; free), a venue for exhibitions, advice and resources on various aspects of sustainable living.

South of the main street, a number of pretty thoroughfares rise up to the town's intriguing **castle** (private), a modern residence fashioned out of the medieval ruins. The other obvious landmark is the three-storeyed tower of the massive **St Mary's church**, an ancient site that was heavily "restored" by the Victorians. Fortunately, the church's original Norman font escaped the worst of their efforts. Follow Mill Lane, on the western flank of the castle, or Church Street, from the front of St Mary's, for the relatively easy two-hour ascent of **Carn Ingli** (Hill of Angels), once the core of an active volcano. The peak was inhabited perhaps as recently as Roman times – certainly, the stone embankments of the Iron Age hillfort and the nearby Bronze Age hut circles prove that this was some sizeable community before that. The hill's name comes from the belief that St Brynach lived here in quiet contemplation, with the angels as his companions.

The coast

Either side of Newport, the Coast Path runs through some sublime scenery. To the west of town, the path edges around the nodule of Dinas Head (also known as Dinas Island), en route to Fishguard. Two miles west of the Parrog, the most popular Dinas beach is the northeast-facing stretch at **CWM-YR-EGLWYS**, where the scant seafront ruins of the twelfth-century **St Brynach's church** are all that survived a huge storm on the night of October 25, 1859, when the rest of the church and some 114 ships at sea were wrecked.

The walk around Dinas Head offers splendid views over the huge cliffs and the thousands of nesting sea birds. On the other side of the "island", three-quarters of a mile west of Cwm-yr-Eglwys via the path through Cwm Dewi, or two and a half miles around the Coast Path and the headland, is the grey sand beach of **Pwllgwaelod**, accessible by car off the A487 through the dour village of Brynhenllan. Sadly, the *Sailors' Safety Inn*, where a light was kept burning to help the ships' navigation, closed after 401 years in 1994. It is now being converted into B&B accommodation. Next door, the *Old Sailors* tea room and restaurant is open throughout the summer season.

The segment of Coast Path to the east of Newport, running to the fringes of Cardigan at St Dogmael's, is perhaps the wildest stretch of the whole path. The only part accessible by car is at the spectacularly folded cliffs of **Ceibwr Bay**, eight miles from Newport near the pretty pastel village of **MOYLEGROVE** (Trewyddel). Any section along here is comparatively hard going: the path plummets and climbs along the ridged coast, passing rocky outcrops, blowholes, caves, natural arches, ancient defensive sites and thousands of sea birds.

Nevern, Pentre Ifan and Castell Henllys

Only a little more than a mile by road to the east of Newport, but about double that along the pleasant riverside walk, the straggling village of **NEVERN** (Nanhyfer) is darkly atmospheric, with a couple of intriguing sights. The ruined and overgrown **castle**, a thirteenth-century replacement of a Norman construction on the site of an earlier Welsh fortress, sits high above the village on a bluff. Below, the brooding bulk of the **church of St Brynach**, founded in the sixth century and with an intact Norman tower, has numerous features of interest. Before entering the churchyard, notice the parishioners' mounting block, for getting on and off a horse. The churchyard is roofed by ancient yews, giving it a dank, dark presence. Note the second tree on the right, the famous "**bleeding yew**", so called for the brown-red sap that oozes mysteriously from its bark. Legend has it that it will continue to bleed until a Welsh lord of the manor is reinstated in the village castle – unlikely, given its tumbledown state. Also outside the church, you can see the stunning **Great Cross**, an inscribed tenth-century Celtic masterpiece, some 13ft high, just by the main doorway. The interior of the church is no less interesting. If you stand at the back, you can easily divine how the chancel has been built 1° out of alignment with the nave, supposedly to represent Christ's inclined head on the cross. In the windowsills of the south transept, there are two ancient inscribed stones: one, the **Maglocunus Stone**, with Latin and Ogham inscriptions from about the fifth century AD, and the other, the **Cross Stone**, inscribed with a very early Celtic cross.

Lanes to the south of Nevern lead to the well-signposted cromlech at **Pentre Ifan**. This vast burial stone, with its sixteen-foot arrowhead topstone precariously balanced on large stone legs, dates back over four thousand years. The views from here are superb, situated as it is on the cusp of the stark, eerie Mynydd Preseli and the pastoral rolls of the countryside to the east. A couple of miles east of Nevern, signposted off the A487, the Iron Age hillfort of **Castell Henllys** (Easter–Oct daily 10am–5pm; £3) is undergoing archeological excavation that is turning up more and more of its past. Some recreated huts, complete with thatch, have been built on their prehistoric foundations and, throughout the summer, there are ample chances to try ancient skills, from basket weaving to rare animal husbandry. Sculpture trails through the woods and river valley bring to life the tales of the *Mabinogion*.

Practicalities

Newport is without doubt the best base in north Pembrokeshire. The cheerful national park **tourist office** (April–Sept Mon–Sat 10am–5.30pm; ☎01239/820912) is on Long Street, as is the **post office**, outside of which are boards full of local information. The wholefood shop, *Bwydydd Cyflawn*, on East Street has news of less mainstream events. **Bike rental** is available in town from the *Llysmeddyg* guesthouse, East Street (☎01239/820008).

There's plenty of **accommodation** here. The new youth hostel (☎01239/820080; ①) is a classy conversion of the old school on Lower St Mary Street. A mile south of town, there's a great independent bunkhouse at *Brithdir Mawr* (☎01239/820164; ①) on Ffordd Cilgwyn, at the bottom of the slopes of Carn Ingli. For cheapish B&B, there's *2 Spring Hill*, off the Parrog Road (☎01239/820626; ②) or *Hafan Deg*, off Long Street (☎01239/820301; ②). If your budget is a bit bigger, don't miss the superb *Cnapan Country House* on East Street (closed Feb; ☎01239/820575; ④). The nearest **campsite** is the *Morawelon* (☎01239/820565), just west of town at the Parrog. **Food** and **drink** is also plentiful: unbeatable are the exquisite meals, made from fresh local and even wild produce, at the *Cnapan Country House* (see above). Otherwise, there are solid pub classics, including a good veggie menu, at the *Royal Oak* on Bridge Street, good Indian meals, with Kashmiri specialities, at the *Llwyngwair Arms*, on East Street and great daytime snacks from the *Fronlas Café* and the *Fountain House Foods* deli on Market Street.

Elsewhere on Mynydd Preseli, the *Trewern Arms Hotel* in Nevern (☎01239/820395; ③) is a classy place to stay and eat, while above Ceibwr Bay near Moylegrove, *Cwmcornell* (☎01239/881691; ②) is a pleasant farmhouse B&B.

Cwm Gwaun and the inland hills

The valley of the burbling Afon Gwaun is one of the great surprises of Pembrokeshire. Surrounded as it is by bleak shoulders of bare mountain, the steep, wooded sides and lush vegetation of Europe's oldest glacial vale come as a complete contrast. Even if the locals weren't reputed to live by the pre-1752 Julian calendar, there would still be something other-worldly and timeless about Cwm Gwaun.

The B4313 leaves the skirts of Fishguard, heading southeast into the valley. At the first tiny settlement of **LLANYCHAER**,cross the river and head up the very steep lane to reach the **church** and "**cursing**" **well** of the lost settlement of **Llanllawer**, a few hundred yards further on. The well had a pre-Christian reputation for offering curses and ill omens if you left a bent pin, although most pilgrims sought miraculous cures, here especially for eye conditions. The lane running east opposite the well and church leads to seven large standing stones – the longest megalithic alignment in Wales – in **Parc y Merw** (the Field of the Dead), just short of Trellwyn Farm. Back on the main road, nearly a mile beyond Llanychaer, a lane branches off the B4313 to the left, soon crossing the river near a picnic site, from where there are some good walks up into the old oak forests that line the valley. Before long, the scattered settlement of **PONTFAEN**, complete with its timewarp pub (see p.194), is reached. If you double back on yourself at the *Dyffryn Arms*, following the lane that crosses the river and rises up a sharp hill, you soon reach Pontfaen's exquisitely restored **church**, dedicated, as are so many round here, to St Brynach. The circular graveyard indicates that this was a pre-Christian site of worship, before the church was traditionally founded by the wandering Breton saint in 540 AD. In the graveyard, there are two impressive stone crosses, dating from between the sixth and ninth centuries. By the mid-nineteenth century, the church was in ruins and it took the initiative and wealth of the Arden family, who moved to the adjoining Pontfaen House in the 1860s, to restore it. The intricate interior is notable for its squint, enabling all the congregation, including those in the "cheap" seats, to see what was going on, and a delicious early twentieth-century copy of a Fra Angelico *Madonna* painting.

Back on the lane that follows the Afon Gwaun, a further two miles brings you to the quite delightful **Gerddi Penlan-Uchaf** (Easter–Dec daily 9am–dusk; £1.75), a set of hillside gardens cut through by a stream with wonderful views over the valley. Their speciality lies in the thousands of miniature flowering and alpine plants, together with some impressive dwarf conifers.

It is further south and east that the brooding nature of the Mynydd Preseli makes itself most apparent. This is bleak, invigorating countryside, the wild, open hills scattered with the relics of ancient civilizations and, more often than not, the remains of dead sheep. On the southern slopes, near the village of **MYNACHLOG-DDU**, you'll see the characteristic Preseli blue stone, which was used to construct Stonehenge, some 140 miles away, between 2000 and 1500 BC. The main range of the Preselis lies just north of the village, crossed by an ancient trackway, in use for at least 3,500 years, known as the **Golden Road**. This is best reached from the Croesfihangel tumulus, on a minor lane a mile southwest of the village of Crymych, or, at the other end, at Bwlch-Gwynt, a mile south of Tafarn-y-Bwlch on the B4329. The track connects many of the Preselis' cairns and ancient sites, such as **Beddarthur**, an eerie stone circle that is supposed to be the great king's burial place, **Foeldrygarn** ("the Hill of Three Cairns"), with its hugely impressive Iron Age ramparts and hut circles and **Carn Menyn**, probably the quarry from which the majority of the Stonehenge boulders were mined.

Quarrying the stones of Preseli has gone on for thousands of years, and more modern examples can be seen near the weird little village of **ROSEBUSH**, just off the B4313 to the west of Mynachlog-Ddu. The bizarre nineteenth-century Klondike atmosphere of the place – complete with corrugated iron shacks – is partially explained by the fact that it was built quickly as a would-be resort by the Victorians on the arrival of the railway. Follow the path due north out of the village past the old slate quarries, mined into this century, through the coniferous blandness of Pantmaenog Forest and up onto the Golden Road. An alternative route, on the eastern edge of the forest, leads to the highest point of the mountain range (and, indeed, of Pembrokeshire), at **Foel Cwmcerwyn** (1760ft). This was the site of a legendary battle between King Arthur and his followers and the giant boar, Twrch Trwyth, as detailed in the *Mabinogion*. Topped by a Bronze Age cairn, the rounded hill sits above **Craig y Cwm**, the last glacial valley (c. 8000 BC) in the area.

From the *Tafarn Newydd* crossroads near Rosebush, the B4329 continues south towards Haverfordwest, with a right turn after about two miles signposted for **Llys-y-Frân**, a 187-acre reservoir and attendant country park. The modern visitor centre contains a surprisingly upmarket restaurant, *Merlin's Pantry* (booking essential on ☎01437/532694 or 532273), a useful shop and **bike rental** (March–Oct; ☎01437/532694).

Practicalities

The **Preseli Visitor Centre** at Rosebush is a decent start for leaflets and booklets about the area. Worth buying is the National Park's *Walking in the Preseli Hills* (£2.45). **Bike rental** is available either in Newport or Llys-y-Frân (see p.191 and above). **Accommodation** is varied: on the far side of the Cwm Gwaun from the Gerddi Penlan-Uchaf is the supremely relaxing *Tregynon Country Farmhouse Hotel* (☎01239/820531; ④), overlooking the valley and offering the highest standards of comfort and cuisine. Younger in outlook, just half a mile to the east, is the lively *Gellifawr* (☎01239/820343; ③): self-catering apartments and serviced accommodation complement the excellent bar, where you'll find sturdy meals and a regular line-up of music and entertainment. Also in the Cwm Gwaun, there's the excellent *Gwesty Penlan Oleu* (☎01348/881314; ②), a mile south of Llanychaer. **Camping** is easy enough – there's loads of good common land watered by trickling springs, or, if you need your home comforts, the *Gwaun Vale Touring Park* (☎01348/874698) is on the Fishguard side of Llanychaer.

For even more remote stays, *Yethen-Isaf* (☎01437/532256; ③) is a cheerful farmhouse B&B just over a mile west of Mynachlog-Ddu and handy for walks along and around the Golden Road. Rosebush makes for a good base – the *Old Post Office* (☎01437/532205; ③) is a great B&B and restaurant, particularly noted for its vegetarian specialities, and there's always the corrugated-iron *Tafarn Sinc* (*Zinc Tavern*) in which to while away an evening. Alternatively, just up the road at the B4313/B4329 crossroads, the *Tafarn Newydd* (*New Inn*) hosts frequent folk and other music sessions. There's also a campsite, the *Rosebush Caravan &*

Camping Park (March–Oct; ☎01437/532206) in the village. Pubs in the area worth checking out are *Gellifawr* (see above), *Tate's* at *Tafarn Newydd*, near Rosebush, and the *Bridge End Inn* at Llanychaer; all serve food. Pure **drinking**, however, is best done at the rustic, remote *Dyffryn Arms* at Pontfaen, where you can enjoy good company in an old-fashioned living room.

travel details

Unless otherwise stated, frequencies for trains and buses are for Monday to Saturday services; Sunday averages 1–3 services, though the main routes are more frequent and some routes have no Sunday service at all.

Trains

Carmarthen to: Cardiff (6 daily; 1hr 40min); Ferryside (11 daily; 10min); Fishguard Harbour (1 daily; 55min); Haverfordwest (10 daily; 40min); Kidwelly (10 daily; 15min); Llanelli (hourly; 25min); London (2 daily; 4hr 30min); Milford Haven (hourly; 1hr); Narberth (8 daily; 25min); Pembroke (8 daily; 1hr 10min); Swansea (hourly; 45min); Tenby (8 daily; 45min); Whitland (hourly; 15min).

Fishguard Harbour to: Cardiff (2 daily; 2hr 20min); Swansea (2 daily; 1hr 30min).

Haverfordwest to: Cardiff (7 daily; 2hr 30min); Carmarthen (12 daily; 40min); Milford Haven (11 daily; 20min); Swansea (10 daily; 1hr 30min).

Llanelli to: Cardiff (6 daily; 1hr 20min); Carmarthen (hourly; 25min); Llandeilo (5 daily; 40min); Llandovery (5 daily; 1hr); Llandrindod Wells (5 daily; 1hr 45min); Llanwrtyd Wells (5 daily; 1hr 25min); Pembrey & Burry Port (hourly; 5min); Shrewsbury (5 daily; 3hr 30min); Swansea (hourly; 20min).

Tenby to: Cardiff (2 daily; 2hr 35min); Carmarthen (8 daily; 45min); Lamphey (8 daily; 17min); Narberth (8 daily; 20min); Pembroke & Pembroke Dock (8 daily; 20 & 25min); Penally (8 daily; 2min); Swansea (8 daily; 1hr 35min); Whitland (8 daily; 30min).

Whitland to: Cardiff (11 daily; 2hr); Carmarthen (hourly; 15min); Haverfordwest (10 daily; 25min); Milford Haven (10 daily; 40min); Narberth (8 daily; 10min); Pembroke (8 daily; 50min); Swansea (hourly; 1hr); Tenby (8 daily; 30min).

Buses

Carmarthen to: Aberaeron (6 daily; 1hr 40min); Aberystwyth (3 daily; 2hr 35min); Cardigan (hourly & 2 journeys Sun; 1hr 30min); Cenarth (10 daily; 1hr 5min); Drefach Felindre (7 daily; 50min); Haverfordwest (7 daily; 55min); Kidwelly (8 daily; 25min); Lampeter (6 daily; 1hr 10min); Laugharne (hourly; 35min); Llanarthne (4 daily; 30min); Llandeilo (5 daily; 35min); Llandovery (5 daily; 1hr 15min); Llansteffan (5 daily; 20min); Manorbier (4 daily; 1hr 25min); Nantgaredig (5 daily; 20min); Narberth (6 daily; 40min); Newcastle Emlyn (hourly; 1hr); New Quay (4 daily; 1hr 30min); Pembrey (4 daily; 30min); Pembroke (6 daily; 1hr 40min); Pendine (hourly; 50min); Saundersfoot (4 daily; 45min); Swansea (hourly; 1hr 30min); Tenby (5 daily; 1hr); Trelech (6 daily; 45min).

Fishguard to: Cardigan (hourly; 50min); Haverfordwest (hourly; 45min); Newport (hourly; 30min); St David's (7 daily; 50min); Trefin (7 daily; 35min).

Haverfordwest to: Broad Haven (5 daily; 15min); Cardigan (hourly; 1hr 40min); Carmarthen (7 daily; 55min); Dale (2 daily Tues & Fri; 35min); Fishguard (hourly; 45min); Manorbier (hourly; 1hr 10min); Marloes (Tues & Fri 1 bus; 35min); Narberth (6 daily; 15min); Newgale (hourly; 20min); Newport, Dyfed (hourly; 1hr 10min); Pembroke (hourly; 50min); St David's (hourly; 50min); Solva (hourly; 40min); Tenby (hourly; 1hr 25min).

Llandeilo to: Carmarthen (6 daily; 35min); Llandovery (8 daily; 35min); Talley (Tues & Fri 1 daily; 20min).

Milford Haven to: Dale (school service; 25min); Marloes (school service; 40min); Pembroke (hourly; 40min).

Pembroke to: Bosherston (3 daily Mon–Fri; 1hr); Carmarthen (4 daily; 1hr 40min); Castlemartin (3 daily; 30min); Freshwater East (2 daily Mon–Fri; 10min); Haverfordwest (hourly; 50min); Manorbier (hourly; 20min); Milford Haven (hourly; 40min); Pembroke Dock (numerous; 10min); Saundersfoot (2 daily; 50min); Stackpole (2 daily Mon–Fri; 50min); Tenby (hourly; 40min).

Pembroke Dock to: Carew (5 daily; 10min); Pembroke (numerous; 10min); Saundersfoot (5 daily; 45min); Tenby (5 daily; 1hr).

Tenby to: Amroth (hourly; 40min); Carew (7 daily; 35min); Carmarthen (5 daily; 1hr); Haverfordwest (hourly; 1hr 25min); Manorbier (hourly; 20min); Narberth (4 daily; 55min); Pembroke (hourly ; 40min); Pembroke Dock (5 daily; 1hr); St Florence (hourly; 12min); Saundersfoot (every 30min; 15min).

CHAPTER THREE

POWYS AND THE DEE VALLEY

T he great tranche of inland mid-Wales is often viewed as little more than a corridor by which to reach the coast. Nothing could be further from the truth, for some of Wales' most enjoyable towns and scenery are to be found here, even if not everyone has yet discovered this secret.

The vast county of **Powys** takes up a full quarter of Wales, its southern end dominated by the **Brecon Beacons National Park**, stretching from the moody heights of the Black Mountain in the west, through the gentler Beacons themselves, and out to the English border beyond the confusingly named Black Mountains. The main centres within the Beacons are Abergavenny (see Chapter One, p.62), in the far southeast, and the small city of **Brecon**, a curious mix of traditional market town, army garrison and often very pretty tourist centre.

The bleaker part of the Beacons lies to the west, around the raw peaks of the **Black Mountain** and **Fforest Fawr**. A few roads cut through the glowering countryside, connecting popular attractions such as the immense **Dan-yr-ogof caves**, opera prima donna Adelina Patti's gilded home and theatre at nearby **Craig-y-nos** and the quite stunning caves and waterfalls around the walking centre of **Ystradfellte**. Walkers are equally well catered for in settlements like **Crickhowell** and **Talgarth**, small towns set in quiet river valleys.

At the northern corner of the National Park, the border town of **Hay-on-Wye** draws in thousands to see the town's dozens of bookshops, housed in warehouses, the old castle and outdoor yards. West of Hay, the peaks of the **Mynydd Eppynt** now form a vast training ground for the British army, on the other side of which lie the old spa towns of Radnorshire – earthy **Llanwrtyd Wells**, moribund **Llangammarch Wells**, the gritty centre of **Builth Wells** and twee **Llandrindod Wells**. The countryside to the north, crossed by spectacular mountain roads such as the **Abergwesyn Pass** from Llanwrtyd, is barely populated and beautiful – quiet, occasionally harsh country, dotted with ancient churches and introspective villages, from the border towns of **Presteigne** and **Knighton**, home of the flourishing **Offa's Dyke path** industry, to inland centres like **Rhayader**, the nearest centre of population for the grandiose reservoirs of the **Elan Valley**.

Montgomeryshire is the northern portion of Powys, similarly underpopulated and remote as its two southern siblings. In common with most of mid-Wales, country towns such as the beautiful **Llanidloes** has a healthy stock of old hippies amongst its population, resulting in a greater-than-expected presence of health-food shops, healing groups and arts activity. To the west, the inhospitable mountain of **Plynlimon** is flecked with boggy heathland and gloomy reservoirs, beyond which is the popular and hearty town of Machynlleth, stranded out on a limb of Powys (see

The Cambrian Coast, p.282). The eastern side of Montgomeryshire is home to the anglicized old county town, **Montgomery**, between the robust town of **Welshpool**, on the English border, and the downbeat centre of **Newtown**, worth visiting only for devotees of early socialist **Robert Owen**, who was born there. The northern segment of the county is even quieter, with regional centres like **Llanfyllin** and **Llanrhaeadr-ym-mochnant** that are little more than villages, leaving the few crowds seen around here to cluster along the banks of **Lake Vyrnwy**, a flooded-valley reservoir which has harmoniously moulded itself into the landscape around it.

Immediately north of Powys is the mountainous strip of land stretching up the **Dee Valley**, an area that combines northern ruggedness (it's a well-defined route into Snowdonia) with the smoother border countryside of Powys and the Marches. Though **Chirk Castle** is the only significant, extant Marcher fortress, it remains a potent reminder of the centuries after the Norman conquest of England, when powerful barons fought the Welsh princes for control of these fertile lands. The Dee Valley remained more firmly Welsh than the Marches, and three hundred years after the arrival of the Normans was the site of the first big revolt against them. From his base near **Corwen**, Wales' greatest hero, Owain Glyndŵr, attacked the property of a nearby English landowner, sparking a fourteen-year campaign which, at its height, saw Glyndŵr ruling most of Wales by means of Parliaments held on the Cambrian coast (see Chapter Four, p.284). Little remains in the valley to commemorate the era, and most people drive through oblivious of its heritage. **Llangollen** is the valley's main draw, with an international *eisteddfod* folk music festival each July and a broad selection of ruins, rides and rambles to tempt visitors throughout the rest of the year.

Getting around

Road transport in Powys and the Dee Valley is fairly easy, with the swift A40 and A438 running from Gwent and England to Carmarthen, Brecon and the west. Further north, the A44 heads into Radnorshire from Leominster in Herefordshire. The A458 heads off the north Wales-bound A5 at Shrewsbury down to Welshpool and Montgomeryshire. Stay on the main A5 for access to Llangollen and the Dee Valley. This makes getting to the mountains easy, but tends to force **cyclists** onto quieter roads such as the B4401 through the Vale of Edeyrnion, and the narrow lanes at the head of Glyn Ceiriog.

Public transport takes more forward planning. **Train** services are restricted to a stop at Chirk on the Chester–Shrewsbury line, the Heart of Wales line from Shropshire to Swansea via Knighton, Llandrindod Wells, Llanwrtyd Wells and smaller stops in between and the Shrewsbury–Machynlleth route through Welshpool and Newtown. Larger centres such as Brecon, Llanidloes, Rhayader, Builth Wells, Hay-on-Wye and Llangollen have no stations. For them, and for the rest of this huge area, sporadic **bus** services (including school and post services) provide the only access. Staples of the mid-Wales bus scene include the two-hourly #94 from Wrexham, through Llangollen, Corwen, Bala and on to Dolgellau on the Cambrian coast, and the twice-daily #47, which runs up the spine of southern Powys from Brecon through Builth to Llandrindod Wells, where it meets connections for Newtown, Welshpool and the north. Nearby towns such as Wrexham, Abergavenny, Machynlleth and, over the border, Oswestry, provide useful intersection points. Excellent free maps – the *Powys Bus and Rail Guide* and the *Clwyd Public Transport Guide* – are obtainable from libraries, tourist offices and main post offices, giving details of operators and their different services.

POWYS

Aside from the new industrial county boroughs, the only Welsh county with no coastline is **Powys**, extending from the fringes of the Glamorgan valleys south of the Brecon Beacons, through the sparsely populated lakelands of Radnorshire and up to the open moorland of the Berwyn Mountains. The county shares all of its eastern border with England, with fingers of rural Shropshire and Herefordshire poking into the Welsh landscape. Powys has only been a county since local government reorganization in 1974, but its name harks back to a fifth-century Welsh kingdom. The modern county is an amalgamation of three old ones: Brecknockshire (centred around Brecon and the Beacons), Radnorshire and Montgomeryshire.

The biggest tourist draws hereabouts are the **Brecon Beacons National Park**, the spa towns of **Radnorshire** and the bibliophilic border town of **Hay-on-Wye**. These are all in the southern half of the county, but there's plenty elsewhere for the adventurous visitor. Glassy lakes, remote hill walking, cheerful little towns and rumps of ancient Celtic history appear throughout, as do centres dedicated to watching the graceful red kite, in its only UK natural habitat, and numerous initiatives in green tourism, from quirky festivals to coracle-building holidays.

Brecon

BRECON (Aberhonddu) is a sturdy county town at the northern edge of the Beacons, whose proliferation of well-proportioned Georgian buildings bears testimony to its past importance, but it's for the town's proximity to the national park that most people come here. A Roman fort was built near here, but the town only started to grow with the building of a Norman castle and Benedictine monastery, founded in 1093 on the banks of the Honddu River, which gives the town its Welsh name. To the dual strands of military and ecclesiastical importance was added the status of regional market centre and cloth weaving town. In the seventeenth-century Civil War, the townsfolk unequivocally demonstrated their neutrality between the forces of Parliament and the Crown by demolishing most of the castle and large sections of the town walls, dissipating the appeal for either side of seizing their town.

Today, many fair-weather walkers base themselves here and explore the well-waymarked hills to the south of the town, including **Pen y Fan**, the highest, most challenging peak in south Wales. Brecon is also a good base for sedentary tourists, with an appealing jumble of architecture and a good social scene.

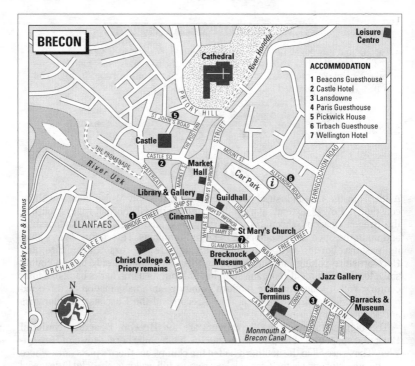

Information and accommodation

The **tourist office** (Easter–Oct daily 10am–6pm; Nov–Easter Tues–Sun 9.30am–5.15pm; ☎01874/622485) and **National Park office** (Easter–Oct daily 9.30am–5.30pm) share the same building in the Lion Yard car park off Lion Street, next to the cattle market. The tourist office includes a bureau de change and holds details of local bus services, which leave from The Bulwark, and also provides details of the town's annual **jazz festival** (☎01874/625557), held over a long weekend in mid-August. For details of gigs and other local events, look in the window of *F H Jones* newsagents in The Bulwark or on the boards in the Market Hall foyer on High Street Superior.

Accommodation

Brecon is a compact town with much **accommodation** to suit all pockets, and Llanfaes, across the river from the main town, has plenty of smaller hotels and B&Bs on its main street. Be warned, though, that rooms in Brecon can be tricky to come by during the jazz festival.

HOTELS AND GUESTHOUSES

Beacons Guest House, 16 Bridge St, Llanfaes (☎01874/623339). Rambling converted town house in an excellent position. Good, cheap evening meals also available. ③.

Castle Hotel, Castle Square (☎01874/624611). Large and sumptuous hotel built into the castle ruins, overlooking the Usk. ⑤.

Lansdowne Hotel, 39 The Watton (☎01874/623321). Classy town-centre hotel in a handsome Georgian corner house. ④.

Llanfaes Guest House, Llanfaes (☎01874/611115). Exclusively lesbian and gay retreat in a pleasant Georgian town house. Phone for details. ③.

Paris Guest House, 28 The Watton (☎01874/624205). Smart Georgian house converted into a low-key, friendly town-centre hotel. ③.

Pickwick House, St John's Road (☎01874/624322). Warm and welcoming town-house B&B near the cathedral, with excellent home-cooked evening meals on offer. ③.

Tirbach Guest House, 13 Alexandra Rd (☎01874/624551). Small and pleasant B&B behind the cattle market. ②.

Wellington Hotel, The Bulwark (☎01874/625225). Imposing old coaching inn that dominates the town's main square. ④.

HOSTELS, BUNKHOUSES AND CAMPSITES

Brynich Caravan and Camping Park, Brynich (☎01874/623325). Situated a mile east of town, just off the A40, overlooking the town and the river.

Cantref Bunkhouse, *Cantref Pony Trekking Centre*, near Llanfrynach (☎01874/665223). Overlooking the Cynrig River, two miles southeast of Brecon. Dormitory-style accommodation with kitchen and showers. Also takes campers, who can pitch tents in the grounds. ①.

Cwmgwdi Farm, two miles from central Brecon (☎01874/622034). Very basic – and quiet – campers' field, on the leftmost lane from Llanfaes' Ffrwdgrech Road.

Llwyn-y-Celyn youth hostel, Libanus, seven miles southwest of Brecon (☎01874/624261). Isolated farmhouse hostel, just off the A470 and main bus route to Merthyr. Camping permitted. Closed Dec to mid-Feb. ①.

The Held Bunkhouse, Cantref, Brecon (☎01874/624646). Basic, but comfortable and warm hostel accommodation a mile south of Brecon's western suburb of Llanfaes (take the Bailhelig Road). ①.

Ty'n-y-Caeau youth hostel, Groesfford, just over two miles east of Brecon (☎01874/665270). The nearest YHA hostel to Brecon, reached via the path (Slwch Lane) from Cerrigcochion Road in town or a mile from bus stops at either Cefn Brynich lock (Brecon–Abergavenny buses) or Troedyrharn Farm (Brecon–Hereford buses). Closed Dec–Feb. ①.

The Town

Buses decant their passengers in **The Bulwark**, Brecon's imposing central square, flanked by the solid-red sixteenth-century tower of the otherwise unremarkable **St Mary's church**, an assortment of old-fashioned shop frontages and the elegant Georgian portico of the **Wellington Hotel**.

At the junction of The Bulwark and Glamorgan Street is the neo-Grecian frontage of the **Brecknock Museum** (Mon–Sat 10am–1pm & 2–5pm; April–Sept also Sun; free), where a display of local trades includes a recreated smithy and a collection of agricultural implements unique to the area. More interesting are the walk-through history of Wales and a nineteenth-century assize court, last used in 1971 and preserved in all its ponderous splendour, overseen by the high judge's throne as if judgements came from God himself. Back near the entrance is a collection, dating back as far as four hundred years, of painstakingly carved Welsh love spoons that were betrothal gifts for courting Welsh lovers.

Running east from The Bulwark is **The Watton**, overlooked by the foreboding frontage of the South Wales Borderers' **barracks**, opposite which is its **museum** (April–Sept Mon–Sat 9am–1pm & 2–5pm; Oct–March Mon–Fri 9am–1pm & 2–5pm; £1), packed with mementoes from the regiment's three-hundred-year existence. Amongst the gung ho bravado, most noticeable are the tales of the 1879 Zulu War when 140 Welsh soldiers defended against an attack by 4000 Zulu warriors. Further along The Watton, Watton Chambers houses the new **Oriel Jazz** gallery (Easter–Oct Mon & Tues 11am–5pm, Wed–Sun 11am–7pm; Oct–Easter daily noon–5pm; free). Capitalizing on Brecon's astonishingly successful annual jazz festival, the gallery presents a fascinating romp through the archives of twentieth-century music, from the slavery rhythms of West Africa, through New Orleans, Chicago and New York to Europe, with rare video footage of some of the jazz greats. From The Watton, a series of small streets runs down to the new canal centre at the northern terminus of the **Monmouth and Brecon Canal**, where afternoon cruises aboard the *Dragonfly* (☎0831/685222; £4) ease their way out of town for an enjoyably relaxed round trip.

North and west of The Bulwark are a cluttered grid of streets, packed with Georgian and Victorian buildings. The High Street Inferior is the main route northwest, passing the **Sarah Siddons** pub, converted from the 1755 birthplace of the great actress. High Street Inferior quickly comes to a car-congested crossroads. Straight ahead, Ship Street descends down to the **River Usk**, the bridge crossing the Usk next to the point where the smaller Honddu River flows in from the north. Over the Usk, the southern suburb of **Llanfaes** is best known for its Dominican **friary**, whose ruined thirteenth-century church is now the centrepiece of **Christ College** school, on the immediate western side of the Usk. The main road continues through Llanfaes and out to the A40 bypass roundabout and the unlikely home of the **Welsh Whisky Visitor Centre** (daily 9am–5pm; £2), where you'll find Welsh gin, whisky and even *Taffski* vodka, a little-known commodity and considerably better than you might think. The two main whiskies (*chwisgi*) are a robust standard *Sŵn-y-Mor*, or "sound of the sea", and a fine malt called the *Prince of Wales*. The visitor centre – with the aid of a ghostly robotic monk called Dafydd – takes you through the history of the nation's whisky production, which reputedly dates back to the fourth century AD and a monastic distillery on Bardsey Island on the Llŷn peninsula. You learn, for instance, that Jack Daniel, eponymous hero of bourbon production, was a Cardiganshire man, and get to sample and buy the products.

From the town centre crossroads, High Street Superior goes north, past the long **Market Hall**, home of a twice-weekly produce market (Tues & Fri) and, on the third Saturday of each month, an excellent **craft market**. The road becomes The Struet, running alongside the rushing waters of the Honddu. Off to the left, Priory Hill and, a few yards further on, a footpath (signposted "Public Conveniences") climb up to the stark grey buildings of the monastery settlement, centred on the **cathedral**, or Priory Church of St John the Baptist. The building's dumpy external appearance belies its lofty interior, graced with a few Norman features intact from the eleventh-century priory that was built here on the site of a probable earlier Celtic church. The hulking Norman font sits at the western end of the nave, near the entrance and the unusual stone cresset, a large boulder indented with thirty scoops in which to place torches. Of the many family monuments in the nave, the most interesting is the **Games monument** (1555), in the southern aisle, made up from three oak beds and depicting an unknown woman whose hands remain intact in prayer, but whose arms and nose have been unceremoniously hacked off. The fine vaulting in the elegant choir is the nineteenth-century work of prolific restorationist Gilbert Scott, who worked on St Asaph and St David's cathedrals, and designed St Pancras Station in London. There's a new, and mildly interesting, **heritage centre** (Easter–April, Oct & Nov Mon–Sat 10.30am–3pm; May–Sept Mon–Sat 10am–5pm; free) open in a converted six-teenth-century tithe barn in the cathedral close.

Between the cathedral and the River Usk, the few remains of the town's **castle** are moulded into the walls of the *Castle Hotel*. The end result is a powerful, if bizarre, amalgam that looks its best from along **The Promenade** by the River Usk, reached from the town-centre side of the river bridge. In high summer, motor and rowing boats can be rented along the river bank.

Eating and drinking

As an important regional centre first and foremost, Brecon has always been well served for **food** and **drink**. It's a lively and cosmopolitan town, although some of the pubs in the near vicinity of the barracks are definitely worth avoiding.

Restaurants and cafés

Beacons Guest House, 16 Bridge St, Llanfaes (☎01874/623339). Open to non-residents for excellent, inexpensive lunches, teas and dinners, many inspired by traditional Welsh recipes.

Brecon Tandoori, Glamorgan Street (☎01874/624653). Traditional curry house just along from the old Shire Hall, behind The Bulwark.

Castle Hotel, Castle Square (☎01874/624611). Worth investigating for the good-value fixed dinner menu in this enjoyable restaurant in the town's smartest hotel.

Coracle Café, High Street Inferior. Friendly place with a good daytime menu of snacks and inexpensive, hearty meals.

La Brasseria, 22a High St Superior (☎01874/611313). Old Spanish-style upstairs brasserie, big on oak beams and a solid, reasonably priced fish and meat menu.

The Oak, 12 The Bulwark (☎01874/625501). Great daytime eatery that transforms into a stylish, enjoyable evening restaurant serving some excellent, inexpensive local dishes.

Watergate Fish Bar, Ship Street. Brightly lit traditional chip shop, with tables so you can eat in, almost on the bridge itself.

Pubs

Boars Head, Ship Street. Two very different bars: the front is basic and the best place to meet locals, whereas the back bar is loud and resembles a youth club.

Bull's Head, The Struet. Small and cheery locals' pub, with views over the Honddu River and towards the cathedral. Good-value food and regular live music and quizzes.

Gremlin Hotel, The Watton. Ancient pub with an informal atmosphere and great selection of bar snacks and larger meals (not Sun and Mon evenings).

Old Cognac, High Street Inferior. No-nonsense town pub, offering cholesterol-packed lunchtime food.

Sarah Siddons, High Street Inferior. Named after the famous actress, born here when the pub was known as the *Shoulder of Mutton*. A replica of Gainsborough's aloof portrait of her now forms the pub sign. A busy, popular pub, often full of off-duty soldiers.

Wellington Hotel, The Bulwark. Surprisingly unstuffy hotel bar, a frequent venue for live music, especially jazz.

Activities and entertainment

Just off the A470 (turn off at Libanus), five miles southwest of the town, the **Brecon Beacons Mountain Centre** (daily March–June & Sept–Oct 10.30am–5pm; July &

August 10am–6pm; Nov–Feb 10.30am–4.30pm; ☎01874/623366) sits on a windy ridge, amongst gorse heathland, overlooking some of the most inspiring scenery in the Beacons. As well as an excellent café, there are interesting displays on the flora, fauna, geology and history of the area, together with a well-stocked shop of maps, books and walking gear. Waymarked walks, both locally around the lofty heath and across the river valley to the more challenging peaks of Corn Du and Pen y Fan, lead away from the centre. Buses leave Brecon for Merthyr, with a stop at Libanus school, from where it is a one-mile uphill walk along the lane next to the church up to the centre. Four miles southeast of town, between the villages of Llanfrynach and Pencelli, the **Water Folk Canal Centre** has a small museum (Easter–Oct Mon–Thurs, Sat & Sun 10am–5.30pm; £1.50) stuffed with canal art and memorabilia and, more excitingly, also runs horse-drawn barge trips (Easter–Oct Wed, Sat & Sun noon & 3pm; August daily noon & 3pm; £3).

The town is well served for sports and recreational facilities: the old-fashioned *Coliseum* **cinema** is on Wheat Street (☎01874/622501), near the central crossroads, and there's an indoor **swimming pool** and impressive new leisure centre a mile northeast of the centre on the Cerrigcochion Road at Penlan (☎01874/623677). *Kevin Walker Mountain Activities*, 74 Beacons Park (☎01874/625111), organize hill walking, survival courses, caving, rock-climbing and abseiling trips. For **bike rental**, the *Beacons Experience*, near the Mountain Centre at *Forest Lodge Farm*, Libanus (☎01874/636799) will deliver and collect its flashy mountain bikes within the Brecon area.

The Brecon Beacons

With the lowest profile of Wales' three national parks, the **Brecon Beacons** are the destination of thousands of urban walkers largely from the industrial areas of south Wales and the West Midlands of England. Spongy hills of heather and rock tumble and climb around river valleys that lie between sandstone and limestone uplands, peppered with glass-like lakes and villages that seem to have been hewn from one rock. Known for their vivid quality of light, the hills of the Beacons disappear and re-emerge from hazy blankets of cloud, with shafts of sun sharpening lush green fields out of a dullened patchwork.

The National Park straddles Powys from west to east, covering 520 square miles. Most remote is the area at the far western side, where the vast, open terrain of **Fforest Fawr** and the **Black Mountain** form miles of tufted moorland and bleak, often dangerous peaks in the north, tumbling down to a region of porous limestone in the south. Here is a rocky terrain of rivers, deep caves and spluttering waterfalls, especially around the village of **Ystradfellte** and in the chasms of the **Dan-yr-ogof caves**.

East of Brecon, the series of interlocked peaks known as the **Black Mountains** stretch all the way to the English border, offering the region's most varied scenery, with the wide valley of the River Usk, home to the main settlement of **Crickhowell** and the beautiful double castle at **Tretower**, alongside almost impossibly green hills. Lying underneath the northern bluff of the mountains is the pleasant border town of **Hay-on-Wye**, at the point where the mountainous Brecon Beacons dissolve into the softer contours of Radnorshire.

BRECON BEACONS NATIONAL PARK

Black Mountain

The most westerly expanse of upland in the national park is known as the **Black Mountain** (Mynydd Ddu), rising between the A4069 and A4067, eight miles south of Llandovery (see p.144). Although the mountain is named in the singular, it covers an unpopulated range of barren, smooth-humped peaks that break suddenly at rocky escarpments towering over quiet streams and glacial lakes. This area provides the most challenging and exhilarating walking in south Wales and has long been popular with trippers from the Valleys, just a few miles south. Paths cross the wet, wild landscape from Dan-yr-ogof in the east, from the soaring ruins of **Carreg Cennen Castle** (see p.143), just short of Llandeilo in the west, from Tyhwnt, near Ystradgynlais, in the south and, in the north, from the hamlet of **LLANDDEU-SANT**, seven miles south of Llandovery, home to a charming YHA **hostel** (☎01550/740634; ①) in the former village pub. Three miles west of Llanddeusant, you can **camp** at the pleasant *Pont Aber Inn* (☎01550/740202) on the main A4069. The best walks from Llanddeusant run along wooded gulches and moorland bluffs to the twin glacial lakes of **Llyn y Fan Fach** and **Llyn y Fan Fawr**. Llyn y Fan Fach features in one of Wales' most oft-told myths of a beautiful maiden, together with her herd of magic cattle, who rose from the lake to marry a local farmer. The maiden's father had sanctioned the union only on the condition that if the farmer struck his daughter three times, she would return to the lake. Such occasions inadvertently occurred, the final blow being either when he slammed a gate and hit her or when he shook her at a funeral for laughing. The maiden silently left the man and, with her cattle, disappeared beneath the lake's icy waters once more. The round trip from Llanddeusant to both the lakes is around ten miles, and provides often bleak and lonely walking through valleys cut between purple hills, slashed with tumbling streams. This is classic glacial scenery: occasional mounds and moraines of rock debris indicate the force of the ice pushing through the valleys. Such heaps sometimes grew to a size large enough to form a natural dam, building up a lake, such as Llyn y Fan Fach, in its wake.

From Llyn y Fan Fach, a precarious path leads around the top of the escarpment, following the ridge to **Fan Brycheiniog** (2630ft), above the glassy black waters of Llyn y Fan Fawr. A remote path heads from here to the cross-moor road, two miles away.

The Fforest Fawr

Covering a vast expanse of hilly landscape between the Black Mountain and the central Beacons southwest of Brecon, **Fforest Fawr** (Great Forest) seems something of a misnomer for an area of largely unforested sandstone hills dropping down to a porous limestone belt in the south. The "forest" tag refers more to the old definition of a forest as land used as a hunting ground.

The hills rise up to the south of the A40 west of Brecon, with the A4067 Sennybridge–Ystradgynlais road piercing the western side of the range and the A470 Brecon–Merthyr road defining the Fforest's eastern limit. Between the two, a twisting mountain road rises up out of the fertile valley of the Senni River three miles south of Sennybridge, straining up to cross the bleak plateau towards the top of Fforest Fawr and descending into the limestone crags around the hamlet of **YSTRADFELLTE**, little more than a handful of houses, a church and a pub, the popular *New Inn*. It is, however, a phenomenally popular centre for walking, as a result of the dazzling countryside on its doorstep. Lush, deep ravines – a total contrast to the barren mountains immediately to the north – carve their way through the limestone ridge south of the village, with great pavements of bone-white rock littering fields next to cradling potholes, disappearing rivers and crashing waterfalls. As a classic limestone landscape, the Ystradfellte district is recognized as one of the most impressive in the British Isles.

A mile south of Ystradfellte, the River Mellte tumbles into the dark and icy mouth of the **Porth-yr-ogof** (White Horse Cave), emerging into daylight a few hundred yards further south. It's a mighty sight, as the clear water tumbles into a gaping hole overhung by a great shelf of limestone. A signposted path heads south from the Porth-yr-ogof car park and into the green gorge of the River Mellte. Continue for little more than a mile to the first of its three great waterfalls, **Sgwd Clun-Gwyn** (White Meadow Fall), where the river crashes 50ft over two huge, angular steps of rock before hurtling down course for a few hundred yards to the other two falls, the graceful **Sgwd Isaf Clun-Gwyn** (Lower White Meadow Fall), and, a little further on, the mighty **Sgwd y Pannwr** (Fall of the Fuller).

The path continues through the foliage to the confluence of the rivers Mellte and Hepste, half a mile further on. A quarter of a mile along the Hepste is the most impressive, and most popular, of the area's falls, the **Sgwd yr Eira** (Fall of Snow), whose rock below the main tumble has eroded back six feet, allowing people to walk directly behind a dramatic twenty-foot curtain of water – particularly dazzling in afternoon or evening sunlight, when it glitters like a million shooting stars. There's a shorter signposted path to Sgwd yr Eira from just above Sgwd Isaf Clun-Gwyn, and an even shorter direct two-mile walk from the village of **Penderyn**, off the A4059 three miles north of Hirwaun, reached by regular buses from Aberdare. There's a cosy **youth hostel** (☎01639/720301; ①) at **TAI'R HEOL**, half a mile south of Ystradfellte and just a short walk from Porth-yr-ogof. Just up the lane towards Ystradfellte, you can **camp** at *Penllwyn-Einon Farm Bungalow* (☎01639/720542), or in numerous informal spots in the woods.

Dan-yr-ogof Showcaves and Craig-y-nos

Six miles of upland forest and squelchy moor lie between Ystradfellte and the **Dan-yr-ogof Showcaves** (April–Oct daily 10am–4pm; Nov–March phone for details; ☎01639/730284 or 730693; £5.95), off the A4067 to the west. Only discovered in 1912, they claim to form the largest system of subterranean caverns in western Europe, and, although relentless marketing has turned them into something of an overdone theme park, the caverns are truly awe-inspiring in their size.

A path to the first series of caves, reached around a hideous park of plastic dinosaurs, leads through a warren of caverns, framed by stalactites and frothy limestone deposits spewing, frozen, over the crags and walls. Highlight of the bewildering subterranean trip is the **Dan-yr-ogof** cave itself, the longest showcave in Britain. Even better is the trip along the path through the downbeat recreated Iron Age "village", which leads to the opening of a series of caves that culminate in the **Cathedral Cave**. En route, the visitor passes through a winding succession of spookily lit caverns, where water cascades relentlessly down the walls and crusts of thin stalactites, looking like spun pasta squeezed through the rock, hang above. Light and sound come together in the final cave, the 150-foot-long, 70-foot-high cathedral, in the shape of a swelling classical soundtrack and dancing light show that succeeds, almost despite its inherent tawdriness, in impressing the visitor. The third cave to see is reached along a fearful path behind the dinosaur park, clinging precariously to a cliff edge. **Bone Cave** was known to be inhabited by prehistoric tribes, so the owners have fenced off an assortment of dressed-up mannequins in the cave for an accompanying son et lumière show that makes Iron Age woman look like a reject from *Miss Selfridge*.

By the main car park for the complex is the Dan-yr-ogof **trekking centre**, which arranges horse rides, and also has a **hotel** (number as above; ③), and **campsite**. Less commercialized camping is available just up the road at the *Tafarn-y-Garreg* pub (☎01639/730236), or up the track behind at *Maes-yr-eglwys Farm* (☎01639/730347). Unless you want to get an early start on the caves, or are using it as a base for walking, there's little here to make you stay.

A quarter of a mile south of the cave complex is the spiky shape of the nineteenth-century **Craig-y-nos Castle**, a grand folly built in 1842 and fancifully extended from 1878, when it was bought by Adelina Patti, the celebrated Italo-American opera singer. In her forty years of residence, she turned the place into a Disneyesque castle, even adding a gaudy, scaled-down version of the Drury Lane opera house for performances. After years of careless development, the castle was bought out in 1994 by enthusiasts headed by Welsh opera diva, Dame Gwyneth Jones, and is currently being renovated to reopen as a spectacular country opera house – a sort of Welsh Glyndebourne – by 1999; for now, groups can go on a tour of the restored theatre if booked in advance (☎01639/730205). Some 44 acres of the grounds have been turned over to the **Craig-y-nos Country Park** (unrestricted entry), whose car park and information centre is the starting point for signposted and leafleted walks around a landscaped site along the banks of the young River Tawe.

The central Beacons

Far more popular for walking and pony trekking than the wet and wild Black Mountain and Fforest Fawr, the **central Beacons**, grouped around the two highest peaks in the national park, are easily accessible from Brecon, just six miles to the north. This is classic old red sandstone country: sweeping peaks rising up out of glacial scoops of land. Although the peaks never reach 3000ft, the terrain is unmistakably, and dramatically, mountainous.

Pen y Fan (2907ft) is the highest peak in the Beacons, indeed in all south Wales. Together with **Corn Du** (2863ft), half a mile to the west, they form the most popular ascents in the park, particularly along the well-trampled muddy red path that starts from Pont ar Daf, half a mile south of Storey Arms on the A470 midway between Brecon and Merthyr Tydfil. This is the most direct route from a road, where a comparatively easy five-mile round trip gradually climbs up the southern flank of the two peaks. A longer and generally quieter route leads up to the two peaks from the "Gap" route, the pre-nineteenth-century (and possibly Roman) main road that winds its way north from the Neuadd reservoirs, through the only natural break in the sandstone ridge of the central Beacons to the bottom of the lane that eventually joins the main street in Llanfaes, Brecon, as Bailihelig Road. Although the old road is no longer accessible for cars, car parks at either end open out onto the track for an eight-mile round-trip ascent up Pen y Fan and Corn Du from the east.

The Black Mountains

The easternmost section of the national park is the area around the **Black Mountains**, not to be confused with its singular namesake forty miles west. Far

A CIRCULAR WALK AROUND CORN DU AND PEN Y FAN

Note: The OS Outdoor Leisure 1:25,000 map #12 (Brecon Beacons West & Central) is recommended

The two biggest peaks of the Brecon Beacons attract vast numbers of walkers, most of whom take one of the shortest routes from the A470 south of Brecon. The alternative route detailed here is far longer – some eight miles, taking at least four hours – but infinitely more rewarding.

It starts at the car park by the late Victorian Neuadd reservoirs (SO 032179). Go through the gate and head down left through a gully and up onto the top of the grassy dam that once held the water of the lower, smaller reservoir, which was drained in 1985 when new safety restrictions made it too expensive to upgrade. Go to the end, through the muddy gap and up the hill in front, keeping the plantation forest (much of which is partly cleared) on your left-hand side. Keep to the fairly well-defined track and, when the forest ends, continue up the sharp gradient ahead, keeping the little stream gully on your left. This is the toughest and steepest part of the walk, but before too long you're up on the top of a windy ridge, commanding wide views over the reservoirs, the Beacons and way beyond. Head right along a well-defined path along the ridge top. The slope to the right becomes gradually sharper and more cliff-like as you continue over tiny streams that course down to the valley below. When the ridge on which you're walking narrows to a thin spit, views to the left down the completely uninhabited Cwm Crew are delightful. Corn Du and Pen y Fan are now looming in the foreground – follow the obvious path that strikes up the sandstone ridge to the first summit. Note how eroded the main path from the A470 is when you meet it just short of the peak.

Follow the obvious route from the summit of Corn Du down and up again to the peak of Pen y Fan, the highest point in south Wales. From both, the views over the mountains and valleys to Brecon are awesome. You can continue beyond Pen y Fan up to the next summit, Cribyn, and then descend to the Gap, where the wall of hills is breached by a track that may have been a Roman through route. Alternatively, without missing too much, you can take a right by the stream in the valley between Pen y Fan and Cribyn, following the rough track around the base of Cribyn to meet the Gap track. Turn right and continue along above the Neuadd reservoirs, turning right at the stream gulch to return to the car park.

quieter than the central belt of the Brecon Beacons, the Black Mountains combine some of the awesome remoteness of Fforest Fawr with the dry terrain and excellent walking of the central Beacons.

The wide valley of the River Usk divides the central Beacons from the Black Mountains, whose sandstone range rises to better defined individual peaks than can be found in the western end of the national park. The only exception to the unremitting sandstone is an isolated outcrop of limestone, long divorced from the southern belt, that peaks due north of Crickhowell at Pen Cerrig-calch (2302ft).

The Black Mountains have the feeling, unlike the Black Mountain or Fforest Fawr, of a landscape only partly tamed by human habitation. Tiny villages, isolated churches and delightful lanes are folded into the undulating green landscape. The most popular and rewarding areas to walk are in the east of the mountains, along the lane past Llanthony Priory (see p.68) and along the southern band of peaks, easily reached from Abergavenny (see p.62) and Crickhowell, notably Pen Cerrig-celch, Table Mountain and the Sugar Loaf. The mass of rippling hills in the centre and to the north are less easy to reach, although a couple of good paths cross the contours.

Llangorse, Talybont, Talgarth and Bronllys

Sheltering in the western lee of the Black Mountains, a mile from the pristine village of **LLANGORSE** (Llangors), the reed-shored **Llangorse Lake** (Llyn Syfaddan) washes its way around a low contour in the mountains, and was noted for its miraculous properties (blood-red water, groaning sounds and mythical lost city) in medieval times, but it's a rather more pedestrian affair today. A popular outdoor recreational centre, the lake hosts rowing, canoeing, fishing, windsurfing and yachting, as well as mountain-bike and caravan rental and the *Lakeside* **campsite** (☎01874/658226). There is the mediocre *Lakeside* bar and restaurant by the lake, but you'd be better off ambling into the village to sample the excellent food at the *CXVII Castle Inn*. The friendly *Red Lion* (☎01874/658238; ③), on the corner of the lane leading down to the lake, does superb food and decent B&B.

The wide, fertile vale of the Usk flows south of Llangorse, passing alongside the Monmouth and Brecon Canal, sitting on a shored-up bank of land above tidy little **TALYBONT-ON-USK**, a village top-heavy with bridges that reveal much about transport history: a disused rail bridge cuts across the main street near an aqueduct that carries a canal over the Caerfanell River, a tributary of the Usk dammed to form the reservoir two miles away. A few yards up the canal is a classic example of an old swingbridge, and another lane heads south from the village to the 323-acre **reservoir**, built to supply water to Newport, and crowded in by steep, conifer-forested hillsides. The lane continues up onto the rocky hillsides, past the waterfalls on the Nant Bwrefwr and beyond to the isolated and hauntingly beautiful **Neuadd reservoirs** in the north, a good starting point for walks to the summits of Pen y Fan and Corn Du along the old "Gap" road (see walk on p.209), or, to the south, the busier and more popular **Pentwyn** and **Pontsticill** (aka Taf Fechan) **reservoirs**. Car parks, snack bars and signposted forest walks form the bulk of most people's experience of these latter two reservoirs, although two eastbound paths at either end of the Pontsticill reservoir enable escape from this in favour of a fairly steep climb up the rocky slopes for wonderful views over the lakes. The hamlet of **PONTSTICILL**, behind the dam at the southern end of the lower lake, is only three miles north of urban Merthyr Tydfil (see p.83). Below the settlement, the tiny **Brecon Mountain Railway** (Easter–Oct mostly daily; ☎01685/722988) shuttles passengers along a two-mile section of track on the eastern bank of the reservoir and down to Pant, just north of Merthyr.

Regular Brecon–Crickhowell **buses** stop at Talybont. Amongst the village **pubs**, the *White Hart* is enjoyably basic and the *Star* (☎01874/676635; ③) more inspired in its choice of food, jazz and theme nights, range of beers and good **B&B**. You can **camp** at Welsh Water's *Filter House* at the top end of Talybont Reservoir (☎01874/676307 or 676605), south of the village. **Bike rental** is available from the *Talybont Venture Centre* in the Old Shop (☎01874/676458), while groups of five or fewer can rent a **boat** on the canal, bookable at the *Travellers' Rest* pub (£48 a day, £30 half-day; ☎01874/676401), south of Talybont on the B4558.

The town of **TALGARTH**, five miles north of Llangorse, is a spirited and friendly village built around its unusual town hall and the brooding bulk of **St Gwendoline's church** tower, constructed in the fourteenth century but harking back to Talgarth's position as a defence centre against the Norman invasion. The *Tower Hotel*, The Square (☎01874/711253; ③), is the town's main centre for eat-

A CIRCULAR WALK AROUND THE EASTERN BEACONS

Starting at the Blaen-y-glyn car park (SO 064169), on the lane between Talybont and Pontsticill/Merthyr, cross the road and take the track opposite, past rapids and falls along the River Caerfanell, down to the right. Continue for about 600 yards, over a concrete bridge, and take the left path at the fork. This heads uphill, with the plantation forest to your left (and a good comparison with the natural woodland across the valley to the right). Continue into the forest and take the left fork where the path splits into three. After about 300 yards, you come to a clearing, where you take a sharp left over the stream and continue past the picnic tables, fording another stream and taking a sharp right uphill to a fence and stile. Turn right along the forest track, then left at the Torpantau car park entrance, and head up the steep bank for about a third of a mile – the views over the valley of Glyn Collwn are superb here. At the corner of the forest, bear slightly right, away from the stream. It's a hard climb up to the ridge of Craig y Fan Ddu, straight ahead, but well worth it for some stunning vistas. The path swings left, shortly approaching the lip of the slopes to the right. Keep the ridge immediately to your right, cross the stream, and continue across the boggy moorland, still climbing gently. After about a mile, there's a short descent to Bwlch y Ddwyallt, where five paths converge.

Take the first right path, and, after 100 yards or so, strike left, crossing below a peat bog. Cross a stream and head towards the bottom of the rocky edge ahead. A monument, lying between two heaps of twisted metal, marks the spot of a wartime RAF plane crash. Climb up the slope to the top of the ridge, and then walk along its rim in a southeasterly direction, keeping the quarried cliffs to your right. After half a mile, you'll reach a spur of land with steep slopes either side. Head straight on, down the steep grassy slope in front, across a patch of moor and then right, following a fence, down into the valley. Cross the stile and turn left along the river path, past some little waterfalls. At the footbridge, you can either cross the river and return by the original path, or continue on this bank, past numerous falls and pools. Either way, the road and car park are reached in about 700 yards.

ing, drinking and **B&B**. There's also a cheerful independent hostel, *Joe's Lodge* (☎01874/711845; ①) on the Hay Road. The *Bridge End Inn*, over the bridge from the *Tower*, is good for live music and a cheerful atmosphere, while the superb *Book Shop Café*, an outpost of Richard Booth's Hay empire (see p.215), is good for snacking while perusing travel literature and maps.

Between Talgarth and the neighbouring village of **BRONLLYS** is **Bronllys Castle**, of which only a large twelfth-century cylindrical tower remains – climb to the top for stunning views up the Llynfi River valley and beyond to the light-washed peaks of the Black Mountains. There are some great places to **eat** and **sleep** around here: just north of Bronllys, the *Honey Café*, open daily until 10pm, has been around since 1935 and has newsy noticeboards. Heading up the A470 brings you to the relaxing, fifteenth-century *Griffin Inn* (☎01874/754241; ⑤), serving delicious local dishes, *Llangoed Hall* (☎01874/754525; ⑧), a luxurious mansion once owned by Laura Ashley's husband, and *Trericket Mill* (☎01982/560312; ①/②), where there's good B&B and bunkhouse accommodation.

Three miles south of Talgarth, the hamlet of **PENGENFFORDD** is a good base for walks in the mountains, including up to the vast nearby Iron Age hillfort of **Castell Dinas**, whose 2500-year-old-ditches and grass ramparts sit 1500ft up in a magnificent position under an outlying crop of the mountain range, commanding views far down the valley of the Rhiangoll river. The site's combined practicality for shelter, defence and settlement were used again when a medieval castle was built to complement Tretower at the other end of the valley, but a few isolated bits of rubble are all that remain. The *Castle Inn* (☎01874/711353; ③), a popular base for walkers for its camping, B&B, food and drink, sits at its base on the main road. *Upper Trewalkin Farm* (☎01874/711349; ③), up in the lanes between Pengenffordd and Talgarth, is a brilliant farmhouse B&B with staggering views over Castell Dinas and the Black Mountains.

Tretower

Rising out of the valley floor, dominating the view from both the A40 and A479 mountain road, the solid round tower of the **castle and court** (April–Oct daily 9.30am–6pm; Nov–March Mon–Sat 9.30am–4pm, Sun 2–4pm; £2.20; CADW) at **TRETOWER** (Tre-twˆr), was built to guard the valley pass. The bleak thirteenth-century round tower replaced an earlier Norman fortification, and in the late fourteenth century a comparatively luxurious manor house was built a couple of hundred yards away over a sheep-filled field, gradually being expanded more over the ensuing years. In the summer, Shakespeare and contemporary plays are acted out in the inspirational surroundings of the court (details ☎01874/730279). The court has been fully restored, with its family rooms and ostentatious beam-ceilinged Great Hall facing in on the central cobbled courtyard and square sandstone gatehouse. With much of the work still under way, exposed plaster and beams give a good insight into late medieval building methods. An open-air gallery and wall walk enable the visitor to view the site on the upper level. An enjoyable self-guided Walkman tour takes the visitor around the site.

Crickhowell

One of the liveliest bases in the Black Mountains, **CRICKHOWELL** (Crucywel), on the northern shore of the wide and shallow Usk, has a grand seventeenth-century **bridge** with thirteen arches visible from the eastern end and only twelve from the west, spawning many a local myth. Bridge Street rises from the river and up to the uninspiring mound of the ruined **castle** and the wide **High Street**. New Road runs parallel to Bridge Street from the river, passing the steeple of the town's fourteenth-century **church of St Edmund**. There really isn't that much to see in the town, but its spectacular northern backdrop is **Table Mountain** (1481ft), whose brown cone presides over the rolling green fields below. The best access is along the path that goes off by the electricity substation past The Wern off Llanbedr Road, and at the summit there are remains of the 2500-year-old hillfort (*crug*) of Hywel, from which the town, tumbling down the slopes below into the Usk Valley, takes its name. An alternative, and far shorter, route heads up alongside the stream behind the *Perth-y-pia* bunkhouse (see below). The views are amongst the best in the area. Many walkers follow the route to the north from Table Mountain, climbing two miles up to the plateau-topped limestone hump of **Pen Cerrig-calch** (2302ft).

Crickhowell has many facilities in quite a compact space. The enthusiastic **tourist office** (April–Oct daily 10am–1pm & 2–6pm; ☎01837/812105) is in Beaufort Chambers on Beaufort Street. **Accommodation** is abundant, with the grandiose coaching inn, the *Bear Hotel* on Beaufort Street (☎01873/810408; ④), and the cheerfully relaxed *Dragon* on the High Street (☎01873/810362; ③); for cheaper B&B, try *Greenhill Villa* on Beaufort Street (☎01873/811177; ③) or *Tˆy Gwyn* (☎01873/811625; ③) on Brecon Road, opposite the Porth Mawr, an impressive stone gatehouse.

There's also the town-centre *Riverside Park* **campsite** on New Road (☎0873/810397). A mile north of town, just beyond the turning for the delightful village of **LLANBEDR**, is the superb *Perth-y-pia* (☎01873/810050; ①/②), an elevated outdoor centre offering excellent B&B and hostel accommodation and home-cooked evening meals; there's also camping just opposite at *Ty-mawr* (☎01873/810164). Across the river from Llanbedr, *Gellirhydd Farm* (☎01873/810466; ②) offers great B&B and the chance to learn all kinds of woodcraft.

There's no shortage of places to **eat** and **drink** back in Crickhowell: for lunch, there are daytime snacks at the *Corner House* tea room on Beaufort Street, or the the *Cheese Press* on the High Street. Evening food is almost universally available in the town's pubs: the *Bear Hotel* (see above) wins legions of awards for its heavenly, pricier-than-average bar and restaurant food; the local delicacies on offer in the *White Hart* on Brecon Road are cheaper, and there's the similar but staid *Six Bells* on New Road. Hearty, if pricey, Welsh cuisine is available at *Tŷ Croeso* (☎01873/810573), across the Usk a mile west of Crickhowell at The Dardy, near Llangattock. Down by the town bridge, the *Bridge End* pub, part of which is an old tollhouse, is a very fine bet for excellent food, including some impressive vegetarian selections. Llanbedr boasts the cheerful *Red Lion*.

The *Crickhowell Mountain Gear* shop, next to the market cross at 1 High St (☎01873/810020), sells all of the predictable caving and walking paraphernalia, while *Mountain and Water*, in the Riverside Centre on New Road (☎01873/811887), offer canoeing, kayaking, climbing, orienteering, mountain activities and **bike rental**, for which you should phone in advance.

Hay-on-Wye

The sleepy border town of **HAY-ON-WYE** (Y Gelli), at the northern tip of the Brecon Beacons, is known to most people for one thing – books. Hay saw its first second-hand bookshop open in 1961 and has since become a bibliophile's paradise, with just about every spare inch given over to the trade, including the old cinema, houses, shops and even the ramshackle stone castle. There are now over twenty bookstores here, the largest containing around half a million tomes.

Hay, as a border town full of non-local folk, has little indigenous feel, although its setting amongst soft mountains, together with its creaky little streets, maintain an unhurried charm. It's a fascinating place to visit, bursting alive in the summer with riverside parties, travelling fairs and a vast shifting population. In the last week of May, all fashionable London literary life decamps to Hay for the **Hay Festival of Literature** (☎01497/821217), held in venues around the town. The atmosphere at this time is superb, although accommodation gets booked up well in advance. At any time of the year, the area surrounding Hay makes staying in the town a sensible option. One of the most awesome mountain roads in south Wales south of the town climbs up into the Black Mountains and under the glorious viewpoint at Hay Bluff before descending into the Gospel Pass (see p.69) and Vale of Ewyas (see p.67). This is wonderful walking country, although the little ribbon of road laid seemingly casually across the springy moor can get horribly congested in high summer.

Arrival and information

Buses stop by the Oxford Road car park, next to the **tourist office** (Easter–Oct daily 10am–1pm & 2–5pm; Nov–Easter daily 11am–1pm & 2–4pm; ☎01497/820144),

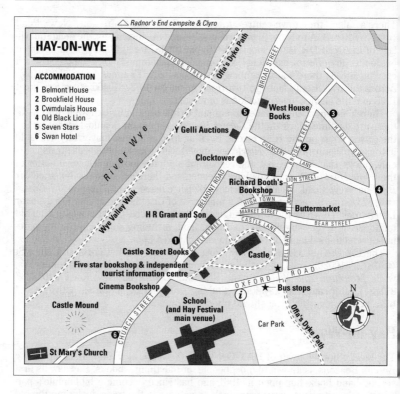

HAY-ON-WYE

ACCOMMODATION
1 Belmont House
2 Brookfield House
3 Cwmdulais House
4 Old Black Lion
5 Seven Stars
6 Swan Hotel

Radnor's End campsite & Clyro

BRIDGE STREET

Offa's Dyke Path

BROAD STREET

West House Books

HEOL Y DWR

BROOK STREET

Y Gelli Auctions

CHANCERY LANE

Clocktower

LION STREET

Richard Booth's Bookshop

HIGH TOWN

ST JOHN'S PL

Buttermarket

BEAR STREET

H R Grant and Son

MARKET STREET

CASTLE LANE

CASTLE STREET

BELL BANK

River Wye

Wye Valley Walk

Castle Street Books

Five star bookshop & independent tourist information centre

Castle

OXFORD ROAD

Cinema Bookshop

Bus stops

School (and Hay Festival main venue)

Offa's Dyke Path

CHURCH STREET

Castle Mound

Car Park

N

Swan Hotel

St Mary's Church

---

housed in a grim craft centre. They can recommend from the plentiful local **accommodation**, which gets booked up long in advance for the festival. **Bike** (and **canoe**) **rental** is available from *Paddles & Pedals*, yards away on Castle Street (☎01497/820604). There's a **laundry** in Oxford Terrace, behind the castle.

Accommodation

Belmont House, Belmont Road (☎01497/820718). Classy guesthouse on the continuation of Broad Street. ②.

Brookfield House, Brook Street (☎01497/820518). Small, friendly B&B off Lion Street. ②.

Cwmdulais House, Heol-y-dwr (☎01497/820640). Cheerful B&B on the back road behind Lion Street. ②.

Old Black Lion, Lion Street (☎01497/820841). Captivating thirteenth-century inn, which favours candlelight in the evenings. Excellent accommodation. ③.

Old Post Office, Llanigon, two miles south of Hay (☎01497/820008). A wonderful seventeenth-century vegetarian B&B, which also rents out bikes and is well placed for local walks, including the Offa's Dyke Path (see p.228). ②.

Radnors End campsite (☎01497/820780 or 820233). A 5-min walk from town, across the Wye bridge and on the road to Clyro. A beautiful setting overlooking Hay, with showers and washing machine on site.

Seven Stars, Broad Street (☎01497/820886). Popular town pub near the clock tower, with a good range of bedrooms. ③.

RICHARD BOOTH AND THE HAY BOOK BUSINESS

Richard Booth, whose family originates in the area, opened the first of his Hay-on-Wye second-hand bookshops in 1961. Since then, he has built an astonishing empire and attracted other booksellers to the town, turning it into the greatest market of used books in the world. There are now over twenty such shops in the minuscule town, the largest of which – Booth's own flagship – contains around half a million volumes.

Whereas so many mid-Welsh and border towns have seen populations ebb away over the past fifty years, Hay is booming on the strength of its bibliophilic connections. Booth views this transformation of a hitherto ordinary little market town as a prototype for reviving an agrarian economy, depending on local initiatives and unusual specialisms instead of handouts from vast statutory or multinational corporations. He is unequivocal in his condemnation of bulky government organizations such as the Wales Tourist Board and the Development Board for Rural Wales, which, he asserts, have done little to stem the flow of jobs and people out of the region but which have succeeded instead in lining the pockets of a chosen few. This healthy distaste for hefty bureaucracy, coupled with Hay's geographical location slap on the Wales–England border and Booth's own self-promotional skills, led him to declare Hay independent of the UK in 1977, with himself, naturally, as king. He appoints his own ministers and offers "official" government scrolls, passports and car stickers to bewitched visitors. Although such a proclamation of UDI carries no weight officially, most of the people of Hay seem to have rallied behind King Richard and are delighted with the publicity, and visitors, that the town's continuing profile attracts.

King Richard continues to take his self-appointed role seriously, pumping out a series of tracts and pamphlets on subjects dear to his heart, from the predictable rallying cries against supermarket developments to criticism of the town's high-profile annual literary festival, founded on the basis of Hay's bibliophilic reputation. Amongst the egotism and occasional self-righteousness, Booth hits many targets accurately, and his criticism of the homogenization and consequent decline of rural communities due to crass actions by government and big business is a theme to which many have subsequently been drawn.

The Town and around

Don't come to Hay if you don't like books, as they are the chief concern of this small market town. The best bookshop to start sampling the spirit of the town is up the gated track towards the castle opposite the Oxford Road car park, where you'll find Richard Booth's self-styled **independent tourist information centre** and **Five Star bookshop**, with racks of overspill books under canopied covers outside, together with honesty boxes for payment. The shop itself specializes in an unlikely mix of sci-fi, horror, leisure and tourism, including many a tract containing the Thoughts of King Richard. Here – or from the official tourist office – you can pick up the invaluable free *Hay-on-Wye Booksellers & Printsellers* leaflet, detailing all of the town's literary concerns. Just beyond the *Five Star* bookshop is the **castle**, a fire-damaged Jacobean mansion built into the walls of a thirteenth-century fortress, and owned – like just about everything in Hay – by Richard Booth. The ruling monarch lives in part of the castle, affected by fires in 1939 and 1978, although his wife runs the *Castle Bookshop*, a very sedate collection of fine art, antiquarian and photography books – in another part of the mansion. If you go from the tourist office to the bottom of Oxford Road and turn left into Castle Street, you come immediately to the **Hay Cinema Bookshop**, housed in the old town cinema and particularly good for new remaindered books at very low prices.

A small bookshop-lined alleyway leads from the gated track to Castle Street, where **H R Grant and Son** at no. 6 and **Castle Street Books** at no. 23 are the best in town for contemporary and historical guides and maps, the former selling works pertaining to nineteenth-century diarist Reverend Francis Kilvert and his winsome journals (see below). Beyond the colonnaded **Buttermarket** at the top end of Castle Street, **Richard Booth's Bookshop**, 44 Lion St, is the largest shop in Hay, a huge, draughty warehouse of almost unlimited browsing potential. Lion Street dips down to Broad Street at the clock tower near **Y Gelli Auctions** (☎01497/821179), with regular sales of books, maps and prints. Further along tree-lined Broad Street is **West House Books**, best for Celtic and women's works.

A road passes over the River Wye and climbs the hill towards **CLYRO**, little more than a mile away. Sheltering behind the busy A438, the village is home to a couple of small commercial art galleries trading on the strength of Clyro's connections with nineteenth-century wandering parson Francis Kilvert. Although he was vicar of Clyro for only seven years (1865–72), the village, its idyllic surroundings and its precisely recorded inhabitants featured prominently in his published diaries, drawing a steady trickle of pilgrims to see the place ever since.

The A438 heads south, through the one-horse hamlet of **LLOWES**, whose dowdy church of St Meilig houses a superb three-ton seventh-century Celtic cross. A mile further, a lane to the right climbs to **MAESYRONNEN**, where the low-roofed barn chapel, built in 1696, is the oldest surving Nonconformist worship house in Wales. If it's locked, and you want to see the whitewashed interior, with its old benches and stacked wooden pulpit, get the key from the Old Post Office in Ffynnon Gynydd, a mile up the lane.

Eating , drinking and entertainment

As a centre for walking, as well as the ubiquitous book trade, Hay is very well served for **food and drink** outlets. There are some good restaurants, and the pubs span the entire spectrum, from rustic bars little changed in decades to foodie haunts and cheerful places where you will often find **live music**.

Blue Boar, Castle Street. Tasteful wood-panelled bar on the corner with Oxford Road. Excellent beer and reasonable summer food.

Granary, Broad Street (☎01497/820790). Unpretentious, moderately priced bistro, excellent for vegetarian food and local produce.

Kilvert Court Inn, Bull Ring. Warm and friendly locals' pub, with a fine and imaginative menu. In summer, there's live Celtic, world and other music outdoors in the marquee most Thursdays and occasionally at the weekend.

Old Black Lion, Lion Street (☎01497/820841). Beautiful, olde-worlde pub that avoids any hint of kitsch. Superb, award-winning meals in the bar, or more robust fare in the pricier restaurant.

Pinnochio's, Broad Street (☎01497/821166). Relaxed, popular and reasonably priced Italian restaurant, with a delightfully convivial atmsophere on a warm summer's evening.

Swan Hotel, Church Street. Good downstairs bar, popular for its pool tables and games machines. Hearty, good-value bar snacks also available.

Three Cocks Hotel, Three Cocks, five miles southwest of Hay on the A438 (☎01497/847215). A stuffy hotel with a tasty Belgian restaurant on its ground floor. Expensive, though.

Three Tuns, Broad Street. Time-warped pub with a dusty, flagstoned bar filled with disorganized mounds of memorabilia. Go easy on the lethal draught local cider.

The Wells towns

Straddling the old border of Brecknockshire and Radnorshire, around fifteen miles north of Brecon, are the four spa towns of mid-Wales, strung out along the Heart of Wales rail line and the main A483. Up until the eighteenth century, all were obscure villages, but then came the great craze for spas, and anywhere with a decent supply of apparently healing water joined in on the act. Royalty and nobility spearheaded the fashion, with spas such as Llandrindod gaining a reputation for licentiousness and a general air of lawless reverie. Come the arrival of the railways, the four Welsh spas became the domain of everyone, although each had its own clientele and appealed to different social groups. The westernmost, **Llanwrtyd Wells** was a popular haunt of the Welsh middle classes in the nineteenth century, locked in mountainous countryside at the foot of the eerily bleak **Mynydd Eppynt** range. From here, the River Irfon winds up into the mountains towards the hamlet of **Abergwesyn**, from which a narrow road climbs up, before dropping down into Tregaron (see p.269). Four miles east along the river, the waters of tiny, nondescript **Llangammarch Wells** contain barium chloride, a popular Victorian remedy for rheumatism and heart problems.

East of here, the larger town of **Builth Wells** is best known nowadays as the home of the huge Royal Welsh Showground, but far prettier – although considerably more twee and anglicized – is **Llandrindod Wells** to the north, whose spa is the only one of the four in any state of decent repair. There are some excellent and fairly gentle walks around Llandrindod, as well as some beautiful, isolated churches – notably, at **Cefnllys** and **Disserth**.

Llanwrtyd Wells and around

Of the four spa towns, **LLANWRTYD WELLS** is the most appealing. It's friendlier, livelier, more Welsh, more unspoiled and in more beautiful surroundings than the other three. This was the spa to which the Welsh – farmers of Dyfed alongside the Nonconformist middle classes from Glamorgan – came to great *eisteddfodau* in the valley of the Irfon. The town shows obvious signs of its Victorian heyday, especially in the tall nineteenth-century town houses that line the streets.

Main Street runs through the town, crossing the turbulent Irfon River just below the town's main square. On the opposite side of the main road, a lane winds for half a mile along the river to the *Dolecoed Hotel*, built near the original sulphurous spring. Although the distinctive aroma had been noted in the area for centuries, it was truly "discovered" in 1732 by the local priest, Theophilus Evans, who drank from an evil-smelling spring after seeing a rudely healthy frog pop out of it. The spring, named **Ffynon Droellwyd** (Stinking Well), can still be sniffed out in the fields beyond the hotel, now erupting around a dome-shaped extension behind the neat red-and-white spa buildings, in the process of restoration.

Back in Llanwrtyd Wells proper, the A483 crests over a hill immediately north of the town, descending to the **Cambrian Woollen Mill** (Mon–Fri 8.30am–4.30pm; £3), a fairly unrewarding factory tour through the process of Welsh tweed production. There is a shop (free entry) on site, also open at weekends.

Practicalities

Llanwrtyd's **tourist office** is in *Tŷ Barcud* on the Square (Easter–Oct daily 10am–5pm; ☎01591/610666); it has all the usual facilities and also doubles as a **red**

kite centre, with lots of information on this distinctive bird of prey. **Accommodation** includes the boisterous *Neuadd Arms* in the main square (☎01591/610236; ③), which also rents out **bikes**, the solidly Victorian *Belle Vue Hotel* a few yards away (☎01591/610237; ③), and the cheaper *Cerdyn Villa*, Station Road (☎01591/610635; ②). The *Stonecroft Inn* in Dolecoed Road (☎01591/610332; ①/③) is a superb pub – with great food and regular live folk, R&B and rock music – with B&B facilities and a small, self-catering **hostel** annexe. There's another independent hostel three miles southeast of town at *Caban Cwmffynnon* (☎01591/610638; ①), just beyond the hamlet of **Cefn-gorwydd**, which is also the base of *Dinefwr Treks* for biking, bird-watching and pony-trekking trips. The *Drovers' Rest* **restaurant** (☎01591/610246), by the river bridge, serves wholesome, traditional Welsh dishes and snacks. The *Belle Vue* also provides cheap, hearty food, as does the *Neuadd Arms*, host to a wide range of bizarre and entertaining annual events, including a Man vs Horse race, a Saturnalian shindig in mid-January, a Drovers' Walk, a town festival in the first week of August, walking expeditions, a snorkelling competition in a local bog, a beer festival in November and a New Year's Eve torchlight procession through the town.

Mynydd Eppynt and Llangammarch Wells

The gorgeous scenery around the town of Llanwrtyd Wells is one of its biggest attractions, nowhere more evident than in the country to the south, where the remote **Crychan Forest** and the doleful mountains of the **Mynydd Eppynt** make up the northern outcrops of the Brecon Beacons, most dramatically along the roads that snake across the moors from the towns of Garth and Builth. The bulk of the Eppynt has been appropriated by the British Army, as evidenced by the many red flags flying stiffly, signs warning you not to stop or touch anything and, saddest of all, the spooky **Drovers' Arms**, midway between Garth and Upper Chapel on the B4519, once a welcome respite for those droving cattle across the mountains and now a boarded-up wreck. Thankfully, another old drovers' inn, the gas-lit *Griffin* (☎01982/552778; ④), on the B4520 between Upper Chapel and Builth, is thriving.

The B4519 descends dramatically from the Eppynt above a beautifully isolated valley, the **Cwm Graig Ddu**, from where the views over miles of soft farmland and rippling hills are overwhelming. At the bottom of the hill, a lane forks left, soon to join the River Irfon that winds to **LLANGAMMARCH WELLS**, where it meets the Cammarch River. A mile before the village is the exquisite black-and-white timbered **Lake Hotel** (☎01591/620202; ⑤), the home of the now-defunct barium well that attracted Lloyd George and foreign heads of governments searching for cures, and probably the best reason to come here. The village is excellent for fishing, but singularly dull otherwise.

Abergwesyn and the Pass

Although the drovers' roads and inns across the Mynydd Eppynt are now forbidden territory, the most spectacular of the drovers' routes is thankfully still open. The lane from Llanwrtyd meets up with another road from Beulah at the riverside hamlet of **ABERGWESYN**. From here, a quite magnificent winding thread of a road – the **Abergwesyn Pass** – climbs up alongside the dwindling river, leaving it at the perilous **Devil's Staircase** and pushing up through dense conifer forests to wide, sparse valleys bereft of any sign of human habitation, framed by craggy peaks, bubbling waterfalls and blotches of gorse and heather. At the little bridge over the tiny Tywi River, a track heads south past an isolated, gas-lit **youth hostel** (April–Sept; ☎01974/298680; ①) at **DOLGOCH**. On the other side of the river, a new road channels past the thick forest on to Llyn Brianne (see p.147), a couple of miles further on. This is as remote a walking holiday as can be had in Wales – paths lead from Dolgoch, through the forests and hillsides to the tiny chapel at **SOAR-Y-MYNYDD** and beyond, over the mountains to the next hostel at **Tŷ'n-y-cornel** (☎01222/222122; ①), five strenuous miles from Dolgoch.

From Dolgoch, the Abergwesyn Pass continues over the massive, wide terrain, before dropping down along the rounded valley of the Berwyn River and into Tregaron (see p.269). Although the entire Llanwrtyd–Tregaron route is less than twenty miles in length, it takes a good hour to negotiate the twisting, narrow road safely. The old drovers, driving their cattle to Shrewsbury or Hereford, would have taken a good day or two over the same stretch.

Builth Wells and around

Very much the spa of the Welsh working classes, **BUILTH WELLS** (Llanfair ym Muallt) still caters to its locals. An earthy agricultural town that has little to detain you, it's a useful centre for transport, cheap accommodation and entertainment, and can make a reasonable base for exploring the area around.

The most pleasant area in Builth is the verdant stretch along the Wye, below the architecturally undistinguished High Street, where you'll find the multi-purpose **Wyeside Arts Centre** (☎01982/552555), converted out of the town's Victorian Assembly Rooms right by the Wye bridge. On the other side of the river, Builth's major modern source of prosperity, the **Royal Welsh Showground** (☎01982/553683), hosts numerous agricultural events, together with monthly flea markets and occasional specialized collectors' fairs. The massive **Royal Welsh Show**, a giant coming-together of all matters agricultural, takes place in mid-July.

Practicalities

Builth Road **train station** is nearly three miles north of the town and inaccessible by public transport. **Buses** depart from the car park alongside the river bridge, in which the **tourist office** (Easter–Oct daily 10am–6pm; Nov–Easter Mon–Sat 10am–5pm; ☎01982/553307) is to be found. **Bike rental** is from *Builth Wells Cycles* at Fairleigh on Smithfield Road (☎01982/552923).

Accommodation comes cheap: the *White Horse* on the High Street (☎01982/553171; ③) is also the liveliest pub in town, and, at the top of the High Street, *The Owls* B&B (☎01982/552518; ②) has an excellent reputation. There are numerous cheap daytime cafés, and pubs such as the *Lion Hotel* (☎01982/553670; ③) on Broad Street, near the bridge, and the *White Horse* (which also hosts regular live music and quizzes) that provide decent evening **food**. There's a great farmhouse B&B, *New Hall Farm* (☎01982/552483; ③), in Llanddewi'r Cwm, a mile and a half south of town. Five miles northwest of Builth at Llanafan-fawr, *Greenwood Courses* (☎01597/860469) offers traditional residential training in all kinds of woodcraft, with all food, walks and coracle trips included in the cost.

Cilmeri

In the centre of **CILMERI**, an unassuming village that straggles along the main A483 road and rail line between Builth and Llanwrtyd, the *Prince Llywelyn* pub seems incongruously placed as a reminder of Welsh martyrdom in a fairly anglicized corner of eastern Wales. A hundred yards further up the main road towards Llanwrtyd and all becomes clear when you catch sight of a large, pointed granite boulder on a small hillock, said to be the spot at which, in December 1282, Llywelyn ap Gruffydd (the Last), was killed by English troops as he was escaping from the abortive Battle of Builth, four miles away. On realizing who they had killed, it is said that the English soldiers hacked off Llywelyn's head, whereupon it was dispatched to London and paraded victoriously through the city's streets. The English tablet by the monument calls Llywelyn "our prince". Its Welsh equivalent, tellingly, describes him as *ein llyw olaf* – "our last leader". Semantics aside, you are unlikely ever to see the monument without someone's fresh flowers adorning it.

Llandrindod Wells and around

If anything can sum a town up so succinctly, it is the shiny new plaque at **LLAN-DRINDOD WELLS** (Llandrindod) train station, commemorating the 1990 "Revictorianization of Llandrindod station". The town has not been slow to follow suit, peddling itself as Wales' most upmarket Victorian inland resort as if the very life of the place depended upon it.

It was the railway that made Llandrindod, arriving in 1864 and bringing carriages full of well-to-do Victorians to the fledgling spa. Llandrindod blossomed, new hotels were built, neat parks were laid out and the town came to rival many of the more fashionable spas and resorts over the border. Even now, after faintly gloomy Builth, the town can seem like a salty breath of fresh air. Its fine nineteenth-century buildings have been swabbed and sandblasted, ornate cast-iron railings restored, and the spa brought back to some kind of life. There is plenty of accommodation in the town, a good range of things to do and the surrounding countryside – like all of mid-Wales – offers an endless variety of excellent walks.

Arrival, information and getting around

The **train station** (☎01597/822053) is in the heart of town, between the High Street and Station Crescent. **Buses** also depart from outside. The **tourist office** on Temple Street (April–Oct Mon–Fri 9am—6pm, Sat & Sun 10am—1pm & 2–6pm; Nov–March daily 10am–1pm & 2–5pm; ☎01597/822600) holds details of the different local bus companies, their routes and times, and will also recommend and book accommodation. For a wider view of festivals and gigs in the area, consult the posters in the *Herb Garden* veggie restaurant (see p.222) or *Van's Good Food Shop*, sheltering behind a brilliant red frontage that looks more like a gaudy Victorian traction engine, on Middleton Street, connecting Station Crescent and Spa Road. The town's largest annual event is, no surprise, August's **Victorian Festival**, which culminates in a firework extravaganza over the town lake. The longer-established annual town **eisteddfod** takes place in early October. **Market day** is Friday. **Bike rental** is from the *Greenstiles Bike Shed* (☎01597/824594), behind the station on the High Street.

Accommodation

As the major tourist centre for the past 130 years in all of rural mid-Wales, Llandrindod is well served for hotels, B&Bs, restaurants and cafés, even if its strait-laced past is reflected in the notable lack of pubs.

Disserth Farm, Disserth, three miles southwest of Llandrindod (☎01597/860277). Campsite in a beautiful riverside setting, next to the lovely village church.

Drovers Arms, Howey, almost two miles southwest of town (☎01597/822508). Superb inn, with fine beer, food and accommodation. ③.

Greylands, High Street (☎01597/822253). A tall Victorian redbrick house in the town centre, near the station and all amenities. ②.

Griffin Lodge Hotel, Temple Street (☎01597/822432). Cheerful hotel in a sturdy Victorian house. ③.

Kincoed Hotel, Temple Street (☎01597/822656). Well-appointed old town-centre hotel, opposite *Kwik Save* supermarket. ③.

Metropole Hotel, Temple Street (☎01597/822881). Elegant and large old spa hotel, the centrepiece of the town, with an excellent indoor swimming pool and a refined dining room that's open to non-residents. ⑤.

Rhydithon, Dyffryn Road (☎01597/822624). One of the smartest and friendliest guesthouses in town, just off the High Street. ②.

The Town

Llandrindod's Victorian opulence is still very much in evidence in the town's grandiose public buildings, especially the lavishly restored **spa pavilion** inside the pleasant **Rock Park**, with its trickling streams and well-manicured glens. European Union regulations prohibit the use of the Llandrindod spa taps in the café inside, and if you're desperate to taste the waters, you'll have to settle for a chalybeate fountain outside that spouts the stuff. A walk from the pavilion leads to "**Lovers' Leap**", a recreated bit of Victorian nonsense that's just a fake cliff with mediocre views over the river. The architecture around the park entrance is Llandrindod at its most confidently Victorian, with large, elaborately carved terracotta frontages and expansive gabling, and the **High Street** runs from here to the town centre, containing good record, antique, book and junk shops.

Behind the tourist office on Temple Street, you'll find the small town **museum** (April–Sept daily except Wed 10am–12.30pm & 2–4.30pm; Oct–March Mon–Tues & Thurs–Fri 10am–12.30pm & 2–4.30pm, Sat 10–12.30pm; free), where the exhibition is largely dedicated to excavated remains from the Roman fort at Castellcollen, a mile northwest of Llandrindod; kitsch Victoriana make up the bulk of the rest of the collection, including a large group of dolls. A new **red kite gallery** has been fitted out upstairs, with television linkups to local nests and some stunning photos of airborne majesty. Next to the museum is a glutinous **grotto**, a nineteenth-century whimsy built by a local doctor. West of Temple Street is Spa Road, a left turn off which leads down to the **Grand Pavilion**, home of tea dances and other genteel pursuits.

Cefnllys

One of the most popular walks from Llandrindod heads east from the town, along Cefnllys Road, though some beautiful wooden pockets to the banks of the River Ithon at **CEFNLLYS**, just under two miles away. A car park by the river leads on to **Shaky Bridge**, whose name dates from when just two planks of wood connected the two banks – a more solid structure is in evidence today. On the other side of the Ithon, the castle mound rises to the right and you'll see the dumpy witch's-hat spire of the thirteenth-century **St Michael's church** ahead. In Victorian times, the rector removed the church roof to persuade the few remaining parishioners to travel into up-and-coming Llandrindod instead for worship.

There was an outcry and a collection, and the roof was restored just two years later; photographs in the church show this strange period in its history. Back on the Llandrindod side of the river, **Bailey Einon Wood** is a designated nature reserve running three-quarters of a mile along the river, with some enchanting walks through its open glades.

Disserth

The other outlying former parish of Llandrindod is **DISSERTH**, lying a couple of miles to the south of the town, off the A483 at Howey, where the **church of St Cewydd** lies beside the Ithon in one of its most pastoral stretches. Resembling a fat medieval barn with a squat stone tower attached, the church escaped the restorative zeal of the Victorians, leaving its seventeenth-century wooden box pews intact, many with family names still discernible. The 1687 triple-decker pulpit, looking more like an auctioneer's lectern, is a rare survivor of pre-Victorian days.

Where the lane to Disserth heads west off the A483 at Howey, another lane also climbs up into the **Carneddau Hills**. About two miles after leaving the main road, a number of paths leave the lane and delve south into the rocky terrain, where glacial features like moraines and abandoned blocks of stone litter the landscape.

Eating and drinking

Aspidistra, Station Crescent. Decent daytime café, serving cheap and wholesome sandwiches and snacks. Inexpensive.

Dillraj, Emporium Buildings, Temple Street (☎01597/823843). Extremely classy, but not overpriced, Indian restaurant, opposite the tourist office. Moderate.

Franky's, Temple Street (☎01597/823727). Garish cellar bar-cum-bistro, compensated for by the good range of reasonable pizzas.

Herb Garden, Spa Road (☎01597/824737). New, inexpensive vegetarian eatery offering good, wholesome meals and snacks, together with occasional culinary theme evenings.

Llanerch Inn, Llanerch Lane. Central Llandrindod's only pub, and an excellent one. It's a cosy sixteenth-century inn that predates most of the surrounding town, with lots of pub games and a solid menu of good-value, well-cooked classics.

North and East Radnorshire

Before the reorganization of British counties in 1974, Radnorshire was the most sparsely populated in England and Wales, and it's still a remote area, especially in the north and east. In the northwest, **Rhayader** is the only settlement of any real size, and, although fairly plain to look at, is an excellent base, with some friendly pubs. Most people stay here in order to explore the wild, spartan countryside to the west of the town, a hilly patchwork of waterfalls, bogland, bare peaks and the four interlocking reservoirs of the **Elan Valley**, built at the turn of the century and displaying a grandiose Edwardian solidity.

The countryside to the northeast of Rhayader is slightly tamer, and lanes and bridle paths delve in and around the woods and farms, occasionally brushing through minute settlements like the village of **Abbeycwmhir**, whose name is taken from the deserted Cistercian abbey that sits below in the dank, eerie valley of the Clywedog Brook. The hills roll eastwards towards the English border and some of the most intact parts of **Offa's Dyke**, the eighth-century King of Mercia's border with the Welsh princes. The handsome town of **Knighton**, perched right on the border, is at the centre of the 177-mile path that runs along the dyke and is well geared-up for walkers and cyclists, with good accommodation, cheery pubs and cafés. Seven miles south, inches from England, the dignified little town of **Presteigne** contains a few reminders of its former importance as a county capital. The River Lugg flows through Presteigne from the Radnorshire hills, passing the isolated church at **Pilleth**, where Owain Glyndŵr captured Sir Edmund Mortimer, agent of the English king, in 1402.

Rhayader and around

RHAYADER (Rhaeder Gwy, literally "waterfall on the Wye") has boomed this century as mid-Radnorshire's principal base for the spectacular hills and reservoirs of the Elan Valley. Although the waterfall invoked by the town's name virtually disappeared when the town bridge was built in 1780, the Wye still frames the town centre, running in a loop around the western and southern sides. Rhayader was a centre of the mid-nineteenth-century "**Rebecca Riots**", when local farmers disguised themselves in women's clothing in order to tear down tollgates that were prohibitively expensive for itinerant and local workers.

Rhayader's handsome four main streets – named North, South, East and West – meet at a small town clock tower. Fifty yards up East Street from the clock tower, there's a tiny **folk museum** (Sat 10am–1pm & 2–5pm; Easter–May also Mon & Tues 2–5pm; June to mid-July also Fri 2–5pm; mid-July to Sept also Mon, Wed & Fri 2–5pm; free), good for its examination of the building of the local reservoirs in the Elan Valley, as well as an enjoyably haphazard clutter of agricultural and industrial artefacts from the area. Three miles north of town, just off the A470, is the lovely **Gilfach Farm nature reserve**, showpiece of the Radnorshire Wildlife Trust. Within the 418 acres, there are meadows, oak forest, moorland and river habitats supporting a huge variety of wildlife and flora. The restored longhouse farm has now been kitted out as a **visitor and exhibition centre** (April–Sept Fri–Sun 10am–5pm; £1.50), showing live video footage from ten nests around the reserve.

Practicalities

Buses stop in the main Dark Lane car park, opposite the **tourist office** (April–Oct daily 10am–6pm; Nov–March Fri & Sat 10am–5pm; ☎01597/810591) that shares its building with a leisure centre. Rhayader has always been well serviced for visitors, and eighteenth-century coaching inns still line the main streets. More modern **accommodation** includes the *Bryncoed* B&B on Dark Lane (☎01597/811082; ②), opposite the tourist office, the *Elan Hotel*, West Street (☎01597/810373; ③), or *The Mount*, East Street (☎01597/810585; ②), a friendly B&B and the base for *Clive Powell Mountain Bikes*, from which you can rent **bikes** or join an organized trip around the tracks of mid-Wales – there's also a shop outlet (☎01597/811343) opposite the B&B. Alternative bike rental is supplied by the *E T James Garage* on East Street (☎01597/810481 or 810396). On the outskirts of town, off South Road (the A470 from Builth), *Gigrin Farm* (☎01597/810243; ②) is a fine B&B, **camping** spot and official red kite feeding centre. Almost two miles northeast of town, off the Abbeycwmhir Road, is *Beili Neuadd* (☎01597/810211; ③), a relaxing farmhouse B&B. There's a campsite at *Wyeside* (☎01597/810183), a few hundred yards north of town off the A44, and a **laundry** on East Street.

Despite having a population of less than two thousand, there are twelve **pubs** in Rhayader, most offering reasonable pub food. Try the old-fashioned *Cornhill Inn* on West Street, or, over Bridge Street in the small hamlet of **LLANSANTF-FRAED CWMDEUDDWR**, usually shortened to Cwmdeuddwr, the tiny, ancient *Triangle*, whose toilets are on the other side of the street, and where darts players must stand in a special floor hole for fear of spearing the roof. More upmarket, the *Brynafon* **restaurant** (☎01597/810735), half a mile south on the road to Builth Wells, is good for evening meals.

Elan Valley

Until the last decade of the nineteenth century, the untamed countryside west of Rhayader received few visitors, although the poet Shelley did holiday here: his honeymoon retreat at Nantgwlyllt was amongst the couple of dozen buildings submerged by the waters of the **Elan Valley** reservoirs, a nine-mile-long string of four lakes built between 1892 and 1903 to supply water to the rapidly growing industrial city of Birmingham, 75 miles away; in the 1950s, a supplementary reservoir at Claerwen, to the immediate west, was opened (see opposite). Although the lakes enhance an already beautiful and idyllic part of the world, the colonialist way in which Welsh valleys, villages and farmsteads were seized and flooded to provide water for England is something the tourist boards prefer to gloss over. The natural resentment against this has perhaps been best expressed by poet R S Thomas in his soulful elegy, *Reservoirs*:

> *There are places in Wales I don't go:*
> *Reservoirs that are the subconscious*
> *Of a people, troubled far down*
> *With gravestones, chapels, villages even;*
> *The serenity of their expression*
> *Revolts me, it is a pose*
> *For strangers, a watercolour's appeal*
> *To the mass, instead of the poem's*
> *Harsher conditions. There are the hills,*
> *Too; gardens gone under the scum*
> *Of the forests; and the smashed faces*
> *Of the farms with the stone trickle*
> *Of their tears down the hills' side.*

The "watercolour's appeal" of the Elan Valley is, nonetheless, extremely strong, not only for the landscape but the profusion of rare plants and birds – red kites especially – in the area. From Rhayader, the B4518 heads southwest four miles to **ELAN** village, off the main road, a curious collection of stone houses built in 1909 to replace the reservoir constructors' village that had grown up on the site. Just below the dam of the first reservoir, **Caban Coch**, the **Elan Valley visitor centre** (mid-March to Oct daily 10am–6pm; free), incorporates a tourist office (☎01597/810898), and a permanent exhibition that is sensitive to the English Victorian imperialism that built the reservoirs, stressing just how grim conditions were in nineteenth-century Birmingham, how rich the wildlife and flora around the lakes are and even how some of the water is now drunk in Wales. Frequent guided **walks** and even **Land Rover safaris** head off from the centre. The only place to **stay** here is the *Elan Valley Hotel* (☎01597/810448; ③), an imposing neo-Colonial pile on the Rhayader side of Elan village, which attracts a youngish clientele with its fine food and drink and regular programme of music, literary and storytelling weekends and parties.

From the visitor centre, a road tucks in along the bank of Caban Coch to the **Garreg Ddu** viaduct, where a road winds along the bank for four spectacular miles to the vast, rather chilling 1952 dam on **Claerwen Reservoir**. More remote and less popular than the Elan lakes, Claerwen is a good base for the serious walker, who can follow a path from the far end of the dam and walk the harsh but beautiful eight miles or so across the mountains and past smaller, natural lakes to the abbey of Strata Florida (see p.270). Alternatively, the path that skirts around the northern shore of Claerwen leads across to the lonely **Teifi Pools**, glacial lakes from which the Teifi River springs.

Back at the Garreg Ddu viaduct, a more popular road continues north along the long, glassy finger of **Garreg Ddu** reservoir, before doubling back on itself just below the awesome **Pen-y-garreg** dam and reservoir; if the dam is overflowing, the vast wall of foaming water is mesmerizing. At the top of Pen-y-garreg lake, it's possible to drive over the final, or more properly the first, dam on the system, at **Craig Goch**. This is the most-photographed of all the dams, thanks to its gracious curve, elegant Edwardian arches and neat little green cupola. The lake beyond it is fed by the Elan River, which the road crosses just short of a junction. A bleak, invigorating moorland pass heads west from here to drop into the eerie moonscape of Cwmystwyth (see p.279), while the eastbound road funnels into a beautiful valley back to Rhayader. On the way back, fork off the Elan Valley Road in Rhayader on to the smaller Aberystwyth Road.

Abbeycwmhir

ABBEYCWMHIR (Abaty Cwm Hir) seven miles from Rhayader, takes its name from the abbey whose sombre ruins lie behind the village. Cistercian monks founded the abbey in 1146, planning one of the largest churches in Britain, whose 242-foot nave has only ever been exceeded in length by the cathedrals of Durham, York and Winchester. Destruction by Henry III's troops in 1231 scuppered plans to continue the building, however. The sparse ruins of what they did build – a rocky outline of the floorplan – lie in a conifer-carpeted valley alongside a gloomy green lake, lending weight, if only by atmosphere, to the site's melancholic associations. Llywelyn ap Gruffydd's body, after his head had been carted off to London, was rumoured to have been brought here from Cilmeri in 1282, and a new granite slab, carved with a Celtic sword, lies on the altar to commemorate this last native prince of Wales. It should look incongruous, but somehow it only adds to the eerie presence of the ruins and the village.

Presteigne and around

A tiny, old-fashioned place, whose architecture reeks of its former status as county town, **PRESTEIGNE** (Llanandras) lies snugly between the B4362 town bypass and the River Lugg, the border with England, which flows under the seventeenth-century bridge at the bottom of the handsome Broad Street. Just before the bridge, the solid parish **church of St Andrew** contains Saxon and Norman fragments, as well as a sixteenth-century Flemish tapestry. To the left of the main entrance to the churchyard are twin gravestones that give an insight into the morals of the early nineteenth century. The original stone commemorates one

Mary Morgan, who gave birth to a bastard child in 1805, her father persuading her to murder it; he then sat on the jury that condemned her to death. A sanctimonious inscription records that she was "unenlightened by the sacred truths of Christianity" and "became the victim of sin and shame and was condemned to an ignominious death". Opposite is a later stone erected in repentance by the townsfolk, inscribed "He that is without sin among you, let him first cast a stone at her".

Broad Street heads up to the main crossroads, with the High Street forking west and Hereford Street to the east. On the corner of Hereford and Broad streets is the nineteenth-century Italianate Assembly Rooms, also housing the town's library. Down the much prettified Broad Street, the old Shire Hall, a handsome 1829 building, houses the district **museum** (May–Oct Tues & Sat 10.30am–1pm & 2.30–5pm; July & Aug also Thurs; 20p), a beguiling and unpredictable collection of dusty relics from the area's past.

Along the main streets – Hereford Street in particular – there are some enjoyably musty second-hand book and antique shops, and the High Street contains the town's most impressive building, the Jacobean **Radnorshire Arms**, built as a private home for John Bradshaw, a signatory on the death warrant of Charles I, before becoming an inn in 1792.

Practicalities

Buses from Knighton, Kington and Leominster stop outside the *Radnorshire Arms* or just around the corner in Station Road. The **tourist office** (April–Sept daily 10am–6pm; ☎01544/260193) is on the High Street, just near the town hall. More esoteric information can be found yards away in Broad Street, at the *Tee-pee* second-hand shop, or further down the same street at the *Many Hands* craft shop. **Accommodation** spans period luxury at the *Radnorshire Arms* (☎01544/267406; ⑥) to the no-nonsense *Farmers Inn* (☎01544/267389; ③) on Hereford Street. You can **camp** for £1 at *Gumma Farm* (☎01547/560243), two miles west on the road to Discoed, or there's a fuller site, including caravans, at Rockbridge Park (☎01547/560300), half a mile nearer town on the banks of the River Lugg.

Many people "dropped out" here in the 1960s and 1970s, and today it's a centre for folk and traditional music: the August bank holiday sees a **festival** (details ☎01544/267163), organized by the excellent free music paper *Broad Sheep*, in venues around town, while regular music strikes up in the Memorial Hall, the Royal British Legion on Hereford Street and the *Farmer's Inn* on Hereford Street. This is the town's liveliest pub, and serves decent **food**. Alternatively, eat at cafés on the High Street, the old-fashioned *Barley Mow* on Hereford Street or the enjoyably laid-back *Hat Shop* restaurant and bar (☎01544/260017) at 7 High St.

Old and New Radnor

OLD RADNOR seems cut out of a hillside just off the A44 six miles southwest of Presteigne, and was once the home of King Harold, killed at the Battle of Hastings by William the Conqueror's troops. The site of his castle is down the lane running southeast from the large, very English-looking **church**, overlooking a wooded vale. Inside the church, a massive eighth-century font on four stone feet is the most remarkable legacy. Opposite the church, the rambling fifteenth-century *Harp Inn* (☎01544/350655; ③) has been magnificently restored from its earlier use as a farm cottage.

NEW RADNOR, just over two miles to the west, was built as a small Norman settlement and then planned, in the thirteenth century, to be expanded into a major city and capital of Radnorshire. The project faltered, confirming Wales' antipathy towards large settlements, instead of the more common feature of scattered farmsteads. Today, you enter the village from the A44 to the southeast, past a Victorian steeple erected to honour local dignitary Sir George Cornewall Lewis. This is the only feature of the village that seems to suggest any kind of metropolitan status, as the couple of streets are deathly quiet, lined with a couple of reasonable pubs, the best of which is the surprisingly lively *Eagle* on Broad Street (☎01544/350208; ②/③), which has B&B and dorm accommodation, serves perry (a potently alcoholic pear drink), hosts regular gigs, has a good menu and is the base for various local outdoor pursuits, including caving and paragliding.

North of New Radnor, the deep-clefted valleys and wooded hillsides of **Radnor Forest** offer some of the region's best walking. The most popular route is along the driveable track that forks north off the A44 just over a mile west of New Radnor, leading into a thick forest and to the rushing cascade of the **Waterbreak-its-neck** waterfall, at its foaming best in winter.

Knighton

A town that straddles King Offa's eighth-century border as well as the modern Wales–England divide, **KNIGHTON** (Tref-y-clawdd, "the town on the dyke") has come into its own as the most obvious centre for those walking the **Offa's Dyke Path**. Located almost exactly halfway along the route, Knighton, although without many specific sights, is a lively, attractive place that easily warrants a stopoff.

So close is Knighton to the border that the town's **train station** and its accompanying hotel are actually in England. From here, Station Road crosses the River Teme into Wales and climbs a couple of hundred yards into the town, joining the pretty Broad Street at Brookside Square. Further up the hill is the town's Victorian, alpine-looking clock tower, where Broad Street becomes West Street and the steep High Street soars off up to the left, past rickety Tudor buildings and up to the mound of the old **castle**. In West Street, the excellent **Offa's Dyke Centre** also houses the **tourist office** (April–Oct daily 9am–5.30pm; Nov & Feb–March Mon–Fri 9am–5pm, Sat & Sun 10am–3.30pm; Dec & Jan Mon–Fri 9am–5pm; ☎01547/528753). Looming high above Knighton, a mile off the A4113, the **Powys County Observatory** (tours daily 11am & 2pm; July & Aug daily except Wed; Sept–June Sun only; £2.90; ☎01547/520247) has a planetarium, camera obscura and solar telescope, and runs tours, evening groups and courses – phone for details.

Accommodation is plentiful and geared towards the backpacking market. There's the basic but cheerful *Red Lion* on West Street (☎01547/528231; ②), *The Lanterns* (☎01547/528922; ②) on the High Street, or the *Fleece House* B&B (☎01547/520168; ③) and the *Plough Hotel* (☎01547/528041; ③), both on Market Street. The *Plough* offers limited **camping**, or there are tent fields at *Panpwnton Farm* (☎01547/528597), over the river and half a mile up the lane that forks left at the station (note the fading letters "ER" in the forest above, planted for the present Queen's coronation in 1953), or the remote *Cwmgilla* (☎01547/528387), a mile above the main road to Rhayader. For **eating and drinking**, it's hard to beat the comfortable *Horse and Jockey* at the town end of Station Road, which has a vast menu for lunch and early evening, serves huge, tasty pizzas until 11pm and packs in live music and discos as well. You might also find folk and jazz in the *Plough*. The local **bike rental** firm, *Wheely Wonderful* (☎01568/770755), is over the border in Shropshire at Petchfield Farm, Elton, near Ludlow; they will deliver to Knighton if you're without a car.

OFFA'S DYKE

George Borrow, in his classic *Wild Wales*, notes that once "it was customary for the English to cut off the ears of every Welshman who was found to the east of the dyke, and for the Welsh to hang every Englishman whom they found to the west of it". Certainly, **Offa's Dyke** has provided a potent symbol of Welsh–English antipathy ever since it was created in the eighth century as a demarcation line by King Offa of Mercia, ruler of the whole of central England. It appears that the dyke was an attempt to thwart Welsh expansionism.

The earthwork – up to twenty feet high and sixty feet wide – made use of natural boundaries like rivers in its run north to south, and is best seen in the sections near Knighton in Radnorshire and Montgomery. Today's England–Wales border crosses the dyke many times, although the basic boundary has changed little since Offa's day. The glorious **long-distance footpath**, opened in 1971, runs from Prestatyn on the north Clwyd coast for 177 miles to Sedbury Cliffs, just outside Chepstow in Gwent, and is one of the most rewarding walks in Britain – neither too popular to be unpleasantly crowded, nor too similar in its landscapes. The path is maintained by the Offa's Dyke Association, whose headquarters is in the *Offa's Dyke Centre* in Knighton (see p.227).

Montgomeryshire

The northern part of Powys is made up of the old county of **Montgomeryshire** (Maldwyn), an area of enormously varying landscapes and few inhabitants. The best base for the spartan and mountainous southwest of the county is the solid little town of **Llanidloes**, less than ten miles north of Rhayader, a base for ageing hippies on the River Severn (Afon Hafren), which arrives in the town after winding through the dense **Hafren Forest** on the bleak slopes of **Plynlimon**.

From Llanidloes, one of Wales' most dramatic roads rises past the chilly shores of the **Llyn Clywedog** reservoir, squeezed into sharp hillsides, and up through the remote hamlets of **Staylittle** and **Dylife**. This stark, uplifting scenery contrasts with the gentler, greener contours that characterize the east of the county, where the muted old county town of **Montgomery**, with its fine Georgian architecture, perches above the border and Offa's Dyke. The Severn runs a few miles to the west, near the impeccable village of **Berriew**, home of the bizarre **Andrew Logan Museum of Sculpture** and below the dank hilltop remains of **Dolforwyn Castle**. Further south, the Severn runs in a muddy channel through drab **Newtown**, good only as a transport interchange and for followers of **Robert Owen**, the pioneer socialist.

In the north of the county, **Welshpool** forms the only major settlement, packed in above the wide flood plain of the Severn. An excellent local museum, the impossibly cute toy rail line that runs to **Llanfair Caereinion**, good pubs and reasonable hotels make the town a fair stop for a day or two. On the southern side of Welshpool is Montgomeryshire's one unmissable sight, the sumptuous **Powis Castle** and its exquisite terraced gardens. The very north of the county is pastoral, deserted and beautiful. The few visitors that there are throng **Lake Vyrnwy** and make their way down the dead-end lane to the **Pistyll Rhaedr** waterfall, leaving the leafy lanes and villages like **Llanfyllin** and **Llanrhaeadr-ym-mochnant** intact for those searching for peace, cheerful pubs and good walking.

Llanidloes and around

Thriving when so many other small market towns seem in danger of atrophying, the secret of success for **LLANIDLOES** seems to be in its adaptability, from rural village to weaving town and, latterly, a centre for artists, craftsfolk and assorted alternative lifestylers. One of mid-Wales' prettiest and most welcoming towns, the four main streets meet at the black-and-white **market hall**, built on timber stilts in 1600, allowing the market – now long since moved – to take place on the cobbles underneath. Running parallel with the length of the market hall are China Street and Long Bridge Street, the latter good for interesting little shops, like the very browsable *Nature Gallery* art store. Off Long Bridge Street to the left is Church Street, which opens out into a yard surrounding the dumpy parish **church of St Idloes**, whose impressive fifteenth-century hammerbeam roof is said to have been poached from Abbey Cwmhir.

Going west from the market hall is Short Bridge Street, a line of fine architecture that runs down to the River Severn, past two imposing nineteenth-century chapels – one Zionist, one Baptist – staring across the road at each other, seemingly waiting for the other to blink. Heading the other way from the market hall is Great Oak Street, the town's most important and attractive thoroughfare. Facing each other at the bottom of the street are the **town hall**, home of the tourist office, originally built as a temperance hotel to challenge the boozy **Trewythen Arms** opposite. A plaque on the hotel commemorates Llanidloes as an unlikely seeming place of industrial and political unrest, when, in April 1839 Chartists stormed the hotel, dragging out and beating up special constables who had been dispatched to the town in a futile attempt to suppress the political fervour of the local flannel weavers. The town's wonderfully eclectic **museum** (Easter–Sept daily 9.30am–5pm; Oct–Easter daily except Sun; free) forms part of the tourist office complex in the town hall. The diverting collection of old local prints and mementoes, including pictures of boomtown Dylife (see below), pale beside the stuffed two-headed lamb, born locally in 1914. Also housed in the museum is a **red kite centre**, with live transmission from nests in the Hafren Forest. Great Oak Street is also home to a branch of **Laura Ashley**'s empire, whose mission to wrap the world in floral fabric started just up the road in **Carno**.

Practicalities

Llanidloes is a good base, with friendly pubs and restaurants and plenty of places to stay. China Street curves down to the car park from where all **bus** services operate. The **tourist office** is part of the town hall at the bottom of Great Oak Street (hours as above; ☎01686/412605). For news of alternative events – like the **Fancy Dress Night**, on the first Friday of July, when the pubs open late, the streets are cordoned off and virtually the whole town gets kitted out – pick up the free monthly community paper, the *Llani Gazette*, or visit the excellent *Llanidloes Resource Centre* on Great Oak Street. At the bottom of the road is the area's best **bookshop**, *Great Oak*, with loads of Celtic and Welsh-interest stuff and a barn full of good new and second-hand fiction.

 Accommodation spans the delightful *Red Lion Hotel* (☎01686/412270; ④) and the genteel *Unicorn* (☎01686/413167; ③), both on Long Bridge Street, and the chintzy *Mount Inn* (☎01686/412247; ③), and handsome *Severn View* B&B (☎01686/412207; ②), both on China Street. You can camp at *Dol-llys Farm* (☎01686/412694), on the northern fringe of town.

Among the many options for **food**, there's wholesome vegetarian fare in the laid-back *Great Oak Café* on Great Oak Street, the cheap and hearty *Traveller's Rest* on Long Bridge Street or, for a bit of a treat, the *Orchard House* on China Street (☎0686/413606). Most of the **pubs** here serve food, for which the lively *Red Lion* has the best reputation, while the *Stag* on Great Oak Street, and the *Angel* on the High Street are less touristy than most others. The most laid-back of the lot is the *Crown*, towards the top of Long Bridge Street. There's also award-winning food available in the cheerful *Blue Bell Inn*, four miles down the A470 in the village of **LLANGURIG**.

Llyn Clywedog, Plynlimon, Dylife and Staylittle

Four miles northwest of Llanidloes, the beautiful **Llyn Clywedog reservoir** was built as recently as the 1960s and has settled well into the folds of the Clywedog Valley. At its southern end, this modern concrete dam is Britain's tallest (237ft), towering menacingly over the remnants of the **Bryntail lead mine**, through which a signposted path runs. The roads along the southern shores of Clywedog wind around into the dense plantation of **Hafren Forest**, the only real sign of life and vegetation on the bleak, sodden slopes of **Plynlimon** (Pumlumon Fawr). There is a car park at **RHYD-Y-BENWCH**, in the heart of the forest, from where walking paths fan out, the most popular being a six-mile round trip following the infant River Severn up through the trees, past a waterfall and out to its source, a saturated peat bog on the side of one of the harshest terrains in Wales.

Plynlimon is bleak and difficult walking if you are venturing beyond the fairly well-trodden path to the Severn's source. Water oozes everywhere in this misty wilderness, with four other rivers – the Wye included – rising on its tufted slopes. The rivers Hengwm, Llechwedd-mawr and Rheidol have been dammed on Plynlimon's western side to form the desolate, black-watered reservoir of **Nant-y-Moch**, reached by road via Ponterwyd (see p.277). There is little sympathetic landscaping here, the lake looking nothing more than the flooded valley that it is.

GLYNDŴR'S WAY

A fairly new long-distance footpath, **Glyndŵr's Way** weaves its 123 miles through Montgomeryshire and northern Radnorshire countryside well reputed for the solitude that it offers. Running from Knighton in the south, the path climbs up into the remote hills to the northwest before turning south four miles south of Newtown. From here, the path plunges through the pastoral hills and past only occasional settlements towards Abbeycwmhir, where it again turns and heads north towards Llanidloes and Llyn Clywedog, passing the 103 lofty turbines of the Penrhyddlan and Llidiartywaun Windfarm, the largest in Europe. From Llyn Clywedog, the path heads across the mine-scarred mountains around Dylife and down into Machynlleth. It then ducks back inland, along the A489 for a few miles before dipping down into the hills, up over the A470 and across its bleakest stretch: the wet and wild upland moor south of the A458. Through the Dyfnant Forest, Glyndŵr's Way zigzags down to the shores of Lake Vyrnwy, eastwards along the River Vyrnwy and over its last few miles to Welshpool.

Well signposted all the way, Glyndŵr's Way is far quieter than Offa's Dyke path, both in the number of settlements en route and the number of people attempting it. Varied scenery includes barren bog, exhilarating uplands, reservoirs, undulating farmland and sections of river-valley walking.

The hamlet of **STAYLITTLE** (Penfforddlas) – whose English name comes from a village blacksmith who was so quick at shodding horses his smithy became known as *Stay-a-little* – is above the Clywedog River at the northern end of Llyn Clywedog. Just north of the village, the mountain road to Machynlleth forks left, running past the plunging ravine of the Twymyn River to the north. Old mine workings herald the approach to **DYLIFE**, or "Place of Floods", a lead-mining community of around two thousand people in the mid-nineteenth century, with a reputation as a lawless, licentious gambling pit. The mine closed in 1896, and the population has since dwindled to around just twenty, although this increases when walkers and devotees of good beer and food flock to the old *Star Inn* (☎01650/521345; ③) during the warmer months. Good walks from Dylife include up to Pen-y-crogben, the mine-clad slope that rises to the south of the village, and west to **GLASLYN**, or "blue lake", and the reedy shores of **Bugeilyn**. The superb **Glyndŵr's Way** footpath (see opposite), crosses this patch on its way to Machynlleth. A popular viewpoint on the road two miles west of Dylife has been furnished with a cheery memorial to broadcaster and author **Wynford Vaughan-Thomas** (1908–87), whose outstretched slate hand points out to the dozens of rippling peaks and verdant valleys.

Montgomery and around

The tiny town of **MONTGOMERY** (Trefaldwyn) is Montgomeryshire at its most anglicized. It lies at the base of a **castle** on the Welsh side of Offa's Dyke and the present-day border. The castle was started in 1233 by the English king, Henry III, and today's remains are not on their own worth the steep climb up the lane at the back of the town hall, although the view over the lofty church tower, handsome Georgian streets and the vast green bowl of hills around the town is wonderful. The impressively symmetrical main thoroughfare – well-named Broad Street – swoops up to the perfect little redbrick **town hall**, crowned by a pert clock tower. Facing the town hall, Arthur Street goes down to the right and the **Old Bell museum** (April–July & Sept Wed–Fri & Sun 1.30–5pm, Sat 10.30am–5pm; Aug Mon–Fri & Sun 1.30–5pm, Sat 10.30am–5pm; 50p), an unusually enjoyable local history collection of artefacts from excavations, scale models of local castles, an old workhouse exhibition and mementoes from Montgomery civic life.

At the other end of Broad Street, the rebuilt tower of Montgomery's parish **church of St Nicholas** dominates the snug proportions of the buildings around it. Largely thirteenth-century, the highlights of its spacious interior include the 1600 canopied tomb of local landowner, Sir Richard Herbert, and his wife, Magdalen. They lie in prayer on top, with their eight (apparently angelic) children (including Elizabethan poet George Herbert) in beatific kneeling positions behind them. Under the couple lurks a shrouded cadaver. The two medieval effigies on the floor at the end of the tomb are of uncertain origin, although the farther one is though to be of Sir Edmund Mortimer ("revolted Mortimer", as Shakespeare had him), son-in-law of Owain Glyndŵr, brother-in-law of Hotspur and once Constable of Montgomery Castle. Equally impressive are the elaborately carved fifteenth-century double screen and accompanying loft, believed to have been built from sections removed from an abbey over the border in Cherbury.

Montgomery is near one of the best preserved sections of **Offa's Dyke**, which the long-distance footpath shadows either side of the B4386 a mile east of the town. Ditches almost twenty feet high give one of the best indications of the dyke's original look and, to the south of the main road, the England–Wales border still exactly splices the dyke, twelve hundred years after it was built. If you want to **stay** here, the rambling *Dragon Hotel* (☎01686/668359; ④), by the town hall, has a swimming pool and is dependable, if rather pompous. Better options are *Bronwylfa* (☎01686/668630; ③), a beautiful white Georgian town house on Broad Street, or *Little Brompton Farm* (☎01686/668371; ③), two miles south of town and handy for the Offa's Dyke path. For **food** and **drink**, head for *The Checkers* pub, opposite *Bronwylfa* on Broad Street, livelier and younger than the *Dragon*.

Berriew

North of Montgomery, just five miles southwest of Welshpool, the neat village of **BERRIEW** (Aberrhiw) is more redolent of the black-and-white settlements over the English border than anywhere in Wales, its Tudor houses grouped prettily around a small church, the shallow waters of the Rhiw River and the posh *Lion Hotel* (☎01686/640452; ⑤).

Just over the river bridge, the **Andrew Logan Museum of Sculpture** (May–June & Sept–Oct Sat, Sun & Bank Holiday Mon 2–6pm; July & Aug Wed–Sun 2–6pm; £1.50) makes for an incongruous attraction in such a setting, with a good selection of the notable British modern sculptor's work. Andrew Logan is the man who inaugurated the great drag-and-grunge ball known as the *Alternative Miss World Contest* in the 1970s, launchpad of the formidable Divine's career, from which astounding costumes and memorabilia form a large chunk of the exhibits at the museum. There's also Logan's oversized horticultural sculpture, including giant lilies encrusted with shattered mirrors and vast metal irises that rise to scrape the roof, as well as his smaller-scale jewellery and model Goddesses that only add to the sublime camp of the exhibition.

Dolforwyn Castle

The A483 continues southwest through the valley, with occasional glimpses of the River Severn and in almost constant proximity to the reed-filled **Montgomery Canal**. Just before the road bridge swings suddenly over to cross them both six miles southwest of Montgomery, there's a small right turn leading up to the *Dolforwyn Hotel* and the gaunt remains of unsignposted **Dolforwyn Castle**. Described by Jan Morris as "the saddest of all the Welsh castles", this was the very last fortress to be built by a native Welsh prince on his own soil – Llywelyn ap Gruffydd in 1273 – as a direct snub to the English king, Edward I, who had expressly forbidden the project. Llywelyn built his fortress and started to construct a small adjoining town as a Welsh fiefdom to rival the heavily anglicized Welshpool, just up the valley. Dolforwyn only survived for four years in Welsh hands before being overwhelmed after a nine-day siege by the English, and the castle was left slowly to rot. In the past twenty years, the remains have been excavated, and significant portions of the fragile old castle have emerged on the wind-blown hilltop, with its astounding views over the Severn valley, four hundred feet below. The small left turning after the hotel leads down to the entrance to Yew Tree Cottage, otherwise identified by a rusty corrugated-iron shack and twin gates. The track leading up is a public path that winds its way up to the lonely ruins. The path circles around the castle and heads north, coming to a stile after a hundred yards or so. Crossing this, and heading diagonally across the field towards the track and another stile, the path brushes past the fragmentary earthwork remains of Llywelyn's lost market town.

Newtown

NEWTOWN (Y Drenewydd), despite its name, was founded in the tenth century around a small castle, growing steadily until its population explosion in the nineteenth century as a centre for weaving and textiles. As in so many other places, the town's traditional industry has all but disappeared, and it hasn't really found anything to replace it. Although the centre of town is bland enough not to cause offence, it's not a terribly stimulating place and hardly one in which to linger – although you might find yourself making transport connections here, and there is an excellent theatre, the **Hafren** (☎01686/625007), and a strong music scene.

Of Newtown's sights, the High Street is home to the **W H Smith** chain of newsagents, housing a small and reasonably interesting **museum** (Mon–Sat 9.30am–5.30pm; free) about the company and its growth from 1792. A block west, the car park where you'll find the bus depot and tourist office is also home to **Oriel 31** (Mon–Sat 10am—5pm; free), a great gallery of imaginative temporary exhibitions, classes and occasional live music, poetry readings and storytelling. On Severn Street, opposite the nineteenth-century red terracotta **clock tower**, is the house in which early socialist **Robert Owen** was born in 1771, now open as a **Memorial Museum** (Mon–Fri 9.45–11.45am & 2–3.30pm, Sat 10–11.30am; free) that explains this remarkable man's life. The museum's visitors' book indicates just how much of a shrine the place has become, with a roll call of socialist politicians and trade unionists scrawling their thanks for Owen's work in its pages. Displays include Owen's own notebooks and ledgers, contemporary paintings of his communities in America and New Lanark, and newspaper records of establishment disdain for his work.

ROBERT OWEN

Robert Owen (1771–1858) was born in Montgomeryshire in the late eighteenth century, but left Wales to enter the Manchester cotton trade at the age of eighteen and swiftly rose to the position of mill manager. His business acumen was matched by a strong streak of philanthropy towards his subordinates. Fundamentally, he believed in social equality between the classes and was firmly against the concept of competition between individuals. Poverty was something he believed could be eradicated by cooperative methods. Owen recognized the potential of building a model workers' community around the New Lanark mills in Scotland and joined the operation in 1798, swiftly setting up the world's first infant school, an Institution for the Formation of Character and a model welfare state for its people.

Owen's ideas on cooperative living led to his building up the model community of New Harmony in Indiana, USA, which he established between 1824 and 1828, before handing the still struggling project over to his sons. Before long, and without the wisdom of its founder, the idealistic tenets of New Harmony collapsed under the weight of greed, ambition and too many vested interests. Undeterred, Owen, by now back in Britain, was encouraging the formation of the early trade unions and cooperative societies, as well as leading action against the 1834 deportation of the **Tolpuddle Martyrs**, a group of Dorset farm labourers who withdrew their labour in their call for a wage increase. Owen's later years were dogged by controversy, as he lost the support of the few sympathetic sections of the British establishment in his persistent criticism of organized religion. He gained many followers, however, whose generic name gradually changed from Owenites to socialists – the first usage of the term. Owen returned to Newtown in his later years, and died there in 1858.

Over the river at 5–7 Commercial St, the **Textile Museum** sits above six cramped old weavers' cottages (May–Sept Tues–Sat 2–5pm; free). Exhibits show the dramatic ebbs and flows of the town's staple trade, from the flannel and hand-loom factories of the 1790s, through the social unrest and industrial decline of the 1830s and 1840s (Wales' first Chartist demonstration took place here in 1838), the revival of trade thanks to Pryce Pryce-Jones' world-first mail order service and its subsequent dwindling to nothing by 1935. Pryce-Jones' **Royal Welsh Warehouse** – an industrial cathedral that dominates the eastern approach to the town centre – is now a deadbeat shopping centre.

Five miles north of Newtown, the mock-Tudor **Gregynog Hall** was the home from 1920 of Gwendoline and Margaret Davies, aesthete sisters who inherited a vast fortune from their port-building father and spent much of it on a world-class art collection, most of which now resides in Cardiff's National Museum of Wales (see p.99). Gregynog became their headquarters for an artistic revival, including the establishment of a world-famous small press, which is up and running once more. It is now an extra-mural outpost of the University of Wales, offering public courses in Welsh language and culture and hosting an annual music **festival** in late June. **Guided tours** (June–Sept Mon–Sat 11am & 3pm; £2) lead you through the hall and its splendid grounds and gardens, although you can wander around the latter two at any time.

Two miles north of town, on the A483 to Welshpool, there's a great **quad biking** centre at *Severn Valley Quad Trekking*, Broniarth Farm (☎01686/625560).

Practicalities

Newtown's **train station** is on the southern edge of the town centre, and a path heads straight up past the ugly Victorian parish church of St David and up Back Lane to the car park that serves both as the **bus station** and as temporary home to the **tourist office** Portakabin (Easter–Oct daily 10am–5.30pm; ☎01686/625580). For information of gigs and festivals – like the superb **Mid Wales May Festival** (☎01686/621975), a weekend of music, poetry, storytelling and street theatre – check out the *Ian Snow* craft and clothing shop, 1 The Cross.

If you have to **stay** in Newtown, your best bet is the *Plas Canol* guesthouse, between the station and the town centre on New Road (☎01686/625598; ②). The mock-Jacobean *Pheasant Inn* on Market Street (☎01686/625966; ②) does good B&B, as well as cheap and tasty **lunches** and real ales. *Yesterdays* (☎01686/622644; ③),˙ behind the clock tower in Severn Square, also offers decent B&B and super Welsh speciality dishes.The best traditional food, plus great pasta and pizza, is at the comfortable *Courtyard* on Severn Street. You won't be stuck for **pubs** – there are loads, even if most are eminently avoidable. The *Lion Inn*, near the clock tower, is good for live music, late drinking and discos, while Commercial Street's *Bell Hotel* and Severn Street's *Sportsman* host regular live folk, R&B and blues.

Welshpool

Three miles from the English border, eastern Montgomeryshire's chief town of **WELSHPOOL** (Y Trallwng) was formerly known as just Pool, its prefix added in 1835 to distinguish it from the English seaside town of Poole in Dorset. It's not a very Welsh place, lying in the anglicized valley of the River Severn (Afon Hafren) and with a history that depended largely upon the patronage of English landlords and kings. The town's new bypass has cleared its streets of excessive traffic, and left a number of well-proportioned roads crowned with some Tudor and many good Georgian and Victorian buildings. But it's for sumptuous **Powis Castle**, one of the greatest Welsh fortresses, that Welshpool is on most people's agenda.

Arrival, information and accommodation

The pompous neo-Gothic turrets of the old Victorian **train station** (its modern replacement is directly behind) sit at the top of Severn Street, which leads down into the town centre. The **tourist office** is at the northern edge of the town in the *Flash Leisure Centre*, Salop Road (daily 9.30am–5.30pm; ☎01938/552043), twenty minutes' walk from the central town crossroads. By car, it's just off the bypass at the first Welshpool exit on the road from England.

There is plenty of B&B **accommodation** in town, with a dozen or so along the Salop Road; of them all, *Montgomery House* (☎01938/552693; ②) is the surest bet. Other places include *Severn Farm* on Leighton Road (☎01938/553098; ③), just beyond the industrial estate to the east of the station, which will also let you pitch a **tent**; *Dysserth Hall* (☎01938/552153; ③), opposite Powis Castle along a small lane running off the Berriew Road, or right at the heart of town at the main crossroads, the traditional, rather upmarket coaching inn, the *Royal Oak* (☎01938/552217; ⑤). There are two superb farmhouse B&Bs just north of town: *Gungrog House* (☎01938/553381; ③) and, a little further towards the village of **Guilsfield** (Cegidfa), *Lower Trelydan Farm* (☎01938/553105; ③).

The Town

Arriving at Welshpool's modern **train station** gives a false sense of what to expect from the town, which is much more attractive than the modern mess around the rail lines would lead you to believe. Two hundred yards along Severn Street, a humpback bridge over the much-restored **Montgomery Canal** hides the canal **wharf**, from where gaudily painted boats will chug you up the navigable section for a few miles and a couple of hours (☎01938/553271). There's also an old wharfside warehouse here that has been carefully restored as the **Powysland Museum** (Mon, Tues, Thurs & Fri 11am–1pm & 2–5pm, Sat & Sun 2–5pm; also May–Sept Sat & Sun 10am–1pm; free), an impressively wide collection looking at the local area throughout history. Of special interest is the display about the impact of the Black Death here, when half the town's population died, and Roman remains from the now obliterated local Cistercian abbey of Strata Marcella.

Right at the centre of town are the crossroads, where the Georgian **Royal Oak Hotel** acts as a firm reminder of the junction's importance on the old coaching route. Broad Street is the most architecturally interesting of the streets leading off from here, with the ponderous Victorian town hall and its dominating clock tower overlooking some fine Tudor and Jacobean town houses. On New Street, behind the *NatWest* bank, is an early eighteenth-century circular **cockpit** you can wander around. Broad Street changes name five times as it rises up the hill towards the tiny Raven Square terminus station of the **Welshpool and Llanfair Light Railway**, half a mile beyond the town hall. The eight-mile narrow-gauge line (April–Sept daily 10am–4pm; ☎01938/810441) was open to passengers for less than thirty years, closing in 1931, but now scaled-down engines once more chuff along the appropriately modest valleys of the Sylfaen Brook and Banwy neu Einion River to the almost eerily quiet village of **LLANFAIR CAEREINION**, a good daytime base for walks and pub food at the *Goat Hotel*. The **post office**, opposite the church, stocks free leaflets of some good local circular walks.

Eating and drinking

Welshpool's four main streets are home to most of the town's **eating** and **drinking** establishments. The best restaurant in town is the moderately priced *Justin's Hideaway* in the *Park House* cellars on the High Street (closed Sun; ☎01938/555006), but the *Shilam Tandoori* at 13 Berriew St (☎01938/553431) is also good. Many of the town's pubs do lunchtime food with some, notably the *Talbot* in the High Street, serving excellent evening meals as well. Cheap and filling breakfasts, lunches and teas are served in the *Buttery*, opposite the town hall on the High Street. Other good pubs for evening entertainment include the small, dark *Mermaid* on the High Street and the *Powys Arms* up Salop Road, with live music, quizzes and karaoke.

Powis Castle

In a land of ruined castles, the sheer scale and beauty of **Powis Castle** (April–June, Sept & Oct Wed–Sun 11am–5pm; July–Aug Tues–Sun 11am–5pm; £6, or £4 gardens and museum only; NT), a mile from Welshpool up Park Lane, is the real reason for coming to the town. On the site of an earlier Norman fort, the castle was started in the reign of Edward I by the Gwenwynwyn family; to qualify for the site and the barony of De la Pole, they had to renounce all claims to Welsh princedom. In 1587, Sir Edward Herbert bought the castle and began to transform it into the Elizabethan palace we see today.

Inside, the **Clive Museum** – named after Edward Clive, son of Clive of India, who married into the family in 1784 – forms a lively account of the British in India, through diaries, notes, letters, paintings, tapestries, weapons and jewels, although it is the sumptuous period rooms that impress most, from the vast and kitsch frescoes by Lanscroon above the balustraded staircase to the mahogany bed, brass and enamel toilets and decorative wall hangings of the state bedroom. The elegant Long Gallery has a rich sixteenth-century plasterwork ceiling overlooking winsome busts and marble statuettes of the four elements, placed in between the glowering family portraits.

The **gardens**, designed by Welsh architect William Winde, are spectacular. Dropping down from the castle in four huge stepped terraces, the design has barely changed since the seventeenth century, with a charmingly precise orangery and topiary that looks as if it is shaved daily. Summertime outdoor concerts, frequently with firework finales, take place in the gardens.

Llanfyllin and around

The hills and plains of northern Montgomeryshire conceal a maze of deserted lanes and farm outposts along the contours that swell up towards the north and the foothills of Denbighshire's Berwyn Mountains. The only real settlement of any size is **LLANFYLLIN**, a peaceful but friendly hillside town, ten miles northwest of Welshpool in the valley of the River Cain, and the best-equipped place in the area to stay. The High Street is a busy centre of bright pubs, cafés, shops and a weekly Thursday market. Narrow Street forks off from here, climbing to the restored **well of St Myllin**, who has reputedly looked after inhabitants of his town since the sixth century by curing the ailment of any Llanfyllin citizen. From here, views over the town, its unusual plain redbrick church (few churches were built in eighteenth-century Wales) and the looming Berwyn Mountains, are delightful.

Llanfyllin has plenty of places to **stay**: the *Cain Valley* on the main High Street (☎01691/648366; ③) is an old coaching inn, and there's B&B at *The Chestnuts*

(☎01691/648179; ②). Just west of the town is the splendid *Bodfach Hall* (closed Oct–Easter; ☎01691/648272; ④), set in gorgeous grounds. There's a fine **restaurant** on the High Street in the shape of *Seeds* (☎01691/648604), with a three-course set dinner menu including good vegetarian options. Alternatively, there's cheap eating at *Eagles* café on the High Street, or good pub food in the back bar of the *Cain Valley* (see above), far less snooty than the posh front area. The *New Inn* is the least touristy of the High Street's pubs.

The Tanat and Rhaeadr valleys

Parallel to the valley of the River Cain, three or four miles to the north, are the luscious valleys of the Afon Tanat and its tributary, the Rhaeadr. It's a sparsely populated, little-changed backwater, a beguiling area set against the looming Berwyn Mountains.

For a place so near the English border, **LLANRHAEADR-YM-MOCHNANT** is surprisingly Welsh in its language and appearance. The small, low-roofed village, six miles north of Llanfyllin, is best remembered as the serving parish of Bishop William Morgan, who translated the Bible into Welsh in 1588 (see p.380), an act which ensured the survival of the old tongue. The village has two great pubs – the *Three Tuns* and *Wynnstay Arms*, and excellent B&Bs at *Plas-y-Llan* (☎01691/780236; ③) and *Rose Cottage* (☎01691/780398; ②). For **bike rental** with a difference, Llangedwyn Mill in the village of Llangedwyn, three miles east, is the home of *Swallow Tandems* (☎01691/780050), Britain's only tandem specialist.

Llanrhaeadr lies at the foot of the wild walking country of the southern Berwyn Mountains. A lane from the village courses northwest alongside the Rhaeadr River, through an increasingly rocky valley for four miles, before coming to an abrupt halt at **Pistyll Rhaeadr**, supposedly Wales' highest waterfall at 150ft. The river tumbles down the crags in two stages, flowing under a natural stone arch that has been christened the Fairy Bridge. When it's quiet, tame chaffinches swoop and settle all around this enchanting spot, although the charms are a little hard to appreciate amid the crowds on a warm summer Sunday. Right by the car park, the summer-only *Tan-y-Pistyll* licensed café and B&B (☎01691/780392; ③) is nothing special, but its location is superb.

The B4396 runs east from Llanrhaeadr, along the Tanat Valley and through the village of **LLANGEDWYN**. A mile or so after the village, few tourists make it up one of the left turns leading to **SYCARTH**, only a mile from the English border, but one of the most Welsh of all shrines; a grass mound marks the site of Owain Glyndŵr's ancestral court, reputedly a palace of nine grand halls. Bard Iolo Goch immortalized this Welsh Shangri-la as a place of "no want, no hunger, no shame / No-one is ever thirsty at Sycarth".

Just to the east of Sycarth, the English–Welsh border tightly encircles the 740-foot limestone crag of **Llanymynech Rocks** (now a nature reserve), before cutting down to run right through the middle of the village of **LLANYMYNECH**. Indeed, the divide runs slap through the village's *Lion Hotel* – not so long ago, thanks to the now dead Welsh ban on licensing on the Sabbath, half the pub had to remain "dry" on Sunday, while the other (English) half downed beer with gusto. Just over the road, the *Bradford Arms* does superb bar and restaurant food.

The B4391 hugs the river as far as the soporific little **LLANGYNOG**, where it heads north into the Berwyn Mountains and Denbighshire. The village, cowering under the rocky screes of Craig Rhiwarth, is a low-key walkers' base. The lane by the bridgeside fish-and-chip shop leads to a stunning four-mile hike over the top of Y Clogydd and down to the elfin charms of Pistyll Rhaeadr (see above). Less strenuously, you can walk two miles further up the Tanat Valley to the hamlet of **PENNANT MELANGELL**, sitting low in a quiet valley of sheer sides and sparkling brooks, the site of one of Wales' most enduring legends. The eighth-century saint Melangell was praying in the valley when a hare being chased by a hunt pack led by Prince Brochwel took refuge in her skirts. The hounds drew to a sudden stop before her and fled howling. The prince drew his horn to his lips to call them, only to find himself unable to remove it. The prince was so moved by her gentle humanity that he granted her the valley, in which she built a religious community. The idyllic little **church** (May–Oct daily 10am–6pm; Nov–April daily 10am–4pm) that sits there today dates from the eighth century, although the site was one of worship and spiritual significance way before. Inside, the twelfth-century shrine (the oldest known in Britain) and supposed effigy of St Melangell lie beneath an exquisite barrel roof. Her grave is in the semicircular *cell y bedd* at the back of the church. Intact Norman features include a window in the main church, the doorway at the back, the south door porch and the font. By the Norman doorway at the back, a locally discovered whale bone is mounted on the wall.

Lake Vyrnwy

A monument to the self-aggrandizement of the Victorian age, **Lake Vyrnwy** (Llyn Efyrnwy) combines its functional role as a water supply for Liverpool with a touch of architectural genius, in the shape of the huge nineteenth-century dam at its southern end and the Disneyesque turreted straining tower which edges out into the icy waters. It's a magnificent spot, and a popular centre for walking and bird-watching. A commemorative stone at the eastern end of the dam arrogantly celebrates "taking and impounding the waters of the Rivers Vyrnwy, Marchnant and Cowny", which flooded a village of four hundred inhabitants in the process.

Vyrnwy was the first of the massive reservoirs that mid-Wales came to host, constructed during the 1880s. The village of Llanwddyn was flattened and rebuilt at the eastern end, people receiving compensation of just £5 for losing their homes. The story is told, somewhat apologetically, in the **Vyrnwy Visitor Centre** (daily 10.30am–5.30pm; Jan–March Sat & Sun only; free), which combines with the **tourist office** (same hours; ☎01691/870346) and an RSPB centre, located in the cluster of buildings on the western side of the dam. **Bike rental** is available from *Mandy's Tea Shop* (☎01691/870377), in the workshops by the visitor centre or, more cheaply, from the *Bethania Adventure Centre* (☎01691/870615), in the boathouse near the dam, which also offers **river rafting** and **sailing** trips.

If you want to **stay** near the lake, there's the grand *Lake Vyrnwy Hotel* (☎01691/870692; ⑤), overlooking the waters above the southeastern shore. It's a mite pricy, but if you just want a look, it serves a full afternoon tea in a chintzy lounge overlooking the lake. There's farmhouse B&B at *Tyn-y-maes* (☎01691/870216; ③), a couple of miles east of the new village of **Llanwddyn** on the B4393. Alternatively, there's the sublime ivy-draped *Cyfie Farm* (☎01691/648451; ③), just over a mile south of **Llanfihangel-yng-Ngwynfa**.

THE DEE VALLEY

Northern Powys peters out on the stark slopes of the Berwyn Mountains, on the other side of which lies the charming valley of the wide, meandering **River Dee**.

Llangollen, along with the smaller towns of Bala and Corwen, grew up partly as a market centre, but also served the needs of cattle drovers who used the passage carved by the river through the hills as the easiest route from the fattening grounds of northwest Wales to the markets in England. Long before rail and road transport pushed the dwindling numbers of drovers out of business at the end of the nineteenth century, they had already been joined by early tourists. Most made straight for Llangollen, where the ruins of both a Welsh castle and a Cistercian abbey lent a gaunt Romantic charm to a dramatic gorge naturally blessed with surging rapids. The arrival of the train, in the middle of the nineteenth century, made Llangollen a firm favourite with tourists from the mill towns of northwest England, but also opened up **Corwen** and **Bala**, market towns making the best of the new opportunities for income. The train line closed in the 1960s and Corwen slipped back into its former role, but Bala has become one of Wales' top watersports venues, a centre for windsurfing and white-water kayaking. Between the two, the **Vale of Edeyrnion** slumbers at the foot of the fine walking country of the Berwyn range. Between Llangollen and the English border, the Dee is joined by one of its major tributaries, the River Ceiriog, which flows, parallel to and south of the Dee, down the peaceful valley of **Glyn Ceiriog** to the Marcher fortress of **Chirk Castle**.

Chirk and Glyn Ceiriog

Like the Berwyn foothills over the county border in Montgomeryshire, **Glyn Ceiriog** and its surrounds are blissfully quiet and starkly beautiful. Tiny lanes wind up from Llanrhaeadr-ym-Mochnant and the Tanat Valley to a tranquil stretch that's occasionally – and very optimistically – promoted as the "Little Switzerland of Wales".

Chirk and Chirk Castle

The Normans founded **CHIRK** (Y Waun) almost a thousand years ago, their motte remaining as a small tree-covered mound at the southern end of this pleasant but dull village with long views up the valley to the Berwyn hills. Chirk's minor architectural features are laboriously explained on the *Chirk Town Trail* leaflet (available free from tourist offices in the region), so you're better off with its companion, the *Chirk Bridges Trail* (2 miles; 1hr; negligible ascent) which circles Thomas Telford's towering 1801 aqueduct carrying the Llangollen Canal seventy feet above the river. The route is sporadically indicated by a red hand, the principal element on the local lairds' coat of arms and the source of all the "Hand" hotels which dot the region.

For the last 400 years, the Myddleton family have occupied the massive drumtowered **Chirk Castle** (July & Aug daily except Sat Castle noon–5pm, garden 11am–6pm; April–June & Sept daily except Mon & Sat; Oct Sat & Sun only; £4; NT), squatting ominously on a rise half a mile to the west of Chirk. Roger Mortimer began the construction of this Marcher fortress at the behest of Edward I during the thirteenth century, and it eventually fell to the Myddletons. The approach to the castle is guarded by a magnificent Baroque **gatescreen**, the finest work done by the Davies brothers of Bersham, who wrought it between 1712 and 1719. The ebullient floral designs are capped by the Myddleton coat of arms, with a pair of wolves reproduced atop the cage-like gateposts (perhaps a memorial to one of the last wolves in Wales, said to have kept watch over the moat in the 1680s). From the gates, a mile-and-a-half-long avenue of oak leads up to the castle, an austere-looking place, softened only by the mullioned windows. The original plan was probably to mimic Beaumaris Castle (see p.411), started just a couple of months earlier, but it lacks Beaumaris's purity and symmetry. The east and west walls are both incomplete, stopping at the half-round towers midway along the planned length, and the towers have been cut down to wall level, probably after the Civil War, when taller towers would have been vulnerable to mortar attack. Internal modifications have been no less extensive, leaving a legacy of sumptuous rooms reflecting sixteenth- to nineteenth-century tastes, many returned to their former states after some Victorian meddling by Pugin in the 1840s.

After touring the house, you should try to leave an hour spare to explore the beautiful ornamental gardens or to trace the section of Offa's Dyke that runs across the front of the house, though it was flattened in 1758 for use as a cart track.

Glyn Ceiriog

Chirk Castle guards the entrance to the Glyn Ceiriog valley, for centuries an important route into the heart of Wales and over the Berwyns into Snowdonia. These days it is the minor B4500 which runs beside the river for five miles through the hamlet of Dolywern to the slightly larger **GLYN CEIRIOG**, home to the **Chwarel Wynne Slate Mine** (Easter–Oct daily 10am–5pm; £2.50). The half-hour underground tour and tatty museum are engagingly low-key, but if you are making for Snowdonia, you'd be better to save your money for the more spectacular tours under Blaenau Ffestiniog (see p.336).

It's another four miles to **LLANARMON DYFFRYN CEIRIOG** (usually referred to as Llanarmon DC), an appealing small village consisting of nothing but a church, a post office and some excellent accommodation catering to walkers. From February to November, the mountain-leader owners of *Gwynfa* (see below) run *Hillwalk Wales*, guided hillwalks for all abilities (£10 a day; ☎01691/600287) and a series of residential weekend courses. From Llanarmon DC, you can link up with the walk described on p.257, by taking the road heading northwest opposite the church. After five miles, you reach the memorial stone mentioned.

Practicalities

Trains on the Shrewsbury to Wrexham main line stop at Chirk's train station midway along the half-mile-long Station Avenue. **Buses** stop in the centre of Chirk and infrequently penetrate the Glyn Ceiriog valley as far as Llanarmon DC. *Berwyn Bikes* (☎01691/718845) rents **mountain bikes** in Glyn Ceiriog village. The many high-quality country **inns** in the region are an attraction in themselves, and all serve good **food**.

Ddol-Hir, Glyn Ceiriog (☎01691/718681). Small riverside caravan and campsite on the B4500 a mile west of the village.

Glyn Valley Hotel, Glyn Ceiriog (☎ & fax 01691/718896). Modest inn serving reasonably priced bar meals. ④.

Golden Pheasant Hotel, Llwynmawr (☎01691/718281, fax 718479). Traditional eighteenth-century rod-and-gun country hotel, with pleasant rooms, gradually undergoing modernization. Food is served in both the formal restaurant and wood-beamed bar. ⑤.

Gwynfa, Llanarmon DC, 200 yards along the Llanrhaeadr road (☎01691/600287). Attractive, comfortable non-smoking B&B, the home base for *Hillwalk Wales* (see above).Vegetarian breakfasts and four-course evening meals for £10. Closed Dec & Jan. ③.

Hand Hotel, Church Street, Chirk (☎01691/773472, fax 772479). Sixteenth-century coaching inn with fully fixtured, modernized rooms. Substantial breakfast included, and full dinners served in the restaurant. The warren of small bars all serve real ales. ⑥.

Hand Hotel, Llanarmon DC (☎01691/600666, fax 600262). Sixteenth-century converted farmhouse with a wood-beamed bar. Try to get one of the older but less well-appointed rooms rather than those in the modern extension. ⑦.

The Lodge, Halton (☎01691/774424). Spacious, tastefully decorated rooms in a secluded Georgian mansion a mile north of Chirk, just off the A5. ⑤.

Tŷ Gwyn, Llanarmon DC (☎01691/600229). Comfortable B&B with inexpensive meals on prior request. ③.

West Arms, Llanarmon DC (☎01691/600665, fax 600622). Ancient farmhouse-turned-inn with a gorgeous inglenook fireplace and some characterful rooms. Morning tea and a hearty breakfast, plus sumptuous dinners and affordable bar meals. ⑨.

The Woolpack Inn, Pandy, a mile west of Glyn Ceiriog (☎01691/718382). Gently modernized old mill with decent rooms, a restaurant and a bar with lined with real-ale pumps. ⑤.

Llangollen and around

LLANGOLLEN, seven miles northwest of Chirk, is in both setting and character the embodiment of a Welsh town, clasped tightly in the narrow Dee Valley between the shoulders of the Berwyn and Eglwyseg mountains. Along the valley's floor, the waters of the River Dee (Afon Dyfrdwy) cut a wide arc around the base of **Dinas Brân**, a conical tor surmounted by the ruins of a native Welsh castle. At the apex of the bend, the Dee licks the angled buttresses of Llangollen's weighty Gothic bridge, which has spanned the river since the fourteenth century. On its south bank, half a dozen streets, their houses harmoniously straggling up the rugged hillsides, are labelled in both Welsh and English, and form the core of the scattered settlement flung out across the low hills.

As the only river crossing point for miles, Llangollen was an important town long before the early Romantics arrived at the end of the eighteenth century, when they were cut off from their European Grand Tours by the Napoleonic Wars. Turner came to paint the swollen river and the Cistercian ruin of **Valle Crucis**, a couple of miles up the valley; John Ruskin found the town "entirely lovely in its gentle wildness"; and writer George Borrow made Llangollen his base for the early part of his 1854 tour detailed in *Wild Wales*. The rich and famous came not only for the scenery, but to visit the celebrated **Ladies of Llangollen**, an eccentric pair of lesbians who became the toast of society from their house, **Plas Newydd**. But by this stage some of the town's rural charm had been eaten up by the works of one of the century's finest engineers, Thomas Telford, squeezing both his **London–Holyhead trunk road** and the **Llangollen Canal** alongside the river. Canal trips run east to his majestic nineteen-span **Pontcysyllte Aqueduct** over the Dee, while steam-hauled trains now ply the reconstructed track west towards the head of the canal at the Horseshoe Falls. If none of this is energetic enough, try the panoramic day-long walk along the limestone escarpment to the north of town (see p.247).

Llangollen's functional-looking streets can seem little different from any other Welsh town, but its rural environs are home to a wealth of historical sites, making this a very popular base throughout the summer, particularly in early July when the town struggles to cope with the thousands of visitors to Wales' celebration of worldwide folk music, the **International Music Eisteddfod** (see p.245).

Arrival, information and getting around

Buses are the only form of public transport to reach Llangollen, with local services (and the daily Wrexham–London *National Express* coach) stopping on Market Street. The nearest **train station** is five miles away at Ruabon, and passed by frequent buses on the Llangollen–Wrexham run. With your own vehicle, the most spectacular way to approach Llangollen is over the 1350-foot Horseshoe Pass (A542) from Ruthin.

The **tourist office** (Easter–Oct daily 10am–6pm; Nov–Easter 9.30am–5pm; ☎01978/860828) is fifty yards south of the bridge and less than a hundred yards from the bus stop on Market Street. Alternative information is available at the *Earth Mother* New Age shop on Oak Street. Buses in the immediate locality are very infrequent, so you might as well resign yourself to **getting around** on foot – no great hardship as Valle Crucis, the most distant sight, is only a mile and a half along the towpath. There is no **bike rental** in Llangollen itself, but *Berwyn Mountain Bikes* (☎01691/718845), four miles south in Glyn Ceiriog, will deliver.

Accommodation

Finding **rooms** in Llangollen can be a chore in the middle of summer, especially during the Eisteddfod, though this is alleviated by people letting out one or two bedrooms in the peak period. The tourist office can book you into these as well as ordinary guesthouses. These are dotted all over the valley, though many of the cheaper ones are on Hill Street heading up towards Plas Newydd.

Hotels and guesthouses

Bodidris Hall, seven miles north of Llangollen on the A5104 (☎01978/790434, fax 790335). Secluded luxury in a largely Tudor building in nine acres of grounds, with log fires, oak beams and an award-winning restaurant. ⑧.

Bryn Howel, Trevor, two miles east off the A539 (☎01978/860331, fax 860119). One of Llangollen's better hotels, though the assiduous courting of the conference set strips it of some of its charm. Beautiful grounds and good facilities including sauna, solarium, free trout fishing and a top-class restaurant (see p.249). Some cheaper two-night deals. ⑨.

Cefn-y-Fedw, Garth, Trevor, five miles from Llangollen (☎01978/823403). Excellent non-smoking farmhouse B&B. Take the A539 to Trevor then left at the *Australia Arms* and continue straight ahead, following signs for Penycae. Closed for lambing Nov–April. ③.

Gales, 18 Bridge St (☎01978/860089, fax 861313). Very comfortable and central guesthouse above a great restaurant. En-suite rooms with TV and Laura Ashley decor. ④.

Hafren, Berwyn Street (☎01978/860939). Good non-smoking B&B, at the bottom of this price category with shared bathroom and no single supplement, along the A5 to Corwen. ③.

Jonkers, 9 Chapel St (☎01978/861158). A couple of compact but appealing rooms, one with a four-poster, under the eaves of a café. Great if you like ancient uneven floors, poky corridors and a shared bathroom. ③.

Mrs Adams, 2–3 Aberadda Cottages, Hill Street (☎01978/860770). One of the cheapest central B&Bs with en-suite rooms, at the bottom of this price code. Non-smoking. ③.

Mrs Lewis, 1 Bodwen Villas, Hill Street (☎01978/860882). Bargain, central B&B. ②.

The Old Vicarage, Bryn Howel Lane, three miles from Llangollen (☎01978/823018). Very comfortable and spacious country guesthouse by the Dee. Take the A5 east, turn left at *Aqueduct Inn*, then left after the bridge. ③.

The Royal Hotel, Bridge Street (☎01978/860202, fax 861824). Good traditional nineteenth-century hotel by the bridge in town. ⑦.

Walton House, Queen Street (☎01978/860825). Decent basic B&B that's about as cheap as it gets in Llangollen. ②.

Hostels and campsites

Eirianfa, Berwyn Road (☎01978/860919). Fully featured riverside holiday park almost a mile west of the town on the A5.

Llangollen YHA hostel, Tyndwr Road (☎01978/860330, fax 861709). High-standard hostel in a Victorian manor that's also one of the YHA's principal activity centres (see "Activities", p.249). It is a mile and a half east of town – go along the A5 towards Shrewsbury, turn right up Birch Hill, then right again. Open all day, April–Oct. ①.

Mile End Mill Bunkhouse, Mile End Mill, Berwyn Road (☎01978/869043). Clean, basic accommodation in three- or four-bed dorms for £6 (£8 en suite) overlooking the canoe slalom site a mile west of town. ①.

Wern Isaf Farm (☎01978/860632). Simple farmhouse campsite just under a mile up Wern Road. Turn right over the canal on Wharf Hill.

The Town

Few visitors can resist admiring the view up the valley from the parapet of the **town bridge** which, though widened and strengthened over the years, has spanned the river since the fourteenth century. Below it, the Dee pours through the fingers of shale which make up the unimaginatively dubbed "Town Falls" rapids, an occasional venue for canoe slaloms.

The bridge runs onto Castle Street, which heads due south past the tourist office to the **European Centre for Traditional and Regional Cultures**, or ECTARC (May–Sept Mon–Sat 10am–6pm, Sun 11.30am–5.30pm; Oct–April Mon–Sat 10am–5pm, Sun 11.30am–4.30pm; ☎01978/861514; free). Primarily a centre for folk studies, it also presents occasional performances and six-monthly displays drawing on each of the fifteen EU countries in turn. Bibliophiles should cross the road to *Maxim's* café above which Hay-on-Wye book emperor Richard Booth (see p.215) has opened a cavernous second-hand **bookshop**. Further along Castle Street, the small, basement **Post Office Museum** (daily 9am–5.30pm; £1) offers a bitty but moderately diverting display of letter writing and delivery paraphernalia. Some exquisite nineteenth-century nibs, inkstands and seals stand out from the ancient mail delivery bags and massed ranks of first-day covers.

Llangollen takes its name from the **Church of St Collen** on Church Street, off Castle Street (sporadically open during church hours, but key available at the nearby *Hand Hotel*). Dedicated to a sixth-century saint, the church features a fine fifteenth-century oak hammerbeam roof, said to have come from Valle Crucis (see p.247). The graveyard is of equal interest for the triangular railed-off monument to Mary Carryll erected by her mistresses, the Ladies of Llangollen (see below), who are also buried with her in the churchyard and commemorated on the other two sides of her pillar.

Plas Newydd

Standing in twelve acres of formal gardens, half a mile up Hill Street from the southern end of Castle Street, the two-storeyed mock-Tudor **Plas Newydd**, Butler Hill (April–Oct daily 10am–5pm; £1.80) was, for almost fifty years, home to the celebrated **Ladies of Llangollen**. Lady Eleanor Butler and Sarah Ponsonby were a lesbian couple from Anglo-Irish aristocratic backgrounds, who tried to elope together at the end of the eighteenth century. After two botched attempts dressed in men's clothes, they were grudgingly allowed to leave in 1778 with an annual allowance of £280, enough to settle in Llangollen, where they became the country's most celebrated lesbians – though apparently they were affronted by the suggestion that their relationship was anything other than chaste. Regency society was captivated by their "model friendship" in what Simone de Beauvoir called "a peaceful Eden on the edge of the world". Despite their desire for a "life of sweet and delicious retirement", they didn't seem to mind the constant stream of gentry who called on them. They found the Duke of Wellington a "charming young man, hansom, fashioned tall and elegant" and commemorated his visit in typically self-absorbed manner by engraving "E.B & S.P. 1814" over the mantelpiece in the Oak Room. Walter Scott was also well received, though he found them "a couple of hazy or crazy old sailors" in manner, and like "two respectable superannuated clergymen" in their mode of dress. Thomas de Quincey humoured the ladies, if only to bend their favour towards his friend Wordsworth, who had displeased them by referring to their house as "a low roofed cot" in an inelegant poem he had composed in the grounds.

THE LLANGOLLEN INTERNATIONAL MUSIC EISTEDDFOD

Llangollen is heaving in summer, but never more so than during the second week of July, when for six days the town explodes into a frenzy of music, dance and poetry. The **International Music Eisteddfod** comes billed as "the world's greatest folk festival" but unlike the National Eisteddfod (see "Annual events" in *Basics*), which is a purely Welsh affair, the Llangollen event draws amateur performers from thirty countries, all competing for prizes in their chosen disciplines. Throughout the week, impromptu dances and choral performances burst into being anywhere that a group of people can congregate, often blocking traffic. Competitive performances are concentrated in the main venue, the **Royal International Pavilion**, on the north bank just west of the Gothic bridge, but performers occasionally present their works at other sites around the town, Plas Newydd and Valle Crucis included. When the day's competition is over, headlining stars often pack out the pavilion: Luciano Pavarotti and his 200-strong entourage fronted up in 1995 on the fortieth anniversary of his first performance here.

The festival has been held in its present form since 1947, when it was started more or less on a whim by one Harold Tudor to soothe the social wounds of WWII. Forty choirs from fourteen countries performed at the first (entirely choral) event, and it expanded, drawing praise quickly, from Dylan Thomas, who declared that "the town sang and danced, as though it were right". Today over 12,000 international musicians, singers, dancers and choristers descend on this town of 3000 people, further swamped by up to 150,000 visitors. While the whole setup can seem oppressive, there is an irresistible *joie de vivre* as brightly costumed dancers walk the streets and fill the fish-and-chip shops.

Unless you are going specifically for the Eisteddfod, the week beginning the second Tuesday of July is a good time to stay away. Accommodation should be booked at least a year in advance, though **tickets** (☎01978/860236, fax 861300) for all but the headlining shows can be obtained much closer the time, often on the day itself. Access to the site, with no guarantee of a seat, costs as little as £4 a day.

Gifts of sculpted wood panelling formed the basis of the riotous friezes of gloomy woodwork that weigh on your every step around the modest black-and-white timbered house, and most of the rooms have been left almost empty, so as not to hide the panelling. This does make it a little sterile, with only one upper room being devoted to a few of the ladies' possessions, and printed boards covering their life story.

The north bank of the Dee

Wherever you are in Llangollen, the hills echo to the shrill cry of steam engines easing along the **Llangollen Railway** (April–Oct 3–8pm daily; winter Sat, Sun & school holidays; ☎01978/860979; £6 return). Shoehorned into the north side of the valley, it runs from Llangollen's time-warped station west past Glyndyfrdwy, near the Horseshoe Falls, as far as Carrog six miles up the valley, and eventually will go as far as Corwen. Operating along a restored section of the disused Ruabon–Barmouth line, belching steam engines creep along the river bank, hauling ancient carriages which sport the liveries of their erstwhile owners. The railway recently gained some notoriety by offering steam train funerals, the body or ashes being loaded on a train equipped for a mobile wake. Local opposition – founded on fears that rail fanatics would have their ashes thrown in the fire box to be distributed over the valley – has scuppered plans for the time being. The occasional driver-experience courses, letting you behind the controls of a steam loco (£120 for 2hr) are proving less controversial. You can dine on the train, too (see p.249)

A short riverside walk from the station leads to **Lower Dee Mill**, Mill Street (daily 10am–5pm; combined ticket valid all day £7), an ugly light industrial building converted to house three widely divergent museums. Fanfare is reserved for the **Doctor Who Museum** (individually £4), one man's mission to preserve the fantasy of this enduring British sci-fi TV drama. If you grew up with the programme you'll love it, but don't expect any chilling encounters: the only-just-animated Hall of Monsters serves only to confirm how shabby and low-tech the Daleks, Silurians, Axons and Sea Monsters were, the original costumes seemingly slapped together from lampshades and bubble-wrap.

Train buffs will be drawn to **Model Railway World** (£3), where demonstrations of die-casting and model-building give way to an extensive collection of large layouts – some of them token-operated – in every imaginable scale. The **Boat Museum** (£1) has the broadest appeal, admirably explaining the construction of the Llangollen Canal in the context of Britain's canal building mania at the end of the eighteenth century. Until the coming of the railway in 1865, the waterway was the only means to carry slates from the quarries on the Horseshoe Pass. Designed as a water supply for the Shropshire Union Canal, it was one of Britain's finest feats of canal building: from the artificial **Horseshoe Falls**, a crescent-shaped weir built in 1806 to feed water into the canal, its architect, Thomas Telford, managed to avoid using locks for the first fourteen miles. He did this by building the thousand-foot-long **Pontcysyllte Aqueduct** 126ft above the river, at **Froncysyllte**, four miles east, employing long cast-iron troughs supported by stone piers – a bold move for its time. Diesel-driven licensed narrowboats run from **Llangollen Wharf**, Wharf Hill (summer Sat & Sun noon; July & Aug daily; £5.50), a two-hour one-way trip returning by road. Alternatively you can drive to Froncysyllte on the A542 – or walk the towpath – and take a forty-minute narrowboat ride with *The Ribbon Plate* (April–Sept daily except Mon 11am & 3pm; July & Aug hourly; £1) across the aqueduct and back, turning a blind eye to the nearby chemical plant. More committed narrowboaters can rent one for the day from *Trevor Wharf Services* in Froncysyllte (☎01978/821749; £55–70).

Castell Dinas Brân

It is the view both ways along the valley which justifies a 45-minute slog up to **Castell Dinas Brân** (Crow's Fortress Castle), perched on a hill 800ft above the town, and reached by a path by Llangollen Wharf. The lure certainly isn't the few sad vaulted stumps which stand in poor testament to what was once the district's largest and most important Welsh fortress. Built by the ruler of northern Powys, Prince Madog ap Gruffydd Maelor, in the 1230s, the castle rose on the site of an earlier Iron Age fort. Edward I soon took it as part of his first campaign against Llywelyn ap Gruffydd (see p.432), and the castle was left to decay, John Leland, Henry VIII's antiquarian, finding it "all in ruin" in 1540.

Although not much to look at, it is a great place to be when the sun is setting, imagining George Borrow translating seventeenth-century bard Roger Cyffyn:

> *Gone, gone are thy gates, Dinas Brân on the height!*
> *Thy warders are blood-crows and ravens, I trow;*
> *Now no-one will wend from the field of the fight*
> *To the fortress on high, save the raven and the crow.*

A WALK FROM LLANGOLLEN

Note: This walk is not easy to follow without the OS Landranger #117 map

Climbing up to Dinas Brân, you get a fair idea of what is in store on Llangollen's **Precipice Walk** (14 miles; 7hr; 1800ft ascent), which traces the crest of the wonderful limestone escarpment formed by Trevor and Eglwyseg rocks. One of the most dramatic sections of the Offa's Dyke Path – though not the dyke itself – follows the base of these cliffs, but the tops make a far better walk, offering superb views down into the Vale of Llangollen and across the Berwyn Range to the south. Since the eastern half of what is effectively a circuit around Ruabon Mountain is the least interesting part, the walk is described anti-clockwise so the best can be experienced when you're freshest. Although it is certainly a long walk, the worst of the climbing is quickly over and fine weather makes it a superb outing.

Start the walk on a narrow tarmac path over the canal from Llangollen Wharf signposted up towards the ruins of **Castell Dinas Brân**. From the castle the route ahead unfolds, down the north flank towards the tarmacked road which runs below the escarpment forming part of the Offa's Dyke Path. Turn right at the road and head east along it for three miles, always taking any left turns and keeping the open land of Ruabon Mountain on your left. Half a mile past Hafod Farm turn left to Bryn-Adda following a Public Footpath sign. The route then heads roughly north over dense heather to the forestry plantation at Newtown Mountain and on to the road near Mountain Lodge. Just past the entrance to the lodge, turn west up towards the top of the moor and the head of the valley known as World's End. Follow the southern perimeter of a plantation and pick up the path, which then follows the escarpment south back to Llangollen. The easiest way back is to continue past Dinas Brân to the end of Trevor Rocks, then follow the road down to town.

The Eisteddfod site, Valle Crucis Abbey and Eliseg's Pillar

Walking west from the town bridge the Eisteddfod site soon hoves into view heralded by the architecturally controversial but nonetheless impressive **Royal International Pavilion**. The 6000-seat white plastic structure was designed to evoke the shape of the traditional marquee formerly erected on the site each year, but looks more like some giant armoured reptile dropped from a great height into the green valley. Outside the Eisteddfod season, the auditorium acts as a concert venue and sports hall, the foyer operates as a **gallery** (Mon–Fri 10am–4pm; free) with reputable changing exhibitions of international fine art and north Welsh crafts, and side rooms host workshops ranging from alternative medicines to Chinese brush painting.

Following the A542 or the canal towpath a mile west, you pass Llangollen's **Motor Museum** (Easter–Oct daily 10am–5pm; Nov–Easter Mon–Fri 10am–12.30pm & 1.30–5pm; £1.50), a shed full of lovingly restored not-so-vintage cars and vans, but it's more rewarding to follow the road another half-mile to the gaunt remains of **Valle Crucis Abbey** (April–Sept daily 10am–5pm; £1.70; CADW), in Glyn y Groes (Valley of the Cross). In 1201, Madog ap Gruffydd Maelor of Dinas Brân chose this majestic pastoral setting for one of the last Cistercian foundations in Wales, as well as the first Gothic abbey in Britain. Despite a devastating fire in its first century, and a company of far-from-pious monks, it survived until the Dissolution in 1535. The church fell into disrepair, after which the monastic buildings, in particular the monks' dormitory, were employed as farm buildings. Later,

THOMAS TELFORD (1767–1834)

The English poet Robert Southey dubbed **Thomas Telford** the "Colossus of Roads" in recognition of his pre-eminence as the greatest road builder of his day, if not the greatest ever. Throughout the early years of the nineteenth century, he managed some of the most ambitious and far-reaching engineering projects yet attempted, and there was seldom a public work on which his opinion wasn't sought.

Born in Scotland, he was apprenticed to a stonemason in London where he taught himself engineering architecture, eventually earning himself a position working for the Ellesmere Canal Company, who were planning a canal to link the Severn, Dee and Mersey rivers. His reputation was forged on the **Pontcysyllte Aqueduct**, part of the **Llangollen Canal** which, though one of his earliest major projects, was recognized as innovative even before he had completed it. Though lured away to build the Caledonian Canal in Scotland and St Katherine's Docks in London, he continued to work in Wales, reaching the apotheosis of his road-building career by pushing the **London–Holyhead Turnpike** through Snowdonia.

After the 1800 Act of Union between Britain and Ireland, a good road was needed to hasten mail and to transport the new Irish MPs to and from parliament in London. What is now the A5 was wedged into the same valley as Telford's Llangollen Canal, then driven right through Snowdonia with its gradient never exceeding 1:20. The combination of its near-level route and the high quality of its well-drained surface cut hours off the journey time, but the Dublin ferries left from Holyhead on the island of Anglesey separated from the mainland by the Menai Strait. Telford's solution and his greatest achievement was the 580-foot-long **Menai Suspension Bridge**, strung 100ft above the strait to allow tall ships to pass under. Though the idea wasn't completely novel, the scale and the balance of grace and function won the plaudits of engineers and admiring visitors from around the world.

Turner painted the abbey, imaginatively shifting Dinas Brân a couple of miles west onto the hill behind.

Though less impressive than Tintern Abbey (see p.55), Valle Crucis does greet you with its best side, the largely intact west wall of the church pierced by the frame of a rose window. At the opposite end, the equally complete east wall guards a row of six graves, one of which is said to contain Owain Glyndŵr's resident bard, Iolo Goch. There are displays on monastic life upstairs, reached by a detour through the mostly ruined cloister and past the weighty vaulting of the chapterhouse.

The cross that gives the valley its name is the eight-foot-tall **Eliseg's Pillar** (unrestricted access; CADW), four hundred yards north by the A542. Erected to a Prince of Powys in the ninth century by his great-grandson, it originally stood 25 feet high but was smashed during the Civil War in the 1640s. The stump remains, but you can now only see half of the full 31 lines glorifying the lineage of the Princes of Powys, which Celtic scholar Edward Llwyd translated from the remaining pieces in 1696.

Eating, drinking and entertainment

Though not extensive by city standards, Llangollen boasts a fairly good selection of **restaurants** and no shortage of **cafés** around town. Picnic ingredients are best sought at the *Blas Da* food emporium on Castle Street next to the tourist office.

Outside Eisteddfod week, there's not a great deal of **nightlife**, but local bands do play from time to time and it is always worth checking if there is anything going on at the Eisteddfod site or at ECTARC.

Restaurants and cafés

Berwyn Belle (☎01978/860583). Enjoy an expensive four-course dinner on the Llangollen Railway (see p.245) as it inches its way to Carrog and back. Runs Sat 7.30pm and Sun 1pm roughly May–Sept & Dec.

Cedar Tree Restaurant at the *Bryn Howel Hotel*, Trevor (☎01978/860331). Formal, award-winning restaurant with great views of Dinas Brân across the lawns.

Gales Wine Bar, 18 Bridge St (☎01978/860089). Old church pews, large helpings of delicious home-made bistro-style food and one of the most extensive wine cellars around.

The Gallery, 15 Chapel St (☎01978/860076). Friendly restaurant serving a good range of pizza and pasta dishes.

Jonkers Coffee Shop, 9 Chapel St. A quiet non-smoking café with books and newspapers and very good food served in the dim interior or the walled garden. Open daily and for dinner Fri & Sat.

The Woolpack Restaurant, 13 Church St (☎01978/860300). Opposite *Gales* and in direct competition with it, *The Woolpack* offers a slightly more formal approach for just a pound or two more, though midweek there are often three-course specials for under £10.

Pubs and entertainment

Bull Hotel, Castle Street. Lively and central town pub (with a beer garden) that's the main gathering place for Llangollen's youth.

Dee Bar,*The Royal Hotel*, 1 Bridge St. Very youthful and lively, especially at weekends.

Royal International Pavilion, Abbey Road (☎01978/860111). Year-round venue for sporadic and predominantly choral or classical concerts.

Hand Hotel, 26 Bridge St. Straightforward local pub where you can listen to the male voice choir in full song at 7.30pm on Mon & Fri.

Jenny Jones, Abbey Road (☎01978/860653). Good pub with mixed clientele most nights, live country and western music on Wed and jazz on Thurs.

Jonkers (see "Accommodation"). Tiny and typically packed venue for occasional poetry readings and noted folk bands. Book early.

Prince of Wales, Berwyn Street. The place to be on Wed night for local rock.

Wynnstay Arms, 20 Bridge St. A child-friendly bar divided into several smaller rooms, with good beer.

Activities

The climb up to Dinas Brân and the Panorama Walk (see box) both make for excellent walks with magical valley views, but require considerably more effort than the gentle riverside walk along Victoria Promenade to Riverside Park, a modest grassy expanse with a **novelty golf course** (90p) where you are required to steer your ball around mini versions of local beauty spots: the Pontcysyllte Aqueduct, the Horseshoe Falls, Valle Crucis, Plas Newydd . . . you get the idea.

The bouncy but less-than-menacing waters of the Dee are perfectly suited to the modest **rafting trips** (£8 an hour) operated by *J J Canoeing & Rafting*, Mile End Mill, Berwyn Road (☎ & fax 01978/860763), which also offers **kayaking** and guided **mountain-bike** tours.

Llangollen's YHA hostel (see "Accommodation", p.243) operates as an **activity centre**, offering plenty of short, introductory sessions in kayaking, caving, rock climbing, mountain biking and sailing. Two-day residential courses typically cost £70–90, with the week-long "Wet and Wild" extravaganza of canoeing, sailing, gorge walking and windsurfing priced at £225.

Corwen and around

In the early fifteenth century, Welsh rebel Owain Glyndŵr set out from **CORWEN**, eight miles west of Llangollen, to wrest back all Wales from the English barons (see p.284). There is precious little to commemorate this fact, only the shape of a dagger incised into a grey-stone lintel of the south porch of the thirteenth-century **church of St Mael and St Julien**, known as **Glyndŵr's Sword**. The Welsh hero, local landowner and scourge of Henry IV is said to have cast the "sword" in anger at the townspeople from atop the hill behind. It actually predates him by half a millennium, but you can still keep his prowess in mind as you follow a path leading up between dry-stone walls from the road to the right of the post office up to the **viewpoint**. Before doing that, take a look around the near-circular churchyard with its well-preserved Celtic cross and gravestone with indentations for penitents' knees. Inside the church, there is a fine Norman font.

In Glyndŵr's time and probably before, Corwen was an important cattle drovers' town. The two main routes out of north Wales – one from Anglesey and the Llŷn peninsula, the other from Ardudwy and Harlech – met here for the final push to the English markets. The arrival of the train killed off the cattle trade but not the town itself, which for a century became an important junction of the Barmouth and Rhyl train lines. Now a quiet market town, it does have a couple of sights nearby, including two fine ancient churches (see below). Glyndŵr aficionados will probably be interested in the thirty-foot-high truncated cone of **Owain Glyndŵr's Mount**, on the south bank of the Dee just over three miles east on the road to Llangollen, where he is supposed to have stood on lookout for his enemies. He may well have done so, but the earthworks are more likely to be a Norman motte-and-bailey castle.

Corwen's charms don't justify stopping overnight, although the *Corwen Court*, London Road (closed Dec–Feb; ☎01490/412854; ②), is a B&B with a difference: converted from a police station and courthouse, the cells are now single rooms, and the doubles are converted from the sergeant's family's quarters. If that doesn't suit, the welcoming *Powys House Estate*, Bonwm, a mile east on the A5 (☎01490/412367; ③), has its own swimming pool and tennis court; and *Mrs Jones*, Tyn Llidiart, Carrog Road (☎01490/412729; ③) has non-smoking rooms and the most outstanding breakfasts this side of anywhere.

Buses on the Llangollen–Bala route stop in the centre of Corwen.

Capel Rûg and Eglwys Llangar

Taking its name from the Welsh word for heather, **Capel Rûg** (April–Sept Tues–Sat 10am–2pm & 3–5pm; £1.70; CADW), a mile west of Corwen on the A494, is one of Wales's best examples of an unmolested seventeenth-century church. Along with the Gwydyr Uchaf Chapel, near Llanrwst (see p.315), it gives a charming insight into worship three hundred years ago, when mass was a private clerical devotion, with the congregation kept behind rood screens.

Rûg didn't entirely escape, but much here is as it was built in 1637 by the former privateer and collaborator on William Morgan's Welsh Bible (see p.380), William

Salusbury. The plain exterior design gives no hint of the richly decorated interior: wooden angels support a roof patterned with stars and amoebic swirls, and a painting of a skeleton said to represent the transient nature of life and the inevitability of death. Informative displays in the ticket office give more details of the building's use.

Your ticket to Capel Rûg also entitles you to an escorted visit from there to another little-changed church, **Eglwys Llangar** (normally locked, phone Capel Rûg for tour times, usually 2pm), a mile to the south off the B4401, which dates back to the fourteenth century or earlier. Parish boundary changes in 1853 made this church redundant, saving its extensive fifteenth-century wall paintings and seventeenth-century figure of death from obliteration. The interior woodwork is wonderful, from the beamed roof and minstrels gallery down to the eighteenth-century box pews.

The Vale of Edeyrnion

If you are not in a hurry to get from Corwen to Bala, take the quiet B4401 along the Dee through the peaceful villages of the Vale of Edeyrnion: Cynwyd,

---

A WALK ON THE BERWYNS FROM CYNWYD OR LLANDDERFEL

Note: The OS 1:50,000 Landranger #125 map is recommended for this walk

Henry II's 1165 expeditionary force encamped on the Berwyn Hills until forced to flee back to England from the guerrilla tactics of Owain Gwynedd and the Welsh weather. Legend has it that the king beat his retreat along the ancient high-moor trackway, thereafter known as Ffordd Saeson (Englishman's Road). Whether he did or not, the path makes for a good route up onto these lonesome rocky heather-clad outcrops. The **walk** (10 miles; 5–6hr; 2500-ft ascent) follows part of Ffordd Saeson starting from Cynwyd beside *Y Llew Glas* (The Blue Lion) pub, passing the YHA hostel up through a forest to the deep heather moorland pass of **Bwlch Cynwyd** (1700ft). An alternative to this direct route forks right a hundred yards after the youth hostel and leads past a waterfall and serene lake, before rejoining the main path. From Bwlch Cynwyd, the circular route leads south, but if the skies are clear, the lone summit of **Moel Fferna** (2067ft), a mile or so to the north, makes a rewarding detour. South from Bwlch Cynwyd, follow the path beside the fence for a couple of miles across desolate, somewhat featureless land to the summit of **Pen Bwlch Llandrillo Top** (2037ft), then drop down the other side to an ancient drovers' road. Known locally as the Maid's Path, it was once the harvest-time route for girls heading east from Llandrillo, sometimes as far as Llanarmon Dyffryn Ceiriog, five miles from here (see p.240). If you don't have your own transport, try walking over the Berwyns from the Vale of Edeyrnion into Glyn Ceiriog: it is the closest you'll get to experiencing what the drover's life must have been like.

Near where you meet the drovers' road, a much later traveller is commemorated by a stone to "A Wayfarer 1877–1956, a lover of Wales". In the days before knobbly tyres and gas mono-shock suspension systems, one W M Robinson rode up here by bicycle, unwittingly laying the groundwork for scores of mountain bikers now following his lead along the bridleways. A metal box nearby contains a book to record your visit.

The cairned summit of **Cadair Bronwen** (2575ft), a mile and a half south of the memorial, is the only place in Wales where you can pick cloudberries (sharp-tasting orange blackberries); otherwise head east for Glyn Ceiriog or west for the Vale of Edeyrnion. After half a mile on the westerly path, a sign points to Llandrillo, while an unsigned path forks right to Cynwyd.

Llandrillo and Llandderfel. None of the villages is particularly interesting, but any can act as a base for walks on the largely undiscovered Berwyn Range to the east (see p.251), where you can walk all day without seeing a soul.

The road passes a couple of the best country hotels in the area, a simple campsite and a **YHA hostel**, *The Old Mill* (May–Sept; ☎01490/412814; ①), in the hamlet of Cynwyd, two miles south of Corwen. Walkers who don't fancy the youth hostel might prefer the comfortable *Fron Gogh Farmhouse* a mile and a half south of Cynwyd (☎01490/440418; ④) with moderately priced meals, or the nearest **campsite** *Hendwr Caravan Park* (April–Oct; ☎01490/440210), a further half-mile south. This is just one of several which dot the river flats through the valley.

The Berwyns are equally accessible from **LLANDRILLO** where, after a day in the hills, you can luxuriate in the elegant Georgian surroundings of *Tyddyn Llan Country House*, on the B4401 towards Bala (☎01490/440264; ⑧) and eat in its highly rated, expensive restaurant. For sheer grandeur, though, you can't beat the handpainted and intricately carved Victorian interiors of *Palé Hall* (☎01678/530285, fax 530220; ⑨), three miles on and just outside Llandderfel, where the ageing Queen once stayed – a great place for a splurge. If your budget won't stretch to these kind of prices, there's also the *Bryntirion Inn* (☎01678/530205; ④), where you turn off the B4401 to get to *Palé Hall*, which has free fishing for guests.

In **LLANDDERFEL**, the large stone house at the fork in the road at the far end of the village is *Bronwylfa* (April–Nov; ☎01678/530207; ③), where you are greeted with tea and *bara brith*. A mile further along the B4401, and only two miles short of Bala, *Melin Meloch* (March–Nov; ☎01678/520101; ③) is partly built from a converted thirteenth-century watermill beside the Dee, and will provide moderately priced communal meals by arrangement.

Bala

Easily reached either via the A494 from Corwen or over a spectacular mountain pass from Montgomeryshire's Lake Vyrnwy, the little town of **BALA** (Y Bala), at the northern end of Wales' largest natural lake, **Llyn Tegid** (Bala Lake), is a major watersports centre with a modest sideline in remote walks on little-visited hills. If neither of these are of interest, there's little point in stopping here. The four-mile-long body of water is perfect for **windsurfing** in particular, with buffeting winds whipping up the valley formed by the Bala geological fault line, which slices thirty miles northeast from the coast, up the Talyllyn Valley, and between the Aran and Arenig mountains flanking the lake.

Bala's second lake, **Llyn Celyn**, five miles west of town, isn't very much smaller than Llyn Tegid but is very much an artificial affair, created to supply Liverpool, in England, with its drinking water. A modern chapel on the shore commemorates the valley-bottom village of Capel Celyn (flooded to create the reservoir) and its former inhabitants.

The Town

The narrow town sits slightly back from the lake edge, perhaps to avoid the catastrophe which, according to two legends, drowned the old town which stood where the lake now is. One tells of someone forgetting to put the lid on the well which, during the night, overflowed covering the valley and town. A more entertaining story records the fate of the quasi-legendary prince Tegid Foel, who was warned by a voice that, because of his cruelty to his people, "Vengeance will come". On the birth of his son, he held a banquet at which a hired harpist heard a voice saying "Vengeance has come". A bird led him away onto a hill where he slept, waking to find the town submerged beneath the lake which took the prince's name.

Bala has a role in Welsh history which far outweighs its current status. The district was of only minor importance before the eighteenth century, the Romans having built a fort at the southern end of the lake (not open to the public), and the Normans having erected a motte, now tree-covered and known as **Tomen-y-Bala**, on Heol y Domen off the northern end of the High Street (keys from the council offices, 22–24 High St) which gives a panoramic view over the town. But it was wool – and socks in particular – that brought the town its fame. Until the Industrial Revolution killed the trade, most men and women in the town were involved in knitting, even clothing George III, who wore Bala stockings for his rheumatism. During this period, the people of Bala became noted for their pious-

---

THOMAS CHARLES AND MICHAEL D JONES

During the seventeenth and eighteenth centuries, the religious needs of the Welsh were being poorly met by the established Church. None of the bishops were Welsh, few were resident, and most regarded their positions as stepping stones to higher appointments, and so the preachings of the newly emerging Nonconformists – Quakers, Baptists and, later, Calvinist and Wesleyan Methodists – were welcomed by the people. Congregations swelled from the middle of the eighteenth century, but conversion didn't get into full swing until the effects of itinerant religious teachers improved literacy and the strident sermons of native Welsh-speakers fired their enthusiasm. There were already over twice as many chapels as Anglican churches when the chief protagonist of Methodism in Wales, **Thomas Charles**, gave the movement a massive boost through the founding of the British and Foreign Bible Society, a group committed to distributing local-language Bibles worldwide.

He had already reprinted Bishop Morgan's 1588 original Welsh translation (see p.380), but was down to his last copy when 16-year-old Mary Jones (see p.290), the daughter of a poor weaver from the other side of Cadair Idris, arrived on his doorstep. She had saved money for six years to buy a Bible from Thomas Charles and, in 1800, walked the 25 miles to Bala, barefoot some of the way, prompting Charles to found the society.

Despite the rise in Nonconformism, many of the more pious converts sought greater freedom to worship as they pleased, in a land where they felt free; something denied them in Wales by the oppression of both the English Church and State. The reformist preacher **Michael D Jones** came to Bala enlisting recruits for his model colony outside Wales, and accordingly, he helped them found *Y Wladfa*, "The Colony", a Welsh enclave in Chubut Valley, Patagonia: in 1865 he transported 153 Welsh settlers, mostly from Bala, to Argentina, to set up a radical colony where Nonconformism and the Welsh language kept a tight rein. This was the start of a 3000-strong community (and the world's first society to give women the vote), which grew until 1912, when immigration stopped and linguistic assimilation accelerated. Jones stayed in Wales, setting up the Bala-Bangor Theological College and leading campaigns for Welsh causes, and many now regard him as "the father of modern Welsh nationalism".

ness and followed the preachings of Nonconformist ministers Thomas Charles and Michael D Jones (see box, p.253). Charles is buried a mile south in the churchyard at Llanycil; his statue stands outside the Presbyterian church on Tegid Street, and a plaque locates his former home at 68 High St, in what is now a *Barclays* bank. A nearby plaque records Mary Jones' walk (see box, p.253).

The only other thing to do is ride the **Bala Lake Railway** (mid-April to Sept; ☎01678/540666; £5.50 return, £3.50 single), which starts half a mile south of Bala on the other side of the lake and runs for four miles along the route of the former Ruabon–Barmouth standard-gauge line, which closed in 1963. It's one of Wales' least interesting narrow-gauge runs, but you can ride the renovated north Wales slate quarry trains down the far side of the lake to Llanuwchllyn. The *Eagles Inn*, ten minutes' walk from Llanuwchllyn station, serves excellent bar meals, and you could even stick around to hear the local male voice choir rehearse in the village hall at 7.30pm on Thursdays.

Practicalities

The best approach to Bala is the A4212 from south of Blaenau Ffestiniog over the wild uplands between the twin peaks of Arenig Fawr and Arenig Fach. Unfortunately, this can't be done by public transport as Bala's only **bus** is the #94, which runs from Llangollen through the Vale of Edeyrnion (see p.257) to Dolgellau stopping on High Street. The **tourist office**, Pensarn Road (April–Oct daily 10am–6pm; ☎01678/521021), is half a mile south along High Street in the same building as the Penllyn Leisure Centre.

Accommodation

Bala and its immediate vicinity have plenty of places to **stay** or you can make the most of the surrounding countryside by staying in the Vale of Edeyrnion (see p.257), northeast of the town.

HOTELS AND GUESTHOUSES

Abercelyn, half a mile south of Bala on the A494 (☎01678/521109). A fine country house in an eighteenth-century former rectory. Closed Jan. ④.

Fron Feuno Hall (☎01678/521115). Gracious country house with a vast lounge overlooking Llyn Tegid and comfortable, spacious rooms. Lots of thoughtful little touches make it all the more appealing. Delicious evening meals by arrangement. Closed Dec & Jan. ⑥.

Traian, 95 Tegid St (☎01678/520059). Good-value, very welcoming central guesthouse with shared bathrooms. ②.

White Lion Royal Hotel, 61 High St (☎01678/520314). In the last century, both Queen Victoria and George Borrow chose the *White Lion*. It is still the best in town, even if the breakfasts are no longer the sumptuous spreads described by Borrow. ⑤.

HOSTELS AND CAMPSITES

The Coach House, Tomen Y Castell on the A494, a mile and a half north of Bala (☎01678/520738). Superior self-catering bunkhouse with small dorms (£6.50) and communal lounge and cooking areas. Very reasonable meals are available on request and duvets can be rented (£1) if you haven't brought a sleeping bag. ①.

Glanllyn, four miles south of Bala on the A494 (☎01678/540227). Family campsite across the lake, with watersports gear for rent. March–Oct.

Pen-y-Bont, on the B4402 Llandrillo road (☎01678/520549). The nearest campsite, by the outlet of the lake. Open April–Oct.

Tyn Cornel (☎01678/520759) four miles west along the A4212. Simple riverside campsite geared towards paddlers from the nearby Tryweryn slalom site. April–Oct.

Eating and drinking

Guests at the local country guesthouses and B&Bs can't go wrong with the meals offered in-house, but Bala still has its fair share of decent **restaurants** and **pubs**.

Neuadd y Cyfnod, 2 High St (☎01678/521269). This cavernous and grandly decorated old school hall serves good-value no-nonsense fare such as a £5 all-day breakfast.

Plas Coch High Street (☎01678/520309). Excellent moderately priced à la carte dinners in this traditional hotel.

Plas Yn Dre, 29 High St (☎01678/521256). Friendly licensed restaurant popular with locals for the broad choice and the Welsh lamb speciality.

The Ship, 30 High St. Good drinking pub with three-course bar meals for around a fiver.

White Lion, High Street. Ancient coaching inn and the best place to drink in town, a favourite with both locals and rosy-cheeked hill walkers huddled around the inglenook fireplace. Decent bar meals, too.

Watersports

Slalom kayak fans can make for the National White Water Centre at **Canolfan Tryweryn** (☎01678/521083), below the Arenig mountains, four miles west up the A4212. When water is released – typically around 200 days a year – it crashes down a mile and a half through the slalom site where frequent competitions take place on summer weekends. When the site is free, the centre organizes the only thrilling **white-water rafting** trips in Wales (£10 for 20min, or £140–190 for a 2-hr group experience). Proficient **kayakers** can also take to the water (£4.50 a day for canoeing association members, £10 others). Gear rental is available.

Down on the shores of Llyn Tegid by the tourist office, *Bala Adventure & Watersports Centre* (☎ & fax 01678/521059) runs courses in windsurfing, open-water kayaking and sailing. They're mostly aimed at groups but you can get individual instruction for around £35 a day. Once you're proficient you can take to the water, although on top of rental fees (starting at £12 for a kayak) you have to pay to get on the lake – £3 for sailing and £2.20 for canoeing or fishing.

travel details

Unless otherwise stated, frequencies for trains and buses are for Monday to Saturday services, Sunday averages 1–3 services, though the main routes are more frequent and some routes have no Sunday service at all.

Trains

Knighton to: Crewe (2 daily; 1hr 35min); Llandovery (4 daily; 1hr 40min); Llandrindod Wells (4 daily; 40min); Llanwrtyd Wells (4 daily; 1hr 5min); Shrewsbury (4 daily; 55min); Swansea (4 daily; 3hr 10min).

Llandrindod Wells to: Crewe (2 daily; 2hr 20min); Knighton (6 daily; 40min); Llandovery (4 daily; 1hr); Llanwrtyd Wells (4 daily; 30min); Shrewsbury (4 daily; 1hr 40min); Swansea (4 daily; 2hr 20min).

Welshpool to: Aberystwyth (6 daily; 1hr 30min); Birmingham (7 daily; 1hr 30min); Machynlleth (7 daily; 55min); Newtown (8 daily; 20min); Pwllheli (3 daily; 3hr); Shrewsbury (8 daily; 25min).

Buses

Bala to: Corwen (7 daily; 25min); Dolgellau (7 daily; 35min); Llandrillo (6 daily; 20min); Llangollen (6 daily; 55min).

Brecon to: Aberdulais (3 daily; 1hr 5min); Abergavenny (6 daily; 55min); Builth Wells (3 daily ; 40min); Craig-y-nos/Dan-yr-ogof (4 daily; 30min); Crickhowell (6 daily; 25min); Hay-on-Wye (6 daily; 45min); Hereford (5 daily; 1hr 45min); Libanus (6 daily; 8min); Llandovery (2 daily; 40min); Llandrindod Wells (3 daily; 1hr); Merthyr Tydfil (6 daily; 35min); Newport (5 daily; 1hr 50min); Pontypool (6 daily; 1hr 20min); Sennybridge (4 daily; 15min); Swansea (5 daily; 1hr 25min); Talgarth (6 daily; 25min); Talybont (5 daily; 15min).

Chirk to: Llangollen (5 daily; 20min); Oswestry (hourly; 25min); Wrexham (hourly; 40min).

Corwen to: Bala (7 daily; 25min); Denbigh (every 2hr; 1hr); Llangollen (6 daily; 20min); Ruthin (every 2hr; 30min).

Knighton to: Ludlow (5 daily; 45min); Newtown (Tues & Thurs 3 buses; 1hr); Presteigne (school bus and 3 on Thurs; 25min).

Llandrindod Wells to: Abbeycwmhir (1 postbus daily Mon–Fri; 2hr); Aberystwyth (Tues, Thurs & Sat 1 bus; 1hr 45min); Brecon (3 daily; 1hr); Builth Wells (hourly; 20min); Cardiff (1 daily; 3hr); Disserth (2 daily; 15min); Elan Village (1 postbus daily Mon–Fri; 35min); Hay-on-Wye (Wed & Sat 1 daily; 1hr); Hereford (1 daily; 2hr); New Radnor (Fri & Sat 1 daily; 30min); Newtown (3 daily; 1hr 15min); Rhayader (3 daily; 30min).

Llanfyllin to: Llanwddyn for Lake Vyrnwy (school bus; 20min); Oswestry (4 daily; 45min); Welshpool (1 daily Mon–Fri; 40min).

Llangollen to: Bala (6 daily; 55min); Chirk (5 daily; 20min); Corwen (6 daily; 20min); Wrexham (at least hourly; 30min).

Llanidloes to: Aberystwyth (1 daily; 1hr); Dylife (2 postbuses daily; 30min); Newtown (9 daily; 35min); Ponterwyd (1 daily; 40min); Shrewsbury (4 daily; 2hr); Welshpool (5 daily; 1hr 15min).

Llanwrtyd Wells to: Abergwesyn (postbus; 15min); Builth Wells (2 daily; 45min).

Oswestry (Shropshire) to: Chirk (hourly; 25min); Llanfyllin (4 daily; 45min); Welshpool (5 daily; 55min); Wrexham (hourly; 1hr 30min).

Shrewsbury (Shropshire) to: Llanidloes (4 daily; 2hr); Montgomery (3 daily; 50min); Welshpool (7 daily; 45min).

Welshpool to: Berriew (7 daily Mon–Sat; 15min); Llanidloes (6 daily; 1hr 15min); Llanfyllin (1 daily Mon–Fri; 40min); Llanymynech (5 daily; 30min); Montgomery (school bus; 25min); Newtown (7 daily; 35min); Oswestry (5 daily; 55min); Shrewsbury (7 daily; 45min).

CHAPTER FOUR

THE CAMBRIAN COAST

Cardigan Bay (Bae Ceredigion) takes a huge bite out of the west Wales coast, leaving behind the Pembrokeshire peninsula in the south and the Llŷn peninsula in the north. Between them lies the Cambrian coast, a loosely defined mountain-backed strip, periodically rent by tumbling rivers, which stretches up from Cardigan to Harlech and the shores of Tremadog Bay.

Before the railway and better roads were built during the nineteenth century, the awkward barrier of the Cambrian Mountains served to isolate this stretch of coast from the rest of Wales, and only narrow passes and cattle-droving routes pushed through the rugged terrain to get to the markets in England. Today, large sand-fringed sections are peppered with low-key coastal resorts, peopled in the summer by families from the English Midlands. The presence of English-dominated resorts and the influx of rat-race refugees to this staunchly nationalistic part of the country has, in the past, fuelled local antipathy. Protests tend to rally around incomers reluctant to use of the Welsh language – in 1993, for instance, there were threats to raze several English-run shops for refusing to display bilingual signs in their windows – but tensions seem to have eased a little since, and those foreign settlers who learn the language and actively support their adoptive land usually integrate successfully.

The Cambrian coast starts where the rugged seashore of Pembrokeshire ends, continuing in much the same vein of great cliffs, isolated beaches and swirling sea birds, punctuated with *sarnow*, stony offshore reefs largely exposed at low tide. North of the spirited town of **Cardigan**, the coast breaks at some popular seaside resorts – the best being **Llangranog** and **New Quay** – before the tiny and ordered Georgian harbour town of **Aberaeron**, recently designated the seat of the new county borough of Ceredigion.

A verdant **inland** alternative to the coastal resorts follows the River Teifi, which meets the sea at Cardigan and meanders through lush meadows past a clutch of small towns, prominent among them the stalwart market centre of **Newcastle Emlyn**, the lively university town of **Lampeter** and the charmingly old-fashioned community of **Tregaron**.

The coastal and inland routes connect at the robust and cosmopolitan "capital" of mid-Wales, **Aberystwyth**, built on the estuary of the **Rheidol**, a fast-falling river with dramatic ravines that make for great walking country. A narrow-gauge railway, an attraction in itself, climbs out of Aberystwyth to the popular tourist honeypot of **Devil's Bridge**, where three bridges, one on top of the other, span a turbulent chasm of waterfalls.

Although on a western limb of Powys, this chapter includes **Machynlleth**, at the head of the Dyfi estuary and a magical place, the seat of Owain Glyndŵr's putative fifteenth-century Welsh parliament and still a thriving market centre. Just outside the town is the **Centre for Alternative Technology**, Britain's most impressive showpiece for sustainable living and renewable energy resources.

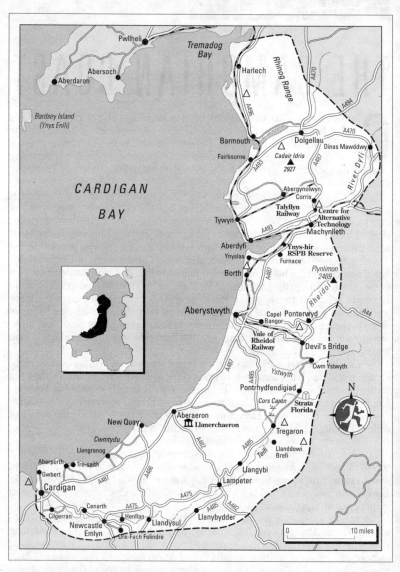

The main road continues due north from Machynlleth, but trains and the small-er coast road skirt west around **Cadair Idris**, the monumental mountain that dominates the southern third of the **Snowdonia National Park**. Each of its crag-fringed faces invites exploration, but it is best approached from the south where the narrow-gauge Talyllyn rail line reaches the tiny settlement of **Abergynolwyn**, a great base for the minor sights of the **Dysynni Valley**. Cadair Idris' northern

---

ACCOMMODATION PRICE CODES

Throughout this guide, hotel and B&B accommodation is priced on a scale of ① to ⑨. Category ① only applies to youth hostels; for the rest, the number indicates the **lowest price** you could expect to pay per night for a **double room in high season**. The prices indicated by the codes are as follows:

① under £20	④ £40–50	⑦ £70–80
② £20–30	⑤ £50–60	⑧ £80–100
③ £30–40	⑥ £60–70	⑨ over £100

---

flank slopes down to the market town of **Dolgellau**, at the head of the scenic Mawddach estuary, and linked by waterside path to the likable resort of **Barmouth**. The coastal strip then broadens out with complex dune systems protecting the approaches to **Harlech** and its castle, the southernmost link in Edward I's chain of thirteenth-century castles, perched high on its rocky promontory. Views from its fractured battlements sweep north towards the mountains of Snowdonia and west to the Llŷn peninsula.

Getting around

The most relaxing way to get fairly swiftly to and along the Cambrian coast is on the mid-Wales **train** line from Shrewsbury in England through to Machynlleth. Here the line splits: one branch runs south to Aberystwyth where you can pick up the Vale of Rheidol line to Devil's Bridge; the other swings north, calling at 25 stations in under sixty miles before it terminates at Pwllheli on the Llŷn (see p.357).

Buses run almost parallel to the trains, also extending south to Cardigan and inland to all towns of any size. There's also the express *TrawsCambria* service from Swansea to Bangor through Aberystwyth, Machynlleth, Dolgellau and Porthmadog. Many of the villages bypassed by the regular services rely on a skeletal network of **postbuses** (see *Basics*, p.26) working out of Aberystwyth and Machynlleth, though the most remote aren't served by public transport at all.

Detailed information on bus and train services as far south as Machynlleth appears in the Gwynedd and Ceredigion regional transport guides, available at tourist offices.

From Cardigan to Aberaeron

The southern section of Ceredigion coastline is enormously popular, combining safe beaches, lively market towns, some great coastal walking and a resident pod of bottlenose dolphins. Although some of the larger towns, particularly **Aberporth**, have lost much of their scenic splendour under relentless waves of holiday homes and caravan parks, many of the coast's other settlements manage to cling onto some of the salty charm that makes them so popular: **New Quay** is a delightful hillside town, while smaller places like **Llangranog**, **Penbryn**, **Mwnt** and **Gwbert** neatly juxtapose superb countryside and sweeping beaches, and the primly ordered **Aberaeron**, with its fine harbour, is quite unlike anywhere else on the coast.

Just inland, at the mouth of the Teifi, is the old county town of **Cardigan**, scarcely thrilling but pretty, cheerful and with an excellent range of pubs, accommodation and entertainment, as well as a sizeable travelling and New Age community.

The main A487 road runs parallel to the coast, meeting the sea at Aberaeron., and forms the basis of the regular #550 bus service linking the larger seaside villages and towns along this stretch.

Cardigan and around

An ancient borough and port until the Teifi Estuary silted up in the last century, **CARDIGAN** (Aberteifi) was founded by the Norman lord Roger de Montgomery around its castle in 1093. The town is at the lowest bridging point of the Teifi estuary, rising up on the river's northern bank from its medieval bridge, its gracefully simplicity making it the town's most attractive feature. The castle mound sits at the bridge's town end, with Bridge Street sweeping up a hill around it and becoming the picturesque High Street, off which run pavement-less thoroughfares, crammed with buildings from different periods. The High Street snakes past a good range of pubs and shops to the angular, turreted oddity of the **Guildhall**, with the Welsh flag skewered adamantly to its grey frontage. Through the Guildhall courtyard is the town's **covered market**, a typically eclectic mix of fresh food and some good-quality craft and second-hand stalls. A couple of hundred yards up Pendre from the Guildhall, Bath House Road dips down to the left and the redoubtable **Theatr Mwldan**, whose imaginative programme of art, theatre, cinema and music, together with a great café and the tourist office, make it an essential stop.

Priory Street leads down the hill from the Guildhall, past the council offices and tiny town **museum** (Mon–Fri 10am–5pm; free), mainly concerned with fishing memorabilia. Beyond lies Finch Square, with the bus terminus and some good pubs and cafés.

A mile out of town along the Teifi River is the large **Welsh Wildlife Centre** (daily 10am–5pm; £2.25), encompassing several important habitats – reedbeds, meadows, marshes and untouched oak woodland – for otters, badgers, butterflies and birds, including Wales' largest resident group of Cetti's Warblers. An uncomfortable combination of viewing hides and adventure playgrounds, the place seems torn between entertaining families and interesting enthusiasts, a lack of direction exemplified by an architecturally striking but inappropriate curved-glass **visitor centre** (closed Nov–March; ☎01239/621600).

Practicalities

Cardigan is just beyond the northern end of the Pembrokeshire Coast Path (see p.159), which terminates at Poppit Sands on the other side of the Teifi Estuary. The helpful **tourist office** (Easter–Sept daily 10am–6pm; Oct–Easter Mon–Sat 9am–5pm; ☎01239/613230) is in the foyer of *Theatr Mwldan* on Bath House Road, although details of the many local green festivals and meetings are usually posted on the bulletin boards at the *Hungry Tummy* wholefood café, upstairs in the entrance hall of the market.

There's plenty of **accommodation**, with numerous B&Bs along the Gwbert Road, off North Road: *Brynhyfryd* (☎01239/612861; ③), at the town end, and *Maes-a-Môr* (☎01239/614929; ②), just up in Park Place, are the best. On the High Street, the old-fashioned *Black Lion* pub (☎01239/612532; ③) has pleasant rooms and serves good meals. With your own transport, try the fifteenth-century *Rosehill Farm* in Llangoedmor, a mile and a half east of town (☎01239/612019; ③), which boasts a gorgeous riverside setting and excellent evening meals. The nearest YHA **hostel** (☎01239/612936; March–Oct only; ①) is four miles away at Poppit Sands, reached in high summer (July & Aug) by the #407 bus, which otherwise stops two miles short at St Dogmaels. **Camping** is allowed in the hostel grounds.

For **eating** and **drinking**, the café at *Theatr Mwldan*, open every day in summer and on performance evenings, serves cheap vegetarian dishes and local specialities. More substantially, *Jackets*, 58 North Rd (☎01239/615206), serves pizzas, potatoes, kebabs and pies and runs a free delivery service, while the licensed *Homely Kitchen* café on Pendre (☎01239/621863) serves good budget meals, and the *Rose of India* on Priory Street (☎01239/614891) dishes up reasonable curries. The *Red Lion* (*Y Llew Coch*), at the bottom of The Pwllhai near Finch Square, is the town's liveliest **pub**, with a pool room and live rock music at weekends, while the *Eagle*, at the southern end of the town bridge, serves the best pub food. The large and friendly *Angel Hotel* on St Mary Street hosts weekend **discos**.

The southern coast

One of the most popular stretches of coastline in the whole country, the rippled cliffs, expansive beaches and hedged lanes of the Ceredigion coast attract thousands of visitors every year, many of them keen to appreciate the tranquil ten miles of **Heritage Coast** from Ynys Lochtyn, near Llangranog, to New Quay.

The Gwbert Road heads out of the neat Cardigan suburbs before descending to the estuary edge and the straggling seaside village of **GWBERT**, whose eighteen-hole golf course is the only reason for staying here – in which case, the soulless but smart *Gwbert Hotel* (☎01239/621241; ⑥) is your best bet. More likely, you might spend an hour at the **Cardigan Island Coastal Farm Park** (daily dawn–dusk; £1), half a mile beyond the hotel, which boasts farmyard creatures both domestic and exotic and the chance to spot fur seals on a coastal walk overlooking **Cardigan Island**. The walk continues to the isolated hamlet of **MWNT**, whose exquisite sandy beach, cliffs and tiny, whitewashed fourteenth-century church are all under the custody of the National Trust.

The most popular stopping-off point on this stretch of coast has to be **ABERPORTH**, an elderly resort built around two adjoining bays, neither of them particularly pretty. The town's holiday resort status has long since robbed it of charm, and though it's packed full of places to stay, you're far better off pushing on to the infinitely preferable hamlet of **TRE-SAITH**, a mile east. This rewarding spot has a compact beach and, just around the rocks, a sandy cove with its own natural after-sea shower – a waterfall crashing down from the River Saith above. There are **dinghy races** from the beach on summer Sundays, and at low tide you can walk around to the wide, sandy, National Trust beach at **PENBRYN**. The numerous **places to stay** include the non-smoking *Iscoed* (☎01239/810030; ③), heading down into the village, and the hilltop *Bryn Berwyn* (☎01239/811126; ③), both ten minutes' walk from the beach .

Just along the coast, three miles northeast of Tre-Saith, **LLANGRANOG** is the most attractive village on the Ceredigion coast, wedged in between hills covered with bracken and gorse. The main, very narrow, streets wind their way to the tiny seafront, well geared up for tourists with a good range of cafés, B&Bs, pubs and sporting activities. The beach can become horribly congested in midsummer, however, at which times it's better to head over to **Cilborth Beach**, reachable along the coast at low tide or on a cliff path leading along glorious National Trust headland to **Ynys Lochtyn** and a couple of other remote beaches. In Llangranog, you can **stay** at the excellent 350-year-old *Ship Inn* (☎01239/654423; ③), or the earthier *Pentre Arms* (☎01239/654345; ③) which also has one very cheap single room (£12.50); both do good food. Between Penbryn and Llangranog is the *Maesglas* caravan park (☎01239/654268), which takes tents.

From Llangranog, you can walk along the coast path towards New Quay Head, where seasonal flowers swathe wind-blasted hillsides and cliffs that drop dramatically into clear seas. The cave-walled beach at **CWMTYDU** is glorious, approached along tiny lanes dropping in hairpin bends from above. Here you'll find *Cwmtydu Trekking Centre* (May–Oct daily; ☎01545/560494) which runs well-priced one- or two-hour hacks. Between Cwmtydu and the handsome village of **LLWYNDAFYDD** is a complex of self-catering cottages at *Neuadd* (☎01545/560324). In Llwyndafydd itself, just down the lane, the popular *Crown Inn* (closed Sun evening in winter) is deservedly noted for its beers and range of food.

New Quay

Along with Laugharne in Carmarthenshire, **NEW QUAY** (Cei Newydd) lays claim to being the original Llareggub in Dylan Thomas' *Under Milk Wood* (see p.150). Certainly, it has the little tumbling streets, prim Victorian terraces, cobblestone harbour, pubs and dreamy isolation that Thomas so successfully invoked in his play. In the height of the tourist season, however, the quiet seclusion can be hard to find, although even at these times, the town maintains a charm lost in so many of the other Ceredigion resorts. Although there is a singular lack of excitement in New Quay, it does make a great base for coastal walks and the odd boat trip, and outside the summer it is *the* place to be on New Year's Eve, when virtually the whole town gets kitted out in fancy dress and spends most of the night locked in the pubs or dancing out in the streets.

The main road cuts through the upper, residential part of town, past Uplands Square, from where acutely inclined streets swoop down to the pretty **harbour**, formed by its sturdy stone quay, and small curving **main beach**. Back from the beach, the higgledy-piggledy lines of multi-coloured shops and houses comprise the **lower town**, the more traditionally seaside part of New Quay, full of cafés, pubs and beach shops.

It's easy to escape the bustle, though. The northern stretch of beach soon gives way to a rocky headland, **New Quay Head**, where an invigorating path steers along the top of the sheer drops to **Bird Rock**, aptly named for the sheer profusion of razorbills and guillemots nesting here, and beyond to Cwmtydu. A route plan is available from the tourist office (see below).

Practicalities

Buses to New Quay stop on Park Street, just around the corner from Uplands Square and close to some reasonably priced **B&Bs**. These include the *Elvor* on George Street (☎01545/560554; ③), *The Moorings* on Glanmor Terrace (☎01545/560375; ③) and the *Seahorse Inn* on Margaret Street (☎01545/560736; ③). Pricier are the lovely seventeenth-century *Black Lion Hotel*, Glanmor Terrace (☎01545/560209; ④), and, on the edge of town overlooking the harbour, the ugly but luxurious *White House* (☎01545/560968; ④), which has a swimming pool and

---

DOLPHINS AND DANGER

One of only two pods in Britain, the Cambrian coast's **bottlenosed dolphins** are one of New Quay's major attractions, and can often be seen frolicking by the harbour wall, particularly when the tide is full and the weather calm. There are also several **boat trips** geared around potential sightings. The pleasure jaunts run by *New Quay Boat Trips* (Easter & late-May to Sept daily; ☎01545/560375 after 6pm; 20min £1, 1hr £2.50;) are the cheapest, but chances are better on the two-hour, ranger-led *Heritage Coast Cruises* (summer only Wed 10am; book in advance through the tourist office; £4) which, weather permitting, meet weekly at the tourist office. Dedicated naturalists might consider *Wildlife Cruises* (☎01545/580444; £10 for 2hr, £18 4hr, £32 8hr) which go further offshore and up along the heritage coast on data-gathering exercises; again, these have a ranger on board.

Although this stretch of coast is comparatively clean, Cardigan Bay's sea creatures are in constant danger from PCBs, inadequately treated sewage, monofilament fishing nets and noise from jetskis and powerboats, as well as occasional disasters like the 1996 *Sea Empress* oil spill at Milford Haven (see p.175). To get some idea of the results, visit the **Bird & Wildlife Hospital**, a couple of miles inland of New Quay at Cross Inn, half a mile down the lane opposite the *Penrhiwgaled Arms* (May–Sept Tues, Thurs & Sat 2–4pm; rest of year by appointment; ☎01545/560462; donations), a voluntary organization working with oil-soaked birds and diseased and damaged seals and dolphins. The dedicated couple who run the place are usually happy to answer questions and show you their work.

---

sauna. There's a quiet caravan and tent **campsite** a mile down the B4342 at *Wern Mill* (☎01545/580699), just outside the grim village of **Gilfachreda**.

Hidden among New Quay's innumerable cheap **cafés** are places like the *Mariner's Café*, by the harbour wall, which has an espresso machine, a rarity in these parts. Most of the **pubs** serve food, the best being the *Seahorse* and the *Black Lion* (see above for both) – the latter with regular live folk music – and the traditional, beery *Dolau Inn* on Church Street.

The **tourist office** is centrally located at the junction of Church Street and Wellington Place (April–June & Sept daily 10am–5pm; July & Aug daily 10am–6pm; ☎01545/560865). You can rent canoes, surfskis and windsurfers from *New Quay Marina Watersports* down by the main beach, and go pony trekking at *Plas-y-Wern Riding Stables* (☎01545/580156), a couple of miles out of town on the B4532. Four-hour **fishing trips** (☎01545/560375; £10) leave several times a day from the beach, and the town's **yacht club** (☎01545/560516) welcomes visitors. Details of the numerous **dolphin-watching** boats trips are given in the box above.

Aberaeron and around

New Quay may share its name with a town in Cornwall, but **ABERAERON**, seven miles up the coast, has more of a Cornish air, its large, deep harbour encased by pastel-shaded Georgian houses built virtually from scratch in the early nineteenth century by the Reverend Alban Gwynne. After the 1807 Harbour Act paved the way for port development, Gywnne spent his wife's inheritance dredging the Aeron Estuary as a new port for mid-Wales and constructing a formally planned town around it – reputedly from a design by John Nash.

Georgian planning is most evident around the central **Alban Square**, with graceful terraces of quoin-edged buildings and the odd pedimented porch, all writ small in keeping with the Ceredigion coast. From there, the grid of narrow streets stretches away to the sea at **Quay Parade**, the neat line of ordered, colourful houses on the seafront.

Sadly, despite its architectural beauty, Aberaeron is almost unique amongst the Ceredigion resorts for its unappealing **beach** – its north end all stones and rubbish, its south end only marginally better. Consequently, the most agreeable activity in Aberaeron is just to amble around the waterfront, taking in the child-oriented attractions. Right on the harbour in Cadwgan Place, the **Hive on the Quay** (late-May to mid-Sept daily 11am–1pm & 2–5pm; £1) combines an exhibition of bees and a twenty-minute video on the life of a honey bee with chances to sample honey-based products, including delicious ice cream; it also has a good restaurant (see below). The moderately diverting **Sea Aquarium**, past a several old fishermen's houses at 2 Quay Parade (Easter–Oct 10am–5pm; £2.50), has a tide pool of local fish and a good shark video. The cluster of ageing stone buildings at the southern end of town house **Clôs Pengarreg** (summer daily 10am–6pm; rest of year Mon–Fri 10m–4pm), a better than average collection of craft shops.

Llanerchaeron

While you're in Aberaeron, head three miles east along the A482 and check out **Llanerchaeron** (Easter fortnight & mid-May to early Oct Mon, Tues, Thurs & Sun 10am–4pm; £2). The partially renovated remains of a late-eighteenth-century, Welsh country estate, it is a remarkable example of a type of holding once common in these parts. The National Trust has embarked on a ten-year project to restore the Nash-designed main house and a range of domestic buildings, gradually opening them to the public. Until then, you're restricted to the grounds, though these in themselves are almost a time capsule of horticultural history, with walled gardens, early greenhouses and hotbeds whose underground heating is styled on Roman hypocausts. A rare opportunity to see behind the scenes of a restoration, the most rewarding time to visit is at 2pm on Thursdays and Sundays in July and August for one of the volunteer-run guided **tours** (70p). The #202 bus from Aberaeron to Lampeter passes within a mile of the site.

Practicalities

Buses stop on the A487, here known as Bridge Street, from where it is a five-minute walk along Market Street and Quay Parade to the **tourist office** (July & Aug daily 10am–6pm; Easter–June & Sept daily 10am–5pm; Oct–Easter Mon–Sat 10am–5pm; ☎01545/570602). There is a good supply of decent budget **accommodation** in and around Aberaeron, but little in the way of luxury. Cheapest of the lot, with good if showerless rooms from £13, is *Llys Aeron*, almost a mile inland on Lampeter Road (☎01545/570276; ②). For a little more style, try the *Hazeldene*, South Road (☎01545/5706532; ③), a quality B&B in a former sea captain's house ten minutes' walk from the town centre, one of whose rooms sports a water bed. Alternatively, try the tastefully decorated *Castle Hotel* on Market Street (☎01545/570205; ③), the welcoming and attractive *Fairview*, overlooking the harbour at 3 Cadwgan Place (☎01545/571472; ③), or *Moldavia*, 7–8 Bellevue Terrace (☎ & fax 01545/570107; ④), a beautifully decorated B&B with a large conservatory, a walled garden full of plants, and rooms with sea views. The best local **campsite** is the clifftop *Wide Horizons* (☎01545/570043), just over a mile south on the A487.

For **food**, try the moderate *Arosfa*, 8 Cadwgan Place (☎01545/570120), an evening and Sunday-lunch restaurant serving traditional and invented Welsh dishes along with mainstream offerings. The *Hive on the Quay* has a good fish restaurant (☎01545/570445) with some European regional dishes, *Pier Cottage* on Ship Street (☎01545/570132) has pleasant tea rooms with a frequently changed blackboard menu and sunny garden, and *The Apple Pie*, 35 Alban Square, is a good bakery-cum-deli-cum-café. The town's **pubs** include *The Monachty Arms Hotel*, 7 Market St (☎01545/570389), with its harbourside beer garden, and the *Black Lion*, Alban Square, which has a good range of guest real ales and Irish music most Thursday nights. Otherwise, **entertainment** is restricted to the free *Hymns on the Quay*, sung outside the tourist office at 7.30pm on Sundays in August.

The tourist office has route plans for local walks – including the **cliff path** to Cei Bach with its ancient church (usually closed) – and a National Trust shop. For summer **horse riding**, contact *Gilfach Holiday Village*, Llwyncelyn, two miles south along the A487 (☎01545/580288; £7 an hour).

The Teifi Valley

The Teifi is one of Wales' most eulogized rivers – for its rich spawn of fresh fish, its otter population, its meandering rural charm and the coracles that were a regular feature from pre-Roman times – and flows through some gloriously green and undulating countryside to its estuary at Cardigan. Small towns have grown up along its course, each hubs of enterprise in their time – witness the numerous water-driven mills in the valley – but mostly bypassed by the Industrial Revolution, making them perfect draws for alternative-lifestyle types spilling over from the New Age heartland of Powys.

The river is tidal almost as far up as the massive ramparts of **Cilgerran Castle**, four miles below the falls at **Cenarth**. Upstream, it flows around three sides of another fortress at **Newcastle Emlyn**, and also takes in the proudly Cymric university town of **Lampeter**. Beyond here, the river passes through a different, harsher scenery for eleven miles from **Tregaron**, a town Welsh in its language, feel and flavour, and a good base for nearby **Llanddewi Brefi**, with some spectacular walks up into the Abergwesyn Pass (see p.218) and the reedy bogland of **Cors Caron**. The river's infancy can be seen in the austere town of **Pontrhydfendigaid**, famous for its annual eisteddfod, and the nearby ruins of **Strata Florida Abbey**, beyond which the river emerges from the dark and remote **Teifi Pools**.

Cilgerran

Just a couple of miles up the Teifi from Cardigan is the attractive village of **CILGERRAN**. Behind the wide main street are the massive ramparts of the **castle** (April–Oct daily 9.30am–6.30pm; Nov–March daily 9.30am–4pm; £1.70; CADW), founded in 1100 at a commanding vantage point on a high wooded bluff above the river, then still navigable for seagoing ships. This is the legendary site of the 1109 abduction of Nest (the "Welsh Helen of Troy") by a lovestruck Prince Owain of Powys. Her husband, Gerald of Pembroke, escaped by slithering down a toilet waste chute through the castle walls.

The massive dual entry towers still dominate the castle, and the outer walls are some four feet thicker than those facing the inner courtyard. Walkways high on the battlements – not for those suffering vertigo – connect with the other towers. The outer ward, over which a modern path now runs from the entrance, is a good example of the keepless castle evolving throughout the thirteenth century. Any potential attackers would be waylaid instead by the still evident ditch and outer walls and gatehouse, of which only fragmentary remains can be seen. Another ditch and drawbridge pit protect the inner ward underneath the two entry towers. The views over the forested valley towards the pink and grey Georgian fantasy castle of **Coedmore**, on the opposite bank, and towards Cardigan, are inspiring. If the castle is closed, get the key from the adjoining Castle House.

A footpath runs down from the castle to the river's edge and display boards telling the story of the emigrants to America, for whom Cardigan was the last sight of home, and the history of the Teifi valley industries, particularly quarrying, brick making and coracle fishing. Guided two-hour Canadian **canoe trips** (☎01239/71039; £7) through the wooded valley leave from the quay during the summer months.

Cenarth

A tourist magnet since the nineteenth century, **CENARTH**, seven miles upstream from Cardigan, is a pleasant spot, but hardly merits the mass interest it receives. The secret is that the village's main asset, its **waterfalls**, are close to the main road, ideal for lazy visitors. The low but impressive cataracts are a result of the Teifi being split by rocks, as it tumbles and churns its way over the craggy limestone. The path to the falls runs from opposite the *White Hart* pub and past the **National Coracle Centre** (Easter–Oct daily except Sat 10.30am–5.30pm; £1.50), a small museum with intriguing displays of original coracles from all over the world, half of them from Wales. Many of the exhibits date from the last two centuries, their hazel and willow shells covered in treated calico, but there are several older, more traditional ones cloaked in ox hide. Your entry fee also entitles you to visit the restored seventeenth-century **flour mill** (same hours) by the falls' edge. The adjacent *Three Horseshoes* pub serves good beer and bar meals.

Newcastle Emlyn and around

An ancient farming and droving centre, **NEWCASTLE EMLYN** (Castell Newydd Emlyn) still retains a distinctly agricultural feel, particularly on Fridays, the loud and busy market day. The swooping meander of the Teifi River made the site a natural defensive position, first built on by the Normans. The "new" **castle**, of which only a few stone stacks and an archway survive, replaced their fortress in the mid-thirteenth century. Although the ruins aren't impressive, the site, surrounded on three sides by the river flowing through a valley of grazing sheep and rugby fields, is gently uplifting and quintessentially Welsh. The castle is tucked away at the bottom of dead-end Castle Terrace, which peels off the main street by the squat little stone **town hall**, topped by a curiously phallic cupola.

Although there are few other sights in the town there are at least some great pubs, and with its unhurried charm and fabulous scenery, it's a good base from which to explore the surrounding area.

Practicalities

Newcastle Emlyn's **tourist office** (Easter–Oct Mon–Sat 9.30am–5.30pm; ☎01239/711333) and the tiny *Attic* **theatre** are both located in the miniature town hall on Bridge Street. Inexpensive, central B&B **accommodation** is available at the old-fashioned *Plough* on Emlyn Square (☎01239/710994; ②), and the cheerful *Pelican Inn* on Sycamore Street (☎01239/710606; ②), which also does tasty all-day food. Further out, the *Maes-y Derw Guest House* (☎01239/710860; ③), half a mile towards Cardigan on the A484, with spacious Edwardian rooms, a restaurant and private fishing, is charming, as is *Fedwen Guest House*, Waungilwen, Velindre, Llandysul (☎01559/37142; ②), three miles towards the *Museum of the Welsh Woollen Industry* (see below), set in five acres of grounds.

The best place to **eat and drink** is the deservedly popular *Bunch of Grapes*, a stylish bar on Bridge Street, with guest real ales and live music most Thursdays. You can get a good lunch and coffee at the licensed *Snapdragon* (closed Sun; ☎01239/710404), down by the Teifi, while straightforward boozing is enjoyable at the *Ivy Bush*, a gnarled old Welsh local on Emlyn Square, or the *White Hart* on Sycamore Street.

Museum of the Welsh Woollen Industry, Teifi Valley Railway and Ffostrasol

The lower Teifi's prolific past as a weaving centre is best seen in the village of **DREFACH FELINDRE**, five miles southeast of Newcastle Emlyn. At the turn of the century, this was at the centre of the wool trade, with 43 working mills in and around the village. Today the National Museum of Wales' **Museum of the Welsh Woollen Industry** (April–Sept Mon–Sat 10am–5pm; Oct–March Mon–Fri 10am–5pm; £2.50), housed in a vast Edwardian mill, does a fine job of evoking the days when a full workforce churned out flannel shirts for miners or khaki for World War I soldiers' uniforms. Displays of old photographs and mementoes set the tone for the main exhibit, long rooms full of carding and twisting machines, Jacquard looms and machinery for processes you never imagined existed. Natural dyeing is treated in some depth, along with fleece-to-fabric demonstrations of various working methods. The museum is at the hub of twenty miles of paths, packed into a two-mile radius, along which workers walked to the mills.

A mile to the north at **HENLLAN**, the volunteer-run **Teifi Valley Railway** (Easter–Oct & Christmas daily; ☎01559/371077; £3.50) operates seven daily steam- and diesel-hauled trains along a mile and a half of narrow-gauge track. Seven miles further on, at the junction of the B4571 and the A486, the hamlet of **FFOSTRASOL** only merits a special visit during the first or second week in July, when it plays host to the annual *Gŵyl Werin y Cnapan* (☎01239/858955), one of the largest **Celtic folk festivals** held anywhere.

Lampeter

Eighteen miles from Newcastle Emlyn, **LAMPETER** (Llanbedr Pont Steffan) is the home of possibly the most remote university in Britain, and certainly one of the oldest. The St David's University College, now a constituent of the University of Wales, was the country's first university college, founded in 1822 by the Bishop of St David's to aid Welsh students who couldn't afford the trip to England to receive a full education. With a healthy student population (albeit one comprised substantially of theologians, many of them involved in Islamic studies), together with large numbers of resident hippies, the small town, with a permanent population of less than 2000, is well geared up for young people and visitors.

There's not a great deal to see in Lampeter, and what you are able to visit is fairly low-key. **Harford Square** forms the hub of the town and is named after the local landowning family who were responsible for the construction of the early nineteenth-century **Falcondale Hall**, now an opulent hotel, on the northern approach to Lampeter. Around the corner is **Y Galeri**, a showcase for the work of local artists, at the back of the *Mulberry Bush* health-food shop at 2 Bridge St.

The main buildings of the **University College** lie off College Street, and include C B Cockerell's original stuccoed quadrangle of buildings from 1827, modelled along the lines of an Oxbridge college. The motte of Lampeter's long-vanished **castle**, tucked right underneath the main buildings, forms an incongruous mound amidst such order. The High Street is the most architecturally distinguished part of town, its eighteenth-century coaching inn, the *Black Lion*, dominating the streetscape; you can see its old stables and coach house through an archway. The former town hall provides access to the new municipal buildings on Market Street, which contain a minute civic **museum** (Mon–Thurs 9am–1pm & 1.45–4.30pm; free), mainly comprising curly old photographs of the town.

If you are in the area around the Whitsun bank holiday weekend (usually late May) and have a taste for folk and world music, dance, country pursuits and abundant wassailing, then make for the **Llanfair Spring Fair** (☎01239/698313), held four miles north of Lampeter at Llanfair Clydogau.

Practicalities

Lampeter makes a good base – it's a lively town, there are frequent gigs and theatre performances and enough pubs and cafés for any visitor. It's also in excellent **cycling** country, where the surrounding terrain is gentle enough for inexperienced bikers. There are no bike rental places in town, though you might be able to pick up a cheap second-hand cycle from the nameless store next to *Ralph's Bakery* on College Street. There is a **tourist office** of sorts (Mon–Fri 9am–5pm; ☎01570/422426) in the new civic buildings. It doesn't book **accommodation**, but rooms are easy to find: noticeboards in the *Mulberry Bush* wholefood shop (see above) carry information about local B&Bs and longer lets. Alternatively, there's a good B&B, *Haufan*, 6 Station Terrace (☎01570/422718; ③), behind University College, and hotel accommodation in the recently refurbished *Black Lion* on the High Street (☎01570/422172; ⑤). The best accommodation, though, lies slightly out of town: *Pantcelyn* (☎01570/434455; ③), a couple of miles west at Llanwnnen, has good rooms and will do evening meals, and the abundantly appointed *Falcondale Country House Hotel* (☎01570/422910; ⑥), a Victorian mansion in fourteen acres of parkland a mile out on the Aberaeron road, which picks up the top end of the market. There's a **campsite** five miles northeast at *Moorlands*, near Llangybi (☎01570/493543). Just off the B4343, running up the Teifi Valley towards Llanddewi Brefi, is one of the area's best farmhouse B&Bs at *Pentre Farm* (May–Oct; ☎01570/493313; ③), near Llanfair Clydogau, five miles from Lampeter.

There are plenty of decent places to **eat** in town. Cheap and popular with students is the *Cottage Garden* restaurant, opposite the university on College Street and, well up the cholesterol scale there's *Lloyds* on Bridge Street, an upmarket fish-and-chip shop and restaurant, open until 9pm. Also on Bridge Street and fairly studenty is the friendly *King's Head* pub, with a wide-ranging menu and some very well-kept beer. Make sure you at least stick your head in *Conti's Café* on Harford Square. The food is cheap and none too spectacular, but the surroundings are wonderfully decayed, plastered with ageing accolades for the café's rich dairy ice cream. Out of town, real-ale fiends will love the *Ram Inn*, a sixteenth-century drovers' inn a mile east in Cwmann, while foodies should head four miles beyond to Harford and *Seguendo di Stagioni* (☎01558/650671). Local, in-season produce dictates the table d'hôte menu of this superb, justly expensive Italian restaurant, where beautiful preparation and exquisite flavours don't preclude hearty helpings.

Tregaron and around

On the cusp of the lush Teifi Valley and the gloomy moors rising above it, the neat small town of **TREGARON**, ten miles northeast of Lampeter, has a tendency to enchant passing visitors. It feels almost untouched by the late twentieth century, and seems a bastion of the Welsh language and culture in an area that has suffered galloping anglicization over recent decades.

All roads to Tregaron lead into the spacious market square, hemmed in by solid eighteenth- and nineteenth-century buildings, of which the most impressive must be the classically symmetrical old drovers' inn, the **Talbot Hotel**. The square and the inn were the very last points of civilization that drovers saw before they headed out of town on the wild Abergwesyn Pass (see p.218), which rises above the town en route to Llanwrtyd Wells and beyond. The pristine **statue** in the centre of the square is of Henry Richard (1812–88), the founder of the Peace Union, forerunner of the League of Nations and, subsequently, the United Nations. On the corner of the market square and Dewi Road is the *Rhiannon* craft design centre, a wonderful shop stocking jewellery fashioned from Welsh gold and other materials in Celtic designs, as well as goods made of slate and various Welsh-interest books.

The river running through the middle of Tregaron is the Brennig, a babbling tributary of the Teifi which meanders through a wide, flat valley into the eerie wetland of **Cors Caron** (Tregaron Bog), two miles north. This is one of the most prodigious areas for wildlife in Wales, a national nature reserve of peat bog, home to marsh grasses, black adders, buzzards and even the occasional red kite. There's a limited walkway along the disused rail line, but to really see the bog you'll need to follow the three-mile circuit along both the railway and the river; call ahead to reserve the necessary permit (☎01974/831671) and pick it up when you are in the vicinity.

Practicalities

Buses arrive at the market square, by the Henry Richard statue. There's a small **tourist office** (Mon–Fri 9.30am–5pm; ☎01974/298144) in the council offices in Dewi Road, just off the main square, but only irregularly is anyone in attendance. The choice of **accommodation** isn't wide. The *Talbot Hotel* on the square (☎01974/298208; ④) is much better for eating and drinking than sleeping, so you're better off a mile up the Aberystwyth road at *Neuaddlas* guesthouse (☎01974/298965; ③). Three miles northeast is the remote Blaencaron **youth hostel** (April to early Sept; ☎01974/298441; ①), perfectly positioned for walks on the towering moorland above the tiny stream.

There are a couple of **cafés** along the road to Aberystwyth, including the cheap and wholesome *Country Kitchen* by the river bridge. Bar meals are served at the *Clwb Rygbi* on the Aberystwyth road and in the *Talbot Arms*. For plain **drinking**, hit *Y Llew Coch* by the river bridge, a young pub with a pool table and bar games.

Llanddewi Brefi

The Dewi Road from Tregaron runs south past a cottage hospital and along the Teifi to the tight little village of **LLANDDEWI BREFI**, where the present thirteenth-century **church of St David** is home to one of Wales' most persistent legends. A convocation of 118 Welsh churchmen met here in 519 AD and summoned Dewi Sant (Saint David). As he began to speak, the ground beneath him shuddered ominously and suddenly rose, giving him a natural platform, upon which the church now sits, from where he was able to continue speaking. Part of the church wall consists of two discernible stones with fragmentary Latin inscriptions carved on them. These were broken up by an illiterate eighteenth- or nineteenth-century mason from a single memorial that dated from within a century of David's death – the first recorded mention of the Welsh patron saint. The graveyard has a cool and contemplative atmosphere, and contains a memorial to a local man rejoicing in the name of Ajax Ajax, and inside the church are some interesting stones, one with Ogham inscriptions. Either of the village's two creaky pubs – the *Foelallt Arms* and the ancient *New Inn* – are great places to booze away an evening.

Pontrhydfendigaid and Strata Florida

Six miles northeast of Tregaron, the last village on the Teifi is gloomy **PONTRHYDFENDIGAID** ("Bridge near the ford of the Blessed Virgin"), a grey-stoned cluster remarkable only for its annual May eisteddfod in the village pavilion. The infant Teifi flows in from the east, followed by a road that, after a mile, reaches the atmospheric ruins of the mighty **Strata Florida Abbey** (April–Sept daily 10am–5pm; £1.70; Oct–April unrestricted entry), bucolically located in the *Ystrad Fflur*, "the valley of the flowers". This Cistercian abbey was founded in 1164, swiftly growing into a centre for milling, farming and weaving, and becoming an important political centre for Wales. In 1238, a dying Llywelyn the Great, fearful that his work of unifying Wales under one ruler would disintegrate, summoned the lesser Welsh princes here to command them to pay homage to his son, Dafyd.

The church here was vast – larger than the cathedral at St David's and, although very little survived Henry VIII's Dissolution of the Monasteries, the huge, Norman west doorway gives some idea of its dimensions. Fragments of one-time side chapels include beautifully tiled medieval floors, and there's also a serene cemetery, but it's really the abbey's position that impresses most, in glorious rural solitude against wide open skies and fringed with a scoop of sheep-spattered hills. A twisting yew tree reputedly shades the spot where Dafydd ap Gwilym, fourteenth-century bard and contemporary of Chaucer, is buried.

The narrow lane running due east from Strata Florida leads to Tyncwm, a farm with bridleways to the drenched grass and craggy outcrops around the **Teifi Pools**, a series of sombre lakes where the Teifi River rises. This is stern, but rewarding, walking country where you may be tempted to strike out over the rocky, squelchy moorland down to the Claerwen Reservoir (see p.225).

Aberystwyth

The liveliest seaside resort in Wales, and capital of the sparsely populated middle of the country, **ABERYSTWYTH** is an essential stop along the Ceredigion coast. With one of the most prestigious colleges of the University of Wales and the National Library both in the town, there are plenty of cultural and entertainment diversions here, as well as an array of Victorian and Edwardian seaside trappings. As a town firmly rooted in all aspects of Welsh culture, it's an enjoyable and relaxed place to gain a clear insight into the nation's psyche.

The precursor of Aberystwyth is the inland village of **Llanbadarn Fawr**, the seat of Wales' oldest bishopric between the sixth and eighth centuries. It grew around the thirteenth-century castle as Llanbadarn, minting its own coins and becoming a major headquarters for Owain Glyndŵr's revolutionaries in the Middle Ages. The *Cymdeithas yr Iaith* (Welsh Language Society) was founded in 1963 and is still located here, and the National Library was begun here in 1907. It was no surprise that, after decades of Liberal domination, the Aberystwyth-dominated Ceredigion and Pembroke North constituency finally plumped for a Plaid Cymru MP in the 1992 election, thus turning the whole west coast – from Anglesey to the bottom of Cardigan Bay – Plaid green on the political map.

As a seaside resort, Aberystwyth is hard to beat. Two long, gentle bays curve round between two rocky heads: Constitution Hill to the north, and Pen Dinas to the south above the town harbour marina where both the Rheidol and Ystwyth rivers end their journeys through the valleys of Aberystwyth's hinterland (see p.276). The town rises up towards the east from the flat plains in between the two, peaking at Penglais, where the graceful Portland stone buildings of the university gaze over the town.

Arrival and information

Aberystwyth's twin **train stations** (one for mainline trains and one for the Vale of Rheidol line) are adjacent to each other: the former on Alexandra Road, a ten-minute walk from the seafront on the southeastern side of the town centre, the latter reached either through the main station or down a short access road to the side. **Local buses** stop outside the station, with **long-distance** ones using the depot further down the road by the entrance to the park. In addition, Aberystwyth acts as the hub of three **postbus** services which penetrate the town's hinterland. One service runs inland up the southern side of the Vale of Rheidol to Devil's Bridge and Cwmystwyth; a second follows the Vale's northern side to Capel Bangor and Capel Dewi; and the third runs south into the villages of the Aeron Forest, Llangwyryfon and Blaenpennal. All leave from Chalybeate Street at the back entrance to the post office at around 7.30am and 2.30pm.

The busy **tourist office** (daily 10am–5pm; ☎01970/612125), which can help with accommodation and sell you tickets for local events, is a ten-minute stroll from Alexandra Road, straight down Terrace Road towards the seafront.

Accommodation

As in all major seaside towns, there are hundreds of **places to stay**, so beds are generally quite reasonable and easy to find. The tourist office will only give infor-

ABERYSTWYTH

△ Machynlleth

◁ Cliff Railway

▷ Cardigan, Lampeter

ACCOMMODATION
1 Brendan Guesthouse
2 Bryn-y-don
3 Cymerau
4 Four Seasons
5 Groves
6 Helmsman
7 Richmond
8 Sinclair
9 Yr Hafod

University College of Wales

National Library of Wales

Bronglais Hospital

Sports Ground

Town Hall

Cinema

Train Station

Vale of Rheidol Railway

Bus Station

Pier

Pavilion

Library

Market

Theatre

St Michael's

Castle

University College of Wales

War Memorial

Rummers

PENGLAIS ROAD

LLANBADARN ROAD

PLASCRUG AVENUE

PARK AVENUE

NORTH ROAD

QUEEN'S ROAD

MARINE TERRACE

TERRACE ROAD

NORTHGATE ST

POPLAR ROW

NORTH PARADE

ALEXANDRA ROAD

MILL STREET

PIER ST

EAST GATE

DARKGATE STREET

BRIDGE ST

HIGH ST

SOUTH ROAD

NEW PROMENADE

MARINE TER

NEW ST

PORTLAND ST

PORTLAND ROAD

QUEENS INN RD

GRAYS INN RD

TREFECHAN RD

PENPARCAU ROAD

River Rheidol

N

yds   0   300

mation on accommodation verified by the Wales Tourist Board, so, if desperate, or if the B&Bs offered are too pricey, there are a couple of reasonable places in the streets down towards the castle and others along South Marine Terrace.

Hotels and guesthouses

Brendan Guest House, 19 Marine Terrace (☎01970/612252). One of the better budget seafront B&Bs, with some en-suite rooms. ③.

Bryn-y-don, 36 Bridge St (☎01970/612011). Spirited and charming guesthouse with shared-bathrooms, a hundred yards or so up from the station. ③.

Conrah Country House Hotel, Chancery, Rhydgaled (☎01970/617941, fax 624546). Elegant Georgian house in 22 acres of grounds with luxurious rooms, sauna and heated indoor pool, three miles south along the A487. ⑧.

Cymerau, 8 New St (☎01970/617590). About the cheapest B&B around, with good, standard rooms and hearty breakfasts. ②.

Four Seasons, 50–54 Portland St (☎01970/612120, fax 627458). Comfortably decorated, upmarket Victorian town house behind the seafront, with an award-winning restaurant. ⑦.

Groves, North Parade (☎01970/617623, fax 627068). Welcoming town-centre hotel serving evening meals. All rooms have bathrooms. ⑤.

Helmsman, 43 Marine Terrace (☎ & fax 01970/624132). Tall seafront guesthouse in the middle of the curving Promenade. Book early for a sea view. ③.

Richmond, 44–45 Marine Terrace (☎01970/612201, fax 626706). Comfortable, family-run seafront hotel, with a full complement of en-suite rooms. ⑤.

Sinclair, 43 Portland St (☎ & fax 01970/615158). Small and beautifully modernized Victorian guesthouse benefiting from the intimacy of its size, and serving good evening meals. No smoking allowed. ④.

Yr Hafod, 1 South Marine Terrace (☎01970/617579). Compact, cheerful and recently reno-vated B&B south of the castle, the best of the bunch on the seafront. ③.

Campsites and self-catering

Aberystwyth Holiday Apartments, 9 Northgate St (☎01970/612878). Self-contained, self-catering flats let by the week.

Glan-y-mor Leisure Park, Clarach Bay (☎01970/828900). The best of the caravan parks in Clarach Bay, on the other side of Constitution Hill, to the north of Aberystwyth. It has cara-vans for rent and tent pitches.

Midfield, Southgate, Penparcau (☎01970/612542). Campsite just off the A4120 (A487) south of town. Free showers and games area.

University of Wales, Penglais (☎01970/621960 or 621961). Self-contained flats and B&B (£28) available during the student vacations on the university's Penglais site and also down by the seafront. Campus facilities include two sports halls and a heated swimming pool.

The Town

Constitution Hill (430ft) overshadows the northern end of the long Promenade, where it rises sharply away from the rocky beach. It is a favourite jaunt, crowned with a tatty jumble of amenities that includes a café, picnic area, telescopes and an octagonal **camera obscura** (Easter–Oct daily 10am–5.30pm; free), a device pop-ular in the pre-TV era and affording close-up and long-shot views over the town, the surrounding mountains and bays, plus a vista of the hordes of caravans to the north, looking like legions of tanks poised for battle. The existing structure was built in the 1980s on the ground plan of the original, but expanded to make it the largest of its type in the world. If you don't fancy the invigorating walk up, you can take the clanking 1896 **cliff railway** (Easter to mid-July & Sept–Oct daily 10am–6pm; mid-July to Aug daily 10am–9pm; £2 return) from the grand terminus building at the top of Queen's Road, behind the Promenade.

From the bottom of Constitution Hill, the **Promenade** – officially Marine Terrace – arcs away to the south, past ornate benches decorated with snakes, a continuous wall of hotels and guesthouses, a prim bandstand and a shingle beach. Terrace Road peels off to the left, almost immediately reaching the **Amgeuddfa Ceredigion** (Ceredigion Museum), atmospherically housed in the ornate Edwardian *Coliseum* music hall (Mon–Sat 10am–5pm; free). Mementoes of the building as a theatre and cinema give a sense of place to an otherwise disparate collection, on three floors, including cosy reconstructed cottages, dairies complete with all manner of separating and churning equipment, a nineteenth-century pharmacy, exhibits on the local geology, and a surprisingly interesting look at the history of weights and measures.

Marine Terrace continues round to the spindly **pier**, beyond which a John Nash-designed turreted **villa** dominates the seafront. Dating from 1790, the villa was extended massively in the 1860s as a hotel designed to soak up the anticipated masses arriving on the new rail line, but when the venture failed, it was sold in 1872 to the fledgling university, whose property it remains. The Promenade cuts around the front of the building to a rocky headland, where the **castle** ruins (unrestricted access) stare blankly out to sea. The thirteenth-century fortress, built by Edward I as part of his conquest of Wales, is more notable for its breezy position than for the buildings themselves, of which the two outer gates are the most impressive remains. South of the castle is the quieter, sandy beach along South Marine Terrace, which peters out by the wide **harbour**, the mouth of the Rheidol and Ystwyth rivers.

A couple of blocks inland from the Promenade, you'll find the terminus of the **Vale of Rheidol railway** (see p.276) on Alexandra Road, and, above in the former station restaurant, the fascinating **Aberystwyth Yesterday** exhibition (April–Oct daily 10am–5pm; Nov–Feb daily noon–3pm; free), a compulsive ragbag of hundreds of old local photographs, costumes and period furniture.

North Parade meets up with Queen's Road at the bottom of Northgate Street, which winds east, becoming Penglais Road as it climbs the hill towards the university's main campus and the **National Library of Wales** (Mon–Fri 9.30am–6pm, Sat closes 5pm; free). Housed in a massive white Edwardian building overlooking the town, the library's fine manuscripts include the oldest extant Welsh text, the twelfth-century *Black Book of Carmarthen*, and the earliest manuscript of *The Mabinogion*. Temporary exhibitions in the corridors and Gregynog Gallery are invariably excellent, as is the permanent **A Nation's Heritage**, giving a well-rounded introduction to the history of the written word and printing in Wales, with highlights like the first Bible in Welsh, printed in 1588. Tickets (☎01970/623816) need to be obtained for entry into the Reading Room, which boasts an enormous range of texts, maps, photos and documents, including, as one of the UK's six copyright libraries, copies of every new book published in Britain.

Eating, drinking and entertainment

Aberystwyth's cultural and gastronomic life is an ebullient, all-year-round affair, thriving on students in term time, visitors in the summer and a large esoterically inclined community at all times. As well as a varied range of **pubs** and **restau-**

rants, this is the best place for Welsh **music** and a lively centre for theatre and cinema. For a slice of Edwardian gentility, take afternoon tea in any of the seafront hotels along the Promenade.

Restaurants and cafés

Bistro 33, 33 North Parade (☎01970/615332). Airy restaurant whose varied international menu concentrates on fresh and wholefood ingredients. Closed Sun.

Le Casablanca, 26 Eastgate St (☎01970/617024). Cheap and cheerful Mediterranean restaurant with a lively atmosphere and reasonable food. Bring your own alcohol.

Corners, corner of Mill and Queen streets (☎01970/611024). Appealing bistro with no-nonsense lunches, good (if unadventurous) dinners and decent coffee. Closed Sun & Mon.

Gannets Bistro, 7 St James Square (☎01970/617164). Small restaurant that makes delicious and imaginative dishes from local farm and sea produce. Closed Tues.

Pipers, 26 Alexandra Rd (☎01970/624270). Unpretentious, moderately priced Italian restaurant also serving a broad range of British food.

Royal Pier Tandoori, the Pier (☎01970/624888). Swish, romantic but affordable end-of-pier restaurant, with views over the twinkling bay. Serves a good range of curries and bargain lunchtime specials for £5.

The Stop Inn, 12a Baker St (☎01970/625719). Tucked down an alleyway off Baker Street, this inexpensive pasta joint makes some of Aberystwyth's best pizza.

Y Graig, 34 Pier St (☎01970/611606). Quirky wholefood café with a drinks licence, great atmosphere and eclectic clientele.

Yeskins, 49 North Parade (☎01970/615374). Daytime wholefood restaurant with a gallery. Everything is made to order so service tends to be a bit slow; you can bring your own booze to while away the wait.

Pubs

Bay Hotel, Marine Terrace. Student pub with regular discos, open until 1am.

Bear, below the *Marine Hotel*, Marine Terrace. Cellar bar on the seafront, usually packed with students and young people, particularly on Fri for live Welsh music.

Boar's Head, Queen's Road. Friendly, lively gay-leaning pub.

Castle Hotel, South Road. Harbourside pub built in the style of an ornate Victorian gin palace. Live local folk bands at weekends and a good bar menu with vegetarian specialities.

Pier Hotel, Pier Street. Endearing old town pub, its lounge entrance up a tiny side alley.

Rummers, Bridge Street, by the River Rheidol bridge. Popular pub and wine bar with outside seating by the river and live music Thurs–Sun.

Ship and Castle, corner of Vulcan and High streets. Nautical-style bar, with a good range of beer, cider and food. Hosts regular Welsh and Irish folk music, best on Wed.

Weston Vaults, Thespian Street/North Parade. Unpretentious and popular with students.

Y Cŵps (*Coopers Arms*), Llanbadarn Road. Firmly Welsh local, evident from the green, white and red exterior. Fun and friendly, with regular Welsh folk and jazz nights.

Entertainment

Aberystwyth Arts Centre, the University, Penglais (☎01970/623232). The town's main venue for arthouse cinema, touring theatre, classes, events and wide-ranging temporary exhibitions. Hosts the annual Welsh International Film Festival jointly with the *Commodore Cinema* (usually second week in Nov; ☎01970/617995).

Commodore Cinema, Bath Street (☎01970/612421). Screens mainstream current releases.

Theatr y Castell, St Michael's Place/Vulcan Street (☎01970/624606). Venue for local amateur productions and a few touring companies.

Listings

Banks All major banks are along Great Darkgate Street and North Parade.

Bike rental *Red Dragon*, Exchange Stores (☎01970/880588) in Capel Bangor, five miles east on the A44 operates a delivery and collection service to Aberystwyth.

Books *Siop y Pethe*, North Parade, has a huge array of Welsh-interest books, magazines and music in both Welsh and English. There is also a good bookshop in the Aberystwyth Arts Centre, though *Galloways*, on Pier Street, has a wider range. *Ystwyth Books*, near the Market Hall on Princess Street, also sells maps and second-hand records.

Festivals Friends of the Earth/Greenpeace Festival takes place annually in June (☎01970/627302), a Festival of the Countryside in late June/early July, a Traditional Jazz Festival in Sept (☎01970/627302), the two-week Aberystwyth International Music Festival in late July (☎01970/622889) and a Poetry Festival in mid-July (☎01970/622889).

Gay, Lesbian and Bisexual Line (Tues 6–8pm; ☎01970/615076).

Male Voice Choir *Cor Meibion* rehearse at the Tabernacle Chapel on Mill Street (Thurs 7.45–9.30pm; ☎01970/624494).

Post office 8 Great Darkgate St.

Sport *Plascrug Leisure Centre* (☎01970/624579), off the Llanbadarn Road, has two indoor pools, sauna, solarium, squash and tennis courts, indoor pitches and multigym. The *University Sports Centre* (☎01970/622280) is open to the public in the summer vacation.

Around Aberystwyth

Aberystwyth's sights run out long before it's time to hit the restaurants and nightlife, so there is every reason to go exploring beyond the town. Immediately inland is the **Vale of Rheidol**, a region of forested glades and remote villages, easily accessed by road or, more enjoyably, rail – the narrow-gauge steam train which serves the area is a draw in itself. Tourist attractions like **Devil's Bridge**, where the line terminates, are also obviously popular, although there are numerous other lesser-known beauty spots whose charms require only a little more imagination to discover.

The coast north of Aberystwyth also has its devotees, principally sunseekers drawn to the beach at **Borth** and the dunes close to the mouth of the Dyfi Estuary. Nature buffs will prefer to head further northeast to the RSPB's **Ynys-Hir Nature Reserve**, with its complex series of bird habitats.

The Vale of Rheidol

Inland from Aberystwyth, the Rheidol River winds its way up to a secluded, wooded valley, where occasional old industrial workings have moulded themselves into the contours, rising up past waterfalls and minute villages. It's a glorious route, and by far the best way to see this part of the world is on board one of the trains of the **Vale of Rheidol Railway** (April–Oct; ☎01970/625819; £10 return), a narrow-gauge steam train that wheezes its way along twelve miles of sheer rock faces climbing six hundred feet in the process. It was built in 1902, ostensibly for the valley's lead mines but with a canny eye on its tourist potential. Today, the line is privately run, with between two and four trips offered daily.

If you'd rather drive, the easiest way is to take the A4120 along the south side of the valley direct to Devil's Bridge (see p.278) or the A44 along the north side; the two meet at Ponterwyd. The tiny hamlet of **CAPEL BANGOR**, five miles east of Aberystwyth along the A44, has little to recommend it but for the *Rheidol Riding Centre* (☎01970/880863) where you can hack for around £7 an hour, the 300-year-old *Tynllidiart Arms* noted for its Belgian bottled beers and summertime draught cider, and the nearby **Cwm Rheidol Reservoir**, reached by a narrow riverside route off the main road. This is the final element in a small, showpiece hydro-electric scheme that starts high in the headwaters of the Rheidol River at the Nant-y-moch Reservoir. An **information centre** (daily 10.30am–4.15pm; free), run by privatized electricity generator *PowerGen*, explains the scheme's signifi-cance and a visit is essential to appreciate the free 45-minute tour of the **power station** and neighbouring **fish farm** (April–Oct daily 10.30am–4.30pm) a stone's throw up the road.

Slight remains of old lead workings are evident on the banks of the reservoir, although the valley's mining legacy is better seen further along, as the road begins to narrow before finally disappearing into a wood as a mud track. From here, paths rise either side of the river to overlook the burned orange spoil, vivid-ly coloured water and bright plants, fitted snugly into their green landscape. A sharp path on the south side of the river climbs up to Rhiwfron halt on the Rheidol railway (see above), and an even more punishing route from the northern bank scrambles up over the mines and into the sombre little village of **YSTUMTUEN**, a former lead-mining community whose school has been converted into a basic **YHA hostel** (April–early Sept; ☎01970/890693; ①).

Llywernog Silver-Lead Mine and Ponterwyd

Travelling eastbound, the A44 winds up into **galena** country, tucked between the bleak moorland of Plynlimon (see p.230) and the rugged mountains to the south. The silver-rich lead ore was found throughout the region and scores of mines sprang up, each plugging away at the lode until waterlogging made the mines uneconomic. In the boom years, the latter half of the 1800s, the whole of northern Ceredigion was a mini-Klondike, attracting speculators and oppor-tunists by the trainful. The remains – waste tips scarring hillsides and shafts pockmarking former sites – lie all around, most now hidden amongst the exotic evergreens of the Rheidol Forest. They can be visited on wonderful walks from the **Bwlch Nant-yr-Arian visitor centre** (Easter–Sept Mon–Fri & Sun 10am–5pm, Sat 12.30–5pm, closes 6pm July & Aug; free), perched above a mag-nificent valley scooped out of the wooded hillsides, seven miles east of Capel Bangor.

The soft contours of the forest make it difficult to imagine how stark the valley once looked. A truer picture unfolds a mile further east with the impressive bar-renness around the **Llywernog Silver-Lead Mine** (Easter–Oct daily 10am–6pm; ☎01970/890602; £3.95 including underground tour), which opened in the 1740s and closed in the early years of this century. Decay was well advanced when the place reopened in the early 1970s, but the site has expanded consistently over the years in a satisfyingly rough manner. A low-key mock-up of a working mine, hous-ing an interesting museum, leads onto a collection of rusted machinery and the dank, dark mine itself, visitable on a great thirty-minute underground tour. Topside, you can pan for "fool's gold" or dowse for veins of galena.

The largest settlement to spring up around the mines was **PONTERWYD**, a mile from Llywernog on the banks of the Rheidol. There's nothing of interest here; indeed, one of the funniest sections in George Borrow's *Wild Wales* tells of his night in the inn at Ponterwyd – now the *George Borrow Hotel* – when the pompous Englishman met his match in a pugnacious landlord, who, even in 1854, was complaining about the numbers of unimaginative tourists ignoring his and other local villages and flocking instead flocking to Devil's Bridge.

Devil's Bridge

Folk legend, idyllic beauty and travellers' lore combine at **DEVIL'S BRIDGE** (Pontarfynach), a tiny settlement twelve miles east of Aberystwyth – reached by road (A4120) or the Vale of Rheidol railway – built solely for the growing visitor trade of the last few hundred years

The main attraction is the Devil's Bridge itself, where three roads – the A4120, the B4343 and the B4574 – converge and cross the churning River Mynach yards above its confluence with the Rheidol, to form three bridges, one on top of the other. The road bridge in front of the striking, but distinctly antiquated, *Hafod Arms* hotel (☎01970/890232; ④) is the most modern of the three, dating from 1901. Immediately below it, wedged between the rock faces, are the stone bridge from 1753 and, at the bottom, the original bridge, dating from the eleventh century and reputedly built by the monks of Strata Florida Abbey (see p.270). To see the bridges – and it is worth it, as they make a truly remarkable sight – you have to enter the turnstiles on either side of the modern road bridge. With your back to the hotel, the right-hand side (50p) is the shorter route, signposted to the Punch Bowl. Slippery steps lead down to the deep cleft in the rock, where the water pounds and hurtles through the gap crowned by the bridges. The Punch Bowl is the name given to a series of rock bowls scooped by the sheer power of the thundering river, which rushes through past bright-green mossy rocks and saturated lichen.

On the opposite side of the road is a ticket office (Easter–Oct daily 9.30am–6.30pm) – pay £2 or pass through turnstiles (£1) when closed – which opens out onto a path leading down into the valley and ultimately to the crashing **Mynach Falls**. The scenery here is magnificent: sharp, wooded slopes rising away from the frothing river, with distant mountain peaks surfacing on the horizon. A platform overlooks the series of falls, from where a set of steep steps takes you further down to a footbridge dramatically spanning the river at the bottom. From the platform, and from here, views over the confluence of the two rivers and towards the **Gyfarllwyd Falls** are awesome. Be warned, however, that Devil's Bridge has been a seriously popular day excursion for centuries, with no sign of its attraction waning. In order to escape some of the inevitable congestion, it is wisest to come here at the beginning or end of the day, or out of season.

The railway terminates at a tinpot brown and cream shack, just by Devil's Bridge **post office**, which has some worthwhile booklets on local walks. For **accommodation**, there's the *Hafod Arms* (see above) or *Ewbarfe Farmhouse* (☎01970/890251; ③), a mile north on the A4120, where you can also get a decent evening meal. Reasonably priced **camping** is offered at *Woodlands Caravan Park* (☎01970/890233) by the petrol station, just beyond the bridges.

The *Hafod Arms* serves **food**, as do a couple of simple cafés, but you're better off six miles west along the A4120 at the *Halfway Inn*, just beyond the spectacularly positioned village of **PISGAH**. Beers, ciders and hearty local dishes are served up along with Welsh folk choirs, jazz and special events.

THE PARSON'S BRIDGE WALK

Note: The OS Landranger #135 "Aberystwyth" map makes route finding a lot easier.

The **Parson's Bridge Walk** (6 miles; 3–4hr; 1000ft ascent) is one of the most popular and rewarding outings from Devil's Bridge, taking in a broad swathe of the Rheidol scenery: mine workings, woods and waterfalls. Unfortunately, it does involve a little road walking, so get this over with first by taking the A4120 a mile and a half north to a small church on the left. The path to the right of the church leads down to the Parson's Bridge, an unusual modern glass-fibre structure thankfully replacing a predecessor which only just spanned the narrow fissure of churning water.

The path now climbs gently towards the south across farmland, eventually meeting a narrow lane which winds into the former lead-mining village of **Ystumtuen**. Head south from the village past the YHA hostel to the end of the lane and take the track straight ahead, which drops down almost to river level through oak woods revealing views across to the falls below Devil's Bridge. Swing west following the contour through recently felled forest to meet the lane running the length of the valley bottom. Mine scars on the right and modest falls to the left herald the narrow footbridge across the Rheidol. Take this and turn sharp right to begin the stiff climb up to the railway, which you eventually cross close to Devil's Bridge.

The Vale of Ystwyth

The Ystwyth River runs pretty much parallel to the Rheidol, a couple of miles to the south. Four miles south of Devil's Bridge is the drab village of **PONTRHYDYGROES**, once the centre of local lead-mining activity. The B4574 climbs out of the village and past the delightful country estate of **Hafod**, once the seat of a great house belonging to the wealthy Johnes family. In the late eighteenth century, Thomas Johnes commissioned a mansion here in the Picturesque style; it was added to by John Nash, amongst others, and contained a library full of Welsh manuscripts, but was ravaged by a terrible fire in 1807. The replacement sumptuous house was demolished in 1962 as an unsafe ruin, and all that remains is the beautiful estate Johnes landscaped and forested two hundred years ago. The church, off the B4574, is the best place to start on the waymarked trails through the estate leading down to the river. Johnes' larch forest, broken by trickling streams, monumental relics and planted glades, swoops down to the Ystwyth River, less than a mile from the church car park. A bridge spans the river, where paths fan out either way along its banks or up through the tiny valley of the Nant Gau.

Continuing east, a small road grinds up the hill into the bizarre moonscape surrounding **CWMYSTWYTH**, a small, semi-derelict village at the bottom of a valley of old lead mines, deserted in the late nineteenth century when the mines were exhausted. As the river shimmers past, the view is one of abandoned shafts, tumbledown cottages, twisted tramways and grey heaps of spoil littering spartan hillsides. The isolated road continues to climb the uninhabited slopes, before dropping down into the Elan Valley (see p.224) and its reservoirs.

North from Aberystwyth

The A487 runs north from Aberystwyth towards Machynlleth, slicing between the mountains to the east and the flat lands bordering the vast Dyfi Estuary. The seaward plain is one of the most surprising landscapes in Wales, at its heart a raised bog, **Cors Fochno**, visible from the main road but seen much better from the rail line or the coastal B4353. This short road, lined by towering sand dunes – by far the tallest things aroun – sneaks past **Borth**, a dreary but serviceable town stretching for nearly two miles along the seafront, to the national **nature reserve** at **Ynyslas**, the best place to explore the dunes themselves.

Inland, attractions worth heading off the A487 for include the roadside village of **Furnace** with its eighteenth-century iron foundry, now open as a museum, and **Ynys-hir**, an RSPB nature reserve with an impressive range of bird habitats.

Borth and Ynyslas can be reached from Aberystwyth on buses #511, #512, #520 and #524. The #514 to Machynlleth runs through Furnace and Ynys-hir.

Borth and Ynyslas

The drab resort of **BORTH**, five miles north of Aberystwth off the B4353, is basically one long street, desolate in winter and heaving solid in the summer. As it was built solely for holiday-makers, the only occupants of its austere, washed-out Victorian houses are pubs, restaurants, tacky shops and B&Bs, interspersed with the odd caravan and campsite. The shallow **beach** is good for safe swimming, though, and if you've got kids you could take them to see caged creatures at the **Animalarium** half a mile off High Street near the train station (daily April–Sept 10am–6pm; Oct 11am–4.30pm; £2.75). **B&Bs** are plentiful – try the *Glanmor* (☎01970/871689; ③) on the High Street – or there's an Edwardian **youth hostel** (☎01970/871498, fax 8718271) at the northern end of High Street, and the *Ynys Fergi* **campsite** on the road to the Animalarium.

To the north, the flat landscape meets the formidable sand dunes that line the southern side of the Dyfi Estuary. The road follows the coast a couple of miles to **YNYSLAS**, entrance to the dramatic estuary-side **Ynyslas nature reserve** (£1 per car), most notable for its birdlife. In winter, wading and sea birds nest among the dunes and mudflats; while in summer, butterflies flit around vibrant sand plants growing in the grass. The views here are dramatic: for once, a Welsh vista almost uncluttered by mountains, panning over the sky, estuary and seascape, and across the river to the colourful huddle of Aberdyfi (see p.286). The **visitor centre** (Easter–Sept daily 10am–4pm; ☎01970/871640) can point you to the short circular dune walk or half a mile along the beach to the **fossilized forest**. At low tides, the sands near the water's edge are studded with the petrified stumps of a dozen or so 5000-year-old trees, a reminder that the coast was some twelve miles away when these trees were in their prime. A less prosaic explanation tells of a drowned land known as Cantre'r Gwaelod which was protected by sea walls and floodgates. Their keeper, Seithenyn, happened to get drunk the night of an almighty storm and the sea burst through, drowning a thousand people and their settlements.

Furnace and Ynys-hir

The Borth road rejoins the A487 a couple of miles south of the hamlet of **FURNACE** which, as its name suggests, grew principally as an industrial centre, firstly around silver refining and then iron smelting. Both activities centred around the **Dyfi Furnace** (unrestricted access), a barn-like building constructed to harness the power of the Einion River, with a waterwheel driving the bellows.

The adjacent narrow lane follows the river through a forest and out into the idyllic **Cwm Einion**, known as "Artists' Valley" because of its popularity with nineteenth-century landscape painters. From the *Ty'n-y-cwm* tea room a mile and a half east, walks head up into the deserted foothills of Plynlimon (see p.230), across the spongy moors and through conifer forests to the remote glacial lakes of **Llyn Conach** and **Llyn Dwfn**, three miles away.

Half a mile north of Furnace, a short lane runs seaward to *Ynys-hir Hall* (see p.284) and the RSPB's **Ynys-hir Nature Reserve** (April–Oct daily 9am–dusk; Nov–March daily 10am–dusk; £2, free to members). The thousand-acre site, comprising five rich and distinct habitats, drips with diversity. Redstarts, pied-fly-catchers and warblers flit about the ancient hanging oak woodland so typical of mid-Wales; cormorants flock to the estuarine salt marshes; red-breasted mer-sangers and elusive otters inhabit the freshwater streams and pools; remnant peat bogs are a riot of wild flowers in spring; and winter brings water rails to the reed beds to join the herons. The attractions are obvious to the birders who return time and again to the network of hides, but there's enough along the one- or two-hour designated trails to interest anyone.

Southern Cadair Idris and the Dyfi and Talyllyn valleys

The southern coastal reaches of Snowdonia National Park are almost entirely dominated by **Cadair Idris** (2930ft), a five-peaked massif standing defiant in its isolation. Tennyson claimed never to have seen "anything more awful than the great veil of rain drawn straight over Cader Idris", but catch it on a good day, and the views from the top – occasionally stretching as far as Ireland – are stunning. During the last Ice Age, the heads of glaciers scalloped out two huge cwms from Cadair Idris' distinctive dome, leaving thousand-foot cliffs dropping away on all sides to cool, clear lakes. The largest of these amphitheatres is Cwm Gadiar, the **Chair of Idris**, which takes its name from a giant warrior poet of Welsh legend, although some prefer the notion that Idris' Chair refers to a seat-like rock formation on the summit ridge, where anyone spending the night (specifically New Year's Eve, say some) will become a poet, go mad or die.

Cadair Idris' southern limits are lapped by the broad expanse of the Dyfi Estuary, which in turn bleeds into the grand scenery of the **Dyfi Valley**, "one of the greenest corners of Europe". Focal point for the valley is the genial town of **Machynlleth**, a candidate for the Welsh capital in the 1950s and site of Owain Glyndŵr's embryonic fifteenth-century Welsh parliament. The area is rife with the B&Bs and businesses of the New Agers who have flocked to this corner of Wales since the late 1960s, and in the hills to the north, the renowed, cooperatively run **Centre for Alternative Technology** makes for one of the most interesting days out in Wales.

Small-time coastal resorts are sprinkled around the region, the pick of them being **Aberdyfi**, though many prefer to press on to **Tywyn** and ride the **Talyllyn Railway**, justly one of Wales' most popular narrow-gauge lines, running seven miles up the **Talyllyn Valley** to **Abergynolwyn** at the foot of Cadair Idris, and only a short distance from the dilapidated thirteenth-century **Castell-y-Bere** and the inland cormorant colony at **Craig yr Aderyn**.

A well-co-ordinated network of trains, steam rail lines and buses make **getting around** the area easy. The very useful, summer-only *Dyfi Sherpa* ticket (£7.50;

Harlech △   Coed y Brenin & Blaenau Ffestiniog △   △ Bala

AROUND CADAIR IDRIS

▽ Aberystwyth

☎01286/679535), allows a circuit from Tywyn using the Talyllyn Railway to Abergynolwyn, the #30 bus to Machynlleth and the bus or mainline train back to Tywyn. Available from train stations and tourist offices, it can also be bought on the bus at Machynlleth.

Machynlleth and around

Shortlisted for Welsh capital in the 1950s and site of Owain Glyndŵr's embryonic fifteenth-century Welsh parliament, **MACHYNLLETH** (pronounced Mah-hun-cthleth) has an air of importance hardly borne out by its population of a couple of thousand.

It is difficult to imagine a nation's capital consisting essentially of just two inter-secting streets, but that is the basis of Machynlleth. The A489 enters the town from the east becoming the wide main street, **Heol Maengwyn**, busiest on Wednesdays when a lively **market** springs up out of nowhere. Heol Maengwyn comes to an end at a T-junction, under the fanciful gaze of a fussy **clock tower**, erected in 1873 by local landowner, the Marquess of Londonderry, to commemorate his son and heir's coming of age.

Glyndŵr's partly fifteenth-century **Parliament House** (Easter–Sept daily 10am–5pm; other times by arrangement on ☎01654/702827; free) sits halfway along Heol Maengwyn, a modest looking black-and-white-fronted building concealing a large interior. Displays chart the course of Glyndŵr's life, his military campaign, his downfall, and the 1404 parliament in the town, when he controlled almost all of what we now know as Wales and even negotiated international recognition of the sovereign state. The sorriest tales are from 1405 onwards when tactical errors and the sheer brute force of the English forced a swift retreat and an ignominious end to the great Welsh uprising.

Opposite the Parliament House, a path leads into the landscaped grounds of **Plas Machynlleth**, the elegant seventeenth-century mansion of the Marquess of Londonderry. Its solitude is entirely intentional: in the 1840s the Marquess bought up all the surrounding buildings and had them demolished, and rerouted the main road away from his grounds. The house is now home to **Celtica** (daily 10am–6pm; £3.95) which sets out to be both a resource for all matters Celtic and an evocation of the Cymric spirit. The latter is attempted in the theatrical "Celtic Experience", a lightweight series of audiovisual tableaux and dioramas tracing the Celts over the last 3000 years. While successfully painting a picture of a modern, living Celtic race, its rather pointed omission of non-Celtic aspects of Welsh society is questionable: there isn't a black face anywhere, for instance. It also falls into the archetypal Welsh trap of conjuring up a mystical, lyrical past only to spill into romantic sentimentality, aided by the use of some particularly mawkish special effects. Nevertheless, it is a spirited show, and the final rousing chorus is satisfactorily uplifting to tempt you upstairs, where you can listen to recordings of six Celtic languages – Welsh, Irish Gaelic, Scottish Gaelic, Manx, Cornish and Breton – and take in a lower-key and more substantial presentation of Celtic history.

Around the corner in Heol Penallt, almost opposite the parish church, is **Y Tabernacl** (Mon–Sat 10am–4pm; ☎01654/7073355; free), a beautifully serene old chapel converted into a cultural centre. Home to the small collection of the **Wales Museum of Modern Art**, it also hosts films, theatre and the August **Gŵyl Machynlleth** festival (☎01654/703355), which combines classical music, debate, theatre and some folk music.

A mile and a half northeast of town at **PENEGROES**, you can see how stone-ground flour was once made at **Felin Crewi** (April–Oct Tues–Sun 10.30am–5pm; £1.85), one of the last working water mills in Wales, with a sixteenth-century mill building.

Practicalities

The **train station** is a five-minute walk up the Heol Penallt/Doll from the clock tower. Most **buses** leave from the bus depot opposite, while the **postbus** services which loop inland pick up at the post office on Heol Maengwyn at 7.20am and 3.55pm. You can **rent bikes** from *Greenstyles Cycles*, Heol Penallt (☎01654/703543) at £8–12 per day, £16 for a tandem. The **tourist office** (Easter–Sept daily 10am–6pm; Oct–Easter daily 10am–5pm; ☎01654/70240) is next to the Parliament House on Heol Maengwyn.

Accommodation is plentiful. There's the faded grandeur of the *Wynnstay Arms* (☎01654/702941; ⑤), on Heol Maengwyn, and the earthier *Glyndŵr Hotel* (☎01654/703989; ②) towards the station on Heol Doll, while central, serviceable B&Bs include the *Maenllwyd* (☎01654/702928; ②) and the slightly cheaper *Brondre* (☎01654/702422; ②), both on Newtown Road, the eastward extension of Heol Maengwyn. Further out, there's the friendly *Cwm Dylleth* (☎01654/702684; ②) a mile and a half southeast at **Forge**; luxurious country-house accommodation and fine modern cuisine at *Ynys-hir Hall*, (☎01654/781209, fax 781366; ⑨), close to the Ynys-hir Nature Reserve (see p.281) at Egwysfach, six miles southwest on the A487; a **campsite** three miles north near the Centre for Alternative Technology at *Llwyngwern Farm* (☎01654/702492); and a **youth hostel** (see p.286) five miles away at Corris.

There are plenty of **cafés**, **restaurants** and **pubs** in the town, including a great wholefood shop and café, *Siop y Chwarel*, owned by the Centre for Alternative

OWAIN GLYNDŴR

No name is so frequently invoked in Wales as that of Owain Glyndŵr (*c.* 1349–1416), a potent figurehead of Welsh nationalism ever since he rose up against the occupying English in the first few years of the fifteenth century.

Little is known about the man described in Shakespeare's *Henry IV, Part I* as "not in the roll of common men". There seems little doubt that the charismatic Owain fulfilled many of the mystical medieval prophecies about the rising up of the red dragon. He was of aristocratic stock, and had a conventional upbringing, part of it in England of all places. His blue blood – he was directly descended from the princes of Powys and Cyfeiliog – furthered his claim as Prince of Wales, and as a result of his status, he learned English, studied in London and became a loyal, and distinguished, soldier of the English king, before returning to Wales and marrying.

Wales in the late fourteenth century was a turbulent place. The brutal savaging of Llywelyn the Last and Edward I's stringent policies of subordinating Wales had left a discontented, cowed nation where any signs of rebellion were sure to attract support. Glyndŵr became the focus of the rebellion through a parochial problem: his neighbour in Glyndyfrdwy, the English Lord of Ruthin, seized some of his land and when the courts failed to back him, Glyndŵr took matters into his own hands. With four thousand supporters and a new declaration that he was Prince of Wales, he attacked Ruthin, and then Denbigh, Rhuddlan, Flint, Hawarden and Oswestry, before encountering an English resistance at Welshpool. However, whole swathes of north Wales were his for the taking. The English king, Henry IV, despatched troops and rapidly drew up a range of severely punitive laws against the Welsh, even outlawing Welsh-language bards and singers. Battles continued to rage, with Glyndŵr capturing Edmund Mortimer, the Earl Marcher, in Pilleth in June 1402. By the end of 1403, he controlled most of Wales.

In 1404, Glyndŵr assembled a parliament of four men from every commot in Wales at Machynlleth, drawing up mutual recognition treaties with France and Spain. At Machynlleth, he was also crowned king of a free Wales. A second parliament in Harlech took place a year later, with Glyndŵr making plans to carve up England and Wales into three as part of an alliance against the English king: Mortimer would take the south and west of England, Thomas Percy, Earl of Northumberland, would have the Midlands and North, and Glyndŵr himself Wales and the Marches of England. The English army, however, concentrated with increased vigour on destroying the Welsh uprising, and the Tripartite Indenture was never realized. From then on, Glyndŵr lost battles, ground and castles and was forced into hiding; dying, it is thought, in Herefordshire. The draconian anti-Welsh laws stayed in place until the accession to the English throne of Henry VII, a Welshman, in 1485. Wales became subsumed into English custom and law, and Glyndŵr's uprising becoming an increasingly powerful symbol of frustrated Welsh independence. Even today, the shadowy organization that surfaced in the early 1980s to burn the holiday homes of English people and English estate agents dealing in Welsh property has taken the name *Meibion Glyndŵr*, "The Sons of Glendower".

Technology, on Heol Maengwyn. Lunch is good at the otherwise bland *White Lion* on Heol Pentrerhedyn, near the clock tower, but better at the rather upmarket *Wynnstay Arms*, which also serves surprisingly reasonable evening meals. Less formal, but very good for food, is the *Dyfi Forester Inn* on Heol Penallt. The *Glyndŵr Arms*, on Heol Doll, features local music at the weekends, although the liveliest pub in town is a bikers' haunt, the *Skinners Arms* on Heol Penallt.

Centre for Alternative Technology and Corris

Since its foundation in the middle of the oil crisis of 1974, the **Centre for Alternative Technology** (CAT), or *Canolfan y Dechnoleg Amgen* (daily 10am–5pm, displays open to 7pm in summer; £4.95, £5.50 July & Aug, discounts to those arriving by bike or public transport), just over two miles north of Machynlleth off the A487, has become one of the biggest attractions in Wales. In just over twenty years, seven acres of a once-derelict slate quarry have become an almost entirely self-sufficient community, generating eighty percent of its own power from wind, sun and water. But this is no back-to-the-land hippie commune. Right from the start, the idea was to embrace *sustainable* technology – and the on-site equipment, much of it developed and built here, reflects the centre's achievements in this field – and, most importantly, to promote its application in urban situations.

Whole houses have been constructed to showcase energy-saving ideas and to demonstrate how they can be built with minimal skills and local materials. Composting toilet systems and a natural reed-bed filtration system produce superb rich soil, much needed for the organic gardens, and drinkable water. Many of the hands-on exhibits are self-explanatory, but the ebullient fifty-strong staff – many living communally, all receiving identical (very low) wages – are happy to explain the concepts.

All this earnest education is leavened with flashes of pzazz. A **water-balanced cliff railway** (April–Oct) whisks the visitor 200ft up to the main site from the car park, a "mole hole" – a human-sized earth tunnel with authentic sounds and and textures – forces an appreciation of insect life, and a new "transport maze" confuses all except those who understand sound transport policy. It's also a beautiful site, sensitively landscaped using local slate and wood, and you can easily spend half a day sauntering around it. There's plenty for kids to do, the wholefood restaurant turns out delicious organic food, and the excellent bookshop stocks a wide range of alternative literature.

Primarily, though, this is a living community which exists more to educate by example than entertain. Residential **courses** are offered (details from CAT, Machynlleth, Powys SY20 9AZ; ☎01654/702400), the most popular being a guide to building your own energy-efficient home, but even a brief visit will fascinate and inspire.

Corris

The spirit of the Centre for Alternative Technology is carried higher up the valley to **CORRIS**, a small slate-mining settlement which, after decades of decline, is beginning to reform itself. Almost thirty years of self-help have finally borne fruit with the opening of the **Corris Railway and Museum** (mid-July to Aug daily 11am–5pm; late May to mid-July & Sept daily 2–4pm; other times by appointment; ☎01654/761624; £1) which once moved slate and passengers from the main line at Machynlleth to the quarries at Corris. The line closed in 1948 when the bridge over the Dyfi was washed away, and since 1970 volunteers have raised money to rebuild the track. By summer 1997, two-thirds of a mile of track will be operational, initially with diesels, and later with Welsh-built steam locos.

Elsewhere, there's the Corris Craft Centre on the A487, a former slate mine now home to **King Arthur's Labyrinth** (daily 10am–5pm; £3.85), a rather contrived 45-minute tour based around the ancient Welsh stories of the Mabinogion. Led by someone dressed as a monk, the boat trips into the various dank caverns that comprise the labyrinth are fun, but the half-baked *son et lumière* tableaux, hampered by poor sound and visuals, dilute the power of the magical tales. One for the very bored only.

The run-of-the-mill Craft Centre also houses the local **tourist office** (Easter–Oct daily 10am–5.30pm; ☎01654/761244) and can point you down the hill to the *Canolfan Corris* **youth hostel** on Old Road (April–Oct; ☎ & fax 01654/761686; ①). Occupying a former village school, the hostel is an enthusiastically and ecologically run concern, with large subdivided dorms, some family rooms and tent space; you can cook for yourself or have very reasonable, healthy meals made for you. Alternatively, you'll find **B&B** rooms and **bar meals** at the *Briach Goch Hotel* (☎01654/761229; ③) on the A487.

Aberdyfi

On a blustery winter's day, the battened-down Victorian seafront terraces of **ABERDYFI**, at the mouth of the Dyfi Estuary on its northern shore, can seem almost suicidally forlorn. But in the summer, the streets come alive and Aberdyfi is transformed into understated and likable resort, whose sheltering horseshoe of mountains, dotted with a pleasing jumble of houses, provides a mild climate for the summer crowds drawn by the beach and watersports. Canoes and sailboards can be rented on the beach from *Short Dŵr Dyfi Watersports* (☎01654/710065), but there isn't much else to do here: even swimming is pretty much off limits though a new sewage pipeline to the treatment station at Tywyn has improved matters considerably.

In the mid-nineteenth century, the town, with its seamlessly joined eastern neighbour **Penhelig**, built shallow-draught coastal traders for the inshore fleet, a past remembered in the small historic and **maritime display** in the tourist office Wharf Gardens (see below). Sticking to outdoor pursuits, there's a pleasant coastal walk east to the wooded **Picnic Island** starting at The Green, a manicured lawn in Penhelig. The path follows the inappropriately named Roman Road, a relatively modern path cut into the low coastal cliffs and crossing a couple of short bridges to well-sited rest spots on promontories. Appetite whetted, you might like to take in the fourteen acres of rock and water gardens, mature trees, heathers and woodland wild flowers which comprise **Plas Penhelig Gardens** (April to mid-Oct Wed–Sun 2.30–5.30pm; £1.50), immediately behind the *Penhelig Arms*.

Practicalities
Aberdyfi is served by two equally convenient **train** stations, the request-only Penhelig, half a mile east, and Aberdyfi, half a mile west of the **tourist office** at Wharf Gardens (Easter–Oct daily 10am–6pm; ☎01654/767321), near where the #29 **bus** stops.

The best budget **accommodation** here is the friendly, non-smoking *Cartref Guest House*, Penrhos (☎01654/767273; ③) near Aberdyfi train station, and the summer-only *Brodawel*, on Tywyn Road (☎01654/767347; ③), opposite the members-only golf course a mile north of town; both do evening meals for under a tenner. Also good are *Sea Breeze*, 6 Bodfor Terrace (☎01654/767449; ③), along the waterfront in town, and *Ceunant*, Aberdyfi Road (☎01654/767264; ②), a welcoming cheapie three miles east towards Machynlleth.

Penhelig is home to a couple of top-class small hotels. The *Penhelig Arms Hotel* (☎01654/767215, fax 767690; ⑦), near Penhelig train station, is particularly noted for its excellent restaurant with extensive wine list, while the Edwardian *Plas Penhelig Country House Hotel*, a mile up the road behind (closed Dec to mid-March; ☎01654/767676, fax 767783; ⑧), is justifiably proud of its magnificent public areas, seven-acre estuary-front gardens and traditional table d'hôte menu.

Lighter **meals** are offered at the good-value *Old Coffee Shop*, 13 New St (closed Jan), built into the cliff behind the *Britannia Hotel*, with home-made cakes and inexpensive lunches, and *The Grapevine Restaurant*, 1 Chapel Square (☎01654/767448), where you can get bistro favourites. In the evening, *The Dovey Inn* on Sea View Terrace has the best bar meals and, along with the *Britannia*, the liveliest atmosphere.

Tywyn and the Talyllyn Railway

Despite four miles of sandy beach, **TYWYN** (The Strand), three miles north of Aberdyfi, is really only of interest as a base for the Talyllyn and Dysynni valleys (see p.288). At the east end of High Street, the five-foot-high **Ynysmaengwyn** or St Cadfan's Stone, within the Norman nave of the **Church of St Cadfan** (daily 9am–5pm, later in summer, church tour Wed 5pm), bears the earliest example of written Welsh, dating back to around 650 AD, but that's about as far as things to see go.

Tywyn's saving grace is the **Talyllyn narrow-gauge railway** (April–Oct daily; ☎01654/710472; £7.50 return), which belches seven miles inland through the delightful wooded Talyllyn Valley to Nant Gwernol. From 1866 to 1946, the rail line was used to haul slate from the Bryn Eglwys quarry near Nant Gwernol to Tywyn Wharf station, then just four years after the quarry's closure, rail enthusiasts took over the running of services, making this the world's first volunteer-run railway. The round trip (at a maximum 15mph) takes two hours, but you can get on and off as frequently as the schedule allows, taking in some fine broadleaf forest **walks**. The best of these starts at Dôlgogh Falls station, where three trails (maximum 1hr; leaflet 30p) lead off to the lower, mid-and upper falls. At the end of the line, more woodland walks take you around the site of the old slate quarries. In mid-August each year, the schedule is disrupted by the "Race the Train" event, when runners attempt to beat the train on its thirteen-mile trip to Abergynolwyn and back. Some do.

The **Narrow-Gauge Museum** (open when trains are running; 50p) at Tywyn Wharf station boasts half a dozen locos and some oddball rolling stock culled from the ruins of other lines – including a shunter from the *Guinness* brewery in Dublin – but equally venerable machinery still works the line. Of the original Talyllyn rolling stock, two steam engines and all five of the oak and mahogany passenger carriages still run up to Nant Gwernol.

Practicalities

The three main roads in Tywyn – the High Street, Pier Road and the Aberdyfi road – meet at the **train station**, which also acts as the main **bus** stop. The **tourist office** is on the High Street (Easter–Oct daily 10am–1pm & 2–6pm; ☎01654/710070), Pier Road makes for the beach, and the Aberdyfi road heads south past the Talyllyn narrow-gauge train station (Tywyn Wharf) two hundred yards away. **Bike rental** is available for £8 a day from *J Gray Jones*, 37 High St (☎01654/710525).

Decent **accommodation** can be found at the *Ivy Guest House*, opposite the tourist office on the High Street (☎01654/711058; ②), or the cheaper, non-smoking *Glenydd Guest House*, 2 Maes Newydd (☎01654/711373; ②), two hundred yards from the beach off Pier Road. For something a little nicer, try the summer-only *Pant-y-Neuadd*, Aberdyfi Road (☎01654/711393; ③), an old country house half a mile south on the A493. Of the many **campsites** in the area, the handiest is *Ynysmaengwyn Caravan Park* (April–Sept; ☎01654/710684), a mile out on the Dolgellau road.

The best **food** in town is at the moderately priced *The Proper Gander*, High Street (☎01654/711270), serving imaginative lunches, teas and great desserts all day, and à la carte meals on Thursday, Friday and Saturday evenings. *Y Gegin Fach* (☎01654/710229) on College Green, the eastern extension of High Street, is handy for filling up with basic, inexpensive food.

The Talyllyn and Dysynni valleys

The **Talyllyn and Dysynni valleys** form a two-pronged fork pointing southwest towards the sea. The handle is formed by the Talyllyn Valley, which starts at the northeast by Minffordd and is followed by the Dysynni River (Afon Dysynni) as far as Abergynolwyn. Here the valley splits into two, some ancient geological upheaval having forced the river to abruptly switch its course north, forming the Dysynni Valley and leaving its original course beside the Talyllyn Railway all but dry. Although a quick tour around the sites won't take more than a day, the area has some good accommodation, making it an ideal choice for a relaxing couple of days exploring.

The Talyllyn Valley is served by the #30 bus, running from Tywyn to Abergynolwyn, continuing to Minffordd (where you can catch #2 to Dolgellau) and Machynlleth. The Talyllyn narrow-gauge railway runs from Tywyn to Abergynolwyn station half a mile short of the village, or to Nant Gwernol, just past the village but off the road. **Accommodation** is scattered throughout the two valleys, but the only **restaurants** are those attached to hotels. Campsites tend towards the simple: farmers' fields with or without showers.

The Talyllyn Valley

From Tywyn, the road up the **Talyllyn Valley** runs parallel to the Talyllyn Railway (see above), meeting it at Dolgoch Falls, the site of some wooded walks and the *Dolgoch Falls Hotel* (March–Oct; ☎01654/782258; ④), where moderately priced meals (£13.50) are available. You'll find cheaper accommodation at the superb farmhouse B&B, *Tan-y-Coed-Uchaf*, half a mile further on (March–Oct; ☎01654/782228; £30), just two miles short of the twin valleys' largest settlement, **ABERGYNOLWYN**, comprising a few dozen quarry workers' houses, two pubs

WALKS ON CADAIR IDRIS FROM MINFFORDD

Note: The OS Outdoor Leisure 1:25,000 map of "Cadair Idris/Dovey Forest" is highly recommended for all these walks, although the OS Landranger 1:50,000 "Dolgellau" map will do.

The steepest and most dramatic ascent of Cadair Idris follows the **Minffordd Path** (6 miles; 5hr; 2900ft ascent), a justifiably popular route that makes a full circuit around the rim of **Cwm Cau**, probably the country's most dramatic mountain cirque.

The path starts just west of the *Minffordd Hotel* at the junction of the A487 and the B4405. From the car park, follow the signs along an avenue of horse chestnuts and up through the woods, heading north. You will reach a fork: take the left path that wheels around the end of Craig Lwyd into Cwm Cau, and before you reach the lake, fork left and climb onto the rim of Cwm Cau, following it round to **Penygadair** (2930ft; see also p.295), the highest point on the massif. Here there's a circular shelter and a tin-roofed hut originally built for dispensing refreshments to thirsty Victorians, and now affording none-too-comfortable protection from wind and rain.

The shortest descent follows the summit plateau northeast, then down to a grassy ridge before ascending gradually to **Mynydd Moel** (2831ft) and a magnificent view down into a cwm containing the waters of Llyn Arran. The descent starts beside the fence, crossed just before the summit, and follows it south all the way to the point below Cwm Cau where the uphill path forked.

On a good day, an **extended route** (9 miles; 7hr; 2900ft ascent) makes a more pleasurable descent and leaves your knees in better shape for the next day's walk. This follows the ridge around to **Gau Graig** (2240ft), finally dropping off the northernmost of the two spurs and swinging east to the road. Follow the A487 southwest until the old road branches right, then follow this parallel to the main road right back to Minffordd.

– including the *Railway Inn* (☎01654/782279) with the best range of real ales for miles around – and the great little *Riverside Guesthouse and Café*, Cwrt (☎01654/782235; ②) serving all-day breakfasts, and full meals for residents. It has a limited number of bargain **tent** sites.

The Dysynni Valley branches northwest here, but the Talyllyn Valley continues northeast past the basic *Cedris Farm* **campsite** (☎01654/782280), a mile northeast of Abergynolwyn, and two miles further on to the serene **Tal-y-Llyn Lake**. The chief interest here is the fifteenth-century **St Mary's church** on the southern shores of the lake, a fine example of a small Welsh parish church, unusual because of its chancel arch painted with an alternating grid of red and white roses, separated by grotesque bosses.

The lake itself is frequently stocked with brown trout and, occasionally, migratory sea trout and salmon. The classy, angling-oriented *Tynycornel* hotel (☎01654/782282, fax 782679; ⑧) issues fishing permits (£12 a day), and rents dinghies (£16) and tackle (£10); it also boasts a sauna, mountain bikes for guests and an excellent but expensive restaurant open to non-residents. On a tighter budget, try the adjacent sixteenth-century *Pen-y-Bont* (☎01654/782218, fax 782666; ④), which offers a good bar, an affordable restaurant and £12-a-day **mountain bikes**.

It's a further two miles northeast to the start of one of the best routes up Cadair Idris (see box) from **MINFFORDD**, made up of only the informal *Minffordd*

Hotel (March–Nov; ☎01654/761665, fax 761517; ⑥), an eighteenth-century farm-house and coaching inn, open to non-residents for traditional British dinners (Thurs–Sat), and two low-cost **campsites**: *Cwmrhwyddfor Farm* (☎01654/761380), half a mile northeast, and *Dôl Einion* (☎01654/761312), a couple of hundred yards southwest. *Dolffanog Fawr* (☎01654/761247; ④), a seventeenth-century farmhouse B&B, is under a mile to the southeast near the north end of Tal-y-Llyn Lake.

The Dysynni Valley

The **Dysynni Valley** has more to offer in the way of sights, even though the lack of public transport makes it difficult to get to. A mile and a half northwest of Abergynolwyn, a side road cuts northeast to the hamlet of **LLANFIHANGEL-Y-PENNANT** and the scant ruins of the native Welsh **Castell-y-Bere** (unrestricted access; CADW), a fortress built by Llywelyn ap Iorwerth (Llywelyn the Great) in 1221 to protect the mountain passes. After being besieged twice in the thirteenth century, this castle – one of the most massive of the Welsh castles – was consigned to seven centuries of obscurity and decay. There's still plenty to poke around, with large slabs of the main towers still standing, but it's primarily a great place just to sit or picnic, with good views to Cadair Idris and Craig yr Aderyn (see below). Half a mile northeast of the castle, you pass the ruined **Tyn-y-ddôl** (unrestricted access), once the home of Mary Jones, famed for her 1800 bible-buying walk to Bala (see box on p.253), an event commemorated by a plaque in the remains of the house. Tyn-y-ddôl marks the beginning of a path (10 miles; 7hr; 2900-ft ascent) up Cadair Idris, though a longer and far less exciting one than those described in the box on p.289.

Three miles seaward from Tyn-y-ddôl, along the Dysynni Valley road, around thirty breeding pairs of cormorants colonize **Craig yr Aderyn** (Birds' Rock), a 760-foot-high cliff four miles from the coast. As the sea has gradually withdrawn from the valley, the birds have remained loyal to their home, making this Europe's only inland cormorant nesting site. Watch them return in V-formation at dusk from the negligible remnants of an Iron Age fort on top of Craig yr Aderyn reached by an east path (2 miles; 1hr; 750-ft ascent) from two miles west of Abergynolwyn where the *Llanllŵyda* **campsite** (☎01654/782276) lies conveniently by the start of the footpath up Craig yr Aderyn. Choughs and peregrine falcons share the rock in winter, and the occasional red kite can crop up at any time of year.

A couple of miles further down the valley a road cuts right to *Peniarth Uchaf*, (☎01654/710804, fax 712044; ⑤), a wonderful, very formal guesthouse set in expansive grounds. Half a mile on you meet the coast road (at this stage 2 miles inland) at Llanegryn, where the little church on the hill half a mile northwest of the village (open daily) has an unexpectedly beautifully rood screen, probably carved in the fifteenth century, which is said to have been carried overnight from Cymer Abbey (see p.293) after its dissolution. Just over two miles north of Llanegryn, at Llangelynnin, is another ancient church (open daily): a mainly eleventh-century building on the foundations of an eighth-century structure, and bare but for a few basic pews and a horse bier. Just outside the porch is the grave of Abram Wood, patriarch of *Y Teulu Wood*, a clan of Romanies who settled in Wales at the beginning of the eighteenth century.

Northern Cadair Idris and the Mawddach Estuary

In 1824, Wordsworth found the Mawddach "a sublime estuary". Some years later, John Ruskin concurred, deeming the waterside road he followed here "the most beautiful walk in the world". Romantic hyperbole perhaps, but these broad tidal flats gouging deep into the heart of the mid-Wales mountains create dramatic backdrops from every angle. With the sun low in the sky and the tide ebbing, the constantly changing course of the river trickles silver through the golden sands.

But the colour of the sands isn't just an illusion: they really do contain gold, though not enough for gold-mining company *Rio Tinto Zinc*, who thankfully abandoned their plans to dredge for the stuff in the early 1970s. Spasmodic outbursts of gold fever still occasionally hit the region's main town, **Dolgellau**, but most people are content to come here for some excellent walking up Cadair Idris and along the estuary, or to hit the beaches. The low-key **Fairbourne** and shoddy but relatively alive **Barmouth** are the main lures.

Fairbourne

The tiny, decaying resort of **FAIRBOURNE**, on the southern side of the Mawddach Estuary, was developed in the late nineteenth century as the country estate of the chairman of the McDougall's flour company. It sports one of the finest beaches in Wales and great views along the coast and across the estuary. Mr McDougall would undoubtedly be dismayed at the state of the town today, but it does have one attraction, the steam-hauled **Fairbourne Railway** (Easter–Sept 9 daily; £3.75 return). This makes a pleasant alternative route across the estuary to Barmouth, starting across the road from the **train station** and running a mile to a connecting **passenger ferry** (Easter–Oct; 90p single, £1.50 return) which takes you the rest of the way.

There is little reason not to press on from Fairbourne, but there are several handy **B&Bs** and the non-smoking *Cyfannedd Uchaf Farmhouse* (☎01341/250526; ③), which serves excellent meals, high above the estuary two miles east towards Arthog then a further two miles south along a narrow road.

Dolgellau

Its distance from England and its historical position in the heartland of Welsh nationalism should make **DOLGELLAU** (pronounced Dol-gethl-aye) the Welshest of towns, but the town's architecture draws more from nineteenth-century England: a dour series of small squares – all with English names – clustered around the solid granite neo-Georgian facades of Eldon Square, built to lure Victorian tourists from across the border to marvel at Cadair Idris and the Mawddach Estuary.

It is a much older town than appearances suggest, lying at the junction of three Roman roads which converged on a now-vanished military outpost. It was here in 1404 that Owain Glyndŵr assembled the last Welsh parliament and later signed an alliance with Charles VI of France for providing troops to fight against Henry

IV of England. Seventeenth-century Quakers sought freedom from persecution here, and in the 1860s Dolgellau became the focus of numerous gold rushes, drawing wave after wave of prospectors to pan the estuary or blast levels into Clogau shale or mudstone sediment under the Coed y Brenin Forest. The quartz veins yielded some gold, but in quantities too small to make much money.

Today Dolgellau is a far from exciting place, but the town and its environs make a logical base for some wonderful walks, notably an easy stroll along the Mawddach Estuary and a strenuous hike up Cadair Idris.

Arrival, information and accommodation

Dolgellau has no train station but is well served by **buses** from Bala, Barmouth and Machynlleth, which all pull into Eldon Square. The building known as Tŷ Meirion houses the **tourist office** (Easter–Oct daily 10am–1pm & 2–6pm; Nov–Easter Mon & Thurs–Sun 10am–5pm; ☎ & fax 01341/422888), along with the Quaker Interpretive Centre (see below).

There is very little commendable **accommodation** in Dolgellau itself, but plenty of great places scattered around about, some so close to Cadair Idris that you can start your hike at the back door.

HOTELS AND GUESTHOUSES

Aber Café, Smithfield Street (☎01341/422460). Very friendly B&B above a decent café. ②.

Borthwnog Hall, three miles west of Dolgellau on the A496, towards Bontddu (☎01341/430271, fax 430682). Small country house with its own art gallery superbly located on the northern shores of the Mawddach Estuary, with log fires and great meals. Take the #94 bus. ⑥.

Clifton House Hotel, Smithfield Square (☎01341/422554). Good-value hotel built in an ex-police station and jail. The basement cells are used as a restaurant. ④.

Dwy Olwen, Coed y Fronallt, Llanfachreth Road (☎01341/422822). Peaceful guesthouse in landscaped gardens a 10-min walk from the centre. Cross the Big Bridge and turn right. ②.

George III Hotel, Penmaenpool, four miles west of Dolgellau (☎01341/422525). Superb seventeenth-century hotel right by the Mawddach Estuary (bus #28). Some rooms are in former train station buildings. Top food and drink (see p.295). ⑧.

Ivy House, Finsbury Square (☎01341/422535). Licensed guesthouse a few yards southeast of Eldon Square, with a restaurant and cellar bar. ③.

Penmaenuchaf Hall, Penmaenpool, four miles west of Dolgellau (☎ & fax 01341/422129). Grand house formerly home to a Lancashire cotton magnate; now operating as a classy hotel with beautiful decor, a full-size billiard table and free angling for trout and salmon. It's pricey for one night but very competitive for short breaks. ⑧.

Tan-y-Fron, Arran Road (☎01341/422638). Non-smoking B&B with en-suite rooms and an associated campsite, a 10-min walk east along Arran Road. Closed Dec & Jan. ③.

Troed-y-Gader, Cader Road (☎01341/422556). One of the cheapest places around but it is a mile and a half out – past *Ivy House* and left at the *Shell* station. ②.

Tyddyn Mawr Farmhouse, Islawrdref, three miles southwest of Dolgellau (☎01341/422331). Eighteenth-century farmhouse on the slopes of Cadair Idris at the foot of the Pony Path. Great value at the low end of this category with all rooms en suite. ④.

Tŷ Nant, Cader Rd, Islawrdref, three miles southwest of Dolgellau (☎01341/423433). Simple, comfortable B&B, with a campsite, perfectly sited right at the foot of the Pony Path. ②.

Tŷ Saf Farmhouse, Llanfachreth (☎01341/423261). Small, comfortable seventeenth-century guesthouse in three acres of grounds close to the Precipice Walk. Great £12 communal dinners and generous breakfasts. ④.

HOSTELS AND CAMPSITES

Bryn-y-Gwyn Campsite, Cader Road (☎01341/422733). A basic tents-only site less than a mile southeast of Dolgellau.

Caban Cader Idris, Islawrdref, three miles southwest of Dolgellau (☎01248/600478). Twenty-bed bunkhouse at the foot of the road leading up to Kings YHA hostel. Beds at £6 a night. ①.

Kings YHA hostel, Penmaenpool, four miles west of Dolgellau (March–Oct; ☎01341/422392, fax 422477;). Large country house a mile up a wooded valley off the #28 Tywyn bus route (last bus around 7pm). This is an ideal base for the Pony Path up Cadair Idris. ①.

Tan-y-Fron Campsite, Arran Road (☎01341/422638). Well-appointed and reasonably priced camping and caravan site next to the B&B.

Tŷ Nant, Cader Rd, Islawrdref, three miles southwest of Dolgellau (☎01341/423433). Simple field campsite (£1.50 per person) with pay-to-use shower facilities shared by a simple bunkhouse. £3 gets you a bunk space (bring your own mat and bedding) and the use of a gas cooker, pots and pans.

Vanner Abbey Farm (☎01341/422854). Attractive camp and caravan site by Cymer Abbey.

The Town

Today Dolgellau's only central diversion is the **Quaker Interpretive Centre**, in the tourist office (see above), which uses a series of explanatory panels to tell of the local Quakers' (the Society of Friends) well-recorded sufferings before the 1689 Act of Toleration that put a stop – at least legally – to persecution for their pacifist Nonconformist views, non-attendance at church and non-payment of its tithes. At a trial in Bala in 1679, this last sin earned a group of Friends a prison term, a further encouragement to those thinking of following the two thousand Welsh Quakers who had already fled to the United States and started the Pennsylvania towns of Bangor, Bryn Mawr and others. The building also houses a national park exhibition.

Prospecting declined after the gold rushes of the late nineteenth century, but the hopeful still occasionally open up an ore vein. Try your hand on a three-hour-long **Gold Mining Tour** (April–Oct daily 9.30am–4pm; reduced hours in winter; ☎01341/423332; £9.50), which leaves from the **Welsh Gold Visitor Centre** (April–Oct daily 9am–7pm; reduced hours in winter; free) by the Big Bridge. The half-mile underground walk is fun, but barely justifies the expense: you see some real goldiggers at work, operating the milling and separating equipment, but most of the tour is designed for visitor amusement, with a staged blasting and the opportunity to chip away at the rock for a few minutes. Don't expect to find any nuggets: it usually takes two tons of ore to recover an ounce of metal and the shiny stuff in your rock chips is more than likely iron pyrites (fool's gold). Booking is advisable, and you should arrive early to grab a front seat in the minibus, as the views of the Coed y Brenin Forest en route to the mine are lovely.

Around Dolgellau

Long before the Victorian gold frenzy, the Romans had discovered flecks of gold in the Mawddach silt, then thirteenth-century Cistercian monks, based at **Cymer Abbey** (April–Oct daily 9.30am–6.30pm; Nov–March Mon–Sat 9.30am–4pm, Sun 2–4pm; £1.20; CADW), two miles north of Dolgellau, were given "the right in digging or carrying away metals and treasures free from all secular exaction". The fine location at the head of the Mawddach Estuary is typical of this austere order, but unfortunately the surrounding caravan site mars the effect of the remaining Gothic slabs. A path beside the abbey makes an alternative approach to the Precipice Walk (see box overleaf).

Precious metal was also the raison d'être for **BONTDDU**, four miles west along the A496 towards Barmouth, the source of gold used in royal wedding rings for the Queen and Charles and Di. You can't visit the site as it is still in operation, so the only gold you'll see now is in the springtime blooms at **Farchynys Cottage** (May–Sept Tues, Wed & Thurs 11am–5pm; £1) in the four acres of established garden and natural woodland.

There's more tranquillity a few miles southwest of Dolgellau at **Cregennan Lakes**, a serene local beauty spot set against a backdrop of brooding mountains. For something more boisterous, there's superb year-round pony trekking from **Abergwynant Trekking Centre** (☎01341/422377; £12 for 2hr), at Penmaenpool four miles west of Dolgellau on the A493.

Eating, drinking and entertainment

As with accommodation, most of Dolgellau's good **eating** takes place out of town, typically in the better hotels. Indeed, the only reason to hang around town in the evening is to take in rehearsals for one of the town's two **choirs**: the mixed *Côr Gwerin y Gader* which meets at The Vestry, Tabernacle Chapel, Cader Road (Mon 8pm), and the male voice *Côr Meibion Dolgellau*, at Ysgol y Gader (Wed 8pm).

Bwyty Dylanwad Da, 2 Smithfield St (☎01341/422870). The best restaurant in town, with creative, affordable dishes and great desserts served in simple surroundings. Closed Feb.

Fronoleu Farm Restaurant, Tabor, a mile east of Dolgellau off the Arran Road (☎01341/422361). Licensed restaurant in eighteenth-century Quaker farmhouse with live harp playing Tues, Thurs & Sat. Bar meals also available.

WALKS AROUND DOLGELLAU

Note: No map is needed for the first three walks; the OS Outdoor Leisure 1:25,000 map of "Cadair Idris/Dovey Forest" is recommended for the fourth, although the OS Landranger 1:50,000 "Dolgellau" map will do.

TORRENT WALK

The attractive lowland **Torrent Walk** (2 miles; 1hr; 100-ft ascent), follows the course of the Clywedog River as it carves its way through the bedrock. Stroll downstream past the cascades to the *Clywedog Tea Garden*, where you can eat home-baked scones in a riverside garden before starting back. Bus #2 can take you the two miles east along the A470, from where it's a hundred yards or so down the B4416 to a sign on the left-hand side marking the beginning of the walk.

PRECIPICE WALK

The not remotely precipitous **Precipice Walk** (3–4 miles; 2hr; negligible ascent) is very easy-going, simple to follow and has great views to the 1000-foot ramparts of Cadair Idris and along the Mawddach Estuary – best in late afternoon or early morning sun. The path makes a circuit around Foel Cynwch, starting three miles north of Dolgellau off the Llanfachreth road just near the Big Bridge. Bus #33 runs twice daily on Tuesdays and Fridays only, from Dolgellau to the car park by the start of the walk. From the car park turn left down a sideroad then left again up a track, following the signs all the way. On the shores of Llyn Cynwch, the path splits. Take the left fork along the shores then follow the contour around the bracken- and heather-covered Foel Cynwch back to the lake and return along the approach route. If you don't coincide with the bus, a path beside Cymer Abbey (see p.293) is the next best approach to this walk.

George III, Penmaenpool (see "Accommodation", p.292). Superb spot for an afternoon drink, a bar meal or something gamey and expensive from the à la carte menu.

Penmaenuchaf Hall, Penmaenpool (see "Accommodation", p.292). High-quality modern British cuisine in tasteful surroundings, though the service and food don't quite warrant the high prices. The £4 cream teas are well worth it, though.

Stag Inn, Bridge Street. Straightforward town-centre pub with good beer and a garden.

Tyn-y-Groes Hotel, Glanllwyd, four miles north of Dolgellau (☎01341/440275). Hospitable hotel in the Coed y Brenin forest. Good beer washes down fine bar meals or you can opt for the à la carte restaurant.

Y Sospan, Queen's Square (☎01341/423174). Dependable café/bistro behind the tourist office, serving good coffee, decent daytime meals and better dinners (booking necessary).

Barmouth and around

The best approach to **BARMOUTH** (Abermo) is the one created for the nine-teenth-century English Midlands sea-bathers, the rail bridge from the south over 113 rickety-looking wooden spans across the Mawddach River estuary. On the face of it, this tight little town, tucked into the shadow of steep cliffs and lapped by both estuary and sea, should be the jewel of the Cambrian coast, but years of shabby development have lumbered it with too many heavy buildings and sad pleasure-beach attractions. Keep your eyes out to sea or make for the hills behind the town, though, and it's a fine stop for a night or two.

PENMAENPOOL–MORFA MAWDDACH WALK

Beside the Mawddach Estuary's broad sands, a disused rail line makes for easy going on the **Penmaenpool–Morfa Mawddach Walk** (8 miles one way; 3hr; flat), starting at the car park by the Big Bridge in Dolgellau and passing Penmaenpool on its way to Morfa Mawddach. The first two miles are the least interesting, so it makes sense to catch the #28 bus to the **RSPB Nature Information Centre** (Easter–May Sat & Sun noon–4pm; June to mid-Sept daily 10am–5pm; free) in an old rail signal box at Penmaenpool, just by a wooden toll bridge (daily 8am–7pm; cars 25p, pedestrians 2p) linking the two banks of the estuary. From there the path hugs the estuary bank all the way to Morfa Mawddach, from where you can walk across the bridge to Barmouth (see above) or catch the bus back to Dolgellau. Another good scheme is to take the bus to Morfa Mawddach and walk back to Penmaenpool.

PONY PATH

If the weather is good and you are well kitted out, don't miss the classic **Pony Path** (6–7 miles; 4–5hr; 2500ft ascent), a straightforward and enjoyable route which starts from the car park at Tŷ Nant, three miles southwest from Dolgellau along the Cadair Road. Turn right, then right again at the telephone box, following the path to "Cader Idris". Already the views to the craggy flanks of the massif are tremendous, but they disappear as you climb steeply to the col where you turn left on a rocky path to the summit shelter on **Penygadair** (2930ft; see also p.289). The descent is either by the same route or (with some care and considerable efforts to minimize erosion) by taking the first part of the Fox's Path down to Llyn y Gadair. From the summit, go northeast to a grassy plateau then north to a couple of cairns and down to Llyn y Gadair. By the lake, forsake the rest of the Fox's Path in favour of a less obvious route heading off from the northwest corner of the lake, eventually meeting the Pony Path again. Note that there are no buses up Cadair Road.

Barmouth was once a shipbuilding centre, and a maritime air lingers at the quay at the south end of town, departure point for a **passenger ferry** to Fairbourne (Easter–Oct; as frequently as custom demands; 90p single, £1.50 return) and several sea angling and sightseeing trips (enquire on quay). In late June each year, the highly competitive **Three Peaks Race** starts here, a two-to-three-day amateur yachting event entailing navigation to Caernarfon, the English Lake District and Fort William in Scotland, and a run up the highest peak in each country.

The quay is also where you'll find the **RNLI Lifeboat Museum** (daily 10am–5pm; free), with its workaday exhibition of lifesaving paraphernalia; and the **Tŷ Gwyn Museum** (July–Sept Tues–Sun 10.30am–5pm; free), a medieval tower house where Henry VII's uncle, Jasper Tudor, is said to have plotted Richard III's downfall. First recorded in a poem around the middle of the fifteenth century, the house was thought to have been destroyed until renovations in the 1980s revealed its identity. It now contains displays on the Tudor dynasty, as well as a shipwreck museum.

On the hill behind, the **Tŷ Crwn Roundhouse** (same hours as Tŷ Gwyn) acted as a lockup for drunken sailors in the eighteenth century, and was reputedly built circular to prevent the devil lurking in any corners and further tempting the incarcerated mariners. It now houses some old photos of Barmouth.

Practicalities

Buses from Harlech and Dolgellau stop on Jubilee Road, near the **train station** and just a few yards from the **tourist office** (Easter–Oct daily 10am–6pm; ☎01341/280787).

In winter, the office displays a list of available **accommodation**, but in summer, there's no shortage. There are also loads of places to **camp**, the closest – and least afflicted with fixed caravans – being *Hendre Mynach*, Llanaber Rd (March–Oct; ☎01341/280262), just off the beach a mile north of town. For something simpler, try *Cefn Ddu* (☎01341/430644), a cheap, tent-only site with showers, down by the estuary, just west of Bontddu.

HOTELS AND GUESTHOUSES

Awelon, Ffordd Gellfechan (☎01341/280254). Central and very friendly, this is the best of Barmouth's cheapies. ②.

Bay View, 6 Porkington Terrace (☎01341/280284). Not quite as much of a bargain as other places in town, but a dependable place to rest your head. ③.

Bryn Melyn Hotel, Panorama Road (☎01341/280556, fax 280276; ④), comfortable, traditional, mountainside noted for its fine estuary views and proximity to the Cambrian Way walking route. ④.

The Gables, on Mynach Road (☎01341/280553). Ten minutes' walk north, a characterful place that's very welcoming to walkers.③.

Holme Lea, 4 Marine Rd (☎01341/281419). Another budget B&B that's pretty decent. ②.

Just Beds, Bryn-Teify, King Edward Street (☎01341/281165). As implied, you get the bare minimum here – there's no breakfast, but you're welcome to use the kitchen. ①.

Llwyndû Farmhouse, Llanaber, two miles north of Barmouth (☎01341/280144, fax 281236). One of the finest farmhouse B&Bs in Wales, with en suite rooms in the seventeenth-century farmhouse building – complete with mullioned windows and inglenook fireplace – and adjacent converted barn, plus delicious evening meals in the candlelit dining room. ⑤.

Wavecrest Hotel, 8 Marine Parade (☎01341/280330). Antique-furnished seafront hotel. ③.

WALKS FROM BARMOUTH

The best lowland walk on the Cambrian coast, the **Barmouth–Fairbourne Loop** (5 miles; 2–3hr; 300-ft ascent) makes a superb circuit around Barmouth and Fairbourne, with fine mountain, estuarine and coastal views all the way. The route can be done with almost no walking at all using the rail line to Fairbourne, the Fairbourne narrow-gauge railway and the ferry across the mouth of the estuary, but walking allows for seemingly infinite variation. The route first crosses the rail bridge (30p toll) to Morfa Mawddach station, follows the lane to the main road, crosses it onto a footpath that loops around the back of a small wooded hill to Pant Einion Hall, then follows another lane back to the main road near Fairbourne. Turn north for 400 yards, then left down the main street of Fairbourne to the sea, walk north along the beach and you can catch the ferry back to Barmouth. Any desired extension to the walk is best done from Morfa Mawddach, where the route described meets the Penmaenpool–Morfa Mawddach Walk (see p.295). Follow it for a mile to Arthog where a small road and a mesh of paths lead up past waterfalls to the beautiful **Cregennan Lakes** (NT).

The **Panorama Walk** (10min) is more famous, but apart from the fine estuary view, its chief quality is its brevity, the viewpoint being only yards away from the nearest road. By taking in **Dinas Oleu** (Fortress of Light), the cliffs immediately above Barmouth, which became the National Trust's first property in 1895, it can be turned into a decent walk (3 miles; 2hr; 400-ft ascent). Essentially the route follows Gloddfa Road opposite *Woolworth's* on the High Street onto the exposed clifftops, where there is a map of the reserve. Go through the metal gate and follow the path past Frenchman's Grave to a road where you turn left to the Panorama Viewpoint. Return by the same route.

EATING, DRINKING AND ENTERTAINMENT

Among the usual cheap cafés that litter a down-at-heel resort, there are quite a few decent places to eat. The *Llwyddû Farmhouse* and *Wavecrest Hotel* (see above) both serve good meals to non-residents, or try *Brambles* on Church Street (☎01341/280038) for British and French evening meals and very popular Sunday lunches. Also on Church Street is the *Indian Clipper* (☎01341/280252), a great south Asian balti house which serves plenty of vegetarian dishes, while on the harbour front you'll find the low-key *Anchor Restaurant*, with mammoth French sticks, pancakes and pavement tables, and the neighbouring *Isis*, good for pizza and vegetarian food.

The **entertainment** scene has less to offer, with only a couple of decent pubs and the odd pretty awful holiday-season club. Your best bets are *The Last Inn* on Church Street (☎01341/280530), a cosy bar in a former cobbler's shop, where you can also get a good pub meal, and *Tal y Don* on the High Street, a traditional and friendly pub with well-kept real ales.

Ardudwy

North of Barmouth, the coast opens out to a narrow coastal plain running a dozen miles towards Snowdonia and flanked by the heather-covered slopes of the Rhinog Mountains, five miles inland. This is **Ardudwy**, a land which Giraldus Cambrensis described as "the rudest and roughest of all the Welsh districts", a contention hard to reconcile with a fertile strip used as a fattening ground for black Welsh cattle on their way to the English markets, and now tamed by caravan sites and golf courses.

No modern road crosses the Rhinogs to the east, but until the early nineteenth-century building of coach roads, the existence of two mountain passes (see box overleaf) made this a strategic and populous area, as the number of minor Neolithic burial chambers and small Iron and Bronze Age forts demonstrate. Further up the coast, the town of **Harlech** was built as one link in Edward I's chain of magnificent fortresses. It is the only sizeable town in the region, followed in importance by **Llanbedr**, from where a road runs west to the camping resort on Shell Island, and another rises east, splitting into two delightful remote valleys.

Bus #38 services the coast from Barmouth to Harlech, then inland to Blaenau Ffestiniog. The Cambrian coast train line covers the same route to Harlech, from where it makes for Porthmadog on the Llŷn peninsula (see p.342).

Llanddwywe and Dyffryn Ardudwy

Two of the most accessible and impressive Neolithic sites in Ardudwy are in the contiguous twin villages of **LLANDDWYWE** and **DYFFRYN ARDUDWY**, five miles north of Barmouth. Turn right opposite the church in Llanddwywe and continue for a mile to get to **Cors-y-Gedol Burial Chamber** (unrestricted entry), a large capstone on deeply embedded uprights. The communal **Dyffryn Ardudwy Burial Chamber** (unrestricted entry; CADW), just off the road in Dyffryn Ardudwy, is more substantial. Two supported capstones lie amongst a bed of small boulders, the base stones of a mound thought to have been a hundred feet long. Finds from the dig here in the early 1960s are on display at the National Museum in Cardiff.

If you are travelling by train, get off at Talybont, walk north to visit the two sites and rejoin the line at Dyffryn Ardudwy, a walk of three miles in all. Just beyond Dyffryn Ardudwy station is the southern entrance to the **Morfa Dyffryn National Nature Reserve**, a coastal dune system stretching up to Shell Island (see below) notable for its flora, particularly the marsh helleborine. This is a fragile zone and permission for access must first be obtained from the Countryside Council for Wales (☎01248/372333).

There's a great place to **stay** on the main road in Dyffryn Ardudwy: *Glan y Wern* (☎01341/247580; ②) offers attractive rooms in the main house or cottage annexe, and organic breakfast – with ingredients from the garden – cooked by a former chef at the Centre for Alternative Technology. Delicious evening meals are available, as are pottery and t'ai chi classes.

The new "Dolgellau" OS map shows several routes with public foot access over the moors to the east. Most are ancient drovers' tracks and excellent for long lonely walks, especially if you're equipped with Shirley Toulson's *The Drovers' Roads of Wales* (see *Contexts*, p.470). The longest and most challenging of the tracks forms part of the old Harlech-to-London road which crosses the tiny and remote Pont Scethin, a favourite with postcard and calendar photographers.

Llanbedr and around

LLANBEDR, three miles north of Dyffryn Ardudwy, is home to the **Maes Artro Village** (school holidays daily 10am–5.30pm; £3), with its distinctly missable aquarium and Village of Yesteryear. Other than that, its YHA **hostel**, Plas Newydd (☎01341/241287, fax 241389; ①), right in the centre and open from mid-February to October, makes it a reasonable place to stay, as do the *Victoria Inn* (☎01341/241213; ④) with its beer garden, good bar meals and à la carte dinners, and the excellent *Llew Glas Brasserie* (☎01341/241555). There's also the crowded, caravan-free **campsite** (mid-March to Oct; ☎01341/214217) and restaurant on **Shell Island**, or Mochras, two miles away (£4 per car in summer, £3 in winter). A peninsula at anything other than high tide, you reach the island by a tidal causeway, then you can swim, examine the wild flowers or scour the beach for some of the two hundred varieties of shell found here. At low tide you can see a line of rocks in the sand leading out towards Ireland, known as Sarn Badrig (St Patrick's Causeway) and traditionally thought to be the road to a flooded land known as "The Low Hundreds", whose church bells still ring from below the water. Some imagination may be needed to hear this, but you can easily pick out what is probably a glacial lateral moraine, particularly from the top of the Rhinogs, from where it often appears to divide the ocean into two shades of blue.

East of Llanbedr, a narrow road follows the Artro River six miles to the waters of Llyn Cwm Bychan, deep in the heather and angular rocks of the Rhinog range. There's a basic **campsite** at the head of the lake, and paths up to the **Roman Steps** – most likely a medieval packhorse route, made of flat slabs cutting through the range – onto Rhinog Fawr (see box overleaf). Branching off the Cwm Bychan road, an even narrower and more picturesque road leads to **Cwm Nantcol**, the next valley south, where you can park at the ancient farm of **Maes-y-garnedd**, the birthplace of Colonel John Jones, brother-in-law of Oliver Cromwell and signatory to Charles I's death warrant, and a starting point for the Rhinog walks (see box overleaf). There is no public transport up either valley.

North of Llanbedr the A496 climbs gently for a mile or so to **Chwarel Hên Llanfair** (Easter to mid-Oct daily 10am–5pm; £2.50), a small slate quarry visited on a self-guided underground tour that doesn't hold a candle to those in Blaenau Ffestiniog. A few yards further on, a small road branches down to **Llandanwg**, a great place to get out onto the dunes, with a small, typically locked church that has to be periodically dug out of the sand by youth scheme workers so that the occasional service can be held.

Harlech

It's hard to dislike **HARLECH**, three miles north of Llanbedr. The time-worn castle dramatically clinging to its rocky outcrop alone raises it above its neighbours, and the buildings of this small town, cloaking the hill behind the fortress, command one of Wales' finest views over the dunes of Morfa Harlech across Cardigan Bay and beyond to the Llŷn. There's not a lot to do here, but there are good beaches nearby, and the narrow streets harbour surprisingly good places to eat and sleep.

Arrival, information and accommodation

Harlech's **train** station is on the main A496 under the castle. Most **buses** call both here and on High Street a few yards from the **tourist office**, Gwyddfor House (Easter–Oct daily 10am–6pm; ☎01766/780658). *Theatr Ardudwy* (☎01766/780667) on the main road occasionally puts on a decent play and has the only cinema in the district. There's **accommodation**, in town and around, to suit

WALKS ON THE RHINOGS

The northern Rhinogs offer some surprisingly tough walking. At under 2500ft they are not giants, but the large rough gritstone rocks hidden in thick heather make anything but the most well-worn paths hard going and potentially ankle-twisting. Besides, Rhinog Fawr is completely within the Rhinog National Nature Reserve and, while no permit is needed, the thin soil and fragile nature of the environment demand that you don't stray. The rewards are long views across Cardigan Bay, a good chance of stumbling across a herd of feral goats and a strong sense of achievement. The two walks described here start at the head of different valleys (see "Llanbedr and around", p.298), but share a common summit, that of Rhinog Fawr. Ambitious walkers might try combining the two (10 miles; 7hr; 3700-ft ascent), using paths that only approximately follow those marked on the OS Landranger #124 "Dolgellau" map or the Outdoor Leisure #19 map.

CWM BYCHAN WALK #1

The **Cwm Bychan walk** (5 miles; 3–4hr; 1900-ft ascent) starts at the car park in Cwm Bychan, following signs up through a small wood then out onto the open moor and up to the misnamed **Roman Steps**. These guide you up to the pass, Bwlch Tyddiad, giving views east to Bala and beyond. Continue a couple of hundred yards past the large cairn to a smaller one signalling a much less well-defined path leading south and steeply up. Beyond Llyn Du the terrain gets steeper still, and you may have to use your hands to finally reach **Rhinog Fawr** (2362-ft). The standard route is then to retrace your steps, but in good weather you can descend the same way you came for a few hundred yards and seek out a line running northwest from the shoulder towards Gloyw Llyn. From there, with some effort, you can pick up a path to the head of Llyn Cwm Bychan.

CWM BYCHAN WALK #2

The second **walk** (6–7 miles; 5–6hr; 2900-ft ascent) starts by the farmhouse at the head of Cwm Nantcol and makes a fairly rugged circuit over Rhinog Fawr and Rhinog Fach. Follow the track north from the car park to the house, into the fields and over the stile, then turn northeast and walk gradually towards the base of the rocky southwest ridge, following the white marker posts. Eventually the path turns north to a cairn on the skyline, then east following more cairns up the ridge to the summit trig point of **Rhinog Fawr** (2362-ft).

To approach Rhinog Fach you first have to make an arduous descent into Bwlch Drws Ardudwy (The Pass of the Door of Ardudwy). In 1773 Thomas Pennant found "the horror of it far exceeding the most gloomy idea that could be conceived of it. The sides seem to have been rent by some mighty convulsion into a thousand precipices." That might be a bit overstated, but describing the route between these precipices is all but impossible. From the summit of Rhinog Fawr head southeast towards a couple of cairns, then with Rhinog Fach ahead of you keep left, descending on whatever looks like it has had the most use. Eventually you'll reach the col, where you cross the stone wall and start on a fairly clear line up **Rhinog Fach** (2236ft). Explore the summit ridge to get the best views either way, then descend to Cwm Nantcol by first walking to a rocky ledge overlooking Llyn Hywel to the south. From here you should be able to see a scrappy path running very steeply down to the lake on the right-hand edge of the ledge. You'll have to use your hands at times and there are sections of scree, but you're soon on a clear path that skirts north around the base of Rhinog Fach towards Bwlch Drws Ardudwy. When it reaches the path through the pass, turn left and follow it back to Cwm Nantcol.

all pockets, and a reasonable summer-only **campsite**, *Min y Don* (☎01766/780286), only three minutes' walk towards the beach, left out of the station then first right.

HOTELS AND GUESTHOUSES

Aris Guesthouse, 4 Pen y Bryn (☎01766/780409). Friendly guesthouse with a great view, just above the town – past the *Lion Hotel*, then second left. ③.

Byrdir, High Street (☎01766/780316). Reliable small hotel with some en-suite rooms and meals available, 50yd from the tourist office. Closed Nov. ③.

Castle Cottage, Pen Llech (☎01766/780479). Cosy informal hotel with the trappings of a place charging twice as much, and consequently often booked well ahead. Excellent meals and a comfortable bar. Closed Feb. ⑤.

Godre'r Graig (☎01766/780905). Standard rooms in a B&B very convenient for the station on the other side of the level crossing. ②.

Gwrach Ynys Country Guesthouse, Ynys, Talsarnau, two miles north of Harlech (☎01766/780742). Comfortable and justifiably popular country house on the coastal flats with en- suite rooms, good home-cooked meals and plenty of advice on local walks. Open March–Nov. ④.

Maes-y-Neuadd, Talsarnau, three miles north of Harlech (☎01766/780200, fax 780211 substantially modernized country-house hotel, parts of which date from the fourteenth century. The expensive meals have garnered all manner of accolades. ⑨.

Tremeifion, Talsarnau, three miles north of Harlech (☎01766/770491). Luxury, non-smoking vegetarian guesthouse in three acres of grounds. B&B and half-board deals are available, the latter including evening meals made almost entirely from organic produce, and served with organic wine. ④/⑦.

Tyddyn-y-Gwynt, two miles above the town (☎01766/780298). Farmhouse with standard rooms, run by friendly local people. Take the road past the *Lion Hotel*, head straight at the crossroads and turn left at *Bryn Gwyn Cottage*. ②.

The Town

Although blessed with some of the coast's best beaches, it is the substantially complete **castle** (April–Oct daily 9.30am–6.30pm; Nov–March Mon–Sat 9.30am–4pm, Sun 11am–4pm; £3; CADW), squatting on its 200-foot bluff, that is Harlech's strength. Started in 1285 as one of Edward I's Iron Ring of monumental castles (see p.397), it was built of a hard Cambrian rock, known as Harlech grit, hewn from the moat where sheep now peacefully graze. One side of the fortress was originally protected by the sea, now receded and leaving the castle dominating a stretch of duned coastline.

The castle has seen a lot of action in its time: it withheld a siege in 1295, was taken by Owain Glyndŵr in 1404, and the youthful, future Henry VII – the first Welsh king of England and Wales – withstood a seven-year siege at the hands of the Yorkists until 1468, when the castle was again taken. It fell into ruin, but was put back into service for the king during the Civil War, and in March 1647 it became the last Royalist castle to fall.

The first defensive line comprised the three successive pairs of gates and portcullises built between the two massive half-round towers of the **gatehouse**, where an exhibition now outlines the castle's history. Much of the castle's outermost ring has been destroyed, leaving only the twelve-foot-thick curtain walls rising up 40ft to the exposed battlements, and only the towering gatehouse prevents you walking the full circuit. The inner ward was never completed but corbels and inset fireplaces give clues to the original domestic functions.

Outside the castle, a modern equestrian **statue** depicts a scene from *The Mabinogion* recalling a semi-mythical era long before Edward's conquest. The heroic giant and king of the British, Bendigeidfran (Brân the Blessed), ruled the court at Harlech, which needed to ally itself with the Irish. Bendigeidfran's sister Branwen (White Crow) married the king of Ireland and bore him a son, Gwern, but war soon broke out and Gwern was killed. Sorrowful uncle and dead nephew are **The Two Kings** of the sculpture's title.

Eating and drinking

Castle Cottage, High Street (☎01766/780479). Limited choice two- and three-course dinner menu featuring the likes of smoked haddock in leek sauce. Very good, informal service, cosy surroundings and moderate prices. Wed–Sat only in winter, but Sun lunch served in summer.

Hung Yip, High Street. Straightforward but good, cheap Chinese meals.

Lion Hotel. About the liveliest pub in Harlech, with hand-pumped ales and good home-cooked bar meals. Just up from the central crossroads.

Plâs Café, High Street (☎01766/780204). Licensed café and restaurant with a good range of inexpensive to moderate food and one of the finest views around. Sit in the glass-fronted dining room, or the garden if the weather is fine.

Yr Ogof, High Street (☎01766/780888). Highly commendable bistro-style place a few yards north of the centre, with bentwood chairs and a good-value range of inventive vegetarian and meaty dishes.

travel details

Unless otherwise stated, frequencies for trains and buses are for Monday to Saturday services; Sunday averages 1–3 services, though the main routes are more frequent and some routes have no Sunday service at all.

TRAINS

Aberdyfi to: Barmouth (8 daily; 30min); Machynlleth (8 daily; 20min); Porthmadog (6 daily; 1hr 20min); Pwllheli (6 daily; 1hr 40min); Tywyn (8 daily; 5min).

Aberystwyth to: Birmingham, England (7 daily; 3hr); Borth (9 daily; 12min); Machynlleth (6 daily; 30min); Shrewsbury (7 daily; 2hr).

Barmouth to: Aberdyfi (8 daily; 30min); Harlech (6 daily; 30min); Machynlleth (8 daily; 1hr); Porthmadog (6 daily 45min).

Harlech to: Barmouth (6 daily; 30min); Birmingham (5 daily; 4hr 15min); Machynlleth (6 daily; 1hr 20min); Porthmadog (7 daily; 20min).

Machynlleth to: Aberdyfi (8 daily; 20min); Aberystwyth (9 daily; 30min); Barmouth (6 daily; 55min); Birmingham (7 daily; 2hr 30min); Harlech (6 daily; 1hr 20min); Porthmadog (6 daily; 1hr 45min); Shrewsbury (7 daily; 2hr).

Tywyn to: Aberdyfi (7 daily; 5min); Barmouth (7 daily; 25min); Harlech (6 daily; 1hr); Machynlleth (7 daily; 30min); Porthmadog (6 daily; 1hr 10min).

BUSES

Aberaeron to: Aberystwyth (hourly; 40min); Carmarthen (5 daily; 1hr 30min); Lampeter (7 daily; 35min); New Quay (hourly; 20min).

Aberdyfi to: Machynlleth (4–6 daily; 25min); Tywyn (4–6 daily; 10min).

Aberystwyth to: Aberaeron (hourly; 40min); Borth (hourly; 25min); Caernarfon (1 daily; 2hr 40min); Cardigan (5 daily; 2hr); Carmarthen (1 daily; 2hr 35min); Devil's Bridge (2 daily; 40min); Dolgellau (5 daily; 1hr 25min); Machynlleth (5 daily; 45min); New Quay (hourly; 1hr); Ponterwyd (7 daily; 30min); Pontrhydfendigaid (1 daily; 55min); Tregaron (3 daily; 1hr); Ynyslas (5 daily; 30min).

Barmouth to: Dolgellau (12 daily; 20min); Harlech (9 daily; 25min).

Cardigan to: Aberaeron (6 daily; 1hr 10min); Aberporth (hourly; 25min); Aberystwyth (5 daily; 2hr); Carmarthen (hourly; 1hr 30min); Cilgerran (8 daily, 10min); Dre-fach Felindre (hourly; 30min); Newcastle Emlyn (hourly; 25min); New Quay (hourly; 1hr).

Dolgellau to: Aberystwyth (5 daily; 1hr 25min); Barmouth (12 daily; 20min); Llangollen (6 daily; 1hr 30min); Machynlleth (6 daily; 35min); Porthmadog (6 daily; 50min); Tywyn (6 daily; 50min).

Fairbourne to: Dolgellau (6 daily; 20min); Tywyn (6 daily; 35min).

Harlech to: Barmouth (9 daily; 25min); Blaenau Ffestiniog (4 daily; 35min).

Lampeter to: Aberaeron (7 daily; 35min); Carmarthen (8 daily; 1hr 10min); Llanddewi Brefi (Mon 1 bus, Tues, Thurs & Fri 4 buses; 25min); Pontrhydfendigaid (Tues 3 buses; 50min); Tregaron (Mon 1 bus, Tues, Thurs & Fri 4 buses; 30min).

Machynlleth to: Aberdyfi (4–6 daily; 25min); Aberystwyth (5 daily; 45min); Corris (10–20 daily; 12min); Dolgellau (6 daily; 35min); Llangollen (6 daily; 2hr 55min); Tywyn (4–6 daily; 35–45min).

New Quay to: Aberaeron (hourly; 20min); Aberporth (hourly; 40min); Aberystwyth (hourly; 1hr); Cardigan (hourly; 1hr).

Tregaron to: Aberystwyth (3 daily; 1hr).

Tywyn to: Aberdyfi (4–6 daily; 10min); Abergynolwyn (4 daily; 15min); Corris (4 daily; 30min); Dolgellau (6 daily; 50min); Fairbourne (6 daily; 35min); Machynlleth (4–6 daily; 35–45min).

CHAPTER FIVE

SNOWDONIA AND THE LLŶN

What the coal valleys are to the south of the country, the mountains of **Snowdonia** (Yr Eryri) are to the north: the defining feature, not just in their physical form, but in the way they have shaped the communities within them. Trapped between the brash coastal resorts in the north and the thinly inhabited hill tracts of mid-Wales to the south, this mountainous kernel is north Wales' crowning glory, a tightly packed bundle of soaring cliff faces, jagged peaks and plunging waterfalls.

Snowdonia is the heart – and undisputed highlight – of the massive **Snowdonia National Park** (Parc Cenedlaethol Eryri), an 840-square-mile area which extends north and south, beyond the bounds of Snowdonia and this chapter, to encompass the Rhinogs, Cadair Idris (see p.281) and 23 miles of superb Cambrian coastal scenery. It is this little section, little more than ten miles by ten, that most people mean when they refer to Snowdonia: staggeringly beautiful and home to Wales' highest mountain, **Snowdon** (Eryri),where winter snows cling to 3000-foot peaks well into April.

Not surprisingly the massif is the region's focus, and there are enough mountain paths to keep even the most jaded walking enthusiast happy for weeks. But Snowdonia isn't all walking. Small settlements are dotted in the valleys, making great bases or places to rest. Chief among them are **Betws-y-Coed** and **Llanberis**, the latter linked to Snowdon's summit by mountain rail, while others, like **Beddgelert** and **Blaenau Ffestiniog**, are former mining or quarry towns still brimming with interest.

West of here, the mountain landscape gently bleeds into the gentler rockiness of the **Llŷn peninsula**, which juts into the Irish Sea at almost a right angle to the Cambrian Coast. Linked to Snowdonia by the magnificent narrow-gauge **Ffestiniog Railway**, its first settlement is the harbour town of **Porthmadog**, with its neighbour, the Italianate dream village of **Portmeirion**. The Welsh castle at **Criccieth** and the museum devoted to Lloyd George a couple of miles away are the only reasons to pause before Wales ends in a flourish of small coves around **Abersoch** and **Aberdaron**. Finally, roads loop back along the Llŷn to the tip of the north coast where **Caernarfon**, the heart of one of the most nationalist, Welsh-speaking areas in the country, is overshadowed by its stupendous castle.

Getting around

Getting to the fringes of Snowdonia from elsewhere in Wales is not a problem: mainline **trains** run along the coast to nearby Bangor, while the Conwy Valley line

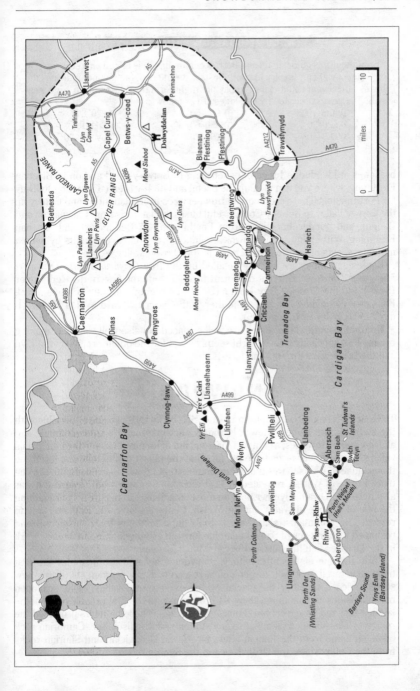

ACCOMMODATION PRICE CODES

Throughout this guide, hotel and B&B accommodation is priced on a scale of ① to ⑨. Category ① only applies to youth hostels; for the rest, the number indicates the **lowest price** you could expect to pay per night for a **double room in high season**. The prices indicated by the codes are as follows:

① under £20	④ £40–50	⑦ £70–80
② £20–30	⑤ £50–60	⑧ £80–100
③ £30–40	⑥ £60–70	⑨ over £100

---

branches at Llandudno Junction penetrating to Betws-y-Coed and on to Blaenau Ffestiniog, where you can pick up the useful and highly scenic Ffestiniog Railway for Porthmadog. There are frequent **bus** services from Llandudno and Conwy up the Conwy Valley to Betws-y-Coed, useful buses to Llanberis from Caernarfon and Bangor, and good connections from Porthmadog to Beddgelert and Blaenau Ffestiniog. Within Snowdonia, towns are linked every one to two hours by *Sherpa* minibuses, except for the poor service in the Ogwen Valley.

Routes and times are all fully detailed on the free *Gwynedd Public Transport Maps and Timetable*. Current **discount fares** include the **Gwynedd Red Rover** (£4.20) and the *Crosville* **Day Rover** (£5.70), both good for one day's bus travel. For those combining bus and train, there's the **North & Mid Wales Rover** (1-day £15.50, 2-day £23, 3-day £36).

Roads throughout the region are well surfaced but also well travelled, making cycling less appealing than it might seem, except for the quieter roads on the Llŷn and the bridleways through the forests.

SNOWDONIA

To Henry VIII's antiquarian, John Leland, **SNOWDONIA** seemed "horrible with the sight of bare stones"; now it is widely acclaimed as the most dramatic and alluring region in Wales, a compact, barren land of tortured ridges dividing glacial valleys, whose sheer faces belie the fact that the tallest peaks only just top three thousand feet. It was to this mountain fastness that Llywelyn ap Gruffydd, the last true "Prince of Wales", retreated in 1277 after his first war with Edward I; it was also here that Owain Glyndŵr held on most tenaciously to his dream of regaining the title of "Prince of Wales" for the Welsh. Centuries later, the English came to remove the mountains; slate barons built huge fortunes from Welsh toil and reshaped the patterns of Snowdonian life forever, as men looking for steady work in the quarries fled the hills and became town dwellers.

From the late eighteenth century, Snowdonia became the focus for the first truly structured approach to geological research. Early proponents of this new science pieced together the glacial evidence – scoured valley walls, scalloped mountainsides and hanging valleys – to come up with the first reliable proof of the last Ice Age and its retreat ten thousand years ago. These pioneers produced the rock-type classifications familiar to any students of the discipline: Cambrian rock takes its name from the Roman name for Wales, Ordovician and Silurian rocks from the Celtic tribes, the Ordovices and the Silures.

Botanists found rare alpine flowers, writers produced libraries full of purple prose, and Richard Wilson, Paul Sandby and J M W Turner all came to paint the landscape. Soon, those with the means began flocking here to marvel at the plunging waterfalls and walk the ever-widening paths to the mountaintops. Numbers have increased rapidly since then, and thousands of hikers arrive every weekend for some of the country's best walks over steep, exacting and constantly changing terrain. Recognizing the region's scientific importance, as well as its scenic and recreational appeal Snowdonia became the heartland of Wales' first, and still largest, national park (see box below).

The last Ice Age left a legacy of peaks ringed by cwms – huge hemispherical bites out of the mountainsides – while the ranges were left separated by steep-sided valleys, a challenge for even the most fly-footed climber. The most striking monument, and understandably the clear focus, is **Snowdon**, reached by superb climbs and a cog railway from the former slate town of **Llanberis**. But the other mountains are as good or better, often far less busy and giving unsurpassed views of Snowdon. The **Glyders** and **Tryfan** are particular favourites and best tackled from the **Ogwen Valley**. The walkers' hamlets of **Capel Curig** and **Pen-y-Pass** have a suitably robust atmosphere, though many more prefer the comforts of the nearby Victorian resort of **Betws-y-Coed**. Elsewhere, settlements tend to coincide with some enormous mine or quarry. Foremost among these are **Beddgelert**, whose former copper mines are open to the public, and **Blaenau Ffestiniog**, the "Slate Capital of North Wales", where two mines open their caverns for underground tours.

If you are serious about doing some **walking** – and some of the walks described here are serious, especially in bad weather (Snowdon gets 200 inches of rain a year) – you need a good map such as the 1:50,000 OS *Landranger* #115 or the 1:25,000 OS *Outdoor Leisure* #17. Walking conditions are often posted on the doors or noticeboards of outdoor shops and tourist offices, but you should consult the local mountain weather forecast. There are also premium-rate phone weather forecasts: *Weathercall* (☎0891/505315) providing an up-to-date summary of north Wales' weather conditions and a forecast for the next few days, and *Mountaincall* (☎0891/505330) which concentrates on hill-country conditions in the Snowdonia National Park (☎0839/500449).

SNOWDONIA NATIONAL PARK

The oldest and largest of Wales' national parks, **Snowdonia National Park** (Parc Cenedlaethol Eryri) was set out in 1951 over 840 square miles of northwest Wales – all the way from Conwy to Aberdyfi – to encompass the Rhinogs, Cadair Idris and 23 miles of the Cambrian coast. Jagged mountains predominate, but the harsh lines come tempered by broadleaf lowland woods around calm glacial lakes, waterfalls tumbling from hanging valleys and complex coastal dune systems. However, you won't find total wilderness: 25,000 people, predominantly Welsh-speakers, live in the park and another fourteen million people come here each year to tramp almost 2000 miles of designated paths. In apparent contradiction to its name, the national park is 75 percent privately owned by the Forestry Commission and National Trust. However, trespass isn't usually a problem as long as you keep to the ancient rights of way that conveniently cross private land where needed. Many of the most popular areas are National Trust land where access is unrestricted.

Roewen & Conwy △   △ Conwy & Llandudno

Trefriw Wells

Penyrhelgi-du

Llyn Cowlyd
Reservoir

Trefriw

A470

A458

River Conwy

Llanrwst

Llyn Crafnant
Reservoir

Gwydir
Castle

Gwydir
Chapel

A5

GWYDIR
FOREST

Capel Curig   △ Capel Curig

River Nantgwryd

A5

Tŷ Hyll

Swallow
Falls

River Llugwy

Moel
Siabod

Betws-y-Coed

A470

Capel Garmon

Capel Garmon
Burial Chamber

Lledr Valley △

A470

Pont-y-Pant

Fairy Glen
Conwy Falls

A5

River Machno

Dolwyddelan

Dolwyddelan

Pentre-bont

Tŷ Mawr

Ty'n y Coed Uchaf

River Conwy

△ Llangollen

Roman Bridge

Penmachno

A470

Llechwedd Slate Caverns

Gloddfa Ganol Slate Caverns

Blaenau
Ffestiniog

N

A496

A470

Ffestiniog

CENTRAL SNOWDONIA

▽ Bala & Dolgellau

Accommodation inside the Snowdonia National Park is strictly limited, and most is on the fringes. The main exception is Betws-y-Coed, a village packed with guesthouses, all of them filling up early during the busy summer season. Elsewhere in Snowdonia are B&Bs, hostels, bunkhouses and basic campsites, mostly geared towards walkers and climbers. In all, there are seven **YHA hostels** within ten miles of Snowdon's summit, and a further half-dozen other budget places. Even with a medium-sized backpack, walking from one to another makes a welcome change from the usual circular walks.

Betws-y-Coed and around

Sprawled out across a flat plain around the confluence of the Conwy, Llugwy and Lledr valleys, **BETWS-Y-COED** (pronounced Betoos-ah-Coyd) should be the perfect base for exploring Snowdonia. Its riverside setting, overlooked by the conifer-clad slopes of the **Gwydyr Forest**, is undeniably appealing, and the town boasts the best selection of hotels and guesthouses in the region, but after an hour moochng around the outdoor equipment shops and drinking tea you are left wondering what to do. None of the serious mountain walks start from here, and, while there are a couple of easy strolls (see box) up river gorges leading to the town's two main attractions, the **Conwy Falls** and **Swallow Falls**, these can get depressingly busy in the height of summer. That said, its much-touted role as "the gateway to Snowdonia" means it is hard to avoid.

The quieter valleys in the vicinity can often be a lot more appealing. The rail line from the coast comes up the **Conwy Valley** past **Llanrwst**, five miles north of Betws-y-Coed, a town graced by a fine bridge attributed to Inigo Jones and a couple of beautifully decorated chapels. The train continues south from Betws-y-

△ A5 to Swallow Falls, Capel Curig & Bangor   △ Gwydir Castle, Llanrwst & Conwy

Miners Bridge

GWYDYR FOREST

River Llugwy

Pont-y-Pair Bridge

Motor Museum

Railway Museum

Riverside Campsite

OLD CHURCH ROAD

St Michael's Church

Suspension footbridge

Bus stops

St Mary's Church

Beics Betws

Train Station

Llanrwst & Conwy

Capel Garmon

ACCOMMODATION

1 Aberconwy House
2 Bryn Afon Guesthouse
3 The Ferns Guesthouse
4 Glan Llugwy
5 Henllys Old Courthouse
6 The Riverside
7 Swn-y-Dwr

N

River Conwy

BETWS-Y-COED

0   yds   800

Waterloo Bridge

A470 to Lledr Valley & Blaenau Ffestiniog ▽ ▽ A5

Coed up the **Lledr Valley**, a wonderfully scenic journey passing the lonely **Dolwyddelan Castle**, on its way to the slate town of Blaenau Ffestiniog. Further to the southeast, a minor road leads to **Penmachno** and the house of William Morgan, the translator of the Bible into Welsh. Walkers bound for the high hills will be heading west beside the **Llugwy River** to the mountain centre of Capel Curig and beyond to Llanberis and the Ogwen Valley. Most of the land around Betws-y-Coed and along the Conwy Valley was part of the Gwydyr Estate owned by the Wynn family, descended from the kings of Gwynedd and the most power-ful dynasty in the region until the male line died out in 1678; several place names are reminders of the family's might.

Llanrwst is the largest town in the district and operates as a hub for the local **bus** system. Some services terminate, requiring a change onto buses to Betws-y-Coed and Penmachno or Trefriw, Roewen, Conwy and Llandudno. If you are only planning to stop at Llanrwst and then the coastal resorts, **trains** from the station at the north end of town are faster and more comfortable.

Arrival and accommodation

Betws-y-Coed is arranged in a flat triangle bounded by the Conwy and Llugwy rivers and the A5, which forms the town's main street, running west from the Waterloo Bridge to the Pont-y-Pair bridge. Access is easy, either by train or bus from the north coast, or by car along the A5 from Llangollen, and frequent buses continue towards the peaks around Snowdon. The **train station** is just a few paces across the grass from the **tourist office**, Royal Oak Stables (Easter–Oct daily 10am–6pm; Nov–Easter daily 9am–1pm & 2–4pm; ☎01690/710426, fax 710665), where displays give a quick overview of conservation work in Snowdonia. **Buses**, which fan out to Penmachno, the Ogwen Valley, Llanberis, Conwy and Llandudno, stop outside St Mary's Church on the main street.

Accommodation

The town has plenty of **accommodation**, but has to cope with an even larger numbers of visitors pushing prices up in the summer. Expect to pay a pound or two more than in other towns in Snowdonia and don't be surprised to find the places listed full if you arrive late in the day. There are two nearby **youth hostels**, at Capel Curig and in the Lledr Valley. The closest **campsite** is *Riverside Caravan & Camping Park* (Easter–Oct; ☎01690/710310), right behind the station. Walkers and climbers who want direct access to the mountains need to make for Capel Curig (see p.319) or Llanberis (see p.324).

Aberconwy House, Llanrwst Road (☎01690/710202). Friendly Victorian guesthouse over-looking the Llugwy Valley. Cross the suspension bridge behind the station if you're on foot or take the A470 towards Llanrwst. ③.

Bryn Afon Guesthouse, Mill Street (☎01690/710403). Popular if fairly standard guesthouse just over the Pont-y-Pair bridge from the main road. ③.

Cae'r Berllan, on the A470 towards Llanrwst (☎01492/640027). A sumptuous country guesthouse in an ivy-clad sixteenth-century manor almost three miles from Waterloo Bridge. Excellent, moderately priced à la carte and set menus are also available to non-guests. ④.

The Ferns Guesthouse, Holyhead Road (☎01690/710587). Licensed non-smoking guest-house an easy walk across the footbridge into town. All the rooms are en suite. ③.

Glan Llugwy, on the A5 towards Capel Curig 300 yards beyond Pont-y-Pair (☎01690/710592). One of the cheapest B&Bs, with TVs in rooms. ②.

Henllys Old Courthouse, Old Church Road (☎01690/710534). Non-smoking guesthouse in a former Victorian magistrates courthouse, with comfortable single rooms in the old holding cells and views over the River Conwy. Healthy breakfasts and very good dinners served. March–Oct. ⑤.

Penmachno Hall, Penmachno (☎01690/760207). Superior country guesthouse with stylish, comfortable rooms, on the edge of Penmachno and right by the entrance to Tŷ Mawr Wybrnant. The hospitable hosts offer good meals made with garden vegetables, and often join you for dinner. ⑤.

The Riverside, Holyhead Road (☎ & fax 01690/710650). The cheapest place for bed and continental breakfast, above the restaurant of the same name a few yards towards Capel Curig from the Pont-y-Pair bridge. Nice non-smoking rooms, some with baths, and discounts for the restaurant . ①/②.

Swn-y-Dwr, Mill Street, just past *Bryn Afon* (☎01690/710648). Popular, non-smoking guesthouse, over the Pont-y-Pair bridge. ③.

Tan-y-Foel, Capel Garmon (☎01690/710507, fax 710681). A sixteenth-century farmhouse that ranks as the best small country hotel in the district with eight acres of grounds, extensive views, a heated indoor pool and superb dinners for around £25. Take the A470 towards Llanrwst then turn right after two miles. Non-smoking. ⑧.

Tŷ Gwyn, on the A5 (☎01690/7103383). Cosy old coaching inn with wood-beamed rooms, a bar that is hard to leave and some top-notch food. Half a mile east of the centre just over Waterloo Bridge. There are a couple of cheaper rooms, but you'll need to book well ahead. ④.

White Horse Inn, Capel Garmon (☎ & fax 01690/710271). Pleasant rooms just over a mile from Betws-y-Coed, above a 400-year-old village inn with a popular bar and restaurant (see "Eating and drinking"). ④.

The Town

The settlement of Betws-y-Coed is first recorded during the fifth or sixth century, when a monastic cell was founded, earning the town its name of "oratory in the forest". Apart from some lead mining, it remained a backwater until 1808, when road improvements brought the Irish Mail this way. As part of the A5 construction, Telford completed the graceful **Waterloo Bridge** (Y Bont Haearn) in 1815, giving quicker access and luring landscape painters David Cox and J M W Turner, who in turn alerted the leisured classes to the town's beauty. Anglers keen to exploit the richly stocked pools came too, but it was the arrival of the train line in 1868 that really lifted its status from coaching station to genteel resort, an air the town vainly tries to maintain. Today it's mainly a centre for walkers, although there are a few sights worth seeking out. All camera-wielding visitors at some time end up at the **Pont-y-Pair Falls**, a low cataract where the waters of the River Llugwy thunder over assorted boulders and funnel under the adjacent Pont-y-Pair bridge. Relaxing on the stone slabs which surround the falls, it is hard to generate much enthusiasm for the fourteenth-century **St Michael's church** (key from the Railway Museum, or the tourist office in winter), most interesting for the twelfth-century font and a carved effigy of an armoured knight, whose inscription identifies him as Gruffydd ap Dafydd Goch, the grandson of Llywelyn ap Gruffydd's brother, Prince Dafydd.

Just a few paces away, the **Conwy Valley Railway Museum** (Easter–Oct daily 10.15am–5.30pm, Nov–Easter Sat & Sun 10.30am–4.30pm; £1) is a fairly dull collection of memorabilia and shiny engines, slightly enlivened by a model of a Welsh slate quarry and the opportunity for kids to take a short ride on a miniature train or tram. If internal combustion interests you more than steam, the **Motor Museum** (Easter–Oct daily 10am–6pm; £1.30), a couple of hundred yards away behind the tourist office, is a marginally better bet. The half-dozen classic bikes and fifteen cars on display change frequently, but expect the likes of a 1934 Bugatti Straight 8 and a Model T Ford.

Activities

The most leisurely thing to do in Betws-y-Coed is to join a **guided walk** from outside the tourist office (5–6hr; May–Sept Thurs–Sun 10am; £3). For the more ambitious, *Snowdonia Mountain Guides* (☎01690/710720), contactable through the *Climber and Rambler* shop opposite Pont-y-Pair bridge, runs day courses in **guided mountain walking** (£32), **scrambling** (£37–42), **rock climbing** (£32–45), **abseiling** (£32–35) and **gorge walking** (£32), and longer excursions at all levels; prices include use of all specialized equipment.

Mountain bikes can be rented from *Beics Betws* (☎01690/710766) on Church Hill at the top of the road beside the post office, with information on routes through the Gwydyr Forest obtainable from the tourist office (£2). The nearest **horse riding** is at *Ty Coch Farm* (2hr £15; ☎01690/760248), seven miles south of Betws-y-Coed in Penmachno. **Anglers** with a rod licence and their own tackle can try hooking salmon and sea trout on stretches of the Conwy right in town (£18–24 for 24hr; mid-March to mid-Oct Mon–Fri) and brown and American brook trout on Llyn Elsie in the hills just south (£13 a day). For details and permits contact Mr Parry (☎01690/710232) at the *Tan Lan* bread shop next to the post office.

Eating and drinking

For a town so geared to tourism that you can hardly turn around without knocking someone's cream tea onto the floor, there are surprisingly few places to **eat**. Guesthouses offering meals will often be your best bet, although most of the **pubs** serve snacks and basic meals as well as beer.

The Buffet Coach Café, The Old Goods Yard. Basic café with home-made snacks inside (or outside) a 1940s railway carriage at the station.

Dil's Diner, Station Approach (☎01690/710346). Greasy spoon café beside the train station, a great place for breakfast or to fill up after a day in the hills. It often closes at around 5pm in winter, but stays open till around 9 or 10pm in summer.

The Riverside, Holyhead Road (☎ & fax 01690/710650). One of the town's best restaurants, small and convivial with an imaginative menu of well-prepared food and a good wine list. Not too expensive, either.

The Stables, *Royal Oak Hotel*, High Street (☎01690/710219). Currently the town's hottest bar, with good beer and bar food, and jazz on summer Thursdays.

Tŷ Gwyn, on the A5 (see "Accommodation"). The best place to eat in town, whether you want a pub meal or table d'hôte. Menus usually include game and local fish, as well as good vegetarian dishes and delectable desserts. Prices are inexpensive to moderate.

White Horse Inn, Capel Garmon (see "Accommodation"). An excellent evening retreat, with cosy bars, good beer, home-cooked bar meals and a restaurant serving fine, moderate to expensive country cooking from Wed to Sun.

The Llugwy Valley: Swallow Falls and the Gwydyr Forest

The **Swallow Falls** (a mistranslation of *Rhaeadr Ewynnol* or "foaming cataract") lie two miles west along the A5 towards Capel Curig. Its proximity to the road and obvious photogenic qualities make it one of the region's most-visited sights, but it is no more than a straightforward, pretty waterfall with the occasional mad kayaker scraping down the precipitous rock. Pay your 40p and you can walk down to a series of viewing platforms.

Less than a mile beyond, the road crosses the river passing **Tŷ Hyll** (Easter–Oct daily 9.30am–5pm; Nov–Easter Mon–Fri variable hours; 50p), known as the "Ugly House" for its chunky appearance. Decked out with period furniture and surrounded by a forest full of easy paths, it is also the headquarters of the *Snowdonia National Park Society*, an environmental campaigning group which lobbies to preserve the region's ecological and social integrity.

From here, a small sideroad climbs north into the evergreens of the **Gwydyr Forest**, an area best explored by mountain bike but pleasant enough on foot. The **Miners' Trail** (3 miles; 2hr; minimal ascent), from a lakeside parking area a mile or so northeast of Tŷ Hyll, gives a focus to a forest walk though you would have to be pretty keen on defunct lead workings to get much out of it. From Tŷ Hyll, the A5 follows the River Llugwy upstream past a number of roadside cataracts, most notably opposite *Cobden's Hotel*, and on to Capel Curig.

The Conwy Valley: Capel Garmon, Llanrwst and Trefriw

Fed by the water of the Machno, Lledr and Llugwy rivers, the Conwy River leaves Betws-y-Coed along its broad pastoral corridor to the sea at Conwy (see p.394) flanked on the left by the bald tops of Snowdonia's northern and eastern bulwark, the mighty Carneddau range. More manageable hills lie to the east where Neolithic dwellers left their mark at the **Capel Garmon Burial Chamber** (unrestricted access; CADW), a heavily reconstructed multi-chambered communal burial site built between 2500 and 1900BC. The site – actually only some rough stones lining a series of linked pits – is a five-minute signposted walk across farmland two miles southeast of Betws-y-Coed and half a mile south of the tiny hilltop village of **CAPEL GARMON**, chiefly distinguished for the excellent *White Horse Inn* (see p.312 and above) and the valley views from the cemetery across the road.

Llanrwst and around
LLANRWST, five miles north of Betws-y-Coed, is the largest and most economically important town in the valley. Not striking, nor especially large, it does have a working-town feel and was once the largest wool market in north Wales and a centre for harp manufacture. It still retains its Wednesday and Friday livestock markets, and the general one on Tuesday.

Inigo Jones is said to have spent his early years here, so it isn't entirely unlikely that the great seventeenth-century architect was at least partially responsible for the town's most noted sight, the slender humpback **Pont Mawr** (Big Bridge) normally attributed to him. It undoubtedly bears his mark: three graceful arches and beautifully proportioned symmetry, combined with engineering techniques which were extremely advanced for their time. The bridge carried all the cross-river traffic in the area before the building of Telford's bridges at the estuary of the Conwy and upstream at Betws-y-Coed, and its single lane still struggles in summer.

Claims that Jones also had a hand in the design for **Gwydyr Chapel** (open daily) are harder to verify. He was certainly known to landowner Richard Wynn – Jones' father and grandfather were tenants on the Wynn estate – who in 1633 commissioned the elaborate chapel to be attached to the Church of St Grwst. A riot of alabaster, carved memorials and seventeenth-century brasses set off a huge stone coffin, said to be that of Llywelyn ap Iorwerth ("the Great"). The beautiful rood screen in the main body of the church was salvaged when the former Maenan Abbey, Wales' largest Cistercian house, was dissolved by Henry VIII. Its paltry remains can be seen in the grounds of the expensive *Maenan Abbey Hotel*, two miles to the north of Llanrwst.

Half a mile away across the river from the chapel is Richard Wynn's ancestral home, **Gwydyr Castle** (daily 10am–5pm; £2.50), actually a low-slung manor house begun in 1492 on the site of a fortified house a century older. Despite substantial additions in the sixteenth and nineteenth centuries, with parts plundered from the post-dissolution Maenan Abbey, the ivy- and wisteria-covered building is a model of early Tudor architecture. Its core is a three-storey solar tower, whose windows relieve the gloom of the great halls, each with enormous fireplaces and stone-flagged or heavy timber floors. Most of the original fittings and superb Tudor furniture were sold off in 1921 by the then owner, the Earl of Carrington, and much of the rest of the house was ruined in a fire a few months later. The house is currently in the early years of three-decade restoration programme and, in line with its baronial nature, the furnishing is kept simple – tapestries cover the solid stone walls, a few tables and chairs are scattered about and there's some fine painted glass. Fortunately some of the original furnishings have been tracked down. By mid-1997, the highlight will be the Dining Parlour, one of the country's finest examples of a room of any period, initially installed by Richard Wynn around 1642 and again attributed to Inigo Jones. The complete set of heavily carved oak panels, Baroque doorcase and fireplace, and abundant gilded Spanish leather was bought during the 1921 sell-off by American newspaper magnate William Randolph Hearst and shipped across the Atlantic. New York's Metropolitan Museum acquired it in 1956 and kept it boxed up for forty years until the recent agreed sale. Until then, the Dutch Garden with its fountain, peacocks and Cedars of Lebanon dating back to 1625, is the main attraction – on fine days at least.

A few hundred yards from his home, Richard Wynn built his own private **Gwydyr Uchaf Chapel** (key from the adjacent Forestry Commission office, Mon–Fri 8.30am–5pm; free; CADW) in 1673. The plain exterior is in striking contrast to the unashamedly Baroque interior, with its roof beams cut into angelic figures. The inward-facing pews are unusual, but it is the painted ceiling which is really outstanding, depicting the Creation, the Trinity and the Day of Judgement.

Llanrwst centres on the tiny Ancaster Square, linked by Denbigh Street to the town's main **train station**. **Buses** stop on Watling Street, which branches off midway along Denbigh Street. Since it's so close to Betws-y-Coed, few people will want to stay in Llanrwst, but there is decent **accommodation** along Main Street with comfortable rooms and a friendly welcome at *Pickwick's* (☎01492/640275;

WALKS FROM BETWS-Y-COED

The best two walks from Betws-y-Coed follow narrow river gorges. Neither is circular, so unless you plan to hitch, consult bus timetables first to avoid a long wait for the infrequent services.

The **Conwy Gorge walk** (3 miles; 1hr 15min; descent only) links two of the district's best-known natural attractions, **Fairy Glen** and the **Conwy Falls** (see opposite), by way of a cool green lane giving glimpses of the river through the woods. The best approach is to forgo the forty-minute walk along the A5 towards Llangollen and take the #49 bus (five times daily) to the *Conwy Falls Café*. After viewing the Falls, walk a hundred yards back along the road towards Betws-y-Coed, then follow a path parallel to the river through the trees. After about half an hour, you'll see the gate to Fairy Glen on your left. Returning to the main path, continue to the *Fairy Glen Hotel*, where you can cross the river by Beaver Bridge, turn right and follow a minor road back to town.

The car park on the north side of the Pont-y-Pair bridge marks the beginning of the **Llugwy Valley walk** (6 miles; 2hr 30min; 600-ft ascent), a forested path following the twisting and plunging river upstream to Capel Curig. With the A5 running parallel to the river all the way, there are several opportunities to cut short the walk and hitch or wait for the bus back to Betws-y-Coed. Less than a mile from Pont-y-Pair you first reach a ford where the Roman road Sarn Helen crossed the river, then pass the steeply sloping **Miners' Bridge**, which linked miners' homes at Pentre Du on the south side of the river to the lead mines in the Gwydyr Forest. The path follows the river on your left for another mile – though path maintenance sometimes means you have to cut up into the pines – to a slightly obscured view of **Swallow Falls**. Detailed maps available from the tourist office show numerous routes back through the Gwydyr Forest, or you can continue half a mile to the road bridge by Tŷ Hyll and follow the right bank to Capel Curig, passing the scant remains of the Caer Llugwy, a Roman fort, and a couple more treacherous rapids: The Mincer and Cobden's Falls.

③)), above the tea rooms of the same name, and opposite at *The Eagles Hotel* (☎01492/640454; ④)), which offers almost 200 gourmet sandwiches and moderately priced meals. For lighter **meals**, cross Pont Fawr to the *Tu Hwnt i'r Bont Tearooms* (Easter–Oct) in a fifteenth-century stone cottage next to the bridge, or pick up picnic requisites from the well-stocked delicatessen *Blas ar Fwyd*, 25 Station St, at the north end of town.

Trefriw and Llyn Crafnant

Judging by the brochures scattered all over north Wales, you would think that the only thing in the small village of **TREFRIW**, two miles north of Llanrwst, is the **Woollen Mills** (Easter–Oct Mon–Fri 9.30am–5.30pm; free). It isn't, but its demonstrations of late-nineteenth-century weaving methods, using power from the stream outside, certainly make for a more compelling visit than other mills around north Wales.

In the second century, Romans garrisoned in the now barely discernible camp of Canovium on the banks of the Conwy were the first to make a fuss over the iron-rich waters of **Trefriw Wells** (Easter–Oct daily 10am–5.30pm; Nov–Easter Mon–Sat 10am–5pm, Sun noon–5pm; £2.65), a mile and a half north of the village. A robust pair of gentlemen's and ladies' bathhouses, complete with slate tubs, were built around 1700, but the spa vogue didn't get into full swing until the

Victorian era when health-seekers flocked upriver from Conwy. The wells waned along with the fashion, but are open again for interesting, if laboured, twenty-minute self-guided tours during which you can sample the waters. A signposted road back in the village close to the woollen mills leads three miles southwest to **Llyn Crafnant**, a calm reservoir hemmed in by mountains, and one of the more popular local beauty spots.

Conwy Falls, Fairy Glen and Penmachno

None of the attractions of Betws-y-Coed can compete with getting out to the gorges and waterfalls in the vicinity, and walking is the ideal way to see them (see box opposite). The final gorge section of the River Conwy, a couple of miles above Betws-y-Coed, is one of the most spectacular things to see, the river plunging fifty feet over the **Conwy Falls** into a deep pool. After slotting 50p in the turnstile beside the *Conwy Falls Café* (reached by the #49 bus five times daily), you can view the falls on the right and a series of rock steps to the left originally cut as a kind of primitive fish ladder, now superseded by a tunnel through the rock on the far side.

After carving out a mile or so of what kayakers regard as some of north Wales' toughest whitewater, the Conwy negotiates a staircase of drops and enters the **Fairy Glen**, a cleft in a small wood which takes its name from the Welsh fairies, the *Tylwyth Teg*, who are said to be seen hereabouts. A short lane from the Beaver Bridge beside the *Fairy Glen Hotel* leads to a car park from where a short path (20min each way; 50p) leads to the glen, on the A470 to Blaenau Ffestiniog.

Penmachno

The River Machno enters the Conwy just above the Conwy Falls at the end of its short run down through the small village of **PENMACHNO** from the surrounding hills. Just above the confluence, the waters once provided the motive power for the **Penmachno Woollen Mill** (daily 10am–5pm; free) where panels on the weaving process, and half a dozen ageing looms producing uninspired patterned cloth, feebly attempt to lure you into the shop.

The mill shares its car park with **Ty'n y Coed Uchaf** (April–Sept Thurs–Sun noon–5pm; Oct Thurs, Fri & Sun noon–4pm; £1.70; NT), a 35-acre smallholding reached along a twenty-minute path. The property, along with Tŷ Mawr Wybrnant (see below) and vast tracts to the east, was part of the fabulously rich Penrhyn Estate until 1951 when the land was gifted to the government in lieu of capital taxes. Twenty thousand acres of agricultural land now make up the Ysbyty Estate, where the National Trust is endeavouring to maintain a rural community partly by funding projects to replace dry-stone walls and re-lay hedges in the traditional manner. Pick up the free leaflet available in the car park to find some fine examples of both walls and hedges, protecting ancient fields rich in wild flowers and insect life threatened on agricultural land elsewhere.

The estate's centrepiece is its nineteenth-century Welsh **farmhouse** and outbuildings. Although inhabited until 1990, the house had not been structurally altered since 1916; electricity and gas were never connected and there was no piped water, nor even an indoor toilet. Careful restoration has been undertaken in the three small rooms, only slightly erasing the ghosts of generations of past tenants whose fine rustic furniture still fills every corner. A coal range shoehorned into an inglenook, a Welsh dresser arrayed with patterned plates and prim ornamentation lend a slightly formal air partly displaced by the short, personal guided tour.

Five miles on, and two and a half miles beyond Penmachno village at the end of a long drive, stands the isolated little cottage of **Tŷ Mawr Wybrnant** (times and prices as for Ty'n y Coed Uchaf). Here Bishop William Morgan, the man who first translated the Bible into Welsh (see p.380), was born in 1545 and lived until his teenage years when he decamped to Gwydir Castle to pursue his education. The original cottage was altered markedly over the years but has now been restored to something like its sixteenth-century appearance, all bare stone and beams, and a gaping fireplace supporting a huge, sagging beam dating back to the thirteenth century. Star attraction is the collection of Bibles and prayer books, including a Morgan original. Despite this, virtually the only people who come here are those who come to pay homage to the man who not only furthered Protestantism in Wales but probably saved the language.

The Lledr Valley

The train line up the Conwy Valley from Betws-y-Coed follows the twists of the beautiful **Lledr Valley** to Blaenau Ffestiniog, the river flowing through deciduous and pine forests that give way to the smooth, grassy slopes of the Moel Siabod before you bore through over two miles of slate – the longest rail tunnel in Wales. Take this trip while you can: the line is endangered by privatization and the recent closure of its current funder, the Trawsfynned nuclear power station.

The A470 runs parallel to the river from Betws-y-Coed to Blaenau Ffestiniog. Five miles south of Betws-y-Coed you come to Pont-y-Pant station, where the Roman road Sarn Helen crosses the river on a clapper bridge and follows the river to Dolwyddelan. The Lledr Valley **YHA hostel** (April–Aug; ☎01690/750202; ①), across the field from the station, is an ideal starting point for a walk up Moel Siabod (see box, p.320) and also accommodates **campers** for half the adult rate.

A mile further on is **DOLWYDDELAN**, a village well placed for the southern approach to Moel Siabod and only a mile east of lonely **Dolwyddelan Castle** (April–Oct daily 9.30am–6.30pm; Nov–March Mon–Sat 9.30am–4pm, Sun 2–4pm; £1.70; CADW), commanding the head of the valley. Llywelyn ap Iorwerth ("the Great"; see p.432) may well have been born here, since his father was reputedly responsible for its construction at the end of the twelfth century. The strategic site, on the important route from Aberconwy to the north and Ardudwy to the south, was soon turned against him when Edward I took the castle, refortified it and used it to further subdue the Welsh. By the end of the fifteenth century, it had become redundant and lay abandoned, until the Wynns of Gwydir treated it to a suitably Victorian reconstruction, complete with the fanciful battlements and a new roof. Today, all it shelters is a small exhibition on native Welsh castles, and gives a panoramic view from between its castellations.

If you want to stay around here, the castle custodian runs the nearby *Bryn Tirion Farm* B&B (☎01690/750366; ③), a **campsite** and, from October to March, a **bunkhouse** (①), for which you need your own sleeping bag. Back in the centre of Dolwyddelan, *Elen's Castle Hotel* (☎01690/750207; ②) has rooms and a bunkhouse (①), and serves good inexpensive bar food and pricier meals. The best **pub** is the cosy, welcoming *Y Gwydyr*, where Sunday lunch is served in summer.

Capel Curig and the Ogwen Valley

Tantalizing glimpses of Wales' highest mountains flash through the forested banks of the Llugwy as you climb west from Betws-y-Coed on the A5. But Snowdon, the mountain which more than any other has become a symbol of north Wales for walkers, mountaineers, botanists and painters alike, eludes you until the final bend before **Capel Curig**. This tiny walkers' village makes a perfect base for the two valleys which plunge westwards deep into the mountains. The A4086 follows Nant Gwryd southwest to the Snowdon massif (see p.328) while the A5 prises apart the Carneddau and Glyder ranges to the northwest, forging through the **Ogwen Valley** to tatty **Bethesda**, home to one of Wales' last surviving slate quarries.

As you cross the watershed between the Llugwy and Ogwen rivers, the frequently mist-shrouded Carneddau range to the north glowers across us at the Glyder range and its triple-peaked **Tryfan**, arguably Snowdonia's most demanding mountain. This forms a fractured spur out from the main range and blocks your view down the valley, the twin monoliths of Adam and Eve that crown Tryfan's summit picked out on the skyline. The courageous or foolhardy make the jump between them as a point of honour at the end of every ascent. West of Tryfan the road follows a perfect example of a U-shaped valley, carved and smoothed by rocks frozen into the undersides of the glaciers that creaked down **Nant Ffrancon** ten thousand years ago.

Capel Curig

The tiny, scattered village of **CAPEL CURIG**, six miles west of Betws-y-Coed, competes with Llanberis (see p.324) to be Wales' major centre for outdoor enthusiasts. There is scarcely a building here which isn't of some use either as inexpensive accommodation, a mountain-gear shop or just a place to replenish the body. Foremost among them is **Plas-y-Brenin: The National Mountaineering Centre** (☎01690/702214, fax 702394), a quarter of a mile along the A4086 to Llanberis from the town's main road junction, built around a former coaching inn and hotel, and now running nationally renowned residential courses in orienteering, canoeing, skiing and climbing. There are daily mountain weather forecasts in reception. If you're just passing through and don't have your own equipment, the two-hour abseiling, canoeing and dry-slope skiing sessions held during July and August (£7.50) may be of interest. Kids who want a full day taster of canoeing, skiing and abseiling can be left on the "All Day Adventure" (£17.50), though adults are welcome too. There is also a state-of-the-art climbing wall open throughout the year (daily 10am–11pm; £2 during the day, £3 on evenings and weekends), and the opportunity to hear talks or watch slide shows of recent expeditions (usually Mon–Thurs & Sat 8pm; free). Plas-y-Brenin doesn't rent out **mountain bikes**; for those you'll need to visit *Clogwyn Mountain Bikes* (☎01690/720210; £13 a day) at *A5 Services* petrol station half a mile along the A5 from the junction.

Despite Capel Curig's popularity, the only major walk is up Moel Siabod (see box overleaf), but the village acts as a base for the Ogwen Valley and Snowdon. The road to the valley runs four miles southwest past **Dyffryn**, the farm written about by Thomas Firbank (see "Books" in *Contexts*), to the *Pen-y-Gwryd Hotel* (see p.333). The A498 continues south to Beddgelert, past the best view of the east

A WALK FROM CAPEL CURIG

If you approached Capel Curig from the west, you won't have looked twice at the rounded grassy back of **Moel Siabod** (2862ft), but its eastern aspect is another matter – a challenging ridge rising up to afford a magnificent summit view of the Snowdon Horseshoe.

The mountainous section of the **east ridge walk** (5 miles; 4hr; 2200ft) is circular and brings you back into the Llugwy Valley. The route starts from opposite the YHA hostel in Capel Curig, crossing the concrete bridge and following the right bank downstream past the falls by *Cobden's Hotel* to the Pont Cyfyng road bridge (30min), an alternative starting point for the walk. Taking the road south, turn right on the second path signposted to Moel Siabod. The path quickly rises out of the valley and keeps to the left of the mountain, past a disused slate quarry and across some boggy land, before the long scramble up the east ridge. Once found, the path is fairly clear, but it weaves around outcrops past places where a moment's inattention could be perilous. The summit is flat and uninteresting, so once you've admired Snowdon, turn northeast and follow the craggy summit ridge which eventually starts to drop across grass to the moors below, soon rejoining your ascent route for the hike back to Pont Cyfyng.

An alternative, if you are prepared to carry all your gear or chance the public transport system to get back to Capel Curig, is to approach the summit by the route described, then retrace your steps down the ridge, and descend through the pine forest above Dolwyddelan into the Lledr Valley (see p.318).

face of Snowdon, while the A4086 branches west to Llanberis, passing Pen-y-Pass, the start for the best-known Snowdon walks.

Practicalities

The only **buses** servicing Capel Curig are the #19, which runs between Llandudno and Llanberis, and the #65, which links Bangor and Llanrwst. If neither suits, you can always walk the six miles along the Llugwy River from Betws-y-Coed (see box, p.318).

Once here, there are plenty of **places to stay**, though none is especially luxurious. Best are *Bron Eryri* (☎01690/720240; ③), a comfortable and welcoming B&B half a mile outside the village towards Betws-y-Coed, and the *Bryn Tyrch Hotel* (☎01690/720223; ③), also on the A5 but closer to the main road junction. There's also limited accommodation at *Plas-y-Brenin* (see p.319; ③), while cheaper options include *Llugwy Guesthouse* on the A4086 (☎01690/720218; ②) and the simple yet comfortable *Bryn Glo* (☎01690/720215; ②), a mile towards Betws-y-Coed. The cheapest option in the village is the **YHA hostel** (mid-Feb to mid-Dec; ☎01690/720225, fax 720270; ①), 500 yards along the A5 towards Betws-y-Coed.

During the day, walkers tend to patronize either the *Pinnacle Café*, grafted onto the post office and general store at the main road junction, or the *Snowdonia Café*, next to the YHA: both serve substantial portions at low prices. In the evening they retire to the warm and lively bar at the *Bryn Tyrch Hotel* (see above). The inexpensive **meals** here are huge, and predominantly vegetarian – indeed, this is one of the very few establishments in the whole of Snowdonia to make any real attempt to please vegans. Everyone who isn't at the *Bryn Tyrch* is in the bar at *Plas-y-Brenin*.

The Ogwen Valley

Five miles west of Capel Curig the gentle **Ogwen Valley** fills with the waters of Llyn Ogwen, a post-glacial lake formed behind time-compacted moraine left by the retreating ice. At its western end stands **IDWAL COTTAGE**, the only settlement in the valley and so small it isn't named on maps. Comprising just a mountain rescue centre, a snack bar and a YHA hostel clustered around a car park, the main reason to come here is to make some of Wales' most demanding and rewarding walks (see box overleaf), or start the easier twenty-minute walk to the magnificent, classically formed cirque, **Cwm Idwal**.

The evidence of glacial scouring is so clear here that you wonder why it took geologists so long to work out the process that created these hollowed faces and scored rocks. In 1842, Darwin wrote of his visit with the geologist Alan Sedgewick eleven years earlier, recalling that "neither of us saw a trace of the wonderful glacial phenomena all around us". The cwm's scalloped floor traps the beautifully still **Llyn Idwal**, which reflects the precipitous grey cliffs behind, split by the jointed cleft of Twll Du, **The Devil's Kitchen**. Down this channel, a fine watery haze runs off the flanks of **Glyder Fawr**, soaking the crevices where early botanists found rare arctic-alpine plants (see *Contexts*, p.449); the main reason for designating Cwm Idwal as Wales' first **nature reserve** (NT) in 1954. More common species carpet the reserve in early summer but have to compete with grazing sheep who destroy all but the comparatively luxuriant fenced-off control areas. Geomorphologists pay more attention to the twisted rocks beside the Devil's Kitchen, one of the few places where you can see the downfolded strata of what is known as the Snowdon syncline, evidence that the existing mountains sat between two much larger ranges some 300 million years ago. To their left, the smooth inclines of the Idwal Slabs act as nursery slopes for budding rock climbers: good for some half-hearted "bouldering" for the ill-equipped.

An easy well-groomed path leads up to the reserve from the car park, where the café (daily 8.30am–5pm; later on summer weekends) will sell you a nature trail booklet for 60p. A five-minute walk down the valley from the car park, the road crosses a bridge over the top of **Rhaeadr Ogwen** (Ogwen Falls), which cascades down this step in the valley floor. Before you put your camera away, look under the road bridge, where you'll see a simple mortarless arch of a bridge, part of the original packhorse route that followed the valley before Telford pushed the Holyhead road through.

Practicalities

Depending on the season and school holidays, two or three **buses** run along the valley daily between Betws-y-Coed and Bangor, three or four more running east from Idwal Cottage in summer, usually inconveniently timed. There's a footpath parallel to the fast and busy road, following the five-mile-long packhorse route that runs the length of the valley from Capel Curig to Idwal Cottage. **Accommodation** in the valley is limited. Two and a half miles west of Capel Curig, the *Williams Barn*, Gwern-y-Gof Isaf Farm (☎01690/720276; ①), has a self-catering bunkhouse and cheap **campsite**, or there's the smaller *Gwern Gof Uchaf* campsite, a mile further west, and the *Idwal Cottage* **YHA hostel** (March–Oct; ☎01248/600225, fax 602952; ①), at the western end of Llyn Ogwen, five miles from Capel Curig. Residents can get meals at the hostel, otherwise the valley is self-catering and has no shops.

WALKS FROM OGWEN: TRYFAN, THE GLYDERS AND THE CARNEDDAU

Note: The OS Outdoor Leisure 1:25,000 map of "Snowdonia" is highly recommended for all these walks, though the latter half of the Carneddau walk is omitted. The 1:50,000 Landranger #115 covers the whole area.

THE GLYDERS

Tourists climb Snowdon but mountain connoisseurs almost invariably prefer the sharply angled peaks of the **Glyders**, with their challenging terrain, an entertaining high-level jump, cantilevered rocks and views back to Snowdon. The sheer number of good walking paths make it almost impossible to choose one definitive circular route. The individual sections have therefore been defined separately giving the greatest flexibility. **All times given are for the ascents**: expect to take approximately half the time to get back down.

TRYFAN

If you've got the head for it, the **North Ridge of Tryfan** (3002ft) (1 mile; 1hr–1hr 30min; 2000-ft ascent) is one of the most rewarding scrambles in the country. It's not as precarious as Snowdon's Crib Goch, but you get a genuine mountaineering feel as the valley floor drops rapidly away and the views stretch further and further along it. The route starts in the lay-by at the head of Idwal Lake and goes left across rising ground, until you strike a path heading straight up following the crest of the ridge to the summit. Anyone who has seen pictures of people jumping the five-foot gap between Adam and Eve, the two chunks of rhyolitic lava which crown this regal mountain, will wonder what the fuss is about until they get up there and see the mountain dropping away on all sides. In theory the leap is trivial, but the consequences of overshooting would be disastrous.

There are two other main routes up Tryfan. The first follows the so-called **Miners' Track** (2 miles; 2hr; 1350-ft ascent) from Idwal Cottage, taking the path to Cwm Idwal then, as it bears sharply to the right, keeping straight ahead and making for the gap on the horizon. This is **Bwlch Tryfan**, the col between Tryfan and Glyder Fach, from where the **South Ridge** of Tryfan (800 yards; 30min; 650-ft ascent) climbs past the Far South Peak to the summit. This last section is an easy scramble. The second route, which is more often used in descent, follows **Heather Terrace** (1.5 miles; 2hr; 2000-ft ascent), which keeps to a fault in the rock running diagonally across the east face. The start is the same as for the north ridge, but instead of following the ridge, you cut left, heading south until you arrive between the South and the Far South Peaks. A right turn then starts your scramble for the summit.

GLYDER FACH

The assault on **Glyder Fach** (3260ft) begins at Bwlch Tryfan, reached either by the Miners' Track from Idwal Cottage or by the south ridge from Tryfan's summit. The trickier route follows **Bristly Ridge** (1000 yards; 40min; 900-ft ascent) which isn't marked on OS maps but runs steeply south from the col up past some daunting-looking towers of rock. In good conditions, it isn't that difficult, and saves a long hike southeast along a second section of the **Miners' Track** (1.5 miles; 1hr 30min; 900-ft ascent), then west to the summit, a chaotic jumble of huge grey slabs thatmany people don't bother climbing up, preferring to be photographed on a massive cantilevered rock a few yards away.

GLYDER FAWR

From Glyder Fach, it is an easy enough stroll to **Glyder Fawr** (3280ft) (1 mile; 40min; 200-ft ascent), reached by skirting round the tortured rock formations of **Castell y Gwynt** (The Castle of the Winds) then following a cairn-marked path to the dramatic summit of frost-shattered slabs angled like ancient headstones.

Glyder Fawr is normally approached directly from Idwal Cottage, following the **Devil's Kitchen Route** (2.5 miles; 3hr; 2300-ft ascent) past Idwal Lake, then to the left of the Devil's Kitchen, zigzagging up to a lake-filled plateau. Follow the path to the right of the lake; then, where paths cross, turn left for the summit.

A **southern approach** to Glyder Fawr (3 miles; 2hr 30min; 2100-ft ascent) leaves from beside the YHA hostel at Pen-y-Pass (see p.332), following a "courtesy path" marked by red flashes of paint. It rises steeply behind the hostel heading north-west, but turning north for the summit to avoid straying onto the screes on the flanks of the neighbouring mountain, Esgair Felen.

THE CARNEDDAU RANGE

The appearance of the **Carneddau Range** could hardly be in greater contrast to the jagged edges of the Glyders. These peaceful giants, which present the longest stretch of ground over three thousand feet in England and Wales, form a rounded plateau stretching to the cliffs of Penmaenmawr on the north coast. The sound of a raven in the neighbouring mist-filled cwms, and the occasional wild pony, can often be your only company on inclement days, but in fine weather the easy walking and roof-of-the-world views make for a satisfying day out. Though the tops are fairly flat once you're up there, getting to them can be a hard slog. The start from Idwal Cottage is the most strenuous, requiring a long push up the shaley south ridge from the stile beside the road bridge at the foot of Ogwen Lake. If you can, avoid this in favour of a fine **Carneddau loop** (9 miles; 5hr; 3500-ft ascent) starting from the lay-by at the head of the lake near Tal y Llyn Ogwen farm, and taking in the range's four mighty southern peaks. The path keeps to the right of the farm, then follows boggy land by a stream towards its source, Ffynnon Lloer, before turning left up the east ridge of **Pen yr Ole Wen** (3212ft), with its magnificent view down into Nant Ffrancon and back to Tryfan. In clear weather, you can see the route running north past Carnedd Fach, past what looks to be a huge artificial mound, to **Carnedd Dafydd** (3425ft). After a short easterly descent, the path skirts the steep Ysgolion Duon cliffs, then climbs over stones to the broad, arched top of **Carnedd Llywelyn** (3491ft), the highest of the Carneddau and surpassed in Wales only by two of Snowdon's peaks, Yr Wyddfa and Crib-y-ddysgl. For little extra effort, enthusiasts can conquer **Yr Elen** (3152ft), a short distance to the northeast, but most will be content with the easterly descent to **Craig yr Ysfa**, a sheer cliff which drops away into **Cwm Eigiau**, a vast amphitheatre to the north. Continuing with care, skirt around the north of Ffynnon Llugwy reservoir and climb to the grassy top of **Penyrhelgi-du** (2733ft), from where there is a steady broad-ridged descent to the road near Helyg. The mile back west to the starting point is best done on the old packhorse route running parallel to the A5, and linked to it occasionally by footpaths.

If you are considering one-way walks, several other possibilities present themselves, the most appealing of which is the full ridge walk from here linking up with the Roman road which links Rowen to Aber (see p.401).

Llanberis and Snowdon

Mention **LLANBERIS**, ten miles west of Capel Curig, to any mountain enthusiast and **Snowdon** immediately springs to mind. The two seem inseparable, and it's not just the five-mile-long umbilical of the **Snowdon Mountain Railway** (see p.332), Britain's only rack and pinion railway bonding the town to the summit, nor the popular path running parallel to it (see box, p.330). This is the nearest you'll get in Wales to an alpine climbing village, its single main street thronged with weather-beaten walkers and climbers decked out in Gore-Tex and Fibrepile, high fashion for what is otherwise a dowdy town. Most are Snowdon-bound, others are just making use of abundant budget accommodation and the best facilities this side of Betws-y-Coed.

At the same time Llanberis is very much a Welsh rural community, albeit a depleted one now that slate is no longer being torn from the flanks of Elidir Fawr, the mountain separated from the town by the twin lakes of Llyn Padarn and Llyn Peris. The quarries, which for the best part of two centuries employed up to three thousand men to chisel out the precious slabs, closed in 1969, leaving a vast staircase of sixty-foot-high terraced platforms as a testament to their labours. At much the same time proposals were tabled for a power station to be built on the site of the former quarries. Environmentalists – as often as not the same middle-class English second-home owners who had pushed property prices beyond the means of the local people – were incensed that this fragile spot on the fringes of the national park could be desecrated. The people of Llanberis, still reeling from the closure of the quarries, had no such qualms. In the end both parties were pacified: the project went ahead underground.

Arrival, information and accommodation

With no train or *National Express* services, the easiest way here is on **bus** #77 from Bangor, bus #88 from Caernarfon or the summer-only *Sherpa* buses #19 or #95. All stop along High Street outside either of the two outdoor equipment shops, both just a few steps from the town's **tourist office**, 41b High St (Easter–Sept daily 10am–6pm; Oct daily 10am–4pm; Nov–Easter Wed–Sun 10am–4pm; ☎01286/870765).

There's a wealth of low-cost **accommodation** and **campsites** in or close to town, as well as up at Pen-y-Pass (see p.332). Luxurious places are harder to find, so if you have your own transport and don't mind being a few miles further from the mountain, you might prefer to stay in places listed under Caernarfon (see p.357) or Bangor (see p.402).

Hotels and guesthouses

Alpine Lodge Hotel, 1 High St (☎ & fax 01286/870294). Traditional and friendly licensed guesthouse with comfortable rooms, all with private facilities, and bunkhouse accommodation let on a B&B basis. ②/③.

Dolafon Hotel, High Street (☎ & fax 01286/870933). Appealing, well-priced B&B in its own grounds, with spacious, comfortable rooms and delicious evening meals. ③.

Dolbadarn Hotel, High Street (☎ & fax 01286/870277). Reasonable rooms in a former coaching hotel that's one of the oldest buildings in the village, now operating its own pony-trekking centre. ③.

Erw Fair, High Street (☎01286/872400). Large house with newly decorated rooms, all with TVs, and hearty breakfasts with locally made sausages. Rates drop dramatically in winter. ③.

Graigfryn, Penisarwaun, three miles northwest of Llanberis (☎01286/871007). An exclusively vegetarian and vegan wholefood, non-smoking B&B in a Victorian farmhouse. Home-grown vegetables are used in the three-course evening meals. ③.

The Heights, 74 High St (☎01286/871179, fax 872507). B&B catering primarily to the walking and climbing set, with comfortable rooms and dorms (see "Hostels" below). Downstairs is the liveliest bar and restaurant in town, and a climbing wall. ③.

Padarn Lake Hotel, High Street (☎01286/870260, fax 870007). One of Llanberis' larger, full-facility hotels with lake views from some of the spacious and pleasant rooms, and a restaurant and bars downstairs. ⑤.

Plas Coch, High Street (☎01286/872122). Pleasant low-cost B&B with some mountain-view rooms. The inexpensive evening meals, with traditional Welsh and vegetarian options, are excellent. ③.

Hostels, bunkhouses and campsites

Cae Gwyn Campsite, Nant Peris, 2 miles southeast of Llanberis (☎01286/870718). Fairly basic water-and-showers campsite towards Pen y Pass, almost opposite the *Vaynol Arms*. Budget-minded climbers and mountain bikers make up the bulk of the clientele.

Gallt-y-Glyn, half a mile northwest of Llanberis on the Caernarfon Road (☎01286/870370). Reasonable six-berth dorms in the annexe of a traditional hotel. There are no self-catering facilities but breakfast is included and bar meals are available. Take the #88 bus, and a sleeping bag and towel. ①.

Gwastadnant B&B, Bunkhouse and Camping, Nant Peris (☎01286/870356). The closest accommodation to Pen y Pass with a pleasant and friendly B&B, a bunkhouse with self-catering facilities and three-tier bunks at £3–4 a night and a small campsite across the road for £2.50. It is three miles east of Llanberis, beyond Nant Peris. ①/②.

Hafod Lydan Campsite, Capel Goch Road. A pound-a-night site in a farmer's field, with no showers, a quarter of a mile beyond the Llanberis YHA hostel.

The Heights (see "Hotels and guesthouses" above). Accommodation in eight-bed dorms with bedding and towels provided but no self-catering facilities. Bed only £7, B&B £10.50. ①/②.

Jesse James' Bunkhouse, Buarth y Clytiau, Penisarwaun (☎01286/870521). The original bunkhouse, large, clean, non-smoking and well run by a mountain guide for thirty years. Beds are £6.75 a night, and you'll need a sleeping bag and towel. Separate and slightly more luxurious self-contained accommodation is also available for £9–10. Take the A4086 two miles towards Caernarfon, turn right onto the B4547 and continue for a mile. ①.

Llanberis YHA hostel, Llwyn Celyn (☎01286/870280). Well-appointed but not especially atmospheric YHA hostel, a 700-yard uphill slog along Capel Goch Road off High Street. ①.

Pritchard's Camping, Nant Peris (☎01286/870494). Pretty much identical to *Cae Gwyn Campsite*, but 200 yards closer to Llanberis.

Rhydau Duon Farmhouse, Brynrefail, two miles northwest of Llanberis (☎01286/870744). A small rural group-activity centre with a friendly communal feel and a range of bunkhouse and B&B accommodation. Canoeing and rock-climbing instruction is also available. Take the B4547 towards Bangor, first right into Brynrefail, cross the river then second right. ①–③.

The Town and around

One dramatic tower and assorted scattered remains are all that is left of thirteenth-century **Dolbadarn Castle** (unrestricted access; CADW), perched on its rock between Llyn Peris and Llyn Padarn where it guards the entrance of the Llanberis Pass. Its construction, though undocumented, is usually attributed to Llywelyn ap Iorwerth ("the Great") though its circular keep is more redolent of a

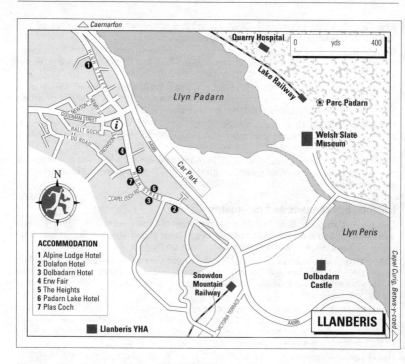

Caernarfon

Quarry Hospital

0   yds   400

Lake Railway

Llyn Padarn

✿ Parc Padarn

Welsh Slate Museum

HIGH STREET
NEWTON
GOODMAN STREET
RALLT GOCH
TY DU ROAD

(i)

Car Park

CAPEL COCH RD

Llyn Peris

Capel Curig, Betws-y-coed

N

ACCOMMODATION
1 Alpine Lodge Hotel
2 Dolafon Hotel
3 Dolbadarn Hotel
4 Erw Fair
5 The Heights
6 Padarn Lake Hotel
7 Plas Coch

Snowdon Mountain Railway

Dolbadarn Castle

VICTORIA TERRACE

A4086

LLANBERIS

■ Llanberis YHA

Norman Marcher fort than a native Welsh castle. Close up, there's not a lot to look at, but, viewed across Llyn Padarn and framed by the grey crags of the Pass behind, it is easy to see why both Richard Wilson and Turner came to paint it.

The road opposite the Mountain Railway terminus, at the east end of town, runs a few yards past the castle to the grounds of the **Parc Padarn** (Llyn Padarn Country Park; unrestricted access), where lakeside oak woods are gradually recolonizing the discarded workings of the defunct Dinorwig Slate Quarries, formerly one of the largest slate quarries in the world. Equipment and engines which formerly hauled materials up inclined tramways have been partly restored and punctuate the paths which link the levels chiselled out of the hillside.

The fort-like complex of buildings at the base of the main tramway was once used as the quarry's maintenance workshops and now houses the **Welsh Slate Museum** (Easter–Oct daily 9.30am–5.30pm; £2.50). The fifty-foot-diameter water wheel that once powered cutting machines through a cat's cradle of lineshafts, countershafts and flapping belts still turns, but no longer drives the machinery. Though most of the equipment dates back to the early part of this century, it was still in use until the quarries closed and is quite familiar to the former quarry workers who demonstrate their skills at turning an inch-thick slab of slate into six, even eight, perfectly smooth slivers. The slate was delivered to the slate-dressing sheds by means of a maze of tramways, cranes and rope lifts, all kept in good order in the fitting and repair shops. As you pass through, look out for the scales used to calculate the price each rock cutter would be paid for his work, before the typical deductions for the amount of rope and gunpowder he used to extract the diverse types of slate. Some of these are displayed nearby and range from mottled burgundy and bottle green to every shade of grey.

To keep everything in working order, the craftsmen here operate an ageing foundry, producing pieces for the scattered branches of the National Museum of Wales, as well as repairing the rolling stock which plies the adjacent **Llanberis Lake Railway** (July & Aug 4–11pm daily; March–June & Sept to early Oct 3–6pm daily except Sat; £3.90 return). The original railway, which from 1843 to 1961 transported slate and workers between the Dinorwig quarries and Port Dinorwig on the Menai Straits, was sold for scrap. Enthusiasts subsequently relaid a tame two-mile stretch to Pen-y-llyn along the shores of Lake Padarn. The smoking tank engine takes about forty minutes for the round trip, and although there's nothing much to do at the other end, you can at least catch a different train back and break your journey halfway at the **Cwm Derwen Visitor Centre** (open when trains are running; 60p) which illustrates the history of the woodland that spreads up the slopes behind the rail tracks. You're really better off just walking around the old slate workings and through the ancient woodlands of Coed Dinorwig slowly, making for the period-furnished **Quarry Hospital** (May–Sept 10am–4.45pm; free), where the resident surgeon patched up gruesome injuries from gunpowder blasts and falling rock.

In 1974, five years after the quarry closed, work began hollowing out the vast underground chambers of the **Dinorwig Pumped Storage Hydro Station**. Unlike most power stations, this is a net drain on the national grid, able to instantly produce electricity to cope with the early-evening increase in demand. Within ten seconds it can be wound up to its maximum power output (1800 Megawatts), achieved by letting the contents of the Marchlyn Mawr reservoir rapidly empty through the turbines into Llyn Peris; then, when the demand lessens, pumping it up again. If you can bear the thinly disguised electricity industry advertisement which precedes it, there's an hour-long minibus tour down through rock-hewn tunnels to the powerhouse below. For this, you need to call at **Dinorwig Discovery** (Feb & Nov Tues–Thurs & Sun 10.30am–3.30pm; March–May, Sept & Oct daily 10am–4pm; June–Aug daily 9.30am–5.30pm; £5) by the lake on the A4086 which bypasses the town centre. Tours depart every half-hour or so; while you wait you can visit the Mammoth Exhibition, tolerably interesting displays on glaciation and its effect on Snowdonia's geology, flora and fauna centred on a replica of a huge woolly mammoth.

Eating, drinking and entertainment

While Llanberis isn't spilling over with good places to **eat**, it does have something to suit all pockets. Pretty much all there is lies on the High Street, where you'll find couple of likeable **pubs**. To broaden the choice, Bangor and Caernarfon are both only eight miles away.

Arthur's Café, next to *Dolafon Hotel*, High Street. Basic café with no-nonsense dishes, including a good Welsh rarebit.

Y Bistro, 43–45 High St (☎01286/871278). The best restaurant for miles around, offering expensive but generous two-, three- and four-course set meals from a bilingual menu, all served with canapés on home-made bread. Booking recommended. Closed Sun.

The Heights, 74 High St (☎01286/871179). Excellent-value pizza, meat, vegetarian and vegan meals, and one of the liveliest bars in town. Full of climbers and walkers.

Pete's Eats, 40 High St (☎01286/870358). Outdoor types flock here for top-value basic meals of gut-splitting proportions and a few more delicate dishes. Summer daily to 8pm; winter Mon–Fri till 5pm, Sat & Sun till 8pm.

Prince of Wales, 38 High St. Ordinary local pub which comes to life on Saturday night when you can join in with the Welsh singing led by the resident electric-organist.

Vaynol Arms, Nant Peris, two miles east of Llanberis. Cosy pub, the only one before Pen-y-Gwryd, with good beer and a convivial atmosphere. Full of locals midweek, and climbers and campers from across the road at weekends.

Activities

By far the most popular activity around Llanberis is simply getting out on foot. This is principally on Snowdon (see box, p.330), whose vast steep-sided cwms have become the summer playground for rock athletes picking their way up impossibly sheer faces. If you're not equipped or confident enough to go **climbing** or **scrambling** by yourself, engage the services of one of the many mountain guides based around Llanberis: *Gwynedd Mountaineering Services*, Pant y Celyn, 13 Stryd y Ffynnon, Llanberis (☎01286/871128), and *High Trek Snowdonia*, Tal y Waen, Deiniolen (☎01286/871232), both offer good packages.

When inclement weather forces climbers in off the crags, the keen ones make straight for the bouldering room in *The Heights* (£1; see "Accommodation") or the huge indoor climbing wall at **Beacon Climbing Centre**, three miles west from Llanberi Ceunan in Waunfawr (Mon–Fri 11am–10pm, Sat & Sun 10am–10pm; ☎01286/650045; £3.50).

With so many precipitous mountains, Llanberis is ideally suited for **paragliding**. The longest-standing operator is *Enigma: The Snowdonia School of Paragliding*, 1 Stryd-y-Llyn, Cwm-y-Glo (April–Oct; ☎01286/870940, fax 872507) which offers solo flights from £45 and offer tandem flights – where you are effectively a passenger strapped to an instructor – from £30; *Snowdon Gliders: The Mountain Paragliding Centre*, Cefn yr Ynys, Mynydd Llandegai (☎ & fax 01248/602581), is comparable.

If you're looking for something less specialized, *Padarn Water Sports and Activities Centre*, Parc Padarn (☎01286/871762), offers the broadest range of both **watersports** and land-based activities, mostly but not entirely oriented towards groups, with half-day courses in canoeing, abseiling, climbing and orienteering starting at £18; gear rental is also available.

As well as being one of the most popular walking routes up Snowdon, the **Llanberis Track** (see box on p.330) is designated a bridleway, making it, the Snowdon Ranger Path and the Pitt's Head Track to Rhyd-Ddu, open for **cyclists**. A voluntary agreement exists restricting access to and from the summit between 10am and 5pm from June to September, but otherwise these paths are open. Unfortunately, there is no bike rental in Llanberis, so you'll have to pick one up in Betws-y-Coed (see p.313). You can also take a **horse** up onto Snowdon's lower slopes (£10 an hour, £40 a day) from *The Dolbadarn Pony Trekking Centre* at the *Dolbadarn Hotel* on High Street (☎01286/870277).

Snowdon

The highest British mountain south of the Scottish Grampians, the **Snowdon** massif (3650ft) forms a star of shattered ridges with three major peaks – Crib

Goch, Crib-y-ddysgl and Y Lliwedd – and the summit, **Yr Wyddfa**, crowning the lot. If height were its only quality, it would be popular, but Snowdon also sports some of the finest walking and scrambling in the park, and in the winter, the longest season for ice climbers and cramponed walkers. Its Welsh name, Eryri, is derived from either *eryr* (land of eagles) or *eira* (land of snow); since the eagles have long gone, the latter is more appropriate, with winter snows a feature well into April.

Some hardened outdoor enthusiasts dismiss Snowdon as overused, and it certainly can be crowded. A thousand visitors a day press onto the postbox-red carriages of the Snowdon Mountain Railway (see p.332), while another fifteen hundred pound the well-maintained paths to make this Britain's most-climbed mountain. Opprobrium is chiefly levelled at the train for its mere existence, and at the abominable concrete-bunker summit **café** for selling the country's highest pint of beer. But at least there's a warm place for walkers to rest, and those unable to walk up have the chance of seeing the mighty **views** over most of north Wales – and even across to Ireland on exceptionally clear days.

There is no longer a tumulus on the top of Snowdon, but the Welsh for the highest point, *Yr Wyddfa*, means "The Burial Place" – near proof that people have been climbing the mountain for millennia. More recently, early ascents were for botanical or geological reasons – 500-million-year-old fossil shells can be found near the summit from when Snowdon was on the sea bottom – but the Welsh naturalist Thomas Pennant came up here mainly for pleasure, and in 1773 his description of the dawn view from the summit in his *Journey to Snowdon* encouraged many to follow. Some were guided by the Snowdon Ranger from his house on the south side (now a YHA hostel), but the rapidly improving facilities in Llanberis soon shifted the balance in favour of the easier Llanberis Path, a route later followed by the railway. This remains one of the most popular routes up, though many prefer the three shorter and steeper ones from the Pen-y-Pass car park at the top of the Llanberis Pass. By far the most dramatic, if also the most dangerous, is the wonderful Snowdon Horseshoe, which calls at all four of the high peaks.

Legends, painters and poets

From the departure of the Romans until the tenth century, Welsh history comes down to us leavened with equal measures of myth, and populated with the shadowy figures of Arthur, Gwrtheryn (Vortigern) and Myrddin (Merlin). Glastonbury in England lays a powerful, though not incontestable, claim to being the location of Arthur's court and burial place, but his British (as opposed to Anglo-Saxon) blood gives him a firm place in Welsh hearts; and in Wales, Snowdon is always held to be his home. It was on top of Dinas Emrys, the seat of Gwrtheryn's realm at the foot of the south ridge near Beddgelert, that that most potent symbol of Welsh independence, the **Red Dragon**, earned its colours. The Celtic king, Gwrtheryn, was trying to build a fortress to protect himself from the Saxons but each night the earth swallowed the building stones, a phenomenon that Myrddin divined to be due to two dragons sleeping underground: one white, the other red. When woken, they engaged in an unending fight which Myrddin pronounced to symbolize the Red Dragon of Wales' perpetual battle with the White Dragon of the Saxons.

Arthur's domain was higher up the mountain. Llyn Llydaw aspires to being the pond where Bedivere threw King Arthur's sword, Excalibur, while thirteen hun-

WALKS ON SNOWDON

Note: The OS Outdoor Leisure 1:25,000 map of "Snowdonia" is highly recommended for all these walks.

LLANBERIS PATH

The easiest and longest route up Snowdon, the **Llanberis Path** (5 miles to summit; 3hr; 3200-ft ascent), following the rail line, is widely scorned by the sort of serious hiker who wouldn't use the railway or take tea at the summit café. The path starts opposite the *Royal Victoria Hotel* and out of sight of the summit which gradually comes into view as you rise towards the midway point and **Clogwyn Du'r Arddu** (The Black Cliff, or "Cloggy" to its friends), an ominous sheet of rock which frames a small lake. Today, climbers sprint up the face, which caused an early exponent to lament, "No breach seems either possible or desirable along the whole extent of the west buttress. Though there is the faintest of faint hopes for a human fly rather on the left side." The path next passes Clogwyn station, from where you get a great view down onto the Llanberis Pass, which soon disappears from sight as the path gets steeper, passing the low remains of stables where mule trains used to rest. **Bwlch Glas** (Green Pass) is marked by the "Finger Stone" where the Snowdon Ranger Path (see below) and three routes coming up from Pen-y-Pass join the Llanberis Path for the final ascent to **Yr Wyddfa**. Llanberis Path is the route used by the annual Snowdon Race which takes place on the second Saturday in July, with the leading runners recording times of only a little over an hour for the combined ascent and descent.

THE MINERS' TRACK

The **Miners' Track** (4 miles to summit; 2hr 30min; 2400-ft ascent) is the easiest of the three routes up from Pen-y-Pass. Leaving the car park, a broad track leads south then west to the former copper mines in Cwm Dyli. Dilapidated remains of the crushing mill perch on the shores of Llyn Llydaw, a tarn-turned-reservoir with one of the worst eyesores in the park, an above-ground pipeline slicing across Snowdon's east face to the power station in Nantgwynant. Skirting around the right of the lake, the path climbs more steeply to the lake-filled Cwm Glaslyn, then again to Upper Glaslyn, from where the measured steps of those ahead warn of the impending switchback ascent to the junction with the Llanberis Path.

PIG TRACK

The stonier **Pig Track** (3.5 miles to summit; 2hr 30min; 2400-ft ascent) is really just a shorter and steeper variation on the Miners' Track, leaving from the western end of the Pen-y-Pass car park and climbing up to **Bwlch y Moch** (the Pass of the Pigs), which gives the route its name. Ignore the scramble up to Crib Goch (part of the Snowdon Horseshoe) and traverse below the rocky ridge looking down on Llyn Llydaw and those pacing the Miners' Track, content that you're already 500ft up on them. They'll soon catch up, as the two tracks meet just before the zigzag up to the Llanberis Path.

SNOWDON HORSESHOE

Some claim that the **Snowdon Horseshoe** (8 miles round; 5–7hr; 3200-ft ascent) is one of the finest ridge walks in Europe. The route makes a full anticlockwise circuit around the three glacier-carved cwms of Upper Glaslyn, Glaslyn and Llydaw. Not to be taken lightly, it includes the knife-edge traverse of **Crib Goch**. Every summer's day, dozens of people find themselves straddling the lip, empty space on both sides, and wishing they weren't there. In winter conditions, an ice axe and crampons are the minimum requirement. The path follows the Pig Track to Bwlch y Moch, then pitches right for the moderate scramble up to Crib Goch. If you balk at any of this, turn back. If not, wait your turn, then painstakingly pick your way along the sensational ridge to **Crib-y-ddysgl** (3494ft), from where it is an easy descent to Bwlch Glas and stiffer ascent to Yr Wyddfa. Having ticked off Wales' two highest tops, turn southwest for a couple of hundred yards to a marker stone where the Watkin Path (see below) drops away to the east. Follow it down to the stretched saddle of **Bwlch-y-Saethau** (Pass of the Arrows), then onto the cairn at Bwlch Ciliau from where the Watkin Path descends to Nantgwynant. Ignore that route, continue straight on up the cliff-lined northwest ridge of **Y Lliwedd** (2930ft), then descend to where you see the scrappy but safe path down to Llyn Llydaw and the Miners' Track.

SNOWDON RANGER PATH

Many of the earliest Snowdon climbers engaged the services of the Snowdon Ranger, who led them up the comparatively long and dull but easy **Snowdon Ranger Path** (4 miles to summit; 3hr; 3100-ft ascent), on the now unfashionable south side of the mountain. The path starts from the Snowdon Ranger YHA hostel (see Beddgelert "Accommodation" p.334) on the shores of Llyn Cwellyn, five miles northwest of Beddgelert. To the left of the hostel, a path leads up a track then ascends, steeply flattening out to cross sometimes boggy grass, eventually skirting to the right of the impressive Clogwyn Du'r Arddu cliffs (see "Llanberis Path", above). This is another steep ascent which eventually meets the Llanberis Path at Bwlch Glas.

PITT'S HEAD TRACK

The **Pitt's Head Track** (4 miles to summit; 3hr; 2900-ft ascent) has two branches, one starting from Pitt's Head Rock, two and a half miles northwest of Beddgelert, the other from the National Park car park in Rhyd-Ddu, a mile beyond that. They join up after less than a mile's walk across stony, walled grazing land, and after crossing a kissing gate continue to the northwest up to the stunning final section along the rim of Cwm Clogwyn and the south ridge of Yr Wyddfa.

WATKIN PATH

The most spectacular of the southern routes up Snowdon, the **Watkin Path** (4 miles to summit; 3hr; 3350-ft ascent), is also the one with the greatest height gain. From Bethania Bridge, three miles northeast of Beddgelert in Nantgwynant, the path starts on a broad track through oaks opening up to long views of a series of cataracts. Ascend beside these to a disused inclined tramway where the track narrows before reaching the natural amphitheatre of Cwm Llan. The ruins of the South Snowdon Slate Works only temporarily distract you from **Gladstone Rock**, at which, in 1892, the 83-year-old Liberal statesman, then in his fourth term as British Prime Minister, officially opened the route. A narrower path wheels left around the base of Craig Ddu, then starts the steep ascent past Carnedd Arthur to Bwlch Ciliau, the saddle between Y Lliwedd (see "Snowdon Horseshoe" above) and the true summit (Yr Wyddfa), then turning right for the final climb to the top. The Watkin Path can be easily turned into a loop by descending the top section of the Pitt's Head Track then continuing down Bwlch Main to the saddle and cutting east into Cwm Llan and down.

dred feet above, Bwlch-y-Saethau (The Pass of the Arrows) was where a wayward arrow mortally wounded Arthur, while on the point of vanquishing his nephew Modred. The remains of Carnedd Arthur, just below Bwlch Ciliau on the Watkin Path (see box, p.331), are claimed as his burial site, but it is probably a fairly modern cairn. Another burial place is that of one of Arthur's victims, Rhita Gawr, whose now-vanished tumulus gave Snowdon's highest point, Yr Wyddfa, its name.

Throughout the eighteenth and nineteenth centuries, anywhere with Arthurian associations proved an irresistible magnet for all manner of writers and painters. Thomas Gray added to both the mystery of the place and its Celtic symbolism in his ode *The Bard*, in which the last Welsh bard hurls himself off the summit while fleeing Edward I's marauding army, but the painter Richard Wilson had already beaten him to the task. His *Snowdon from Llyn Nantlle* had already planted the pre-Romantic seeds from which grew a vast, and still growing, body of work capturing the mountain's changing moods from every conceivable angle.

The Snowdon Mountain Railway

The **Snowdon Mountain Railway** (mid-March to Oct 6–25 trains daily; ☎01286/870223; summit return £14) was completed in 1896, and carriages, some dating back to the nineteenth century, pushed by seventy-year-old steam locos still climb to the summit in just under an hour. The three-thousand-foot, mostly one-in-eight struggle up five miles of the most heavily maintained track in Britain follows the shallowest approach to the top of Snowdon. It starts at the eastern end of Llanberis opposite the *Royal Victoria Hotel*, and climbs past the summertime swimming hole at Bishop's Falls to the summit **café**, designed in 1936 by Portmeirion architect Clough Williams-Ellis on what must have been a rough Monday morning. The café currently has a licensed bar and a post office where you can buy a "Railway Stamp" (10p) to affix to your letter – along with the usual Royal Mail one – thereby entitling you to use the highest postbox in the UK and enchant your friends with a "Summit of Snowdon – Copa'r Wyddfa" postmark. In bad weather, trains terminate at Clogwyn station, a thirty-minute walk from the top.

Times and type of locomotive vary with demand and season, but whether hauled by steam or diesel the full round trip takes two and a half hours, with half an hour on top. You can only book on the day, and in summer tickets are frequently sold out by 11am. If you walk up by one of the routes detailed in the box on p.330, you can still take the train down. Standby tickets back to Llanberis (£6) are sold at the summit if there are seats, but round-trippers get priority.

The Llanberis Pass and Pen-y-Pass

The steady Llanberis Path which grinds up Snowdon's gentlest ascent may be the most popular single route up the mountain, but more walkers start from the lofty saddle at the top of the **Llanberis Pass**, the deepest, narrowest and craggiest of Snowdonia's passes, running five miles east from Llanberis. At its head is the YHA hostel, café and car park which make up **PEN-Y-PASS**, the base for The Miners' Track, the Pig Track and the demanding Snowdon Horseshoe (see box, p.330). These all leave from the car park, while a route up Glyder Fawr (see box, p.323) follows a "courtesy path" to the west of the hostel.

Frequent #19 and #95 *Sherpa* **buses** travel daily to Pen-y-Pass, the latter being the recommended approach from the Llanberis side even if you have a car, since the Pen-y-Pass car park is almost always full and costs £4. Use the free "park and ride" facility at the bottom of the pass close to the *Vaynol Arms*.

The only **accommodation** at Pen-y-Pass is the YHA **hostel** (Jan–Oct; ☎01286/870428, fax 872434; ①), open from 1pm each day, with free parking, plus videos on climbing and kayaking. A mile east is the nearest **pub** with accommodation, the *Pen-y-Gwryd Hotel* (Jan & Feb weekends only; ☎01286/870211; ④), a wonderfully rustic place with ageing furniture, magnificent Edwardian bathrooms, an outdoor sauna, and a lot of muddy boots in the bar. Amongst others, the first successful expedition up Mount Everest in 1953 stayed at the hotel while doing final equipment testing, and took time out to sign the ceiling: Edmund Hillary, Chris Bonnington, Doug Scott and Portmeirion designer Clough Williams-Ellis are all there. The Everest team also brought back a piece of the mountain, which now sits in pride of place on the bar. If you stay, expect a congenial though somewhat regimented atmosphere and lots of plain home cooking.

Beddgelert and around

Almost all of the prodigious quantity of rain which falls on Snowdon spills down the valleys on its south side: either into the Glaslyn River in Nantgwynant or the Colwyn River in Nant Colwyn. At their confluence, just before they jointly crash down the bony **Aberglaslyn Gorge** towards Porthmadog, the few dozen hard grey houses making up **BEDDGELERT** huddle together in some majestic mountain scenery.

If you tire of the view from the village, it is easy enough to get out on one of the longer walks described in the box on p.335. A shorter and more celebrated excursion takes you four hundred yards south, along the right bank of the Glaslyn, to the spot that gives the village its name, **Gelert's Grave** (*bedd* means "burial place"), where a railed-off enclosure in a field marks the final resting place of Prince Llywelyn ap Iorwerth's faithful dog, Gelert, who was left in charge of the prince's infant son while he went hunting. On his return, the child was gone and the hound's muzzle was soaked in blood. Jumping to conclusions, the impetuous Llywelyn slew the dog, only to find the child safely asleep beneath its cot and a dead wolf beside him. Llywelyn hurried to his dog, which licked his hand as it died. Sadly, the story is an all-too-successful nineteenth-century fabrication, conjured up by a wily local publican to lure punters. The real source of the name is probably the grave of Celert, a sixth-century British saint who is supposed to have lived hereabouts, possibly near **Dinas Emrys**, a wooded mound a mile up Nantgwynant on the A498, where Vortigern's fort once stood, and legend has it, dragons once fought (see p.329).

There's little enough to see now, except for the red-brown stain on the hillside opposite identifying the **Sygun Copper Mine** (Easter–Sept Mon–Fri 10am–5pm, Sat 10am–4pm, Sun 11am–5pm; Oct–Easter daily 11am–4pm; £4.25), whose ore drew first the Romans, then nineteenth-century prospectors here. The dilapidated remains of what was once the valley's prime source of income have now been restored and made safe for the cool (9°C) 45-minute guided tour up through the multiple levels of tunnels and galleries, accompanied by the disembodied voice of a miner telling of his life in the mine. After the tour, you are free to potter around the ore-crushing and separation equipment, or ask the guide to point you over the hill towards the foot of the Aberglaslyn Gorge (see p.335).

Practicalities

Beddgelert sits on two **bus** routes: the #95 Caernarfon *Sherpa* and the #97 to Portmeirion and Porthmadog. All stop near the road bridge over the Colwyn River, the effective centre of town and just a few yards away from the **National Trust Shop and Information Centre**, Llywelyn Cottage (April–Oct daily 10am–5pm; ☎01766/890293) which is the nearest thing in the village to a tourist office. You can **rent bikes** from *Beics Beddgelert* (☎01766/890434) at the Beddgelert Forest Campsite (see below).

Accommodation

Bed and breakfast **accommodation** is abundant. Most of the houses near the bridge and along the Caernarfon road let rooms, though if you're wanting to make an early start on the Snowdon walks you'll find the hostels better sited.

HOTELS AND GUESTHOUSES

Ael-y-Bryn, Caernarfon Road (☎ & fax 01766/890310). Central guesthouse with good views and inexpensive home-cooked evening meals. ③.

Beddgelert Antiques and Tea Rooms, Waterloo House (☎01766/890543). Three attractive en-suite rooms above the restaurant and tea rooms, directly opposite the bridge. ③.

Colwyn (☎01766/890276). Central 300-year-old cottage guesthouse with comfortable en-suite rooms. A separate two-person self-catering cottage is also let by the week. ③.

Plas Colwyn (☎01766/890458). Non-smoking guesthouse by the bridge, with inexpensive home-cooked evening meals in licensed restaurant. ③.

Royal Goat Hotel (☎01766/890224). Large central hotel with sporty leanings – fishing, horse riding and golf available to guests – and a residents-only bar. ⑥.

Sygun Fawr Country House, three-quarters of a mile northeast off the A498 (☎01766/890258). A partially sixteenth-century house in its own grounds that's the pick of the local hotels. A sauna and good evening meals add to the attraction. Closed Jan. ⑤.

HOSTELS AND CAMPSITES

Beddgelert Forest Campsite (☎01766/890288). Excellent and reasonably priced campsite a mile out on the Caernarfon road. Here you can brush up your compass work on the site's orienteering course in the forest before testing it on the hills. Open all year.

Bryn Dinas Bunkhouse (☎01766/890234). Fully self-catering £6-a-night bunkhouse, right at the foot of the Watkin Path (see Snowdon box, p.331) three miles northeast of Beddgelert on the A498. A sheet and blankets are supplied. ①.

Bryn Gwynant YHA hostel (☎01766/890251, fax 890479). Beautifully sited hostel in Nantgwynant four miles northeast of Beddgelert on the A498. It also has a campsite where you can use the hostel's facilities for half the adult rate. Daily April–Oct, weekends Nov–March. ①.

Cae Du Camping (☎01766/890595). Simple summer-only site less than a 10-min walk towards Capel Curig on the A498.

Snowdon Ranger YHA hostel (☎01286/650391, fax 650093) Former inn five miles north-west of Beddgelert on the Caernarfon road at the foot of the Snowdon Ranger Path (see Snowdon box, p.331). April–Oct. ①.

Eating and drinking

Beddgelert Antiques and Tea Rooms, Waterloo House (see "Accommodation", above). (☎01766/890543). Attentive service, cosy surroundings and an evening menu rich in game. Good daytime tea rooms too.

Lyn's Café and Tea Garden, Church St (☎01766/890374). Decent tea rooms with garden seating, offering substantial daytime meals and moderately priced dinners.

Prince Llewelyn, Smith Street. Convivial atmosphere around the fire or out in the sun, in a central pub serving good real ales.

Riverside Garden Restaurant (☎01766/890551). Central restaurant with a waterside terrace serving hearty breakfasts, moderately priced meals and cream teas.

Tanronnen, on the south side of the bridge. Likeable pub with decent beer and bar meals.

WALKS FROM BEDDGELERT

As you might expect for a village sited at the southern point of the Snowdon massif, there are a couple of ascents of Snowdon starting near Beddgelert, listed in the Snowdon box (see p.330). Otherwise the following walks are the best ones to do from the village.

THE ABERGLASLYN GORGE

An easy walk follows the short but very picturesque **Aberglaslyn Gorge** (4 miles; 2hr 30min; 600ft ascent) returning to the copper mines (see p.333) on a path up Cwm Bychan between Mynydd Sygun and Moel y Dyniewyd. Take the right bank of the river, past Gelert's Grave, crossing over the bridge onto the disused track-bed of the Welsh Highland narrow-gauge rail line. This gently graded path then hugs the left bank for a mile down to Pont Aberglaslyn, with the more adventurous Fisherman's Path just below it, giving a closer look at the river's course through chutes and channels in sculpted rocks. From the road bridge at Pont Aberglaslyn road bridge – the tidal limit before The Cob was built at Porthmadog (see p.342) – you can retrace your steps, follow the A498 back on the far bank, or head north up Cwm Bychan on a path near the exit of the disused railway tunnel. It is about a two-mile valley walk to the copper mines from where a track follows the left bank of the River Glaslyn to Beddgelert. You can do the walk in reverse by setting off from the top level of the copper mines at the end of the guided tour. Ask the guide for directions.

MOEL HEBOG

From Beddgelert you are unlikely to have missed the lumpish **Moel Hebog** (Bald Hill of the Hawk; 2569ft) to the west of the village. It is the highest point on a fine panoramic **ridge walk** (8 miles; 5hr; 2800ft ascent) which also takes in the lesser peaks of Moel Lefn, and Moel yr Ogof (Hill of the Cave), named after a refuge for Owain Glyndŵr when fleeing the English in 1404 after his failed attempt to take Caernarfon Castle. The final forest section can be a bit disorientating, even in good weather, so make sure you have your compass.

Start half a mile northwest of the centre of Beddgelert on the A4085, where Pont Alyn crosses the river to *Cwm Cloch Isaf Farm*. Follow the signs to a green lane, which soon leads up onto the broad northeast ridge, keeping left of the Y Diffwys cliffs. The summit cairn is joined by two walls, the one to the northwest leading down a steep grassy slope to Bwlch Meillionen, from where you can ascend over rocky ground to Moel yr Ogof, or descend to the right, then skirt left in a probably fruitless attempt to locate the difficult-to-find Glyndŵr's Cave. From the top of Moel yr Ogof, it's a clear route north to Moel Lefn, then down to a cairn from where you can plan your descent. The easiest line is to Bwlch Cwm-trwsgl, near the highest point of the Beddgelert Forest, where a stile over a wire fence leads into the forest. Both OS 1:25,000 "Snowdonia" and 1:50,000 #115 "Snowdon" maps then show a clear, though not always easy-to-follow, route to the *Beddgelert Forest Campsite*, where you turn right and tramp a mile along the A4085 to Beddgelert.

Blaenau Ffestiniog and around

Snowdonia's most southerly major settlement, **BLAENAU FFESTINIOG** cowers at the foot of stark thousand-foot mountains thickly strewn with discarded heaps of splintered slate. *Blaenau* means "head of the valley", in this case the lush Vale of Ffestiniog, a dramatic contrast to this seemingly forbidding place. Blaenau Ffestiniog attracts some of Snowdonia's worst weather,and when clouds hunker low in the great cwm and rain sheets the grey roofs, grey walls and grey paving slabs it can become a terrifically gloomy place unlike anywhere else on earth. Fortuitously, this is a great place to be in the rain – on days when every tourist office in north Wales is packed with wet visitors wondering what to do, Blaenau Ffestiniog is at its most dramatic, and besides, its slate mines will keep you dry.

Thousands of tons of slate per year were once hewn from the labyrinth of underground caverns below the town, but these days only two mines manage to keep ticking over, aided by the good income made from their **tours** (see opposite). Sometimes it feels as though little has changed here since the late 1960s, the last time the mines were really profitable, but the loss of a steady income has hit the town hard: its population has dropped to less than half its 1910 peak of 12,000, unemployment is high, almost all the Nonconformist chapels are just discarded shells, and *Ar Werth* (For Sale) signs have sprouted everywhere. For now, the town's economy leans on tourism, generated by its mine tours and the fact that it's the junction of two of the finest train journeys in the country: the narrow-gauge **Ffestiniog Railway** which winds up from Porthmadog (see p.345), and the Lledr Valley rail line to Betws-y-Coed (see p.318).

THE CURSE OF THE RHODODENDRON

It is against the pervasive greyness of Blaenau Ffestiniog that Snowdonia's **rhododendron** invasion is most evident. Come in June and July and many of Snowdonia's valleys are a riot of lilac and purple blooms. There's no doubting their aesthetic appeal but these choking mats of foliage rank high on ecologists' hate lists. In their native Himalayas they grow into trees, but in Britain, where they've spread from the cultivated gardens of grand houses, they've become a noxious weed. Native flora can't compete with the dense canopy which cuts out so much sunlight that nothing can grow underneath, a major threat to native birds and insects which thrive in more open scrub. Volunteer action groups periodically target particular areas, blitzing a valley by digging out all the plants, but the rhododendron is proving difficult to contain.

Arrival and accommodation

By **car**, Blaenau Ffestiniog is most dramatically approached from the north along the Lledr Valley, climbing over the Crimea Pass between the Manod and Moelwyn mountains and plunging down into the town's shattered landscape. The **train station** on the High Street serves both the Ffestiniog line from Porthmadog and mainline train services from Betws-y-Coed, and also houses the **tourist office** (April–Oct daily 10am–6pm; ☎01766/830360). **Buses** stop either in the car park around the back or outside *Y Commercial* pub on High Street.

Many of Blaenau Ffestiniog's visitors ride the train up from Porthmadog, visit a slate mine and leave, and this is reflected in the limited range of **accommodation**. There are good hotels, like the upmarket *Queen's Hotel*, right by the station at 1 High St (☎01766/830055, fax 830046; ⑤), *The Don*, 147 High St (☎01766/830403; ②), and *Afallon*, almost a mile south of the tourist office on Manod Road (☎01766/830468; ②). A mile or so south along Manod Road (the A470), *Cae Du* (☎ & fax 01766/830847; ④) is a comfortable seventeenth-century beamed farmhouse, beautifully sited at the end of a long drive. Five miles further there's *Tyddyn Du*, Gellilydan (☎01766/85281; ③), an old farmhouse with a separate cottage suite reached on bus #35. The nearest **campsites** are *Bryn Tirion* four miles north in the Lledr Valley (see p.318) and *Llechrwd* (☎01766/590240), a similar distance southwest in Maentwrog.

The Town and mines

It is difficult to get a real feeling of what slate means to Blaenau Ffestiniog without a visit to one of the town's two slate mines, a mile or so north of town on the Betws-y-Coed road (bus #140, hourly when the mines are open) both of which present entertaining and informative insights into the rigours of a miner's life.

The more packaged of the two is the **Llechwedd Slate Caverns** (March–Sept daily 10am–5.15pm; Oct–Feb daily 10am–4.15pm; single tour £5.95, both tours £9.15), slightly closer to the town and spectacular enough to be chosen as the setting for the first ever Welsh language film, *Y Chwarelwr* (The Quarrymen) in 1935. You can walk around the reconstructed Victorian mining village, watch slate being split, shaped and engraved, and visit *The Miners Arms* pub for nothing, but to visit some of the 25 miles of tunnels and sixteen working levels you need to take one of two tours.

The **Miners' Tramway Tour** takes you by a small train a third of a mile along one of the oldest levels, cut in 1846, disembarking a couple of times to admire the enormous Cathedral Cave and the open-air Chough's Cavern – both tilted at 30° to follow the slate's bedding plane – as you are plied with facts on slate mining. The awe-inspiring scale of the place justifies going on the tour even without the unconvincing tableaux of Victorian miners at work chained high up in the tops of the caverns. On the more dramatic **Deep Mine Tour** you're bundled onto specially designed carriages and lowered to one of the deepest parts of the mine down a 1-in-1.8 incline – Britain's steepest underground inclined railway. After donning waterproofs and headgear, you head off into the tunnels, guided by an irksome taped spiel of someone pretending to be a Victorian miner. That said, the content is good, concentrating on the working and social life of the miners who in winter never saw daylight, taking their breaks in a dank underground shelter known as a *caban*. The long caverns angling back into the gloom become increasingly impressive, culminating in one filled by a beautiful opalescent pool.

Visitors more inclined to exploring at their own pace are better served at the **Gloddfa Ganol Slate Mine** (mid-July to Aug daily except Sat 10am–5.30pm; Easter to mid-July, Sept & Oct Mon–Fri 10am–5.30pm; £5), slightly further along the same road from Blaenau Ffestiniog. It is hailed as the world's largest slate mine, quite believable as you wander across a vast and supremely desolate plateau of slate waste bounded by modern open-cast workings. The setup in the **main mine** is much like that at Llechwedd, though there are no trains and no pressured schedule, so you can amble around and soak up the feel of the place. The walk in, down a level tunnel, follows taped explanations through fourteen caverns, past mannequins dressed as miners and lamps probing the darker recesses of caverns 240ft deep. It is worth saving time to explore the workings above ground. Huge pieces of mining and earth-moving equipment are dwarfed by the scale of the open-cast pit visible from windows in either the tame **heritage centre** or one of the **two museums**. The first of these relates some of the history and changing fortunes of Blaenau Ffestiniog, along with examples of the multifarious uses of slate; the second presents a mainly photographic exhibition on the Manod Slate Quarry, two miles east of here, which was requisitioned during World War II for the storage of national treasures. You can't visit the site, which is now empty, but the museum tells of the vast chambers which were levelled, strengthened, ventilated and heated before most of the collections of the National and Tate galleries, pieces from the British Museum and, some say, the Crown Jewels were secretly transported here in chocolate delivery vans.

As at Llechwedd, the surface buildings house demonstrations of slate splitting and cutting, but don't let it distract you from the excellent **Quarrymen's Cottages**, a faithful reproduction of a three-cottage terrace, each two-up-two-down decorated in a different period: 1885, World War I and World War II.

THE WELSH SLATE INDUSTRY

Slate is as much a symbol of north Wales as coal is of the south: it too peaked around the turn of the twentieth century and shaped society for a century or more, drawing thousands from the impoverished hills to the relative wealth of the new towns which sprang up around the quarries.

Slate derives its name from the Old French word *esclater*, meaning "to split", a perfect description of its most highly valued quality. Six hundred million years ago, what is now north Wales lay under the sea, gradually accumulating a thousand-foot-thick layer of fine-grained mud. In the collision zone of converging continental plates, the deposits were subject to immense pressures which caused the massive folding and mountain-building; the shale then metamorphosed into the purplish Cambrian slates of the Penrhyn and Dinorwig quarries (see p.406 and p.327) and the hundred-million-year-younger blue-grey Ordovician slates of Ffestiniog (see p.337).

The Romans recognized the potential of the substance, roofing the houses of Segontium (see p.360) with it, and Edward I used it extensively in his Iron Ring of castles around Snowdonia (see box, p.397). But it wasn't until around 1780 that Britain's Industrial Revolution took hold, leading to greater urbanization and a demand for roofing slates. As cities grew during the nineteenth and early twentieth centuries, millions of tons of slate were shipped around the globe, primarily for use as a cheap and durable roofing material. Hamburg was re-roofed with Welsh slate after its fire of 1842, and it is the same material that still gives that rainy-day sheen to interminable rows of English mill-town houses.

By 1898, Welsh quarries – run by the English, like the coal and steel industries of the south – were producing half a million tons of dressed slate a year, almost all of it from Snowdonia. At Penrhyn and Dinorwig, mountains were hacked away in terraces, sometimes rising 2000ft above sea level, with teams of workers negotiating with the foreman for the choicest piece of rock and the selling price for what

You can also dish out for the hour-long **LandRover Tour** (book at the reception; £3) which dives into the mountain, climbs up through six levels past the remoter chambers and disgorges you at a wonderful vantage point with views over the vast heaps of discarded slate around Blaenau Ffestiniog.

Both these quarries, as well as all their now-deceased kin, dispatched their dressed and packed product, on the first leg of its journey to the markets around the world, down to Porthmadog, thirteen miles away on the **Ffestiniog Railway** (see p.345). Whether you're heading to Porthmadog or just want to ride the train, it is well worth considering doing part of the journey on foot (see box overleaf).

About a mile down the track the train stops at Tanygrisiau station, a short walk from the powerhouse for the **Ffestiniog Pumped Storage Power Station**, with a mildly diverting **information centre** (mid-July to Aug daily 10am–4.30pm, Easter–June, Sept & Oct closed Sat; free) and hour-long **guided tours** (hourly on the half-hour; £2.50) around rows of humming machinery and up to the Stwlan Dam, a buttressed structure in the hills above, visible throughout the Vale of Ffestiniog, that holds back the upper reservoir. Check with the tourist office to see if these tours are still running, as there are rumours that they may stop once the station becomes remotely operated from Dinorwig in Llanberis.

---

they produced. They often slept through the week in damp dormitories on the mountain, and tuberculosis was common, exacerbated by slate dust. At Blaenau Ffestiniog, the seams required mining underground rather than quarrying, but conditions were no better; miners even had to buy their own candles, their only light source. Few workers were allowed to join *Undeb Chwarelwyr Gogledd Cymru* (The North Wales Quarrymen's Union), and in 1900 the workers in Lord Penrhyn's quarry at Bethesda went out on strike. For three years they stayed out – Britain's longest ever industrial dispute – but failed to win any concessions. Those who got their jobs back were forced to work for even less money as a recession took hold, and although the two World Wars heralded mini-booms as bombed houses were replaced, the industry never recovered its nineteenth-century prosperity, and most quarries and mines closed in the 1950s.

Welsh slate was firmly established as the finest in the world at the 1862 London Exhibition, where one skilled craftsman produced a sheet 10ft long, 1ft wide and a sixteenth of an inch thick – so thin it could be flexed. Slate is now produced worldwide and although none beats the quality of north Wales' output, this is little compensation as the region struggles to compete with inferior but cheaper Spanish slate. Until recently, the Snowdonia National Park Board insisted on local slate for roofing, but pressure from the European Union now forces them to accept slate "equivalent in colour, texture and weathering characteristics". The last criterion is a moot point, as the Spanish industry is barely thirty years old, but in the meantime slate is being shipped from Spain while Welsh slate lies in the ground and unemployed quarrymen kick their heels. The quarries which do survive produce relatively small quantities, much of it used for floor tiling, road aggregate or an astonishing array of ashtrays and coasters etched with mountainscapes. More memorable are the roadside fences made from lines of broken, wafer-thin slabs, the beautifully carved slate fire surrounds and mantelpieces occasionally found in pubs and houses, and Westminster Abbey's memorial to Dylan Thomas which is made entirely of Penrhyn slate.

Eating, drinking and entertainment

Good **food** isn't especially abundant in Blaenau Ffestiniog, though *Caffi Glen*, 36 High St, does simple all-day breakfasts and snacks, and there's a decent café, *Y*

WALKS FROM BLAENAU FFESTINIOG

The following two walks can both be done from Blaenau Ffestiniog, but involve a fairly dull first mile easily avoided by catching the Ffestiniog Railway or driving to the reservoir at Tanygrisiau.

The gentler walk down into the **Vale of Ffestiniog** (4–5 miles; 2–3hr; descent only) follows the train line to its 360° loop, through sessile oak woods and past several cascades all the way to Tan-y-bwlch. It is easy-going, and has some great views south to the Rhinogs (see p.300) and west to the Glaslyn estuary, and includes a ride back on the train; check the times at Tanygrisiau station and buy your ticket when you start to ensure a place on the return train. From the station, turn right past the Tanygrisiau information centre then take the second left, not the road beside the reservoir but the next one following the footpath signs. Cross the train line, then pass a car park on your left before turning left down a track and skirting behind the powerhouse. The path then sticks closely to the train line, occasionally crossing it. Even when there are several paths you can't go far wrong if you keep the train lines in sight. *The Grapes* pub at Maentwrog, half a mile from Tan-y-bwlch, is a great place to while away the time until the next train (or the one after that).

The second walk, a circuit of the peaks of **Moelwyn Mawr, Moelwyn Fach and Cnicht** (13 miles; 7hr; 4000ft), is tougher, longer and best left for a fine day. Even then, navigation isn't always easy, and you need both the *Landranger* #115 "Snowdon" map and the *Landranger* #124 "Dolgellau" map (the *Outdoor Leisure* 1:25,000 maps #17 and #19 are better still). These factors make this group far less popular than either Snowdon or the Glyders, but given the right conditions it can be a great walk past masses of old slate workings up onto some respectably lofty tops with panoramic views of southern Snowdonia.

From the station in Tanygrisiau, turn right past the information centre, then follow the road as it doubles back north away from the reservoir. After a couple of hundred yards, turn left at a T-junction onto a track up to a car park. Follow the footpath signs past the disused quarries in Cwmorthin, swinging west up to Bwlch-y-Rhosydd (not named on *Landranger* map), a small plateau strewn with slate waste and long-discarded slate-built workshops. The route from here up **Moelwyn Mawr** (2526ft) starts behind the largest building heading south up an old incline, skirting left around a quarry eventually reaching the northeast ridge route to the summit. From there to **Moelwyn Fach** (2333ft) is straightforward, heading south down a generally easy ridge to Bwlch Stwlan then up the west ridge.

From Moelwyn Fach, turn west and follow the ridge to the hamlet of Croesor. If you have transport this makes a good starting point, cutting three miles off the walk since you avoid the stretch from Tanygrisiau to Bwlch-y-Rhosydd and back.

A road to the left of the disused chapel in Croesor leads to a stile from where the route up **Cnicht** (2260ft) is clearly signposted. From this angle, you are looking along the southwest-to-northeast ridge line of the mountain, giving it the triangular shape which earns it its rather fanciful "Matterhorn of Wales" nickname. The climb up is not really difficult, but it is steep in places. A series of almost equally high summits then give way to a shallow descent towards Llyn yr Adar. Just before the lake, a path cuts right and makes a gradual undulating southeast descent back to Bwlch-y-Rhosydd, from where you retrace your steps to Tanygrisiau.

Fuddai, by the information centre at Tanygrisiau serving Welsh specialities. For something more substantial you're limited to the moderate *Myfanwys*, 4 Market Place (☎01766/830059), *The Firefly*, 38 High St (☎01766/830097), for hearty Greek and Italian, or the tasty dishes at the *Queen's Hotel* (see "Arrival and accommodation", p.337). Most locals frequent *Grapes* at Maentwrog, four miles south down the A496, a pub with a game-rich restaurant, *Flambard's* (☎01766/590208), and massive bar meals – leave room for the desserts if you can.

The *Wynnes Arms*, a short walk south of *Afallon* guesthouse, is Blaenau Ffestiniog's best traditional **pub**, though the newer *Queen's Hotel* has rapidly gained a dedicated clientele. About the only other thing to do in the evening is to listen to a **male voice choir**. The *Brythoniaid* choir rehearses at Ysgol y Moelwyn on Wynne Road near the hospital (Thurs 7.30pm); *Côr Meibion y Moelwyn* uses the Old Salem Chapel in Rhiw, half a mile north of the tourist office on the A470, then left as the road narrows (Tues & Fri 7.30pm).

South of Blaenau Ffestiniog

Blaenau Ffestiniog is surrounded by slate waste on three sides. The fourth drops away into the bucolic **Vale of Ffestiniog**, best explored using the Ffestiniog Railway (see p.345), or on the first walk described in the box opposite.

Heading south from Blaenau Ffestiniog, the A470 runs through the village of **Llan Ffestiniog** (Ffestiniog on maps, just Llan locally), three miles away, broadly following what is left of the old Great Western Railway route which ran across the broad open moors of the Migneint to Bala. Rusted rails run as far as the greatest blot on the National Park's landscape, the defunct **Trawsfynydd Nuclear Power Station** a further four miles south. Trains removed the last of the fuel rods in 1995, but it's going to take 130 years to safely clear and landscape the area. In the meantime, cursory nature trails have been created around the plant and a visitor centre dispenses half-truths and irrelevant "facts". Both are best avoided.

With the eastern flanks of the Rhinogs (see p.300) on the right, the A470 continues south to Dolgellau – past the *Rhiw Goch Ski Centre* (daily 9.30am–10pm), where two hours' dry-slope skiing costs £11 – through **Coed y Brenin** (The King's Forest). Economics dictate that this vast plantation comprises row upon row of pines but there is the occasional patch of deciduous wood and some fine waterfalls. The best way to see them is to drop in to the **visitor centre** (Easter & June to early Sept daily 10am–5pm; early Sept to Oct daily 11am–4pm; ☎01766/540569; £1 per car) and **rent a bike** (£3 per hour) or go **orienteering** (30p). Wildlife enthusiasts can make for the **observation hide** (£10 key deposit from visitor centre) to view fallow deer and woodland birds at dawn and dusk.

THE LLŶN

The **Llŷn**, an undulating spur from Snowdonia's mountainous heartland, takes its name from an Irish word for "peninsula", an apt description for this most westerly part of north Wales, which, until the fifth century, had a significant Irish population. The cliff-and-cove-lined finger of land juts out south and west, separating Cardigan and Caernarfon bays, its hills tapering away along the ancient route to **Aberdaron** where pilgrims sailed for **Ynys Enlli (Bardsey Island)**. Ancestors of those last Irish inhabitants may have been responsible for the numerous hillforts and cromlechs found on the Llŷn, particularly the hut circle of **Tre'r Ceiri** hillfort. But today it is the beaches, not prehistoric remains, that lure people to the south-coast family resorts of **Cricieth**, **Pwllheli** and **Abersoch**, and unless you want to rent windsurfers or canoes, it's preferable to make for the much quieter coves punctuating the north coast or press on along the narrow roads that dawdle down towards Aberdaron.

The Llŷn is approached through one of two gateway towns linked by the A487, an effective boundary between Snowdonia proper and the peninsula. **Porthmadog**, nestling into the crook of the elbow formed by the Cambrian coast and the Llŷn, is primarily of interest for its proximity to the private dream village of **Portmeirion**, reached on Wales' finest narrow-gauge train line, the **Ffestiniog Railway**. The Llŷn's northern coast comes to an abrupt end at the mouth of the Menai Strait, guarded by the magnificent fortress which forms the centrepeice of **Caernarfon**, a good base for both the Llŷn and central Snowdonia.

Not even in Snowdonia does it feel more remote than the tip of the Llŷn, and nowhere in Wales is more staunchly Welsh: road signs are still bilingual but the English is frequently defaced; on the Llŷn proper, Stryd Fawr is used instead of High Street, and in most local shops you'll only hear Welsh spoken. There are pockets that are being bought up by English second-home owners and other immigrants, many of whom make no attempt to learn the language, and something like twenty percent of all houses on the Llŷn are either holiday homes or weekend retreats. But the peninsula remains defiantly Welsh, seven decades after the meeting in Pwllheli that saw the formation of the Welsh nationalist party, Plaid Cymru. It is also a stronghold of the shadowy *Meibion Glyndŵr*, or "Sons of Glendower" (see *Contexts*, p.444) whose incendiary tactics remain legendary despite a recent quiet spell.

The bountiful caravan parks can seem unappealing to campers and often only accept families and couples, but a local ruling allows anyone with a field to run a campsite for one month a year, and through the summer they spring up everywhere. Trains and *National Express* buses both serve Criccieth and Pwllheli, leaving an extensive network of infrequent buses to cover the rest. Better still, the peninsula's quiet narrow lanes through rolling pastoral land are ideal for cycling, and you can rent bikes in Pwllheli. If you want to do a little walking on the peninsula, check out the *Llŷn Footpath Network* package (£1.75), containing eight linear walks which can all be made circular by bus using the timetable included. It's a nice idea incompletely executed, so with a head for maps you may be better off devising your own walks.

It is also worth noting that the region known as Dwyfor – essentially the main body of the Llŷn, Porthmadog and Beddgelert – was the last place in Wales to ban drinking on Sunday. Only after the seven-yearly plebiscite in 1996 was the ruling overturned and pubs allowed to open their doors on the Sabbath.

Porthmadog and around

The Vale of Ffestiniog and Beddgelert's Glaslyn River meet the sea at Tremadog Bay where the Cambrian Coast makes a sharp left to become the south side of the Llŷn. The bustling town of **PORTHMADOG** drapes itself around the northern shore of Traeth Bach, the mountain-backed common estuary, sadly making little

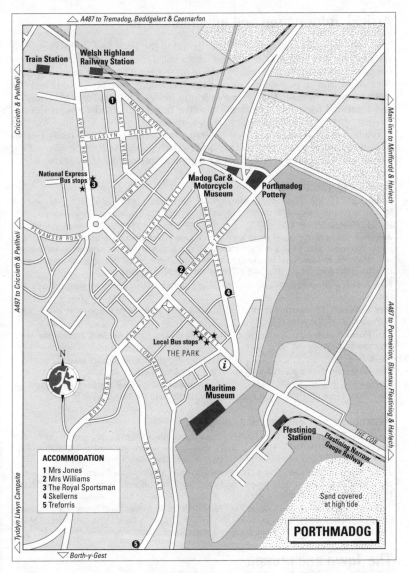

△ A487 to Tremadog, Beddgelert & Caernarfon

Train Station

Welsh Highland Railway Station

◁ Criccieth & Pwllheli

▷ Main line to Minffordd & Harlech

❶

MADOG STREET

EAST AVENUE

GLASLYN STREET

AVENUE ROAD

National Express Bus stops ★ ❸

NEW STREET

Madog Car & Motorcycle Museum

Porthmadog Pottery

◁ A497 to Criccieth & Pwllheli

PENAMSER ROAD

CHAPEL STREET

HIGH STREET

MADOG STREET

SNOWDON STREET

❷

❹

▷ A487 to Portmeirion, Blaenau Ffestiniog & Harlech

BANK PLACE

HIGH STREET

N

Local Bus stops ★★ ★★

THE PARK

ℹ

LOMBARD STREET

WELSH ROAD

GARTH ROAD

Maritime Museum

Ffestiniog Station

Ffestiniog Narrow Gauge Railway

THE COB

ACCOMMODATION

1 Mrs Jones
2 Mrs Williams
3 The Royal Sportsman
4 Skellerns
5 Treforris

◁ Tydyn Llwyn Campsite

❺

▽ Borth-y-Gest

Sand covered at high tide

PORTHMADOG

of its wonderful position. It was once the busiest slate port in north Wales but now only rates as a pleasant enough town to use as a base for a night or two. Two things it does make a fuss about are the Italianate folly of **Portmeirion**, two miles east of the town, and the wonderful **Ffestiniog Railway** that originally carried down slates from Blaenau Ffestiniog through thirteen miles of verdant mountain scenery to Porthmadog-made schooners for export.

Arrival, information and accommodation

The mainline **train** station is at the north end of the High Street; the Ffestiniog station is located down by the harbour, about half a mile to the south. In between the two, there's the helpful **tourist office** on the High Street (Easter–Oct daily 10am–6pm; Nov–Easter daily except Tues 10am–5pm; ☎01766/512981) and the stops for both *National Express* **buses** from Chester, Liverpool and Manchester, and local bus services. Note that Dolgellau buses go inland through Coed-y-Brenin: take the train if you want to stick to the coast.

While limited budgets are well catered for, there's not much really decent **accommodation** without pressing on to Criccieth (p.348) or Harlech (see p.299), unless you're prepared to splash out for a night at the swanky *Hotel Portmeirion* .

Hotels and guesthouses

Golden Fleece Inn, Tremadog, a mile north of Porthmadog (☎01766/512421). The best bet for pub accommodation with pleasant rooms above an excellent bar. ③.

Hotel Portmeirion, Portmeirion (☎01766/770228, fax 771331). Elegant individually designed suites in the hotel or in serviced cottages throughout Portmeirion village. The more expensive suites will strain your credit, but it is worth asking about deals on low-season, midweek and weekend breaks. The most atmospheric of the cottages are often booked months in advance for popular times. Tennis and a heated outdoor pool. ⑧.

Mrs Jones, 57 East Ave (☎01766/513087). Very comfortable guesthouse near the train station. ②.

Mrs Williams, 12 Snowdon St (☎01766/512635). One of the town's best-value B&Bs, right at the bottom of the price code. ③.

The Royal Sportsman, Avenue Road (☎01766/512015). About the best hotel in the town, near the train station. ④.

Skellerns, 35 Madog St (☎0766/512843). The cheapest guesthouse around, near the Ffestiniog train station a 2-min walk north from the tourist office. ②.

Treforris, Garth Road (☎01766/512853). Large house overlooking the harbour to the west. Take Bank Place off High Street then left onto Garth Road – a 15-min walk in all. ②.

Bunkhouse, self-catering and campsite

Eric's Bunkhouse, 2 miles north of Porthmadog on the A498 to Beddgelert, opposite *Eric Jones' Café* (see "Eating"). Rock climbers' bunkhouse where you can get a mattress for around £2 a night and a flasher one next door with kitchen and shower for £4.50.

Hotel Portmeirion (see above). The hotel also runs fully equipped luxurious self-catering accommodation (two to eight people) let by the week, or half-week in winter. Four-berth cottages cost from £300 to £500 a week.

Tyddyn Llwyn, Black Rock Road (☎01766/512205). High-standard family campsite on a grassy hillside with all facilities and a bar on site. A 15-min walk along the road to Morfa Bychan following Bank Place southwest off High Street. March–Oct.

The Town and around

Porthmadog would never have existed at all without the entrepreneurial ventures of a Lincolnshire MP named William Alexander Madocks, who named the town and its elder brother Tremadog, a mile to the north, after both himself and the Welsh Prince Madog, who some say sailed from the nearby Ynys Fadog (Madog's Island) to North America in 1170. In 1805, Madocks fancied he could get himself some good grazing land by draining a thousand acres of estuarine mudflats here;

he bought Ynys Fadog, built an earth embankment, then started on Tremadog. The towns prospered and, buoyed by their success, Madocks embarked on a project to enclose a further 7000 acres by sealing off the Glasyln estuary with a mile-long embankment known as The Cob, southeast of present-day Porthmadog. Madocks died before the project came to fruition, but the Glaslyn River was rerouted and soon scoured out a deep watercourse close to the north bank, ideal for a slate wharf. This was the first of several which, boosted by the completion of the Ffestiniog Railway in 1836, spread along a waterfront thick with orderly heaps of slate and the masts of merchant ships. The boom time has long since slowed, and slate traffic had ceased by the middle of the twentieth century; now only a few dozen pleasure yachts grace the harbour.

The waterfront is still the most interesting place to wander, not least because the last surviving slate shed contains the recently refurbished **Maritime Museum** (Easter & June–Sept daily 10am–6pm; £1). Amongst the obligatory ships in glass cases, panels tell of the town's shipbuilding role and its importance in carrying slate around the world.

Just across the harbour, the Ffestiniog Railway (see below) begins its ascent, but Porthmadog has a second narrow-gauge line, the far less interesting **Welsh Highland Railway** (Easter & mid-May to Sept 6–8pm daily; £1.75), running from just near the train station along a mile of track.

On rainy days, head for the northeastern end of Snowdon Street, where you can throw a pot, paint a plate or dip a candle at the **Porthmadog Pottery** in Snowdon Mill (Mon–Fri 9.30am–5pm; July & Aug daily), or admire the bodywork on show next door at the **Madog Car & Motorcycle Museum** (Easter–Oct Mon–Sat 10am–5pm; £1.50). The gleaming collection of exclusively British bikes and cars, from the 1920s through to the mid-1960s, includes a lovely belt-driven 1924 Sunbeam and a 1948 water-cooled Scott Flying Squirrel.

All the sand and water around Porthmadog might leave you hankering for a swim. **Black Rock Sands**, three miles west at **MORFA BYCHAN**, is the best beach, a long swathe of golden sands, not unpleasantly bordered by caravan sites, although there are plans for 800 chalet-style holiday homes in the near future. The #96 bus goes there in summer, or there's a Criccieth-bound footpath along the coast starting on Lôn Cei (Quay Lane) at the back of the harbour and reaching Black Rock Sands by way of **BORTH-Y-GEST**, a small former boat-building village enveloping a picturesque harbour a mile south of Porthmadog. There's nothing to do there but enjoy the estuary views and eat at the waterfront *Sea View Restaurant* (☎01766/512720), really more a pleasant café.

The Ffestiniog Railway

Without a doubt, the **Ffestiniog Railway** (Easter–Oct 4–10 times daily; Nov–Easter mainly weekends; return to Blaenau Ffestiniog £11.40, single £5.70, less for shorter journeys) ranks as Wales' finest narrow-gauge rail line, twisting and looping up 650ft from Porthmadog to the slate mines at Blaenau Ffestiniog, thirteen miles away. The gutsy little engines make light of the steep gradients and chug through stunning scenery that ranges from broad estuarine expanses and the deep greens of the Vale of Ffestiniog, only fading to grey on the final approaches to the slate-bound upper terminus at Blaenau Ffestiniog.

When the line opened in 1836, it carried slates from the mines down to the port with the help of gravity, horses riding with the goods, then hauling the empty carriages back up again. Steam had to be introduced to cope with the 100,000 tons of slate a year that Blaenau Ffestiniog was churning out in the late nineteenth century, but the slate-roofing market collapsed between the wars and passengers were carried instead, until 1946 when the line was finally abandoned. Most of the tracks and sleepers had disappeared by 1954 when, encouraged by the success of the Talyllyn Railway (see p.287), a bunch of dedicated volunteers began to reconstruct the line, only completing the entire route in 1982.

Leaving Porthmadog, trains cross The Cob then stop at Minffordd, a jumping-off point for the Cambrian coast line and the mile-long walk to Portmeirion (see below). A mile further on, Penrhyn station presents the possibility of a four-mile walk through the woods of Coed Llyn y Garnedd to either the third station, Plas Halt, from where it is a short stroll to *The Grapes* pub at Maentwrog (see p.340), or the nearby fourth station at Tan-y-bwlch. Short nature trails spur off from Tan-y-Bwlch, as does the longer Vale of Ffestiniog walk (see p.340) which passes Dduallt station by the spiral on its way to Tanygrisiau, the start of the Moelwyn/Cnicht walk (see p.340). You can get on and off as frequently as the timetable allows, and the journey is included in the *North and Mid Wales Rover* ticket (see *Basics* p.23); you must pay £2 each way for bikes, but call first to confirm. Sit on the right of the carriage going up to get the best view of the scenery.

At the Ffestiniog Railway station in Porthmadog's High Street, a small but interesting **museum** (open when trains are running; free) presents the history of the line and exhibits some of the original rolling stock, including horse wagons.

Portmeirion

The other main lure of Porthmadog, apart from the Ffestiniog Railway, is the unique Italianate private village of **PORTMEIRION** (daily 9.30am–5.30pm; £3.20 in summer, £1.60 in winter), set on a small rocky peninsula in Tremadog Bay, three miles east near Minffordd. You can visit the village by train: both the mainline and Ffestiniog trains, as well as buses #1 and #2, stop in Minffordd, from where it is a 25-minute walk to Portmeirion. You can also walk from Porthmadog in an hour following the footpath parallel to the Ffestiniog line across The Cob.

Perhaps best known as "The Village" in the 1960s British cult TV series *The Prisoner*, Portmeirion is the brainchild of eccentric architect Clough Williams-Ellis and his dream to build an ideal village which enhances rather than blends in with the surroundings, using a "gay, light-opera sort of approach". The result certainly is theatrical: a stage set with a lucky dip of unwanted buildings arranged to distort perspectives and reveal tantalizing glimpses of the sea or the expansive sands behind.

In the 1920s, Williams-Ellis began scouring Britain for a suitable island – he believed only an island could provide the seclusion for his project – but having found nothing he could afford, was gratified to be offered a piece of wilderness four miles from his home, Brodanw House, at Garreg (see below). A house already on the site was turned into a hotel, the income from it providing funds for Williams-Ellis's "Home for Fallen Buildings". Endangered buildings from all over Britain and abroad were broken down, transported and rebuilt, every conceivable style being plundered: a Neoclassical colonnade from Bristol, Siamese figures on Ionic columns, a Jacobean town hall, a Buddha, and the Italianate touches, a Campanile and a Pantheon. Williams-Ellis designed his village around a Mediterranean piazza, piecing together a scaled-down nest of loggias, grand porticoes and tiny terracotta-roofed houses, and painting them in pastels: turquoise, ochre and buff yellows. Continually surprising, with hidden entrances and cherubs popping out of crevices, the ensemble is eclectic, yet never quite inappropriate.

Long-term structural considerations were evidently not foremost in William-Ellis's mind during the construction and the place soon fell into a state of tattiness, but a programme of renovation replaced and Portmeirion is again looking spruce. More than three thousand visitors a day come to ogle in summer when it can be a delight; fewer in winter when it is just plain bizarre. And for one weekend in September, Portmeirion hosts *The Prisoner* convention when fans book the place out to re-enact scenes as best they can – though, as much of the series was shot in the studio, the juxtaposition of Portmeirion's buildings doesn't match that of The Village.

Sometimes dismissed as the grandest folly of all and a symbol of Britain's fascination with eccentrics, Portmeirion at least supports William-Ellis's guiding principle that natural beauty and profitable development needn't be mutually exclusive. Architectural idealism aside, it was always intended to be self-sustaining, much of the finance coming from the opulent waterside *Hotel Portmeirion* (see p.344). In the evening, when the village is closed to the public, patrons get to see the place at its best: peaceful, even ghostly. The hotel also takes up many of the cottages that make up the village, so much of your time will be spent outside, or popping into the shops selling *Prisoner* memorabilia or gaudy Portmeirion pottery. Guests and visitors can eat at the expensive hotel-restaurant (see p.348), but most will be content with a couple of cafés, or better still, bring a picnic and find a spot on the easy paths that lace the dell and its cloak of exotic forest.

Clough Williams-Ellis's talents are also in evidence four miles northeast of Portmeirion at his ancestral home of **Brodanw House** (daily 9am–5pm; £1.50), near Garreg, where whimsical topiary creates a formal, yet not quite manicured, setting for a solid Welsh stone house. The house itself is closed to the public, leaving only the gardens and some of the grounds, visited by following the "To the Tower" sign opposite the entrance. A ten-minute woodland walk brings you to the outlook tower, with expansive views of Porthmadog and the Moelwyns.

Eating, drinking and entertainment

Allport's, corner of Snowdon and Madoc streets. Ordinary-looking fish-and-chip shop deemed the "Best in Wales" in 1995.

Brodanw Arms, Llanfrothen, five miles northwest of Porthmadog. Slate-floored traditional inn known locally as *Y Ring* and currently the only pub anywhere near Porthmadog with any live entertainment. Sat night usually sees live music and occasional comedy, while Thurs & Sun are typically the preserve of local folkies. Real ales, pool tables, a beer garden, kids' play area and decent bar meals should please just about everyone.

Eric's Café, a mile east of Tremadog on the A498 (☎01766/512199). Good solid standard food wolfed down by climbers of the Tremadog crags across the road. There's a good noticeboard, a small stock of climbing gear and guidebooks for sale, and Eric runs an indoor climbing wall across the road (£1.50). Usually open to 6pm, later on summer weekends.

The Golden Fleece Inn and Bistro, Tremadog. An ancient coaching inn on Tremadog's main square with a cramped "cave bar" serving inexpensive bar meals around the fire or out in the courtyard. There's a blackboard bistro menu in the moderately priced restaurant out the back.

The Harbour Restaurant, High Street, opposite the tourist office (☎01766/512471). Not surprisingly, seafood dominates the menu in this simply decorated but very good restaurant. Open daily in summer, Thurs–Sat in winter.

Passage to India Tandoori, 26a Lombard St (☎01766/512144). Typical curry restaurant menu disguises the fact that this is one of the best such places around. It is across the park, west of the High Street.

Portmeirion Restaurant, *Hotel Portmeirion* (☎01766/770228). Delightful, expensive hotel restaurant with views across the Traeth Bach sands. Inventive modern cuisine employs local game and seafood. Jacket and tie are required in the evening.

The Ship, Lombard Street. Popular pub noted for its good beer, its bar meals and the highly praised but reasonably priced Cantonese -and Peking-style restaurant upstairs.

The Ship and Castle, High Street. Make up your own mind as to whether this youthful pub with lively jukebox lives up to its local moniker, "The Shit and Hassle".

Yr Hen Fecus, Lombard Street (☎01766/514625). Imaginative, moderately priced eating, including some decent vegetarian dishes, served in café-style surroundings.

Criccieth and around

When sea-bathing became the Victorian fashion, English families descended on the sweeping sand and shingle beach at **CRICCIETH** (sometimes Cricieth), five miles west of Porthmadog. Aided by the rail line, they built the long terraces of guesthouses that grew up behind the beach, which subsequently decayed and were reborn in recent years as retirement homes. These days, beach-bound holiday-makers go further west, leaving a quiet amiable resort which curiously abounds with good places to stay and great restaurants, making it a suitable touring base for the peninsula and Porthmadog.

There's not much to see or do here, apart from visiting David Lloyd George's childhood home a mile or so to the west at Llanystumdwy (see p.350), and the battle-worn **Criccieth Castle** (late March to Sept daily 10am–6pm; unrestricted access in winter; £2.20; CADW), dominating the coastline with what remains of its twin D-towered gatehouse. The castle was started by Llewelyn ap Iorwerth in 1230, but strengthened and finished by Edward I, who took it in 1283, and his successors. During his 1404 rebellion, Owain Glyndŵr grabbed it back, only to raze it and leave little remaining besides a plan of broken walls and the gatehouse. It is a great spot to sit and look over Cardigan Bay to Harlech in the late afternoon, but leave time for the fairly workaday exhibition on Welsh castles and a wonderful animated cartoon based on the twelfth-century Cambrian travels of Giraldus Cambrensis (see box on p.350) in the ticket office. If all you want are wonderful views, those from the top neighbouring hill are free, just as good and are set off by the hulking castle.

If you are here during the third week of June, you might want to attend the week-long **Criccieth Festival** of jazz and classical music taking place at various venues around town (☎01766/522778 for bookings). Some events are hosted by **Capel Celfyddyd**, Marine Terrace (Tues–Sun 10am–6pm; donations), a nineteenth-century chapel converted into an art gallery and showing predominantly local artists.

Practicalities

Both *National Express* **buses** from the north Wales coast and frequent local buses from Porthmadog and Pwllheli stop at Y Maes, the open square at the centre of town flanked by The Green. **Trains** on the Cambrian coast line stop a couple of hundred yards west, out past the **tourist office**, 30 Stryd Fawr (May–Sept Mon–Sat 10.30am–6.30pm, Sun 2–6pm; ☎01766/533515), which can help you find **accommodation**, though with so many good choices you shouldn't have any difficulty. For such a small town, good **restaurants** are surprisingly abundant and offer the best range of eating on the peninsula.

Hotels and guesthouses

Bron Eifion Country House Hotel (☎01766/522385, fax 522083). Beautiful Victorian country house full of carved Oregon pine and set in five acres nearly a mile west of the centre of town. ⑨.

Craig-y-Môr, West Parade (☎01766/522830). Well-appointed rooms, some with excellent sea views, and home-cooked meals for around £12. Closed Nov–Feb. ③.

Moelwyn, 27–29 Mona Terrace (☎01766/ 522500). Unfussy en-suite rooms with sea views and TVs. Above one of the best restaurants in town, with discounted meals for guests. Closed Jan–March. ④.

Muriau, Lôn Fel (☎01766/522337). Excellent-value seventeenth-century gentleman's residence with a congenial, if slightly formal atmosphere, large tasteful rooms overlooking formal lawns and £12 evening meals. ③.

Mynydd Ednyfed, Caernarfon Road, a mile north on the B4411 (☎01766/523269). Luxurious country-house hotel with cheerful, floral but not over-fussy rooms and a strong sporting bent. There's a tennis court, gym and solarium on site, and shooting and fishing catered for. Classy, moderately priced food, too. ⑥.

Seabank Hotel, Marine Terrace (☎01766/522255). One of Criccieth's cheapest waterfront guesthouses, 200 yards west of the castle and with a good bar. ②.

Trefaes Guesthouse, Y Maes (☎01766/523204). Excellent guesthouse with attractively furnished rooms hung with good Welsh art. All rooms have private facilities and TVs. Full Welsh breakfasts are served, though the emphasis is on vegetarian cuisine, and you can drink your own wine at dinner. ③.

Bunkhouse and campsite

Mynydd Du (☎01766/522533). Simple campsite a mile towards Porthmadog on the A497. April–Oct.

Tyddyn Morthwyl Farm and Caravan Park (☎01766/522115). Not the closest but the nicest campsite, on the Caernarfon road, a little over a mile north of Criccieth. A bargain price (£2 per person) includes hot showers and there's a spacious bunkhouse in converted farm buildings for £4 a night. Book ahead and bring a sleeping bag.

Eating and drinking

Blue China Tearooms, Marine Terrace. The pick of the bunch for daytime coffee and cake.

Bron Eifion Country House Hotel (see above). Expensive, innovative and highly rated cuisine; strong on steak and seafood.

Cadwalader's, Castle Street. Watch the legendary thick rich ice cream being made right in front of you at the original of several *Cadwalader*'s emporia all over north Wales.

Lion Hotel, The Green. Popular town pub with a good beer garden and live and varied entertainment on Tues and Sat evenings.

Moelwyn (see above). International menu with superb seafood and a comprehensive wine list in airy non-smoking surroundings with great sea views. Three-course Sun lunches for £9.

Mynydd Ednyfed, Caernarfon Road (see above). Tasty and carefully presented food in a country-house hotel a mile north of town. Moderate prices.

Poachers Restaurant, 66 Stryd Fawr (☎01766/522512). Second-string French-style café-restaurant with a three-course dinner for under £7 if you eat before 7pm (not Sat).

The Prince of Wales, Stryd Fawr. The best of the town's pubs: a multi-room local with a couple of guest beers, inexpensive bar meals and live music most Tues evenings.

Tir-a-Môr, 1–3 Mona Terrace (☎01766/523084). Perhaps the pick of the town's restaurants: not strictly Italian, but with a large range of reasonably priced Italian-influenced dishes and an extensive wine list. It is just downhill from the square in the centre of town. Evening only, closed Sun.

Llanystumdwy

Though born in Manchester, the Welsh nationalist, social reformer and British Prime Minister David Lloyd George (1864–1945) lived in his mother's home village of **LLANYSTUMDWY**, a mile west of Criccieth, until 1881, when he was nearly eighteen. He grew up in Highgate House, the home of his uncle, the village cobbler, which is now part of the **Lloyd George Museum** (Easter–May Mon–Fri 10.30am–5pm; June Mon–Sat 10.30am–5pm; July–Sept daily 10.30am–5pm; Oct Mon–Fri 11am–4pm; £2.50). A fairly dull collection of gifts, awards and caskets honouring Lloyd George with the freedom of various cities illustrate the great man's popularity, and the museum's displays are full of anecdotes and little-known facts about him, with weighty and hagiographic explanatory panels and a couple of short films giving a broad sweep of his life.

The video presentations demonstrate some of his talent as a witty and powerful orator, but only hint at the figure described by Churchill as "a man of action, resource and creative energy, [who] stood, when at his zenith, without a rival".

Read between the lines to get a sense of the betrayal felt by many Welsh nationalists as his interest turned from the politics of Wales to those of Westminster.

Rustic late nineteenth-century beds and dressers furnish Lloyd George's wooden-floored two-up, two-down house, in a garden laid out much as it would have been in Lloyd George's day. Before ambling through the garden, walk down the path towards the River Dwyfor, beside which Lloyd George is buried under a memorial – a boulder and two simple plaques designed by Portmeirion designer Clough Williams-Ellis (see p.346). Bus #3 runs from Porthmadog and Criccieth, through the village on its way to Pwllheli.

Pwllheli

PWLLHELI (pronounced something like "Pootl-heli") nearly became famous: if Manchester, 120 miles away, had won its bid to host the Olympic Games in 2000, the new marina here was earmarked as the yachting venue. Occasional races and regattas now keep the boating fraternity happy as the town dejectedly returns to its position as the market town for the peninsula, a role it has maintained since 1355, when it gained its charter. There's little to remind you of the town's age though, as the oldest building only dates back to the early seventeenth century and almost everything else is Victorian. There's really no reason to stop here, but this is the end of the line for buses and trains so you probably will, at least briefly.

Pwllheli's one defining feature is its Welshness. Even in the height of summer, you'll hear far more Welsh spoken here than English and perhaps wish you'd made more of an attempt to learn some. It was at the *Maesgwyn Temperance Hotel* (now a pet shop on Y Maes, marked with a plaque) during the National Eisteddfod in August 1925 that six people, three from *Byddin Ymreolwyr Cymru* (the Army of Welsh Home Rulers) and three from *Y Mudiad Cymreig* (The Welsh Movement) met to form Plaid Cymru. Pwllheli also has one of the few exclusively Welsh-language bookshops in the country, *Llên Llŷn* , on Y Maes, owned by writer Alun Jones.

You might as well move on unless you are drawn to either the small-thrill roller coasters and heated pools of *Butlin's* **Starcoast World** (April–Oct and sporadically in winter daily 10am–10pm, last admission 4pm; £5.50, winter £4), three miles towards Criccieth, or the **field archery and shooting range** at the *Llanbedrog Archery Centre* (daily 10am–dusk; archery £17 a session, shooting £25hr; by appointment on ☎01758/740810), just off the A499 in Llanbedrog.

Practicalities

The town spreads out from Y Maes, the central square where *National Express* and local **buses** pull in. The **train station**, northern terminus of the Cambrian coast line, stands a few yards to the east, opposite the **tourist office**, Station Square (daily 10am–6pm; Nov–March closes 5pm; ☎01758/613000). You can **rent mountain bikes** during the summer at £10 a day from *Llŷn Cycle Centre*, 2 Ala Rd (☎01758/612414).

The best of the local **accommodation** is scattered around Pwllheli, but in the centre try *26 Stryd Fawr* (☎01758/613172; ②), with TVs in all rooms, or, four hundred yards away, *Llys Gwyrfai*, 14 West End Parade (☎01758/614877; ③), a comfortable guesthouse with sea views, rooms with baths and home-cooked meals.

The best place to stay in the vicinity is *Plas Bodegroes* (March–Oct; ☎01758/612363; ⑤), a very comfortable Georgian country house set in parkland at Efailnewydd, two miles northwest of Pwllheli on the A497, and serving superb meals. Non-smokers are well catered for at *Hen Ficerdy*, Abererch (March–Oct; ☎01758/612162; ③), a former country vicarage with great views of Cardigan Bay, a mile northeast of Pwllheli on the A499 (turn left at the chapel); or try *Gwynfryn Farm*, just over a mile north of Pwllheli (☎01758/612536; ②), a working dairy farm-cum-B&B with comfortable rooms, self-catering units and a low-cost, high-summer **campsite**. The farm is up Gaol Street, left of the Salem Chapel, branch left, then straight on until the entrance is signposted on the left. Other campsites include the expensive *Hendre Caravan Park*, Efailnewydd (March–Oct; ☎01758/613416), a mile northwest on the A497.

If you have the money, *Plas Bodegroes* (see above; dinner only and closed to non-guests on Mon) could present you with the best **eating** you'll experience in Wales. Five smallish courses of innovative, beautifully presented food with wine won't give you much change out of £40, but expect to be well pleased. Diners with lighter purses can eat moderately priced Italian at *Pompei*, 53 Stryd Fawr (☎01758/614944), Spanish at the appealing *Tapas Restaurant*, 6 Lower Ala Rd (☎01758/614069), or anything from mussels in garlic sauce to pizza at the inexpensive *Mariner Bistro* on Station Square.

For **drinking**, Pwllheli's best bet is the 400-year-old *Penlan Fawr*, 3 Penlan St, where there's occasional live music, and summer barbecues in the beer garden. Locals and those in the know tend to head four miles southwest to **LLANBEDROG** where there are two great pubs, both serving fine inexpensive meals: the *Glyn-y-Weddw Arms*, Ty Du on the A499 and the friendly *Ship Inn*, Bryn-y-Gro, half a mile further on, with a very popular summertime beer garden.

Abersoch and around

After the distinctly Welsh feel of Pwllheli, **ABERSOCH**, seven miles southwest along the coast, comes as a surprise. This former fishing village pitched in the middle of two golden bays has, over the last century, become a largely anglicized resort, catering largely to comfortably-off boat owners. Abersoch now ranks as one of the country's major dinghy-sailing centres, the odd foreign entrant to the numerous regattas throughout the summer lending a mildly cosmopolitan air to the place and fuelling its haughty opinion of itself.

Such high self-esteem isn't really justified, but at high tide the harbour is attractive, and the long swathe of the Town Beach is a fine spot even if it is barely visible under the beach towels at busy times. A short walk along the shore shakes off most of the crowds, but a better bet is to make for three-mile-long **Porth Neigwl** (Hell's Mouth), two miles to the southwest, which ranks as one of the country's best surf beaches – beware of the undertow if you are swimming. Around town the needs of yachties and surfers are catered for with a couple of chandlers and more surf shacks than anywhere north of the Pembrokeshire coast. Sun-seekers should head a mile north to a fine stretch of beach backed by *The Warren* holiday park.

Bus #18 can take you to **Llanengan**, a short walk from the beach of Porth Neigwl, where you can also visit the gorgeous twin-aisled fifteenth-century **St Engan's Church** (instructions for obtaining the key are inside the porch), with its two altars and two rood screens, integral parts of decoration that have been little changed by the eighteenth- and nineteenth-century reformist zeal that altered most other churches. Llanengan is also home to the *Sun Inn* (see below), a cosy pub serving great bar meals, and with a pleasant beer garden.

Practicalities

Buses from Pwllheli make a loop through the middle of Abersoch stopping by the **tourist office**, Lôn Pen Cei (Easter to mid-Sept daily 10.30am–5pm; winter daily noon–2pm; ☎01758/712929). To continue to Aberdaron by bus, you have to take a Pwllheli-bound service as far as Llanbedrog, then change onto the #17.

There is no shortage of **places to stay** in Abersoch, the cheapest being *Trewen*, Lôn Hawen, just off Lôn Sarn Bach (☎01758/712755; ②), and *Ganllwyd*, Gwydryn Drive (☎01758/713590; ②). On Lôn Sarn Bach are the excellent *TŷDraw*(☎ & fax 01758/712647; ③), *Angorfa Guest House*, (closed Dec; ☎01758/712967; ③), and the comfortable, very professional *Neigwl Hotel* (☎01758/712363; ⑦). Two and a half miles south of Abersoch, the road through Sarn Bach and Bwlchtocyn goes to the luxurious *Porth Tocyn* country-house hotel (Easter to mid-Nov; ☎01758/713303, fax 713538; ⑨), with an outdoor pool and great views of Cardigan Bay.

Almost all **campsites** around Abersoch are family-oriented places, so groups need to look especially responsible to be admitted. One of the best such places is the *Seaside Camping Site*, Lôn Golff (☎01758/712271), overlooking the Town Beach and golf course. A slightly looser rein is given at the simple *Bryn Cethin Bach*, Bwlchtocyn (☎01758/712285), nearly two miles south.

Abersoch is increasingly well supplied with decent **places to eat**, including *Mañana*, Lôn Pen Cei, a casual Mexican-Italian-influenced café-cum-restaurant, *Champers* bistro in the *Vaynol Arms*, Lôn Sarn Bach (☎01758/712770), and the restaurant at *St Tudwal's Inn* (☎01758/712539). The moderate *Neigwl Hotel* (see above) produces consistently good four-course meals in decent quantities, while *Porth Tocyn* (Easter to mid-Nov; see above), dishes up top-class five-course meals and a Sunday buffet lunch. For **snacks**, take afternoon tea at *Oriel Fach*, Stryd Fawr, or load up on wholefood quiche at *The Tasty Food Shop*, Lôn Pen Cei. **Drinking** is done at the *Sun Inn* at Llanengan (an ancient pub a mile or so southwest of Abersoch, also serving great bar food), the *Vaynol Arms* on Lôn Pen Cei, and *The Brig* in the *Harbour Hotel* on Lôn Sarn Bach.

If baking on the beach isn't active enough, rent a sailboard or kayak at the Town Beach or *The Warren*, or windsurfers, surfboards and wet suits from *Abersoch Watersports*, Lôn Pont Morgan (☎01758/712483) by the harbour. Throughout the summer, fishing trips can be organized through the *Craft and Angling Centre*, The Harbour (☎01758/712646) and you can go pony trekking with *Llanbedrog Riding Centre*, Abersoch Road, Llanbedrog (☎01758/740267) just over two miles north along the A499.

Aberdaron and around

Travelling through undulating pasture to the small lime-washed fishing village of **ABERDARON**, two miles short of the tip of the Llŷn, you really feel that you are approaching the end of Wales. The village, now comprising just a few dozen houses, was little more than an inn and a church during the millennium from the sixth century, when it was the last stop on a long journey for pilgrims to Ynys Enlli or Bardsey Island (see p.355), tucked away around the headland. Just back from the water, the fourteenth-century stone *Y Gegin Fawr* (Great Kitchen) served as the pilgrims' final gathering place before the treacherous crossing, and now operates as a café; the twelfth-century **church of St Hywyn** on the cliffs behind the stony beach still serves its original purpose, and was ministered by Wales' greatest living poet, R S Thomas (see box below), until he retired in 1978.

In the early years of his retirement, Thomas lived five miles east of Aberdaron in a cottage in the grounds of **Plas-yn-Rhiw** (April–Sept daily except Sat noon–5pm; £2.50; NT), a Regency manor house on Tudor foundations at the western end of Porth Neigwl. The slate-floored, stone-walled Plas-yn-Rhiw was derelict when bought in 1938 by Thomas' friends, the moneyed Keating sisters, and restored with the help of Portmeirion architect Clough Williams-Ellis, whose off-

---

R S THOMAS

The reclusive poet R(onald) S(tuart) Thomas, hotly tipped as the possible recipient of the 1997 Nobel Prize for Literature, is something of a Welsh anti-hero. Born in Cardiff in 1913, he was ordained into the Church in Wales at the tender age of 23, and spent all of his working life as a minister, in some of the rural parishes of mid-Wales, in Caergybi/Holyhead and, most famously, for his last couple of working decades as the parish priest in Aberdaron, the last parish on the fiercely Welsh Llŷn peninsula. He has remained there through his retirement.

Thomas' first volume of poetry, *The Stones of the Field*, was published in 1946. He remained a virtual unknown through the publication of his next two volumes, and it was not until 1955 that recognition started to come with the publication of his fourth tome, *Song at the year's turning: Poems 1942–1954*, which included an introduction by John Betjeman. Since then, the poet's output has been consistent and regular, with some of his better-known collections including *The Bread of Truth* (1963) and *Not that he brought Flowers* (1968). A good starter anthology of his work – *Selected Poems* – is published by Bloodaxe.

The poetry of R S Thomas is dark and spartan, illuminated with regular shafts of visionary light. His most common themes include religion, and Christianity in particular, rural and pastoral strands and the poet's eternal topic of love in human relationships. But it is in his Welsh themed work that Thomas most savagely and thrillingly hits the mark. A belligerent advocate of Welsh as a language and culture (even if he most commonly writes in English), he is nonetheless gloomy about its direction and future, as this short extract from *A Welsh Testament* (1961), dealing with the contradictory emotions of his birthright nationality, demonstrates:

I never wanted the drab rôle
Life assigned me, an actor playing
To the past's audience upon a stage
Of earth and stone; the absurd label
Of birth, of race hanging askew
About my shoulders. I was in prison
Until you came; your voice was a key
Turning in the enormous lock
Of hopelessness. Did the door open
To let me out or yourselves in?

beat touch is evident in the flattened arches and a Gothic doorway rescued from a castle being demolished. Unlike most National Trust mansions, this is a manageable and relaxed place, filled with rustic furniture, like a 1920s oil stove used by Honora Keating until her death in 1981, and the same sister's accomplished watercolours. All the rooms are interesting, but the upstairs sitting room is perhaps most notable for its six-foot-thick wall containing a fireplace, a spiral staircase and a window nook overlooking gorgeous gardens almost overgrown with fuchsias, hydrangeas, roses and wild flowers..

Having made your way out as far as Aberdaron, it's an idea to use this as a base for exploring the narrow lanes at the end of the peninsula leading to the National Trust property around **Mynydd Mawr**, the hill overlooking Bardsey Sound. A minor road weaves west to Braich-y-Pwll, two miles west of Aberdaron, from where a short path heads down the cliffs to the ruins of St Mary's church, the crossing point at the end of the Pilgrim's Way. The road continues from here to the top of Mynydd Mawr, from where the medieval patchwork of ancient fields which make up the tip of the Llŷn is clearly visible.

Alternatively, head two miles north to the clean, safe and secluded bay of **Porth Oer**, known as "Whistling Sands" for the white sands which squeak as you walk on them. The rare #17B bus runs here in the summer.

Practicalities

Without your own transport, the only way to get to Aberdaron is to catch the infrequent #17 **bus** from Pwllheli. **Accommodation** is fairly limited. The cheapest option is *Brynmor* (☎01758/760344; ②), a hundred yards up the road to Porth Oer; the central *Ty Newydd Hotel* (☎01758/760207; ⑥) is the most comfortable. A mile or so outside Aberdaron, *Pennant* (☎01758/760610; ③) makes a good base, especially since you can **rent bikes** there: coming from Pwllheli, turn right at the bottom of the hill, right again after fifty yards, then continue straight on until you see the sign. Continuing on the same road for half a mile and forking right, you come to a very good non-smoking guesthouse, *Carreg Plas* (☎01758/760308; ③). The nearest of many decent **campsites** is *Dwyros*, up the hill on the way to Mynydd Mawr. The seasonal *Mur Melyn* (no phone), midway between Aberdaron and Porth Oer off the eastbound B4413, is a little quieter. Tap-in-a-farmer's-field sites abound, including a couple of good ones along the road to Rhiw, a fine one overlooking Porth Neigwl, just below Plas-yn-Rhiw, and a couple more on the approach road to Mynydd Mawr.

For light **meals**, try the tea rooms at the back of *Hen Blas Crafts* in the middle of the village. For bar snacks and full dinners, there's the *Ty Newydd Hotel* (see above).

Ynys Enlli (Bardsey Island)

Bardsey Island or **Ynys Enlli** (The Island of the Currents) rises out of the ocean two miles off the tip of the Llŷn, separated from it by a strait of churning unpredictable water. This national nature reserve has been an important pilgrimage site since the sixth century, when Saint Cadfan set up the first monastery here: three visits were proclaimed equivalent to one pilgrimage to Rome. Legend claims Bardsey as "The Isle of Twenty Thousand Saints", most likely remembering not saints, but vast numbers of pilgrims who came to die at this holy spot. By the twelfth century, Giraldus Cambrensis was already claiming that "the bodies of a vast number of holy men are buried there", and that "no one dies there except in extreme old age, for disease is almost unheard of". Numerous other stories tell of the burial place of Myrddin (Merlin) and the former Bishop of Bangor, St Deiniol, but the only hard evidence is the remaining **bell tower** of the thirteenth-century Augustinian Abbey of St Mary and a few Celtic crosses scattered around it. After the Dissolution of the monasteries in 1536, piracy became the focus of the island's economy for over a century, gradually giving way to agriculture and fishing.

Interesting though the abbey ruins and subsequent buildings are, most visitors come to watch **birds**, as there are a dozen or so species of nesting sea birds here – Manx shearwaters, fulmars, guillemots – and an astounding number of vagrants that turn up after being blown off course by storms. Few other people bother to make the journey, since **boats** are dependent on tides, winds and a viable load of passengers; contact the *Bardsey Island Trust* (☎01766/514774) which often runs a Saturday boat from Pwllheli (£15), or *Elwyn Evans* (April–Oct; ☎01758/730654; £15), which runs trips daily from Porth Meudwy, a tiny cove half a mile south of Aberdaron, giving three hours on the island. There are a few cottages rented by the week from the *Trust*, but no other facilities on the island.

The north Llŷn coast

Sprinkled with small coves and sweeping beaches between rocky bluffs, the **north Llŷn coast** is a dramatic contrast to the busier south. It has few settlements of any size, leaving quieter beaches – Porth Ysgadan by Tudweiliog and Traeth Penllech by Llangwnnadl – easily accessible using the #8 bus from Pwllheli and a short walk.

Nefyn and Porth Dinllaen

The only settlements of any size on the north coast are a pair of villages overlooking beautiful sweeping bays. **NEFYN** is the larger, but it doesn't have a lot to recommend it. Holiday-makers bring the most trade now, but you can learn about the village's herring-fishing past in the mildly diverting **Maritime Museum** (July–Sept Mon–Sat 10.30am–4.30pm; free) inside St Mary's Church. The neighbouring village of **MORFA NEFYN**, a mile to the west, and the adjacent shoreline hamlet of **PORTH DINLLAEN**, both benefit from having lost the 1839 battle to become the terminus for ferries to Ireland. A single Parliamentary vote swung the decision in favour of Holyhead (see p.419), thus saving the tiny hamlet of Porth Dinllaen – recently bought lock, stock and a mile of beach by the National Trust – from that town's fate, and leaving a pristine sweeping bay and the popular waterside *Tŷ Coch Inn*, a refreshing place after a day on the beach. To get there, walk a mile west along the beach from Morfa Nefyn or walk the path across the golf course.

There are a couple of great low-cost **B&Bs** in Morfa Nefyn, a hundred yards towards the beach from the crossroads in the village: *Trigfan*, Lôn Penrhos (☎01758/720584; ②), or *Anya* (☎01758/721209; ②), a couple of doors down. There's also the summer-only *Greenacres* **campsite** along the road to Nefyn.

Tre'r Ceiri and the Church of St Beuno

By far the most interesting prehistoric remains on the Llŷn are those of **Tre'r Ceiri** or "Town of the Giants" (unrestricted access) hillfort, five miles east of Nefyn.

Crowning the entire rounded top of the second-highest of the three Yr Eifl mountains, the hillfort is a massive tumble of rocks, mostly formed into the waist-high walls of about 150 dry-stone hut circles, huddling together from the wind and encircled by a rampart twelve feet high in places. Archeological evidence indicates summer habitation here since the Bronze Age, but the huts are probably only a couple of thousand years old. Locals refer to them as *Cýtiau Gwddelod* or "Irishmen's Huts", possibly recalling the Irish immigrant population on the Llýn in the first few centuries AD, when five hundred people lived on this inhospitable site. Today the ruins command a stunning view over the whole peninsula.

The infrequent #223 bus passes the base of the main path up, which leads off the B4417 a mile west of Llanaelhaearn, itself reached by the hourly buses #12 and #14 from Pwllheli. The steep path makes for a saddle, then bears right, reaching Tre'r Ceiri in under half an hour.

The path to Tre'r Ceiri is also the approach route to the tops of the other two peaks, from where you can look down into Vortigern's valley and the **Nant Gwrtheyrn National Language Centre** (☎01758/750334), in a couple of rows of converted granite quarry cottages. Reached down a narrow track from Llithfaen, three miles east of Nefyn, the centre holds residential courses entirely in Welsh, runs a café and has explanatory leaflets (£1) for its three-mile nature trail.

The last worthwhile stop on the #12 or #14 bus routes to Caernarfon is **CLYNNOG-FAWR**, where the early sixteenth-century **Church of St Beuno** (generally 10am–dusk) is built on foundations laid by Saint Beuno in the sixth century. An important stop for pilgrims heading for Ynys Enlli (see p.355), the present interior still has a spartan monastic interior of whitewash and limestone flags, but also a fine hammerbeam roof with ornamental bosses and a chancel with well-worn misericords.

Caernarfon and around

It was in **CAERNARFON** in 1969 that Charles, the current heir to the throne, was invested as Prince of Wales, a ceremony which reaffirmed English sovereignty over Wales in this, one of the most nationalist of Welsh-speaking regions. Since 1282, when the English defeated Llywelyn ap Gruffydd, the last Welsh Prince of Wales, the title has been bestowed on heirs to the English throne, usually in a ceremony held either at Windsor Castle or in Westminster Abbey in London. But in 1911, the machinations of Lloyd George – MP for Caernarfon, Welsh cabinet minister and future Prime Minister – ensured that the investiture of the future King Edward VIII would take place in the centre of his constituency: a paradoxical move for a nationalist, considering the symbolic implications.

By the time it was Charles's turn, nationalist activism was on the rise and two of the more militant cadres of the so-called Free Wales Army tried to blow up the Prince's train, succeeding only in killing themselves. That day, July 1, is now commemorated by a march through the streets of Abergele, near where the accident happened, led by their successors *Meibion Glŷndwr*, the Sons of Glendower (see p.444). Charles' 25-year commemorative return visit in the summer of 1994 was less than triumphant, a low-key affair most significantly characterized by the local constabulary ruling that the local joke shop risked committing a public-order offence by selling "wingnut" ears and Prince Charles masks.

This is a town where ardent support for Plaid Cymru guarantees the party a seat in Westminster and where the local dialect is barely intelligible even to other

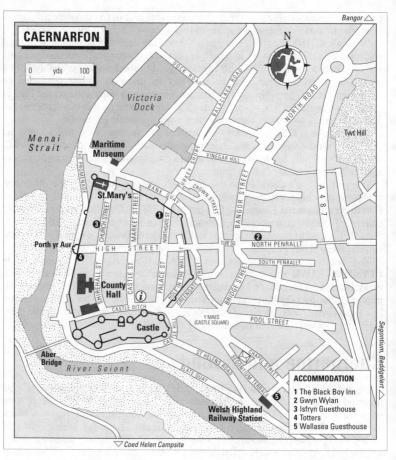

△ Bangor

CAERNARFON

0   yds   100

Menai Strait

Victoria Dock

DOCK ROAD

BALACLAVA ROAD

NORTH ROAD

Maritime Museum

Twt Hill

THE PROMENADE

TURKEY SHORE

VINEGAR HILL

BANGOR STREET

A 487

St.Mary's

BANK QUAY

CROWN STREET

CHURCH STREET

MARKET STREET

NORTHGATE ST

①

Porth yr Aur

HIGH   STREET

TURF SQ

② NORTH PENRALLT

SHIREHALL ST

CASTLE STREET

PALACE ST

HOLE IN THE WALL ST

GREENGATE STREET

SOUTH PENRALLT

BRIDGE STREET

④

County Hall

ⓘ

CASTLE DITCH

Y MAES (CASTLE SQUARE)

POOL STREET

Castle

CASTLE HILL

Aber Bridge

River Seiont

ST HELENS ROAD

SLATE QUAY

SEGONTIUM TERRACE

CHAPEL STREET

Segontium, Beddgelert △

⑤

Welsh Highland Railway Station

ACCOMMODATION
1 The Black Boy Inn
2 Gwyn Wylan
3 Isfryn Guesthouse
4 Totters
5 Wallasea Guesthouse

▽ Coed Helen Campsite

Welsh-speakers. It is also the county town of Gwynedd, a suitable title for what is one of the oldest continuously occupied towns in the country, once the site of the Romans' most westerly legion post. Segontium, on the outskirts of town, was the base of Maximus, the Spanish-born pretender to the imperial throne who was declared Emperor by his British troops in 383 AD, only to undertake an unsuccessful march on Rome.

The remains of Segontium are about as impressive as Maximus' march, but, with its magnificent castle and town walls, Caernarfon is an appealing place, especially if you have recently visited the similar setup in Conwy (see p.394). Apart from the castle, however, there isn't too much to see: you can only walk a small section of the wall and the rest of the town, ripped through by a dual carriageway, has a fairly modern feel. It even fails to exploit its magnificent setting, where the tidal mouth of the River Seiont meets the Menai Strait, allowing buses to clog the central square and lining the prime waterside at the foot of the castle with a huge car park. That said, its position at the point where the Llŷn joins the north coast and good bus connections to Llanberis and Snowdonia, make it a decent base for a couple of days, and there are some diverting sights in the area.

Arrival, information and accommodation

With no train station, the hub of Caernarfon's public transport system is Y Maes (Castle Square), both *National Express* and local **buses** arriving right under the walls of the castle, just a few steps from the **tourist office**, Oriel Pendeitsh, Castle Street (Easter–Oct daily 10am–6pm; Nov–Easter daily except Wed 9.30am–5pm; ☎01286/672232).

While there are a number of cheap places close to the centre, Caernarfon is comparatively short on more upmarket **accommodation**, though the high standard of the farmhouses around about goes some way to redressing the balance. A couple of these – *Ty-Mawr Farm* and *Tŷ'n Rhos* – are in Llanddeiniolen, halfway between Caernarfon and Bangor and detailed in Chapter Six (p.403). The town is well equipped with **campsites**: *Cadnant Valley* (March–Oct; ☎01286/673196) is twenty minutes' walk east of town near the start of the A4086 to Llanberis, and *Coed Helen* (March–Oct; ☎01286/676770), with only five tent sites among the caravans, is slightly closer on foot – cross the Seiont River by the footbridge by the castle and turn left – but further by car – follow the signs from the road junction a mile south of town.

Hotels, guesthouses and hostels

The Black Boy Inn, Northgate Street (☎01286/673023). Characterful but bathless low-beamed rooms in what is said to be the town's oldest building (bar the castle). Newer en-suite accommodation also available. ③.

Chatham Farmhouse, Llandwrog, four miles south of Caernarfon just beyond Saron (☎01286/831257). Attractive and welcoming country guesthouse with a fine inglenook fireplace and nice decorative touches. The evening meals are made with organic vegetables from the garden and you can bring your own wine. ③.

Gwyn Wylan, 7 North Penrallt (☎01286/672902). Basic B&B close to the town centre. ②.

Hafoty, Rhostryfan (☎01286/830144). Small and highly rated B&B in a modernized eighteenth-century farmhouse with well-appointed rooms and a great view of Caernarfon Castle. Take the A487 south through Bontnewydd up the hill to the T-junction where you turn left and follow the signs. ④.

Isfryn Guesthouse, 11 Church St (☎01286/675628). Good-value B&B in the centre; book ahead in summer. Moderately priced three-course evening meals available. ③.

The Old School Bunkhouse, Bwlch Derwyn, Pant Glas, twelve miles south of Caernarfon (☎01286/660701). Comfortable rural B&B and bunkhouse a mile west of the A487, halfway to Porthmadog. Bunkhouse beds are £4.50 a night and inexpensive meals are available. ③.

Pengwern Farm, Saron, three miles southwest of Caernarfon (☎ & fax 01286/830500). Friendly, top-quality non-smoking B&B with en-suite rooms in a rural setting, and farm-fresh evening meals. Take the A487 south across the river then turn right towards Saron – *Pengwern* is just over two miles down on the right. Feb–Nov. ③.

Seiont Manor, Llanrug, 3 miles east of Caernarfon on the A4086 (☎01286/673366). Rustic building remodelled into the region's finest hotel, complete with indoor pool, sauna and use of mountain bikes. Superb, though pricey, French food. ⑨.

Totters, Plas Porth Yr Aur, 2 High St (☎01286/672963). Caernarfon's first and only backpacker hostel, centrally located in a large house divided into six-bunk dorms. Beds with linen go for £9. No self-catering facilities, but a light breakfast is included. Bike rental for £5. ①.

Ty-Mawr Farmhouse, Saron (☎01286/830091). Top-value farmhouse B&B with evening meals and a choice of traditional, vegetarian or wholefood breakfast. Take the A487 south across the river then turn right towards Saron. *Ty-Mawr* is almost three miles on. ③.

Wallasea Guesthouse, 21 Segontium Terrace (☎01286/673564). Low cost and very central, overlooking the Seiont. ②.

The Town

In 1283, Edward I started work on **Caernarfon Castle** (April–Oct daily 9.30am–6.30pm; Nov–April Mon–Sat 9.30am–4pm, Sun 11am–4pm; £3.80; CADW) the strongest link in his Iron Ring (see p.397), and the decisive hammerblow to any Welsh aspirations to autonomy. Until Beaumaris Castle was built to guard the other end of the Menai Strait, Caernarfon was the ultimate symbol of both Anglo-Norman military might and political wrangling. With the Welsh already smarting from the loss of their Prince of Wales, Edward is said to have rubbed salt in their wounds by justifying his own infant son's claim to the title, declaring the future Edward II "a prince born in Wales who could speak never a word of English". The story is almost certainly apocryphal, since Edward's son, though born at Caernarfon, wasn't invested until seven years later.

Edward attempted to appease the Welsh in the building of his castle by paying tribute to aspects of local legend. The Welsh had long associated their town with the eastern capital of the Roman Empire: Caernarfon's old name, Caer Cystennin, was also the name used for Constantinople, and Constantine himself was believed to have been born at Segontium. Edward's architect, James of St George, exploited this connection in the distinctive limestone and sandstone banding and polygonal towers, both reminiscent of the Theodosian walls in present-day Istanbul. The other legend to influence the castle was the medieval *Dream of Macsen Wledig*, in which the eponymous Welsh hero (the Roman legionnaire Maximus) remembers "a fair fortress at the mouth of a river, in a land of high mountains, opposite an island, and a tower of many colours at the fort, and golden eagles on the ramparts". When it came to finishing off the turrets in 1317, Edward III perfected the accuracy of this description by adding eagles – also, ironically, the standard of Owain Gwynedd. These are weathered almost beyond recognition now, but the rest of the castle is in an excellent state of repair, thanks largely to Anthony Salvin's nineteenth-century reconstruction, carried out after Richard Wilson and J M W Turner had painted their Romantic images of it.

As a military monument of its time, the castle is supreme. It was taken once, before it was finished, but then withstood two sieges by Owain Glyndŵr with a complement of only 28 men-at-arms. Entering through the **King's Gate**, the castle's strength is immediately apparent. Between the octagonal towers, embrasures and murder-holes face in on no fewer than five gates and six portcullises, and that's once you have crossed the moat, now bridged by an incongruous modern structure. Inside, the huge lawn gives a misleading impression, since both the wall dividing the two original wards and all the buildings which filled them crumbled away long ago. The towers are in a much better state, and linked by such a honeycomb of wall-walks and tunnels that a visit can be an exhausting experience. The most striking and tallest of the towers is the King's Tower at the western end, whose three slender turrets adorned with eagle sculptures give the best views of the town. To the south, the Queen's Tower is entirely taken up by the numbingly thorough **Museum of the Royal Welch Fusiliers** (sic), detailing the victories of Wales' oldest regiment, with collections of medals, uniforms and a brass howitzer captured from the Russians at the Battle of the Alma in 1854. Crossing the upper ward from here you pass the site of the original Norman motte, now covered in Dinorwig slate as part of the dais for the investiture of the Prince of Wales. Displays on the most recent ceremony, and others since the pageant was moved here in 1911, are presented in the **Prince of Wales Exhibition** in the Northeast Tower, just beyond the dais.

The castle forms one side of Caernarfon's rectangle of **town walls**, almost as complete as those at Conwy (see p.397), but so boxed in by modern buildings that they're far less striking. You can only walk a very short section, at the end of Market Street, close to the Chantry of St Mary, the restored fourteenth-century church built into a corner of the town wall on Church Street. Just outside the walls, Victoria Dock is home to a **Maritime Museum** (Easter & June to mid-Sept daily 11am-4pm; 50p) based in and around the *Seiont II* steam dredger, which is gradually being renovated, and the *Nantlys*, the last ferry to ply the Menai Strait. The only way to get out on the Strait now is on the *Queen of the Sea* (June–Sept daily; ☎01286/672772), a pleasure craft which makes forty-minute excursions (£3) from the quay below the castle.

A ten-minute walk along the A4085 Beddgelert road brings you to the western end of the Roman road from Chester at **Segontium Roman Fort and Museum** (April & Oct Mon–Sat 9.30am–5.30pm; May–Sept Mon–Sat 9.30am–6pm, Sun 2–6pm; £1; CADW). The Romans occupied this five-acre site for three centuries from around 78 AD, though most of the remains are from the final rebuilding after 364 AD. The ground plan is seldom more than shin-high and somewhat baffling, making the museum and displays in the ticket office pretty much essential.

Eating, drinking and entertainment

Caernarfon boasts a number of low-key and likable **restaurants** which may well be the focus of your evening's entertainment, as there is little else except for a smattering of **pubs**. There is really no organized nightlife, everyone heading ten miles north to Bangor. The *Caernarfon and Denbigh Herald*, which comes out on Thursdays, has **gig** information for both Bangor and Caernarfon. For news of alternative social occasions, check out the noticeboard at the New Agey *Lockstones*, in the old **Market Hall** on Palace Street, home to a number of interesting shops and stalls.

Restaurants, cafés and pubs

Anglesey Arms, The Promenade. The sea wall outside makes this the best pub for soaking up the afternoon sun, though it also rates with good real ales and decent bar meals.

The Black Boy Inn (see "Accommodation"). The closest Caernarfon comes to an old-fashioned British pub, with a choice of two low-beamed bars and the best bar meals in town.

Courteney's, 9 Segontium Terrace (☎01286/677290). Eclectic range of excellent food and good wines served in a small room which is often full, especially at weekends. Closed Mon & Tues lunch and all day Sun.

The Gatehouse Restaurant, 20 Palace St (☎01286/674333). Licensed daytime café serving a good range of hearty dishes and good coffee. Turns into a pizza restaurant in the evening.

The Harlequin, Market Hall. Cheery daytime café upstairs in the Market Hall, with good coffee, toasted sandwiches, omelettes and varied vegetarian and meat dishes.

Stone's, 4 Hole in the Wall St (☎01286/671152). Simply decorated brick-walled place serving moderately priced bistro-style meals. The roast pheasant is good, and there's a choice of four vegetarian dishes. Closed Sun.

Tafarn Yr Albert, 10 Segontium Terrace. Bustling local where you might catch a Welsh-language band on a Saturday night.

Y Goron Fach, Hole in the Wall Street. A good range of cask ales in a friendly setting.

Around Caernarfon

One of the most enjoyable ways to get out into Caernarfon's surroundings is to follow either of two **bike paths** along the route of a disused railway: Lôn Las Menai, running north for four miles to Y Felinheri (Port Dinorwig), or Lôn Eifion, heading twelve miles south to Bryncir. Unfortunately, the only bike rental in Caernarfon is limited to guests at *Totters* hostel (see p.359) so the next bet, once it opens in mid-1997, will be the new narrow-gauge **Welsh Highland Railway** (contact the tourist office for details) – not to be confused with the identically named company in Porthmadog – which will run a steam passenger service from St Helen's Road, close to the castle, to Dinas, three miles south along a portion of the line shared by the Lôn Eifion cycle path.

North of Caernarfon

Three miles northeast of Caernarfon, just west of the village of Bethel on the B4366, the **Greenwood Centre** (mid-March to Oct daily 10am–5.30pm; £3.25) sets out to celebrate the life of trees, something it does admirably well. On the fringe of a copse of managed woodland, a large barn has been built using ancient methods and forty tons of green Welsh and English oak trees, its gargantuan beams held together with pine struts and wooden pegs.

Tree and forest ecology is explored through a blend of the scientific, the spiritual (due attention is paid to Celtic tree spirits and the like) and the sensory: you're invited to punch the bark of a redwood to see how soft it is, identify aromatic woods from their smell, and try out an Ethiopian wood pillow. Outside, visitors can turn wood on a foot-operated lathe, try shooting a longbow or simply amble around the wildlife pond, arboretum and forest nursery.

A couple of miles due west, the shores of the Menai Strait hold **Plas Menai: The National Watersports Centre**, Llanfairisgaer (☎01248/670964, or 670597, for the 24-hr brochure request line), a predominantly group-oriented complex with two- to seven-day courses in sailing, windsurfing, canoeing and powerboating.

South of Caernarfon

A much-touted but overrated outing south from Caernarfon is the **Caernarfon Air Museum** (March–Oct daily 9am–5.30pm; £3.50), eight miles south of town at Dinas Dinlle (bus #91), where cases of model aeroplanes help to fill out a small hangar containing half a dozen examples of the real thing. Better reasons to come out here might be the **scenic flights** over Caernarfon (10min; £20) and Snowdon (25min; £35), or the **Dinas Dinlle** Roman and early British oval hillfort at the south end of the beach. The hill has suffered erosion by the sea, removing most of the archeological evidence, and has also been damaged by footsteps, so the path to the top is sometimes cordoned off. If it's not, and your visit coincides with low tide, you might be able to see Caer Arianrhod, a row of rocks named after the girl in *The Mabinogion* who gave birth to Lleu Llaw Gyffer, destined to become Lord of Gwynedd.

The Lôn Eifion bike path veers right to the **Inigo Jones Tudor Slateworks**, Groeslon (Easter–Sept Mon–Fri 9am–5pm, Sat & Sun 10am–5pm; Oct–Easter Mon–Thurs 9am–4.30pm, Fri closes 3.30pm; £2.50), on the A470 six miles south of Caernarfon, a collection of roadside sheds where slate has been fashioned since 1861, when the factory was started by one Inigo Jones, apparently unrelated to the seventeenth-century architect. A large proportion of the inscribed slate plaques adorning public buildings around north Wales were cut here, ample excuse for an interesting calligraphy exhibition. Try your hand at chiselling out a few random chips of slate to appreciate the skill of the carvers here.

travel details

Unless otherwise stated frequencies for trains and buses are for Monday to Saturday services; Sunday averages 1–3 services, though the main routes are more frequent and some routes have no Sunday service at all.

TRAINS

Betws-y-Coed to: Blaenau Ffestiniog (6 daily; 30min); Llandudno Junction (6 daily; 25min).

Blaenau Ffestiniog to: Betws-y-Coed (6 daily; 30min); Llandudno Junction (6 daily; 1hr); Porthmadog by Ffestiniog Railway (Easter–Oct 4–10 daily; 1hr).

Criccieth to: Porthmadog (6 daily; 10min); Pwllheli (6 daily; 15min).

Porthmadog to: Barmouth (7 daily; 45min); Blaenau Ffestiniog by Ffestiniog Railway (Easter–Oct 4–10 daily; 1hr); Harlech (7 daily; 20min); Machynlleth (7 daily; 1hr 40min); Pwllheli (6 daily; 25min).

Pwllheli to: Criccieth (6 daily; 15min); Porthmadog (6 daily; 25min).

BUSES

Aberdaron to: Pwllheli (7 daily; 40min).

Abersoch to: Pwllheli (9 daily; 15min).

Beddgelert to: Caernarfon (6 daily; 30min); Llanberis (4 daily; 40min); Porthmadog (6 daily; 30min).

Betws-y-Coed to: Bangor (2 daily; 50min); Blaenau Ffestiniog (1 daily southbound only; 30min); Capel Curig (7 daily; 15min); Llanberis (3 daily; 40min); Llanrwst (3 daily; 10min); Idwal Cottage (6 daily; 20min); Penmachno (5 daily; 10min).

Blaenau Ffestiniog to: Caernarfon (roughly hourly; 1hr 30min); Harlech (4 daily; 35min); Porthmadog (hourly; 30min).

Caernarfon to: Bangor (every 20min; 30min); Beddgelert (6 daily; 30min); Cardiff (1 daily; 7hr 25min); Criccieth (3 daily; 40min); Llanberis (every 30min; 25min); Porthmadog (at least hourly; 45min); Pwllheli (every 30min; 45min).

Capel Curig to: Bangor (2 daily; 40min); Betws-y-Coed (7 daily; 15min); Idwal Cottage (6 daily; 10min); Llanberis (3 daily; 30min).

Criccieth to: Caernarfon (3 daily; 40min); Llanystumdwy (hourly; 5min); Porthmadog (hourly; 15min); Pwllheli (hourly; 20min).

Idwal Cottage to: Bangor (2 daily; 30min); Betws-y-Coed (6 daily; 20min); Capel Curig (6 daily; 10min).

Llanberis to: Bangor (8 daily; 40min); Beddgelert (4 daily; 40min); Betws-y-Coed (3 daily; 40min); Caernarfon (every 30min; 25min); Capel Curig (3 daily; 30min).

Llanrwst to: Betws-y-Coed (3 daily; 10min); Conwy (every 30min; 40min); Llandudno (every 30min; 1hr).

Nefyn to: Pwllheli (11 daily; 15min).

Porthmadog to: Beddgelert (6 daily; 30min); Blaenau Ffestiniog (hourly; 30min); Caernarfon (at least hourly; 45min); Criccieth (hourly; 15min); Dolgellau (6 daily; 50min); Pwllheli (hourly; 40min).

Pwllheli to: Aberdaron (7 daily; 40min); Abersoch (9 daily; 15min); Caernarfon (every 30min; 45min); Chester (1 daily; 4hr); Criccieth (hourly; 20min); Manchester (1 daily; 5hr 30min); Nefyn (11 daily; 15min); Porthmadog (hourly; 40min).

CHAPTER SIX

THE NORTH COAST
AND ANGLESEY

Wales' **north coast**, and its natural extension, **Anglesey**, encompass not only the geographical extremities of the country, but take in an area exhibiting the extremes of Welsh life. Walking around most of the brash seaside towns along the eastern section of the coast, only the street signs give any indication that you are in Wales at all: further west, there are places where English is seldom spoken other than to visitors. Scattered along the coast, dramatically sited castles work as a superb antidote to low-brow fun-seeking, while head inland and the stark urban ugliness of anglicized towns like **Wrexham** is tempered by the picture-perfect tranquillity of the rural **Vale of Clywd**.

Two major forces shaped the region into what it is today. In the thirteenth century, the might of English king Edward I all but crushed the Welsh princes and forced their armies out of the area, and Edward set about building the Norman castles which finally hammered them into subjugation. Towns grew up around the early castles at **Flint** and **Rhuddlan**, but neither had town walls, leaving the now mostly ruined structures in isolation. The castle at **Conwy**, however, was surrounded by a "bastide" town, the castle's keepers and town's burghers dependent on one another. Conwy was entirely the preserve of the English, thereby economically and politically marginalizing the Welsh who retreated west, to Anglesey, where the English wielded less influence. As a response, Edward sited his final castle at **Beaumaris**, a supreme expression of the militarily advanced concentric design, protecting the entrance to the **Menai Strait**, the treacherous channel that separates the Isle of Anglesey from the mainland.

The second sweeping change came in the late nineteenth and early twentieth centuries, when the benefits of the Industrial Revolution finally loosened the shackles on English mill-town factory workers enough for them to take holidays. Beachfront towns sprang up, catering entirely to the summer visitors who arrived by the trainload to spend one week's annual leave promenading and dancing. The setup isn't too different today, but the ever-present automobile has all but taken over from the train, caravans are as popular as guesthouses and amusement arcades rule. The stretch of coast from **Rhyl** to **Colwyn Bay** epitomizes this tatty image, the hallmarks of the shabby British seaside resort all too apparent. In contrast, Victorian **Llandudno**, always the posher place to stay, remains a cut above the rest, lying at the foot of the **Great Orme** limestone peninsula.

A few surprises come embedded into this matrix of bingo halls and caravan sites. The allegedly miraculous waters at **Holywell** have attracted the hopeful

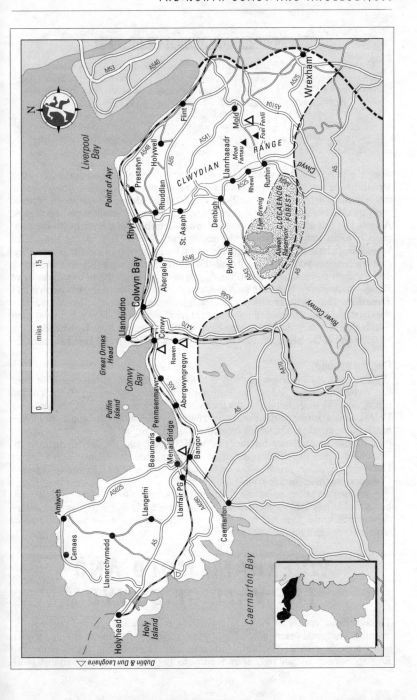

since the seventh century, while two different species of pilgrim make for either **Prestatyn**, to start the 170-mile Offa's Dyke Path along the English border, or for the National Portrait Gallery's collection at **Bodelwyddan**. To the south of here, the Vale Of Clwyd follows a pastoral valley, past Britain's smallest cathedral at **St Asaph**, to a pair of attractive old market towns, **Denbigh** and **Ruthin**. To the east, the Clwydian Range separates the valley from **Mold**, the county town, and **Wrexham**, a base for exploring the industrial heritage sites of the Clwedog Valley.

If it's beaches you want, you'll find that more discerning swimmers and windsurfers shun the mainland coast, heading instead through the university town of **Bangor** to Anglesey. Here, the southwestern resorts of **Rhosneigr**, **Rhoscolyn** and **Trearddur Bay** are the favoured spots, though for scenery there's a lot to be said for the coast along the extensive dune system of **Newborough** and the sea cliffs around **South Stack**, both great for birdwatching. Lastly, the ferries from **Holyhead**, at the western end of the island, provide the fastest route to Dublin and Dun Laoghaire.

Getting around

With the recent conversion of the A55 to a dual carriageway, you can drive from the Welsh border to Bangor or Anglesey in an hour, bypassing all the coastal towns and skirting round the northern reaches of Snowdonia in the process. Unless you take one of the slower alternative routes along the coast, you'll see much more on the **train**, which hugs the coast, linking all the resorts to Bangor, then across to Anglesey for the run to Holyhead and the ferries to Ireland. Travelling along the north coast, then changing onto the Conwy Valley line at Llandudno Junction, provides one of the fastest routes from England to Betws-y-Coed and the heart of Snowdonia.

With the exceptions of *National Express* **bus** services to Bangor and Holyhead, bus travel is much more piecemeal. Services are fairly frequent, detailed where appropriate in the text and in a series of excellent timetables available free at tourist offices and bus stations.

WREXHAM, MOLD AND THE VALE OF CLWYD

The northeast corner of Wales is one of the most widely ignored parts of the country. Thousands skirt around it or drive through en route to the more obviously appealing west. The light industrial hinterland of the towns along the English border are an ugly introduction to the region's largest conurbation,

Wrexham, which struggles to boost its image by packaging its mining and smelting heritage along the **Clywedog Valley**. Nearby **Mold** is a dull market town which seems to merely watch life tick by and deserves only the briefest of stops, but climbing the **Clwydian Range** into the pastoral **Vale of Clwyd** sees things improve dramatically. Nineteenth-century poet Gerard Manley Hopkins eulogized about the valley where he studied for the priesthood, celebrating its beauty in some of his best-loved works, *The Windhover*, *In the Valley of the Elwy* and *Pied Beauty*. The gentle contours and minor sights take time to appreciate, something seldom afforded the valley by visitors to the largest towns, **Ruthin** with its fine set of medieval buildings, **Denbigh**, surmounted by its craggy castle, and the tiny city of **St Asaph**.

Wrexham and the Clywedog Valley

If **WREXHAM** (Wrecsam) is your introduction to Wales, don't be disappointed. It certainly isn't pretty, nor is it characteristically Welsh. George Borrow walked here from Chester in 1854 and observed: "its appearance is not Welsh – its inhabitants have neither the look nor the language of Welshmen". At that time it still hadn't been granted its charter, which it earned three years later in recognition of its increasing commercial importance, predominantly in brick and tile manufacture. Industry was not new to the area, the **Clywedog Valley**, a couple of miles to the south, playing a key role in the early part of the Industrial Revolution and recently being rejuvenated as the town's chief attraction, the jewel in its crown being the National Trust's **Erddig Hall**.

The Town

The town's main draw – other than the Clwyedog Valley – is **St Giles' Church** (Easter–Sept Mon–Fri 10am–4pm; free), its Gothic tower gracefully rising above the kernel of small lanes at the end of Hope Street. Topped off with a steeple in the 1520s, the tower's five distinct levels, stepping up to four hexagonal pinnacles, is replicated at America's Yale University in homage to the ancestral home of the college's benefactor, Elihu Yale, whose tomb is here at the base. The engraved stone in the tower wall near Yale's grave came from the university, the one it replaced now holding up a replica tower there. The church's spacious interior is mainly of interest for the scant remains of the late-fifteenth-century wall painting of *The Last Judgement* above the entrance to the chancel. It is approached through wrought-iron gates installed between 1718 and 1724 by the famed Welsh iron-workers Robert and John Davies of Bersham, also responsible for the striking gates at Chirk Castle (see p.239).

Before heading for the Clywedog Valley, spend twenty minutes in the small but informative **Wrexham County Borough Museum** on Regent Street (Mon–Sat 10am–4pm; free) which focuses on the town's nineteenth-century boom years.

Practicalities

Wrexham has two **train stations**, half a mile apart. Chester, Chirk and Shrewsbury trains call only at Wrexham General on Regent Street, ten minutes' walk northwest of the centre along Hope Street. Services from Liverpool (change at Bidston on the Wirral line) call at General on request then at Wrexham Central in Hill Street, right in the middle of town. Part way along Regent Street, King Street branches off left to the **bus station** where infrequent *National Express* buses (tickets from *Key Travel* on King Street) arrive from Manchester, London and Glasgow and regular **local buses** leave to Chester, Llangollen and Mold. The **tourist office** is on Lambpit Street (April to mid-Oct Mon–Sat 10am–5pm; mid-Oct to March closes 4pm; ☎01978/292015), reached by turning left where Hope Street takes a turn to the right.

Accommodation

There's a reasonable choice of **places to stay** in Wrexham, most of them afford-able if not very exciting. The nearest **campsite** is the pricey *Plassey Leisure Park* (☎01978/780277), nearly four miles south at Eyton, with tent and caravan facili-ties, a swimming pool and a micro-brew pub.

Abbotsfield Priory Hotel, 29 Rhosddu Rd (☎01978/261211, fax 291413). Very comfortable hotel converted from an old priory. A 5-min walk from the town centre – follow Regent Street towards Wrexham General, then turn right into Grosvenor Road. ④.

Aldersey House, 25 Hightown Rd (☎01978/365687). Very good, central rooms without baths in one of the town's cheapest B&Bs. ③.

Grove Guesthouse, 36 Chester Rd (☎ & fax 01978/354288). Reasonably priced guesthouse with a couple of more expensive en-suite rooms. ③.

Littleton, 24 Bersham Rd (☎01978/352867). Comfortable B&B a 10-min walk from central Wrexham with welcoming, garrulous hosts. ③.

Lyndhurst Guesthouse, 3 Gerald St, off Grosvenor Road (☎01978/290802). Comfortable, central rooms, with a very warm welcome and good breakfasts. ③.

The Stableyard, High Street, 5 miles southwest in Bangor-on-Dee (☎ & fax 01978/780642). Attractive rooms and superb meals in a former tavern, in an appealing, ancient village. ③.

Eating and drinking

Wrexham isn't blessed with many great places to **eat**, but there are a few worth trying, along with cheap cafés on Bank Street, a narrow passage off Hope Street, and the odd undistinguished Chinese and curry restaurant. The **pubs** are better; but only just.

Bumble, 2 Charles St. Café above a gift shop, good for sandwiches and more substantial meals. Closed Sun.

Chequers Wine Bar, 7–9 Church St (☎01978/290910). About the best place to eat in town, with moderately priced bistro-style meals served during the day in the downstairs café, and an upstairs wine bar open Thurs–Sat evenings.

Golden Lion, High Street. Noisy pub serving a wide range of beers, including Wrexham Lager, Britain's first lager, brewed since 1882, using the town's naturally soft water supply. Well-prepared bar meals are available.

Horse and Jockey, Hope Street. Characterful, central low-beamed pub, also serving Wrexham Lager.

Plas Coch, Plas Coch Road (☎01978/261470). Three-course meals for around a fiver, a 15-min walk out past Wrexham General.

The Stableyard (see "Accommodation" above). A better bet than any of Wrexham's establishments, with excellent à la carte dishes and a £17 three-course table d'hôte menu.

The Clywedog Valley

The **Clywedog Valley**, which forms an arc around the western and southern suburbs of Wrexham, was the crucible of industrial achievement in the northern Welsh borders during the eighteenth century. Iron production boomed here, thanks to an abundance of ore deposits and cheap water power harnessed from the River Clywedog. As the Industrial Revolution forged ahead, however, coal became a more important energy source than water and factories moved closer to their raw materials, leaving the valley barely disturbed. Though considerable work is still being done, the emphasis is now on a series of modest attractions linked by the seven-mile-long **Clywedog Trail**. It is all a bit heavy on packaged heritage, but no less interesting for that, and you can see all the sights in one long, varied day, making use of the free *Clywedog Valley* leaflet available from tourist offices and any of the sites. With the exception of Minera and Nant Mill, all the sites are within a couple of miles of the centre of Wrexham, and can be visited on foot. The easiest way to see the whole valley from Wrexham is to catch the #10 or #11 bus to Minera, walk the full length of the trail to King's Mill, then catch the #31 the mile or so back into Wrexham. You can also catch the #2B bus between Wrexham and the Bersham Heritage Centre.

The **Minera Lead Mines** (April–July & Sept Tues–Sun 10am–5pm; Aug daily 10am–5pm; £1), four miles west of Wrexham, is the latest to get the heritage treatment. There isn't a lot to see, and many of the surface workings are still incompletely excavated, but the engine house and a pithead derrick have been largely rebuilt, and there's a good patch of reconstructed ore-processing machinery by the small museum in the former ore house. You get a far better impression of the site's layout, though, by walking up onto the hill behind – a heather-clad moor on the fringe of a region known as World's End – and looking back on the valley which, in the eighteenth century, was covered with mines extracting galena, a silver-and-zinc-rich lead ore from the bottom of shafts over 1200ft deep.

From the lead mines, a path leads for almost a mile east along the River Clywedog to the wildlife and local history centre at **Nant Mill** (Easter–Sept Tues–Sun 10am–5pm; Oct–Easter Sat & Sun 10am–4pm; free), where you can pick up leaflets for nature trails leading to a very visible section of **Offa's Dyke** (see p.228) in the woods nearby. The Clywedog Trail runs through the wood to **Bersham Ironworks** (Easter–Sept Tues–Sun 10am–5pm; £1), established in the seventeenth century and expanded by Cumbrian ironmaster John "Iron-Mad" Wilkinson who, in 1775, patented his new method for horizontally boring out cylinders. This produced the first truly circular, smooth bore, perfect for highly accurate cannons – hundreds were made here for the American Civil and Napoleonic wars – and the production of fine tolerance steam-engine cylinders. Engineer James Watt was a big customer: he produced steam engines which made water-powered sites unprofitable and eventually put Bersham out of business. After nearly two centuries of neglect, the remains are now being unearthed, revealing a broad area of mostly knee-high foundations around the centrepiece, the old foundry. This survived largely intact though it saw service as a corn mill and still retains its huge water wheel. The foundations really only serve to help you visualize the layout, which is better explained inside the old foundry and put in context ten minutes' walk away at the **Bersham Heritage Centre** (Easter–Oct Mon–Fri 10am–5pm, Sat & Sun noon–5pm; Nov–Easter closes 4pm; free), which has a room dedicated to Wilkinson.

Erddig Hall

Despite the closure of the ironworks, coal continued to be mined around Bersham until 1986. After World War II, coal tunnels were pushed under **Erddig Hall**, just south of Wrexham (April–Oct Mon–Wed, Sat & Sun; house noon–5pm, 4pm in Oct; garden 11am–6pm, 5pm in Oct; £5.20, "below stairs" & gardens only £3.40; NT), adding subsidence to the troubles of an already decaying building. Ever since the mansion was built in the late seventeenth century, its owners – all seemingly called Simon or Philip Yorke – maintained a conservative building policy which resulted in near decrepitude. Chief culprit was the fourth Simon Yorke, who inherited the estate in 1922 and did almost nothing, failing to instal electricity, running water, gas or a phone and ignoring a chronic damp problem which had the Chinese hand-blocked paper peeling off the walls. The National Trust took charge in the 1970s, since when it has restored the house to its 1922 appearance and returned the jungle of a garden to its formal eighteenth-century plan.

The house itself isn't distinguished, but, as nothing was ever thrown away, the collection of fine furniture and portraits – including one by Gainsborough of the first Philip Yorke – is unusually complete. The real interest, however, lies in the servants' quarters, particularly the Servants' Hall, where specially commissioned portraits of eighteenth- and early-nineteenth-century staff members are accompanied by personalized dedications in verse written by a Yorke – a quite extraordinary display of benevolence. You can also see the blacksmith's shop, stables, laundry, the still-used bakehouse and kitchen.

Put an hour aside for the **walled garden**, saved from the worst excesses of the eighteenth-century landscaping craze despite the attentions of William Emes, a contemporary of Capability Brown, who worked on the surrounding parkland. Manicured box hedges delineate beds planted with pleached lime trees, the walls support some 150 species of ivy, and trained apple trees produce fruit celebrated during the Hall's annual apple festival in October.

To get back to Wrexham from Erddig Hall, head half a mile or so northeast to *Squire Yorke Inn*, from where it's about a mile along the road. If you're keen to see corn being milled, head another mile or so northeast from the *Squire Yorke Inn* to **King's Mill Visitor Centre** (Easter–Sept daily except Mon 10am–5pm; £1).

Mold and around

MOLD (Yr Wyddgrug), ten miles north of Wrexham, enjoys a quiet, almost moribund existence disrupted only by the Wednesday and Saturday markets when stalls take the place of cars along the High Street. In truth, there's no great reason for a visit, though you may as well stop in on the way to **Ewloe Castle**, just four miles to the northeast or approaching the Clwydian Hills to the west.

The town was founded during the reign of William Rufus, though only a bowling green and a copse of beeches atop a mound mark the site of the motte-and-bailey fortifications on **Bailey Hill**, at the top of the High Street. The fort was built for the local Norman lord, Robert de Montalt, who probably gave the town its English name, essentially the same as the Welsh, meaning "The Mound". The commanding view over the River Alyn (Afon Alun) illustrates the strategic importance of the site, first taken by Owain Gwynedd in 1157 and again in 1199 by Llywelyn the Great, constantly shifting between Welsh and Anglo-Norman control until Edward I's hand came down hard on the region. Relative calm prevailed until a period during the Wars of the Roses, when private armies held sway. In 1465, after a skirmish in the town, local lord Rheinallt ap Gruffydd succeeded in capturing the Mayor of Chester and taking him back to the Tower in Nercwys, where he was presented with a pie containing the rope that would be his noose. A revenge party from Chester attempted to raid the Tower but was locked inside and the place subsequently torched by Rheinallt's men.

Henry VII's assumption of the throne, after his victory at the Battle of Bosworth, stamped some stability on the area. In gratitude for her son's victory, Henry's mother, Margaret Beaufort, commissioned the airy Perpendicular **St Mary's Church** on the site of a thirteenth-century church at the foot of Bailey Hill. The original oak roof carved with Tudor roses has been retained in the north aisle, as has a quatrefoil and animal frieze running below the small clerestory windows, though most of the rest was restored by Gilbert Scott last century.

Amongst the predominantly fifteenth- and sixteenth-century stained glass, one more modern, late-nineteenth-century window represents the town's meagre memorial to its most famous son (at least to English-speakers) and Wales' greatest painter, the eighteenth-century landscapist **Richard Wilson**, whose grave is by the church's north entrance. Having spent his childhood here, Wilson studied in Italy for six years, where he painted canvases from the Grand Tour, earning a good enough living to support himself back home while he concentrated on the subject for which he is best known: the mountains of Wales, typically dramatic scenes of Cadair Idris or Snowdon, often incorporating Latin elements into the Romantic panoramas. In the decades before John Ruskin's championing of Turner influenced critical taste, Wilson's style went undervalued, and though he co-founded the Royal Academy in 1768 and later won the acclaim of Ruskin, he died a pauper. The story goes that, in return for a few pints, he painted the two-headed sign for the *We Three Loggerheads* pub outside the Loggerheads Country Park (see overleaf), the third loggerhead being the viewer.

Mold is no Welsh-language stronghold, so it seems ironic that it is **Daniel Owen**, a local tailor and nineteenth-century novelist, who should be commemorated by a statue, outside the library. "Not for the wise and learned have I written, but for the common people" is inscribed below the statue and it was his bluntly honest accounts of ordinary life that made him so unpopular with the Methodist leaders of the community. Writing only in Welsh, Owen became the most prominent writer of the late nineteenth century. A room full of his memorabilia takes up a sizeable portion of the small but effective **museum**, housed in the same building as the town's library and tourist office (hours as for tourist office below; free).

There's little else to see in Mold itself, but three miles west on the A494 (bus #B5), **Loggerheads Country Park** offers forest walks and nature trails with views of the Clwydian Range. Pick up more information at the **visitor centre** by the entrance (Mon–Fri 11am–4.30pm, Sat & Sun 10am–5pm; closes earlier in winter).

Practicalities

Mold has no train station, but regular **bus** services stop behind the cattle market east of High Street. From there it is a five-minute walk down King Street to Earl Road and the **tourist office**-cum-library (Mon & Tues, Thurs & Fri 9.30am–7pm, Wed 9.30am–5.30pm, Sat 9.30am–12.30pm or 4pm in summer; ☎01352/759331).

Accommodation isn't plentiful, but close to the centre you have a choice of the classy *Bryn Awel Hotel*, on Denbigh Road (☎01352/758622; ⑤), five minutes' walk north of the church, or *Glendale Lodge* (☎01352/754001; ③), just past *Theatr Clwyd*. The nearest **YHA hostel** (Easter, July & Aug only; ☎01352/810320; ①) is an ageing affair with unusual three-tier bunks at Maeshafn, four miles southwest of Mold, near Loggerheads Country Park. You can camp here and use the facilities at reduced rates.

If you can't stretch to the moderately priced **meals** at *Chez Colette*, 56 High St (☎01352/759225), there are numerous cheap cafés nearby. *We Three Loggerheads* (see p.371) is the best of the **pubs** for both meals and drinking, while **entertainment** revolves around the region's major arts centre, *Theatr Clwyd* (☎01352/755114), a mile east on the A494. It suffered a major funding crisis after its major patron, Clwyd County Council, was disbanded in 1996, but indications are that it will continue to present quality theatre and cinema – it recently screened the world premiere of *August* starring Welshman Anthony Hopkins, for instance – aided by revenue from the good arts bookshop and café.

Ewloe Castle

If only to put Edward I's monstrous castles into perspective, **Ewloe Castle** (unrestricted access; CADW), four miles northeast of Mold, makes an interesting diversion. Tucked in at the end of a wooded glen, it is so cloaked by sycamore and oak that you almost stumble into the ruins. An English stronghold which fell into Welsh hands around 1146, it was being fortified by Owain Gwynedd as an ambush castle when the Battle of Eulo took place in 1157. According to Giraldus Cambrensis, Henry II's "rash enthusiasm" hindered this first assault on Wales, and his push through the wooded pass resulted in the death of many of his men. In gratitude for his own life, the king contributed funds towards the building of Basingwerk Abbey (see p.383).

In 1210 Llywelyn ap Iorwerth ("the Great") built the apsidal Welsh Tower and his grandson, Llywelyn ap Gruffydd ("the Last"), went on to add two wards, protected by a curtain wall and an outer ditch; but while Ewloe was never of great importance, after the completion of Flint Castle in around 1283, it ceased to have any military significance at all.

Until preservation work was begun in the 1920s, local builders had helped themselves to the masonry, leaving just the shell at the head of a valley filled by the ancient woodland of **Wepre Park** (Parc Gwepra). The **visitor centre** (variable hours; ☎01244/814931) for both park and castle is ten minutes' walk from the latter, and a mile or so from Shotton train station, on the North Coast line, four miles southeast of Flint; walk towards the *Somerfield* supermarket, then turn left up Wepre Drive.

The Vale of Clwyd

To the west of Mold, separated from the English Marches and the industry on Deeside by the soft contours of the broad-backed Clwydian Range, the wide and fertile **Vale of Clwyd** follows the sandstone course of the barely noticeable River Clwyd (Afon Clywedog), from Corwen on the A5 (see p.250) to the coast near Rhuddlan. Linked by quiet roads through a patchwork of small farms, three attractive towns of warm-hued stone sit on hillocks above the valley. None warrants more than a couple of hours' attention, but together they make a good day's diversion and a link between the north coast and the route up the Dee Valley towards Snowdonia.

Churches loom large in the valley. Britain's smallest cathedral dominates the village-sized city of **St Asaph**, at the valley's northernmost tip, but the building is barely larger than the parish church in the ancient market town of **Ruthin**, thirteen miles south. Both these buildings and the ancient village church at **Llanrhaeadr**, midway between them, were modernized in the nineteenth century, but it is the last which remains the Vale's prime example of medieval ecclesiastical architecture. **Denbigh**, four miles south of St Asaph, is better known for its "hollow crown", the high-walled castle ruin which rings the top of the hill behind the town.

The old rail line from Corwen to Rhyl has long since gone, leaving regular **buses** along the A525 between Rhyl and Corwen as the primary transport route.

Ruthin

Though surrounded by modern housing and known primarily as a livestock market town, the centre of **RUTHIN** (Rhuthun), ten miles west of Mold, comprises an attractive knot of half-timbered buildings set between church and castle. It is built on a commanding rise in the Vale of Clwyd, close to lands once held by Owain Glyndŵr, which made it ripe for the first push of his quest for dominion over all of Wales in 1400. The heavily restored red-stone **Ruthin Castle** (not open to public), dating from Edward I's first stint of castle-building, was then home to Lord de Grey of Ruthin, a favourite of Henry IV. Coveting a tract of land above Corwen held by Glyndŵr, de Grey used his influence with Henry to have Glyndŵr proclaimed a traitor and was given the land in return. He was thus the first to suffer when Glyndŵr had himself crowned Prince of Wales and with four thousand followers launched an attack on Ruthin on September 20, 1400. The castle itself held, but the town was razed – though not until Glyndŵr's men had plundered the goods brought by the English to the town's annual fair. The castle went on to resist the Parliamentarians for eleven weeks during the Civil War, eventually falling to General Mytton in April 1646, after which it was destroyed. Over three hundred years later, in 1963, it was partially restored as a hotel (see "Practicalities"), with Italian and rose gardens landscaped around the ancient moat and crumbling ruins. Strictly, the grounds are only open to residents and peacocks, but you can wander through if attending one of the ersatz medieval banquets or drinking in the panelled library bar.

Otherwise, time is better spent browsing the mixed bag of architectural styles around St Peter's Square, the heart of the town's medieval street plan. The northeast corner is dominated by the twin-aisled **St Peter's Church** (daily 9am–4pm or thereabouts), approached through a beautiful pair of 1728 iron gates wrought by the Davies Brothers who also made the gates of St Giles church in Wrexham and Chirk Castle. Impressive though the church gates are, they are upstaged by the ceiling of the north aisle: here, 408 carved black oak panels meet at Tudor Rose bosses. This part of the building dates from the fourteenth century, when it was founded as a collegiate church, but Henry VII reputedly donated the ceiling, possibly from Basingwerk Abbey (see p.383), in gratitude to those who helped him take the English throne. The details can be hard to see, but a switch by the hymn board provides illumination for twenty seconds at a time, and the more intriguing designs – grotesque faces and floral and geometric designs – are reproduced on a panel opposite the door. One of the busts on the north wall is of Gabriel Goodman, who, in 1574, while Dean of Westminster, re-founded the **grammar school** that had been closed by Henry VIII forty years earlier; it still stands behind the church, next to the Christ's Hospital Almshouses, which Goodman built in 1590 as a gift to the town.

Goodman's birthplace in St Peter's Square, Exmewe Hall, is now occupied by a branch of *Barclays* bank, but outside sits an unimpressive chunk of limestone known as **Maen Huail**, testament to the darker side of King Arthur's character. The less-than-convincing story has Arthur and Huail, brother of a Welsh chieftain called Gildas, fighting over the attentions of a woman. Huail pierced Arthur's thigh, giving him a permanent limp, but promised never to mention Arthur's loss of face. Inevitably, though, Huail couldn't resist taunting him about it and an incensed Arthur had Huail beheaded on this stone.

Standing isolated on the other side of the square is one of the many half-timbered buildings around the town. Now the *National Westminster* bank, it was built in 1401 as a courthouse and prison and still retains under the eaves the barely visible stump of the **gibbet**, last used in 1679 to hang a Franciscan friar.

The most-photographed building in Ruthin isn't any of these, but the **Myddleton Arms pub**, built in 1657 in Dutch style and topped by seven dormer windows known as "The Eyes of Ruthin".

Practicalities

Buses from Denbigh, Corwen and Mold all stop on Market Street, running between St Peter's Square and the valley's best **tourist office** (June–Sept daily 10am–5.30pm; Oct–May Mon–Sat 10am–5pm, Sun noon–5pm; ☎01824/703992), 300 yards away inside the *Ruthin Craft Centre*. Ruthin is well provided with **accommodation**. Top of the range is *Ruthin Castle Hotel* (☎01824/702664, fax 704924; ⑧), but the *Castle Hotel* (☎01824/70479; ④), a former coaching inn on the square, and the spacious thirteenth-century wood-panelled *Gorffwystfa* B&B, just around the corner on Castle Street (☎01824/702748; ③), are also very comfortable. Otherwise try *Moelfa* on Denbigh Road (☎01824/702468; ③), or *Ye Olde Cross Keys* (☎01824/705281; ③), five minutes' walk west along the B5105. Out of town on the disused Corwen to Rhyl line, the pleasant *Eyarth Old Railway Station* (☎01824/703643; ④), also serves decent meals; take bus #51 to Llanfair Dyffryn Clwyd, from where it's a half-mile walk. You'll also need transport to get to the seventeenth-century *Three Pigeons Inn* (☎01824/703178; ③) in Graigfechan, a mile east on the A494 Mold road, then three miles south on the B5429. It serves good beer and food, with Sunday barbecues in summer, and has live Welsh and Irish music most Saturday nights. There's a simple **campsite** (March–Oct) tucked in behind.

The range of good **food** in Ruthin itself is very limited. Bar meals are available from the pubs around the square, notably *Ye Olde Anchor Inn* on Rhos Street, and you can get a decent curry at *The India Cottage* (☎01824/707277), tucked up an alley off Clwyd Street. *Ruthin Castle Hotel* has medieval banquets (usually Fri & Sat; ☎01824/703435; £25) and serves cream teas (2.30–5.30pm), but frankly you're better off with a drink in the bar.

If gloomy buildings become too claustrophobic, there are **walks** along the Clwydian Range to Moel Famau and Foel Fenlli (see box below), and **horse riding** at the *Star Farm Riding Centre* (March–Nov; ☎01824/705929) at Llangynafal, four miles north of Ruthin.

WALK TO MOEL FAMAU AND FOEL FENLLI

Walks on Moel Famau and Foel Fenlli both start from Bwlch-Pen-Barras, a pass four miles east of Ruthin at the top of the B5429, once used for the main turnpike route over the Clwydian Range to Mold. The **Offa's Dyke long-distance path** (though not the Dyke itself) runs along these bald tops (*moel*, and its initial mutation *foel*, mean "bare mountain"), following the line of a Bronze Age trading route, past the remains of six Iron Age hillforts surrounding the tops and the Jubilee Tower. Proximity to Liverpool, Chester and Wrexham, and the relatively gentle terrain, make this a popular spot at weekends: stick to weekdays if possible. No public transport comes this way but you can walk two miles up the road from Llanbedr-Dyffryn-Clwyd (bus #B5 from Ruthin) to begin a walk at either of two car parks.

From the first car park (free), right at the top of Bwlch-Pen-Barras, you can make the steep climb southwards to the most impressive of the hillfort sites on 1800-foot **Foel Fenlli** (1 mile return; 40min; 500-ft ascent). Excavations here uncovered 35 hut circles within earthworks three-quarters of a mile across. The height from ditch bottom to bank top reaches 35ft in places, with triple defences on the less easily defended eastern flank. Aerial shots make much more of this than is visible on the ground, but that doesn't detract from the walk.

From the same car park, a broad path leads a mile and a half north to the 1820-foot "Mothers' Mountain", **Moel Famau** (3 miles return; 1–2hr; 650-ft ascent), the highest point in the range, topped by the truncated **Jubilee Tower**. The subject of many a disparaging remark when it was built in 1810 to celebrate George III's fifty-year reign, the top of this Egyptian-style structure was never completed. The planned pyramid was to rise to 150ft but was damaged in a storm in 1860 and only partially repaired in 1970. The ruins may not be much, but on a clear day the views over the Vale of Clwyd as far as Snowdon and Cadair Idris make it all worthwhile.

An alternative, less dramatic, approach to Moel Famau leaves a second car park (£1) half a mile or so down the eastern side of the pass, from where an easy blue-marked path (3.5 miles return; 2hr 30min; 900-ft ascent) or slightly harder red path (2.5 miles return; 2hr; 900-ft ascent) guide you through Corsican pine plantations up the southeastern flank to the tower.

Llanrhaeadr

Just off the A525, four miles north of Ruthin, **St Dyfnog's Church** seems much too large for the tiny hamlet of **LLANRHAEADR**. In the sixth century Saint Dyfnog established a hermitage here on the site of a healing well, and donations from pilgrims funded the building of the present church in 1533. Typically for the area it has twin aisles and, though heavily restored in 1880, drips with original features, including a glorious carved barrel roof with vine-leaf patterns and outstanding stained glass. The **Jesse Window**, at the east end of the north aisle, is considered to be one of the finest examples in Britain. Depicting the descent of Jesus through the House of Israel from Jesse, the father of King David, it draws you in to the Virgin and Child above the central light, surrounded by 21 of their bearded, ermine-robed ancestors, whose names are recorded in medieval Latin. The window is believed to be original, contemporary with the church, though it was removed and stored in an oak chest during the Civil War, which is when its companion in the south aisle is thought to have been destroyed. Fragments that may have belonged to it were found nearby and pieced together to form the west window in the nineteenth century.

Reached on the hourly #51 bus, Llanrhaeadr is an easy trip from Ruthin or Denbigh; or you can **stay** just across the road at the *King's Head Inn* (☎01745/890278; ③), a well-preserved sixteenth-century coaching inn with a wide choice of food and a low-beamed bar.

Denbigh and around

The hilltop castle ruins dominating the Vale of Clwyd eight miles north of Ruthin herald **DENBIGH** (Dinbych), a former bastide town (see p.397) which tumbles down the hill towards the medieval centre. The glove-making industry for which the town was once famed has vanished, leaving it merely hosting Tuesday and Friday markets and servicing the sprawling postwar development on its outskirts.

The market takes place on the broad central section of the High Street, surrounded by a pleasing array of colonnaded medieval buildings. Thankfully, they haven't been over-restored and, together with the more modern structures in their midst, help retain a working town atmosphere. Beside *The Old Vaults* pub on the High Street, Broomhill Lane runs up past the crumbling **Burgess Gate**, the former northern entry to the town, to the vast grassy ward of the ruined **Denbigh Castle** (unrestricted access; CADW).

For a long time, the River Clwyd formed the border of England and Wales, guarded here by an unidentified castle built by Dafydd, brother of Llywelyn ap Gruffydd ("the Last"). This probably gave the town its name, meaning "small fort", though it's more imaginatively attributed to John Salusbury, a medieval knight said to have rid the town of a dragon, triumphantly returning with its head to cries of "Dim Dych!" (No More Dragon!). Dafydd's castle put up strong resistance, but eventually fell, allowing Edward I to erect castles here and at the other key sites of Rhuddlan and Ruthin. By 1282, only the outer defences – the town walls – had been started, under the charge of Henry de Lacy, Earl of Lincoln, who required each of his 63 burgesses to "find a man armed in Denbigh to guard and defend the town". This wasn't enough to repel a Welsh revolt in 1294, which though rapidly suppressed, goaded de Lacy into work on the castle proper, employing many of the concepts already implemented by Edward's architect, James of St George.

The most imposing piece of what remains is the **gatehouse**, its three octagonal towers enclosing an originally vaulted hall, making it one of the finest defensive structures of the era. Entrance is beneath a weathered statue of Edward I in a niche, flanked on the right by the Prison Tower, still showing evidence of five garderobes that discharge into a common cesspit, and the Porter's Lodge Tower on the left. From here, you can walk the only remaining section of the wall, extending as far as the Great Kitchen Tower with its two huge fireplaces. On the far side, the Postern Tower was heavily strengthened after 1294, as were the **town walls** that formed the outer ward branching off at the castle walls. Continue along the short section of wall walk (key from the tourist office) down to the **Goblin Tower** from where, at the end of a six-month-long siege in 1646, Charles I threw the castle keys onto the heads of the all-conquering Roundheads.

In 1563, Elizabeth I sold the castle to her favourite Robert Dudley, Earl of Leicester, who in 1579 chose a site just below the castle for the church that he hoped would supplant St Asaph cathedral. It was never completed, but the shell still stands today as **Leicester's Folly**.

Back on High Street, the sixteenth-century County Hall contains the local library, the tourist office and a small **local history museum** (same hours as tourist office, see below; free) with its impressionistic modern mural of Denbigh running up the stairwell. There's also background on Denbigh's famous sons, such as Humphrey Llwyd who, in the sixteenth century, drew up the first separate map of Wales, published posthumously in 1573. He is commemorated in the **St Marcella's Church** (usually closed), a mile east of the centre on Whitchurch Road. Here the cemetery contains the grave of the bard, satirist and playwright Tom o'r Nant or "Tom of the Dingle", who George Borrow casually refers to as "the Welsh Shakespeare". Tom in his autobiography writes, "As soon as I had learned to spell and write a few words I conceived a mighty desire to learn to write; so I went in quest of elderberries to make me ink."

Less esoterically minded visitors might be tempted in the direction of the **Bracdy Dyffryn Clwyd Brewery** (☎01745/815007) on Chapel Place behind the Market Hall. In only three years of operation it has gained an enviable reputation for its beers, and groups of ten or more can arrange a tour and substantial sampling (£3 each), while individuals are welcome at quiet times. Annoyingly, you can't yet drink the beer in Denbigh, but look out for the bilingual pump-handle clips in pubs around north Wales. The premium *Pedwar Bawd* ("Four Thumbs") is particularly good.

Practicalities

All **buses** stop on the High Street, just along from the combined library, museum and **tourist office** in Hall Square (Mon, Wed & Fri 9.30am–7pm, Tues & Thurs 9.30am–5.30pm, Sat 9.30am–4pm; ☎01745/816313), where you can pick up some useful handouts detailing town walks. **Accommodation** in the centre is pretty much limited to *The Bull Hotel* (☎01745/812582; ③), just beside the tourist office, and *Cayo Guesthouse*, 74 Vale St (☎01745/812686; ③), a couple of hundred yards down the main St Asaph road. If you have your own transport, you should try one of the excellent rural B&Bs in the vicinity. *College Farm* (☎01745/550276; ③), at Peniel three miles southwest of town on the B4501 is good, as is *Fron Haul*

Farmhouse, in Bodfari, four miles northeast along the A543 (☎01745/710301; ③), which also serves good meals. People with dogs are particularly welcome at the friendly and comfortable *Berllan Bach*, Ffordd Las, three miles east at Llandyrnog, at the foot of the Clwydian Range (☎01824/790732; ④), where good country dinners go for around £13 – from the roundabout at the southern end of Denbigh, head east through Llanwfan, past the *Kinmel Arms*, then straight on for another half a mile. The most convenient **campsite** is the *Station House Caravan Park* (☎01745/710372) at Bodfari, reached on bus #14.

There are no outstanding **restaurants** in Denbigh, but you can eat well enough. *The Bull Hotel* provides straightforward bar meals, while kebabs and other Middle Eastern dishes are served at the inexpensive Kurdish *Kürdoğlu's Castle*, 6 Love Lane (☎01745/815156). Finding a decent place to **drink** is no problem: *The Old Vaults* on High Street is good, or make for Back Row, behind High Street, for the *Y Llew Aur* (*The Golden Lion*) and *Y Llew Gwyn* (*The White Lion*). There's another *Golden Lion* five miles southeast at Llangynhafal, where the Saturday evening **Welsh singalongs**, complete with close harmonies, often draw local choral groups. Back in town, the *Hope & Anchor*, 94 Vale St, also has folk evenings every Saturday.

The Clocaenog Forest and Llyn Brenig

The high land to the west of the Vale of Clwyd is rolling sheep country, dissected by narrow lanes and the meandering streams which run off the bleak **Mynydd Hiraethog** moorland to the south. The peaty soil and challenging climate on this 1200-foot high plateau support a delicate ecosystem with cottongrass, marsh marigold, the lilac-white cuckoo flower and the pink lousewort thriving amongst the heath, buzzards wheeling overhead and trout plucking at stoneflies and mayflies. But, as elsewhere in Wales, the evergreens are on the march and, over the last couple of decades, vast areas of "wasteland" have been planted with Sitka Spruce, Japanese Larch and Norwegian Spruce to form the **Clocaenog Forest**. At its heart lies the **Llyn Brenig** reservoir, used in conjunction with the waters of Llyn Celyn near Bala to control the water level in the River Dee and providing modest opportunities for aquatic diversion. Few visitors penetrate the area, except to speed through on the A543, the fastest route from Denbigh to Betws-y-Coed and Snowdonia, but locals flock to the **Llyn Brenig Centre** (mid-March to late Oct daily 10am–5pm; £1 per car), just off the B4501, principally for rainbow **trout fishing**. A permit will set you back £10 for the day and boats can be rented for the day (£17), morning (£11) or afternoon from 3pm (£12). The two-mile lakeside drive north from here leads to *Celtic Adventure: Brenig Watersports* (April–Oct daily 9am–5pm; ☎01490/440408) where you can rent kayaks, open canoes and windsurfers at reasonable rates, or launch your own craft for £3–4 a half-day. Windsurfing and canoeing courses run in summer for around £20 a day: they're mainly aimed at groups but you may be able to tag along. Landlubbers can entertain themselves nearby on the mile-long waymarked forest and moorland **nature trail**.

St Asaph

Five miles north of Denbigh, at the point where the valley opens out onto the north coast flats, the cluster of houses centred on a single main street ranks as

Britain's second smallest city, **ST ASAPH** (Llanelwy). The city of St David's in Pembrokeshire is slightly less populous, but St Asaph boasts the country's smallest **cathedral** (open daily 8am–dusk). It is no bigger than many village churches, standing on a rise above the River Elwy (Afon Elwy) with its squat square tower at the crossing of a broad, aisled nave and a well-lit transept.

The town's Welsh name translates as "the church on Elwy River", a title which dates back to the sixth century when Saint Asaph succeeded the cathedral's founder, Saint Kentigern, as abbot in 570, and became its first bishop. Both are commemorated in the easternmost window in the north aisle of the cathedral. There is almost no record of the place from then until 1282, when Edward I's men stormed through and destroyed the church, leaving the incumbent bishop Anian II, whose effigy is in the south aisle, with the task of building the present structure. That too was attacked in 1402 by Owain Glyndŵr, but this time only the woodwork was lost and soon replaced.

From 1601 until his death in 1604, the bishopric was held by **William Morgan** (see box overleaf), who was responsible for the translation of the first Welsh-language bible in 1588. An octagonal monument to Morgan, in the churchyard on the south side of the cathedral, commemorates the work of Morgan and his fellow translators, including William Salusbury and Gabriel Goodman (see p.374). This is Morgan's only memorial; his grave under the presbytery has been unmarked since Giles Gilbert Scott's substantial restoration in the 1870s.

Around a thousand Morgan bibles were printed – one for every church in the land – of which only nineteen remain, one of them displayed in the north transept. The cathedral also has a handsome collection of psalter and prayer books in an alcove in the south transept, Elizabeth I's 1549 copy of *The Book of Common Prayer* only slightly predating Salusbury's New Testament translation of 1567. Tucked into a recess in one of the columns opposite is an exquisite sixteenth-century ivory Madonna, said to have come from the Spanish Armada, and a plaque nearby commemorates native son and explorer, Henry Morton Stanley.

Contact the Dean in advance (☎01745/583597) for access into the crypt to view the cathedral **treasury**, which, alongside its collection of silverware, contains a Welsh–Greek–Hebrew dictionary compiled in the nineteenth century by Richard Robert Jones, usually known as Dic Aberdaron, a self-taught scholar who reputedly knew fifteen languages and smatterings of another twenty. The son of a fisherman, he was born in Aberdaron (see p.353) in 1780 and lived more or less as a tramp. His tombstone, in the churchyard of St Kentigern and St Asaph's Church at the bottom of the High Street, is engraved with a few lines by Ellis Owen which translate as:

> *A linguist eight times above other linguists – truly he was*
> *A dictionary of every province.*
> *Death took away his fifteen languages.*
> *Below he is now without a language at all.*

Practicalities

The A55 runs close by, but without your own transport you're reliant on local **buses**, which all stop right outside the cathedral. If you plan to **stay** in the region you may be better off at places listed under Denbigh (p.377) or Rhyl (p.385), though you can get good central rooms with showers at the *Kentigern Arms* towards the bottom of the High Street (☎01745/584157; ④). A quarter of a mile away are the

WILLIAM MORGAN AND THE FIRST WELSH BIBLE

Until 1588 only English Bibles had been used in Welsh churches, a fact which rankled Welsh-born preacher William Morgan, who insisted that "Religion, if it is not taught in the mother tongue, will lie hidden and unknown". This was the professed reason behind Elizabeth I's demand for a translation, though her subjects' disaffection could be most conveniently controlled through the church. Four clergymen took up the challenge over a period of 25 years, but it is Morgan who is remembered: working away in Llanrhaeadr-ym-Mochnant (see p.237), he so neglected his duties that he needed an armed guard to get to his services and was said to preach with a pistol at his side.

The eventual translation was so successful that the Privy Council decreed that a copy should be allocated to every Welsh church. Though it was soon replaced by a translation of the Authorized Version, Morgan's Bible differs little in style from the latest edition used in Welsh services today. More than just a basis for sermons, The *Welsh Bible* (*Y Beibl*) served to codify the language and set a standard for Welsh prose. Without it the language would probably have divided into several dialects or even followed its Brythonic cousin, Cornish, into history.

nicely furnished, non-smoking *Chalet* (☎01745/584025; ③) and the plush *Plas Elwy* (☎01745/582263; ⑤), both on The Roe – across the river bridge then right.

Snacks, coffee and picnic supplies are available from the *Farm Shop*, halfway down High Street. For more substantial **meals**, make for the *Kentigern Arms* which, as well as being Denbigh's most appealing pub, serves inexpensive bar food and crispy pizzas; or walk across the High Street to the seventeenth-century former almshouse now operating as St Asaph's best restaurant, the moderately priced *Barrow Alms* (☎01745/582260).

THE NORTH COAST

Wales' northern seaboard elicits strong reactions. The ranks of detractors citing obscenely tacky resorts at its eastern end are matched by files of advocates beholden to the charms of those same towns or drawn to the more highbrow attractions further west. Either way, the English borderlands and the interior of northeast Wales are poor preparation for the **north coast**, which peels away from England at **Deeside**, a wedge of former mining country between the salt marshes of the Dee estuary and the Clwydian Range that has its share of modest offerings – among them **Flint**, where you'll find the first link in Edward I's Iron Ring of castles, and understated **Holywell**, whose quiet attractions include St Winefride's Well, a pilgrimage site of varied fortunes during the last thirteen hundred years.

The next 20-mile stretch of sand constitutes the ugliest piece of coastline in Wales, an endless stretch of cramped caravan parks – there's barely an arm's length between neighbouring caravans – packed each year with fun-seekers from Merseyside and the rest of northern England. The "amusements" liberally scattered along the promenades and beachfronts seem designed to keep you off the beaches: wise counsel even in the hottest weather since the sea here is none too clean. Of the resorts, **Prestatyn**, though uninspiring, is at least notable as the starting, or finishing, point of the Offa's Dyke long-distance path. **Rhyl** is the largest and tackiest, although it's full of good budget accommodation, and enjoys proximity to two inland attractions: the second of Edward I's castles at **Rhuddlan** and the National Portrait Gallery's Welsh outpost at **Bodelwyddan**. **Colwyn Bay** is better, but pales next to its far superior western neighbours, Conwy and Llandudno.

The great sweep of the north coast is interrupted by the Great Orme, a massive limestone hummock that rises above **Llandudno**, queen of the north Wales coast for over a hundred years. Neighbouring **Conwy** is more appealing still, packing more sights than the rest of the coast put together into the girdle of 700-year-old town walls which spur off from the mighty castle. The A55 expressway is held tightly to the coast by the northern fringes of Snowdonia's Carneddau range for the final fifteen miles to **Bangor**, home to north Wales' only university and consequently its liveliest town.

Deeside

The industrial hinterland that spreads over the border from Chester and licks the fringes of Mold and Wrexham can best be avoided by heading directly for **DEE-SIDE**, a narrow littoral flanking the River Dee where it broadens out into an expansive estuary. Its salt-soaked fields support huge numbers of waders and **wildfowl**, who come to feed on the sands and mudflats left by retreating tides. Plovers, oystercatchers and Europe's largest concentration of pintails winter here, pushing the population into six figures. The only designated viewing point is the RSPB's **Point of Ayr** site, two miles east of Prestatyn at the head of the estuary, the now-defunct colliery – the last to close in north Wales – and the off-shore gas terminal discouraging all but the keenest of birders. The route there, along the A548 or the North Coast train line, passes an untidy string of largely uninteresting settlements. The crumbling castle remains at **Flint** should only detain you briefly, though you may want longer to pay homage to St Winefride and her healing waters at **Holywell**, especially if you're drawn to the adjacent minor collection of historic industrial buildings of the **Greenfield Valley Heritage Park**. By car, the easiest way to access Deeside is from the A55, where the westbound *Autolodge* service station, four miles south of Holywell, is home to Deeside's main **tourist office** (Easter to mid-Oct daily 9.30am–5.30pm; mid-Oct to Easter Fri–Sun 9.30am–4.30pm; ☎01244/541597).

Flint

If you are travelling on the North Coast train line, be sure to take one of the regional services which stop at **FLINT** (Y Fflint), seven miles north of Mold, and spend the hour between trains rambling around the yellowish sandstone ruins of **Flint Castle** (unrestricted access; CADW), two minutes' walk over the footbridge from the station. Started in 1277 after the Treaty of Aberconwy, this was the first of Edward I's "Iron Ring" of fortresses (see p.397), standing sentinel over the coastal marshes of the Dee estuary and the once-important shipping lanes into Chester. The ten-foot-thick pockmarked sandstone walls form a square with drum towers at all except the southeast corner, where a small moat and drawbridge separate the castle from the well-preserved Great Tower, or Donjon. Unique in Britain, this was intended as the castle's main accommodation and last place of retreat, and came equipped with its own well. Together with its large grassy outer ward and the adjoining town, the castle formed a unified enclave known as a "bastide" (see p.397). Though Conwy and Caernarfon subsequently received the same treatment, Flint can claim to be the first borough in Wales to receive its charter, in September 1284. Until then, towns didn't really exist in essentially rural Wales.

Perhaps Flint's greatest hour came in 1399 when Richard II was lured here from the safety of Conwy Castle and captured by Henry Bolingbroke, the Duke of Lancaster and future Henry IV. Shakespeare dramatized the event in *Richard II*, when in response to Bolingbroke's, "My gracious Lord, I come but for mine own", the defeated king replies, "Your own is yours, and I am yours, and all". Even Richard's favourite greyhound is said to have deserted him at this point.

During the Civil War, Flint remained Royalist until taken in 1647 by General Mytton, who so effectively dismantled it that only six years later it was practically buried in its own ruins. It was in this condition when Celia Fiennes found it on the brief – and generally displeasing – Welsh leg of her journeys around Britain between 1698 and 1712. She described Flint as "a very ragged place", and things haven't changed much. Unless you have come to spot some of the hundred thousand wintering waders on the Dee estuary, you'll probably want to move on by the hourly **trains** or **buses** which leave from outside *The Raven* pub, a few yards north from the station along Holywell Street, the main coast road.

Holywell and around

For thirteen hundred years a place of pilgrimage, **HOLYWELL** (Treffynnon), just off the A55 four miles northwest of Flint, comes billed as "The Lourdes of Wales", though it doesn't really warrant such a comparison. There are no tacky souvenir stalls and for most of the year there are few pilgrims – in fact there's not even much of a town and what there is is best avoided. The source of all the fuss is **St Winefride's Well** (mid-May to Sept daily 9am–5.15pm; Oct to mid-May daily 10am–4pm; 20p donation) – half a mile from the bus station at the far end of the High Street, then turn right and follow the signs – a spring first recorded by the Romans, who used the waters to relieve rheumatism and gout. This sheds considerable doubt on the veracity of the legend that relates an event from around 660 AD. The virtuous Winefride (*Gwenfrewi* in Welsh) was decapitated here after resisting the amorous advances of Prince Caradoc, and the well is said to have sprung up at the spot where her head fell. When Saint Beuno, her uncle, placed her head beside the body, a combination of prayer and the waters revived her, setting her on track for the rest of her life as an abbess at Gwytherin Convent near Llanrwst.

Richard I and Henry V provided regal patronage, ensuring a steady flow of believers to what became one of the great shrines of Christendom. After the Reformation, pilgrimages – now punishable by death – became more clandestine, and the well became a focal point of resistance to Protestantism. A century and a half later, the Catholic king of England, James II, came here to pray for a son and heir; the eventual answer to his imprecations threatened a Catholic succession and contributed to the overthrow of the House of Stuart.

Pilgrims spent the night praying in the Perpendicular **St Winefride's Chapel** (key from the ticket office; CADW), built around 1500 to enclose three sides of the well. Henry VII's mother, Margaret Beaufort, paid for the construction and earned herself a likeness amongst the roof bosses that depict the life of St Winefride in the ornate, Gothic fan-vaulted crypt that surrounds the well. With the gloom only cut by light from votive candles, she's not that easy to see now.

Though the site's importance has waned considerably, pilgrimages do still take place, mainly on St Winefride's Day, the nearest Sunday to June 22, when a couple of thousand pilgrims are led through the streets behind a relic, part of Winefride's thumb bone. The procession ends by the open side of the crypt where the spring – or at least the outflow of a pump installed after mine working disrupted the spring's source in 1917 – fills a calm pool capacious enough to accommodate the dozens of faithful who dutifully wade through the waters three times in the hope of curing their ailments, a rite also associated with the Celtic baptism by triple immersion. Immersion isn't limited to the procession: anyone, irrespective of their professed beliefs, can take the cure, though most choose to go in the summer "Curing Season", during which there are daily services.

Practicalities

Holywell doesn't have a train station, but a reasonable number of **buses** call at the bus station at the southern end of High Street. From here, head a hundred yards down High Street and turn left to get to the tiny **tourist office**, in the library on North Street (Mon 10am–5.30pm, Tues, Thurs & Fri 10am–7pm, Wed 10am–1pm, Sat 9.30am–12.30pm; ☎01352/713157).

The few old pubs and coffee shops probably won't detain you overnight, but if you are **staying**, by far the best bet is the oak-beamed, partly sixteenth-century *Greenhill Farm* (March–Oct; ☎01352/713270; ③), reached by heading northeast from Winefride's Well on the B5121 for a few yards, then taking the second left opposite the *Royal Oak* pub. *Bryn Beuno Guesthouse*, on Whitford Street (☎01352/711315; ②), is also convenient: uphill from the well, turn right along a small bypass and continue for 300 yards. *The Springfield Hotel* (☎01352/780503, fax 780826; ⑤), just off the A55 expressway southeast of Holywell, caters mainly to business traffic but does have an indoor pool.

The best-value pub **meals** in town are those served at the *Royal Oak* on the B5121, which is also the best place to drink.

Greenfield Valley and Basingwerk Abbey

Trainloads of pilgrims used to arrive at Holywell by a steep branch which once ran off the North Coast line. From St Winefride's Well, a path follows a mile of the old line's bed towards the sea past a series of five ponds, the millraces between them providing power for the copper works and cotton mills whose remains now constitute the **Greenfield Valley Heritage Park**. Most of this area is still being renovated and, until the planned opening of the Lower Cotton Mill in mid-1997, forms little more than a sideshow as you walk the mile down to **Basingwerk Abbey** (unrestricted access; CADW), where Archbishop Baldwin and Giraldus Cambrensis spent a night on their tour in 1188 (see p.350). Most of the extant slabs of stonework are the remains of domestic buildings used by the abbot and twelve monks of the Savignac order, who lived in the abbey on its founding by Ranulph II, Earl of Chester, in 1131. Sixteen years later, the order merged with the Cistercians but went on controlling extensive lands in England and Wales until the Reformation when, in 1537, the abbey was Dissolved and its spoils distributed around the region. There's a little more of the history in the **visitor centre** (April–Oct daily 10am–5pm; free), which is effectively the entrance to the

Greenfields Valley Farm and Museum (same hours; £1.45), north Wales' collection of reconstructed farm buildings from around the region, many being saved from destruction, and preserved here as a working farm where you can feed the animals. Sunday afternoons, when there are workshops, demonstrations and guided countryside walks, are the best times to visit.

With your own transport, it is worth an excursion five miles northwest from Holywell to **Maen Achwyfan**, the "Stone of Lamentation" (unrestricted access; CADW), Britain's tallest Celtic cross. Though the shaft, incised with interwoven latticework, is over 10ft high and crowned with a wheel cross, this thousand-year-old cross is little celebrated and stands alone in a field reached by taking the A5026 to the northwest of Holywell, turning right onto the A5151, following the third exit at the first roundabout and turning right at the junction. The #A19 bus runs past the cross from Holywell, but the long wait involved makes the journey less appealing.

Prestatyn to Colwyn Bay

Almost all the vituperative comments aimed at the north coast land squarely on this unattractive twenty-mile stretch of amusement arcades, bingo halls, caravan sites and negligible beach. Chief culprit **Rhyl** is saved by its proximity to one of Edward I's castles at **Rhuddlan** and the collection of Victorian portraits and furniture at **Bodelwyddan**. **Prestatyn** is little better but significant as the starting point for the Offa's Dyke long-distance path, leaving the more architecturally coherent, if hardly exciting, **Colwyn Bay** as the nicest of the three main resorts.

If you happen to be passing on July 1, call in to **Abergele**, between Rhyl and Colwyn Bay, where supporters of the Free Wales Army march through the streets in memory of two martyrs to the cause (see p.357).

Prestatyn

PRESTATYN, nine miles northwest of Holywell, is a likable enough market town, struggling to compete with its neighbours further along the coast by building the **Nova Centre**, a swimming and leisure complex on the beach (Mon & Tues, Thurs & Fri 5–8pm, Sat & Sun 10am–5pm; school holidays Mon–Fri 1–8pm, Sat & Sun 10am–5pm; £1.40, kids £1). Unless you're desperate to try every manner of aquatic activity, then the **Offa's Dyke Path Centre** (Easter–Sept daily 10am–4pm; winter weekends 10am–3pm) next door may prove more interesting, with its interpretive diagram of the 170-mile route of the Offa's Dyke Path from Prestatyn to Chepstow (see box on p.228) and a stack of leaflets for walkers. The more committed traditionally start at least ankle-deep in the water, then cross the beach past a stone pillar onto Bastion Road. The path then follows High Street, through the main shopping area, to the *Cross Foxes* pub, from where acorn-marked signs guide you up to the hills behind. The view to Snowdonia, Liverpool and, on a good day, Blackpool, makes up for the fact that you won't come across any of the Offa's Dyke earthworks until the path gets south of the River Dee, the route planners rightly preferring the Clwydian Ridge to the scrappy industrial towns of Trevor and Ruabon on the dyke's route.

Trains on the North Coast line stop in the centre of town, close to the bus station and a couple of hundred yards from the **tourist office** in the *Scala* cinema on High Street (April–Sept 9.30am–1pm & 2–5pm; ☎01745/889092). You'll probably want to continue along the coast, but for those preparing for (or recovering from) the long walk there are a few **B&Bs**, all licensed and serving evening meals. From the station, turn towards the sea, then either right along the main A548 for *Roughsedge House*, 26–28 Marine Drive (closed Dec; ☎01745/887359; ③), or left to the equally good *Hawarden House*, 15 Victoria Rd (☎01745/854226; ②); *Traeth Ganol*, 41 Beach Rd West (☎01745/853594; ④), is further out, 100 yards left at the *Nova Centre*, but worth the effort. *Nant Mill Farm* (April–Nov; ☎01745/852360) is a simple grassy **campsite** a mile east along the A548.

Suhail Tandoori (☎01745/856829) serves moderately priced Indian **food** in a converted church near the station on the A548, or try the filled baguettes and lasagne on offer at the inexpensive *Bacchus Café Bistro*, 226 High St (☎01745/856844).

Rhyl and around

Anything you can do in **RHYL** (Y Rhyl), three miles west of Prestatyn, you can do better elsewhere. Apart from using it as a base for visits to **Rhuddlan** and **Bodelwyddan**, there's almost no reason to stay in this decaying Edwardian resort completely disfigured by amusement arcades. While desperately trying to woo back the punters with EU-funded initiatives, it fails on the most basic of requirements: the town doesn't even have a decent swimming beach. Most people rightly prefer the lure of the slides and surfing-wave pool of north Wales' most popular tourist attraction, the **Sun Centre** (mid-April to mid-Sept daily 10am–7pm or later; £3.75) on the Promenade. There's more watery entertainment 400 yards further west at the **Sea Life Centre** (daily 10am–5pm, to 6pm in July and Aug; £4.25) with its tanks full of British coastal aquatic life. Several coastal environments are re-created, but the star attraction is the perspex shark tunnel, where dogfish, basking sharks and various eels leisurely drift all around you until the day's highlight: feeding time. The town's other attraction is bingo.

Practicalities

The **train station** and **bus stops** are close together on Wellington and Russel roads which form the main street. Off here, Bodgor Street runs four blocks to the Promenade and the **tourist office** (April–Sept daily 9am–5pm; Oct–March Mon–Fri 9am–5pm, Sat 10am–1pm & 2–5pm; ☎01745/355068). Competition has forced **B&B** prices down: two central cheapies are *Stoneleigh Guesthouse*, 1 Morlan Park (☎01745/336344; ②), off Bath Street, running between East Parade and Russel Road, and *Gwynfa*, 6 Beechwood Rd (☎01745/353848; ②), off East Parade near the *Sun Centre*. Moving slightly upmarket it's worth trying *Kilkee Guesthouse*, 50 River St (☎01745/350070; ③), and *Medeor Hotel*, 3 Elwy St (☎01745/354489; ③); both are off the right-hand side of Wellington Road, walking west from the tourist office. Despite the vast number of caravan parks, the nearest **campsite** taking tents is *Henllys Farm Caravan and Campsite* (April–Oct; ☎01745/351208), three or four miles west of Rhyl.

Decent **eating** places are almost as abundant as hotels. *Boswell's* on Bodfor Street (☎01745/355492) offers an eclectic range of inexpensive bistro food and a healthy wine and cocktail list, but on a sunny day you are better off at the beachfront *Splash Point*, twenty minutes' walk from the centre on Hilton Drive (☎01745/353783), where you can enjoy monkfish cutlets or chicken burritos in the bar or conservatory or outside on the patio. The reasonably priced *Indian Garden*, 41 Abbey St (☎01745/350092), is the best of the curry restaurants, while pricey *Barratt's*, 167 Vale Rd (☎01745/344138), tops them all with modern French cuisine in Rhyl's oldest house. *Splash Point* is the ideal place for a **drink** on a warm afternoon or evening, but the beer is equally good at the more central and very lively *Caskey's*, 21 Vale Rd. If you want to rent a **bike**, try *Hughes Cycles*, 21 Bodfor St (☎01745/342012).

Rhuddlan

RHUDDLAN lies on the banks of a tidal reach of the Clwyd River (Afon Clywedog), which finally meets the sea at Rhyl, two miles to the north. The town itself seems little more than an insignificant suburb of Rhyl but for the diamond-shaped ruin of **Rhuddlan Castle** (May–Sept daily 10am–5pm; £1.70; CADW), a large and impressive hollow shell surrounded on three sides by a dry moat. Constructed by Edward I during his first phase of castle-building from 1277 to 1282, it was designed as a garrison and royal residence and commands a canalized section of the then strategic river that allowed boats to service the castle and provided water for the huge stone-lined moat. **Gillot's Tower**, by the dockgate, provided protection for the supply ships. The massive towers behind were the work of James of St George, who was responsible for the concentric plan that allowed archers on both outer and inner walls to fire simultaneously. This had become irrelevant by 1648, when Parliament forces took the castle during the Civil War and demolished it.

When Giraldus Cambrensis visited Rhuddlan a hundred years before the construction of Edward's castle, he was put up by David ap Owain, son of Owain Gwynedd, at a castle which once stood on **Twt Hill** (unrestricted access), reached by a footpath to the south of the present castle, now just a low hump in a bow of the river.

Important though the castle was, Rhuddlan earns its position in history as the place where Edward I signed the **Statute of Rhuddlan** on March 19, 1284, consigning Wales to centuries of subjugation by the English that many insist still continues. The ceremony took place on the site of **Parliament House**, on the main street 200 yards to the north. A sign on the building cynically claims that the Statute secured Welsh "judicial rights and independence", despite the fact that Edward laid down the laws by which the Welsh should be governed.

Rhuddlan is served by the frequent #51 **bus** from Rhyl or from the Vale of Clwyd and Bodelwyddan.

Marble Church and Bodelwyddan Castle: the National Portrait Gallery

Barrelling west along the A55 expressway towards the coast, the closest you come to Rhyl is the small village of **BODELWYDDAN**, four miles to the south. There is nothing of interest actually in the small town, but from miles around you can pick out the slender 202-foot limestone spire of **Marble Church**, a quarter of a mile to the east of Bodelwyddan, standing as a beacon over the flat coastal plain. The finely worked Gothic tracery of the spire is the church's most impressive feature; inside, the marble arcades that give the church its nickname and the repulsive, cherubic font are something of a letdown. Local architect John Gibson, the sole pupil of Sir Charles Barry, designed it in the 1850s, his choice of Scottish granite intended to bring to mind the home of Saint Kentigern, the first bishop of nearby St Asaph (see p.378) and, under his alternative name of Saint Mungo, the patron saint of Glasgow.

More samples of Gibson's sculptural work are displayed in the finest art show-case in north Wales, **Bodelwyddan Castle** (April–June, Sept & Oct daily except Fri 10am–5pm; July & Aug daily same hours; Nov–March Tues–Thurs, Sat & Sun 11am–4pm; £4, gardens £2), set amidst landscaped gardens on its hill, half a mile south of Bodelwyddan. Although crenellated and edged with turrets, the castle is substantially a nineteenth-century country mansion built on the site of a fifteenth-century house, its opulent Victorian interiors re-created during its restoration in the 1980s, after sixty years as a girls' school. Williams Hall, a wing of the building, now houses one of four provincial outposts of the **National Portrait Gallery**, specializing in works contemporary with the castle.

Most of the two hundred paintings, which change every few years, are on the ground floor approached through the "Watts Hall of Fame". This long corridor was specially decorated in William Morris style to accommodate not only a chair by Morris, but 26 portraits of eminent Victorians by G F Watts, among them Millais, Rossetti, Browning and Walter Crane. The Billiard Room leads off the cor-ridor and through to the outstanding Dining Room. Two sensitive portraits here highlight the Pre-Raphaelite support for social reform: William Holman Hunt's portrayal of the vociferous opponent of slavery and capital punishment, Stephen Lushington; and Ford Madox Brown's double portrait of Henry Farell, prime mover in the passing of the 1867 Reform Bill, and suffragette Millicent Garrett. Works by John Singer Sargent and Hubert von Herkamer also adorn the room, which, like the others, is furnished with pieces from the Victoria and Albert Museum in London. The table and chairs originally belonged to one Alfred Waterhouse, who designed the superb walnut and boxwood grand piano.

More serious Victorians line the Library which leads on to the Ladies' Drawing Room where a beautiful Biedermeier sofa outshines the paintings of little-cele-brated nineteenth-century women around the walls. The Drawing Room opposite serves as sculpture gallery, with a portrait of John Gibson looking down on his own images of Bacchus and Cupid. From the hall between these two drawing rooms, the Grand Staircase leads upstairs to a more detailed presentation of sig-nificant aspects of nineteenth-century portraiture. Portrait photography and works by female artists get generous coverage along with animal painters; Landseer in particular. The top floor is primarily reserved for temporary exhibitions, though there's also a fun, hands-on Victorian Extravaganza, with rooms devoted to sound transmission and reproduction, optical illusions and the moving image.

The entry fee entitles you to a taped audio tour of the ground floor, which intro-duces the key features but comes padded with wearisome dramatized anecdotes designed to enliven the experience. The machine has no fast-forward button, so turn the sound down and read through the *Visitor Guide* (£1.50) or the adequate information sheets in each room.

The rest of the castle and most of the grounds are given over to an expensive adults-only hotel complex open just to guests, though you can walk through the modest gardens, explore the small maze, and take tea in one of the cafés.

To get here, catch the #51 **bus** from Rhyl, Rhuddlan or anywhere in the Vale of Clwyd, bringing you within ten minutes' walk of both the castle and the church.

Colwyn Bay and around

The A548 coast road west from Rhyl meets the A55 near the imposing nineteenth-century folly of Gwrych Castle and then continues on to **COLWYN BAY** (Bae

Colwyn). The hilly setting and unspoiled Victorian main street gives the place marginally more charm than its eastern neighbours, bolstered by the realistic prospect of an operational pier. Along with many other British piers, Colwyn Bay's suffered three decades of neglect as Britons eschewed their seaside in favour of more glamorous Mediterranean resorts, but a small pier renaissance – 1996 was Britain's "Year of the Pier" – has engendered a number of restoration projects around the country. Colwyn Bay's fledgling but ambitious attempt has seen the opening of a number of shops and a bar on the first few yards of the derelict remains of this once-grand jetty. At its foot you can **rent bikes** and rollerblades cheaply from *Happy Hire* (☎01352/758984) and cycle along the new waterfront cycle path or a mile inland and steeply uphill to the **Welsh Mountain Zoo** (Easter–Sept daily 9.30am–6pm; Oct–Easter daily 9.30am–4pm; £5.50), a fairly traditional zoo high in the woods behind the town, with Californian sea lions, "Chimpanzee World" and the free-flying eagle displays touted as the main attractions. Colwyn Bay runs seamlessly west along the coast into **Rhos-on-Sea**, a resort chiefly notable for the *Harlequin Puppet Theatre* on its Promenade (☎01492/548166), one of the very few remaining marionette shows in the British tradition, with an hour-long daytime family show.

Trains stop on the seafront across the road from the **tourist office**, 40 Station Rd (July & Aug Mon–Sat 9.30am–5.30pm, Sun 10am–1pm; Sept–June Mon–Sat 9.30am–5pm; ☎01492/530478), from where the zoo is well signposted. You're better off **staying** at nearby Llandudno or Conwy, though there's a **campsite** at *Dinarth Hall Farm* in Rhos-on-Sea (☎01492/548203). For **eating**, try the moderately priced, Provençal *Café Niçoise*, 124 Abergele Rd (☎01492/531555), with its two- or three-course *menu touristique*, or *Totem*, 2a Erskine Rd (☎01492/53961), around the corner, serving cheap and tasty vegetarian meals during the day.

Llandudno

The twin limestone hummocks of the 680-foot **Great Orme** and its southern cousin the Little Orme provide a dramatic frame for the gently curving Victorian frontage of **LLANDUDNO**, Wales' most enduring archetype of the genteel British seaside resort. The core of the town occupies a low isthmus between two beachfronts, the less developed West Shore and Llandudno Bay where the older set of promenading devotees can be found huddled in the glass frontages of once-grand hotels. Despite the arrival of more rumbustious fun-seekers, it retains an undeniably dignified air but, as the coast's largest town, steers clear of retirement-home stagnation.

Llandudno's early history revolves around the Great Orme, where Saint Tudno, who brought Christianity to the region in the sixth century, built the monastic cell that gives the town its name. When the early Victorian copper mines looked to be worked out in the mid-nineteenth century, local landowner Edward Mostyn set about a speculative venture to exploit the growing craze for sea bathing with a seaside resort for the upper middle classes. Being MP for the constituency, and having the Bishop of Bangor in his pocket, he was able to tease through Parliament an enclosure act giving himself the rights to develop the land.

Work got under way around 1854 and the resort rapidly gained popularity until the end of the century, when Llandudno had become synonymous with the Victorian ideal of a respectable resort, drawing music stars such as Adelina Patti (see p.208) and Jules Rivière, the French conductor who sat in a gilded armchair facing the audience as he waved his bejewelled ivory baton. Mostyn Street, with its wrought-iron and glass verandahs, was said to have some of the finest shops outside London, patronized by the titled guests staying in the hotels: Bismarck, Napoléon III, Disraeli, Gladstone, and Queen Elizabeth of Romania, who stayed here for five weeks in 1890 and is said to have given the town its motto *Hardd, haran, hedd,* meaning "beautiful haven of peace". It may have been just that in 1890, but today it is bustling, with some less-exalted emporia along Mostyn Street and fewer pretensions amongst the hotel owners.

Arrival, information and getting around

The forlorn **train station** at the corner of Augusta and Vaughan streets is only five minutes' walk down Augusta Street/Madoc Street from the **tourist office**, 1–2 Chapel St (Easter–Sept daily 9am–6pm; Oct–Easter Mon–Fri 9am–5pm; ☎01492/876413). Direct trains come from Chester, those from Bangor and Betws-y-Coed generally requiring a change at Llandudno Junction near Conwy. Chapel Street runs parallel to Mostyn Street, where **local buses** from Bangor, Betws-y-Coed, Conwy and Rhyl stop. Less than ten minutes' walk south, *National Express* buses pull in to the **coach park** on Mostyn Broadway.

The tourist office stocks a free map of Great Orme walking paths, though most people drive or use the tram or cableway (see p.392). Alternative **tours** for those in a hurry include the *Great Orme Tours* of Marine Drive and the summit (April–Sept 3 daily; ☎01492/870870; £3.50) which leave from Prince Edward Square, and the *Magical History Tours* (April–Oct several daily; ☎01248/810345; £1.50) for jaunts around town in horse-drawn buggies. Open-top double-decker buses loop from Llandudno to Conwy and back, run by *The Llandudno & Conwy Tour* (late May to mid-Sept at least hourly 10am–4pm; ☎01492/876606; £5). With more energy you can **cycle** on bikes rented from *West End Cycles*, 22 Augusta St (☎01492/876891), across the road from the train station.

Accommodation

You may well want to stay a day or so, and with over 700 **hotels**, this isn't usually a problem, though in high summer (and especially bank holidays), booking ahead is wise. If you haven't made a reservation, your best bet for inexpensive accommodation is St David's Road, with almost a dozen high-standard, predominantly ③-category guesthouses.

Agar House, 17 St David's Rd (☎01492/875572). A suburban home offering a warm welcome, home-cooked dinners and an award-winning garden. Closed Dec–Feb. ③.

Bodnant, 39 St Mary's Rd (☎01492/876936). Comfortable non-smoking guesthouse. ③.

Bodysgallen Hall, three miles south of town on the A470 (☎01492/584466). One of the top country hotels in Wales in a partly seventeenth-century house surrounded by 120 acres of terraced lawns and gardens. Antique-filled rooms, all beautifully decorated and festooned with flowers, in the house itself and in cottages in the grounds. ⑨.

Bryn Derwen Hotel, 34 Abbey Rd (☎ & fax 01492/876804). Sumptuous yet informal small hotel at the foot of the Orme, with huge Victorian rooms and terrific meals. March–Oct. ⑤.

Cliffbury Hotel, 34 St David's Rd (☎01492/877224). Excellent-value non-smoking hotel with well-appointed rooms. One of the best on this street. ②.

Empire, 74 Church Walks (☎01492/860555, fax 860791). Opulent, slightly over-fussy rooms with every conceivable convenience either in the main building, with sauna and indoor and outdoor pools, or next door in the even better rooms of no. 72. ⑦/⑨.

Fernbank, 9 Chapel St (☎01492/877251). One of the cheapest and best equipped of a string of low-cost hotels just along from the tourist office. ②.

Gwesty Leamore Hotel, 40 Lloyd St (☎01492/875552). One of the few guesthouses in Llandudno actually run by Welsh people. Friendly welcome and good facilities, including satellite TV. Closed Dec–Feb. ③.

Howard Hotel, 16 Central Promenade (☎01492/877881). By serving a continental rather than full breakfast, this basic but spacious old seafront hotel just sneaks into this price category. There are no self-catering facilities, but this is the closest thing in town to a youth hostel. ①.

The Lighthouse, Marine Drive, three miles north of Llandudno (☎ & fax 01492/876819). Fortress-like from outside but attractively furnished within, this lighthouse, 370ft above the Irish Sea, is one of Wales' more unusual places to stay. ⑦.

Orme View Guesthouse, 5 Vaughan St (☎01492/870840). Bottom-end place just a few steps from the train station above *Baxter's Photography*. ②.

St Tudno Hotel, 16 North Parade, just behind the pier (☎01492/874411, fax 860407). Superb, small seafront hotel hidden amongst others of much lower stature, with lavishly decorated rooms, excellent meals and "The Best Hotel Loos in Britain". ⑦.

The Wellington, 12 North Parade (☎01492/876709). Good-value seafront hotel with views across the bay from the front rooms, and good inexpensive meals. ④.

The Town

Much of Llandudno's daytime activity revolves around the Great Orme rising steeply to the north, but first-time visitors are inevitably drawn to the **pier** (open all year; free), jutting out into Llandudno Bay with views back to the limestone cliffs. Once the supreme expression of Llandudno's ornate Victoriana, it was partly destroyed by fire in 1994, but is back in operation, its neat wooden deck overrun in summer with kids clamouring to board the modest fairground rides and deckchair denizens cocking an ear to the taped sounds of some Wurlitzer maestro. Ice-cream and candy-floss outlets abound: a town ordinance bars the sale of such fripperies anywhere else on the waterfront.

From the pier, it's a leisurely ten-minute stroll along The Promenade, with its bank of regal four-storey terraced hotels, to Vaughan Street and the region's premier contemporary art gallery, **Oriel Mostyn**, at no. 12 (Mon–Sat 10am–1pm & 1.30–5pm; free), named after Lady Mostyn, for whom it was built in 1901. The gallery has no permanent collection, but its eight shows a year are usually worth catching, featuring often challenging works by artists of international renown with a particular leaning towards the current Welsh arts scene.

If you have kids to entertain, head down Charlton Street from the gallery to the **Alice in Wonderland Centre**, 3–4 Trinity Square (April–Oct daily 10am–5pm; Nov–March closed Sun; £2.65). Here a twenty-minute taped tour guides you through the "Rabbit Hole", full of amateurish animated models of Mad Hatters and March Hares, and treats you to excerpts from Lewis Carroll's books. Lewis Carroll's association with Llandudno is tenuous but assiduously milked by the town's tourism machine. The writer never visited Llandudno, but Alice Liddell, the inspiration for his books, did – her parents' holiday home now forms the core of the *Gogarth Abbey Hotel* also on the West Shore. The only other sight in town is the **Llandudno Museum**, 17–19 Gloddaeth St (Easter–Oct Tues–Sat 10.30am–1pm & 2–5pm, Sun 2–5pm; Nov–Easter Tues–Sun 2–5pm; £1.50), whose local history exhibits focus on pieces unearthed in the copper mines (see overleaf), Roman artefacts and a rebuilt rural kitchen from Llanberis.

The Great Orme

The top of the **Great Orme** (Pen y Gogarth) ranks as the one spot in north Wales with comparable views to those from the far loftier summits in Snowdonia. In many ways they are superior, combining the seascapes east towards Rhyl and west over the sands of the Conwy estuary to the shores of Anglesey with the brooding quarry-chewed northern limit of the Carneddau range where Snowdonia crashes into the sea. Take a short walk across the rounded top of the Orme to get away from the crowds around the summit car park and it is easy to find somewhere to admire the view as fulmars wheel on the thermals, but it's less easy to see the feral goats which roam all over the mountain.

Formed about 300 million years ago at the bottom of a tropical sea, this huge lump of carboniferous limestone was subject to some of the same stresses that folded Snowdonia, producing fissures filled by molten mineral-bearing rock. Though there are a few minor Neolithic sites dotted over the hill, it was in the Bronze Age that the settlement really developed, when the people began to smelt the contents of the malachite-rich veins, supplying copper – if current speculation turns out to be true – throughout Europe.

The Romans seemed to ignore the Orme's potential, leaving it to early Christian Celts like Saint Tudno. The Vikings later gave the place its name, which derives from Old Norse meaning "worm" or "sea serpent" – just how it might have appeared in the mist to those approaching by sea. Today it is favoured not just by day-trippers here for the view, but also by botanists drawn by the profusion of maritime species: goldilocks aster, spotted cats-ear and spiked speedwell.

Apart from walking, there are three other ways to explore the Orme. Traditionally the most popular is **Marine Drive**, a four-mile circuit cut into the rock high above the coastal cliffs, passing *Pen-trwyn*, a rock-climbing venue with several of Britain's trickiest limestone routes. You can freely walk or cycle around, or make the anticlockwise circuit from just near Llandudno's pier in your own vehicle (£1.50 toll summer 9am–8pm, winter 9am–4pm, otherwise free).

A separate road leads directly from Llandudno up to the cafés and bar at the **Summit Complex** (Easter–Oct daily; Nov–Easter Sat & Sun only; ☎01492/870610), following Old Road from Llandudno. The road up to the summit runs parallel to the mile-long route of the vintage, San Francisco-style **Great Orme Tramway** (April–Sept 10am–6pm; Oct–March 10am–4pm; £3.40 return, £2.40 single), creaking up from the bottom of Old Road, much as it has done since 1902. The third route starts at the base of the pier, close to the start of Marine Drive, where an Italianate colonnade flanks the short road to the **Happy Valley** formal gardens and the **Cabin Lift** (July & Aug daily 10am–5.30pm; Easter–May, Sept & Oct daily 10am–4.30pm; £4.60 return, £4.10 single), which carries you up over the Orme to the Summit Complex, a mile away. At the start it swings over **Ski Llandudno** (variable hours, but generally 10am–6pm), where £12 will get you a couple of hours on the dry slopes (including all equipment), or for a quarter of the price you can make a couple of runs down a 700-yard-long snow-free **Toboggan Run**.

The Great Orme Copper Mines

From the tramway's halfway station, it is just a five-minute walk to the long-disused **Great Orme Copper Mines** (mid-Feb to Oct daily 10am–5pm; £4.20). The history of these ancient workings is more interesting than the tour. The Victorians, who last mined the area, were aware of earlier workings, and until the late 1970s these were assumed to be Roman. Digs in the 1980s, however, uncovered 4000-year-old animal bones which had been used as scrapers up to 200ft down. This is one of the few sites in Britain where mineral veins were accompanied by dolomitization, a rock-softening process that permitted the use of the simple tools available in the Bronze Age. Ease of extraction led to this becoming the pre-eminent copper mine in Europe, and with more excavations continuing in the off-season, it may well turn out to have been the world's largest.

Hard hats are provided on the **guided tour**, which, after a poor explanatory video, takes you down through just a small portion of the tunnels. It's enough, though, to get a feel for the cramped working conditions and the dangers of rock-fall, and to see the burial site of one of three cats thought to have been ritually sacrificed by superstitious miners.

Eating, drinking and entertainment

Llandudno is blessed with the best choice of **restaurants** in north Wales, ranging from budget cafés to one of the most expensive places in the country. Most cluster at the foot of the Great Orme around Mostyn Street, where numerous **pubs** cater to most tastes.

Around the turn of the century, all the best performers clamoured to play Llandudno but today you're lucky to get anything more than faded celebrities plying the resorts throughout the summer. However, with the new *North Wales Theatre* (see below) and the ten-day **Llandudno October Festival** of pop, jazz, opera and classical music (℡0800/834820), things are looking a little rosier. The tourist office can usually give you a good idea of what's on, but we've listed the most promising venues.

Restaurants and cafés

Bodysgallen Hall, three miles south of town on the A470 (℡01492/584466). Top-notch traditional and modern British fare in one of the best country hotels around. Table d'hôte with a selection of over 300 wines – very expensive.

The Garden Room Restaurant at the *St Tudno Hotel*, North Parade (℡01492/874411). One of Wales' best restaurants producing French-style meals with fresh Welsh produce where possible. Three-course lunches are moderately priced but in the evening you get the full five-course extravaganza.

Habit Tearooms, 12 Mostyn St. Rich home-made cakes and inexpensive light lunches are served in this bentwood-chair and pot-plant setting.

King's Head, Old Road. Substantial and tasty bar meals ranging from Welsh rarebit to noisettes of lamb in this low-beamed pub.

Number 1's Bistro, 1 Old Rd (℡01492/875424). One of Llandudno's finer low-key restaurants with imaginative, moderately priced French-styled bistro meals served in a simple dark-wood and deep-burgundy furnished rooms. Closed all day Sun, and Mon lunchtime.

Pinocchio Zorba, 153 Mostyn St (℡01492/860670). Relaxed Greek/Italian place serving well-prepared meze, pizza and pasta. Sun lunch buffet for a fiver.

Richards, 7 Church Walks (℡01492/877924). There's a more formal restaurant upstairs, but the basement bistro is better, with a menu strong on seafood. The goat's cheese salad with plum dressing and the local mullet are particularly good.

Romeo's, 25 Lloyd St (℡01492/877777). Cheery Italian restaurant and pizzeria with fine calzone, excellent espresso and equally good traditional British dishes. Takeaways available.

Sandbach Café, 78a Mostyn St (℡01492/876522). Refined tea rooms above a chocolate shop, with a good array of sandwiches, cakes and daily specials.

Bars and pubs

Barton's, George's Place. Popular under-thirties hangout above a café.

The Carlton, 121 Mostyn St, corner of Gloddaeth Street. Lively town-centre pub with pool table, quiz nights, good beer and fine iron and glass verandahs.

Cottage Loaf, Market Street. Flag-floored pub built from old ships' timbers on top of an old bakehouse. Popular for lunchtime eating, and drinking all day.

King's Head, Old Road, by the bottom of the tramway. Llandudno's oldest pub, where Edward Mostyn and his surveyor mapped out the town. Interesting photos inside.

London Hotel, 131 Mostyn St. Despite the red telephone box inside and the Dick Whittington sign, this is a decent pub with good beer and a family room that turns into a piano bar at night.

Entertainment

Broadway Boulevard, *Grand Theatre*, Mostyn Broadway, corner of Ty'n y Ffridd Road (℡01492/879614). Llandudno's liveliest club, with a host of party nights.

North Wales Theatre (*Theatr Gogledd Cymru*), The Promenade (☎01492/872000). North Wales' premiere live entertainment centre, this new 1500-seat theatre lures touring companies and occasional international acts.

The Palladium, Gloddaeth Street (☎01492/876244). Llandudno's cinema, showing predominantly mainstream blockbusters.

Conwy and around

Until 1991, traffic ground steadily through **CONWY**, four miles southwest along the coast from Llandudno, making a visit thoroughly unpleasant. Now, with the completion of the bypass tunnel under the Conwy River (Afon Conwy), its approaches tucked behind a landscaped embankment, the town enjoys a new tranquillity now only threatened by the increase in visitors drawn by a fine castle and nearly complete belt of town walls. Over the last few years, much tarmac has been replaced with cobbles and shopfronts have been prettified, but despite the addition of an unnecessary and totally fake tall ship beside the quay, it has, for the moment, resisted becoming a heritage museum town. It remains one of the highlights of the north coast, its setting on the Conwy estuary, backed by a forested fold of Snowdonia, irresistible to painters and photographers ever since Englishman Paul Sandby published his *Views of North Wales* in 1776.

In Sandby's day, the Conwy estuary still produced a good living for the families who had held mussel-gathering rights on the sands for centuries, a heritage which goes back long before the foundation of the Cistercian monastery of Aberconwy in 1172. The monastery, where Llywelyn ap Iorwerth ("the Great") died in 1240, was on the present site of the parish church of St Mary and All Saints, but a century later was moved eight miles upriver to Maenan, near Llanrwst, to make way for one of the toughest-looking links in Edward I's chain of fortresses.

Apart from a brief siege during the Welsh uprising of 1294, the bulk of events in Conwy's history occurred at the end of the fourteenth century: Richard II stayed at the castle on his return from an ill-timed trip to Ireland in 1399, until lured from safety by Bolingbroke's vassal, the Earl of Northumberland. Northumberland swore in the castle's chapel to grant the king safe passage, but Richard was taken to Flint (see p.381) and kept captive, Bolingbroke becoming Henry IV. Just two years later, on Good Friday when the fifteen-strong castle guard were at church, two cousins of Owain Glyndŵr, Gwilym and Rhys ap Tudor, took the castle and razed the town for Glyndŵr's cause. Harry Hotspur, Chief Justice of north Wales, rushed from Denbigh (see p.376) to besiege the occupied fortress, eventually doing a deal: nine Welsh were to be handed over then hanged, drawn and quartered in return for the Tudors' freedom. After this, the castle fell into disuse, and was bought in 1627 for £100 by Charles I's Secretary of State, Lord Conway of Ragley, who then had the task of refortifying it for the Civil War. It held out until 1646, only surrendering to Mytton once the town had been taken. At the restoration of the monarchy in 1665, the castle was stripped of all its iron, wood and lead, and was left substantially as it is today.

Arrival and information

Llandudno Junction, less than a mile across the river to the east, serves as the main **train station** for *InterCity* services from Chester to Holyhead, as well as for

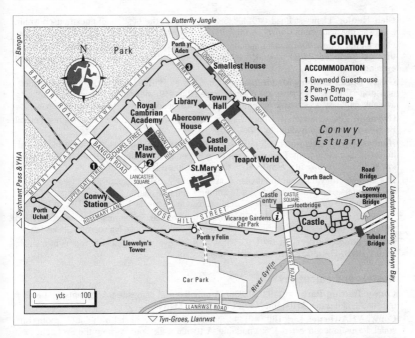

trains heading south to Betws-y-Coed and Blaenau Ffestiniog; only slow, regional services stop in Conwy itself. *National Express* **buses** pull up outside the town walls on Town Ditch Road, as do the open-top double-deckers run by *The Llandudno & Conwy Tour* company (see p.390). Local buses to Bangor, Betws-y-Coed and Llandudno use the stops in the centre, mostly on Lancaster Square or Castle Street.

Walking south from either Conwy station or the Lancaster Square bus stops, skip the Conwy Visitor Centre in favour of the **tourist office** (April–Oct daily 9.30am–6.30pm; Nov–March Mon–Sat 9.30am–4pm, Sun 11am–4pm; ☎01492/592248), which shares the same building and hours as the castle ticket office.

Accommodation

Although the Conwy region offers a fair range of **accommodation** – including the only town-centre YHA hostel in the vicinity – the choice is a bit thin right in the heart of town, and those without the transport to reach the less central places are advised to book ahead in summer.

Hotels and guesthouses

Castle Bank Hotel, Mount Pleasant (☎01492/593888). Licensed, non-smoking hotel with country-house atmosphere and excellent, moderately priced meals. A 10-min walk from the town centre: turn first left outside the town walls on the Bangor road. Closed Jan. ⑤.

Church House, Llanbedr-y-Cennin, five miles south of Conwy (☎01492/660521). Fine, old two-roomed guesthouse with beautiful views. Get off the #19 bus in Tal-y-Bont and walk half a mile west. The *Olde Bull Inn* is nearby (see p.400). ③.

Glan Heulog, Llanrwst Road (☎01492/593845). One of the best small guesthouses within easy walking distance of Conwy on the outskirts of town. Inexpensive meals are served. ②.

Glyn Uchaf, Conwy Old Road, Capelulo, two miles west of Conwy (☎01492/623737). One of the best secluded B&Bs around, backing onto the hills just over Sychnant Pass. Good evening meals. ③.

Gwern Borter Country Manor, Barker's Lane, Rowen (☎01492/650360). Comfortable guest-house on a Conwy Valley farm, just north of Rowen (bus #19) with sauna, gym and pony trekking available and easy access to walks onto the nearby Carneddau range. Meals on request. ④.

Gwynedd Guesthouse, 10 Upper Gate St (☎01492/596537). About the cheapest central B&B and consequently often full. ②.

Henllys Farm, Llechwedd, 1.5 miles west of Conwy (☎01492/593269). Very nice guest-house on a working farm. Turn up Upper Gate Street, bear left along St Agnes Road, then follow signs for Llechwedd – *Henllys* is on the right. Closed Dec–Feb. ③.

The Old Rectory, Llansantffraid Glan Conwy (☎01492/580611, fax 584555). Georgian-style country house, opulently furnished with antiques and fine paintings, overlooking the Conwy estuary, a mile up the Conwy Valley. Creative, expensive meals. Closed mid-Dec to Jan. ⑧.

Pen-y-Bryn, 28 High St (☎01492/596445). Well-appointed, welcoming, non-smoking B&B with private facilities in a central sixteenth-century building above tea rooms. Closed Jan. ③.

Swan Cottage, 18 Berry St (☎01492/596840). Attractive, almost elegant rooms in a small, central B&B. The attic room has great estuary views. ③.

Hostels and campsites

Conwy Touring Park (☎01492/592856). A fully fixtured campsite taking tents, just over a mile south along the B5106 (bus #19). Closed Nov–March.

Conwy YHA Hostel, Lark Hill (☎01492/593571). Brand-new hostel with double rooms and small dorms in a converted 1960s building. A 10-min walk from town up the Sychnant Pass road. Closed Dec to mid-Feb. ①.

Pyllau Gloewen Farm, Tal-y-Bont, 6 miles south of Conwy (☎01492/660504). Conwy Valley farm with B&B facilities, a £7.50 a night bunk barn suitable for walkers and backpackers and an adjacent camp and caravan site. Pick-up available from local train stations. ①/②.

Rowen YHA Hostel, Rowen, a mile up a steep hill above the village (☎01492/650089). Simple but superbly set YHA hostel on the flanks of the Carneddau range, reached by turning right 50 yards past Rowen's pub. Hourly bus #19. Closed Sept–Easter. ①.

The Town

Nowhere in the core of medieval and Victorian buildings is more than two hundred yards from the irregular triangle of protective masonry formed by the town walls. This makes it wonderfully easy to potter around and, though you'll get to see everything you want to in a day, you may well want to stay longer.

Conwy Castle

During their incursions along Wales' north coast, Edward I's Anglo-Norman ancestors had all but destroyed the castle at Deganwy, near Llandudno, but maintaining a bridgehead west of the Conwy River had always eluded them. Accordingly, once over the river in 1283, Edward set about establishing another of his bastide towns. He chose a strategic knoll at the mouth of the Conwy River and set James of St George to fashion a castle to fit its contours. With the help of 1500 men, James took just five years to build **Conwy Castle** (April–Oct daily 9.30am–6.30pm; Nov–March Mon–Sat 9.30am–4pm, Sun 11am–4pm; £3; CADW), now entered through a ticket office and over a modern bridge.

THE "IRON RING"

Dotting the north Wales coast, a day's march from each other, Edward I's fearsome **Iron Ring** of colossal fortresses represents Europe's most ambitious and concentrated medieval building project, designed to prevent the recurrence of two massively expensive military campaigns (see "History" in *Contexts*, p.432). After Edward's first successful campaign in 1277, he was able to pin down his adversary, **Llywelyn ap Gruffydd** ("the Last") in Snowdonia and on Anglesey. This gave him room and time enough to build the now largely ruined castles at **Flint**, **Rhuddlan**, **Builth Wells** and **Aberystwyth**, as well as to commandeer and upgrade Welsh castles, Edward's first attempt at subjugation.

Llewellyn's second uprising, in 1282, was also ultimately unsuccessful, and Edward, determined not to have to fight a third time for the same land, set about extending his ring of fortifications in an immensely costly display of English might. Together with the Treaty of Rhuddlan in 1284, this saw the Welsh resistance effectively crushed. The castles at **Harlech**, **Caernarfon** and **Conwy**, though nearly contemporary, display a unique progression towards the later, highly evolved concentric design of **Beaumaris**. All this second batch, including the town walls of Caernarfon and Conwy, were the work of the master military architect of his age, James of St George d'Espéranche, whose work is now recognized with **UN World Heritage Site** status.

Each of the castles was integrated with a **bastide town** – an idea borrowed from Gascony in southwest France, where Edward I was duke – the town and castle mutually reliant on each other for protection and trade. The bastides were always populated with English settlers, the Welsh permitted to enter the town during the day but not to trade and certainly not carrying arms. It wasn't until the eighteenth century that the Welsh would have towns they could truly call their own.

Overlooked by a low hill, the castle appears less easily defended than others along the coast, but James constructed eight massive towers in a rectangle around the two wards, the inner one separated from the outer by a drawbridge and portcullis, and further protected by turrets atop the four eastern towers, now the preserve of crows. Strolling along the wall-top gallery, you can look down onto something unique in the Iron Ring fortresses, a roofless but largely intact interior. The outer ward's 130-foot-long Great Hall and the King's Apartments are both well preserved, but the only part of the castle to have kept its roof is the **Chapel Tower**, named for the small room built into the wall whose semicircular apse still shows some heavily worn carving. On the floor below, there's a small exhibition on religious life in medieval castles which won't detain you long from exploring the passages.

The rest of the town

Anchored to the castle walls as though a drawbridge, Telford's narrow **Conwy Suspension Bridge** (April–Oct daily 10am–5pm; £1, £2.50 combination ticket with Aberconwy House; NT) was part of the 1826 road improvement scheme, prompted by the need for better communications to Ireland after the Act of Union. Contemporary with his far greater effort spanning the Menai Strait (see p.409), Telford's bridge mimics the crenellations of the battlements above – an attempt to compensate for spoiling the view of the castle painted by J M W Turner in 1802–03. The bridge was used until 1958, when the adjacent new road bridge was built, by which time the demands of modern traffic had inflicted tarmac, signs and street lighting on it. Once threatened with demolition, the bridge has now been restored to an approximation of its original state and is now a footbridge linking the town to the restored **tollhouse**, furnished as it would have been in around 1900. Note the turn-of-the-century toll charges on the board outside.

The approach to the new road bridge has created the only breach in the thirty-foot high **town walls** which branch out from the castle into a three-quarter-mile-long circuit, enclosing Conwy's ancient quarter. Inaccessible from the castle they were designed to protect, the walls are punctuated by 21 evenly spaced horseshoe towers, as well as twelve latrines bulging out from the wall-walk. At present, only half of the distance can be walked in two short sections, the closest and least appealing (castle opening hours only) overlooking a car park. Far superior views over the town to the castle and estuary behind open out from the section of wall which runs down from Porth Uchaf on Upper Gate Street to a spur into the estuary. Here, you come down off the walls by the brightly rigged trawlers, mussel boats and the self-proclaimed **smallest house in Britain** (Easter–June & Sept to mid-Oct daily 10am–6pm; July & Aug daily 10am–9pm; 50p), which was built wedged between two terraces, one of them now demolished. The two tiny rooms combined are only nine feet high and five wide, the door taking up only a quarter of the frontage, so most will have to duck to get in, a problem encountered by the last resident and great-grandfather of the present guardian, a six-foot-three fisherman.

Porth Isaf, the nearby gate in the town walls, leads up Lower High Street to the fourteenth-century timber and stone **Aberconwy House**, Castle Street (April–Nov daily except Tues 10am–5pm; £2, £2.50 combination ticket with the Conwy Suspension Bridge; NT), the oldest house in Conwy and its sole surviving medieval building dating from around 1300. It was built for a wealthy merchant and saw service as a bakery, antique shop, sea captain's house and temperance hotel, somehow managing to survive numerous fires and equally destructive Victorian improvement. Its various incarnations are re-created in rooms furnished with a simple yet elegant collection of Welsh rural furniture on loan from the Museum of Wales. Tours start with an introductory video in the attic, winding up in a kitchen complete with fireside settle, pewter plates and a few hunks of stale bread.

Antiquarians should continue along the High Street to **Plas Mawr** at no. 20, due to reopen in June 1997 after a five-year, £2 million restoration (details on ☎01492/592358; CADW). This is one of the best-preserved Elizabethan town houses in Britain, a Dutch-style house built in 1576 for one of the first Welsh people to live in the town, adventurer and respected entrepreneur Robert Wynne. Though some of the exterior stonework was replaced during renovations in the 1940s and 1950s, much of the interior – including superb moulded plaster ceilings – is conserved original, repairs only being carried out where absolutely necessary.

For over a hundred years, Plas Mawr was home to the **Royal Cambrian Academy**, a group aiming to foster and further art in Wales, now located just behind it in a converted chapel on Crown Lane (Tues–Sat 11am–5pm, Sun 1–4.30pm; Sun 11am–5pm Aug & Sept; £1). The airy, well-lit galleries display work by the Academy members, almost all Welsh or working in Wales, at its best during the annual summer exhibition.

If you're suffocating on history and high art, there's light relief at **Teapot World**, across from Aberconwy House on Castle Street (Easter–Oct Mon–Sat 10am–5.30pm, Sun 11am–5.30pm; £1.50), which packs a thousand pots into one room. Clarice Cliff and the American Rockwood studio are well represented, while Wedgwood, majolica and Bauhaus pieces share space with Art Deco car and train forms, pots emblazoned with anti-slavery and suffragette slogans and items of lewd innuendo.

There's more featherweight entertainment ten minutes' walk north along Castle/Berry Street at the **Butterfly Jungle** (April–Sept daily 10am–5pm; Oct 10am–4pm; £2.85), a hothouse full of bougainvillea, hibiscus and oleander pollinated by some fifty breeds of tropical butterfly, most imported as chrysalises but several bred here.

If you're still stuck for something to do, **river cruises** (March–Oct daily; ☎01492/592284; £3.50) operate from the quay, and there's **pony trekking** from *Pinewood Riding Stables* (☎01492/592256) a mile up Sychnant Pass Road. During the school holidays, hour-long **ghost tours** (nightly 7.30pm; £2) start from the wishing well in Castle Square to trail around the town's spooked sites.

Eating and drinking

For a popular tourist town, Conwy has relatively few **restaurants**, and if you want to sample some really excellent pubs, you've got to get a few miles out of town into the Conwy Valley. **Drinking** in town is less rewarding, and nightlife really isn't a feature here.

Restaurants and cafés

Alfredo's Restaurant, Lancaster Square (☎01492/592381). Good, low-cost pasta dishes and more expensive *secondi piatti* amongst the Chianti bottles.

Anna's Tearooms, 9 Castle St. Slightly pricey, but good-quality tearooms with a good lunchtime menu, located above the *Conwy Outdoor Shop*.

Austrian Restaurant, Conwy Old Road, Capelulo, two miles west over Sychnant Pass (☎01492/622170). Worth making a journey for steaming, fair-priced helpings of goulash and paprika schnitzel. Closed Sun evening and all day Mon.

Edwards, 18 High St. Good deli with a decent salad bar, the place to stock up for picnics.

Pen-y-Bryn Tearooms, 28 High St. Small, non-smoking establishment with the best artery-hardening Welsh teas around and delicious lunches.

The Wall Place, Bishop's Yard, Chapel Street (☎01492/596326). Licensed vegetarian establishment rapidly becoming one of Conwy's trendiest places, with indoor and outdoor seating and cheap, hearty wholefood staples, many of them vegan, and great fruit shakes. Live folk, jazz and Celtic music most Sat evenings for around £3. Closed evenings in winter.

Bars and pubs

Castle Hotel, High Street. Decent bar in this town hotel that's a favourite with the locals.

The Conwy Frigate, The Quay. Former North Sea trawler naffly decked out like a Napoleonic frigate, but a pleasant place to drink in the late afternoon sun.

Groes Inn, Tyn-y-Groes, 2 miles south on B5106 to Llanrwst. Excellent bar meals and cask ales at an atmospheric fifteenth-century pub which claims to be the first licensed house in Wales.

Liverpool Arms, The Quay. Ordinary town pub, but its dockside location makes it a hot venue on warm evenings.

Olde Bull Inn, five miles south in Llanbedr-y-Cennin. Quiet haven serving good bar meals.
Tŷ Gwyn Hotel, Rowen, 5 miles south of Conwy. Village pub in idyllic setting with friendly atmosphere and good garden.
Ye Olde Mail Coach, 16 High St. Spacious neo-olde-worlde pub serving good real ale and bar meals.

Around Conwy

With its marvellous setting and plentiful accommodation, Conwy is the best base for a couple of days exploring the Lower Conwy Valley and the coast around its estuary. It's easy to make a day trip to Llandudno (see p.388), and there's a smattering of other attractive diversions within a few miles' radius. Thousands come here specifically to see **Bodnant Garden** beside the lower reaches of the Conwy, flowing down from Llanrwst and Betws-y-Coed. Conwy also acts as a base for the **Cambrian Way** long-distance walking path to Cardiff (see box). The guesthouses and resturants mentioned in the text are all listed on p.395.

Sychnant Pass and Penmaenmawr

The best short walk from Conwy is on to **Conwy Mountain** and the 800-foot Penmaenbach and Alltwen peaks behind, all giving great views right along the coast. Follow a sign up Cadnant Park off the Bangor road just outside the town walls, then take the road around until Mountain Road heads off on the right towards a hillfort on the summit. This group is separated from the foothills of the

---

THE CAMBRIAN WAY

The ultimate Welsh long-distance path, the **Cambrian Way** nips across the whole country, winding some 274 miles from Cardiff to Conwy. The main feature of the path is its sheer isolation, passing through some of Wales' most spellbinding natural upland scenery, as the route climbs over the Carneddau, the Glyders, the Snowdon massif, Cadair Idris and the Brecon Beacons before dropping down through the Valleys to Cardiff.

This is the most arduous long walk in Wales, and one of the most satisfying, requiring a high degree of commitment even from experienced walkers. Few people attempt to complete the whole walk in one bash, preferring to break it into manageable sections. Fit hikers might do it in two tough weeks but three or even four is more usual. Signposting is erratic en route – if you intend to try the whole path, or any of its sections, A J Drake's *The Cambrian Way: A Mountain Connoisseur's Walk* (see *Contexts*, p.469) is well worth acquiring.

The experience is undoubtedly heightened by spending nights under canvas atop the moors, but with fifteen YHA hostels scattered along the route and B&Bs selected from *Stillwell's National Trail Companion* (see, p.470 in *Contexts*), much of the route can be completed with a roof over your head. Indeed, five hotel owners in Wales have grouped together to divide the path into five segments of six- to seven-day stages. Staying at the hotels, you will be bussed to and from easily walkable sections (around ten miles per day) and provided with electronic navigators, maps and even mobile phones. For details, and free information about the Way, contact the *Cambrian Way Walkers Association*'s effervescent Nick Bointon at Llanerchindda Farm, Cynghordy, Llandovery, Dyfed SA20 0NB (☎01550/750274, fax 750300; see also p.146).

Carneddau range by the narrow cleft of **Sychnant Pass**, traversed by Old Conwy Road, which ducks away from the sea, making an alternative route west, and rejoins the A55 expressway at Penmaenmawr.

The road, served by bus #71, passes the newly opened YHA hostel (see p.396) and the *Pinewood Riding Stables* before dropping into the hamlet of **CAPELULO**. Though you really need the "Snowdon" OS map, Capelulo makes a good starting point for a walk across **Penmaenmawr Mountain**, an important source of stone for axe-making from around 3000 BC. Not surprisingly, the area boasts several Neolithic remains, most notably the misnamed **Druid's Circle** (*Y Meini Hirion*) – marked on the map simply as "Stone Circle" – on the hills behind Penmaenmawr. Of the thirty stones which originally composed the site, only ten survive, but within the ring archeologists found a buried cist containing a food vessel and the cremated remains of a child: possible evidence of a human sacrifice. Folklore has embellished the theme by naming one of the stones, its top scalloped into a cradle shape, the Stone of Sacrifice. Neo-druidic ceremonies still take place here from time to time.

Roewen and Aber Falls

Nine miles west of Conwy on the A55, the otherwise unremarkable *Aber Falls Hotel* signals a sideroad leading inland to the 100-foot **Aber Falls**. Though a torrent after a storm, it can be little more than a trickle in high summer and in the dead of winter can freeze enough to attract ice climbers. The road from the A55 runs a mile through a pretty oakwood valley to a car park at the start of a nature trail. This comprises several footpaths that lead to the Falls, two following the valley with its series of cataracts and cascades, the other cutting up into the pine forests and approaching across a scree slope.

The same road off the A55 continues for two more miles, ending on the northern slopes of the bare Carneddau. From here, a path (6 miles; 2–3hr; 600-ft ascent) follows the low-level route of both a Bronze Age trackway and subsequent Roman road through the Carneddau range to Roewen. For much of the Roman occupation, this was the most important road in Wales, linking the legion's headquarters in Chester – where some of the sandstone paving originally came from – via the now barely visible fort at Canovium, located some two miles southeast of Rowen, to Segontium in Caernarfon (see p.358). The only walkable section these days is the stretch from Aber to Rowen which, along the way, passes a burial chamber, evidence of prehistoric field systems, and far too many power pylons.

The path emerges just behind the superbly set YHA hostel (see p.396) which, together with a post office, the lovely *Tŷ Gwyn* pub and a few houses, comprise the tiny hamlet of **ROEWEN**. The #19 bus links Conwy with Rowen every two hours.

Bodnant Garden

During the months of May and June, the laburnum arch flourishes and banks of rhododendrons are in full and glorious bloom all over **Bodnant Garden** (March–Oct daily 10am–5pm; £4.20; NT), Wales' finest formal garden and one of the most beautiful in Britain, eight miles south of Conwy. Laid out in 1875 around Bodnant Hall (closed to the public) by its then owner, English industrialist Henry Pochin, the garden spreads out over eighty acres of the east of the Conwy Valley. Facing southwest, the bulk of the garden – divided into an upper terraced garden and lower Pinetum and Wild Garden – catch the late afternoon sun as it sets over the Carneddau range, though the limited opening hours mean that visitors only experience this in October. Shrubs and plants provide a blaze of colour throughout the opening season, but autumn is a perfect time to be here, with hydrangeas still in bloom and fruit trees shedding their leaves. You'll need a minimum of two hours to fully appreciate the place. The #25 bus runs here from Llandudno every two hours, calling at Llandudno Junction, or it's a two-mile walk from the Tal-y-Cafn train station on the Conwy Valley line.

Bangor and around

After a few days travelling through mid-Wales or in the mountains of Snowdonia, **BANGOR** makes a welcome change. It's not big; but, as the largest town in Gwynedd and home to **Bangor University**, it passes in these parts for cosmopolitan. The students are the main reason for Bangor's vibrancy, but once they leave for the summer the place thins out with only a trickle of visitors to replace them.

The presence of a large non-Welsh student population inflames the passions of the more militant nationalists in what is a staunchly Welsh-speaking area. Antagonism between students and locals seldom inflates to anything more than drunken slanging matches, but if you've just arrived from one of the largely English-speaking north coast resorts, you'll notice a dramatic change.

In the nineteenth century, the slate industry and road and rail projects brought some urbanization to Bangor. But for well over a millennium before that, the city was solely noted for its see, founded as a monastic settlement by Saint Deiniol in 525 AD. At first, Saint Deiniol only cleared a space in the woods which became known as *Y Cae Onn*, "The Ash Enclosure", only later developing into the present name, a corruption of *bangori*, a type of interwoven wattle fence which presumably demarcated the monastic lands.

Arrival, information and accommodation

All trains on the North Coast line between Chester and Holyhead stop at Bangor's **train station** on Station Road, at the bottom of Holyhead Road. From here Deiniol Road, the town's main street, runs along the bottom of the valley, changing its name to Garth Road and continuing almost to the pier. *National Express* **buses** and local services stop on a short spur of Garth Road, almost opposite *Theatr Gwynedd*. The **tourist office** (April–Sept daily 9.30am–1pm & 2–5.30pm; ☎01248/352786) is inconveniently sited some two miles southeast of town at the *Little Chef* service station by the intersection of the A5 and A55 at Llandegai. Apart from trips to the tourist office and Penrhyn Castle, it is perfectly feasible to walk everywhere, though you could rent a **bike** from *West End Cycles*, 33–35 High St (☎01248/371158).

With its relatively low number of visitors, Bangor doesn't have a huge choice of **places to stay**. Most cheaper accommodation is at the northern end of Garth Road, about twenty minutes' walk from the train station. As usual, many of the better places are out of town and thoroughly inconvenient unless you have your own transport.

Hotels and guesthouses

Dilfan, Garth Road (☎01248/353030). Marginally the best of a row of three serviceable low-cost B&Bs. ③.

BANGOR

ACCOMMODATION
1 Dilfan
2 Eryl Môr
3 Glan Menai
4 Menai Court Hotel
5 Regency Hotel

Menai Strait

Victorian Pier

N

YHA

Theatre Gwynedd

University College

★Bus stops

Bangor Museum & Art Gallery

Cathedral

Recreation Ground

Golf Course

Train Station

0   yds   400

▽ *Caernarfon*

◁ *Menai Bridge & Anglesey*

◁ *University of Bangor : Reichel*

▷ *Penrhyn Castle & ℹ*

Eryl Môr Hotel, 2 Upper Garth Rd (☎01248/353789, fax 354042). Quiet, comfortable, fully licensed hotel with some rooms overlooking Bangor's pier and the Menai Strait. ③.

Glan Menai, Greenbank, Garth Road (☎01248/352802). Good, no-frills budget rooms down towards the pier. ②.

Menai Court Hotel, Craig-y-Don Road (☎ & fax 01248/354200). Bangor's top hotel with plush decor and well-appointed rooms, some with views of Snowdonia or the Menai Strait. ⑦.

Nant-y-Fedw, 2 Tre Felin, Llandegai (☎01248/351683). Extremely welcoming, very comfortable B&B with attractive gardens, en-suite rooms and good evening meals on request. The approach is unprepossessing, down a small turning a quarter of a mile past the entrance to Penrhyn Castle. Booked guests will be met from the train or bus. ③.

Regency Hotel, Holyhead Road (☎01248/370819). Good-value small hotel noted chiefly for its proximity to the train station. ④.

Swn-y-Nant, Caernarfon Road, three miles south of Bangor on the A4087 (☎01248/670792, fax 671140). Attractive rooms in a house that's ideal for kids. The obliging hosts cook lovely meals, keep geese and pigs, and will pick you up from town if you book ahead. ③.

Ty-Mawr Farm, half a mile east of Llanddeiniolen, five miles southwest of Bangor on the B4366 (☎01286/670147). Comfortable B&B on a working farm with views of Snowdonia and very good home-made food. Quality, well-equipped self-catering cottages also available short term outside the school holidays.The infrequent bus #77 (not Sun) stops within half a mile. ③.

Tŷ'n Rhos, Llanddeiniolen, five miles southwest of Bangor (☎01248/670489). Exceptionally good farmhouse accommodation which you'll need to book well in advance. Superb, moderately priced four-course meals. Bus #77 (not Sun). ⑤.

Hostels and campsites

Bangor YHA hostel, Tan-y-Bryn (☎01248/353516, fax 371176). A large house signposted on the right of the A56, 10-min walk east of the centre and reached either by walking along the High Street or taking bus #6 or #7 along Garth Road. Closed late Nov to late Dec. ①.

Treborth Hall Farm, Menai Bridge (☎01248/364399). Simple campsite three miles over the Menai Strait on the A4080.

Tros-y-Waen Farm, off B4547 south of Pentir, 6 miles south of Bangor, towards Llanberis (☎01248/364448). Unremarkable farmhouse B&B surrounded by a quiet low-cost (£4 per tent) campsite with hot showers and a good pub, *The Vaynol Arms*, within walking distance.

University of Bangor: Reichel, Ffriddoedd Road (☎01248/372104). Clean, functional rooms available from late June to late Sept, and over the Easter holidays. ②.

The Town

The university takes up much of upper Bangor, straddling the hill that separates the town centre from the Menai Strait. The shape of the college's main building is almost an exact replica of the **cathedral** (daily 11am–5pm), which boasts the longest continuous use of any cathedral in Britain, easily predating the town. Nowadays only a blocked-in Norman window gives any hint of the see's ancient origins. Though you won't want to spend a lot of time here, it's worth venturing into the cathedral's spacious white-walled interior, particularly to see the sixteenth-century wooden **Mostyn Christ**, depicted bound and seated on a rock.

Little is recorded of the original cathedral until it was destroyed and subsequently rebuilt by the Normans in 1071. Archbishop Baldwin preached here in 1188 while raising support for the Third Crusade, when his chronicler, Giraldus Cambrensis, was shown a double vault by the high altar containing Owain Gwynedd and his brother Cadwaladr. Owain had been posthumously excommunicated by Archbishop Thomas for incest with his first cousin, and the Bishop of Bangor was asked to look for an opportunity to remove the body from the cathedral. He was probably reinterred in the churchyard, though many believe the body lies within the arched tomb in the south transept.

The Norman building was heavily damaged by King John in 1211, a second time by Edward I and then again by Owain Glyndŵr, the various reconstructions resulting in the present thirteenth- to fifteenth-century building, heavily restored by Gilbert Scott in 1866. Outside, there's a **bible garden** with a collection of all the biblical trees, shrubs and flowers capable of withstanding the local climate.

Just over the road, the **Bangor Museum and Art Gallery**, Ffordd Gwynedd (Tues–Fri 12.30–4.30pm, Sat 10.30am–4.30pm; free), offers standard regional museum fare, the snippets of local history enlivened by the refurbished traditional-costume section and the archeology room, containing the most complete Roman sword found in Wales. The most insightful rooms are those devoted to a complete set of furniture from a moderately wealthy Criccieth farm, covering three hundred years of acquisitions, from brooding Welsh dressers to fine Italian pieces. Furniture also forms the basis of the museum's homage to Thomas

Telford, whose favourite chair sits alongside a model of his bridge complete with the web of chains which were stripped off during strengthening in 1935, when they were found to be heavy and unnecessary. The art gallery downstairs has no permanent collection, its temporary displays concentrating on predominantly Welsh contemporary works.

Heading away from the centre, it is not unreasonable to consider walking out to Telford's bridge. Otherwise, you can get a good look at it from Bangor's pristine **Victorian Pier** (20p), which reaches halfway across to Anglesey. The pier, built in 1896, lay derelict for years but has recently been restored and is blessed with just one token amusement pavilion. To get there, either follow Garth Road towards Conwy – a fifteen-minute walk – or work your way down from upper Bangor along College Road, the latter route allowing a detour across a wooded hill known as Roman Camp. Recent digs here have failed to unearth any evidence at all of Roman occupation, but you do at least get a good view of the Strait.

Eating, drinking and entertainment

Bangor has few really good **restaurants**, though as befits a university town there are plenty of places you can fill up reasonably well at modest cost. These are scattered around town, several clustering around the student bedsitland of Upper Bangor along Holyhead Road. High Street is the best zone for grazing or stocking up for a journey, with an abundance of cheap cafés, pasta and sandwich joints.

Restaurants and cafés

Fat Cat Café Bar, 161 High St (☎01248/370445). Breezy modern decor and a moderately priced menu – ranging from massive burgers to salmon and broccoli pasta quills – help pack this place out with students and locals.

Garden, 1 High St (☎01248/362189). Dimly lit Cantonese restaurant serving succulent sesame prawns off a broad, but not overwhelming, menu and weekday lunchtime specials.

Greek Taverna Politis, 12 Holyhead Rd (☎01248/354991). Moderately priced souvlaki and stifado favourites and top-class Greek salads served around the fire, in the airy conservatory or outside in the courtyard. Cheaper meals at the bar and jazz every Mon.

Herbs Cookshop, 307–309 High St. Great daytime vegetarian café with an attached health-food shop and lots to take away. Closed Sun.

Mahabharat, 5–7 High St (☎01248/352802). The best of Bangor's curry houses with very good balti and tandoori dishes.

Menai Court Hotel, Craig-y-Don Road (☎01248/354200). The restaurant of this classy hotel earns the plaudits of foodies for its traditional, expensive British and European dishes and its extensive wine list.

Tandoori Knights, 10 Holyhead Rd (☎01248/364634). All the usual tandoori and balti dishes in a restaurant that often looks closed when it isn't.

Pubs, music and nightlife

Belle Vue, Holyhead Road. Bangor's big student pub, right next to the university and heaving at the weekend.

The Nelson, Beach Road. Reasonable wood-beamed pub with a reputation for good, inexpensive bar meals, tapas and sandwiches.

The Octagon, Dean Street, off High Street. Very mainstream town nightclub.

The Skerries, 374 High St. Lively pub with a decent pint, a relatively up-to-date jukebox and a young crowd.

Tafarn Y Glôb, 7 Albert St. If you've tried to learn any of the language, you can put it to good use at this traditional local where ordering in Welsh is pretty much *de rigueur*. For a pint of beer, try "Un peint o cwrw, os gwelwch yn dda".

Theatr Gwynedd, Deiniol Road (box office ☎01248/351708). Along with its counterpart in Mold, *Theatr Gwynedd* is the most progressive art house in north Wales and is about your only chance of seeing contemporary plays or even slightly offbeat movies.

University Students' Union, Deiniol Road (☎01248/353709). Fly posters around town almost all point you to the *Students' Union*, the venue for any touring rock/pop bands. Usually quiet over the summer break.

The Victoria Hotel, Telford Street, Menai Bridge. The best bet for local live music, across the water in Menai Bridge (see p.409).

Penrhyn Castle

There can hardly be a more vulgar testament to the Anglo-Welsh landowning gentry's oppression of the rural Welsh than the oddly compelling **Penrhyn Castle** (April–June, Sept & Oct daily except Tues noon–5pm; July & Aug daily except Tues 11am–5pm; £4.50 with 50-min recorded tour, £3 grounds & railway museum only; NT), two miles east of Bangor, which overlooks Port Penrhyn from its acres of isolating parkland. Built on the backs of slate miners for the benefit of their bosses, this monstrous nineteenth-century neo-Norman fancy, with over three hundred rooms dripping with luxurious fittings, was funded by the quarry's huge profits.

The responsibility falls ultimately on sugar plantation owner and anti-abolitionist Richard Pennant, First Baron Penrhyn, who built a port on the northeastern edge of Bangor in order to ship his Bethesda slate to the world. But it was his self-aggrandizing great-great-nephew George Dawkins who inherited the 40,000-acre estate, added his ancestor's surname to his own, and with the aid of architect Thomas Hopper spent thirteen years from 1827 encasing the neo-Gothic hall in a Norman fortress complete with monumental five-storey keep.

Many would argue that the vulgarity doesn't stop with the owners but runs right through the fabric of the building, with the abundance of carved slate a further slap in the face to the workers. The decoration is glorious nonetheless, and fairly true to the Romanesque, with its deeply cut chevrons, billets and double-cone ornamentation. Hopper even looked to Norman architecture for the design of the furniture, but abandoned historical authenticity when it came to installing the central heating system, which piped hot air through ornamental brass ducts at the cost of twenty tons of coal a month.

Everything is on a massive scale and no more so than in the Great Hall with its pair of stained-glass Zodiac windows by Thomas Willement. Three-foot-thick oak doors separate subsequent rooms: the Library, with its full-size slate billiard table, and the oppressive Ebony Room, which leads onto the Grand Staircase. Upstairs, the lightness of the original William Morris wallpaper and drapes around the King's Bed are in marked contrast to the Slate Bed, designed for Queen Victoria but declined by her in favour of the Hopper-designed four-poster in the State Bedroom. The family managed to assemble the country's largest private **painting collection**. Much of this remains, especially in the two dining rooms, where there's a Gainsborough landscape amongst the family portraits, Canaletto's *The Thames at Westminster* and a Rembrandt portrait.

Once Richard Pennant had built his port he needed some way of getting the slates down to it. His answer was a horse-drawn tramway, which opened in 1801 and remained in use – though using steam engines by this time – until 1962. Gleaming examples of rolling stock from this and the country's other private industrial railways are on display in the **Industrial Railway Museum** (same hours; entry with castle or grounds tickets), including Lord Penrhyn's luxurious coach linked to a quarrymen's car. Buses #5, #6 and #7 run frequently from Bangor to the gates, from where it is a mile-long walk to the house.

ANGLESEY

Signs welcoming you to **Anglesey** (Ynys Môn) announce this to be *Mam Cymru*, "The Mother of Wales", attesting to the island's former importance as the bread-basket of the region. In the twelfth century Giraldus Cambrensis noted that "When crops have failed in other regions, this island, from its soil and its abun-dant produce, has been able to supply all Wales", and while feeding their less pro-ductive kin in Snowdonia is no longer a priority, the land remains predominantly pastoral, with small fields, stone walls and white houses suggestive of parts of England. Linguistically and politically, though, Anglesey is intensely Welsh. One of the four Plaid Cymru MPs represents the island which, with over seventy per-cent of its population using Welsh as their first language, has one of the country's highest proportions of native speakers. They at least will understand the lines of one of Anglesey's most famous poets, Goronwy Owen, whose eulogy on his homeland translates as "All hail to Anglesey/The delight of all regions/Bountiful as a second Eden/Or an ancient paradise". Judging by the numbers who flock to the island's necklace of fine sandy coves and rocky headlands, many agree with Owen, but just as many charge straight through from Bangor to **Holyhead** and the Irish ferries, missing out on Wales' greatest concentration of prehistoric sites and some superb coastal scenery.

The earliest people on Anglesey were Mesolithic hunters who arrived between 8000 and 4000 BC. Around 2500 BC, a new culture developed among the small farming communities, which was responsible for the many henges and stone cir-cles on the island and held sway until the Celts swept across Europe in the sev-enth century BC, led by their priestly class, the druids. The Celts established themselves so firmly on Anglesey that it was the last place in Wales to fall to the Romans when under Suetonius Paulinus they crossed the Menai Strait in 61 AD. Tacitus recorded the scene:

Women were seen rushing through the ranks of soldiers in wild disorder, dressed in black, with their hair dishevelled and brandishing flaming torches. Their whole appearance resembled the frantic rage of the Furies. The druids were ranged in order, calling down terrible curses. The soldiers, paralysed by this strange spectacle, stood still and offered themselves as a target for wounds. But at last the promptings of the general – and their own rallying of each other – urged them not to be frightened of a mob of women and fanatics. They advanced the standards, cut down all who met them and swallowed them up in their own fires. After this a garrison was placed over the conquered islanders, and the groves sacred to savage rites were cut down.

The vacuum left by the Roman departure in the fifth century was soon filled by the greatest of all Welsh dynasties, the Princes of Gwynedd, who held court at **Aberffraw**. Initially their authority was localized, but under Rhodri Mawr in the ninth century their influence spread over most of Wales as he defeated the

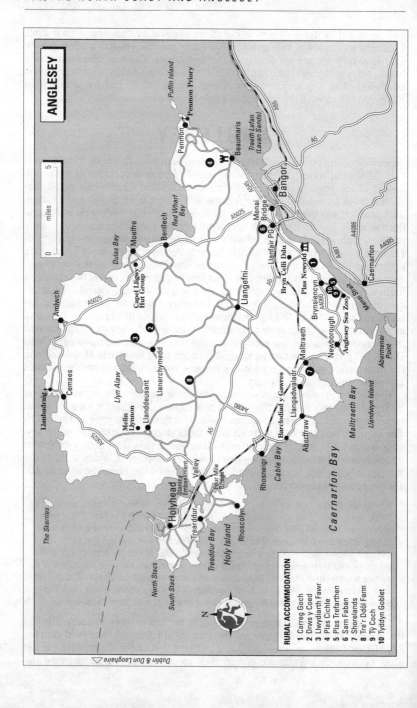

ANGLESEY

Puffin Island

Penmon Priory

Penmon

Beaumaris

Traeth Lafan (Lavan Sands)

Bangor

A55

A5

Red Wharf Bay

Benllech

Moelfre

Dulas Bay

Menai Bridge

A5025

Llanfair PG

A5

Llangefni

A4080

Bryn Celli Ddu

Plas Newydd

Brynsiencyn

Newborough

Anglesey Sea Zoo

Malltraeth

Malltraeth Bay

Llanddwyn Island

Abermenai Point

Caernarfon Bay

Caernarfon

A4085

A4080

Menai Strait

A487

A4086

Amlwch

Capel Lligwy Hut Group

A5025

Llanerchymedd

Llyn Alaw

Llanddeusant

Melin Llynnon

Cemaes

Llanbadraig

Valley

Stanley Embankment

Holyhead

Trearddur

Treaddur Bay

Rhoscolyn

Holy Island

North Stack

South Stack

The Skerries

Four Mile Bridge

Rhosneigr

Cable Bay

Aberffraw

Barclodiad y Gawres

Llangwyfan

Llangadwaladr

miles

0   5

N

▽ Dublin & Dun Laoghaire

RURAL ACCOMMODATION

1 Carreg Goch
2 Drws y Coed
3 Llwydiarth Fawr
4 Plas Cichle
5 Plas Trefarthen
6 Sarn Faban
7 Shorelands
8 Tre'r Ddôl Farm
9 Tŷ Coch
10 Tyddyn Goblet

ANGLESEY'S RURAL B&BS

The island is so compact that, at least if you have your own transport, the choice of **accommodation** should be based on factors other than solely location. There are some excellent moderately prices B&Bs and farmhouses, many of them relatively distant from any recognized sight, but no less appealing for that. Several of the better ones have been listed below and marked on the Anglesey map opposite. See the regional accounts for details.

Carreg Goch, near Llanfair PG (see p.415).

Drws Y Coed, Llanerchymedd (see p.421).

Llwydiarth Fawr, Llanerchymedd (see p.421).

Plas Cichle, Llanfaes, near Beaumaris (see p.411).

Plas Trefarthen, Brynsiencyn (see p.416).

Sarn Faban, Penmynydd Road, Llanfair PG (see p.415).

Shorelands, Malltraeth (see p.417).

Tre'r Ddôl Farm, Llanerchymedd (see p.421).

Tyddyn Goblet, Brynsiencyn (see p.416.

Tŷ Coch, Brynsiencyn (see p.416).

encroaching Vikings, earning thanks from Charlemagne for his efforts. Anglesey again fell to outsiders towards the end of the thirteenth century when Edward I defeated the Welsh princes, sealing the island's fate by building the last of his great castles at **Beaumaris**, by far the most absorbing town on the island.

Getting around the island is easy enough. The train line from Bangor crosses the strait, stopping at the station with the longest name in the world – usually abbreviated to **Llanfair PG** or Llanfairpwll – before continuing to meet the ferries at Holyhead. The rest of the island is covered by a bus network thoroughly detailed in the free *Ynys Môn* public transport timetables.

Menai Bridge and the approaches

Two bridges – both engineering marvels of their time – link Anglesey to the mainland over the **Menai Strait**, a perilous fourteen-mile-long tidal race that in places narrows to two hundred yards, forcing the current up to eight knots as it rushes between Conwy and Caernarfon bays. The view from the mainland over to Anglesey is impressive enough, but outdone by the eastward vistas from the Anglesey shore, the rocky mid-channel islets, some adorned with jetties and small houses, backed by the heartland of Snowdonia.

For centuries before the bridges were built, drovers used these narrows to herd Anglesey-fattened cattle on their way to market in England. Travellers had to wait for low tide to cross Lafan Sands, northeast of Bangor, then find a boat to take them across to Beaumaris, in foggy weather guided only by the sound of church bells. It is no surprise that the Irish MPs, needing transport to Westminster and a faster mail service, pushed for a fixed crossing.

The first permanent connection, in 1826, was Telford's graceful **Menai Suspension Bridge**, the world's first large iron suspension bridge, spanning 579 feet between piers, 100 feet above the water to allow high-masted sailing ships to pass. Almost everything about the project was novel, including the process of lifting the first 23-ton cable into place, which involved a pulley system and 150 men kept in time by a fife band. They celebrated their achievement by running across the nine-inch-wide chain from Anglesey to the mainland.

Robert Stephenson also made engineering history with his **Britannia Tubular Bridge** in 1850, which carried trains across the strait in twin wrought-iron tubes. It burned down in 1970, however, leaving only the limestone piers that now support the twin-deck road and rail bridge to Llanfair PG and Holyhead, bypassing the town of Menai Bridge.

Nestling in the shadow of the older crossing, with a few private islands to break the view across the strait to the mainland, is the town of **MENAI BRIDGE** (Porthaethwy). A short bus ride from Bangor (#53 and #57), it's also little more than half an hour's pleasant walk, with views from the bridge over to the fourteenth-century **Church of St Tysilio** (open mid-July to Aug) on Church Island, where the church's patron saint founded his cell around 630 AD. The island can be reached from the town along Belgian Walk, a causeway and waterside promenade built by refugees during World War I.

There's little else to do in Menai Bridge, but if you have children to entertain, take the B5420 two miles northeast of the village to **Pili Palas** (mid-March to Oct daily 10am–5.30pm; Nov & Dec daily 11am–3.30pm; £3.50), a steamy walk-in butterfly house with up to seventy species, some as big as your hand. British butterflies that are becoming less common in the wild are bred here for release, a venture promoted in the educational material available for kids. An aviary and vivarium complete the setup.

Practicalities

If you plan to **stay** in Menai Bridge, be sure to book ahead at the welcoming, non-smoking *Bwthyn*, 5 Brynafon (☎01248/713119; ③), just off Beach Road, the approach to Belgian Walk, with a couple of nicely decorated en-suite rooms, and locally made sausages for breakfast. The choice of **places to eat** is surprisingly good, the best being *Jodie's Bar & Bistro*, on Telford Road, which runs from the bridge into town (☎01248/714864), with refreshingly original wine-bar food in the cosy main rooms or airy conservatory. Worthy alternatives include decent pub meals at the *Liverpool Arms*, St George's Pier, and two highly rated, moderately priced Chinese places – the central *Sunshine*, Wood Street (☎01248/712808), and *Jade Village* on the A4080 (☎01248/715409), near *Jodie's*. Another good reason to stay is one of the best live **music** venues in the region, *The Victoria Hotel* (☎01248/712309) on Telford Road. Both Welsh- and English-language bands play here, particularly on Wednesdays and weekends, ranging from rock through folk and jazz to Cajun.

Beaumaris

The original inhabitants of **BEAUMARIS** (Biwmares) were evicted by Edward I to make way for the construction of his new castle and bastide town, dubbed "beautiful marsh" in an attempt to attract English settlers. Today the place can still seem like the small English outpost Edward intended, with a grand Georgian terrace (designed by Joseph Hansom, of cab fame) and more plummy English accents than you'll have heard for a while. Many of their owners belong with the flotilla of yachts, an echo of the port's fleet of merchant ships, which disappeared with the completion of the Menai bridges and subsequent growth of Holyhead.

Beaumaris is not only attractive, it boasts more sights than the rest of the island put together. This inevitably brings the crowds here in summer, though even then the evenings, when day-trippers have departed and overnighters are ensconced in their hotel restaurants, are peaceful.

Arrival and accommodation

With no trains, long-distance coaches or tourist office, Beaumaris seems poorly served, but it has a regular **bus** service to Bangor (#53 & #57; infrequent on Sun) and no shortage of decent **places to stay**. For tenters, the nearest **campsite** is *Kingsbridge* (☎01248/490636) not far from *Plas Cichle* (see below).

Hotels and guesthouses

Bishopsgate House Hotel, 54 Castle St (☎01248/810302, fax 810166). High-standard, predominantly business-oriented hotel in an elegant Georgian town house with all the expected facilities and a good restaurant. Closed Jan. ⑤.

Henllys Hall Hotel (☎01248/810412, fax 811511). Victorian country-house hotel, set in 25 acres of woodland walks, with sauna, sunbed, heated outdoor pool, croquet lawns and excellent country cooking. With an eye to the romantic weekend market, several rooms have four-poster beds. ⑦.

Morianfa (☎01248/811083). Spacious unfussy rooms without bathrooms but with fabulous Strait views in an attractive house right on the seafront. June–Sept. ③.

Plas Cichle, Llanfaes (☎01248/810488). The best of the local farmhouse B&Bs with lovely period furnished rooms in a substantial Georgian house a couple of miles from Beaumaris. The welcome is warm and you're encouraged to practise whatever Welsh you've picked up. Book well ahead in high summer. Closed Dec & Jan. ④.

Sea View Guesthouse, 9 Bulkeley Terrace (☎01248/810384). Comfortable, central and non-smoking B&B, the rooms either facing the sea or overlooking the High Street. ③.

Swn-y-Don, 7 Bulkeley Terrace (☎01248/810794). One of the best of the town B&Bs with antique-filled rooms and sea views. ③.

Ye Olde Bull's Head Inn, 18 Castle St (☎01248/810329, fax 811294). The best hotel in Beaumaris, this ancient and luxurious coaching inn was used as General Mytton's headquarters during the Civil War and, in more peaceful circumstances, by Dr Johnson and Charles Dickens. It's got a fantastic restaurant (see "Eating and drinking"). ⑦.

The Town and around

While you can spend an hour or two mooching around the antique shops, enjoying the views across the Strait towards Bangor and along the coast to Llandudno's Great Orme from the stumpy pier, this shouldn't distract from the town's major attractions. There is little doubt that the **castle** remains central to Beaumaris, its water-filled moat and arrow looped ramparts satisfying the British castle archetype more than any other in Wales. The law and order theme continues in the **courthouse** and **gaol**, both offering their own angle on Welsh subjugation. In good weather, a cruise out around **Puffin Island** or a wander along the nearby coastline close to **Penmon Priory** may suit better.

The Castle
Beaumaris Castle (April–Oct daily 9.30am–6.30pm; Nov–March Mon–Sat 9.30am–4pm, Sun 11am–4pm; £2.20; CADW) is the most picturesque of Edward's

gargantuan fortresses, built in response to Madog ap Llywelyn's capture of Caernarfon in 1294. Its architect, James of St George, produced a symmetrical octagonal form, his finest and most highly evolved expression of concentric design. Lacking the domineering majesty of Caernarfon, Conwy or Harlech, its low outer walls seem almost welcoming – until you begin to appreciate the defensive bent of its construction.

Sited on flat land at the edge of town, the castle is approached over a moat and through Moorish-influenced staggered entries at the huge towers of the Gate Next the Sea and the South Gatehouse. The moat originally linked the castle to the sea, now well over a hundred yards away, with a shipping channel allowing boats of up to forty tons to tie up at the iron rings hammered into a protective spur of the outer defences, **Gunner's Walk**. Supplies could be brought in, including corn which was fed into the mill still visible immediately below.

Despite over thirty years' work and ambitious plans for a lavish palace, the castle was never quite finished, leaving most of the inner ward empty and the corbels and fireplaces built into the walls never used. You can, however, explore an unsatisfyingly short section of the **wall walk**, from which archers were able to fire simultaneously from the inner and outer defences, and wander through miles of internal passages in the walls, finding your way to the first floor of the **Chapel Tower** and the small but wonderfully resonant lime-washed chapel, immediately above a small display on "The Castles of Wales".

None of the castle's defences was able to prevent siege by Owain Glyndŵr, who held the castle for two years from 1403, although during the Civil War they did keep out General Mytton and fifteen hundred Parliamentarian troops until the local Royalists were forced to surrender in 1646. At the restoration, the castle was returned to the Bulkeley family, only to be left to fall into ruin before twentieth-century restoration returned some of its glory.

The rest of the town

Almost opposite the castle stands the Jacobean **Beaumaris Courthouse** (Easter & June–Sept daily 11am–4.30pm; May Sat & Sun only; £1.35, joint ticket with gaol £2.80), built in 1614 and the oldest active court in Britain. It is now used only for the monthly Magistrates Court, but until 1971, when they were moved to Caernarfon, the quarterly Assize Courts were held here. These were traditionally held in English, giving the jury little chance to follow the proceedings and Welsh-speaking defendants none against prosecutors renowned for slapping heavy penalties on relatively minor offences. On session days you can go in to watch the trials, now conducted in Welsh, but won't be able to take the recorded tour or inspect *The Lawsuit*, a plaque in the magistrates' room depicting two farmers pulling the horns and tail of a cow while a lawyer milks it.

Many citizens were transported from the courthouse to the colonies for their misdemeanours; others only made it a couple of blocks to the **Beaumaris Gaol**, Steeple Lane (Easter & June–Sept daily 11am–5.30pm, May Sat & Sun only; £2.30 or £2.80 joint ticket with courthouse). When it opened in 1829, this was considered a model prison, its facilities including running water and toilets in each cell, an infirmary and, eventually, heating. Women prisoners did the cooking and were allowed to rock their babies' cradles in the nursery above by means of a pulley system. Advanced perhaps, but nonetheless a gloomy place: witness the windowless punishment cell, the yard for stone-breaking and the treadmill water pump operated by the prisoners. The least fortunate inmates were marched along a first-floor walkway through a door in the outer wall to the gibbet where they were publicly hanged. This was the fate of a certain Richard Rowlands, whose disembodied voice leads the recorded tour of the building and various displays on prison life.

Nearby on Church Street is the **Church of St Mary and St Nicholas**, the only building in Beaumaris approaching the age of the castle. Though ancient enough – started in the twelfth century and rebuilt around 1500 – its chief interest is the coffin in the porch, used as a horse trough for years but originally holding Joan, wife of Llywelyn the Great and daughter of King John of England.

For a more light-hearted half-hour, visit the **Museum of Childhood Memories**, 1 Castle St (Easter–Nov Mon–Sat 10.30am–5.30pm, Sun noon–5pm; £2.75), one man's personal collection amassed over the last thirty years and displaying over 2000 toys dating from the 1840s to around 1970. Highlights among this hoard of dolls, train sets and piggy banks are the musical instruments, an early TV, a stereoscopic viewer and a zoetrope designed in 1850, showing some of the earliest moving images.

Interesting though it is, a fine day might be better spent **cruising** with *Puffin Island Cruises* (Easter–Sept daily 10am–5pm; ☎01248/810251; £3), based in a kiosk at the foot of the pier, which, numbers permitting, will take you for an hour around, but not onto, Puffin Island (see below).

Penmon Priory

One of the earliest monastic sites in Anglesey was on the now uninhabited Puffin Island, four miles northeast of Beaumaris. In Welsh it goes by the name Ynys Seiriol, recalling the sixth-century saint who, on becoming head of the Augustine **Penmon Priory** (unrestricted access; CADW), brought the island community the three-quarters of a mile to Penmon. Saint Seiriol soon became known as the White Saint, not for his unblemished purity, but because his weekly walk to Llanerchymedd to meet Saint Cybi involved journeying with his back to the sun in both directions. Cybi, journeying into the sun from present-day Holyhead, was dubbed the Tawny Saint.

The priory's original wooden buildings were razed by the Danes in the tenth century, but their replacements, the twelfth-century church and the thirteenth-century south range of the cloister, are still standing. Only the church is in good repair and still used, the serene lime-washed nave housing an unusual Norman pillar-piscina – a font gouged from the plinth of a pre-Norman cross still used for Sunday services – and the Penmon Cross, moved here to prevent a thousand years of Welsh weather completely scouring off its plait and fret patterns. There's more patterned stonework in the south transept, approached through a magnificent chevron- and chequerboard-patterned arch. The church's site was chosen for its proximity to the refreshing waters of **St Seiriol's Well**, which now feeds a calm pool and is reached by either the path behind the church, or another opposite the distinctive domed dovecote, built around 1600 to house one thousand pairs of birds.

Three-quarters of a mile beyond the dovecote (£1 toll for cars in summer), a short strait separates Black Point, the easternmost point of Anglesey, from **Puffin Island**, now a nesting point for razorbills, guillemots and puffins, all once permissible food during Lent. Before retiring to the café in the car park at Black Point, take a walk around the headland or past the quarries, where James of St George cut fossil-ridden limestone for Caernarfon and Beaumaris castles, and Telford and Stephenson found the footings for their bridges. The rock was once part of a single mass that included the Great and Little Ormes, eight miles to the east on the mainland.

Getting here is no problem, as the frequent #57 Bangor–Beaumaris **bus** continues to Penmon roughly hourly.

Eating and drinking

There's no need to go hungry in Beaumaris which, for a small place, has a good selection of daytime cafés and several more substantial **restaurants**.

Bottles Bistro, 13 Castle St (☎01248/810623). Cosy restaurant serving a broad range of inexpensive to moderate bistro perennials, including pizza.

Chez Silvia, inside the *Bulkeley Hotel* on Castle Street (☎01248/810415). One of the more refined places to relax over a coffee and admire the sea views. The cakes and coffee are good and the prices modest.

Cottage Restaurant, 10 Castle St (☎01248/810946). The pick of the mid-range restaurants with an imaginative menu of meat and vegetarian dishes and good lunchtime specials, served in a room which partly cantilevers over the street.

Sailor's Return, Church Street. Town pub best known for its excellent bar meals and therefore not too smoky for eating at lunchtimes.

Ye Olde Bull's Head Inn (see "Accommodation", p.411). Beaumaris' top restaurant in the plush wood-beamed rooms of its top hotel. Its immaculately prepared traditional dinners are worth saving up for.

Llanfairpwllgwyngyllgogerychwyrndrobw- llllandysiliogogogoch and the south coast

When Robert Louis Stephenson wrote "to travel hopefully is a better thing than to arrive" he must have been thinking of **LLANFAIR PG**, the village with the longest place name in Britain and little else but for a wool shop and a small train station bearing the famed sign **Llanfairpwllgwyngyllgogerychwyrndrobwllllandysiliogogogoch**. Sadly, "St Mary's Church in the hollow of white hazel near a rapid whirlpool and the Church of St Tysilio near the red cave" is no authentic Welsh tongue twister; simply the fabrication of a Menai Bridge tailor in the 1880s, who added to the original first five syllables in an attempt to draw tourists – as indeed it has.

Coming from Bangor, half a mile before the town you'll probably notice the bronze figure atop the 91-foot-high Doric **Marquess of Anglesey's Column**. The apocryphal story has him declaring to Wellington, on having a leg blown off at Waterloo, "Begod, there goes me leg", to which Wellington drily replied, "Begod, so it do". There hadn't been much love lost between them since the Marquess ran off with Wellington's sister-in-law some years previously. Between 10am and 6pm you can climb the 115 steps up to the Marquess (60p) and share his view across the strait to Snowdonia. His replacement leg is on show at Plas Newydd, close to Bryn Celli Ddu: two good reasons to spend time in the area.

Practicalities

The main reason to stop in Llanfair PG itself is to visit the **tourist office** by the station (Mon–Sat 9.30am–5.30pm, Sun 10am-5pm; closes 5pm in winter;

☎01248/713177), the only one worth its salt on the island. **Trains** continue from Llanfair PG to Rhosneigr and Holyhead, but to visit the rest of the **south coast** you're reliant on the hourly #42 **bus** that passes Plas Newydd and Bryn Celli Ddu, Brynsiencyn and Newborough on its way to Aberffraw and Llangefni (see p.423). No bus continues along the south coast, bus access to Rhosneigr being on the infrequent #25 from Holyhead and the #45 from Llangefni which runs slightly more often. There are several good **places to stay** along the south coast, the closest to Llanfair PG being the *Sarn Faban*, a peaceful country B&B half a mile out on Penmynydd Road (☎01248/712410; ②) – follow the road opposite the *Tŷ Gwyn* pub, bear left where the road curves right and it's on the right. *Carreg Goch*, on the A4080 a mile west of Plas Newydd and Bryn Celli Ddu (☎01248/430315; ③), is also pleasant and convenient.

Bryn Celli Ddu

One of the island's most significant prehistoric sites, **Bryn Celli Ddu** (unrestricted access; CADW), the "Mound of the Dark Chamber", was built by Anglesey's late Neolithic inhabitants four thousand years ago, one and a half miles south. Several seasons of digs have shown it to be an extensive religious site, but today all you can see is a henge and stone circle, later transformed into a passage grave, whose original earthen mound has been replaced by an inept concrete-beam reconstruction. The substantial finds unearthed here – charred bones, arrowheads and spiral-carved stones – are now in the custody of the National Museum in Cardiff. The #42 bus passes within half a mile; otherwise it's an hour-long walk from Llanfair PG.

Plas Newydd

A mile and a half along the road from Llanfair PG to Bryn Celli Ddu is the approach to **Plas Newydd** (April–Sept daily except Sat noon–5pm; Oct Fri & Sun noon–5pm; gardens open an hour earlier; £4; NT). Though now owned by the National Trust, the house remains, as it has been since the eighteenth century, the home of the marquesses of Anglesey. A house had stood on this site since the sixteenth century, but it was the First Marquess's huge profits from Parys Mountain (see p.422) and other ventures that paid for its transformation by James Wyatt and Joseph Potter into a Gothic mansion in the late eighteenth century. Potter designed the pleasing, castellated stable block that almost upstages the modest-looking three-storey house with incongruous Tudor caps on slender octagonal turrets.

Inside, the Gothic Hall, with its Potter-designed fan-vaulted ceiling, leads to the longest and most finely decorated room in the house, the Music Room, originally the great hall. All available space is covered with oil paintings, including one of the First Marquess and another of Lady Paget, his first wife, both by John Hoppner. Despite the Gothic start, Wyatt was given free rein in the rest of the house, and there's a transition to the Neoclassical on entering the Staircase Hall with its cantilevered staircase and deceptively solid-looking Doric columns, actually just painted wood. Predominantly dull paintings line the stairs and the length of the gallery. Several monarchs and most family members are represented, those of the Sixth Marquess and his sister being the work of Rex Whistler, who spent two years here in the 1930s. Persevere through another half a dozen rooms, including Lady Anglesey's pink-and-white bedroom and a former kitchen containing a Whistler exhibition, to reach what is Plas Newydd's glory and Whistler's masterwork, in understandably the most popular room in the house. A whole 58-foot long wall of the Rex Whistler Room is consumed by the magnificent *trompe l'oeil* painting of some imaginary seascape seen from a promenade. At first it seems utterly incongruous but you are soon drawn into the fantasy, your position seeming to shift by over a mile as you walk along, altering your perspective on the mountains of Snowdonia and a whimsical composite of elements. Portmeirion (see p.346) is there, as are the Round Tower from Windsor Castle and the steeple from St Martin-in-the-Fields in London. Whistler himself appears as a gondolier, and again as a gardener in one of the two right-angled panels at either end, which appear to extend the room further.

A few rooms further on you'll find a **Cavalry Museum**, where the prize exhibit is the world's first articulated leg, a synthesis of wood, leather and springs, designed for the First Marquess, who lost his leg at Waterloo. All in all, you'll need to allow a couple of hours for a good look around, and a little longer to take in the Neolithic cromlech located in grounds landscaped by Humphrey Repton in the early nineteenth century. Recover in the former milking parlour, now an excellent tiled tea room serving tasty snacks and light meals.

Anglesey Sea Zoo and Brynsiencyn

Facing Caernarfon across the Menai Strait, seven miles southwest of Llanfair PG, **Anglesey Sea Zoo** (March–Oct daily 10am–5pm; Nov–Feb daily 11am–3pm; ☎01248/430411; £4.50), is one of the most absorbing attractions on Anglesey. Local sea conditions are simulated in wave tanks, and in shallow pools where plaice and turbot, camouflaged against the shingle bottom, are barely visible from the catwalks above. They haven't entirely got away from glass-sided tanks, but most are large and the contents chosen to depict specific environments: tidal flats, quayside and wrecks amongst them. In keeping with the buildings' previous functions as an oyster hatchery and lobster breeding farm, the zoo uses aquaculture to give the lobsters a much greater chance of survival once released into the wild. In summer, the schedule of the #42 **bus** allows for a two-hour visit (Mon–Sat); out of season they may pick you up from **BRYNSIENCYN**, two miles to the north, if you phone ahead. Half a mile southwest of Brynsiencyn, *Plas Trefarthen* (☎01248/43037; ③) is a large, grand Georgian **B&B** in two hundred acres of farmland with magnificent Strait views, a relaxed atmosphere and an acclaimed opera-singing owner, Marian Roberts. Alternatively, try the *Tyddyn Goblet* (☎01248/430296; ②), a characterful farmhouse just off the A4080, and the small, very welcoming *Tŷ Coch* (☎01248/430227; ③). All serve first-class home-made **food**, or you can relax at the end of the road past the Sea Zoo at the *Ferryhouse Café* or *Mermaid Inn*, both with outdoor seating.

Newborough and Malltraeth

Three miles southwest of the Sea Zoo, the end of the Menai Strait is marked by Abermenai Point, a huge sand bar backed by the 600-acre **Newborough Warren** (unrestricted access), one of the most important dune systems anywhere in Britain. As its name suggests, rabbits are common here, as are the otherwise rare thick-horned Soay sheep, Britain's oldest native breed. Since 1948, much of the land has been clad in Corsican and Monterey pine, a commercial operation with ecological benefits – the trees stabilize the ground and provide habitats for goldcrests, warblers and rare native red squirrels, justifying the Warren's designation as a national nature reserve. Three main walking trails, none more than an hour or two's stroll and all very well marked, weave through the pines to **Llanddwyn Island**. In truth a peninsula of rocky coves and sandy beaches, in summer it can be overrun with kids poking around the Twr Mawr (Great Tower), a disused lighthouse built in 1845 in the style of an Anglesey windmill, a row of restored cottages and a thirteenth-century church ruin dedicated to the patron saint of lovers in Wales, Saint Dwynwen. In the fifth century, after her abortive affair with a Welsh prince, Maelon, Dwynwen became a nun and requested that hopeful lovers who make a supplication to God in her name should receive divine assistance.

Entry to the Newborough Warren section of the reserve is from a free car park down a short track from a roundabout, where the A4080 bends north nine miles southwest of Llanfair PG. The main walk from here is out to Abermenai Point (2 miles), but be careful, as rapid tidal changes can quickly cover the broad sandy approach. To get to the reserve's main entrance, continue north along the A4080 for half a mile to **NEWBOROUGH** (Niwbwrch), a town of limited appeal founded by Edward I to rehouse villagers displaced during the building of Beaumaris. From here, a signposted toll barrier (have a couple of pound coins handy) leads to a second car park. Alternatively, get the #42 **bus**.

From 1945 until his death in 1979, the estuarine beaches to the north and around **MALLTRAETH** were the haunt of **Charles Tunnicliffe**, who spent much of his days meticulously producing beautifully detailed wildlife drawings. Birds were always his chief subject, and throughout his fifty-year career he produced thousands of intricate illustrations for other people's works as well as six books of his own, including *Shorelands Summer Diary*, largely researched around Newborough and named after his house in Malltraeth which is now run by a keen birder as a pleasant **B&B** (☎01407/840396; ③). It is located just off the A4080: cross the bridge in the village, turn left at the lay-by, then left again in front of the chapel. Examples of Tunnicliffe's work form a significant part of the *Oriel Ynys Môn* exhibition in Llangefni (see p.423).

Around Aberffraw

The area around Newborough and tiny **LLANGADWALADR**, three miles northwest, was once the seat of the great ruling dynasty of the Princes of Gwynedd who, from the seventh-century reign of Cadfan until Llywelyn ap Gruffydd's death in 1282, controlled northwest Wales, and frequently much of the rest of the country, from this now-quiet corner of Anglesey. Relatively recent finds of the foundations of a great hall are still being uncovered close to Newborough but, for the moment, the most substantial evidence lies in **Llangadwaladr Church** (usually closed except for Sun mornings). When the church was built in the thirteenth century, a memorial plaque, carved in Latin around 625 AD, was incorporated into an inside wall. It reads "Cadfan the King, wisest and most renowned of all kings". Llangadwaladr village takes its name from Cadwaladr, Cadfan's grandson, who subsequently ruled from **ABERFFRAW**, a mile and a half west (buses #42), where the coastal heritage centre, **Llys Llewelyn** (Easter to late Sept Mon–Sat 11am–5pm, Sun 1–5pm; free), has a few explanatory boards on the court and times of the Princes of Gwynedd and a little information on the flora and fauna of the Anglesey coast.

CABLE BAY (Porth Trecastell), two miles northwest of Aberffraw, was the eastern terminus of the first telegraph cable to Ireland, though it is now better known for its good sandy beach popular with surfers and kayakers. On the headland to the north stands the heavily reconstructed remains of the 5000-year-old **Barclodiad y Gawres** burial chamber. Though superior to Bryn Celli Ddu (see p.415), it is more difficult to see, requiring the key from Llys Llewelyn and a torch. Without artificial light, you won't really see the stones carved with chevrons and zigzag patterns the burial chamber shares with Newgrange and other Boyne Valley sites seventy miles across the water in Ireland. No buses pass Barclodiad y Gawres.

Rhosneigr

The weekday roar of fighters from the nearby RAF Valley airfield deafens you long before you reach **RHOSNEIGR**, two miles further north along the coast, an otherwise peaceful Edwardian seaside resort. Rambling over consolidated dunes which back a series of small bays, Rhosneigr remains justifiably popular with English holiday-makers after almost a century of patronage, although space on the beach is these days contested by the dozens of devoted windsurfers who flock here when the wind is right. It is the sort of low-key place you might feel like stopping in for a day or two: if so, you can rent boards and rig from *Funsport*, 1 Beach Rd (☎01407/810899; £25 a day/3-hr beginner's course) and take to the sea or the small Maelog Lake, safer when the wind is offshore.

There's central **accommodation** at *Bryn Maelog* on Chelford Close off the main Maelog Lake Road (☎01407/810285; ②); *Minstrel Lodge* on Station Road (☎01407/810970; ③); and *White Gables B&B* on Maelog Lake Road (☎01407/810863; ③), which welcomes pets and rents **bikes** (£10 a day). There's a **campsite**, *Shoreline Camping* (☎01407/810279), right by the **train station**, a mile north of the clock tower that marks the centre of the town. Rhosneigr has several decent **places to eat**, including *The Honey Pot*, The Square (Winter closed Sun; ☎01407/810302), with both an inexpensive bistro and a moderately priced restaurant; the *Bistro* on the High Street (☎01407/810295), where you can bring your own alcohol; and *Bee Bee's* ice-cream and coffee bar, also on High Street, selling the delicious "Denbigh Farmhouse" ice cream found in discerning outlets all over north Wales.

Holy Island

Holy Island (Ynys Gybi) is blessed with Anglesey's best scenery and cursed with its most unattractive town. The spectacular sea cliffs around **South Stack**, and the Stone Age and Roman remains on **Holyhead Mountain** are just a couple of miles from workaday **Holyhead**, whose ferry routes to Ireland and good transport links mean you'll probably find your way there at some stage.

This hourglass of land adjoins Anglesey's west coast at two points. The more ancient and picturesque approach turns off the A5 at Valley (Dyffryn), crosses the very short Four Mile Bridge and passes the fine beaches at **Rhoscolyn** and **Trearddur Bay** before reaching Holyhead. Most traffic takes the road or rail routes directly to the ferry terminal at Holyhead over the 1200-yard-long Stanley Embankment, built by Telford while working on the A5. Along the way he constructed distinctive octagonal tollhouses used until 1895 when the A5 was Britain's last major toll road. A couple have been converted to houses and one, at the northern end of the Stanley Embankment, now operates as the *Tollhouse Tearooms*.

Getting to Holyhead itself is no trouble, as trains and a fair number of Anglesey's buses go there. Rhoscolyn and South Stack can be reached from Holyhead by the #23 and the #22 respectively. The #4 bus to Holyhead from Bangor and Llangefni is the only really useful service to Trearddur Bay.

Holyhead

HOLYHEAD (Caergybi) is a place of dilapidated shopfronts and high unemployment, the local council's valiant attempts to brighten its image somehow making it even more depressing. In 1727 Swift found it "scurvy, ill-provided and comfortless", while a century or so later George Borrow called it "a poor, dull, ill-lighted town", and, apart from the scurvy and the lighting, little has changed. Fortunately, recent modifications to the ferry terminal and the reasonably well-integrated train and ferry timings mean you shouldn't need to venture into the town proper, but if you do get stuck there are a couple of things to see.

The town's Welsh name indicates the site of a Roman fort – an outpost of Segontium – and home of the sixth-century Saint Cybi. Cybi's cell was built in the protection of the Roman walls and is now marked by the partly thirteenth-century **Church of St Cybi** (sporadically open in summer). Both walls and church have undergone substantial reconstruction, the church gaining stained glass by Edward Burne-Jones and William Morris.

The **Breakwater Country Park** (daily 9am–dusk; free), a couple of miles along Beach Road, is one of the better ways to pass the time if you miss your boat. On the site of an old brickworks, it still holds the remains of a couple of kilns you can mooch about, but is primarily a place to enjoy a bracing clifftop walk to the foghorn station on North Stack (an hour or so return), or on to South Stack (see p.420), an hour's walk beyond.

Practicalities

The **train station**, local and *National Express* **bus stops**, **ferry terminal** and less-than-helpful **tourist office** (daily 10am–6pm; ☎01407/762622) are handily clustered together at the entrance to Holyhead and linked to the town by a pedestrian bridge to London Road. The need of late-arriving ferry passengers has fostered a bunch of poor **B&Bs**, especially those along the A5 into the town, so it's worth searching off the main road, particularly along Walthew Avenue where *Glan Ifor*, no. 8 (☎01407/764238; ②), and *Orotavia*, no. 66 (☎01407/760259; ②), are both simple, but cosy and perfectly serviceable. *Hendre*, Porth-y-Felin (☎01407/762929; ③), is the best of the bunch, a very welcoming former manse with inexpensive evening meals, while the most comfortable **hotel** in town is the *Boathouse Hotel* on Beach Road (☎01407/762094; ⑤), with a good restaurant and bar. If you've got your own transport, head three miles out of town along Walthew Avenue to *Tan-y-Cytiau* (☎01407/762763; ③), a country house nicely set in three acres of grounds on the slopes of Holyhead Mountain; there's also a self-catering cottage sleeping seven in the grounds.

Fast **food** is the staple diet in Holyhead, but you can still eat well; the *Boathouse Hotel* (see above) does succulent fish and seafood dishes, the budget *Omar Khayyam Tandoori,* 8 Newry St (☎01407/760333), serves the tastiest curries for miles around, and the *Castle Bakery*, 83 Market St, is one of the more appealing cafés. For **drinking**, head again to the *Boathouse* (see above), or crawl around the half-dozen bars on Market Street, starting with *The Seventy-Nine* at no. 79.

FERRIES TO IRELAND

Holyhead serves two Irish destinations – Dublin and Dun Laoghaire, six miles south – by two means: traditional **ferries** (3hr 30min) and super-fast **catamarans** which cut the journey down to a little over an hour and a half. *Stena Line* (☎0990/707070) runs to Dun Laoghaire using ferries (sailings currently at 2.15am & 3.30pm) and huge, car-carrying catamarans (currently mid-July to early Sept 4.10am, 8.55am, 1.45pm, 6.25pm & 11.05pm); *Irish Ferries* (☎0990/171717) runs ferries only, berthing in Dublin (sailings currently at 3.45am & 3.45pm). Check in for both ends thirty minutes before departure.

Passenger fares are very competitive, though *Irish Ferries* usually has the edge by a couple of pounds. Typically, the catamarans cost £32 one way for adults in high summer and £26 for the rest of the year; the ferries £27–28 in summer going down to as little as £20 in low season. Even better are the **day-return deals** run by both companies – £8 can get you fourteen hours in Dublin with *Irish Ferries*, provided you get the early boat.

Holyhead Mountain and South Stack

The northern half of Holy Island is ranged around the skirts of **Holyhead Mountain** (Mynydd Twr) which rises 700ft to the west of Holyhead. Its summit is ringed by the remains of the seventeen-acre Iron Age **Caer y Twr** (unrestricted access; CADW), one of the largest sites in north Wales. It seems to have only been used during times of war, as digs haven't unearthed any signs of permanent occupation, just a six-foot-high dry-stone wall enclosure around the ruins of a Roman beacon. In an hour or so you can pick your way up rough tracks from the Holyhead side, but the best approach is by bus #22 or your own transport to the car park at **South Stack** (Ynys Lawd), two miles west of Holyhead. A path (30min) leads from the car park to the top of Holyhead Mountain, though you'll find most people walking the few yards to the clifftop RSPB-run **Ellin's Tower Seabird Centre** (Easter–Sept daily 11am–5pm; free). From April until the end of July, binoculars and closed-circuit TV give an unparalleled opportunity to watch up to 3000 birds – razorbills, guillemots and the odd puffin – nesting on the nearby sea cliffs while ravens and peregrines wheel outside the tower's windows. When the birds have gone, rock climbers picking their way up the same cliff face replace them as the main interest. A twisting path leads down from the tower to a suspension bridge over the surging waves, once the keeper's only access to the now fully automated pepper-pot lighthouse. Though currently out of bounds, there are plans to open the lighthouse to visitors in the future.

William Stanley, who named Ellin's Tower (Twr Elin) after his wife, did most of the excavation work on the **Cytiau'r Gwyddelod** hut circles (CADW), across the road from the South Stack car park. The name translates as the "huts of the Irish" – a common name for any ancient settlement – but evidence from excavations reveals little more than that the builders were late Neolithic or early Bronze Age people. The visible remains comprise nineteen low stone circles – some up to ten yards across – though there seem to have originally been fifty buildings, formed into eight distinct farmsteads separated by ploughed fields.

Trearddur Bay and Rhoscolyn

At the pinch of the hourglass, a couple of miles south of Holyhead, the scattered settlement of **TREARDDUR BAY** (Bae Trearddur) shambles across low grassy hills, around a deeply indented bay of the same name, punctuated by rocky coves. There's no centre to speak of, but it's a much pleasanter base than Holyhead; it even has a good, clean swimming beach sporting a rare European Blue Flag. Watersports equipment can be rented from *Splash Watersports* (☎01407/860318).

If you can afford it, the best **place to stay** is the *Trearddur Bay Hotel*, Lon Isallt (☎01407/860301, fax 861181; ⑨), overlooking the main bay and with a heated indoor swimming pool. On the southern side of the bay, along Ravensport Road, is the cheaper *Seacroft Hotel* (☎01407/860348; ③) and, a mile further on, the *Tyn Rhos Campsite* which, though packed with caravans, takes tents as well.

At the southern tip of the island, a mile or so south of Trearddur Bay, a lane runs down to **RHOSCOLYN**, another scattered seaside settlement, though much smaller and even more appealing. Without your own watersports gear you're a bit stuck, but a limited selection can be rented from *The Outdoor Alternative* (☎01407/860469; ①), a relaxed, simple **campsite** a few yards from the beach which also operates a **self-catering hostel** during school holidays (essentially Easter & Aug). Meals are available on request and staff can organize rock-climbing and kayaking supervision, and point you to some of the best walks around. A few minutes away are the *Old Rectory* (closed Jan & Feb; ☎01407/860214; ⑤), a Georgian country house with outstanding views of the sea, and *The White Eagle*, a good **pub** with a beer garden.

Northern and inland Anglesey

The **northern and eastern sides of Anglesey** tend to be quieter than the south and west; the settlements are clustered behind the sheltered coves which, with the odd rocky headland, make up an appealing (if seldom dramatic) coast. This is primarily family holiday country, though its more thinly spread host of caravan sites make it much less oppressive than the north Welsh coast. None of the resorts is especially notable in its own right but they are well spaced, making cycling between them, or walking the coastal path, an ideal way to get around.

Relying on **buses** is possible, though less rewarding. From Holyhead, the #61 runs to Cemaes and Amlwch, where you can pick up the #62 and #63 to Moelfre, Menai Bridge and Bangor. The #32 links Amlwch to Llanerchymedd and Llangefni. **Accommodation** is detailed under the appropriate town account, but if you are exploring the coast with your own transport you might want to head inland to stay at one of the farmhouses near Llanerchymedd, all of which serve wholesome, hearty dinners. *Drws Y Coed* (☎01248/470473; ③), a comfortable, non-smoking B&B on a working farm a mile and a half east, *Llwydiarth Fawr* (☎01248/470321, fax 470540; ⑤), a spacious, secluded Georgian mansion half a mile north on the B5111, and *Tre'r Ddôl Farm* (☎01248/470278; ③), a welcoming seventeenth-century farmhouse three miles west on the B5112, packed with authentic original features, gorgeously rustic attic rooms and a family suite with laundry facilities, are all recommended.

Melin Llynnon and Cemaes

The main A5025 leaves the environs of Holyhead to follow the island's perimeter clockwise. Along the first northwestern stretch, there's nothing much to justify stopping, although you might be tempted to swing off the road at **LLANDDEU-SANT**, where a signpost points you to **Melin Llynnon** (Easter–Sept Tues–Sat 11am–5pm, Sun 1–5pm; £1.50), Anglesey's only working windmill. At one time, fifty-odd such mills were studded all over Anglesey, grinding away to feed all of north Wales; travelling around the island, over thirty can still be seen, their sail-less stumps either rotting away in field corners or converted (some imaginative-ly) into barns and houses. Only Melin Llynnon, which lay derelict for fifty years, survives in anything like its original form – renovated and restored under the guidance of Lincolnshire millwrights, it is now white-painted, canvas-sailed and once again producing flour. Everything in the mill is wind-powered, even the hoists that lift the grain through trapdoors, and almost extinct milling skills have had to be re-learnt by modern millers who now demonstrate the process and sell the result – in bag and cake form – in a good on-site café.

Wind is also a feature up the road at **CEMAES**, unattractively sandwiched between the ageing Wylfa Nuclear Power Station and a new 24-tower Rhyd-y-Groes Windfarm, but with one of the most attractive harbours on the north coast. Once a major port, Cemaes now serves only the odd trawler and boatloads of yachties drawn by a broad sweep of beach and the most northerly pub in Wales, *The Stag* on High Street.

The headland that forms the eastern side of the bay is surmounted by the tiny and ancient **Llanbadrig Church** (May–Sept daily 10am–noon & 2–4pm), one of only two Welsh churches dedicated to St Patrick. The present structure is main-ly fourteenth-century, but the church's origins date back to the fifth century when Ireland's patron saint is supposed to have been shipwrecked on the small island just offshore and made his way to a cave just below the site of the present church. The church was restored in the nineteenth century by Lord Stanley of Alderley, Bertrand Russell's grandfather, a Muslim who used Islamic imagery in the stained glass.

Cemaes is the most reliable source of **accommodation** along this stretch of coast, with the non-smoking *Treddolphin Guesthouse* (☎01407/710388; ②), 200 yards down Beach Road from *The Stag* (see above), and the *Woburn Hill Hotel*, High Street (☎01407/711388; ③), the most central. Best of all, though, is the licensed Edwardian *Hafod Country House* (March–Oct; ☎01407/710500; ③), with en-suite rooms and excellent meals: at the roundabout on the A5025, at the top of the High Street, turn inland towards Llanfechell and the house is half a mile along. *The Stag* serves up some of the best pub **food** around.

Amlwch

AMLWCH, five miles east of Cemaes, would be just another tiny fishing village but for **Parys Mountain** (Mynydd Parys) a mile or so inland, once the world's largest source of copper. The Ordovices, a great Celtic tribe who occupied north Wales in the Neolithic era, probably began to extract the ore, and the Romans cer-tainly made use of it, but it wasn't until the eighteenth century that production lev-els reached industrial heights. Pollution had become a problem, but people noticed that the iron hulls of ships didn't corrode in the copper-laced harbour waters, fuelling a demand for protective copper sheathing that boosted the mar-ket for Parys copper. International competition in the early nineteenth century saw the town sink back into its role of a fishing port. You can reach the ruined pumping mill on top of Parys Mountain by a path from the car park on the B5111, a mile south of town, just next to the premises of the one company still trying to squeeze a profit from the ravaged heather-and-gorse-clad hulk of the mountain.

Copper was once shipped out by rail along a now disused seventeen-mile line, which local enthusiasts hope to reopen as a steam-hauled tourist route by 2002. Currently there's only the small **Lein Amlwch Museum**, in a former goods shed on Main Road (July to mid-Sept Tues–Sat 10.30am–7pm, Sun 10.30am–5pm; mid-Sept to June Tues–Sat 10.30am–4.30pm, Sun 12.30–4.30pm; £1.50), with a few model train layouts, railway memorabilia and a display on the history of the line.

After visiting so many ancient churches in Wales, **Our Lady Star of the Sea**, a couple of hundred yards along the A5025, to the west of Main Street, comes as something of a novelty. Built in the 1930s of reinforced concrete, the great parabolic ribs of what could be a giant toast rack are supposed to represent an upturned boat, complete with round portholes.

The handiest **accommodation** in Amlwch is at *Bron Arfor* (☎01407/831493; ③), right by the sea at the end of Ffordd Pen y Bonc, which runs opposite the library, and at the *Dinorben Arms*, High Street (☎01407/830358; ③), where you can also get filling pub **food**.

Moelfre and Red Wharf Bay

MOELFRE has a reputation for shipwrecks, though wandering around the peaceful grey-pebbled cove on a sunny day it seems unlikely. An anchor behind the beach was salvaged from the shipwrecked *Hindlea*, which went down in October 1959, exactly a century after the 2700-ton *Royal Charter* foundered, with the loss of 450 lives and nearly £400,000-worth of gold. The dead are remembered by a memorial stone thirty minutes' walk north along the coastal path that starts at the end of the cove, past a small offshore cormorant colony.

The town's only other point of interest lies a mile west off the A5025, where the late Neolithic **Capel Lligwy Hut Group** (unrestricted access; CADW) forms the centrepiece of a site covering three thousand years of human occupation. A five-sided walled enclosure contains the foundations of several circular and rectangular buildings dated to the second and fourth centuries which, along with the hut group on Holy Island, give the best indication of how these people actually lived, rather than how they buried their dead. To the northeast of the main enclosure stands **Capel Lligwy**, a forlorn-looking twelfth-century church, and a short distance to the south is the **Lligwy Burial Chamber** with its 28-ton capstone. All are just a short stroll from the road.

If you want to **stay**, try *Deanfield* (☎01248/410517; ③), 150 yards from the beach on the A5018 south of the village, or the farm **campsite** 500 yards inland from the beach, up the A5018, then along the signposted Ystad Nant Bychan.

A few miles southeast along the coast is **RED WHARF BAY**, a broad and appealing sweep of golden sand backed by the characterful, wooden-beamed *Ship Inn*, one of the best pubs on Anglesey. It is often crowded in summer when you might want to wander down the road to *The Old Boathouse Café & Restaurant* for good meals and great ice-cream sundaes.

Llangefni

About the only reason to come inland is to visit **LLANGEFNI** and the *Oriel Ynys Môn* (Tues–Sun 10.30am–5pm; £2), half a mile along the B5111 from the town (bus #36). This is essentially a tour of the island condensed into one large room, its displays, artefacts and reconstructions conveying something of the island's identity, from the pre-Cambrian substrata through copper mining to the arrival of the Irish Packet Steamers. A corner of the room is a mock-up of Charles Tunnicliffe's Malltraeth studio (see p.417) from which he made many of his detailed wildlife paintings, and elsewhere are finds from archeological digs around the island (though the better ones are in the National Museum in Cardiff), including a well-worn sandstone head carved in the Iron Age.

It is easy enough to continue on from Llangefni, since it's only five miles west of Llanfair PG, and on the #4 bus route to Holyhead and Bangor; if you're stuck, you can **stay** comfortably a mile west of town at *Argraig* (☎01248/724390; ③) – take the B5420 west, then the B4422 south. There are several mainstream **cafés** on the main street, or try one of the wholefood or home-baked dishes on the blackboard menu at *The Whole Thing*, 5 Field St (☎01248/724832).

travel details

Unless otherwise stated frequencies for trains and buses are for Monday to Saturday services; Sunday averages 1–3 services, though the main routes are more frequent and some routes have no Sunday service at all.

TRAINS

Bangor to: Chester, England (25 daily; 1hr 5min); Colwyn Bay (23 daily; 25min); Conwy (7 daily; 20min); Holyhead (20 daily; 30–40min); Llandudno Junction (25 daily; 20min); Rhosneigr (6 daily; 25min); Rhyl (22 daily; 35min).

Colwyn Bay to: Llandudno Junction (35 daily; 6min); Rhyl (35 daily; 10min).

Conwy to: Bangor (7 daily; 20min); Holyhead (8 daily; 1hr); Llandudno Junction (8 daily; 4min).

Flint to: Chester (at least hourly; 15min); Llandudno Junction (at least hourly; 40min); Prestatyn (at least hourly; 15min).

Holyhead to: Bangor (20 daily; 30–40min); Chester (14 daily; 1hr 25min–1hr 40min); Llandudno Junction (20 daily; 1hr); Llanfair PG (7 daily; 30min).

Llandudno to: Llandudno Junction (at least hourly; 10min).

Llandudno Junction to: Bangor (25 daily; 20min); Betws-y-Coed (6 daily; 25min); Holyhead (20 daily; 1hr); Llandudno (at least hourly; 10min); Rhyl (35 daily; 20min).

Llanfair PG to: Bangor (7 daily; 10min); Holyhead (7 daily; 30min).

Prestatyn to: Flint (at least hourly; 15min); Llandudno Junction (at least hourly; 25min); Rhyl (at least hourly; 8min).

Rhosneigr to: Holyhead (7 daily; 10min); Llanfair PG (7 daily; 15min).

Rhyl to: Bangor (22 daily; 35min); Holyhead (7 daily; 1hr 10min–1hr 40min); Llandudno Junction (35 daily; 20min).

BUSES

Bangor to: Beaumaris (every 30min; 25min); Betws-y-Coed (2 daily; 50min); Caernarfon (every 20min; 30min); Capel Curig (2 daily; 40min); Cardiff (1 daily; 7hr 45min); Llangefni (every 30min; 30min); Holyhead (every 30min; 1hr 15min); Llanberis (every 30min; 25min); Menai Bridge (every 30min; 12min).

Beaumaris to: Bangor (every 30min; 25min); Menai Bridge (every 30min; 15min).

Conwy to: Bangor (every 30min; 45min); Llanrwst (every 30min; 40min); Llandudno (every 30min; 20min); Rhyl (every 30min; 1hr 30min).

Denbigh to: Corwen (every 2hr; 1hr); Rhyl (every 30min; 40min); Ruthin (11 daily; 25min); St Asaph (every 30min; 15min).

Flint to: Holywell (every 30min; 10min); Mold (hourly; 30min).

Holyhead to: Amlwch (8 daily; 50min); Bangor (every 30min; 1hr 15min); Cemaes (8 daily; 40min); Chester, England (1 daily, 3hr 30min); Llanfair PG (every 30min; 1hr); Llangefni (every 30min; 45min); Menai Bridge (every 30min; 1hr 5min); Rhoscolyn (4 daily; 15min); Trearddur Bay (every 30min; 1hr 10min).

Llandudno to: Bangor (every 30min; 1hr); Llanrwst (every 30min; 1hr); Rhyl (every 15–30min; 1hr 10min).

Llanfair PG to: Bangor (every 30min; 15min); Holyhead (every 30min; 1hr); Llangefni (every 30min; 15min); Newborough (11 daily; 20min).

Mold to: Chester, England (every 30min; 50min); Ruthin (every 2hr; 45min).

Rhyl to: Llandudno (every 15–30min; 1hr 10min); Ruthin (10 daily; 1hr 10min); St Asaph (every 30min; 25min).

Ruthin to: Corwen (every 2hr; 30min); Denbigh (11 daily; 25min); Mold (every 2hr; 45min); Rhyl (10 daily; 1hr 10min); St Asaph (10 daily; 45min).

St Asaph to: Corwen (every 2hr; 1hr 15min); Denbigh (every 30min; 15min); Rhuddlan (every 30min; 15min); Rhyl (every 30min; 25min); Ruthin (10 daily; 45min).

Wrexham to: Chester (every 15min; 40min); Chirk (hourly; 40min); Llangollen (hourly or better; 35min); Mold (16 daily; 1hr).

FERRIES

Holyhead to: Dublin (2 daily; 3hr 30min); Dun Laoghaire (2 ferries daily; 3hr 30min; 5 catamarans daily; 1hr 40min).

PART THREE

THE
CONTEXTS

THE HISTORICAL FRAMEWORK

THE BEGINNINGS

Before the end of the last **Ice Age** around ten thousand years ago, Wales and the rest of Britain formed part of the greater European whole and the early migrant inhabitants eked out a meagre living on the tundra or a better one amongst the oak, beech and hazel forests in the warmer periods. Most lived in the southeast of Britain, but small groups foraged north and west, leaving 250,000-year-old evidence in the form of a human tooth in a cave near Denbigh in north Wales and a hand axe unearthed near Cardiff.

It wasn't until the early part of the **Upper Paleolithic age** that significant communities settled in Wales, those of the Gower peninsula interring the "Red Lady of Paviland" around 24,000 BC (see p.130). This civilization was far behind those of central France or northern Spain, and remained on Europe's cultural fringe as the melting ice cut Britain off from mainland Europe around 5000 BC. Migrating Mesolithic peoples had already moved north from Central Europe and were followed by **Neolithic colonists**, whose mastery of stone and flint working found its expression in over a hundred and fifty cromlechs (turf-covered chambered tombs) dotted around Wales, primarily Pentre Ifan in Mynydd Preseli (see p.191) and

Barclodiad y Gawres on Anglesey (see p.418). Skilled in agriculture and animal husbandry, the Neolithic people also began to clear the lush forests covering Wales below 2000 feet, enclosing fields, constructing defensive ditches around their villages and mining for flint.

The earliest stone circles – more extensive meeting places than cromlechs – were built at this time and continued to spread over the country as the Neolithic period drifted into the **Bronze Age** around 2000 BC. Through their extensive trade networks, the inhabitants of Wales and the rest of Britain gradually adopted new techniques, changing to more sophisticated use of metals and developing a well-organized social structure. The established aristocracy engaged in much tribal warfare, as suggested by large numbers of earthwork forts built in this and the immediately succeeding period – the chief examples being at Holyhead Mountain on Anglesey and the Bulwalks at Chepstow.

THE CELTS

Celtic invaders spreading from their central European homeland settled here in around 600 BC, imparting a great cultural influence. Familiar with Mediterranean civilization through trading routes, they introduced superior methods of metal-working that favoured iron rather than bronze, from which they forged not just weapons but also coins. Gold was used for ornamental works – the first recognizable Welsh art – heavily influenced by the symbolic, patterned **La Tène** style still thought of as quintessentially Celtic.

The Celts are credited with introducing the basis of modern Welsh. The original Celtic tongue was spoken over a wide area, gradually dividing into Goidelic (or Q-Celtic) now spoken in Ireland and Scotland, and **Brythonic** (P-Celtic) spoken in Wales, Cornwall and later exported to Brittany in France. This highly developed language was emblematic of a sophisticated social hierarchy headed by **druids**, a ritual priesthood with attendant poets, seers and warriors. Through a deep knowledge of ritual, legend and the mechanics of the heavens, the druids maintained their position between the people and a pantheon of over four thousand gods. Most of these were variations of a handful of chief gods worshipped by the great British tribes: the Silures and Demetae in the south of Wales, the Cornovii in mid-Wales and the

Ordovices and Deceangli in the north. Great though the Celtic technological and artistic achievements were, the people and their pan-European cousins were unable to maintain an organized civic society to match that of their successors, the Romans.

THE ROMANS IN WALES

Life in Wales, unlike that in most of England, was never fully Romanized, the region remaining under legionary control throughout its three-hundred-year occupation. **Julius Caesar** made small cross-channel incursions in 55 and 54 BC, kicking off a lengthy but low-level infusion of Roman ideas which filtered across to Wales. This flow swelled a century later when the emperor **Claudius** took the death of the British king Cunobelin (Cynfelyn) as a signal to launch a full-scale invasion in 43 AD which in four years swept across southern England to the frontier of south Wales. Expansionism fomented anti-Roman feeling along the frontier between the Lowland Zone (southern and central England) and the Highland Zone (northern England, Scotland and Wales). Traditionally insular Welsh hill tribes united with their Brythonic cousins in northern England to oppose the Romans, who proceeded to force a wedge between them. The Roman historian **Tacitus** recorded the submission of the Deceangli near Chester, giving us the oldest written mention of a Welsh land. The Romans, held back by troubles at home and with the East Anglian revolt of **Boudicca** (Boadicea), were limited to tentative dabbling in Welsh affairs, sending expeditionary forces against the Silures and the toughest nut, the druid stronghold of Anglesey. The obdurate nature of the Welsh on their back foot kept the Romans at bay until around 75 AD when legionary forts were built at Deva (Chester, England) and Isca Silurium (Caerleon) to act as platforms for incursions west along specially built military roads.

By 78 AD, Wales was under Roman control, its chief fortresses at Deva, Isca Silurium and Segontium (Caernarfon) boasting all the trappings of imperial Roman life: bath houses, temples, mosaics and underfloor heating. Through three centuries of occupation, the Celtic people sustained an independent existence while drawing material comfort from the proximity of Roman cities and auxiliary forts. Elements of Roman life filtered into the Celtic culture: agrar-

ian practices improved, a new religion was partly adopted from the newly Christianized Romans, the language adopted Latin words (*pont* for "bridge", *ffenestr* for "window") and the prevailing La Tène artistic style took on classical Roman elements.

The Roman Empire was already in decline when **Magnus Maximus** (Macsen Wledig) led a campaign to wrest control of the western empire from Emperor Gratian in 383 AD. Maximus' rule was short lived but Wales was effectively free of direct Roman control by 390.

THE AGE OF THE SAINTS

Historical orthodoxy views the departure of literate Latin historians, skilled stonemasons and an all-powerful army, as heralding the **Dark Ages**. In fact, a civic society probably flourished until a century later, when the collapse of trade routes was hastened by the dramatic spread of Islam around the Mediterranean, and Romanized society gave way to a non-Classical but no less structured form of **Celtic society**.

For the next few centuries, **Teutonic barbarian tribes** were struggling for supremacy in the post-Roman power vacuum in southern and eastern England, having little influence in Wales, where the main dynastic kingdoms set to steer Wales' next seven hundred years were taking root. The confusion that surrounds the early years of these dynasties was further muddied in 1136, when Geoffrey of Monmouth published his *History of the Kings of Britain*, portraying **King Arthur** as a feudal king with his court at Caerleon. Victorian Romantics embellished subsequent histories, making it practically impossible to extract much truth from this period.

In the fifth century, the **Irish** (Gwyddyl), who had a long tradition of migrating to the Llŷn and parts of mid-Wales, attacked the coast and formed distinct colonies, but were soon expelled from the north by **Cunedda Wledig**, the leader of a Brythonic tribe from near Edinburgh, who went on to found the royal house of Gwynedd, consolidating the Brythonic language and ostensibly naming regions of his kingdom – the modern Ceredigion and Meirionydd – after his sons. In the southwest, the Irish influence was sustained; the kingdom of Dyfed shows clear Irish origins.

These changes took place against a background of increasing religious energy. Between the fifth and the sixth centuries the **Celtic Saints**, ascetic evangelical missionaries, spread the gospel around Ireland and western Britain, promoting the middle-Eastern eremitical tradition of living a reclusive life. Where their message took root, they founded simple churches within a consecrated enclosure, or *llan*, which often took the saint's name, hence Llanberis (Saint Peris), Llandeilo (Saint Teilo) and many others. In south Wales, **Saint David** (Dewi Sant) was the most popular (and subsequently Wales' patron saint), dying around 589 after a miracle-filled life, during which he made a pilgrimage to Jerusalem and established the religious community at St David's, which had become a place of pilgrimage by the twelfth century.

THE WELSH KINGDOMS

Towards the end of the sixth century the **Angles** and **Saxons** in eastern Britain began to entertain designs on the western lands. The inability of the independent western peoples to unify against this threat left the most powerful kingdom, Gwynedd, as the centre of cultural and political resistance, a position it has retained to this day. The weaker groups were unable to hold the invaders, and after the battle at Dyrham, near Gloucester in 577, the Britons in Cornwall were separated from those in Wales, who became similarly cut off from their northern kin in Cumbria after the battle of Chester in 616.

Though still geographically in a state of change, Wales could by now be said to exist. At this point the racial mix in Wales was probably little different from that to the east where Saxon numbers were small, but Wales was held together by the people's resistance to the Saxons. The Welsh started to refer to themselves as **Cymry** (fellow-countrymen), not by the Saxon term used by English-speakers today, which is generally thought to mean either foreigners or Romanized people. The construction of **Offa's Dyke** (Clawdd Offa) – a linear earthwork built in the middle of the eighth century to mark rather than defend the boundary between Wales and the kingdom of Mercia – gave the Welsh a firm eastern border and allowed them to concentrate on a gradual unification of the patchwork of kingdoms as their coasts were being harried by **Norse and Viking invaders**.

Rhodri Mawr (Rhodri the Great) killed the Viking leader off Anglesey, earning himself the

formal thanks of the Frankish king Charles the Bald (Charlemagne), and helped the country's rise towards statehood through his unification of most of Wales. By this stage, England had developed into a single powerful kingdom for the first time since the departure of the Romans, and though the various branches of Rhodri's line went on to rule most of Wales down to the late thirteenth century, the princedoms were frequently forced to swear fealty to the English kings. Defensive problems were exacerbated by internecine struggles borne of the practice of partible inheritance that left each of Rhodri's sons with an equal part of Wales to control.

Rhodri's grandson **Hywel Dda** (Hywel the Good) largely reunified the country from Deheubarth, his power base in southwest Wales. He added Powys and Gwynedd to his domain, but his most valuable legacy is his codification, compilation and promulgation of the medieval **Law of Wales** (Cyfraith Hywel Dda) at Whitland (see p.150) around 930. Regional customs were fashioned into a single legal system that was only abandoned under the 1536 Act of Union with England. The laws drew more from the tenets of folk law than state edict: farming was conducted communally, the bard was exempt from menial tasks, a husband did not have unrestricted control over his wife (as was the case in much of Europe), and if a family were destitute they were allowed to retain a cooking pot and their harp.

After Hywel's death in 950, anarchy and internal turmoil reigned until his great-great-grandson, **Gruffydd ap Llywelyn**, seized power in Gwynedd in 1039. He unified all of Wales, taking the coronation of the weak English king, Edward the Confessor, as an opportunity to annex some of the Marches in Mercia. Edward's successor, Harold, wasn't having any of this and killed Gruffydd, heralding a new phase of political fragmentation.

THE ARRIVAL OF THE NORMANS

In 1066, the **Normans** swept across the English Channel, killed Harold, the English king, and stormed England. Though Wales was unable to present a unified opposition to the invaders, the Norman king, William, didn't attempt to conquer Wales. The **Domesday Book** – his masterwork of subjugation commissioned in 1085 to record land ownership as a framework for taxation – indicates that he only nibbled at parts of Powys and Gwynedd. Instead, he installed a huge retinue of barons, the **Lords Marcher**, along the border to bring as much Welsh territory under their own jurisdiction as possible. Despite generations of squabbling, the barons managed to hold onto their privileges until Henry VIII's Act of Union over four hundred years later.

The payment of homage by **Rhys ap Tewdwr** the king of Deheubarth, and **Gruffydd ap Cynan** the king of Gwynedd, kept the Welsh borders safe until the death of William I in 1087. His son William Rufus made three unsuccessful invasions of Wales but finally left it to his Marcher lords (now numbering over 140) to advance from their castles into south Wales, leaving only Powys and Gwynedd independent. A lack of English commitment or resources allowed the Welsh to claw back their territory through years when distinctions between English, Normans and Welsh were beginning to blur. One product of this was the quarter-Welsh **Giraldus Cambrensis** (see p.350), who left a valuable record of twelfth-century life in Wales and his opinions on Welsh character. "They are quicker witted and more shrewd than any other Western people", he informs us, a quality which helped them form three stable political entities: Powys, Deheubarth and Gwynedd. The latter, led by **Owain Gwynedd** from his capital at Aberffraw on Anglesey, now extended beyond Offa's Dyke and progressively gained hegemony over the other two. Owain Gwynedd's grandson, **Llywelyn ap Iorwerth** (the Great), who earned his laurels through shrewd campaigning, progressively incorporated the weaker territories to the south into his kingdom and captured several Norman castles to reach the peak of the Welsh feudal pyramid. Manipulating the favours of the English king John, Llywelyn managed to extend his control over southern Powys before a fearful John led two devastating campaigns into north Wales. Llywelyn was humiliated and forced into recognizing John as his heir should Llywelyn's union with John's illegitimate daughter Joan not produce a son. Channelling a now united Welsh opposition against John, Llywelyn struck back and won some degree of Welsh autonomy. Worried that his unified Wales would disintegrate on his death, Llywelyn engineered the smooth succession by commanding his princes to assemble at Strata Florida (see p.270) and pay homage not just to him (as was now his by right) but also to his son, Dafydd. This plan succeeded until after his death, when Wales began to disintegrate to the point where at Dafydd's death in 1246 the country had only nominal unity.

Most of the work of regrouping Wales around one standard fell to Llywelyn the Great's grandson and Dafydd's nephew, Llywelyn ap Gruffydd (Llewellyn the Last).

EDWARD I'S CONQUEST

By 1255, Llywelyn ap Iorwerth's grandson, **Llywelyn ap Gruffydd** (the Last), had won control of Gwynedd. During the next three years he pushed the English out of Gwynedd then out of most of Wales. The English king Henry III was forced to respect Llywelyn's influence and ratified the **Treaty of Montgomery** in 1267, thereby recognizing Llywelyn as "Prince of Wales" in return for his homage. The English monarchy's war with the barons allowed Llywelyn time to politically consolidate his lands which now stretched over all of modern Wales except for Pembrokeshire and parts of the Marches. The tables turned when Edward I succeeded Henry III and began a crusade to unify Britain. Llywelyn had failed to attend Edward's coronation, refused to pay him homage, and at the same time Llywelyn's determination to marry the daughter of Simon de Montfort lost him the support of the south Welsh princes and some Marcher lords. Edward was a skilful tactician and with effective use of sea power had little trouble forcing the already weakened Llywelyn back into Snowdonia. Peace was restored with the **Treaty of Aberconwy** which deprived Llywelyn of almost all his land and stripped him of his financial tributes from the other Welsh princes, but left him with the hollow title of "Prince of Wales".

Edward now set about surrounding Llywelyn's land with castles at Aberystwyth, Builth Wells, Flint and Rhuddlan (see p.397). After a relatively cordial four-year period, Llywelyn's brother Dafydd rose against Edward, inevitably dragging Llywelyn along with him. Edward didn't hesitate and swept through Gwynedd, crushing the revolt and laying the foundations for the remaining castles in his **Iron Ring**, those at Conwy, Caernarfon, Harlech and Beaumaris. Llywelyn, already battered by

Edward's force, was captured and executed at Cilmeri (see p.219), after fleeing from the abortive Battle of Builth in 1282. The **Statute of Rhuddlan** in 1284 set down the terms by which the English monarch was to rule Wales: much of it was given to the Marcher lords who had helped Edward, the rest was divided into administrative and legal districts similar to those in England. Though the treaty is often seen as a symbol of English subjugation, it respected much of Welsh law and provided a basis for civil rights and privileges. Many Welsh were content to accept and exploit Edward's rule for their own benefit, but in 1294 a rebellion led by **Madog ap Llywelyn** gripped Wales and was only halted by Edward's swift and devastating response. Most of the privileges enshrined in the Statute of Rhuddlan were now rescinded and the Welsh seemed crushed for a century.

OWAIN GLYNDŴR

Throughout the fourteenth century, famine and the Black Death plagued Wales. The Marcher lords appropriated the lands of defaulting debtors and squeezed the last pennies out of their tenants, while royal officials clawed in all the income they could from the towns around the castles. These factors and the pent-up resentment of the English sowed seeds of a rebellion led by the tyrannical but charismatic Welsh hero **Owain Glyndŵr**. Citing his descent from the princes of both Powys and Deheubarth, he declared himself "Prince of Wales" in 1400, and with a crew of local supporters attacked the lands of nearby barons, slaughtering the English. Henry IV misjudged the political climate and imposed restrictions on Welsh land ownership, swelling the general support Glyndŵr needed to take Conwy Castle the following year. By 1404 Glyndŵr, who already had control over most of western Wales and sections of the Marches, took the castles at Harlech and Aberystwyth, summoned a parliament in Machynlleth, and had himself crowned Prince of Wales, with envoys of France, Scotland and Castile in attendance. He then demanded independence for the Welsh Church from Canterbury and set about securing alliances with English noblemen who had grievances with Henry IV. This last ambitious move heralded Glyndŵr's downfall. A succession of defeats saw his allies desert him, and by 1408,

when the castles at Harlech and Aberystwyth were retaken for the Crown, this last protest against Edward I's English conquest had lost its momentum. Little is known of Glyndŵr's final years, though it is thought he died in 1416, leaving Wales territorially unchanged but the country's national pride at an all-time high.

THE TUDORS AND UNION WITH ENGLAND

During the latter half of the fifteenth century, the succession to the English throne was contested in the **Wars of the Roses** between the houses of York (white rose) and Lancaster (red rose). Welsh allegiance lay broadly with the Lancastrians, who had the support of the ascendant north Welsh Tewdwr (or Tudor) family. Through the early part of the wars, one Henry Tudor lived with his widowed Welsh mother, Margaret Beaufort, at the besieged Harlech Castle, escaping to Brittany when Yorkist Richard III took the English throne in 1471. Fourteen years later, Henry returned to Wales, landing at Milford Haven, and defeated Richard at the Battle of Bosworth Field, so becoming **Henry VII** and sealing the Lancastrian ascendancy.

Welsh expectations of the new monarch were high. Henry lived up to some of them, removing many of the restrictions on land ownership imposed at the start of Glyndŵr's uprising, and promoting many Welshmen to high office, but administration remained piecemeal. Control was still shared between the Crown and largely independent Marcher lords until a uniform administrative structure was achieved under Henry VIII.

Wales had been largely controlled by the English monarch since the Statute of Rhuddlan in 1284, but the **Acts of Union** in 1536 and 1543 fixed English sovereignty over the country. At the same time the Marches were replaced by shires (the equivalent of modern counties), the Welsh laws codified by Hywel Dda were made void, and partible inheritance gave way to primogeniture, the eldest son becoming the sole heir. For the first time the Welsh and English enjoyed legal equality, but the break with native traditions wasn't well received. Most of the people remained poor, the gentry became increasingly anglicized, the use of Welsh was proscribed and legal proceedings were held in English (a language few peasants understood).

Just as Henry VIII's decision to convert his kingdom from Catholicism to Protestantism was borne more from his desire to divorce his first wife, Catherine of Aragon, than from any religious conviction, it was his need for money not recognition, which brought about the **Dissolution of the monasteries** in 1536. Monastic lands were divided amongst the local gentry, but since Christianity had always been a ritual way of life rather than a philosophical code in Wales, Catholicism was easily replaced by Protestantism. What the Reformation did promote was a more studied approach to religion and learning in general. Under the reign of Elizabeth I, Jesus College was founded in Oxford for Welsh scholars, and the Bible was translated into Welsh for the first time by a team led by Bishop **William Morgan** (see p.380).

With new land ownership laws enshrined in the Acts of Union, the stimulus provided by the Dissolution hastened the emergence of the Anglo-Welsh gentry, a group eager to claim a Welsh pedigree while promoting the English language and the legal system, helping to perpetuate their grasp. Meanwhile, landless peasants continued in poverty, only gaining slightly from the increase in cattle trade with England and the slow development of mining and ore smelting.

THE CIVIL WAR AND THE RISE OF NONCONFORMISM

James I, a direct descendant of the Tudors, came to the throne in 1603 to general popular approval in Wales. Many privileges granted to the Welsh during the Tudor reign came to an end, but the idea of common citizenship was retained, the Council of Wales remaining as a focus for Welsh nationalism. James, fearful of both Catholicism and the new threat of Puritanism – an extreme form of Protestantism – courted a staunchly Anglican Wales and curried the favour of Welsh ministers in the increasingly powerful Parliament. Though weak in Wales, Puritanism was gaining a foothold, especially in the Welsh borders, where William Wroth and Walter Cradock set up Wales' first dissenting church at Llanfaches in Monmouthshire in 1639, to become the spiritual home of Welsh Nonconformism.

The monarchy's relations with the Welsh were strained by **Charles I**, who was forced to levy heavy taxes and recruit troops, but the gentry were mostly loyal to the king at the outbreak of the **Civil War**, which saw the Parliamentary forces installing **Oliver Cromwell** as the leader of the **Commonwealth**. The Puritan support for Parliament didn't go unrewarded and, after Charles' execution, they were rewarded with the livings of numerous parishes and the roots of Puritan Nonconformism spread in Wales. As Cromwell's regime became more oppressive, the Anglican majority became disaffected and welcomed the successful return of the exiled **Charles II**, and the monarchy was restored. Charles replaced many of the clergy in their parishes and passed the Act of Uniformity, requiring adherence to the rites of the Established Church, and so suppressing Nonconformity. The Baptists, Independents and Quakers who made up the bulk of Nonconformists continued to worship in secret, until **James II** passed the **Toleration Act** in 1689, finally allowing open worship, but still banning the employment of dissenters in municipal government; a limitation which remained in force until 1828.

THE RISE OF METHODISM

The propagation of the Nonconformist seed in this fertile soil was less a conscious effort to convert the populace from Anglicanism than to better educate the masses. The late seventeenth century saw a welter of new religious books in Welsh, but with most people still illiterate, religious observance remained an oral tradition. In 1699, the **Society for Promoting Christian Knowledge**, set about establishing schools where the Bible, along with reading, writing and arithmetic, were taught in Welsh as well as English. This met with considerable success amongst the middle classes in anglicized towns, but failed to reach rural areas where children couldn't be spared from farm duties. The next big reformist push came in 1731, when **Griffith Jones** helped organize itinerant teachers to hold reading classes in the evenings and in the quieter winter season, so farmers and their families could attend. Within thirty years, half the Welsh population could read. After Jones' death, **Thomas Charles** of Bala (see p.253) continued his work, establishing Sunday schools and editing the first Welsh Bible to be distributed by the **British and Foreign Bible Society**.

By the middle of the eighteenth century, a receptive and literate populace was ready for three eloquent figures of the **Methodist Revival**, all driven by a strong belief in a resurgent Welsh nation. In contrast to the staid Anglican services, the Methodists held evangelical meetings: **Howel Harris** took his preaching outside or into people's homes, **Daniel Rowlands** converted thousands with his powerful sermons, and **William Williams** became the most important hymn writer in Welsh history. Meanwhile, improved schooling brought about a literary revolution, Welsh re-establishing itself as the vehicle for a vast body of literature which today outweighs the number of speakers.

Until now, Methodism worked within the framework of Anglicanism, but in 1811 the Calvinist Methodists broke away. As the gentry remained with the Established Church, Methodism associated itself with the spiritual and social needs of the masses, becoming a rallying point for the growing sense of disaffection with the traditional rule of the parson and squire. The Chapel became the focus of social life, discouraging folk traditions as incompatible with the Puritan virtues of thrift and temperance. Political radicalism was also discouraged, perpetuating the stranglehold on parliamentary power exercised by the powerful landed elite, the Williams-Wynn, Morgan and Vaughan families in particular. Only property owners were eligible to vote and few were prepared to challenge established dynasties, even when the rare elections took place.

Human rights became an issue in 1776 with the publication of the American Declaration of Independence and a piece by the radical Welsh philosopher, **Richard Price**: *Observations on the Nature of Civil Liberty*. The subsequent calls for a greater degree of democracy – universal suffrage and annual parliaments – increased during the early days of the French Revolution, but little was actually achieved until the next century, when radical Nonconformists were able to exploit the increasing political consciousness of the working class.

WALES AND THE INDUSTRIAL REVOLUTION

Small-scale mining and smelting had taken place in Wales since the Bronze Age, but agriculture remained the mainstay of an economy with a dangerously limited diversity: meat, wool and butter being about the only exports. With the enormous rise in grain prices in the early nineteenth century, Welsh farmers began to diversify and adopted the more advanced English farming practices of crop rotation, fertilizing and stock breeding. Around the same time, acts of Parliament allowed previously common land to be "enclosed", the grazing rights often being assigned to the largest landowner in the district, leaving the previous occupant with few or no rights to its use. This inevitably forced smallholders to migrate to the towns where ever more workers were required to mine the seams and stoke the furnaces, fuelling the **Industrial Revolution**. In the north, **John Wilkinson** started his ironworks at Bersham (see p.370) and developed a new method of boring cylinders for steam engines; while in the south, foundries sprang up in the valleys around Merthyr Tydfil, where methods of purifying iron and producing high-quality construction steel were perfected under the eye of English ironmasters. Gradually the undereducated, impoverished Chapel-going Welsh began to be governed by rich, Church-going, English industrial barons.

Improved materials and working methods enabled the exploitation of deeper coal seams, not just to supply the iron smelters but for domestic fuel and to power locomotives and steamships. As the rich veins of coal deep below the Rhondda valleys were exploited by Welshmen like Walter Coffin and George Insole, south Wales was transformed: rural valleys were ripped apart and quiet hamlets turned into long unplanned rows of back-to-back houses stretching up the valley sides, all roofed in north Wales slate from quarries dug by the Pennant and Assheton-Smith families.

Transportation of huge quantities of coal and steel was crucial for continued economic expansion, and the roads and canals built in the early nineteenth century were displaced around 1850 as the rail boom took hold. Great engineers made their names in Wales: **Thomas Telford** built canal aqueducts and successfully spanned the Menai Strait with one of Britain's earliest suspension bridges; **Isambard Kingdom Brunel** surveyed the Merthyr–Cardiff train line, then pushed his Great Western network almost to Fishguard; and **Robert Stephenson** speeded the passage of trains between London and

Holyhead on Anglesey for the Irish ferry connection.

In mining towns, working conditions were atrocious, with men toiling incredibly long hours in dangerous conditions; women and children as young as six worked alongside them, until this was outlawed by the Mines Act in 1842. Pay was low and often in a currency redeemable only at the poorly stocked, expensive company (Truck) shop. The **Anti-Truck Act** of 1831 improved matters, but a combination of rising population, fluctuating prices and growing awareness of the need for political change brought calls for reform. When it came in 1832, the **Reform Bill** fell far short of the demands for universal suffrage by ballot and the removal of property requirement for voters. This swelled the ranks of the Reformist Chartist movement, and when a petition with over a million signatures was rejected by Parliament, the **Chartist Riots** (see p.223) broke out in northern England and south Wales. The Newport demonstration was disastrous, the marchers walking straight into a trap laid by troops, who killed over twenty men and captured their leader, **John Frost**. Chartism continued in a weakened form for twenty years, buoyed by the **Rebecca Riots** in 1843–43, when guerrilla tactics put an end to tollgates on south Welsh turnpikes.

1850 TO WORLD WAR I

During the latter half of the nineteenth century the radical reformist movement and religion slowly became entwined, despite Nonconformist denial of political intentions. Recognizing that their flock didn't share the same rights as Anglicans, the Nonconformists petitioned for **disestablishment** of the Church in Wales and began to politicize their message. In the 1859 election, tenants on large farms (the only ones permitted to vote) were justifiably afraid of voting against their landowners or even abstaining from voting, and the conservative landowning hegemony held. But as a consequence of the 1867 Reform Act, industrial workers and small tenant farmers got the vote, finally giving a strong working-class element to the electorate, seeing **Henry Richard** elected as Liberal MP for Merthyr Tydfil the following year, the first Welsh member of what soon became the dominant political force. Bringing the ideas of Nonconformity to Parliament for the first time, he spoke eloquently on land reform, disestablishment and the preservation of the Welsh language.

The 1872 Secret Ballot Act and 1884 Reform Act, enfranchising farm labourers, further freed up the electoral system and gave working people the chance to air their resentment of tithes extracted by a Church that didn't represent their religious views. Although several bills were tabled in Parliament in the 1890s, the Anglican church was only disestablished in 1920. The Nonconformist Sunday Schools were meanwhile offering the best primary education for the masses, supplemented, after **Hugh Owen** pushed through the Welsh Intermediate Education Act in 1885, by a number of secondary schools. Owen was also a prime mover in getting Wales' first tertiary establishment started in Aberystwyth in 1872, soon to be followed by colleges at Cardiff (1883) and Bangor (1884). Until they were federated into the University of Wales in 1893, voluntary contributions garnered by Nonconformist Chapels supported the colleges. The apotheosis of "Chapel power" came in 1881 with the passing of the Welsh Sunday Closing Act, enshrining Nonconformism's three basic tenets: observance of the Sabbath, sobriety and Welshness.

THE RISE IN WELSH CONSCIOUSNESS

During the nineteenth century, Welsh language and culture became weakened, largely through immigration to the coal fields from England. English became the language of commerce and the route to advancement; Welsh being reserved for the home and Chapel life of seventy percent of the population. But Welsh was still being spoken in Nonconformist schools when, in 1846, they were inspected by three English barristers and seven Anglican assistants. The inspectors' report – known as **The Treason of the Blue Books** – declared the standards deplorable, largely due to the use of the Welsh tongue, "the language of slavery". This unfair report did some good in fostering free, elementary education at "Board Schools" after 1870, though the public defence of Welsh that ensued failed to prevent the introduction of the notorious "Welsh Not", effectively a ban on speaking Welsh in school.

As the nineteenth-century Romantic movement took hold throughout Britain, the London Welsh looked to their heritage. The ancient tales of *The Mabinogion* were translated into English, the **Welsh Language Society** was started in 1885, *eisteddfodau* were reintroduced as part of rural life, and the ancient bardic order, the **Gorsedd**, was reinvented. But disestablishment remained the cause célèbre of Welsh nationalism which, despite the formation of the **Cymru Fydd** movement in 1886, with its demands for home rule along the lines of Ireland, wasn't generally separatist. Perhaps the greatest advocate of both separatism and Welsh nationalism was **Michael D Jones**, who helped establish a Welsh homeland in Patagonia and campaigned vociferously against "the English cause" (see p.253).

By 1907 Wales had a national library at Aberystwyth, and a national museum was planned for Cardiff, by now the largest city in Wales and laying claim to being its capital – only officially recognized in 1955.

INDUSTRY AND THE RISE OF TRADE UNIONISM

The rise in Welsh consciousness paralleled the rise in importance of the **trade unions**. The 1850s were a prosperous time in the Welsh coal fields, but by the end of the 1860s the Amalgamated Union of Miners was forced to call a strike (1869–71), which resulted in higher wages. A second strike in 1875 failed and the miners' agent, **William Abraham (Mabon)**, ushered in the notorious "sliding scale" which fixed wage levels according to the selling price of coal. This brought considerable hardship to the Valleys, which became insular worlds with strictly ordered social codes and a rich vibrancy borne from the essential dichotomy of the Chapel and the pub. Meanwhile, annual coal production doubled in twenty years to 57 million tons by 1913, when a quarter of a million people were employed. Similarly punitive pay schemes were implemented in the north Wales slate quarries where membership of **Undeb Chwarelwyr Gogledd Cymru** (The North Wales Quarrymen's Union) was all but outlawed by the slate barons. This came to a head in 1900 when the workers at Lord Penrhyn's quarry at Bethesda started Britain's longest ever industrial dispute. It lasted three years but achieved nothing.

From 1885, the vast majority of Welsh MPs were Liberals who helped end the sliding scale in 1902 and brought in an eight-hour day by 1908. The turn of the century heralded the birth of a new political force when **Keir Hardie** became Britain's first Labour MP, for Merthyr Tydfil.

THE TWO WORLD WARS

World War I (1914–18) was a watershed for Welsh society. Seeing parallels with their own nation, the Welsh sympathized with the plight of defenceless European nations and rallied to fight alongside the English and Scots. At home, the state intervened in people's lives more than ever before: agriculture was controlled by the state while food was rationed, and industries, mines and railways were under public control. The need for Welsh food and coal boosted the economy and living standards rose dramatically. Many were proud to be led through the war by Welsh lawyer **David Lloyd George** (see p.350), who rose to the post of Minister of Munitions, then of War, becoming Prime Minister by 1916; but by the time conscription was introduced, patriotic fervour had waned. Many miners, reluctant to be slaughtered in the trenches and resentful of massive wartime profits, welcomed the 1917 Bolshevik Revolution, and though Communism never really took hold, the socialist Labour Party was there to catch the postwar fallout.

Similar dramatic changes were taking place in rural areas, where Welsh farming was embracing new machinery and coming out of nearly a century of neglect. High wartime inflation of land prices and the fall in rents forced some landowners to sell off portions of major estates to their tenants in the so-called "green revolution", breaking the dominance of a rural landed gentry.

The boom time of World War I continued for a couple of years after 1918, but soon the Depression came. All of Wales' mining and primary production industries suffered, and unemployment reached 27 percent, worse than in England and Scotland, which both weathered the Depression better. The **Labour movement** ascended in step with the rise in unemployment, making south Wales its stronghold in Britain. Their stranglehold was challenged by Lloyd George's newly resurgent Liberal Party, but his Westminster-centred politics were no longer trusted in Wales and Labour held firm, seeking to improve workers' conditions: the state of housing was still desperate, and health care and welfare services needed boosting. The Labour Party effectively became the hope that had previously been entrusted to the Chapels and later the Liberals.

A new sense of nationalism was emerging and, in 1925, champions of Welsh national autonomy formed **Plaid Genedlaethol Cymru** (Welsh Nationalist Party) under **Saunders Lewis**, its president for ten years. In one of the first modern separatist protests, he joined two other Plaid members and set fire to building materials at an RAF station on the Llŷn, was dismissed from his post and spent his life in literary criticism, becoming one of Wales' greatest modern writers. Similar public displays and powerful nationalist rhetoric won over an intellectual majority, but the masses continued to fuel the Labour ascendancy in both local and national politics.

Some relief from the Depression came with re-armament in the lead-up to **World War II**, but by this stage vast numbers had migrated from south Wales to England, leaving the already insular communities banding together in self-reliant groups centred on local co-ops and welfare halls.

When war became inevitable, the Labour Party was committed to halting the Fascist threat along with most of Wales. As a result of the demands of the war, unemployment all but disappeared and the Welsh economy was gradually restructured, more people switching from extractive industries to light manufacturing, a process which continues today.

Plaid Cymru were less enthusiastic about the war, remaining neutral and expressing unease at the large number of English evacuees potentially weakening the fabric of Welsh communities. Their fears were largely ungrounded and the war saw the formation of a Welsh elementary school in Aberystwyth and *Undeb Cymru Fydd*, a committee designed to defend the welfare of Wales.

THE POSTWAR PERIOD

Any hopes for a greater national identity were dashed by the Attlee Labour government from 1945 to 1951, which nationalized transport and utilities with no regard for national boundaries, except for the Wales Gas Board. However, under the direction of Ebbw Vale MP, **Aneurin Bevan**, the postwar Labour government insti-

tuted the National Health Service, dramatically improving health care in Wales and the rest of Britain, and providing much-improved council housing.

The nationalized coal industry, now employing less than half the number of twenty years before, was still the most important employer at nationalization, but a gradual process of closing inefficient mines saw the number of pits drop from 212 in 1945 to 11 in 1989, and just one in 1996. Sadly, the same commitment wasn't directed at cleaning up the scars of over a century of mining until after 1966, when one of south Wales' most tragic accidents left a school and 116 children buried under a slag heap at **Aberfan** (see p.82).

In the rural areas, the 1947 Agriculture Act brought some stability to financially precarious hill farmers by stabilizing prices, who were given further protection with the formation of the Farmers' Union of Wales in 1955. A more controversial fillip came from the siting of an aluminium smelter and two nuclear power stations in north Wales, dubious benefits soon eroded by the closure of much of the rural rail system following the Beeching Report in 1963. Despite the switch to light manufacturing and the improved agricultural methods, unemployment in Wales rose to twice the UK average, and women continued to be greatly under-represented.

After its postwar successes, the Labour Party remained in overwhelming control during the 1960s and 1970s, though Plaid Cymru became a serious opposition for the first time, partly due to Labour's reluctance to address nationalist issues. Attlee had thrown out the suggestion of a Welsh Secretary of State in 1946, and not until Plaid Cymru was fielding twenty nationalist candidates in the 1959 election did the Labour manifesto promise a cabinet position for Wales. The position of **Secretary of State for Wales** was finally created in 1964 by the Labour government, led by Harold Wilson, who also created the **Welsh Development Agency** and moved the Royal Mint to south Wales. With Plaid Cymru's appeal considered to be restricted to rural areas, Labour was shocked by the 1966 Carmarthen by-election, when **Gwynfor Evans** became the first Plaid MP. It wasn't until 1974 that Plaid also won in the constituencies of Caernarfon and Meirionydd, and suddenly the Party was a threat, forcing Labour to address the question of devolution. By 1978 Labour had tabled the **Wales Act**, promising the country an elected assembly to act as a voice for Wales, but with no power to legislate or raise revenue. In the subsequent **referendum** in 1979, eighty percent of voters opposed the proposition, with even the nationalist stronghold of Gwynedd voting against.

MODERN WALES

In 1979, the Conservative government of **Margaret Thatcher** came to power, achieving an unprecedented 31 percent of Welsh votes. The 1979 referendum effectively sidelined the home-rule issue and Thatcher was able to implement her free-market policies with an unstinting commitment to privatizing nationalized industries. With 43 percent of the Welsh workforce as government employees, privatization had a dramatic impact. The number of jobs in the steel industry, manufacturing and construction all plummeted, doubling unemployment in five years. Despite this, the Tories held their share of the vote and, because of changes to constituency boundaries, increased their tally of MPs at the 1983 election, while Labour saw their lowest percentage since 1918.

Vast changes in employment patterns signalled the breakdown of traditional valley communities and the labour movement was weakened by successive anti-union measures. None of this broke the solidarity of south Welsh workers during the year-long **Miners' Strike** (1984–85), after which women took a much greater proportion of the work now transferring out of the Valleys onto the south coastal plain. Living standards were still rising and the Welsh were now better off than ever before, but high unemployment and a large rural population meant that average income still lagged behind most areas of England, and despite free medical care the Welsh remained in poorer health. As elsewhere in Britain in the second half of the

twentieth century, the Welsh have turned their backs on the established religions. The chapel has ceased to be the focal point of community life, and something like 4000 churches and chapels are due to close in the next twenty years.

During the 1980s, support for Plaid Cymru shifted back to the rural areas, the party holding all three out of four Gwynedd constituencies after the 1987 election. At the same time, general enthusiasm for the Welsh language increased and a steady decline in numbers of Welsh-speakers was reversed. New Welsh-only schools opened even in predominantly English-speaking areas, and in 1982, S4C, the first Welsh-language television channel, started broadcasting.

Since then, the Tories have landed the country with a succession of variously disinterested, and usually English, Secretaries of State who have done little to further the Welsh cause. Plaid support continues to grow and Wales continues to define a distinct identity which may ultimately be more influential than political allegiances. Certainly voting Labour, once considered the fast-track to Welsh independence, seems a less and less astute move as it lurches right under its leader, Tony Blair, shaking off much of its cherished ideology in the process.

Although it could be argued that Wales is no more in control of its own destiny than any time in the last seven hundred years, many see hope when Welsh independence is viewed in a European context. With devolution for Scotland within a united Europe still an issue, and continuing calls for Catalan and Lombard separation from Spain and Italy respectively, Britain looks ripe for division. But, while Scottish independence appears increasingly possible in the long run, Wales' stronger ties with England – the judicial system in particular – look set to thwart any realistic hopes for some time yet.

CHRONOLOGY OF WELSH HISTORY

250,000 BC	Earliest evidence of human existence in Wales.
9–8000 BC	End of last Ice Age.
6000 BC	Rising oceans separate Britain from Europe.
4000 BC	Agriculturalism becomes widespread in Wales.
2000 BC	Arrival of **Bronze Age** settlers from the Iberian peninsula colonizing Pembrokeshire and Anglesey, while the Gower was settled by people from Brittany and the Loire.
600 BC	**Celts** reach the British Isles: the Goidels settle in Ireland, the Brythons in parts of England and Wales.
43 AD	**Romans** begin conquest of Britain.
61	Suetonius Paulinus attacks north Wales and Anglesey.
78	Roman conquest of Wales completed as Agricola kills druids of Anglesey.
80–100	Caerleon amphitheatre built.
early C4th	Roman departure from Wales.
early C5th	**Cunedda Wledig** arrives from Scotland to conquer north Wales.
C5th–6th	**Age of Saints**.
c.500	St Illtud arrives from Ireland, bringing Christianity and founding Llanilltud Fawr monastery.
c. 589	Saint David (Dewi Sant) dies.
615	Aethelfrith defeats Welsh at Bangor.
616	Battle of Chester – Wales isolated from rest of Britain.
768	Celtic church accepts some of the practices and customs of the Roman Church, including its date for Easter.
c.784	Offa's Dyke (Clawdd Offa) constructed.
844–78	**Rhodri Mawr** rules Gwynedd, later gaining most of the rest of Wales through inheritance and marriage.
C9th–10th	St David's accepts supremacy of Rome.
c.900–50	Hywel Dda rules most of Wales.
C late 10th	Hywel Dda's unified Wales split into four independent principalities.
1039–63	**Gruffydd ap Llywelyn** reunites Wales.
1066	**Normans** invade Wales.
1067	Chepstow Castle started.
1090	First Norman castle at Cardiff.
1094	Normans repelled from Gwynedd and Dyfed.
1115	Norman bishop installed at St David's.
1143	Cistercians found Hendy-gwyn (Whitland) Abbey.
1180–93	St David's Cathedral built.
1188	Archbishop Baldwin (accompanied by Giraldus Cambrensis) recruits for the Third Crusade.
1196–1240	**Llywelyn ap Iorwerth** (the Great) rules as Prince of Gwynedd and later most of Wales.
1215	English barons force King John into signing Magna Carta. Limited rights for Wales.
1246–82	**Llywelyn ap Gruffydd** (the Last) intermittently rules large parts of Wales.
1267	**Treaty of Montgomery** signed by Henry III, ratifying Llywelyn ap Gruffydd's claim to the title "Prince of Wales".
1270–1320	Tintern Abbey built.
1276–77	**First War of Welsh Independence**.
1277	Llywelyn humiliated by signing **Treaty of Aberconwy**. Edward I begins Aberystwyth, Flint and Rhuddlan castles.
1282–83	**Second War of Welsh Independence**. Llywelyn's brother Dafydd rises up against Edward I.
1283	Caernarfon, Conwy and Harlech castles started.
1284	**Statute of Rhuddlan** signed by Edward I.
1294	Revolt of Madog ap Llywelyn.
1295	Beaumaris Castle started.
1301	Edward I revives title of "Prince of Wales" and bestows it on his son, Edward II.
1400–12	Third War of Welsh Independence. **Owain Glyndŵr's** revolt.
1416	Owain Glyndŵr dies in hiding.
1471	Edward IV's Council of Welsh Marches at Ludlow.
1485	Accession of **Henry VII** to throne after landing from exile at Pembroke and beating Richard III at Bosworth.
1536–38	Henry VIII suppresses monasteries.
1536–43	**Acts of Union**: legislation forming the union of Wales and England.

Equal rights but with a separate legal and administrative system conducted wholly in English.

1546 First book printed in Welsh: *Yn y Lhvyyr Hwnn.*

1571 Jesus College, Oxford (the Welsh college) founded.

1588 Translation of complete Bible into Welsh, chiefly by **William Morgan**.

1639 First Puritan congregation in Wales convened at Llanfaches, Gwent.

1642 Beginning of Civil War in England.

1644 **Battle of Montgomery**: first battle of Civil War on Welsh territory.

1646 Harlech and Raglan besieged during the Civil War. Harlech, the last Royalist castle, falls in 1647.

1660 Restoration of the monarchy.

1689 Toleration Act passed, allowing open, Nonconformist worship.

1707 Publication of Edward Lhuyd's *Archaeologia Britannica* initiates foundation of Celtic studies.

1743 Establishment of Welsh Calvinistic Methodist Church.

1759 Dowlais Ironworks started, followed by Merthyr Tydfil iron industry.

1782 Beginning of north Wales slate industry with the opening of Pennant's Penrhyn slate quarry at Bethesda.

1789 First **eisteddfod** for 200 years held at Corwen.

1793–94 Cardiff to Merthyr canal built.

1801 First census. Welsh population 587,000.

1811 Separation of Welsh Methodists from Church of England.

1832 Reform Bill passed in Westminster.

1839 **Chartist** march on Newport fails.

1839–43 **Rebecca Riots** close tollbooths on turnpikes.

1841 Taff Vale Railway built.

1845–50 Britannia Tubular Bridge built.

1859 Liberals win major victory in elections; tenants evicted for voting against their Conservative masters; Nonconformist revival.

1865 Michael D Jones founds Welsh colony in Patagonia.

1872 **University College of Wales** opens in Aberystwyth, followed by Cardiff (1883) and Bangor (1884).

1881 Passing of Welsh Sunday Closing Act.

1884 **Reform Act**. Farm labourers and small tenant farmers get the vote for the first time.

1885 **Welsh Language Society** founded.

1886 Tithe War in north and west Wales.

1893 **University of Wales** established.

1898 Foundation of **South Wales Miners' Federation**.

1900 Britain's first Labour MP, Kier Hardie, elected for Merthyr Tydfil.

1907 Founding of National Museum, Cardiff and National Library, Aberystwyth.

1914–18 World War I.

1916 **David Lloyd George** becomes Prime Minister.

1920 Disestablishment of Church of England in Wales.

1925 *Plaid Genedlaethol Cymru* (Welsh Nationalist Party) formed.

1926 **Miners' strike** and General Strike.

1929–34 Great Depression.

1936 Saunders Lewis and colleagues burn building materials on the Llŷn.

1939–45 World War II.

1951 Minister for Welsh Affairs appointed.

1955 Cardiff declared capital of Wales.

1959 Welsh flag royally accepted as such.

1963 *Cymdeithas yr Iaith Gymraeg* (Welsh Language Society) formed.

1964 James Griffith, first cabinet-level Secretary of State for Wales, appointed.

1966 **Gwynfor Evans**, first Plaid Cymru MP, elected for Carmarthen. Aberfan disaster.

1967 **Welsh Language Act** passed. Limited recognition of Welsh as a formal, legal language.

1974 Local government reorganization, creating eight new counties in Wales.

1979 Referendum on Welsh Assembly. Eighty percent of voters come out against a separate parliament.

1982 Welsh-language TV channel S4C begins broadcasting.

1984–85 **Miners' strike**.

1992 Welsh Language Bill gives Welsh equal status with English in public bodies.

1993 Establishment of the Welsh Language Board.

1994 First Welsh film, *Hedd Wyn*, nominated for an Oscar.

TWENTIETH-CENTURY WELSH NATIONALISM

If any single event can be said to have given birth to Welsh nationalism in the modern sense, it was a meeting amongst Welsh academics at the 1925 eisteddfod in Pwllheli on the Llŷn peninsula. Led by gifted writer Saunders Lewis, the group metamorphosed into **Plaid Genedlaethol Cymru**, the National Party of Wales.

The Welsh identity had always been culturally rich, but was politically expressed only as part of the great Liberal tradition: in the dying years of the nineteenth century, Welsh Liberal MPs organized themselves into a loose caucus roughly modelled on Parnell's Irish parliamentarians and, although the Welsh group was without the clout or number of the Irish MPs, 25 or 30 MPs voting en bloc was serious enough to be noticed. **David Lloyd George** (1863–1945; Prime Minister 1916–22), fiery Welsh patriot and Liberal premier of Great Britain, had embodied many people's nationalist beliefs, although his espousal of greater independence for Wales came unstuck when, ever the expedient politician, he realized the potential difficulty of translating this ideal into hard votes in the industrialized, anglicized south of Wales. During Lloyd George's premiership, the Irish Free State was established, drawing inevitable compar-

isons with the Home Rule demands being less stridently articulated in Scotland and Wales. But the Liberal Party was in sharp decline, nowhere more markedly than in the industrialized swathe of southern Wales, where the populous and radical mining Valleys had deserted the Liberals in favour of new socialist parties. With the urban decline of a steadfast, fiercely pro-Welsh Liberal tradition, and the emergence of the two main parties as class-based warriors at either side of the political spectrum, Welsh nationalism – faced with a persistent slump in the Welsh language – was gradually honed into Saunders Lewis' embryonic political party.

Plaid Cymru – the "Genedlaethol" was soon dropped – had an inauspicious start electorally, polling a total of 609 votes in its first contest in 1929. The party acted more as a pressure group, focused inevitably on the issue of the decline in the Welsh language and inextricably suffused with a romantic cultural air that had little apparent relevance to party politics. As war loomed over Europe in the latter half of the 1930s, Plaid maintained a controversially pacifist stance, winning few new converts. Most sensationally, in September 1936, Saunders Lewis and two other Plaid luminaries, the Rev Lewis Valentine and D J Williams, set fire to the construction hut of a new aerodrome being built on the Llŷn peninsula as part of Britain's build-up to the war. They immediately reported themselves to the nearest police station, attracting huge publicity in the process. Interest in the ensuing trial electrified Wales, causing howls of outrage when the government decided to divert it from sympathetic Caernarfon to the Old Bailey in London. Even recalcitrant nationalist Lloyd George was outspokenly critical of the English decision. The three men were duly imprisoned for nine months, becoming Plaid's first martyrs.

Despite having dwindled throughout the rest of Britain, the prewar Liberal tradition was still strong with the rural majority of Wales, though by the 1951 election this had become just three parliamentary seats out of 36. The **Labour party** was now the establishment in Wales, winning an average of around sixty percent of votes in elections from 1945 to 1966.

National feelings of loss and powerlessness began to take a hold in postwar Wales as the Welsh language haemorrhaged from the country. Although Wales consistently voted Labour, the Conservatives, the most fervently unionist of British political parties, were in power for thirteen years from 1951. Labour's 1945–51 administration had tinkered with a few institutions to give them a deliberately Welsh stance, but the Conservatives – winning only six out of 36 Welsh seats in 1951 – had little time for specifically Welsh demands. Two Welsh Labour MPs, Megan Lloyd George, daughter of the great Liberal premier, and S O Davies, spearheaded new parliamentary demands for greater Welsh independence, presenting a 1956 petition to Parliament, signed by a quarter of a million people, demanding a Welsh assembly. Massive popular protests against the continued flooding of Welsh valleys and villages to provide water for England shook the Establishment. The 1963 formation of the boisterous *Cymdeithas yr Iaith Gymraeg* (the **Welsh Language Society**) created many headlines and attracted a new youthful breed of cultural and linguistic nationalists to the fold. The ruling Conservatives offered token measures in an attempt to lance the rising boil of nationalism: a part-time Welsh Minister was appointed (although the job was always part of another, more important, ministerial brief), Cardiff was confirmed as capital and the Welsh flag authorized as official. The Labour Party, meanwhile, was becoming more distinctively nationalistic, having formed a Welsh Council within the party, from where MPs, trade unionists and ordinary party members began to articulate the need for greater independence. The party stood on a more nationalistic platform than ever before at the **general election of 1964**. As usual, they swept the board in Wales, and finally won throughout the UK as a whole. As promised in their manifesto, the post of **Secretary of State for Wales**, backed by a separate Welsh Office, was created, although with fewer powers than the Scottish equivalent, which had existed since just after the war.

Wales presents a very different proposition from Scotland where early nationalist movements are concerned. Scotland is a far more recent arrival (1707) in the British Union than Wales and still maintains identifiably different education, judicial and legal systems, whereas Wales' are totally subsumed into the English framework. Scotland is also relatively isolated, 400 miles from London, but Wales lies immediately west of large English conurbations: Birmingham, Liverpool and Manchester. Nor is

Scottish nationalism so wrapped in misty-eyed linguistic pride: Gaelic is so thinly scattered that, unlike in Wales, nationalism has far transcended the language issue. Scottish nationalism has gained acceptance in both urban and rural settings, appealing to fiery socialists in Glasgow as much as well-heeled Tories of Grampian. By contrast, Plaid Cymru's support, with a few occasional exceptions, has always been drawn from the rural, Welsh-language strongholds of the west and north.

Despite these inherent drawbacks, it was Plaid Cymru who scored the first, and most dramatic, strike into Westminster. Veteran Labour MP for Carmarthen, Megan Lloyd George, died just a couple of months after the 1966 general election, precipitating a by-election won by charismatic Plaid president, Gwynfor Evans. For Wales, and for Scotland, two countries with a massive in-built majority for Labour and – for once – under a UK-wide Labour government, the nationalist parties provided a safe (and non-Conservative) repository for protest votes. Plaid Cymru and the Scottish National Party both soared in popularity in the wake of the Carmarthen result. Winnie Ewing, for the SNP, captured Hamilton from Labour in a 1967 by-election. Most dramatically, in the heart of socialist south Wales, Plaid ran the Labour government astonishingly close in two by-elections: in Rhondda West (1967) and Caerphilly (1968), the party saw swings of over 25 percent to cut Labour majorities of over twenty thousand to just a couple of thousand. From humble beginnings, it seemed that Plaid's time had come. Its traditional vote in the north and west was soaring, but, more importantly, they were the only party threatening the dominance of Labour in the English-speaking industrial south. It appeared that the party had finally overcome its single-issue status around the Welsh language, and membership ballooned to forty thousand. Welsh nationalism reached new heights at the time of the Prince of Wales' theatrical 1969 investiture at Caernarfon, a gesture resented by many. The cause also gained its first casualties, when two extremist nationalists blew themselves up at Abergele in Clwyd whilst attempting to lay a bomb on the rail line where Prince Charles was due to travel. In some ways, this had a detrimental effect on Plaid's cause, wrongly linking extremism with the more moderate and constitutional methods of the party.

Despite this, the **1970 general election** saw Plaid in more robust mood than had ever previously been justified. The astonishing results of the previous few years led them to believe that they could pick up a clutch of Westminster seats. Yet, despite trebling their 1966 tally to 176,000 votes (11 percent of the poll in Wales), they failed to take any new seats and even lost their place in Carmarthen. The new Conservative government checked Plaid's progress, as protest votes could now safely go to the Labour party. Despite that, Plaid polled well in local elections, even taking control of Merthyr borough council. The Labour party, anxiously watching any inroads into their power base that Plaid could make, embarked on another measured programme of vaguely nationalistic proposals. Supporting bilingual road signs (daubing monoglot English signs was a practice of 1970s nationalists), briefly publishing a Welsh Labour party bilingual magazine, *Radical*, and drawing up plans for a watered-down Welsh assembly were hard-fought tenets of the new Labour party, although many traditionalists felt that these were pandering far too much to nationalist sentiment. The second 1974 election returned Gwynfor Evans in Carmarthen to join two other Plaid Cymru MPs elected in the February election. Plaid's parliamentary band of three was dwarfed by the enormous success of the SNP in Scotland, who had succeeded in getting eleven MPs to Westminster. Furthermore, Plaid's earlier success in the industrialized south had evaporated, and they lost their deposits in 26 of the 36 Welsh seats. Once again, they were a party geographically concentrated in the rural outposts of Wales.

The combined strength of the nationalist parties at Westminster, added to the wafer-thin and dwindling parliamentary Labour majority, meant that the political demands of devolution were high on the government's agenda, as they could ill afford to lose the support, and votes, of the SNP and Plaid Cymru MPs. The ruling Labour government dallied with devolutionary proposals, including setting up the **Wales Development Agency**, supporting the new Wales TUC (Trades Union Congress) and devolving the huge responsibilities of the Department of Trade and Industry in Wales to the Welsh Office in Cardiff. As the Labour parliamentary majority became ever thinner, through the government losing a cache of by-elections, the nationalists' demands became more strident. Eventually, the Labour party put forward bills for Scottish and Welsh assemblies, subject to the result of referenda.

The devolution proposals were simple. Both Scotland and Wales were offered national assemblies, or as broadcaster Wynford Vaughan-Thomas put it, "after its long marriage with England, Wales was being offered, if not divorce, at least legal separation". Campaigning by both sides was fervent, but it was obvious from early on that many Welsh people were suspicious of the proposals. A large number of the eighty percent of the country who did not speak Welsh feared that a Welsh assembly would be the preserve of a new "Taffia", a *Cymraeg* elite. Both north and south Walians worried about potential domination by the other. People feared greater bureaucracy, particularly in the wake of the 1974 local government reorganization when a two-tier system of county and district councils had been imposed on Wales. A third tier, with few apparent powers, was not a terribly attractive proposition. On St David's Day 1979, the Welsh people voted and, by a massive margin (just one-fifth of the 59 percent who voted supported the measure), turned down the limited devolution on offer. In Scotland, the proposals also fell, although a slender majority had voted in favour, but not by the margin required in the bill.

The shock waves were great. Weeks later, the Labour government fell and **Margaret Thatcher**'s first Conservative administration was ushered in. Political nationalism seemed to have gone off the boil, and Plaid Cymru were back to just two MPs representing the northwestern constituencies of Meirionydd and Caernarfon. The early 1980s were dominated by swiftly rising unemployment and a collapse in Britain's manufacturing base. Nowhere was this more evident than in south Wales, where mines and foundries closed and the jobless total soared. Welsh nationalism was suffering an identity crisis, typified by Plaid Cymru's controversial 1981 rewriting of its own constitution to fight for an avowedly "Welsh socialist state", causing some of the more conservative, rural members to quit the party. Basing itself as a republican, left-wing party would, it was believed, bring greater fruit in the populated south. The nationalists suffered by implication from the activities of *Meibion Glyndŵr* (**Sons of**

Glendower), a shadowy organization dedicated to firebombing English holiday homes in Wales. Plaid continued to plough a firmly constitutional and peaceful route to national self-determination, but many people assumed that the bombers received covert support amongst the party's ranks.

Gwynfor Evans might well have lost his Carmarthen seat in 1979, but he was single-handedly responsible for the most high-profile activity of Welsh nationalism in the early 1980s. The Conservative party had fought the general election of 1979 on a manifesto that included a commitment to a Welsh-language TV channel. When plans for the new UK Channel 4 were drawn up, this promise had been dropped. The Plaid Cymru president decided to fast until death, if necessary, as a peaceful protest. It did not take long before this action, gaining enormous publicity in the media, forced the Thatcher government to make a U-turn, and **Sianel Pedwar Cymru** (S4C) was born in 1982. Perhaps the Tories realized the political advantage of bringing Welsh nationalism into the legitimate fold, for the Welsh media industry, long accused of a nationalistic bent, dissipated many angry and impassioned arguments for national self-determination. Many of the most heartfelt radicals ended up in prominent positions within Wales' media.

Like so many other political affiliations and ideals in the 1980s, Welsh nationalism underwent something of a sea change. As the Labour party was routed in the 1983 election, precipitating a rightward slide for the rest of the decade and beyond, Plaid Cymru genuinely began to broaden its base as a radical, multi-layered and mature political force with a firmly socialist and internationalist outlook. They developed serious policies on all aspects of Welsh life, from their traditional rallying calls of language and media to sophisticated analyses of economic policy, the Welsh legal framework and the country's role in the European Union and the wider world. But Welsh devolution – if not outright nationalism – has ceased to be the preserve solely of Plaid Cymru. Two of the three UK-wide parties, Labour and, in particular, the Liberal Democrats, inheritors of the great Liberal tradition, have evolved devolutionary strategies for Wales, Scotland and, to a lesser degree, the regions of England. Each party has a semi-autonomous Welsh branch, with its own

party conference, election broadcasts and manifesto. Even the Conservatives have continued to devolve more governmental decision-making out to the Welsh Office in Cardiff, although this has, ironically, strengthened the nationalist hand. Plaid and the other parties point out that there exists now a huge swathe of government in Wales, overseen by no all-Wales authority, but run instead by unelected bodies, often made up of the government's friends, appointed from Westminster (Parliament) and Whitehall (the civil service). Their call for a Welsh assembly to oversee this vast array of public expenditure is consistently supported by huge majorities in opinion polls.

The Conservatives' two thumping victories in the 1983 and 1987 general elections brought them their largest ever share of Welsh MPs: 14 out of 38 in 1983. This number has fallen ever since, and now Conservative seats in Wales are as patchy as they were in the postwar years. Labour still holds sway as the party of natural government in Wales, commanding over half of the vote, largely on the strength of the sheer weight of population in the southern urban constituencies. The **1992 general election** saw four Plaid Cymru MPs elected to Westminster – their impregnable bastions of Caernarfon and Meirionydd, together with a tenuous hold on their 1987 gain, Ynys Môn (Anglesey) and, in the biggest surprise anywhere in Britain, vaulting from fourth to first place in Ceredigion and Pembroke North, unseating veteran Welsh-speaking Liberal, Geraint Howells. Despite gaining more seats than they had ever before, they still only polled 8.8 percent of votes in Wales, gaining from their peculiarly tight geographical concentration of support. In the rest of Wales, Plaid reached double-figure percentage points in only five other constituencies, and in only one – Gwynfor Evans' old patch of Carmarthen – were they within 25 percent of the winner. With the exception of Carmarthen, it seems that the national party has maximized its parliamentary possibility for the meanwhile.

In many ways, these figures seem to indicate that Welsh nationalism as a political force has reached its modest zenith. However, as this book goes to press, Britain is facing a general election in 1997. The Labour Party, currently predicted to win, has made positive, if contradictory, noises on devolution. A commitment to assembly, coupled with the increasing likelihood of Scottish independence, might have interesting repercussions for Wales. Certainly, with 1996 also seeing the whole of Wales change from the dual system of county and district councils to a single tier of unitary authorities, the argument that an all-Wales forum would be yet another bureaucratic level of government has been largely dissipated.

If Labour does get elected, chances are that Plaid Cymru – with its more sober, less romanticized vision of Welsh nationalism, no longer exclusively based on the language issue – will become the natural repository of protest votes. A taste of this was had in the Pontypridd (1989) and Neath (1991) by-elections, when massive swings from Labour to Plaid Cymru bounced them into second place in a time of Conservative government.

As Plaid Cymru and the opposition British parties plough firmly constitutional paths to devolution or even outright independence, the more extreme nationalist movements, shrouded in anonymity and mystery, have continued to organize. Denouncing Plaid Cymru's leaders as "Westminster apologists", groups like *Meibion Glyndŵr* and the Free Wales Army have run consistent bombing and symbolic vandalism campaigns against offices of state, such as courtrooms and political party headquarters, as well as the more widely known arson campaign against holiday homes in Wales. Since 1979, over two hundred English-owned holiday properties have been torched, a reaction to the lingering death being experienced by many rural Welsh-speaking villages where local people can no longer afford house prices, artificially inflated by their tourist value. Many permanent arrivals who learn the language are made thoroughly welcome, but it is the largely empty properties (up to three-quarters of houses in some villages), filled only occasionally with visitors who make no use of local amenities, that unsurprisingly stir resentment. Other occasional guerrilla tactics include issuing threats to English shop owners and families who, after refusing to display posters in Welsh, were given

an ultimatum to leave Wales. Amongst the tightly knit villages of Gwynedd, the police and security services have had great difficulty finding the culprits, although a few cases have come to trial, resulting in prison sentences of up to twelve years. For a visitor, there is almost no chance of coming across anything more than patches of *Meibion Glyndŵr* graffiti, or slogans exhorting *Cymru Rydd!* (Free Wales!). By far the majority of Welsh people disapprove of, and are even ashamed by, the violent methods of the more radical nationalists, although support for their broader aims – a consolidation of the language, control of holiday homes, houses earmarked for local families – is often confirmed in opinion polls.

In contrast to these more hot-headed eruptions, the channels of constitutional and political nationalism have become more sophisticated in recent years. The success of a television channel in both Welsh and English, together with a bold national programme of Welsh-medium schooling, has brought the first upturn in the language ever recorded in Britain's ten-yearly census. Eighteen long years of Conservative government, which neither Wales nor Scotland has ever voted for, have frustrated the Welsh, who feel that the growth in non-elected bodies overseeing their lives (more acute in Wales than anywhere else in the UK) is an affront to their national democracy. Furthermore, as UK politics become less important, Welsh political leaders are looking beyond Westminster to the parliament and executive of the European Union. The EU chose a converted chapel in the centre of Llangollen to host the office of the *European Centre for Traditional and Regional Cultures* (ECTARC). In 1994, the EU held its inaugural session of the **Council of the Regions**, a forum for the regional components of member states, to which Wales sends three representatives – one Conservative, one Labour and one Plaid Cymru. Plaid's rallying cry of Welsh independence within a Europe of smaller nations and regions may well be setting the agenda in the new millennium.

NATURAL HISTORY OF WALES

A comprehensive account of Wales' land-scapes, land use, flora and fauna would take several books to cover. What follows is a general overview of the effects of geology, human activity and climate on the country's flora, fauna and land management.

Wales is covered with a wide array of sites deemed to be of national or international importance, all seemingly with different designations. The three **National Parks** – Snowdonia, the Brecon Beacons and the Pembrokeshire Coast – comprise almost twenty percent of the country, with another couple of percent incorporated into the five **Areas of Outstanding Natural Beauty** (AONB): the Anglesey coast, the Llŷn coast, the Clwydian Range, the Gower peninsula and the Wye Valley. Smaller areas (from a few acres to large chunks of the Cambrian Mountains) with specific habitats like lowland bogs or ancient woodlands are managed as **National Nature Reserves** (NNRs). Most are widely promoted, usually posted with information boards and threaded with easy, well-signed walking trails. All NNRs contain **Sites of Special Scientific Interest** (SSSIs; aka triple-SIs), a category including around another 700 locations in Wales singled out for special protection. Most are on private land with no right of access.

It must be remembered that nowhere in Wales is untouched, almost every patch of "wilderness" being partially the product of human intervention, thoroughly mapped, mined and farmed. Nor is anywhere free from pollution: the conurbations of England are too close, nuclear power stations and factories dot the countryside and some of the seas are in a terrible state, not least from oil spills such as the 130,000 tonnes the *Sea Empress* leaked into the water around Milford Haven in 1996. That said, several clean-air-loving lichen species – found in few other places in Britain – abound in Wales.

GEOLOGY

Geologists puzzled over the forces that shaped the Welsh landscape for centuries before early nineteenth-century geologist **Adam Sedgwick** and his collaborator (and later rival) **Roderick Murchison** began to unravel the secrets. They were able to explain the shattered, contorted and eroded rocks that form the ancient peaks of Snowdonia, but fought bitterly over rock classification. By naming the **Silurian** rock system (400–440 million years ago) after one of Wales' ancient tribes, Murchison started a trend that continued with the naming of the earlier **Ordovician** system (440–500 million years ago) and the **Cambrian** system (500–600 million years ago given the Roman name for Wales. Anglesey, the Llŷn and Pembrokeshire all have older **pre-Cambrian** rocks; those around St David's are some of the most ancient anywhere.

Wales is packed with mountains, and several areas deserve brief coverage. Between 600 and 400 million years ago **Snowdonia** was twice submerged for long periods in some primordial ocean where molten rock from undersea volcanoes cooled to form igneous intrusions in the sedimentary ocean-floor layers. Snowdon, Cadair Idris and the Aran and Arenig mountains are the product of these volcanoes, with fossils close to the summit of Snowdon, supporting the theory of its formation on the sea floor. After Silurian rocks had been laid down, immense lateral pressures forced the layers into concertina-like parallel folds with the sedimentary particles being rearranged at right angles to the pressure, giving today's vertically splitting sheets of **slate**, the classic metamorphosed product of these forces. It is known that the folded strata that rose above the sea bore no resemblance to today's mountains, the cliff face of Lliwedd on Snowdon showing that the summit was at the bottom of one of these great folds between two much higher mountains. One of these is now known as the **Harlech Dome**, a vast rock hump where the softer Silurian rocks on the surface all wore away and the Ordovician layers below were only saved by the volcanic intrusions, principally Snowdon and Cadair Idris. In between, the Ordovician rocks wore away, exposing the harder Cambrian sand and gritstones of the **Rhinog** range. In the very recent geological past from 80,000–10,000 years ago, these mountains were worked on by the latest series of **Ice Ages**, with glaciers scouring out hemispherical cwms (cirques or corries) divided by angular ridges, then scraping down the valleys, gouging them into U-shapes with waterfalls plunging down their sides.

Snowdonia is linked by the long chain of the **Cambrian Mountains** to the dramatic north-facing scarp slope of the **Brecon Beacons**, south Wales' distinctive east–west range at the head of the south Wales coal field. Erosion of the ancient Cambrian, Ordovician and Silurian rocks which once covered what is now northern Britain and much of the North Sea washed down great river systems, depositing beds of old red sandstone from 350–400 million years ago. These **Devonian** rocks lay in a shallow sea where the molluscs and corals decayed to form carboniferous limestone which in turn was over-laid by more sediment forming millstone grit. Subsequent layers of shale and sandstone were interleaved with decayed vegetable matter, forming a band known as **coal measures**, from which the mines once extracted their wealth. The whole lot has since been tilted up in the north, giving a north to south sequence which runs over a steep sandstone ridge (the Brecon Beacons), then down a gentle sandstone dip-slope arriving at the pearl-grey limestone band where any rivers tend to dive underground into **swallow holes**. They reappear as you reach the gritstone, often tumbling over waterfalls into the coal valleys.

Erosion still continues today, slowly reshaping the landscape, hastened by the Welsh climate.

LAND SETTLEMENT AND USAGE

After the last ice sheet drew back from Wales, the few species which had survived on the ice-

free peaks (nunataks) were in a strong position to colonize, producing an open grassland community more than 10,000 years ago. Birch and juniper were amongst the first trees, followed by hazel. Several thousand years later this had developed into a mixed deciduous woodland including oak, elm and some pine, and in wetter areas damp-loving alder and birch. The Neolithic tribes began to settle on the upland areas, using their flint axes to clear the mountain slopes of their forests. The discovery of bronze and later iron hastened the process, especially since wood charcoal was required for smelting iron ore, and so began the spiralling devastation of Wales' native woodlands. As the domestication of the sheep and goats put paid to any natural regeneration of saplings, more land became available for arable farming. Thin, acidic mountain soils and a damp climate made **oats** – fodder for cattle and horses – about the only viable cereal crop, except in Anglesey which, by the time the Romans arrived in the first century AD, was already recognized as Wales' most important corn-growing land. Cattle rearing was increasingly important on the lusher pastures, and even as late as the twelfth century, Giraldus Cambrensis tells us that "the whole population lives almost entirely on oats and the produce of their herds, milk, cheese and butter".

Giraldus lived at a time when the Normans were pushing into lowland Wales and acting as patrons of the monasteries. Until they were appropriated by Henry VIII in 1536, the seventeen Cistercian houses all kept extensive lands, cleared woods, developed sheep walks and cattle farms. With the Dissolution of the monasteries their lands became part of the great estates which still own large tracts of Wales.

By contrast, the less privileged were still smallholders living simple lives. In the 1770s the travel writer Thomas Pennant noted in his *Tours in Wales* that the ordinary people's houses on the Llŷn were "very mean, made with clay, thatched and destitute of chimneys". The poor state of housing had much to do with the practice of *Tŷ unnos* (literally "one-night house"), supposedly a right decreed by Hywel Dda, in which building a house of common materials close at hand within 24 hours staked your claim on a plot of common land. The practice hadn't completely died out in the 1850s when George Borrow's guide observed, "That is a house, sir, built yn yr hen dull in the old fashion, of earth, flags, and wattles and in one night – the custom is not quite dead."

In the eighteenth century, **droving** reached its peak. Welsh black cattle, fattened on Anglesey or the Cambrian coast, were driven to market in England, avoiding the valley-floor toll roads by taking highland routes that can still be traced. Nights were spent with the cattle corralled in a Halfpenny field next to a lonely homestead heralded by three Scots pines, which operated as an inn. It was a tough journey for men and cattle, but easier than for geese, whose webbed feet were toughened for the long walk with tar and sand.

At home, women ground the corn, aided by mills driven by the same fast-flowing mountain streams that later provided power for textile mills springing up all over the country. The Cistercians had laid the foundations of the **textile industry** for both wool and flannel, but it had generally remained in the cottages, with nearly every smallholding keeping a spinning wheel next to their harp. The same sort of damp climate that made Lancashire the centre of the world's cotton industry encouraged the establishment of a textile industry in Ruthin, Denbigh, Newtown, Llandeilo and along the Teifi Valley, but a lack of efficient transport made them uncompetitive.

The next major shift in land use came with a wave of **enclosure acts** from 1760 to 1820, which effectively removed smallholders from upland common pasture and granted the land to holders of already large estates. With the fashion for grouse shooting taking hold in the middle of the nineteenth century, large tracts of hill country began to be managed as heather moor, with frequent controlled fires to encourage new shoots that the grouse fed on. The people were deprived of their livelihood and access to open country was denied to future generations of walkers.

The mountain building processes discussed above have left a broad spectrum of minerals under Wales. **Copper** had been mined with considerable success since the Bronze Age, and was further exploited by the Romans, who dabbled in **gold** extraction. But it wasn't until the latter half of the eighteenth century that mining became big business, with a rapid expansion in both north and south Wales. **Slate** (see p.338) was hewn from deeper mines and higher moun-

tainsides, while the northern ends of the south Wales valleys echoed to the sounds of the ironworks. The fortuitous discovery of iron ore, limestone for smelting, and coal for fuelling the furnaces made the valleys the crucible of the iron industry, and iron stayed at the forefront here long after richer ore finds elsewhere.

Originally a service industry, **coal mining** soon took over and shaped the development of south Wales for over a century. Further west, the processing of Cornish **copper** financed the development of Swansea, while Llanelli devoted itself to **tin**.

FLORA

Wales supports 1100 of Britain's 1600 native plants – ferns and other moisture-loving species are specially well represented.

Until five thousand years ago, birch, juniper, hazel, oak and elm covered the mountainsides, but devastating forest clearances and a wetter climate have left only a few pockets of native woodland in the valleys, their regeneration threatened by sheep grazing on fresh seedlings. **Pengelli Forest** in Pembrokeshire represents one of Wales' largest blocks of ancient woodland comprising **midland hawthorn** and **sessile oak**, the dominant tree in ancient Welsh forests. Parts of the Severn and lower Wye valleys are well wooded, as is the Teifi Valley where oak, ash and sycamore predominate. Occasionally you still see evidence of **coppicing** – an important and ancient practice common a century ago – where trees are cut close to the base to produce numerous shoots harvested later as small-diameter timbers. Under the canopy, **bluebells** and **wood sorrel** are common, and in the autumn look out for the dozens of species of **mushroom**, especially the delicious but elusive **chantrelle**, found mainly under beech trees.

A far greater area of Wales is smothered in gloomy ranks of **conifers** (predominantly sitka spruce), a product of the twentieth-century monoculture ethic. Forbidding to most birds and too shaded and acidic for wild flowers, they are the object of widespread criticism directed towards the Forestry Commission.

Perhaps the most celebrated of all Wales' plants are the **arctic alpines** that grow away from grazing sheep and goats amongst the high lime-yielding crags and gullies of Snowdonia and the Brecon Beacons, their southernmost limit in Britain. Ever since the ice sheets retreated ten thousand years ago, the warmer weather has forced them towards higher ground, where they cling to small pockets of soil behind rocks. Some get unceremoniously cleaned out by thoughtless climbers trying to push up novel routes, but in the main their spread hasn't changed since they were discovered by seventeenth-century botanists such as Thomas Johnson and Welshman Edward Lhuyd, who found *Lloydia serotina*, a glacial relic more popularly known as the **Snowdon Lily** (though actually a spiderwort), that looks not unlike a small off-white tulip. In Britain, it is found only around Snowdon and then only rarely seen between late May and early June, when it blooms.

The exemplary habitat for arctic-alpines is widely regarded to be **Cwm Idwal** in the Ogwen Valley, where you may get to see some of the more common species, in particular the handsome **purple saxifrage**, whose tightly clustered flowers often push through the late winter snows, later followed by the starry and mossy saxifrages and spongy pink pads of **moss campion**. The star-shaped yellow flowers of **tormentil** are typical of high grassy slopes, and you may also find **mountain avens**, distinguished by its glossy oak-like leaves, and in June when it blooms by its eight white petals. From June to October, purple heads of **wild thyme** cover the ground, providing food for a small beetle unique to Snowdonia.

Sheep prefer the succulent **sheep's fescue**, but competition for the juicier shoots leads to over-grazing and the growth of tough mat-grass which chokes out the **woolly-hair moss**, the **reindeer moss** and the **dwarf willow**, which can otherwise be seen in yellow bloom during June and July. Just below the wind-battered mountaintops you catch the early colonizing species; **alpine meadow grass**, **glacier buttercup**, **mountain sorrel** and **alpine hair grass** among them.

Poor acid soils on the igneous uplands foster the growth of lime-shy purple **heather** – bell, ling, cross-leaved and Scottish are all found – bracken and bilberry which combine with decayed **sphagnum moss** in wetter areas to form peat bogs. Though generally less extensive than upland bogs elsewhere in Britain, the wetlands still support the **bog asphodel** that produces its brilliant yellow spikes in late summer, often in company with the **spotted orchid** and less frequently the tiny **bog orchid**. Insectivorous plants are also found, the **butterwort** (both pale and common varieties) and the **sundew** (long-leaved and round-leaved), which gain nutrients from their poor surroundings by digesting insects trapped on the sticky hairs of their leaves. Limestone uplands such as the Clwydian ridges and parts of the Brecon Beacons are more likely to host less rugged plants, like the **harebell** and the **rock rose**. Streams running off these uplands tumble down narrow valleys hung with ferns and mosses and sometimes scattered with the yellow-flowered **Welsh poppy**.

At sea level, the rivers spawn estuarine "meadows", which in summer are carpeted with bright violet **sea lavender**, followed by a mauve wash of **sea aster** after August. An unusual coastal feature is the dam-formed string of **Bosherston Lakes**, south of Pembroke, where the fresh water supports rafts of white water lilies. Further west, the Pembrokeshire coast is a blaze of colour in early summer, with white-flowered **scurvy grass** and **sea campion**, yellow **kidney vetch** and **celandine**, and blue **spring squill**. **Water crowfoot** is found in fresh water near the coastal footpath, where you can also find the hemispherical lilac heads of **devil's bit scabious**. **Bluebells** and **red campion** cloak Pembrokeshire's islands, while the majority of species mentioned can be found in abundance in Newborough on Anglesey. Here, some of Wales' finest sand dunes are bound by **marram grass**, interspersed with **sea holly**, **sea bindweed** and the odd **marsh helleborine**.

BIRDS

With its long coastline, Wales, as you might expect, abounds in sea birds, and the profusion of islands and its position on the main north–south migratory route make several sites particularly noteworthy. This remains the case despite the massive *Sea Empress* oil spill that contaminated the waters around Milford Haven in early 1996. Wind and tides distributed the oil around the fragile breeding grounds of Pembrokeshire, and some 5000 common scoter were lost, but it could have been a lot worse. Most breeding birds hadn't yet arrived and the worst of the mess was cleaned up before they did. Nevertheless it could be ten years before the place returns to some semblance of normality.

The *Royal Society for the Protection of Birds* (RSPB), Bryn Aderyn, The Bank, Newtown, Powys (☎01686/626678), operates ten sites throughout Wales, half of them on the coast. The islands off the Pembrokeshire coast are incomparable for sea bird colonies, the granite pinnacle of **Grassholm** (RSPB), 12 miles off-shore, hosting the world's third-largest gannet colony with 30,000 pairs. Grassholm can only be visited by prior arrangement after mid-June, but the islands closer to the coast are more accessible (see p.176), **Skokholm** and **Skomer** between them supporting 6000 pairs of **storm petrels** and an internationally significant population of 140,000 pairs of the mainly nocturnal **Manx shearwater**, which spend their winter off the coast of South America. Burrows vacated by the rabbits on the islands also provide nests for puffins, while **razorbills**, **guillemots** (known as *elegug* in Pembrokeshire) and **kittiwakes** nest on the cliffs. Manx shearwaters are also now colonizing **Ramsey Island**, a few miles north, after the eradication of the rats that previously deterred burrow-nesting birds, leaving only the rare **chough**, a red-billed, red-legged member of the crow family. A few pairs of choughs are also found on the important migration stopover, **Bardsey Island**, and at the wonderful **South Stack Cliffs** (RSPB) on Anglesey which, especially from May to July, are alive with breeding guillemots, razorbills and puffins. Like much of the coast, **fulmars** and **peregrine falcons** are also present in respectable numbers, as are **cormorants**, which always nest by the sea, except at Craig yr Aderyn, a cliff four miles inland from Tywyn, where the population is in decline.

The mudflats and saltings of Wales' estuaries provide rich pickings for wintering waders. The **Dee estuary** (RSPB), on the northern border with England, plays host to Europe's largest concentration of **pintail** as well as **oystercatchers**, **knot**, **dunlin**, **redshank** and many others. Numerous terns replace them in the summer months.

Central Wales represents one of Britain's last hopes for reviving the population of **red kites** which, like many other raptors, were traditionally persecuted by gamekeepers and suffered from the use of pesticides, which caused thinning of egg shells. The banning of DDT in the 1960s allowed numbers to increase, but there are still only 100 or so pairs of these fork-tailed

birds left, predominantly in the Elan Valley. However, as with the other persecuted species, the hen harrier, the peregrine falcon and the sparrowhawk, numbers are increasing. Perhaps one day the heights of Snowdonia may again resound to the cry of the eagle which gives the mountains their Welsh name, *Eryri*.

The high country supports larger populations of **kestrels** hovering motionless before plummeting onto an unsuspecting mouse or vole, and golden-brown **buzzards** gently wheeling on the thermals on the lookout for prey which can be as big as a rabbit. Buzzards and peregrine falcons are as happy picking at carrion, but have to compete with sinister black **ravens**, that inhabit the highest ridges and display their crazy acrobatics, often banding together to mob the bigger birds.

Acidic heather uplands between one and two thousand feet provide habitats for the black and red **grouse** whose laboured flight is in such contrast to the darting zigzag of its neighbour, the **snipe**. On softer grassland, expect to find the **ring ouzel**, a blackbird with a white cravat, and the **golden plover**, a bird still common but being threatened, like many others, by the spread of conifer forests, which welcome little except wood pigeons and blackbirds.

After the gloomy pines, it is a delight to wander in relict stands of the ancient oak woodlands, and along the streams the **dipper** and **kingfishers**. On sheltered water you might also find shelduck, Canada geese and three species of swan.

MAMMALS

During the last interglacial period, Wales was warm enough to support hippos and lions, but humans, pressed for space by the expanding ice sheets, killed them off, leaving bears and boars which in turn were dispatched by human persecution. Some of the last beaver lodges in Britain dammed the Teifi in the twelfth century, while half a millennium later wolves disappeared from the land. What remains is a restricted range of wild mammals topped up with semi-wild and feral beasts: shy herds of **ponies** on the Carneddau in Snowdonia and on the Brecon Beacons are rounded up annually, deer occasionally stray from captive herds, and the **goats** in Snowdonia (on the Glyders and the Rhinogs especially) and on the Great Orme at Llandudno are descendants of domesticated escapees.

Generally welcomed by farmers, they forage on the precipitous ledges, thereby discouraging sheep from grazing ventures beyond their capabilities. About the only other large land mammal is the soft-fleeced **Soay sheep** at Newborough Warren on Anglesey.

Though widely acknowledged as the scourge of wildlife, the spread of conifer plantations has seen a surge in the population of the elusive cat-sized **pine marten** which thrives in sitka spruce where their diet of squirrels is readily available. Both pine martens and the more common **polecats** are found in Snowdonia, in the ancient woodlands of Pengelli Forest on the slopes of Mynydd Preseli, in the relict beechwoods of the Brecon Beacons and the coastal dunes where they prey on rabbits. **Polecats**, trapped almost into oblivion in the nineteenth century, have recolonized almost all of Wales and parts of western England over the last fifty years. **Foxes** are still torn apart by dogs in the name of sport but remain widespread, along with the **brown hare**, **stoat** and **weasel**, though the **badger** is rarer and still the subject of persecution through the cruel sport of badger baiting. **Rabbits** seem to be everywhere, and the north American **grey squirrel** has all but dislodged the native red squirrel from its habitat, though it hangs on around Lake Vyrnwy and at Newborough on Anglesey. Of the smaller beasts, **shrews** and **wood mice** abound, and the island of Skomer has a unique subspecies of **vole**.

Otters almost became extinct in Wales some years back, but a concerted effort on the part of the *Otter Haven Project* has seen their numbers climbing in the Teifi and some of the rivers in Montgomeryshire. They remain an endangered species, and perhaps fortunately are seldom seen, but indicate their presence by their droppings.

The waters off the Pembrokeshire Coast around the Marloes peninsula and Skomer Island have been designated a **marine reserve**, though this doesn't cover the **grey seal** breeding colony on the west coast of Ramsey Island, where each year a couple of hundred white-furred pups are born. Sadly, marine pollution is being increasingly detected in the seals' blubber, a worrying sign too for the **dolphins** and **porpoises** inhabiting the coastline.

FISH, REPTILES AND INSECTS

Wales' clean, fast-flowing rivers make ideal conditions for the **brown trout**, a fish managed for sport throughout the country. In Wales, the damming of rivers has seldom cut off spawning grounds, but the fishable limit of the Conwy in particular has been extended by the introduction of a fish ladder around the Conwy Falls. **Salmon** are less common, found mainly in the Usk and the Wye, the only river where it is important as game fish. Along with **roach**, **perch** and other coarse fish, the depths of Bala Lake (Llyn Tegid) claim the unique silver-white **gwyniad**, an Ice Age relic not dissimilar to a small herring, said never to take a lure. Llyn Padarn in Llanberis also notches up a rarity with the freshwater **char**. Conditions for successful fish farming do not exist in Wales, but commercially viable beds of **cockles** still exist on the north coast of the Gower and families still own rights to mus-selling the sands of the Conwy estuary.

With Welsh red dragons dying out along with King Arthur, much smaller lizards and two species of snake are all that remains of Wales' reptiles. The poisonous, triangular-headed **adder** is sometimes spotted sunning itself on dry south-facing rocks, but, except in early spring when it is roused from hibernation, it frequently slithers away unnoticed. The harmless **grass snake** prefers a wetter environment and is equally shy. Easily mistaken for a snake, the **slowworm** is actually a legless lizard and is common throughout Wales, as are **toads** and **frogs** though the rare **natterjack toad** is only found in a few locations.

As for **butterflies**, southern British species – the common blue and red admiral – are abundant in sheltered spots, but aim for the woodland reserves, found dotted all over the country, to find the **dark green fritillary** and its pearl-bordered and silver-washed kin. South Wales is particularly good, with Pengelli Forest home to the rare **white-letter hairstreak** as well as one of Britain's rarest dragonflies, the bright blue **southern damselfly**, and the Gower peninsula harbouring populations of **marbled white butterfly** and the **great green bush cricket**, uncommon anywhere else in Wales. Lastly, Snowdonia has the unique and aptly named **rainbow leaf beetle**.

ECOLOGY AND THE FUTURE

With the smokestack industries now largely absent from Wales and the Valleys mostly devoid of working coal mines, nature (sometimes with the help of schemes to level and replant spoil heaps) is struggling to claw its way back. A verdure inconceivable thirty years ago now cloaks the hillsides, and already the industrial remains are being cherished as cultural heritage; as much a valid part of the "natural" landscape as the mountain backdrops. If you need convincing, climb up to the disused slate workings behind Blaenau Ffestiniog or walk the old ironworks tramways around Blaenafon.

In other areas, much remains to be done to restore the ecological balance. The increasing commercialization of farming has led not just to the damaging application of pesticides and excessive use of nitrogen-rich fertilizers, but to the wholesale removal of **hedgerows and dry-stone walls**, ideal habitats for numerous species of flora and fauna. Conservation groups promote the skills needed to lay hedges and build dry-stone walls, but for every success, another chunk of farmland is paved over with a new by-pass or a meadow is turned over to **conifers**.

The tax incentives which formerly encouraged vast expanses of spruce no longer apply, but economics still favour clear-felling a single species every thirty years or so. The largest forest owner, the Forestry Commission, is keen to shake off its monoculture image and aims to border its forests with a mix of broad-leaved trees and conifers of different ages.

Far from being areas where nature is allowed to take its course, the **national parks** can be their own worst enemies, attracting thousands of people a day. Some attempt is being made to control the effects of tourism through path management and the limited promotion of public transport, but this is more than outweighed by the increasingly aggressive promotion of these regions. Paradoxically, and for all the wrong reasons, **military zones** – Mynydd Eppynt and most of the Castlemartin peninsula, for example – have become wildlife havens away from the worst effects of human intervention.

Wind farms have become a contentious issue in the mid-1990s. Initial enthusiasm for this clean energy has waned as local people complain about the constant drone of the generators, and conservationists battle it out over the relative merits of a nuclear power station that will take 130 years to decommission (as well as several millennia for the fissile material to become safe) and several forests of elegant windmills on top of hills. Friends of the Earth:

Cymru stand firmly in favour of wind power, but have come up against the Campaign for the Protection of Rural Wales (CPRW), Tŷ Gwyn, 31 High St, Welshpool, Powys SY21 7JP (☎01938/552525), one of the main independent environment groups, which is pushing for a ban on any new wind-farm developments favouring promotion of more efficient power usage.

Environmental groups are also keeping a weather eye on offshore **oil** and **gas** exploration, currently much under way off the Welsh coast, particularly in Cardigan Bay. Meanwhile in south Wales, reaction to the *Sea Empress* disaster has turned public opinion away from using Milford Haven or Pembroke Dock to import the dirty but cheap Venezuelan orimulsion to fuel power stations.

One recent success has been the decision not to press ahead with the **Usk Barrage**, which was planned to create a freshwater lake on the outskirts of Newport by damming the estuary, forcing otters and other protected species to abandon the river. Things aren't as rosy on the shores of the Severn estuary nearby, where the popularity of the new second Severn crossing will almost certainly lead to the construction of a fifteen-mile M4 relief road – already named as the M48 – across the environmentally rich Caldicot Levels, destroying several SSSIs. In the last couple of years, the passion and commitment of the anti-roads lobby throughout Britain has arguably had some impact in forcing the government to downsize its road-building schemes, but in the absence of any convincing public transport policy, road construction is likely to continue in a more insidious manner.

The Snowdonia National Park Authority has recognized that sustainable management of farmland is not only ecologically beneficial but that the landscape, with its character largely defined by past farming practices, is worth maintaining in its own right. In response it has set up the **Tir Cymen** (which loosely translates as "well-crafted landscape") scheme, a ten-year government initiative which pays participating farmers for maintaining stone walls, slate fences, earth banks, traditional stone buildings and archeological features. Trial schemes are in place in the southern Snowdonian region of Meirionydd, Dinefwr in Carmarthenshire, and around Swansea and the Gower peninsula.

MUSIC IN WALES

For most people, mention of Welsh music conjures up images of miners in their Sunday best collectively raising the roof of their local chapel, and, despite the near-obliteration of the mining industry, male voice choirs remain a feature of Welsh rural life, with many choirs opening their practice sessions to the public. But Welsh music extends far beyond the dwindling chapels into the country's village halls, clubs, festival sites and pubs, where Dylan Thomas' observation that "we are a musical nation" is often seen, and heard, to be true. In quieter venues, harp players repay their musical debt to ancestors who accompanied the ancient bards (traditional poets and storytellers), while modern folk draws directly from the broader Celtic musical tradition. Exponents of Welsh-language rock have traded in their dreams of commercial success for unabashed nationalism expressed through a multiplicity of styles from punk to electro-pop. Some bands sing in both English and Welsh and there is a fast-growing scene in English-language Welsh rock, which is swiftly gaining both kudos and sales in the late 1990s.

What follows is a general overview of the main styles and a run through the stars, both past and present.

FOLK

The word "folk" translates into Welsh as *gwerin*, but the Welsh word has a much wider meaning than its English counterpart, taking in popular culture as well as folklore. In a Welsh *gwyl werin* (folk festival), you're just as likely to encounter the local rock band as the local dance team, and the whole community will be there – not just committed specialists.

It's often said that the Welsh love singing but ignore their native instrumental music. Welsh folk song has always remained close to the heart of popular culture, with modern folk song-writing acting as the common carrier of political messages and social protest, but traditional Welsh music and dance have had the difficult task of fighting back to life from near-extinction following centuries of political and religious suppression. Unlike their Celtic cousins in

WHERE TO GET INFORMATION

Taplas, the English-language bi-monthly magazine of the folk scene in Wales, is the best source for current events. It's based at 182 Broadway, Roath, Cardiff CF2 1QJ (☎01222/499759).

Cymdeithas Ddawns Werin Cymru (Welsh Folk Dance Society) is also a useful source of events information with an annual magazine and a twice-yearly newsletter, both bilingual. Contact the editor, 10 River View Court, Llandaff, Cardiff (☎ & fax 01222/555055).

The **South Wales Echo** newpaper carries comprehensive daily listings of events in Gwent and mid- and South Glamorgan (☎01222/583583).

The **Museum of Welsh Life**, based at St Fagans, near Cardiff, is a vibrant museum and a vital centre for research and collecting work (☎01222/569441).

Watch out on **posters** for the word *twmpath* – it's the equivalent of a barn dance or ceilidh and is used when Welsh dances are the theme of the night. Calling (dance instructions) could be in Welsh or English, depending on where you are in the country. A *Noson Lwawen*, literally "a happy night", is most likely to be found in tourist hotels and usually offers a harpist, perhaps some dancers and a repertoire of Welsh standards.

For *eisteddfodau*, see main text, below.

Live at Llantrisant, mid-Glamorgan. Pub weekend staged by Llantrisant Folk Club, with limited space but a great party atmosphere. Late April.

Swansea Shanty Festival, West Glamorgan. Growing every year, the sea song and music take place on and around a tall ship in the marina. Early May.

Mid-Wales Festival, Newtown, Powys. The first big outdoor camping event, with an extensive guest list, has concerts at *Theatr Hafren*, and dances and sessions in most of the town's pubs. Mid-May.

Tredegar House Festival, Newport, Gwent. A laid-back and enjoyable weekend at the eighteenth-century country house, good for session players and dancers. Mid-May.

Gwyl Ifan, Cardiff. Welsh for "midsummer", the name of a Nantgarw dance is also the title of Wales' biggest and most spectacular dance festival, staged by Cwmni Dawns Werin Canolfan Caerddyd, with hundreds of dancers giving dis-

plays in Cardiff city centre, Cardiff Castle and St Fagans Folk Museum. Around June 24.

Gwyl Werin y Cnapan, Ffostrasol, Dyfed. The biggest folk event in Wales, hardly known outside the country, has a powerful line-up of bands from Wales and the rest of the Celtic world. Second weekend in July.

Sesiwn Fawr, Dolgellau, Gwynedd. Events indoors and in the streets. Third weekend in July.

Pontardawe International Festival, West Glamorgan – deservedly one of Britain's flagship folk events, with an ambitious line-up of international performers heading for the Swansea Valley town each year. Clever marketing policies and an excellent craft fair have brought local people pouring in as well as the long-distance festival-goers. Third weekend of August.

A number of smaller dance festivals also take place, including **Gwyl Hydref** in Caernarfon on the first weekend of October.

Ireland, Scotland and Brittany, folk musicians in Wales have learnt their tunes from books and manuscripts rather than from older generations of players, and unlike the Celtic music boom of the 1970s, bands concentrating on Welsh tunes were virtually unknown.

This general lack of direction has meant that outside influences have had a considerable bearing on groups forming to play Welsh music, despite the common elements in the repertoire. Language has also been more of a divider in Wales than it has been in other Celtic countries; rock and folk are both great pillars of the Welsh language, but English-speakers have not received the same encouragement to explore their own folk culture within the Welsh framework.

The preservation and nurturing of Welsh-language songs, customs and traditions is vitally important, but the folklore of English-speaking Gower and south Pembrokeshire and the rich vein of industrial material from the valleys is actually in much greater danger of disappearing.

HISTORY

The bardic and **eisteddfod** traditions have always played a key role in Welsh culture. Often

the **bard**, who held an elevated position in Welsh society, was the non-performing composer, employing a harper and a *datgeiniad*, whose role was to declaim the bard's words. The first eisteddfod appears to have been held in Cardigan in 1176, with contests between bards and poets and between harpers, crwth-players (see p.457) and pipers. Henry VIII's **Act of Union** in 1536 was designed to anglicize the country by stamping out Welsh culture and language, and the eisteddfod tradition degenerated over the next two centuries.

The rise of **Nonconformist religion** in the eighteenth and nineteenth centuries, with its abhorrence of music, merry-making and dancing, almost sounded the death knell for Welsh traditions already battered by Henry VIII's assault. **Edward Jones**, *Bardd y Brenin* (Bard to the King), observed sorrowfully in the 1780s that Wales, which used to be one of the happiest of countries, "has now become one of the dullest". Folk music only gained some sort of respectability when London-based Welsh people, swept along in a romantic enthusiasm for all things Celtic, revived it at the end of the eighteenth century. As late as the twentieth century, old ladies who knew dance steps would pull the curtains before demonstrating them, in case the neighbours should see.

The **National Eisteddfod Society** was formed in the 1860s and today three major week-long events are held every year – the International Eisteddfod at Llangollen in July, the Royal National Eisteddfod in the first week of August and the Urdd Eisteddfod, Europe's largest youth festival, at the end of May. The National and the Urdd alternate between north and south Wales.

Eisteddfodau have always tended to formalize Welsh culture because competitions need rules, and such parameter-defining is naturally alien to the free evolution of traditional song

---

VENUES

In the Dyfed and Gwynedd heartland of the language, folk music can be heard in many of the same venues that stage rock events. The language is considered more important than musical categories, and the folk club concept is alien to Welsh-speakers, who never saw the need to segregate music that was a natural part of their cultural life. Folk clubs are found in the anglicized areas and only a few of them feature Welsh music. In the south, check for folk in the general programme at the Welsh cultural clubs in the area: *Clwb Ifor Bach* in Womanby Street, Cardiff (☎01222/232199); *Clwb y Bont* in Taff Street, Pontypridd, Mid-Glamorgan (☎01443/491424); *Clwb Brynmenyn* in Brynmenyn, Mid-Glamorgan (☎01656/725323); and *Clwb Y Triban*, Penallta Road, Ystrad Mynach, Mid-Glamorgan (☎01443/814491).

REGULAR FOLK VENUES IN SOUTH WALES

St Donats Arts Centre (☎01466/792151), in a delightful fourteenth-century Tythe Barn at Atlantic College near Llantwit Major, puts on major folk/roots guests as part of its regular programme.

Llantrisant Folk Club, Cross Keys, High Street, Llantrisant, Vale of Glamorgan (☎01443/226892). International guest list mixed with local sessions centred on Welsh tunes. Weekly, Wednesday.

Penarth Labour Club, Glebe Street, Penarth, Vale of Glamorgan. Guitar-oriented, with regular guests. Weekly, Thursday.

Heritage Folk Club, Llantwit Major Rugby Club, Vale of Glamorgan (☎01446/794461). Weekly, Thursday.

The Hostelry, Llantilio Crossenny, Monmouthshire. Beautiful fourteenth-century pub. Weekly, Thursday.

Four Bars Inn, opposite Cardiff Castle. Big-name international concerts staged by *Taplas* magazine. Monthly, Friday.

Pontardawe Folk Club, Ivy Bush Hotel, Brecon Road, Pontardawe, Vale of Neath. Weekly, Friday.

Boat Inn, Penallt, Monmouthshire. Monthly, last Tuesday.

Halfpenny Golf Club, *The Greyhound*, Llanrhidian, Gower (☎01792/850803). Weekly, Sunday.

Mullighan's Bar, St Mary Street, Cardiff. Irish sessions. Twice weekly, Sunday and Tuesday.

REGULAR FOLK VENUES IN NORTH WALES

ECTARC (the European Centre for Traditional and Regional Cultures) in East Street, Llangollen, Denbighshire (☎01978/861514). Regularly stages international concerts.

Theatr Clwyd, Mold, Flintshire (☎01352/755114). Monthly, first Tuesday.

The Bulkeley Arms, Beaumaris, Anglesey (☎01248/810415). Weekly, Monday.

The London Hotel, Llandudno, Aberconwy (☎01492/876740). Weekly, Sunday.

The Glangasfor, Rhyl, Denbighshire. Weekly, Friday.

The Lex Social Club, Wrexham. Weekly, Thursday.

The Heights, Llanberis, Gwynedd (☎01286/871179). Weekly, Tuesday.

Y Mount Dinas, Llanwnda, Gwynedd. Weekly, Thursday.

and music. When Nicholas Bennett was compiling his 1896 book *Alawon Fy Nghwlad*, still one of the most important collections of Welsh tunes, he rejected a great deal of good Welsh dance music because it did not conform to the contemporary high-art notion of what Welsh music ought to sound like. Despite this frequently heard criticism, *eisteddfodau* have played a major role in keeping traditional music, song and dance at the heart of national culture.

THE HARP

Historically the most important instrument in the folk repertoire, the **harp** has been played in Wales since at least the eleventh century, although no instruments survive from the period before the 1700s, and little is really known about the intervening years. The only surviving music is the famous manuscript of **Robert ap Huw**, written about 1614 in a strange tablature that has intrigued music scholars: five scales were used, but no-one has yet defined satisfactorily how they should sound. In recent years craftsmen have recreated the *crwth* (a stringed instrument which may have been either plucked or bowed), the *pibgorn* (a reed instrument with a cow's horn for a bell) and the *pibacwd* (the primitive Welsh bagpipe). Some groups have adopted these instruments, but their primitive design and performance means they rarely blend happily with modern instruments.

The simple early harps were ousted in the seventeenth century by the arrival of the **triple harp**, with its complicated string arrangement (two parallel rows sounding the same note, with a row of accidentals between them), giving it a unique, rich sound. The nineteenth-century swing towards classical concert music saw the invasion of the large **chromatic pedal harps** that still dominate today, but the triple, always regarded as the traditional Welsh harp, was kept alive by gypsy musicians who preferred to play something portable. A notable, and unique, Welsh harp performance that's well worth catching is the **Cerdd Dant**, where the harpist leads with one tune, accompanying soloists and groups take a counter-tune, and they all end up together on the final note.

MUSICIANS

Undoubtedly the most influential player of recent years is the triple harpist **Robin Huw Bowen**, who has revived interest in the instrument with appearances throughout Europe and North America, and has done tremendous work making unpublished mansucrips of Welsh dance music widely available through his own publishing company. In north Wales, the current pacemakers are **Bob Delyn a'r Ebillion**, whose blend of contemporary Welsh and Breton influences veers over into the rock field: they have even won admiration from *Folk Roots* magazine in England.

New bands like **Moniars** are making a strong showing with young audiences in the north, with a raucous electric bass-and-drums approach to Welsh-language song; the father of Welsh folk, politician/songwriter **Dafydd Iwan**, remains as hugely popular and prolific as ever with his charismatic performances, and songwriter **Meic Stevens** is still producing good work on the borderlines of folk and acoustic rock. Musician **Tudur Morgan** has been involved in some notable collaborations, including working with Irish musician/producer Donal Lunny on *Branwen*, a song and music cycle based on the Welsh *Mabinogion* legend.

Singer/harpist **Sian James**, from Llanerfyl in mid-Wales, has produced two albums so far which have won the acclaim of Welsh- and English-speakers alike. One pacesetter among the women is **Julie Murphy**, born in Essex but now a fluent Welsh speaker, whose Welsh-language work alongside Breton singer **Brigitte Kloareg** in the band **Saith Rhyfeddod** has led to a promising bilingual collaboration with young English hurdy-gurdy expert **Nigel Eaton**. Another quality Welsh-language singer is Cardiff-based **Heather Jones**, who works solo and with fiddlers Mike Lease and Jane Ridout in the trio **Hin Deg**, who blend Welsh song with Welsh/Irish fiddle music.

Close-harmony songs in three or four parts were a feature of life in mid-Wales, where the *plygain* carol-singing tradition still survives at Christmas. Small parties of carol singers, each with their own repertoire, would sing in church from midnight through until the break of dawn on Christmas morning. The group **Plethyn**, which was formed in the 1970s to adapt this style to traditional and modern Welsh songs, still perform occasionally, and member Linda Healey was also involved in the *Branwen* project.

Wales' busiest band is probably **Calennig**, from Llantrisant in Mid-Glamorgan, who blend

RECORD COMPANIES

Sain, the major Welsh recording company, can boast a good number of folk albums and artists in its catalogue, available from Canolfan Sain, Llanddwrog, Gwynedd LL54 5TG (☎01286/831111).

Cwmni Fflach at Llys-y-Coed, Heol Dinbych-y-Pysgod, Aberteifi, Dyfed SA43 3AH (☎01239/614691) is a relative newcomer, with albums by Mabsant and Saith Rhyfeddod among its folk releases.

Steam Pie, at 17 The Grove, Pontllanfraith, Gwent (☎01495/222173), has released albums by The Chartists, Huw and Tony Williams, The Milkshakes and other south Wales-based English-language artists.

Cob Records at 1–3 Brittannia Terrace, Porthmadog, Gwynedd LL49 9NA (☎01766/512170) has an extensive mail-order business. The simplest way for international customers to pay is with *Visa* or *MasterCard* credit cards.

Menter Osian is a new Celtic music mail-order business connected with Gwyl Werin Y Cnapan. They're at Trewerin, Stryd Lincoln, Llandysul, Dyfed SA44 4BU (☎01559/362147). Payments need to be in sterling or *Eurocheques*; it is not yet equipped to accept credit cards.

RECORDINGS

Aberjaber *Aberjaber* and *Aberdaujaber* (Sain). Two albums by a defunct but extremely competent band formed by Cardiff jazz/roots/world musician Peter Stacey, Swansea harpist Delyth Evans and Oxford University graduate Stevie Wishart (viol and hurdy-gurdy), who experimented with Welsh and original instrumental music.

Ar Log *OIVIV* (Sain). Compilation CD of the last two studio albums.

Robin Huw Bowen *Telyn Berseiniol fy Nghwlad* (Teires). Self-produced CD of dance music and airs for the triple harp.

Calennig Dwr *Glan* (Sain). Rocky Welsh dance sets and songs tinged with Breton and Galician influences.

Cilmeri *Cilmeri* (Sain). Long-defunct but well-respected north Wales six-piece, the first band to put a harder Irish-style edge on the music of Wales.

Delyth Evans *Delta* (Sain). Solo album of Celtic harp music by Aberjaber's harpist.

Dafydd Iwan ac Ar Log *Yma O Hyd* (Sain). Compilation CD of two great mid-Eighties albums which celebrated legendary joint tours around Wales by these performers.

Sian James *Distaw* (Sain). Original, modern and traditional songs on harp, keyboard and spine-tingling voice.

Mabsant and Eiry Palfrey *Mabsanta* (Sain). Live show by band and actress celebrating a Welsh Christmas in song and humorous verse.

Y Moniars *I'r Carnifal* (Sain). Debut album from upfront young band.

Tudur Morgan *Branwen* (Sain). Project of songs and music based on the *Mabinogion* legend.

Pedwar Yn Y Bar *Byth Adra* (Sain). Four-piece, also now defunct, which arose from the ashes of Cilmeri and added American and other international influences to Welsh music.

Saith Rhyfeddod *Cico Nyth Cacwn* (Fflach). 1994 album by bagpipers Jonathan Shorland and Ceri Matthews.

Meic Stevens *Er Cof am Blant y Cwm* (Crai). The songwriter's most recent album (1993).

Traditional Plygain parties *Carolau Plygain* (Sain). Few albums are available of Welsh "source" performances, the older generation who handed down their songs, but this Welsh Folk Museum-produced album of Christmas carols from mid-Wales is a gem.

fiery Welsh dance sets with English-language songs from the Valleys and Gower. They tour regularly in Europe, America and New Zealand and have also helped to popularize Welsh dance with a punchy collection of *twmpath* tunes and upfront calling from **Patricia Carron-Smith**.

From the same town come Welsh-language band **Mabsant**, who have also travelled the world with their own tours in the States and Europe, and British Council tours to the Far East. Their strength lies in the powerful voice of **Siwsann George**, also a fine solo singer, and soulful sax work from **Steve Whitehead**.

look set to enrich Britain's musical firmament with their brand of dub-metal, combining trip-hop and hints of jazz with metallist basslines. Their first single, *Enemy Maker*, gave them an instant hit.

WELSH-LANGUAGE ROCK

Whilst English-language Welsh bands have usually enjoyed success by making their nationality an irrelevance, Welsh-language bands have purposely expounded their strong national identity. As a consequence, a unique, self-propagating Welsh-language rock scene has developed, albeit with a widespread lack of major commercial success.

The roots of this thriving, youthful and innovative scene owe much to a musical revolution whose shock waves emanated not from Cardiff or Newport, but from London. The **punk** explosion of 1976 kicked over many of rock's statues, partly thanks to the anarchic fervour of London bands like the **Sex Pistols** and **The Clash** (who made it to the south Wales town of Caerphilly on the ill-fated Anarchy Tour in 1976), but also by virtue of its strong DIY ethic.

Just as labels like Rough Trade, Small Wonder and Cherry Red emerged in London, releasing records that major labels wouldn't, **punk bands** in Wales began releasing their own records. **Trynau Coch**, for instance, set up their own label, Recordiau Coch, attracting attention from the UK music press in the process.

It was in the Eighties, though, that the home-grown Welsh-language pop scene really began to consolidate itself. In 1983, Caernarfon punk band **Anhrefn** (Disorder) set up **Recordiau Anhrefn**, churning out what it called "dodgy compilations of up-and-coming left-field weirdo Welsh bands". This enthusiasm is a trademark of the Welsh-language rock scene. In fact, throughout the Eighties any band that couldn't get some sort of record deal would simply press their own vinyl and sell their records at gigs. The market for the music was small, but the bands made up for it with their have-a-go attitude.

The scene was developing nicely, and in the early Eighties, Radio One DJ **John Peel** – to many, the standard-bearer for underground pop in the UK – became aware of the growing number of Welsh-language bands, and began playing their records on air and inviting them in for sessions. This introduced Welsh music to a Europe-wide audience and proved an important catalyst to new Welsh bands. Peel still features Welsh-language bands broadcasting on Radio One on Saturday afternoon and Sunday evening.

By the Nineties, Welsh-language pop music had established a solid infrastructure of bands, labels and venues. One of the most prolific, eclectic and innovative of these labels is **Ankst**. Started as a part-time venture in 1988, the label is now a full-time concern releasing Welsh-language pop of varied styles. Though the Super Furry Animals (see opposite) have moved on to the big-time Creation records, they're still managed by Ankst along with **Gorky's Zygotic Mynci**, whose eccentric, psychedelic guitar melodies have won over John Cale, apparently one of their biggest fans.

Caernarfon is home to another major promoter of Welsh-language pop, **Crai Records**, a subsidiary of the more folk-oriented **Sain Records**. The label began life in 1989, and its current roster includes the back catalogues of original Welsh punks Anhrefn, folk-roots band Bob Delyn (see "Musicians", p.457), hard-edged Catatonia, ex-Alarm vocalist **Mike Peters** and reggae band **One Style**, who, though based in London, apparently have a strong affinity with Wales.

Other home-grown labels promoting Welsh-language bands include the **Fflach** label in Aberteifi, Dyfed, with their subsidiary **Semtex** specifically for heavy-rock bands. And in Ty Croes, Gwynedd, there's the **Ofn** label, releasing records by experimental, industrial Welsh-

---

WELSH-LANGUAGE RECORD LABELS

For an update of these labels' activities, contact:

Ankst Records, 106 Cowbridge Rd East, Cardiff CF1 9DX (☎01222/235453).

Crai Records, Canolfan Sain, Llandwrog, Caernarfon, Gwynedd (☎01286/831111, fax 831497).

Fflach Records, Llys y Coed, Heol Dinbych y Pysgod, Aberteifi, Dyfed SA43 (☎01239/614691).

Ofn Records, Ein Hoff Le, Llanfaelog, Ty Croes, Gwynedd (☎01407/810742).

SELECTED RELEASES

The following records of English-language Welsh bands should be available
through most high-street record shops.

The Alarm – including a live album and a singles
collection, The Alarm released seven LPs between
1984 and 1991, including those recommended here.

Declaration (IRS). Debut LP full of catchy rock
songs, establishing a simplistic formula they
rarely veered from.

Strength (IRS). Second LP and another big hit.

Standards (IRS). Compilation LP from 1990.

Raw (IRS). Last LP, released in 1991, with a Welsh-
language version released on Crai Records. The
sound of a band ready to split.

Manic Street Preachers

Motown Junk (Heavenly). Essential first single.
Total in-your-face punk rock.

Generation Terrorists (Sony). Debut double LP.
Rock ballads meet punk ferocity and anti-estab-
lishment politics. A great rock record.

Gold Against the Soul (Sony). Second, more
mature and darker LP. Straight-up rock with some
rousing choruses. *From Despair to Where* – also
released as a single – is a classic.

Everything Must Go (Sony). The most mainstream
offering so far, spawning massive hits in the

shape of its title song, *A Design for Life* and *Kevin
Carter*.

K Klass

Universal (Deconstruction/Parlophone). Debut LP
from Wrexham dance act/remix team, featuring
ex-Smiths guitarist Johnny Marr on one track.

Super Furry Animals

Fuzzy Logic (Creation). Highly acclaimed debut
album containing the New Wave charge of *God!
Show Me Magic*, the West Coast *Hometown
Unicorn* and the jaunty, poppy hit *Something for
the Weekend*.

60ft Dolls

The Big 3 (Indolent). A fine debut album from
Newport's pop-meets-garage-band newbies.

Dub War

Enemy Maker (Earache). Top dub-metal sounds.

Catatonia

For Tinkerbell (Crai). Early single lauded as *NME's*
single of the week back in early 1994.

Way Beyond Blue (Blanco y Negro). The latest
long-player bound for critical acclaim on the back
of its first single, *You've Got a Lot to Answer for*.

WELSH-LANGUAGE BANDS

Most major towns in Wales have a Welsh Shop (*Siop Gymraeg*), which will often stock an extensive
Welsh-language music selection. Cob Records in Porthmadog (☎01766/512170) and Bangor
(☎01248/353020) is also worth checking out.

ANKST RECORDS

Various Artists: *A P Elvis, the Fifth Anniversary
Collection*. Featuring 15 tracks from the likes of
Catatonia, Ian Rush, Ffa Coffi Pawb, Gorky's
Zygotic Mynci, Fflaps, Beganifs and Datblygu. A
great introduction to modern Welsh-language pop.

Gorky's Zygotic Mynci: *Tatay*. Debut LP from
this young Carmarthen band, loved by John Cale
and the UK music press. A strange but compelling
brew of gentle balladeering and noisy guitars.

Various artists: *O'R Gad*. Another great Ankst
collection, with 18 tracks.

CRAI RECORDS

Distributed by independent record distributors
Revolver, so available in most independent stores
and mainstream record shops throughout the UK.

Anhrefn: *Rhedeg I Paris*. The godfathers of
Welsh-language rock, with an LP produced by Sex
Pistols producer Dave Goodman. Raw and noisy.

Also by Anhrefn & *Bwtleg*, a live, mono recording from
London's Powerhaus, recorded March 1, 1990. The
official bootleg, with Anhrefn in all their gutsy glory!

Bob Delyn: *Gwbade Bach Cochlyd*. Latest release
from one of Wales' most popular folk roots acts.

Mike Peters: *Back into the System*. Comeback
single for the ex-Alarm vocalist, joined by all-
Welsh band *The Poets*. It sees him taking a more
acoustic path than previously.

Crai Techno. Compilation disc featuring new Welsh
talent, WwzZ, Acid Casuals and Plant o Wyddelwern.

Hen Wlad Fy Mamau: Wonderful 1995 sample
of some of Wales' spunkiest current music makers
in a collection that ranges from steaming triphop,
through lazy world dance beats to soulful soloists
and Celtic harmonies.

OFN RECORDS

Eirin Peryiglus: *Noeth*. Electronic dance/pop
music, released in 1992.

language innovators **Plant Bach Ofnus** (Timid Little Children) and the pop-oriented, electronic **Eirin Peryglus** (Perilous Plums).

The grassroots Welsh **gig circuit** is also healthy, with a lively local pub and club scene. The student unions of Lampeter, Bangor, Cardiff, Swansea or Glamorgan at Treforest universities also regularly put on Welsh bands. Other notable venues are *TJs* in Newport, *Sam's Bar* in Cardiff, the *Ship and Castle* in Caernarfon, *Gassy Jacks* in Cardiff, and the *Tivoli* in Buckley, near Mold.

Welsh-language pop bands can also be found at the **National Eisteddfod**, although this is dominated by more traditional Welsh music.

Welsh-language bands have also been forging links in **Europe**. Bands like Anhrefn, U Thant, Fflaps, Ffa Coffi Pawb and Beganifs have all taken Welsh-language pop to an international audience. Prague has been a particularly fertile ground for Welsh pop and rock, and many Welsh-language bands are eager to take their music abroad, without compromising their lyrical stance.

BOOKS

TRAVEL AND IMPRESSIONS

Dannie Abse, *Journals from the Antheap*. Abse's prose, more accessible than his poetry, succeeds in being wry, serious and provocative at the same time. Much of this volume deals with journeys in his native Wales, which he describes with verve and tongue-in-cheek humour.

George Borrow, *Wild Wales*. Highly entertaining easy-to-read account of the author's walking tour of Wales in 1854, which says as much about Borrow and his ego as it does about Wales and the Welsh, who he treats with benign condescension.

Giraldus Cambrensis, *The Journey Through Wales* and *The Description of Wales*. Two witty and frank books in one volume, written in Latin by the quarter-Welsh clergyman after his 1188 tour around Wales recruiting for the Third Crusade with Archbishop Baldwin of Canterbury. Both superb vehicles for Gerald of Wales' learned ruminations and unreserved opinions, *The Journey* breaks up the seven-week tour "through our rough, remote and inaccessible countryside" with anecdotes and ecclesiastical point-scoring, while *The Description* covers rural life and the finer and less praiseworthy aspects of the Welsh character, summing up with "you may never find anyone worse than a bad Welshman, but you will certainly never find anyone better than a good one".

Tony Curtis (ed), *Wales: The Imagined Nation*. A wonderfully varied selection of essays and wry poetry on a great diversity of topics, including writers such as R S Thomas and Dylan Thomas, together with the representation of Plaid Cymru in Welsh and British media, Wales in the movies, images of Welsh women and the country's indigenous theatre. Learned, often funny, and extremely rich.

Daniel Defoe, *A Tour Through the Whole Island of Great Britain*. Classic travelogue opening a window onto Britain in the 1720s. Twenty pages on Wales.

Trevor Fishlock, *Talking of Wales – A Companion to Wales and the Welsh* and *Wales and the Welsh*. Both rather dated now, but often found in second-hand stores. Vivacious outsider's guides to living in Wales from the ex-Welsh correspondent of the London *Times* newspaper. Both books touch on folklore, humour and politics, and paint an engaging picture of a nation perennially trying to define itself.

Jeremy Moore and Nigel Jenkins, *Wales, The Lie of the Land*. A gorgeous, glossy tome that combines the luscious photography of Jeremy Moore (often seen in the Wild Wales postcard series) and the musings of poet Nigel Jenkins. Spirited, passionate and a fine souvenir of contemporary Wales.

Jan Morris, *The Matter of Wales*. Prolific half-Welsh travel writer Jan Morris immerses herself in the country that she evidently loves. Highly partisan and fiercely nationalistic, the book combs over the origins of the Welsh character and describes the people and places of Wales with precision and affection. A magnificent introduction to a diverse, and occasionally perverse, nation.

H V Morton, *In Search of Wales*. Learned, lively and typically enthusiastic snapshots of Welsh life in the 1930s. A companion volume to his *In Search of England*.

Thomas Pennant, *A Tour in Wales*. First published in 1773, the stories from Pennant's horseback tour helped foster the Romantic enthusiasm for Wales' rugged landscapes.

Peter Sager, *Wales*. Not so much a travel guide as a 400-page celebratory essay on Wales, and especially its people, by a German convert to the cause of all things Welsh. A passionate and fabulously detailed book.

Meic Stephens, *A Most Peculiar People: Quotations About Wales and the Welsh*. A fascinating and varied volume of quotations going back to the century before Christ and up to this decade. As a portrait of the nation, with all of its frustrating idiosyncrasies and endearing foibles, it is a superb example. Most tellingly, it is easy to see how the typical English attitude of sneering at the Welsh is rooted way back in history.

Edward Thomas, *Wales*. Classic 1905 book, in constant reprint. Lyrical and literary ponderings on the Welsh and harsh put-downs on the English. Thomas' grandolinquent opinions, wrapped and couched in his assured and poetical English, are often maddening, but never dull.

George Thomas, *My Wales*, with photographs by Lord Snowdon. Glossy, ponderous coffee-table tome with selections of other writings and the musings of the ex-House of Commons Speaker as well. Fabulous photographs are the main attraction in a book that's better as a souvenir than as a guide.

HISTORY, SOCIETY AND CULTURE

Jane Aaron and others (ed), *Our Sisters' Land: The Changing Identities of Women in Wales*. A series of challenging and well-written essays that delve deep into male-dominated Welsh society, from the home to the political system. Includes personal testimonies and some startling facts about just how entrenched bigotry still is within much of the Welsh establishment.

Leslie Alcock, *Arthur's Britain*. Info-laden assemblage of all archeological and written evidence on the shadowy centuries after the Roman occupation of Britain.

David Berry, *Wales and Cinema: The First Hundred Years*. Thorough examination of this small country's contribution to the big screen, both in terms of stars, directors and writers and its frequent role as subject and setting. From the sublime – some of the superb recent young movies kick-started by S4C – to the ridiculous – Hollywood's take on Wales for blockbusters like *How Green Was My Valley*.

Janet Davies, *The Welsh Language*. The most up-to-date history and assessment of Europe's oldest living language is packed full of readable information, together with plans and maps showing the demographic and geographic spread of Welsh over the ages.

John Davies, *A History of Wales*. Exhaustive run through Welsh history and culture from the earliest inhabitants to the late 1980s, reassessing numerous oft-quoted "facts" along the way. Translated from the original 1990 Welsh edition, it is clearly written and very readable but, at 700 pages, is hardly concise.

Gwynfor Evans, *Land of My Fathers* and *Welsh Nation Builders*. Plaid Cymru's elder statesman first produced the former massive tome in Welsh, translating it into English for publication over twenty years ago. As a thorough and impassioned history, it is hard to beat, although the political viewpoint of the author is always apparent. The latter work engagingly assesses sixty of the greatest contributions to Welsh nationhood.

Geoffrey of Monmouth, *History of the Kings of Britain*. First published in 1136, this is the basis of almost all Arthurian legend. Writers throughout Europe and beyond used Geoffrey's unreliable history as the basis of a complex corpus of myth.

P H Jeffery, *Ghosts, Legends and Lore of Wales*. Excellent, slim and low-cost, if rambling, introduction to Welsh mythology.

Philip Jenkins, *A History of Modern Wales 1536–1990*. Magnificently thorough book, placing Welsh history in its British and European contexts. Unbiased and rational appraisal of events and the struggle to preserve Welsh consciousness, with enough detail to make it of valuable academic interest and sufficient good humour to make it easily readable.

J Graham Jones, *The History of Wales*. The best step forward from our "Historical Framework" section, this concise, easy-paced overview of Welsh life comes with a welcome bias towards social history.

John Matthews, *A Celtic Reader*. Selections of original texts, scholarly articles and stories on Celtic legend and scholarship. Sections on the druids, Celtic Britain and *The Mabinogion*. Assumes a deep interest.

Elizabeth Mavor, *The Ladies of Llangollen*. The best of the books on Wales' most notorious and celebrated lesbian couple. This volume traces the ladies' inauspicious beginnings in Ireland, their spectacular elopement and the way that their Llangollen home, Plas Newydd, became a place of pilgrimage for dozens of influential eighteenth-century visitors. A fascinating story lovingly told.

Jan Morris and Twm Morys, *A Machynlleth Triad/Triawd Machynlleth*. Three-part saga in Welsh and English about Machynlleth, Glyndŵr's capital. Jan Morris remembers the town of 45 years ago, looks at the place today and imagines it as the charmingly self-assured capital of an independent Wales. The book says much about Wales as a whole, and is beautifully written, and often very funny.

John Osmond (ed), *A Parliament for Wales*. Political contributors across the spectrum contribute essays on how they see greater democracy in Wales working. A realistic, sober assessment of some burning contemporary issues.

Trefor M Owen, *The Customs and Traditions of Wales*. Pocket guide to everything from outdoor prayer meetings to the curious Mari Lwyd when men dress as grey mares and snap at all the young girls. Easy to read and fun to dip into.

George Thomas, *Mr Speaker*. The autobiography of Rhondda-born George Thomas, rich-toned ex-Speaker of the House of Commons and now sitting in the Lords as Lord Tonypandy. From his humble beginnings, including the forceful discouragement of speaking Welsh at school, Thomas charts his fascinating career and is particularly interesting for his shattering recollections of the Aberfan disaster and, when Secretary of State for Wales, the 1969 investiture of the Prince of Wales at Caernarfon.

Ned Thomas, *The Welsh Extremist*. A good introduction to the political landscape that has spawned the anti-English bombing campaigns. An evocative argument around the issues of oppression and emancipation.

Patrick Thomas, *Candle in the Darkness: Celtic Spirituality from Wales*. Tales from the "Age of Saints" in Wales, particularly around the numerous Celtic saints who originated here.

Alice Thomas Ellis, *A Welsh Childhood*. Wonderfully whimsical reminiscences of growing up in north Wales. Welsh legends and folk tales form a large part of the backdrop, fermenting excitedly in the young imagination of the popular novelist.

Wynford Vaughan-Thomas, *Wales – A History*. One of the country's most missed broadcasters and writers, Vaughan-Thomas' masterpiece is this warm and spirited history of Wales. Working chronologically through the pre-Celtic dawn to the aftermath of the 1979 devolution vote, the book offers perhaps the clearest explanation of the evolution of Welsh culture, with the author's patriotic slant evident throughout.

Jennifer Westwood, *Albion: A Guide to Legendary Britain*. Highly readable volume on the development of myth in literature.

ART, ARCHITECTURE AND ARCHEOLOGY

Chris Barber and John Godfrey Williams, *The Ancient Stones of Wales*. Comprehensive directory of standing stones and monoliths throughout Wales, together with some of the most potent legends and stories associated with them. Exhaustively researched, if a little difficult to use at times.

CADW, *Wales: Castles and Historic Places*. General chat and rich colour photos of the major CADW sites around the country.

John Harvey, *The Art of Piety: The Visual Culture of Welsh Nonconformity*. Fascinating historical account of the stern-faced chapels which form as instant an image of Wales as any other.

Peter Lord, *Gwenllian: Essays on Visual Culture*. A well-illustrated and enthusiastic set of essays looking at the Welsh visual aesthetic in art from the eighteenth century (the Picturesque) to the present day.

Pevsner and others, *The Buildings of Glamorgan; The Buildings of Clwyd; The Buildings of Powys*. Magisterial series covering just about every inhabitable structure. This project was initially a one-man show, but later authors have revised Pevsner's text, inserting newer buildings but generally respecting the founder's personal tone. Volumes of Dyfed, Gwent and Gwynedd are yet to be published.

T W Potter and Catherine Johns, *Roman Britain*. Generously illustrated account of Roman occupation, written by the British Museum's own curators.

LITERATURE

Leonora Brito, *Dat's Love*. Best of the new black voices emanating from the UK's oldest ethnic minority community in Cardiff Bay. A spicy tale of love and life in a very Welsh cultural melting pot.

Bruce Chatwin, *On the Black Hill*. This entertaining and finely wrought novel follows the Jones twins' eighty-year tenure of a farm on the Radnorshire border with England. Chatwin casts his sharp eye for detail over both the minutiae of nature and the universal human condition, providing a wonderfully gentle angle on Welsh–English antipathy.

Alexander Cordell, *Rape of the Fair Country*; *Hosts of Rebecca*; *Song of the Earth*. Dramatic historical trilogy in the best-seller tradition partly set in the cottages on the site of the Blaenafon ironworks during the lead-up to the Chartist Riots. *This Sweet and Bitter Earth* (Coronet) immortalizes Blaenau Ffestiniog in a lusty slate epic.

John Davies (ed), *The Green Bridge: Stories from Wales*. Absorbing selection of 25 short stories from a broad spectrum of Welsh authors writing in English during the twentieth century, including Dylan Thomas.

Thomas Firbank, *I Bought a Mountain*. One of the few popular books set in north Wales in which Anglo-Canadian Firbank spins an autobiographical yarn of his purchase of most of the Glyder range and subsequent life as a Snowdonian sheep farmer during the 1930s. Generous but patronizing observations about his neighbours and his wife mar an otherwise enjoyable, easy read.

Iris Gower, *Copper Kingdom*; *Proud Mary*; *Spinners' Wharf*; *Black Gold*; *Fiddler's Ferry*; *The Oyster Catchers* – the list goes on. Romantic novels by Wales' most popular author.

Siân James, *Not Singing Exactly*. Dazzling and diverse short-story collection from one of Wales' premier romantic novelists.

Glyn Jones, *The Island of Apples*. Set in south Wales and Carmarthen in the early years of the twentieth century, Jones artfully portrays a sensitive Valley youth's enthralment in the glamour of the district's new arrival.

Gwyn and Thomas Jones (trans), *The Mabinogion*. Welsh mythology's classic, these eleven orally developed heroic tales were finally transcribed into the *Book of Rhydderch* ·

(around 1300–25) and the *Red Book of Hergest* (1375–1425). Originally translated by Lady Charlotte Guest between 1838 and 1849 at the beginning of the Celtic revival.

Lewis Jones, *Cwmardy*. Longtime favourite socialist novel, written in 1937 and portraying life in a Rhondda Valley mining community in the early years of the twentieth century. Followed by its sequel, *We Live*.

Russell Celyn Jones, *Soldiers and Innocents*. Tale of a soldier who deserts from Northern Ireland, kidnaps his five-year-old son and embarks on a voyage of self-discovery which takes him back to the Welsh mining community.

Richard Llewellyn, *How Green Was My Valley*; *Up into the Singing Mountain*; *Down Where the Moon is Small*; *Green, Green My Valley Now*. Vital tetralogy in eloquent and passionate prose following the life of Huw Morgan from his youth in a south Wales mining valley through emigration to the Welsh community in Patagonia and back to 1970s Wales. A best-seller during World War II and still the best introduction to the vast canon of "valleys novels", *How Green Was My Valley* captured a longing for a simple, if tough, life, steering clear of cloying sentimentality.

Catherine Merriman, *State of Desire*. Wry widow's tale, set against the backdrop of the mountains in the southeast Wales Valleys.

Caradoc Pritchard, *One Moonlit Night*. Dense, swirling tale of a young boy's emotional and sexual awakenings in an isolated north Wales village. Full-blooded Welsh prose at its most charged.

Kate Roberts, *The Living Sleep* and *Feet in Chains*, amongst others. One of the best-selling of contemporary Welsh-language writers. These two novels, available in English translation, tell the tales of life in a north Wales slate village.

Ruth Janette Ruck, *Hill Farm Story* and *Along Came a Llama*. Evocative stories about a farming area around Beddgelert.

Dylan Thomas, *Collected Stories* and *Under Milk Wood*. Far better than buying any of the single editions, the *Collected Stories* contains all of Thomas' classic prose pieces: *Quite Early One Morning*, which metamorphosed into *Under Milk Wood*, the magical *A Child's Christmas in Wales* and the compulsive, crackling autobiography of *Portrait of the Artist as a Young Dog*. The language still burns bright in a uniquely robust way. *Under Milk Wood*. is his most popular play, telling the story of a microcosmic Welsh seaside town over a 24-hour period. Reading it does little justice – far better, instead, to get a tape or record version of the play, and luxuriate in its rich poetry or, as Thomas himself described it, "prose with blood pressure".

Gwyn Thomas, *A Welsh Eye*. A partly autobiographical, partly anecdotal view of how it feels to grow up in a small Rhondda town; full of arcane and idiosyncratic wit and much more.

Alice Thomas Ellis (ed), *Wales – An Anthology*. A beautiful book, combining poetry, folklore and prose stories rooted in places throughout Wales. All subjects, from rugby and mountain climbing to contemporary descriptions of major events, are included in an enjoyably eclectic mixture of styles. Possibly the best introduction to Welsh writing.

POETRY

John Barnie, *The City* and *The Confirmation*. One of Wales' best contemporary writers, notable mainly for his mixing of styles from poetry to prose, narration and description. Evocative tales of wartime childhood and stifling parenting, leading to a poignant search for love.

Ruth Bidgood, *Lighting Candles*. Light, elegiac verse inspired by the Welsh landscape. Her interweaving of climate, scenery and emotion is delicately handled, producing fine, and deceptively robust, pieces that stand up as physical description, spiritual discussion or both.

Gladys Mary Coles, *The Glass Island*. Breathtakingly cool and descriptive poetry, much of which is set in the Berwyn Mountains in Clwyd and the hills of north Wales. Her gently probing technique uses discoveries of random objects or sights to spark off musings about their history and derivation.

Gerard Manley Hopkins, *Collected Works*. The religious poetry of this late-nineteenth-century Anglo-Catholic still bears scrutiny today. Much of his best work was inspired by Wales – "the loveable west" – and the metre and rhythm of the Welsh language that he strove to learn. Heartfelt and often profoundly sad, with an exquisite ability to marry the grandeur of the landscape with the intensity of his feelings.

Dafydd Johnson, *Iolo Goch: poems*. All of the surviving poems of Owain Glyndŵr's court bard are shown in translation and context. A fascinating insight into courtly medieval Wales at a time of great national resurgence.

David Jones, *The Anathémata*. Once ranked with Ezra Pound and T S Eliot (who once declared him to be the finest poet then working in the English language), Jones has now been relegated to the footnotes of literary Modernism. A pity, because this long poem – a meditation on the history and mythology of Celtic-Christian Britain – is one of the most ambitious and intelligent pieces of writing to come out of Wales. A refreshing change from the emotive lushness of Dylan Thomas.

T Harri Jones, *Collected Works*. Jones is one of Wales' most prolific twentieth-century writers, pumping out work firmly rooted in his native country. His passion and nationalism seems occasionally naive, although the *hiraeth* for Wales and its rootedness cannot fail to impress.

Meic Stephens (ed), *Oxford Companion to the Literature of Wales*. A customarily thorough volume of Welsh prose, spanning the centuries from the folk tales of *The Mabinogion* to modern-day writings. A succinct and entertaining collection.

Dylan Thomas, *Collected Poems*. Thomas' poetry has always proved less populist than his prose- and play-writing, largely due to its density and difficulty. Many of his lighter poems resound with perfect metre and precise structure, including classics such as *DoNot Go Gentle Into That Good Night*, a passionate yet calm elegy to his dying father.

R S Thomas, *Selected Poems 1946–1968*. A fierce, reclusive Welsh nationalist, Thomas' poetry tugs at issues such as God (he was an Anglican priest), Wales ("brittle with relics") and the family. His passion shines throughout this book, probably the best overview available of his prolific work.

Harri Webb, *Collected Poems* (ed. Meic Stephens). Fine collection of 350 works by a modern-day patriot and poet of biting satire and eloquent expression.

FOOD AND DRINK

CAMRA, *The Best Pubs in North Wales*. A hundred or so top pubs with the emphasis on good beer, produced by the Campaign for Real Ale.

Sarah and Ann Gomar, *Welsh Country Recipes.* Despite leaving out some of the traditional dishes, this bargain book makes amends with its broad scope of more ambitious Welsh recipes.

E Smith Twiddy, *A Little Welsh Cookbook.* Slim hardback neatly covering the traditional Welsh staples: *bara brith*, *cawl*, Glamorgan sausages and *laver bread*.

WILDLIFE AND THE ENVIRONMENT

D and R Aichele, H W and A Schwegler, *Wild Flowers of Britain and Europe.* Superb full-colour identification guide divided by flower colour and subdivided by flower form and habitat. Over 900 species covered but not Wales- or even UK-specific.

Douglas Botting, *Wild Britain: A Traveller's Guide.* Not much use for species identification but plenty of information on access to the best sites and what to expect when you get there. Excellent photos.

Collins Field Guides. Series of thorough pocket-sized identification guides. Topics include insects, butterflies, wild flowers, mushrooms and toadstools, birds, mammals, reptiles and fossils.

William Condry, *A Welsh Country Diary.* Over three hundred brief insights into the intricacies of Welsh country life – from the names of rivers to grass snakes in the garden – seen through the eyes of the longest serving contributor to *The Guardian's* "Country Diary" column.

Michael Leach, *The Secret Life of Snowdonia.* Beautifully photographed coffee-table delvings into the least visible natural sights of Snowdonia from feral goats to the Snowdon lily and a close-up of a raven in its nest.

Les Lumsden and Colin Speakman, *The Green Guide to Wales.* Eco-tourism Cambrian style. A now-dated pocket guide to how to get around Wales with the least damage to the environment and its people. Solid background section on green tourism and good for cooperative and community initiative contacts.

David Saunders, *Where to Watch Birds in Wales.* Enthusiasts' guide to Wales' prime birding locations, along with a bird spotting calendar and a list of English–Welsh–Scientific bird names. Not an identification guide.

Detef Singer, *Field Guide to Birds of Britain and Northern Europe.* Colour-coded sections based on birds' plumage, and 700 beautiful photos back up detailed discussion of behaviour and habitat.

Roger Thomas, *Brecon Beacons National Park – A Countryside Commission Guide.* Superb book, going into huge detail on the beginnings and building of the Beacons, as well as the wildlife and flora that you can expect to see there today. Well-written and hugely informative, whilst remaining essentially personal and enthusiastic.

Martin Walters, *Wildlife Travelling Companion: Great Britain and Ireland.* One of the best amateur books on the flora and fauna of the British Isles, with a few full-colour pages to aid identification, and region-by-region site guide. Twenty pages specifically on Wales, covering South Stack, Newborough Warren, Bardsey, Cadair Idris, Devil's Bridge, St David's Head, Skomer island and more.

OUTDOOR PURSUITS

Bob Allen, *On Foot in Snowdonia.* Inspirational and superbly photographed guide to the hundred best walks, from easy strolls to hard scrambles, in and around the Snowdonia National Park. Well-drawn maps, faultless instructions and a star rating for each walk help you to select your route. An essential guide, perfect but for its weight.

Pete Bursnall, *Mountain Bike Guide: Mid-Wales.* Easy-to-follow pocket guide to a score of biking routes with hand-drawn maps. Due to be followed by a north Wales edition.

Cicerone Guides, *The Mountains of England and Wales; Wales, The Ridges of Snowdonia; Hill Walking in Snowdonia; Ascent of Snowdon; Welsh Winter Climbs; Scrambles in Snowdonia* and others, various authors. Clearly written pocket guides to the best aspects of Welsh mountain activities.

Constable Guides, *Best Walks in Southern Wales; Best Walks in North Wales; Owain Glyndŵr's Way, A Guide to Offa's Dyke,* various authors. More clearly written pocket guides to the best aspects of Welsh mountain activities.

A J Drake, *Cambrian Way: A Mountain Connoisseur's Walk.* Thorough and detailed lightweight guide to Wales' most demanding long-distance path by one of the original proposers of this three-week-long, 274-mile Conwy–Cardiff route along Wales' backbone.

Lawrence Main, *The Dyfi Valley Way*. Comprehensive guide to this long-distance path by one of its creators.

Terry Marsh, *The Mountains of Wales*. A walker's guide to all 183 of the 600-metre peaks in Wales, giving step-by-step descriptions of one or more routes up them all with additional historical references and local knowledge.

Ordnance Survey Pathfinder Guides. Softcover editions for large pockets covering *Pembrokeshire and Gower Walks*, *Snowdonia*, *Anglesey and the Llŷn Peninsula Walks* and *Snowdonia Walks* with 28 routes in each embellished with useful, if plodding, accounts of sights along the way.

Ordnance Survey National Trail Guides. More large, paperback editions full of instructive step-by-step descriptions and additional side-walks from Offa's Dyke North, Offa's Dyke South and Pembrokeshire Coastal Path.

W A Poucher, *The Welsh Peaks*. The classic book on Welsh hill-walking, it is fairly dated now and it is initially awkward to find your way around the 56 routes.

Shirley Toulson, *The Drovers' Roads of Wales with Fay Godwin* and *The Drovers' Roads of Wales II: Pembrokeshire and the South with Caroline Forbes* and *Walking Round Wales: The Giraldus Journey*. The first two are a pair of complementary books giving background material along with instructions on how to trace the routes along which Wales' characteristic black cattle were driven to market in England in the eighteenth and nineteenth centuries. The first book covers the northern two-thirds of Wales with superb shots in black-and-white by photography star Fay Godwin, the much more recent second book covers south Wales with more high-quality photos. *Walking Round Wales* is a very readable guide broken into thirty walks following the route around Wales taken by the twelfth-century clergyman Giraldus Cambrensis and enlivened by his own quirky accounts.

Stillwell's National Trail Companion. Excellent big-pocket directory of reasonably priced accommodation close to some of the more popular UK long-distance paths. Welsh routes include the Cambrian Way, Glyndŵr's Way, the Offa's Dyke Path, the Pembrokeshire Coast Path and the Wye Valley Walk.

OTHER GUIDES

William Condry, *Snowdonia*. A personal guided tour around the Snowdonia National Park dipping into geology, natural history and industrial heritage. The best detailed approach to the region. There's also Condry's *Wales* – as for Snowdonia, but covering the whole country.

David Greenslade, *Welsh Fever: Welsh Activities in the United States and Canada Today*. Essential companion for anyone searching out Welsh and Celtic roots in North America. Commentary on regions from Quebec to San Diego, along with accounts of a hundred individual sites of Welsh or Celtic interest.

Moira K Stone, *Mid Wales Companion*. Wide-ranging though not terribly detailed look at life in the stretch of Wales from southern and eastern Snowdonia down to the Brecon Beacons. The town guides are perfunctory, and it is better for the examination of history (from transport to art), landscape influences and industry.

LANGUAGE

Welsh is spoken widely throughout the majority of the country and as a first language in many parts of the west and north. National TV and radiostations broadcast in it, road signs are written in both Welsh and English, Welsh-medium schools are everywhere, books in Welsh are published at a growing rate of around 400 every year, and magazines and newspapers in the old language are mushrooming. The language's survival, and modest resurgence, is a remarkable story, especially considering the fact that the heart of English culture and its language – the most expansionist the world has ever seen – lies right next door.

In the families of Celtic languages, Welsh bears most similarity to largely defunct Cornish and defiant Breton, the language of the northwestern corner of France. Scots and Irish Gaelic, together with defunct Manx, belong to a different branch of Celtic languages, and, although there are occasional similarities, they have little in common.

The language can be traced back to the sixth century. Through Celtic inscriptions on stones, a section of written Welsh in the eighth-century **Lichfield Gospels**, the tenth-century codified laws of Hywel Dda in neat Welsh prose and the twelfth- and thirteenth-century **Mabinogion** folk tales (believed to have been collated from earlier Welsh writings), it can be seen that Welsh was a thriving language in the centuries up to the Norman invasion of 1066. Moreover, the early language is still identifiable and easily comprehensible for any modern-day Welshspeaker.

English domination since the Norman era has been mirrored in the fate of the Welsh tongue. The Norman lords were implanted in castles throughout Wales to subjugate the natives, with official business conducted in their native French. **Edward I** (1272–1307), who conquered Wales in 1284, was politically sensitive to the power of the language to define a nation, and is said to have promised the Welsh a prince, born in their own country who was unable to speak English. This promise was delivered when Edward made his pregnant wife take up residence in Caernarfon Castle, enabling the king to hold the newborn infant up as a non-Englishspeaking, Welsh-born prince.

Real linguistic warfare came with the 1536 **Act of Union** under Henry VIII. This stated that "from henceforth no Person or Persons that use the Welsh Speech or Language shall have or enjoy any Manner, Office or Fees within this Realm of England, Wales or other the King's Dominion, upon pain of forfeiting the same Office or Fees, unless he or they use and exercise the English Speech or Language". This only legitimized the growing practice of imposing English lords and churchmen on the restless, but effectively cowed, Welsh. Had it not been for **William Morgan**'s 1588 translation of the Bible into Welsh, it is likely that the language would have died. As it was, bringing written Welsh into the ordinary, everyday arena of the public ultimately ensured its survival.

The fate of the language became inextricably linked with its religious use. Right up until the early part of this century, Welsh was actively, even forcefully, discouraged in educational and governmental establishments, but new and Nonconformist religious movements from the seventeenth century onwards embraced the language. The **Industrial Revolution** brought mine owners and capitalists from England into the rapidly urbanizing southeastern corner of Wales, further diluting the language which was, nonetheless, upheld as the lingua franca in the growing numbers of chapels. In the first half of the nineteenth century, it is estimated that over ninety percent of the country's population spoke Welsh, with the remaining ten percent comprising those around the English border, in the small pocket of Pembrokeshire long known as "Little England Beyond Wales" and the wealthier classes throughout Wales, for whom English was part of their badge of status.

In 1854, **George Borrow** undertook his marathon tour of Wales and noted the state of the native tongue throughout. As a natural linguist, he had mastered Welsh and – in typically pompous declamatory fashion – fired questions at people he encountered as to their proficiency in both Welsh and English. The picture he paints is of poorer people tending to be monoglot Welsh, wealthier people and those near the border bilingual. Discouragement of Welsh continued in many guises, most notably in it being forbidden in schools in the latter half of the last century and in the early years of this one. Anyone caught speaking in Welsh had to wear a "Welsh Not", a piece of wood on a leather strap, known as a *cribban*, that would only be passed on if someone else was heard using the language. At the end of the school day, the child still wearing the cribban was soundly beaten. There are still older people in Wales who can remember this barbaric practice, and it is hardly surprising that use and proficiency of the language plummeted. Figures are borne out by the official British census, the first of which was undertaken in 1851, when 90 percent of the country are recorded as speaking the language. Every decade, the figures dipped quite spectacularly – 49.9 percent in 1901, 37.1 percent in 1921, 28.9 percent in 1951 and 18.9 percent in 1981. Then, in 1991, for the first time ever, the percentage of Welsh speakers rose, still around the one-fifth mark but showing the most marked increase amongst the lower age groups, those most able to ensure its future.

The figure of 20 percent (ie half a million people), usually quoted as the current number of Welsh-speakers in Wales, is best seen in its geographical context. Considering the fact that nearly half of the nation's population live in the anglicized regions of Gwent and around Cardiff, the spread of the language becomes clearer. Although it is unusual to hear it regularly in the border counties, it is commonly understood throughout most of West Glamorgan, Carmarthenshire, the northern half of Pembrokeshire, right around Cardigan Bay up to Caernarfon, the Llŷn peninsula and Anglesey and in parts of inland Clwyd, Montgomeryshire and Radnorshire. The northwestern corner, centred on Snowdonia, Anglesey and Llŷn are the real strongholds of Welsh, reflected in these areas' political affiliation to Welsh nationalism.

If Welsh is ending the twentieth century on a more upbeat note than could ever have been predicted thirty or so years ago (when it was believed to be dying out), it is largely due to those campaigning to save it. The campaign dates back to the eisteddfod revivalists of the eighteenth century, although movements with a more political aim are a product solely of this century. The formation of **Plaid Cymru**, the Welsh National Party, in 1925 was largely around the issue of language, as indeed its politics have been ever since. In the early 1960s, concerns about the language reached a zenith in the 1962 radio broadcast entitled *Tynged yr iaith* (The Fate of the Language) by the Plaid founder member, Saunders Lewis. This became a rallying cry that resulted in the formation of *Cymdeithas yr Iaith Gymraeg* (the **Welsh Language Society**) the following year. One of the most high-profile early campaigns was the daubing of monoglot English road signs with their Welsh translations, including any town sign written solely in the anglicized format. As any visitor to Wales sees, nearly all signs are now in both languages. A 1967 Welsh Language Act allowed many forms of hitherto English officialdom to be conducted in either language, stating that Welsh, for the first time in over 400 years, had "equal validity" with English.

Bilingual road signs and tax forms are all well and good, but they could do nothing to stem the linguistic haemorrhage that Wales was threatened with. In the multinational, cross-media world of the late twentieth century, the keys to maintaining and promoting a language were in education and media, particularly television. Following the 1967 act, Welsh-medium education blossomed, with bilingual teaching in all primary schools and for at least a year in all secondary schools. Many secondary schools, particularly in areas traditionally associated with the language, had Welsh as a compulsory subject for five years. Increasing numbers of schools all over the land educate their students in all subjects through the Welsh language. These trends have brought little but sneers from the English establishment, profiling loud complaints from numbers of parents, often English immigrants, who object to their children being "forced" to learn a "dead" language. Although there are still periodic rumbles of discontent, most have come round to the well-founded view that a bilingual

WELSH VOCABULARY

Alban or **ab** Scotland
Amgeuddfa Museum
Ap (ab) Son of
Ar Agor Open
Ar Gau Closed
Ar Werth For Sale
Araf Slow
Bara Bread
Bore Morning
Bore da Good morning
Brecwast Breakfast
Bwrdd Table
Bws Bus
Cân Song
Cenedlaethol National
Crefft Craft
Croeso Welcome
Croglen Rood screen
Cromlech Literally "curved stone", generally used to refer to megalithic burial chambers
Cwm Glacially formed, cliff-backed and often lake-filled bowl in mountains. Also called cirque or corrie
Cyhoeddus Public
Cymdeithas Society
Cymraeg Welsh
Cymraes A Welshwoman
Cymreictod Welshness
Cymro A Welshman
Cymru Wales
Cymry The Welsh people
Da Good
Dewi Sant Saint David
Dim No (as an instruction), nothing

Diolch Thankyou
Diwedd End
Druids Priestly class in pre-Roman Celtic culture, often including administrators and judges
Dŵr Water
Dydd Day
Dyn (ion) Man (men)
Eglwys Church
Eisteddfod Festival
Faint? How much?
Gorsaf Station
Gweddol Fair
Gwely Bed
Gwesty Hotel
Hafod Temporary summer house
Hanner Half
Heddiw Today
Heddlu Police
Heno Tonight
Heol Road
Hiraeth Longing, yearning
Hwyl Spirit
Iaith Language
Iawn Fine
Llech Slate
Llety Lodging place, B&B
Llew Lion (often found in pub names)
Lloegr England
Llwybr Path
Llyfr Book
Marchnad Market
Menyw Woman

Mihangel Michael, as in Llanfihangel
Milltir Mile
Neuadd Hall
Neuadd Y Dref Town Hall
Nofio To swim
Nos da Good night
Noson/noswaith Evening
Noswaith dda Good evening
Olaf Last
Os Gwelwch yn Dda Please
Pêl-droed Football
Pentref Village
Plaid Cymru The Party of Wales
P'nhawn da Good afternoon
Rhiniog Buttress
Saesneg English language
Sais Englishman
Sant Saint
Sarn Causeway
Senedd Parliament
Shwmae Hello
Siop Shop
Sir County, Shire
Stryd Street
Sut ydych chi? (formal) or **Sut ywt ti? (informal)** How are you?
Swyddfa Office
Swyddfa'r Post Post office
Tafarn Pub
Tocyn Ticket
Y, Yr or **'r** The
Yma Here
Ysbyty Hospital
Ysgol School

education (which is, after all, what sixty percent of the world's children receive) actually helps children learn, increasing aptitude for other languages. At the other end of the educational spectrum, Welsh-language courses in the country's universities are growing in popularity and status, meaning that, for pretty much the first time in Wales' history, it is possible to be educated in Welsh from nursery to degree level.

Paralleling Welsh-medium education has been the other modern cornerstone for developing a language – a growth in media. In the mid-1970s, a government report recommended that the putative fourth national TV channel be bilingual in Wales, pulling together (and significantly increasing) periodic Welsh programming on other channels. When plans for Channel 4 were drawn up by the new Conservative administration under Margaret Thatcher in the early 1980s, this recommendation (and her own commitment to uphold this idea) had been dropped. A formidable campaign was launched by *Cymdeithas yr Iaith*, culminating in a hunger strike by Plaid Cymru leader, Gwynfor Evans. Margaret Thatcher, ever an astute politican, realized that creating a Welsh martyr could have dangerous ramifications and the government gracelessly capitulated, giving birth to **Sianel Pedwar Cymru** (S4C) in 1982. Together with the Welsh-language BBC Radio Cymru, S4C has sponsored and programmed enduringly popular Welsh learners' programmes and given the old language greater space than it has ever enjoyed before. Critics would like to believe

that this is a false dawn, but this can easily be dismissed just by touring Wales and seeing the sheer number of Welsh-language classes on offer right across the country, including in some of the most anglicized of border towns. Welsh classes can invariably be found out of Wales too, in language centres across Britain, and universities in Europe and North America.

The Welsh language is both one of Wales' key strengths and its key drawbacks in the quest for some sort of national emancipation. There is still suspicion, occasionally bordering on hostility, towards the Welsh-speaking "elite" who are seen to control the media and local government in the country. Welsh nationalism is so defined by the language that Plaid Cymru has nearly

WELSH PLACE NAMES

The following list is of the most common words that you will see in town and village names. For a brief guide to pronunciation, see "Alphabet", opposite.

Aber Mouth of a river; confluence of two rivers
Afon River
Bach Small, lesser
Bron Slope of a hill
Bryn Hill
Bwlch Mountain pass
Cadair Stronghold, chair
Caer Fort
Canol Centre
Cant Hundred
Capel Chapel
Carreg Stone
Cartref Home
Castell Castle
Clun Meadow
Clwyd Gate, perch
Coch Red
Coed Forest, woodland
Craig Rock
Cyntaf First
De South
Din or **dinas** Fort
Dros Over
Du Black
Dwyrain East

Fawr Big
Fferm Farm
Ffordd Road
Fforest Forest
Gardd Garden
Glas Blue
Glyn Valley
Gogledd North
Gorllewin West
Gwyn White
Gwyrdd Green
Hen Old
Isaf Lower
Llan Clearing, early church
Lle Place
Llwyd Grey
Llyn Lake
Llys Place, court
Maen Stone
Maes Field
Mawr Great
Melin Mill
Melyn Yellow
Merthyr Burial place of saint
Moel Bare or rounded mountain

Môr Sea
Morfa Coastal marsh
Mynydd Mountain
Nant Valley, stream
Newydd New
Nos Night
Pant Vale
Parc Park
Pen Head, top (as of a valley)
Plas Hall, mansion
Pont Bridge
Porth Port, gateway
Rhiw Hill
Rhyd Ford
Taf Dark
Tomen Mound
Traeth Beach
Tref Town
Twr Tower
Ty House
Uchaf Uppermost, highest
Uwch Higher
Wrth Near, by
Ynys Island

always had great difficulty in applying its relevance to those who speak only English, particularly in the urban southeast. Nonetheless, the Welsh language seems to be facing the new millennium in greater heart than could ever have been expected only a few decades ago. The new **Welsh Language Board**, chaired by Lord Dafydd Elis Thomas, the former Plaid Cymru MP, seems robust and confident, although its bite and power have yet to be tested seriously. It is nonsensical to believe that Wales can ever become a primarily monoglot Welsh-speaking nation, but it does seem to be developing well as a model bilingual entity, in which there is room for both languages to thrive together.

ALPHABET

Although Welsh words, place names in particular, can appear bewilderingly incomprehensible, the rules of the language are far more strictly adhered to than in English. Thus, mastering the basic constructions and breaking words down into their constituent parts means that pronunciation need not be anywhere near as difficult as first imagined.

The Welsh **alphabet** is similar to the English, although with seven vowels instead of five, and a different collection of consonants. As well as the same five vowels (a, e, i, o, u), Welsh also has y and w. Most vowels have two sounds, long and short: a is long as in c**a**r, short as in f**a**t; e long as in br**e**r, short as in p**e**t; i long as in s**ea**, short as an t**i**n; o long as in m**o**re, short as in d**o**g; u roughly like a Welsh i; w long as in s**oo**n, short as in l**oo**k; y long as in s**ea** and short as in b**u**n or p**i**n.

In Welsh **adjoining vowels** are common. Ae, ai, aw, ew, iw, oe, oi, ou, wy and yw are the usual forms and are pronounced as the two separate sounds, with, generally, the stress on the first.

There are no letters j, k, v, x and z in Welsh, except in occasional words appropriated and Cymrified from other languages. Additional Welsh consonants are ch, pronounced as in German or as in lo**ch**, dd, pronounced as a hard th as in **th**ose, ff and ph as a soft f as in **f**ive and si as a sh in **sh**oe. The typically Welsh consonant that causes the most problem is the ll, featured in many place names such as **Ll**ango**ll**en. This has no direct parallel in English, although the tl sound in Bent**l**ey comes close. The proper way to pronounce it is to place the tongue firmly behind the top row of teeth and breathe through it without consciously making a voiced sound. Single Welsh consonants are, for the most part, pronounced in similar ways to English. The exceptions are c and g, always hard as in **c**at and **g**ut (never soft as in ni**c**e or ra**g**e) and f, always pronounced as v as in **v**ine.

A further difficulty for those trying to recognize words is the Welsh system of word **mutation**, where a previous word can affect the beginning of a following one, principally to ease pronunciation. Prepositions commonly mutate the following word, turning an initial B into F or M, an initial C into G or Ngh, a D into Dd or N, F into B or M, G into C or Ngh, Ll into L, M into F, P into B, Mh or Ph, T into Th, D or Nh. Thus, "in Cardiff (Caerdydd)" is "y**ng Ngh**aerdydd" (note that the "yn" also mutates to ease pronunciation) and "from Bangor" is "o **F**angor".

WELSH NUMBERS

1 un	13 un-deg-tri	200 dau gant
2 dau (fem. dwy)	20 dau-ddeg	300 tri chant
3 tri (fem. tair)	21 dau-ddeg-un	400 pedwar cant
4 pedwar (fem. pedair)	22 dau-ddeg-dau	500 pum cant
5 pump	30 tri-deg	600 chwe cant
6 chwech	40 pedwar-deg	700 saith cant
7 saith	50 pum-deg	800 wyth cant
8 wyth	60 chwe-deg	900 naw cant
9 naw	70 saith-deg	1,000 mil
10 deg	80 wyth-deg	1,000,000 miliwn
11 un-deg-un	90 naw-deg	
12 un-deg-dau	100 cant	

GLOSSARY OF ARCHITECTURAL TERMS

Aisle Clear space parallel to the nave, usually with lower ceiling than the nave.

Altar Table at which the Eucharist is celebrated, at the east end of the church. When the church is not aligned to the geographical east, the altar end is still referred to as the "east" end.

Ambulatory Passage behind the chancel.

Apse The curved or polygonal east end of a church.

Arcade Row of arches on top of columns or piers, supporting a wall.

Bailey Area enclosed by castle walls.

Barbican Defensive structure built in front of main gate.

Barrel vault Continuous rounded vault, like a semi-cylinder.

Boss A decorative carving at the meeting point of the lines of a vault.

Box pew Form of church seating in which each row is enclosed by high, thin wooden panels.

Buttress Stone support for a wall; some buttresses are wholly attached to the wall, others take the form of a tower with a connecting arch, known as a "flying buttress".

Capital Upper section of a column, usually carved.

Chancel Section of the church where the altar is located.

Choir Area in which the church service is conducted; next to or same as chancel.

Clerestory Upper storey of nave, containing a line of windows.

Corbel Jutting stone support, often carved.

Crenellations Battlements with square indentations.

Crossing The intersection of the nave and the transepts.

Decorated Middle Gothic style, about 1280–1380.

Fan vault Late Gothic form of vaulting, in which the area between walls and ceiling is covered with stone ribs in the shape of an open fan.

Finial Any decorated tip of an architectural feature.

Gallery A raised passageway.

Gargoyle Grotesque exterior carving, usually a decorative form of water spout.

Hammerbeam Type of ceiling in which horizontal beams support vertical pieces that connect to the roof timbers.

Jesse window Stained-glass window depicting the descendants from Jesse (the father of David) down to Jesus.

Keep Main structure of a castle.

Lancet Tall, narrow and plain window.

Misericord Carved ledge below a tip-up seat, usually in choir stalls.

Motte Mound on which a castle keep stands.

Mullion Vertical strip between the panes of a window.

Nave The main part of the church to the west of the crossing.

Ogee Double curve; distinctive feature of Decorated style.

Oriel Projecting window.

Palladian Eighteenth-century classical style, adhering to the principles of Andrea Palladio.

Pediment Triangular space above a window or doorway.

Perpendicular Late Gothic style, about 1380–1550.

Pier Massive column, often consisting of several fused smaller columns.

Portico Colonnade, usually supporting a porch to the building.

Rood screen Wooden screen supporting a Crucifix (or rood), separating the choir from the nave; few survived the Reformation.

Rose window Large circular window, divided into vaguely petal-shaped sections.

Stalls Seating for clergy in the choir area of a church.

Tracery Pattern formed by narrow bands of stone in a window or on a wall surface.

Transept Sections of the main body of the church at right angles to the choir and nave.

Vault Arched ceiling.

INDEX

direct orders from

		UK£8.99	US$14.95	CAN$19.99
Amsterdam	1-85828-218-7	UK£8.99	US$14.95	CAN$19.99
Andalucia	1-85828-219-5	9.99	16.95	22.99
Australia	1-85828-220-9	13.99	21.95	29.99
Bali	1-85828-134-2	8.99	14.95	19.99
Barcelona	1-85828-221-7	8.99	14.95	19.99
Berlin	1-85828-129-6	8.99	14.95	19.99
Belgium & Luxembourg	1-85828-222-5	10.99	17.95	23.99
Brazil	1-85828-223-3	13.99	21.95	29.99
Britain	1-85828-208-X	12.99	19.95	25.99
Brittany & Normandy	1-85828-224-1	9.99	16.95	22.99
Bulgaria	1-85828-183-0	9.99	16.95	22.99
California	1-85828-181-4	10.99	16.95	22.99
Canada	1-85828-130-X	10.99	14.95	19.99
China	1-85828-225-X	15.99	24.95	32.99
Corfu	1-85828-226-8	8.99	14.95	19.99
Corsica	1-85828-227-6	9.99	16.95	22.99
Costa Rica	1-85828-136-9	9.99	15.95	21.99
Crete	1-85828-132-6	8.99	14.95	18.99
Cyprus	1-85828-182-2	9.99	16.95	22.99
Czech & Slovak Republics	1-85828-121-0	9.99	16.95	22.99
Dublin Mini Guide	1-85828-294-2	5.99	9.95	12.99
Edinburgh Mini Guide	1-85828-295-0	5.99	9.95	12.99
Egypt	1-85828-188-1	10.99	17.95	23.99
Europe	1-85828-289-6	14.99	19.95	25.99
England	1-85828-160-1	10.99	17.95	23.99
First Time Europe	1-85828-270-5	7.99	9.95	12.99
Florida	1-85828-184-4	10.99	16.95	22.99
France	1-85828-228-4	12.99	19.95	25.99
Germany	1-85828-309-4	14.99	23.95	31.99
Goa	1-85828-275-6	8.99	14.95	19.99
Greece	1-85828-300-0	12.99	19.95	25.99
Greek Islands	1-85828-310-8	10.99	17.95	23.99
Guatemala	1-85828-189-X	10.99	16.95	22.99
Hawaii: Big Island	1-85828-158-X	8.99	12.95	16.99
Hawaii	1-85828-206-3	10.99	16.95	22.99
Holland	1-85828-229-2	10.99	17.95	23.99
Hong Kong	1-85828-187-3	8.99	14.95	19.99
Hungary	1-85828-123-7	8.99	14.95	19.99
India	1-85828-200-4	14.99	23.95	31.99
Ireland	1-85828-179-2	10.99	17.95	23.99
Italy	1-85828-167-9	12.99	19.95	25.99
Jamaica	1-85828-230-6	9.99	16.95	22.99
Kenya	1-85828-192-X	11.99	18.95	24.99
Lisbon Mini Guide	1-85828-297-7	5.99	9.95	12.99
London	1-85828-231-4	9.99	15.95	21.99
Madrid Mini Guide	1-85828-353-1	5.99	9.95	12.99
Mallorca & Menorca	1-85828-165-2	8.99	14.95	19.99
Malaysia, Singapore & Brunei	1-85828-232-2	11.99	18.95	24.99
Mexico	1-85828-044-3	10.99	16.95	22.99
Morocco	1-85828-040-0	9.99	16.95	21.99
Moscow	1-85828-118-0	8.99	14.95	19.99
Nepal	1-85828-190-3	10.99	17.95	23.99
New York	1-85828-296-9	9.99	15.95	21.99
Norway	1-85828-234-9	10.99	17.95	23.99

around the world

Pacific Northwest	1-85828-092-3	9.99	14.95	19.99
Paris	1-85828-235-7	8.99	14.95	19.99
Poland	1-85828-168-7	10.99	17.95	23.99
Portugal	1-85828-180-6	9.99	16.95	22.99
Prague	1-85828-122-9	8.99	14.95	19.99
Provence	1-85828-127-X	9.99	16.95	22.99
Pyrenees	1-85828-308-6	10.99	17.95	23.99
Rhodes & the Dodecanese	1-85828-120-2	8.99	14.95	19.99
Romania	1-85828-305-1	10.99	17.95	23.99
San Francisco	1-85828-299-3	8.99	14.95	19.99
Scandinavia	1-85828-236-5	12.99	20.95	27.99
Scotland	1-85828-302-7	9.99	16.95	22.99
Sicily	1-85828-178-4	9.99	16.95	22.99
Singapore	1-85828-237-3	8.99	14.95	19.99
South Africa	1-85828-238-1	12.99	19.95	25.99
Soutwest USA	1-85828-239-X	10.99	16.95	22.99
Spain	1-85828-240-3	11.99	18.95	24.99
St Petersburg	1-85828-298-5	9.99	16.95	22.99
Sweden	1-85828-241-1	10.99	17.95	23.99
Thailand	1-85828-140-7	10.99	17.95	24.99
Tunisia	1-85828-139-3	10.99	17.95	24.99
Turkey	1-85828-242-X	12.99	19.95	25.99
Tuscany & Umbria	1-85828-243-8	10.99	17.95	23.99
USA	1-85828-307-8	14.99	19.95	25.99
Venice	1-85828-170-9	8.99	14.95	19.99
Vietnam	1-85828-191-1	9.99	15.95	21.99
Wales	1-85828-245-4	10.99	17.95	23.99
Washington DC	1-85828-246-2	8.99	14.95	19.99
West Africa	1-85828-101-6	15.99	24.95	34.99
More Women Travel	1-85828-098-2	10.99	16.95	22.99
Zimbabwe & Botswana	1-85828-186-5	11.99	18.95	24.99
Phrasebooks				
Czech	1-85828-148-2	3.50	5.00	7.00
French	1-85828-144-X	3.50	5.00	7.00
German	1-85828-146-6	3.50	5.00	7.00
Greek	1-85828-145-8	3.50	5.00	7.00
Hungarian	1-85828-304-3	4.00	6.00	8.00
Italian	1-85828-143-1	3.50	5.00	7.00
Japanese	1-85828-303-5	4.00	6.00	8.00
Mexican	1-85828-176-8	3.50	5.00	7.00
Portuguese	1-85828-175-X	3.50	5.00	7.00
Polish	1-85828-174-1	3.50	5.00	7.00
Spanish	1-85828-147-4	3.50	5.00	7.00
Thai	1-85828-177-6	3.50	5.00	7.00
Turkish	1-85828-173-3	3.50	5.00	7.00
Vietnamese	1-85828-172-5	3.50	5.00	7.00
Reference				
Classical Music	1-85828-113-X	12.99	19.95	25.99
European Football	1-85828-256-X	14.99	23.95	31.99
Internet	1-85828-288-8	5.00	8.00	10.00
Jazz	1-85828-137-7	16.99	24.95	34.99
Opera	1-85828-138-5	16.99	24.95	34.99
Reggae	1-85828-247-0	12.99	19.95	25.99
Rock	1-85828-201-2	17.99	26.95	35.00
World Music	1-85828-017-6	16.99	22.95	29.99

In the USA, or for international orders, charge your order by Master Card or Visa (US$15.00 minimum order): call 1-800-253-6476; or send orders, with complete name, address and zip code, and list price, plus $2.00 shipping and handling per order to: Consumer Sales, Penguin USA, PO Box 999 – Dept #17109, Bergenfield, NJ 07621. No COD. Prepay foreign orders by international money order, a cheque drawn on a US bank, or US currency. No postage stamps are accepted. All orders are subject to stock availability at the time they are processed. Refunds will be made for books not available at that time. Please allow a minimum of four weeks for delivery.

Stay in touch with us!

**ROUGHNEWS is Rough Guides' free newsletter.
In three issues a year we give you news, travel
issues, music reviews, readers' letters and the
latest dispatches from authors on the road.**